Fools, Martyrs, Traitors

LACEY BALDWIN SMITH

Fools, Martyrs, Traitors

THE STORY OF MARTYRDOM
IN THE WESTERN WORLD

NORTHWESTERN UNIVERSITY PRESS
EVANSTON, ILLINOIS

Northwestern University Press
Evanston, Illinois 60208-4210

Originally published in 1997 by Alfred A. Knopf, Inc., New York.
Copyright © 1997 by Lacey Baldwin Smith. Northwestern University Press
edition published 1999 by arrangement with Alfred A. Knopf, Inc.
All rights reserved.

Printed in the United States of America

ISBN 0-8101-1724-X (paper)

Library of Congress Cataloging-in-Publication Data

Smith, Lacey Baldwin, 1922–
Fools, martyrs, traitors : the story of martyrdom in the Western
world / Lacey Baldwin Smith.
p. cm.
Originally published: New York : Alfred A. Knopf, 1997.
Includes bibliographical references and index.
ISBN 0-8101-1724-X (pbk. : alk. paper)
1. Martrydom—History. 2. Martyrs Biography.
3. Traitors Biography. I. Title.
[BL626.5.S65 1999]
179.7—dc21   99-35208
CIP

To my wife and our three adult offspring,
especially Katherine Chandler,
who helped to bring her mother
into the computer age

CONTENTS

ACKNOWLEDGMENTS

Fools, Martyrs, Traitors owes its existence to the encouragement and tolerance of my colleagues, students, and, of course, to she who is always obeyed, my wife, Jean. Robert Lerner read an experimental version of the first chapter and wisely warned me not to give too much away in an introduction; Gary Wills lent his expertise on Socrates; Bill Heyck and Richard Kieckheffer prevented me from treading on too many tender toes in the chapter on Jesus; Jack McLean tactfully cleansed my ethnocentric misconceptions when handling Gandhi; and Peter Hayes guided me into the labyrinth of German history, the Holocaust, and the careers of Dietrich Bonhoeffer and Kurt Gerstein. Lerner, a New Yorker, who remembered his parents talking about Julius and Ethel Rosenberg, did extra duty by reading the section on the Rosenbergs. I am profoundly grateful to all six for their support.

The idea for this book actually began some fifteen years ago as an undergraduate history seminar on martyrs which became affectionately known by students as "Finks, Stinks, and Weirdos." The aim of the course was to excite students about history and expose them to the historical process. Whatever my pedagogical achievements may have been, one accomplishment is indisputable. I, if not my Northwestern students, became fascinated by the subject, and I decided to study and write about the concept of martyrdom, thereby refuting the oft-assumed conflict between teaching and research.

Fools, Martyrs, Traitors

THE DEBATE OVER DEFINITION

Martyrs, *cher ami,* must choose between
being forgotten, mocked, or made use of.
As for being understood—never!
—ALBERT CAMUS,
The Fall

NOT EVEN God, it is said, can change history, but the historian can; his profession requires him to do so. The process entails not so much the deliberate distortion or misrepresentation of the facts—that would be a violation of the rules of the game—as the placement of events in a continuum, giving to human action and thought a past and a future, and creating for history a family of ancestral causes and descendant effects. The past is filled with a host of parentless actors and actions, but of all of history's orphans possibly the martyr is the most lonely and isolated, appearing to us, like both the hero and the traitor, as a two-dimensional stereotype. We find it jarring to imagine the pusillanimous hero, the specious martyr, or the open-hearted traitor. By definition the hero is cleft-chinned and stalwart, the martyr serene-faced and compassionate, and the traitor evil-eyed and conniving. But place martyrs within an historical sequence, relate them to their close cousins the fool and the traitor, assign them siblings and descendants, and ask what personal and cultural interests motivated their sacrifices, and they become complex personalities subject to analysis and criticism. For if a single truism can be claimed for martyrdom, it is that their lot is not an easy one.

Death itself is rarely the stumbling point. The martyr belongs to that select association of men and women who are in such absolute control of their own existence, knowing its exact value, that they are willing to abandon it, flinging life away as if it were no more important than last month's obituary notice. For those of us who cling to this world with the tenacity of a mollusk, the decision to die is both fascinating and repulsive; in one breath, we judge martyrs to be superior mortals, and in the next, delight in questioning their claim to our esteem. The martyr is a profoundly vulnerable species, for, as Erik Erikson said of Mahatma Gandhi, it is easy enough to kill and be killed: what is hard is to "know how to die without killing and to make one's death count for life."[1] The trick is to transform death from a conclusion into a beginning, to make it count; but to do so places the martyr in a peculiarly exposed position. So much depends on the debate over definition, the judgment of history, the cooperation of the executioners, the vagaries of timing and circumstance, and the question of motive.

Who, then, qualifies as a proper martyr? Does the distinction between the fool, the martyr, and the traitor rest solely in the eyes of the beholder? Are all martyrs heroes and all dead heroes martyrs? The term is hopelessly overworked and abused, and the moment the label moves beyond those martyrs carefully scrutinized and calendared by the Catholic Church the word becomes all things to all people—the universal good guy. The martyr suffers, like the hero, from "celebrity hype and political expediency,"[2] not to mention muddled thinking and mercurial fashions. Iraq constructed a 150-foot-high, tiled, domed monument to the fallen heroes of its holy war against Iran, which in turn erected its own "Fountain of Blood," flowing with red water, the central attraction of a cemetery reserved for the martyrs of Islam and the heroes of the country. Saint Paul's Cathedral in London possesses a Book of Martyrs, and not so long ago an American senator publicly claimed an elderly and crippled Jewish tourist thrown to his death off a pleasure liner by Arab terrorists to be a martyr-hero worthy of receiving the Congressional Gold Medal. Christians recognize "red" and "white" martyrs—those who gave their lives as opposed to those who suffered desperately for their faith—and Moslems in India have twenty different ways to achieve the martyr's heaven, ranging from death in defense of Allah and dying while reciting the Koran to being killed by lightning or falling down a dry well.[3]

If society has been lavish in bestowing the martyr's crown, it has been even more confused and quarrelsome about the validity of the title. What is the distinction between a victim and a martyr? Should we confer the honor of martyrdom upon the millions who died in the Nazi holocaust, or were they just unlucky and choiceless people caught in an ideological maelstrom? What of the soldier-hero dead upon the battlefield? Is he a martyr to his country, or is death simply an occupational hazard, a calculated risk for all military personnel? What are we to think of the young man in California who lay down on a railroad track in front of an approaching train to display his passionate opposition to the construction and operation of a nuclear power plant? Trains supplying the plant had always stopped before, but this one didn't, and he lost both legs. Was he any more or less a martyr than the soldier who risks life but in his heart does not expect to die? Or was he just a damn fool? Were those kamikaze pilots of World War II, who flew suicide missions in defense of an emperor who claimed descent from the gods, martyrs or culturally conditioned automatons and overly advertised examples of a society that rated face, reputation, and national honor above life itself?

More disturbing yet, do those Arab terrorists—often only young boys and girls—who in the 1980s drove fire trucks at French and American installations in Lebanon qualify as martyrs, willing sacrifices to Allah, who have earned a guaranteed place in Paradise? Or, as the Western world much prefers, should they be viewed simply as drug-induced sacrificial pawns in a vicious game of power politics? How is society to categorize Dr. Baruch Goldstein, who one Friday morning in February of 1994 fired a hundred and eleven rounds from an automatic rifle into hundreds of Palestinian Moslems kneeling in prayer, killing forty worshipers? Goldstein died a victim of the anger, frustration, and hatred that consumed him, beaten to death by the survivors. Was he a martyr, a terrorist, or a madman? Is he any worse or better than John Brown, who in a series of Sorelian acts of violence and human slaughter deliberately sought to goad the Satanic South into open conflict so it could be destroyed by the North, the ordained instrument of God's ultimate purpose?

The debate and the uncertainty are without end. Should the nineteen-year-old French student, Robert Gerekens, who was pronounced by his headmaster "completely normal" but who in 1970 doused himself in gasoline and set himself on fire in imitation of Jan Palach's incendiary and symbolic protest against the Russian invasion of Czechoslovakia the year before, be ranked as a martyr? He did not ask, he said, for human tears: he took his life "because I could not adapt myself to this world." He wanted his political suicide to be a grim but dramatic protest against the idiocy of war and "the destructive folly of man."[4] Is such a suicidal gesture to be judged sacrificial altruism or deranged egotism?

What of Martin Luther King, whose name stands high in any number of modern martyrologies as the man who spoke for human rights and dignity despite the risk of death? He was gunned down, the victim of human brutality and bigotry, but does this—the manner of his death—make him a martyr? Is it splitting moral hairs to insist on a distinction between assassination by private vengeance and death by official decree? Or what about the unsaintly martyrs, the fashion of whose deaths qualifies them for sainthood but the style of those lives condemns them as criminals? Should the youth who insulted the Roman gods by smashing pagan altars and who was promptly executed for such a desecration be claimed by Christianity as a saint? Does the martyr, as Saint Augustine suggested, possess a higher piety which can turn common vandalism into divine purpose and treason into heroism?[5]

How are we to handle these martyr-traitors? They are the most explosive and difficult of the lot. It is hard enough to judge the naive altruist who steals flowers from a park to give to hospital patients and is charged with theft of public property; it becomes a matter of high politics to decide on modern ideological traitors who in the name of a higher end, be it communism, manifest destiny, or simply free scientific inquiry, betray their country. Why should Guy Fawkes—whose irrational endeavor to blow up king, Lords, and Commons in 1605 in order to further the Catholic faith is still commemorated by equally irrational efforts on the part of British schoolchildren to blow themselves up with fireworks—be branded a traitor but Thomas More and Thomas Becket, equal traitors in the eyes of their kings, be honored as martyrs? Surely the distinction has as much to do with politics and history as with morality and justice; one man's martyr, it would appear, is too often another man's traitor.

The link between the martyr and the traitor has always been close because they possess two essential characteristics in common: neither needs the support or the affirmation of society. Both are either alienated from or rejected by the herd, and both are failures in the eyes of officialdom. The martyr's death clearly constitutes a denial of the existing society—as the young French student said, "I could not adapt myself to this world"; likewise the traitor by definition is a failure:

> Treason never prospers; what's the reason?
> If it prospers, none dare call it treason.[6]

The noble traitor seems to be a contradiction in terms, and the twentieth century has had immense difficulty labeling its Colonel Stauffenbergs, Klaus Fuchses, Dietrich Bonhoeffers, and Ethel and Julius Rosenbergs. History has come to no firm conclusion about the greatest of all high-minded murderers—Marcus Junius Brutus. The medieval world had no doubts about where Brutus belonged: in hell, in company with Judas, for having committed the ultimate political and moral sin—treason to one's lord. The punishment assigned by Dante in the Inferno psychologically fitted their crime: they, along with Cassius, were encased in ice, appropriate bone-chilling suffering for the egotism that had led each to set himself apart from and above the society that had spawned him. The ideological reasons that led to the Ides of March or the possibility that Judas, in selling his soul for thirty pieces of silver, was fulfilling God's will did not bother the Middle Ages one whit: both men were archtraitors and deserved their terrible punishment. By Shakespeare's day Tudor society was willing to accept Brutus as a hero but not, as Marc Antony's dramatic irony displayed, an honorable man. It was not until the eighteenth and nineteenth centuries that Caesar's slayer emerged as a true ideologue, a noble tyrant-slayer and martyr to the cause of republicanism.

The martyr-traitor understandably spawns distaste and debate: the two words together seem for many to be a particularly inappropriate oxymoron. But surely somewhere it is possible to find agreement and locate a martyr upon whom all can agree. What about Joan of Arc, Jeanne la Pucelle (the Maiden), the national heroine of France, in whose honor Charles de Gaulle selected the cross of Lorraine as the symbol of a revitalized France emerging from the ignominy of World War II?[7] She inspired a host of literary giants—Voltaire, Schiller, Anatole France, Mark Twain, G. B. Shaw, and Jean Anouilh—operas by Verdi and Tchaikovsky, and countless films and plays. "A terrible beauty" was born when on Wednesday, May 30, 1431, the English lit the faggots that burned to death a nineteen-year-old illiterate peasant girl from Lorraine. Alexandre Dumas *père* called her "the Christ of France"; Thomas De Quincey, the English essayist, placed her above Milton and Michelangelo because she died "grandly" as only "goddesses would die, were goddesses mortal."[8] Here certainly is unanimity on the part of both the people who lit the flames and those who benefited from her courage.

But does unquestionable courage and simple grandeur in the face of naked political expediency validate a martyrdom? The Catholic Church, when it was finally cajoled into canonizing Joan in 1920, deftly sidestepped the issue. The unadorned facts without reference to the imaginative interpretations and consequences given them by later generations were singularly unpromising for a religious institution that itself 489 years before had enthusiastically found her guilty of heresy and sorcery and had turned her over to the secular powers for punishment with such self-evident delight that it could be, and was, accused of deliberate judicial murder.

France in 1429 was staggering under a political, military, and moral defeat as great as that sustained in 1940. The northern third of the country was occupied by the English and the forces of the French king's vassal the Duke of Burgundy; Paris was in their hands as well as the channel coast from Calais to Brittany. The Valois heir to the throne, the dauphin Charles, on the death of his father in 1422 had been cast aside in favor of his nephew, the nine-month-old son of triumphant Henry Plantagenet of England; and Anglo-Burgundian troops were laying siege to Orléans, the gateway to the south of France. Suddenly there appeared at the discouraged court of the dauphin at Chinon in the unoccupied part of the country a seventeen-year-old girl with a highly developed auditory imagination and a strong preference for male drag, who claimed that her voices and divine guides, later identified as Saint Michael the archangel, Saint Catherine, and Saint Margaret, had bid her tell Charles that he must relieve the siege of Orléans and be crowned king in the ancient cathedral of Rheims—a sure sign that God had determined that France belonged to the Valois, not the English, line. She, Joan, would be the heaven-ordained savior of the kingdom and would drive the "God-damns" back across the channel. If there was a miracle in Joan's life, it happened at Chinon. Her charismatic personality and impregnable conviction galvanized the young prince into action. Orléans was relieved, the English severely defeated, and Charles anointed king at Rheims while Joan stood by. In only nine months she turned the military tide against the enemies of France, and it never ceased to flow until the kingdom, except for Calais, was whole again.

The only part of Joan's prophecy that failed to materialize was the young heroine's triumphant role as the rescuer of France. In May of 1430 the Maid of Orléans was captured by Burgundian forces in a minor skirmish. She was sold to the English at the demand of the University of Paris and Pierre Cauchon, bishop of Beauvais, and tried before an ecclesiastical court, which found her voices either "lies of the imagination, corrupt and pernicious," or apparitions conjured up by "malign and diabolical spirits." She had, the court maintained, blasphemed against God and His sacraments when she said that she wore male garments by divine decree; her assertion that her saints preferred Valois Charles to Plantagenet Henry was sacrilegious; and she was a stubborn schismatic in placing the opinions of her imagined voices above the historic authority of the Church Militant. In the end Joan died at the stake, forced to wear a dunce cap inscribed with the words "Heretica, Relapsa, Apostata, Idolator" because, when faced with the fire, she had recanted and signed an abjuration confessing herself "a miserable sinner," admitting she "falsely pretended" her voices came from saints, angels, and God, and submitting herself to "the correction of our Holy Mother Church and God's good justice." Her recantation was public but not totally convincing, and what happened the next day is one of the many debated mysteries surrounding Joan's life and death. In defiance of her abjuration she again put on male attire. Some sources state she was deliberately tricked into doing so; some argue she was forced by English soldiers; some maintain that she did so from fear that dressed as a woman she would be raped by her jailers; and some say she did so of her own free will because her voices had told her to and because her judges had not kept their promise to remove her fetters and place her in an ecclesiastical jail, not a secular prison surrounded by English soldiers. Whatever the motive, her relapse was fatal, and the English could now prove once and for all that in allowing Joan to burn, God was solidly English, not French. As Bishop Cauchon put it, "We've got her."[9] That same afternoon the court reconvened and declared her "relapsed, heretic and excommunicate," and worthy of the flames.

The documents are equally equivocal as to Joan's state of mind when the following day at 8 a.m. she was turned over to the English and secular authorities at Rouen for burning. The rebellious, mocking mood in which she had signed her recantation was replaced by lamentation and fear: "Alas . . . that my body, whole and entire, which has never been corrupted, will today be consumed and turned to ashes! Ah, I would rather be beheaded seven times than burned!" One disposition, described as "Posthumous Information," even claims that she admitted her voices had lied; they had failed to save her, and she apologized to the English and Burgundians for having killed so many and wishing them in hell.[10] Whatever her terror as she approached the stake, this nineteen-year-old girl, who could only sign her name if her hand was guided and who had fought tenaciously and eloquently throughout her trial to defend her voices and male attire, accepted her inevitable and agonizing death with immense courage. She died, as De Quincey wrote, grandly. Her story is a marvelous fairy tale with a dreadful ending which human imagination and outrage have been trying to change ever since. But despite Paul Claudel's magnificent words to Arthur Honegger's music in *Jeanne d'Arc au Bûcher*—"What Joan could not achieve by force of arms, she is to consummate with her blood"[11]—Joan of Arc did not sacrifice herself in the expectation that her death would help liberate France. No French troops marched against the English shouting revenge for the Maid of Orléans's death; nor did her king lift a finger to save her. Joan died because she would not stop wearing men's clothing and would not renounce the truthfulness and divine origin of revelations and prophecies made to her by inhabitants of the heavenly kingdom, two of whom—Saint Catherine and Saint Margaret—have since been pronounced specious and legendary and have been struck off the calendar of saints by the same institution that finally got around to sanctifying her in 1920. In doing so, however, Rome circumscribed its canonization; it called Saint Joan an exceptionally virtuous and courageous woman but made no mention of her defense of the Catholic faith, let alone the territorial integrity of France. Only in poetry and fiction, it would seem, can political murder be elevated into a martyrdom about which everyone can agree.

Joan of Arc's terror and suffering grip the mind; the injustice of what occurred 566 years ago cries out; but, alas, history runs red with human suffering, and its slaughterhouses, dungeons, prison cells, interrogation rooms, psychiatric wards, and arenas are soaked in pain. Countless men and women have died alone and forsaken simply because they would not adjust their thinking or their actions to their tormentors' will. The unknown martyr must be reckoned in the hundreds of thousands, supremely brave or stubborn individuals, as the case may be, whose names are preserved only in the annals of eternity. But for the chronicler to record, for society to react, and for history to award the martyr's laurels, publicity and choice are central to martyrdom.

T. S. Eliot once wrote that martyrdom is "never an accident" but is always "the design of God."[12] Yet martyrdom for all of its religious and teleological overtones is at heart a public and political spectacle. It is the most dramatic symbol of defiance and condemnation that a man or woman can achieve, a display of individuality sealed and sanctified by death. It strikes at the spiritual sinews of society, placing in question the collective integrity and legitimacy of the dominant group. As such martyrs are the thrice-born product of society, which creates the authority they violate, responds to their so-called criminal behavior, and eventually passes judgment on the meaning of their deaths.

The second half of the nineteenth century was relatively free of martyrs, not so much because there was any scarcity of passionate individuals who maintained that "men were nothing, principles were everything" as because the Western European liberal state—its property owners, its ideologues, and its power brokers—did not feel overly threatened by their presence. Even extreme political deviants were tolerated as "heroes of conscience" and misguided idealists motivated by the purest of impulses, in contrast to the gutter-variety criminal, who acted from greed, laziness, perversity, and immorality. In much of Western Europe, political and altruistic criminals were even accorded preferential treatment, being housed separately from conventional prisoners and allotted milder and less degrading confinement. And why not? They were seen as being morally superior to the common thief, and the very loftiness of their motives shielded them from normal fear of punishment. "To impose harsh penalties," it was argued, "on the nondeterrable" was "both futile and cruel."[13] In such a climate the martyr withered and died. Martyrdom needed dissension and passion, and above all the violent emotional reaction of the legal machinery of state to generate the publicity required and produce the kind of death that could achieve the martyr's purpose.

In order to perform properly, the martyr must be confronted with a simple and immediate choice: conform or die (often unpleasantly). Both elements of the decision—deliberate refusal and positive acceptance of the consequences—must be in the form of a public and legal charade. Had Elizabeth I of England achieved her way, her rival and cousin, Mary Queen of Scots, would never have been proclaimed a martyr by her many supporters. For years Catholic Mary Stuart, as the unwanted and carefully confined visitor south of the border, had been violating English law and outraging Protestant sensibilities, and Elizabeth's preferred solution was to have the lady quietly murdered in bed; but no matter how broadly Bess hinted, she could find no one willing to do the job. Instead, her government's official response to Mary's "treason" was to place the woman on trial—thereby affording her a heaven-sent forum upon which to defend her cause—and then have her publicly executed, an occasion in which the Scottish queen was at her dramatic best, securing for herself a place in the martyr's hall of fame.[14] Likewise, Joan of Arc as a martyr can be said to have been the product of inept English public relations. In purchasing the Maid of Orléans from her Burgundian captors for ten thousand crowns and executing her, the English military transformed a rather embarrassing French peasant girl into an undying heroine. A distraught English soldier exclaimed at her death, "God forgive us; we have burned a saint";[15] more accurately he should have said, "We have created one."

The battle that martyrs have had to fight to metamorphose themselves from condemned criminals into recorded saints has not been confined to the torture chamber, the stake, or the execution block. Martyrs have been at the mercy of time as well as judicial proceedings. The judgment of history has been just as cruel to their image as any failure of will in the struggle with officialdom. As the causes for which and against which they have stood have waned and waxed, martyrs have been forced back into those categories reserved by society for its deviants and misfits—the criminal, the heretic, the psychopath, and the traitor—or, worse, they have been entirely forgotten, denied even a Judas memory. But history has one redeeming feature: it has been highly susceptible—regardless of the cause—to the theatrics of a fine performance; and style remains the key to the martyr's credibility and reputation. Death, like any other human endeavor, is an art, and if martyrs are to prevail, they must die, to use Sylvia Plath's expression, "exceptionally well."[16]

Over the centuries martyrs, particularly the Christian variety, have possessed a clear but demanding historic script for enacting their parts during both the initial legal proceedings and the ultimate test of faith. They had before them the picture of those early Christians who approached death in a Roman arena almost as a calling.[17] Martyrdom as a vocation meant above all else maintaining control over the particulars of death. The splendor of the battle rested not so much in the outcome as in the dignity of the act, and that in turn meant keeping absolute management over the process.

Ever since martyrdom was first conceived as an act of symbolic protest and a necessary means to some transcendent end, many have been called but few, outside of martyrological fiction, have played the role to such perfection that they could achieve the self-control and compassionate detachment of the future Buddha who transformed his body into a hare, shook himself thoroughly lest an innocent flea die in the flames, and jumped into the fire to offer himself as a meal for a hungry beggar.[18] Possibly the ideal as it had been worked out over a millennium and a half was approached in the account of the execution of the English priest Edmund Genings for high treason in 1591. Every word he spoke was a mirror of composure, decorum, and considered choice. He "joyfully saluted the gibbet prepared for him" and, standing upon the ladder with a rope around his neck, conversed politely with his persecutor, a loudmouthed priest hunter named Richard Topcliffe. "Genings, Genings," shouted Topcliffe, "confess thy fault, thy Popish treason, and the Queen by [your] submission no doubt will grant thee pardon." Genings's answer was a paradigm of cool reason, moderation, and propriety. "I know not, Mr. Topcliffe, in what I have offended my dear anointed Princess; for if I had offended her, or any other, in any thing, I would willingly ask her and all the world forgiveness. If she be offended with me without a cause, for professing my faith and religion, because I am a priest . . . I shall be, I trust, excused and innocent before God. I must obey God, saith St. Peter, rather than men, and I must not in this case acknowledge a fault where there is none." Topcliffe in a fury ordered the hangman to "turn the ladder" and bid him cut the priest down while still living. It was then that Genings showed his true mettle and control. As his genitals were being cut off and his belly ripped open, he proved himself to be an absolute master of understatement. In his agony he said in a clear voice, "Oh, it smarts!"[19]

The response of the martyrs to the agony of torture and death by fire and mutilation raises a basic problem for a society such as ours, which views the alleviation of suffering, animal and human, as the highest good. We are profoundly disturbed, as William James noted, by any culture that not only accepts pain as normal but at times actually welcomes it.[20] Of course, possibly the enormous self-control exercised by the martyrs in the face of excruciating pain lies largely in the description of their hagiographers and not in actual fact. There are enough accounts of the desperate efforts of would-be saints to reverse the process of their martyrdom, to struggle out of the flames only to be thrust back with spears and poles, to give strength to our innate suspicion that the picture of the martyr in perfect control of his death is a myth.[21]

Not only is the twentieth century disturbed by the thought of unnecessary suffering, but it is also deeply puzzled by the martyr's response to pain. Dolcino, the archheretic of northern Italy in the early fourteenth century, who was executed with excruciating agony, was reported by a bitterly unfriendly and biased chronicler to have died with extraordinary serenity. In a public and perambulating display, the heretic was systematically mutilated with white-hot pincers "till all his flesh was torn piece-meal from his limbs," but he never dissolved into the mindless raving mass of scorched flesh and nerves desired by his tormentors. "Only when they tore the nose from his face" was he seen "spasmodically to shrug his shoulders," and "a faint sigh" and "a slight contraction" manifested itself in the muscles of his face when the iron burned away his testicles.[22]

What the martyrs experienced in their suffering is beyond our comprehension. Whether they sought and gained, as so many claimed, divinely induced mental and physical inhibitors that permitted them to withstand torments that we can only imagine from brief encounters with the dentist's drill is, like all matters of sensation, beyond documentation. Whether some lucky few were born with extraordinarily high pain thresholds or were able through some psychic and neurological process to change pain into ecstasy are questions that defy answers, because pain is incapable of being shared or measured. As Virginia Woolf has written: "Let a sufferer try to describe a pain in his head to a doctor and language at once runs dry."[23]

Physical pain, it has been said, "is not simply a function of the amount of bodily damage alone"; the response "differs from person to person" and, equally important, from "culture to culture."[24] In one of the few cases where language did not run dry, the seventeenth-century French Huguenot Blanche Gamond was able to record her tortures in words that make it clear that response to pain is not a quantifiable reaction but instead a deeply personal sensation, as much the result of cultural and psychological influences as of physical injury. She was stripped naked to the waist and hung from the ceiling by her wrists, the cord being drawn as tight as her tormentors could manage. She was beaten by six women who kept saying, "Pray now to your God." Suddenly, in the midst of her ordeal, she sensed "the greatest consolation that I can ever receive in my life, since I had the honor of being whipped for the name of Christ." Her experience, she said, transcended words: "Why can I not write down the inconceivable influences, consolations and peace which I felt interiorly?" She had to fall back upon sexual comparisons to express her ecstasy. Her joys "were so great that I was ravished." Her torturers cried out, "We must double our blows; she does not feel them, for she neither speaks nor cries." Blanche's explanation was simple and direct. "How should I have cried, since I was swooning with happiness within?"[25]

Even if we accept the close relationship of pain to ecstasy, our credence is tested further by those heroes of the faith who with perfect timing arranged to expire in the flames with an appropriate message to mankind upon their lips, rejoicing that their suffering would assure them life eternal. The twentieth century is profoundly skeptical of those spiritual athletes who brilliantly enacted a performance in which word, style, and theatrics were all in perfect accord. We sense that such storybook martyrs must be the figment of years of accumulative imagination on the part of hagiographers, unencumbered by historical truth and seeking to dramatize those virtues and strengths essential to their own faith and society. If such paragons actually existed as living men and women, we suspect that reality was far different from their idealized forms. Behind the saintly facade we seek and often find the hidden and secret face of psychotic self-interest, bigotry, and pride. It is only too easy to argue that the martyr was in fact a sick and disjointed personality, as much the hapless product of a divided and floundering society as of the demons of his own mind, scarcely deserving of our admiration, let alone the name of martyr.

Once upon a time society accepted its heroes for what they were—inspirational but rather gaudy and two-dimensional examples of what men and women hold highest: courage, endurance, humility, and compassion. They were golden vessels filled with the essence of divinity and humanity. Today the world is less gullible and a great deal more cynical. We assume the existence of clay feet. It is almost axiomatic that "the greater the genius, the greater the unsoundness."[26] Whisper the words "unconscious motivation," hint at the existence of a martyr personality, or suggest that a "genius" is not someone possessed of special gifts but simply an individual who has in some fashion departed from the norm—an aberration—and the martyr is lucky to survive with a shred of reputation intact.

The dry and brittle parchment upon which the storybook martyr is fictionalized disintegrates the moment it is bent to achieve a three-dimensional effect. The principle of inverse optics operates when viewing martyrs: the more distant they are, the more attractive they appear. Nothing becomes them so splendidly as the glory of their demise, and invariably their lives are recounted backwards—a celebration of death, rarely an understanding of life—and narrated in terms of the heroic perspective of the small voice of conviction pitted against an ocean of bigotry. On close encounter, however, martyrs are found to be twisted, harsh, unyielding people, possessed of what used to be called before the days of psychiatric terminology "cranky" minds—moody, unpredictable, opinionated and self-absorbed.[27] Almost without exception they are people who are willing to do unto others what others have done unto them because they believe themselves to be the possessors of truth for which they are not only willing to die but also willing to have others die. Those who feel within them a sense of uniqueness and destiny; who are obliged to take upon themselves the burdens of mankind—either as social reformers or as spiritual warriors against Satan—who possess a special knowledge of the truth or who concern themselves exclusively with the mystery of eternity and the ultimate meaning of creation, find it difficult to adjust their actions or their thoughts to the normal dilemmas of daily life. Apathy is alien to them, and so, therefore, is tolerance. The price of such absoluteness is dear, for "he who would be friends with God," wrote Gandhi, "must remain alone or make the whole world his friend"; either way, such friendship entails a retreat from normal human contacts.[28] Saint and martyr possess an inner identity that sets them off from the rest of mankind. They are men and women incapable of accepting compromise or accommodating to the needs of others, and more often than not their determination to sacrifice themselves is accompanied by an equal willingness to sacrifice others. They have no need of friend, family, or community.

Martyrs are strong. They make no concessions to the world. They recognize a higher allegiance and on occasion are happy to betray the loyalties that lesser men and women hold sacred. Obsessed with the ultimate pattern of things, martyrs are driven to act upon the knowledge that they are God's or history's instrument for achieving or defending absolute truth. Nevertheless, for all their stalwart qualities and manifest virtues, the martyr retains a disturbing flaw which the rest of mankind is quick to mark. Martyrs by their death present clear evidence that their greatest strength may be their gravest weakness: they cannot live in society with their fellow human beings. "The moral distortions," it has been observed, "of saint and miser differ in quality, not in psychology."[29] What, then, of a martyr's motivation, conscious or otherwise? Behind the heavy veil of humility, piety, and high-minded sacrifice reside what secret demons and unsatiated desires?

Throughout the history of martyrdom one point, at least until the twentieth century, is inescapable: the religious martyr expected to gain by death. The men and women who over the centuries deliberately elected to die for their particular brand of faith, no matter how attractive or distasteful their convictions may have been to prevailing opinion, can be said to have been responding to some variety of self-interest. The early Christian martyrs in particular have been closely scrutinized from that point of view.[30] The absolute certainty afforded by martyrdom of a personal immortality, a reserved seat among the angels and the assurance of an undying place in the memories of their fellow Christians, eternally worshiped as members of God's chosen elite, could be fatally attractive. Whatever the backsliding, drudgery, and insignificance that accompanied their lives on earth, second- and third-century Christian martyrs achieved in death that one uncontroversial act of heroism which made them memorable both in the eyes of God and man. No longer could anyone say their lives had been inconsequential. The lure of martyrdom had not subsided one iota by the end of the seventeenth century, and the author of *A Preparation for Martyrdom*, composed in 1682, could still assure his readers that the heavenly reward for a martyr's death was "even greater than to other saints who did not pass through that Red Sea of blood to the Promised Land."[31] It was on these grounds—too much being received for too little—that Phyllis McGinley in her charming book *Saint-Watching* deliberately excluded the early Christian martyrs: "It's easy to be a martyr. You only have to be it once."[32]

We can understand, even applaud, normal human cravings for a secure place in some highly anthropomorphic heaven perceived as a perfectly structured and idealized version of man's society on earth. But peel back the carefully contrived veneer of stereotyped piety and heroism imposed by hagiographers, and we sense the existence of the dark abyss of psychosis: the agony, the courage, and the distorted logic of personalities that have long since passed spiritual hypochondria by and are well on the road to madness.[33] Our flesh crawls with a mixture of fascination, disbelief, and horror at the picture of Richard Bayfield in 1531 standing in the fire, reaching up without a break in his prayers and yanking off the charred stump of his left arm so that it "fell from his body," or at the image of James Bainham who, half consumed by the flames, assured his audience that he felt "no more pain than if I were in a bed of down."[34] Surely such behavior involved something more than just what the sixteenth century referred to as being "hearty in God's cause."[35] We must be dealing with intensely disturbed men and women, devoured by obsessions, seeking beatification, and constructing for themselves a self-defined and self-achieved immortality which sets up impenetrable walls to guard the soul from doubt and fear. Any absolute triumph over doubt, it has wisely been observed, is an adequate "definition of psychosis."[36]

From the moment martyrdom was first enacted, martyrs have been subjected to various levels of psychoanalytic inspection. Some critics have accused them of having too much enthusiasm for the flames and dismissed them as self-murderers; some have openly branded them as psychopaths, obsessed with a death wish, "martyrs of Satan"; and some have pointed to evidence of masochism, paranoia, and manic depression. Still others have dismissed martyrs as ill-adjusted and pathetic individuals, social rejects, desperately striving to find meaning in life and attempting to draw attention to themselves by the only path open to them. Their tormented behavior, such skeptics argue, is psychologically no different from the exhibitionism of the psychopath who, in his rage against society, guns down dozens of innocent people in order to be noticed, if only briefly in tomorrow's headlines.

The possibility that martyrdom might be only faintly disguised suicide on the part of emotionally disturbed people who were determined, consciously or unconsciously, to end their own lives is a deeply worrisome proposition, because it strikes at the teleological roots of a performance that for many Christians is regarded as being providential. Martyrs are supposed to be humble instruments of divine will, not initiators of their own destruction.

Suicide unfortunately is an act of supreme egotism whether it be viewed psychologically—the most "brutal way of making sure that you will not readily be forgotten"—or theologically—the usurpation of divine authority.[37] Consequently the quickest way to defrock martyrs and deprive them of their laurels has been to accuse them of "tragic show," as the emperor Marcus Aurelius did of the early Christians, or of "Suicide while of Unsound Mind," as did the fourth knight of Thomas Becket in Eliot's *Murder in the Cathedral*.[38] The only really effective rebuttal to such an attack is the one directed at Thomas Thackham in 1557 which accused him of bias and self-interest. Thackham had dismissed Julius Palmer's death at the stake as self-murder, and Palmer's defender wrote, "[I] sayeth that he died a martyr unto the Lord; you say in effect that he ended his life as a castaway and willful destroyer of himself. To be short, the story justifieth the martyrdom. You, to justify yourself, deface the martyr."[39]

Defacing martyrs has had a long and distinguished history, and even the hagiographer John Foxe had to admit that his sixteenth-century Protestant heroes were on occasion far from being normal people. His martyrs, he confessed, seemed at times to be desperately insecure; they lacked any sense of proportion, treating trifles as mountains.[40] Less friendly observers have been struck by the pathological overtones of the words reported to Saint Cyprian: "What is more blessed . . . than to have begun to love one's punishments, after having faith to bear them?"[41] Nor has it gone undetected that numerous hints of masochism and sexual perversion, as much as spiritual ecstasy, underlay the early Christian martyr's attraction for torture and death.[42]

In the hands of the analyst, martyrs have been transformed into hapless psychotics seeking death as a solution or absolution for the guilt, frustration, anger, and insecurity that lay within them. But at least psychotic martyrs can be said to have retained their own individuality and to have possessed their private, if warped, reasons for death. A far worse fate has been reserved for martyrs at the hands of the twentieth-century sociologist who has sought to deprive them not only of their spiritual identity but also of their uniqueness. The martyr is cast as the product and symptom of a certain stage of social development, and the "martyr habit" seen not as a malaise of the soul but as a disease of society, an institutionally induced addiction.[43]

Undeniably, martyrs rarely appear singly. They are usually a group phenomenon, taking strength from their sense of collective identity and representing, in their defiance and denial of the existing order and judicial code, serious rifts within society. Unbalanced and unstable societies experiencing a process of cultural, economic, and political restructuring obviously generate martyrs. But so also do expanding and crusading societies, invigorated by large numbers of highly indoctrinated and motivated people who are willing to die for their faith, for their nation state, or for a political-social ideal. Likewise, decaying or beleaguered societies generate men and women who prefer death, often communal, to surrender or absorption. But having said that it takes two to persecute—martyrs require a peculiar concatenation of political and cultural ingredients and imbalances in order to flourish—one has said very little about why certain individuals deliberately make sacrifices of themselves. Doubtless some societies are more prone to martyrdom than others. Equally obvious, martyrdom can be extraordinarily contagious, but to date no one has been able to prove that the contagion was class oriented, either politically or economically, or that age was in any way a determining factor. The demographic evidence is scarce, but martyrs, young and old, male and female, seem to have come from all walks of life.[44]

The martyr is far too elusive a creature to be caught in the coarse net of social-scientific generalizations or class divisions. Not only do martyrs defy easy categorization, but also much depends on society's definition of abnormal behavior. Is one gentleman martyr, entrapped by the accident of his political and official position, to be equated to one artisan martyr who deliberately brings himself to the attention of the government? Is the Roman slave who refuses to betray her mistress making the same level of sacrifice as the church leader who knows he must die as an example to the faithful? Is the man or woman, minion or master, who is culturally conditioned to admire martyrdom and regards the martyr as the highest role model, the same quality of hero as the psychopathic personality who greedily embraces the flames? Martyrs simply do not lend themselves to an overly socialized or environmentally oriented view of humanity. They remain too individualistic; and that, of course, is the final rub—they can be accused of the sin of pride.

The link between the moral and the psychological has not gone unnoticed, and Ernest Becker in *The Denial of Death* has written that "both sin and neurosis represent the individual blowing himself up to larger than his true size."[45] Pride deprives a person of a sense of proportion and a sense of reality; to use C. S. Lewis's phraseology, it prevents you from "seeing yourself from the outside."[46] The martyr indulges in self-inflation and self-levitation. It is the "self," the "I," that is so difficult to judge and that can be so dangerous to the institution or cause that seeks to harness and use the intense spiritual energy released by martyrdom.

The truth of the confusion is that history crawls with an immense variety of martyrs, every one of whom is somebody's criminal, traitor, psychopath, murderer, or just plain fool. But whatever the label attached or the motives assigned, all martyrs have two things in common: unlike heroes who are products of a consensus society where the quality and worth of their heroic acts are not in dispute, martyrs tend to be the offspring of a society in conflict with itself; and they are very special kinds of villains—they commit offenses of the mind and of the heart, and only rarely do they perpetrate crimes of the body. Martyrs violate the most revered and treasured abstractions that shape and create a society, giving it its uniqueness and vigor. Only inadvertently do they commit crimes against property. They strike at ties of loyalty, allegiance, and sense of collective security, while at the same time they defy society's—at least the ruling elite's—definitions of justice, mercy, honor, love, and duty.

In the final verdict upon the martyr, intent and style are central to the emotional as well as the intellectual response to any given performance. There is, moreover, an inescapable relativity embedded in any final judgment, which must encompass at least four variables: the quality of the motive, the acceptability of the cause, the accidents of timing and circumstance, and the dramatic mode of the death. Only if all four are perfectly attuned and suited to one another can a common death be transfigured into a spectacle of lasting meaning. But despite the variables, we also understand that martyrs are neither simpleminded heroes, spontaneously or accidentally risking or sacrificing their lives for their fellow humans, nor blind victims of happenstance. Choice—sometimes desired, sometimes enforced—and premeditation are all-important, because there is nothing impulsive or accidental about the act of martyrdom. It must be part of some long-term enterprise in which the fashion of the death and the credibility of the martyr are regarded as essential elements in the ultimate success of the venture. There is a profound difference between a willingness to take a risk, even to court destruction, and the deliberate walking into the torture chamber or the fire and purposefully bolting the door on escape. These are the crucial considerations that explain why so many of our favorite and time-honored heroes who have acquired the name of martyr have not found their way into the chapters that follow: they made no special contribution to martyrdom as a concept.

The idea of martyrdom, as it has evolved in the West, does not lend itself to topical analysis; martyrs are too aggressively individualistic to be caged and classified.[47] The human, not the theoretical, components dominate their stories, and the martyrs who appear in this volume have been selected because their lives highlight the complexities of definition and analysis. Only when the drama of their deaths has been narrated and each ordered and paraded as an example of human heroism or folly does the full mystery and fascination of the subject begin to emerge.

Socrates taking the hemlock cup: His sense of timing and instinct for stage center have rarely been matched.

CHAPTER 2

SOCRATES:
THE GENESIS OF MARTYRDOM

Who storms the moss-grown walls of eld
And beats some falsehood down
Shall pass the pallid gates of death
Sans laurel, love, or crown;
For him who fain would teach the world
The world holds hate in fee—
For Socrates, the hemlock cup;
For Christ, Gethsemane.
—D.R.P. MARQUIS,
"The Wages"

*T*HE CONCEPT of martyrdom, as well as the world's first recorded martyr, emerged fully developed from the head of Plato; and to this day Socrates' performance—the cold deliberateness of his actions, the dramatic style of his death, and the purpose for which he died—has stamped and befuddled the history of martyrdom. It is impossible to disentangle the man from the legend, for Socrates is the ultimate historical paradox: a fictionalized reality. He has been studied from a host of perspectives: as the intellectual pillar upon which Plato hung many of his philosophical precepts; as the seminal godfather of authoritarianism and elitism in politics; as the harbinger and herald of the immortality of the human soul; and finally as the man who defined and practiced virtue in a way that had never been done before and who sought to prove that through the exercise of pure reason the individual, even in the face of herd hysteria, unreason, and the interference of the gods, could maintain absolute control over mind and body and destiny. In an oft-reiterated phrase, Socrates was a secular saint.

Such a many-faceted Socrates is, of course, a myth. Historical reality is something quite different, but nobody is agreed on how different.[1] Socrates the man left no records—he would have failed miserably in today's academic environment of publish or perish—and although his trial and execution in 399 B.C. became the cause célèbre of the classical world and his ideas the battleground for partisans and critics alike, the only firsthand accounts of his personality come from the unreliable pens of a handful of youthful and highly biased contemporaries. Plato's literary magic and imagination are largely responsible for the Socratic legend, but he was almost two generations younger than his mentor and at the time of the execution was at home sick in bed. Xenophon, who was probably no older than Plato, wrote a heavy-fisted apologetic about the philosopher, but had left Athens three years before his hero's trial and death. Aeschines of Sphettus was at the death scene, but only a few fragments of his writings remain, mostly about the master's most notorious pupil, Alcibiades. And the opinions of the comic playwright Aristophanes have survived only in the form of his burlesque of Socrates' think factory as a ridiculous assortment of silly sophists with their heads in the clouds. Besides these four accounts, there is an abundance of hearsay exaggerations, doubtful traditions, and the opinions—generally unfavorable—of a number of contemporaries whose views can only be surmised from other people's writings. Many of these bits and pieces eventually found their way into the martyr's first extant biography, little more than an essay in length and a collage of quotations, written over half a millennium after his death.[2] As a corpus of evidence the Socratic sources engender little confidence, and the personality which emerges is so infuriatingly improbable that the reader begins to suspect that the father of martyrdom was too noble by half and deserved the hemlock cup twice over: for his insufferable arrogance as well as his caustic humor and irritating logic.

The human animal from the moment it assumed the disguise of humanity has proved its willingness to die, and men and women have rushed to sacrifice their lives, sometimes carelessly and without thought, sometimes rationally and with deliberation, for a multitude of reasons—to safeguard their beloved, to defend their kin, to satiate and sanctify some power beyond their comprehension, to defend an ideal, or even to prove a point. But Socrates was the first historic individual who, with logic aforethought, elected to die a martyr to a mission that he felt to be both essential to his life on earth and part of a divine and cosmic ordinance decreed from on high, or, as Socrates would more likely have conceived it, from below. Central to that mission were the fashion and timing of his death, which became his passage both to historic immortality and to the eternity of existence beyond the grave.

Socrates lived at a moment that was peculiarly conducive to the invention of martyrdom, for the tiny world that contained him—Athens of the late fifth century B.C.—was undergoing immense social and psychological traumas. In a single lifetime, Socrates' own—469 to 399 B.C.—Athenian society experienced first a spectacular expansion of the intellect accompanied by an explosion of commercial wealth and the development of democratic institutions, and then ignominious military and political collapse. In the midst of a city undergoing unprecedented change resided Athens's self-ordained "gadfly," a man who seems to have been designed by some well-intentioned but otherwise inept deity to be a martyr. As a sage and pre-Christian saint, Socrates violates our sense of decorum. Broad-shouldered, stocky, and muscular—a physique that seems to have been attractive to both sexes—Socrates appears more suited to the locker room than the schoolroom. But behind the snub nose, pop eyes, and satyrish expression resided a devastatingly sharp and witty mind that made no concessions to human folly, and a moral righteousness that is hard to differentiate from pride.

When Socrates was born to a stone craftsman's family sometime around 469 B.C., Athens was on the threshold of two and a half generations of intellectual and political brilliance that filled contemporaries with self-congratulation tinged with acute anxiety and left later generations with a sense of envy and amazement. The age of Periclean Athens, of Sophocles and Euripides, of Herodotus and Thucydides, was taking shape. So also was the Delian League, which supplied the wealth and commerce that made possible the Parthenon, which a grateful city dedicated to its patron goddess, and the series of walls that protected the Acropolis and linked it with the port of Piraeus. As Athens grew from a petty city-state into a Mediterranean naval power and converted her confederacy of island allies into a commercial empire, she clashed with her military and political rival, Sparta. The conflict started when Socrates was only ten, but the ravens of war were not fully uncaged until 433 B.C. when the truth of Thucydides' observations was realized: "War gave birth to every kind of inequity. . . . There was no reconciling force—no promise binding, no oath that inspired awe."[3] Twenty-seven years later, when Socrates was sixty-three, the struggle ended in defeat and political humiliation for Athens. An embittered and deeply shaken and divided polis, looking for the traitor within its gates who could have sapped the moral strength of a city that only a generation earlier had confidently laid the cornerstone to the Parthenon, found an outlet for its paranoia in the trial and execution of Socrates. By a vote of 360 to 140 Socrates' fellow citizens decreed his execution for "refusing to recognize the gods recognized by the state" and "introducing other new divinities. He is also guilty of corrupting the youth."[4] Embedded in these graceless and imprecise words stands a twisted edifice of mutually interlocking private and public motives that led to Western history's first martyrdom.

Socrates had about him two qualities that earned him the enmity, as well as the admiration, of nearly everyone who knew him, and which almost guaranteed him a martyr's crown. He possessed an "iron self-sufficiency" that set him off from his fellow Athenians.[5] He seems to have had no need for or any particular respect for the social and political milieu in which he lived or for the good opinion of those around him. And Plato attributed to him a second characteristic—an infallible gift for attracting attention.[6] His sense of timing and instinct for stage center have rarely been matched.

Socrates started his teaching career as one of a number of sophists who practiced their pedagogical craft in the markets and gymnasiums of the city, but with Socrates there was a difference. He charged nothing for his wisdom, and he spent the last decades of his life ruthlessly demonstrating the shallowness of his colleagues' philosophies and the fallacies of their logic. There was little love lost between Socrates and the other sophists, who not only trained the sons of tradesmen and artisans in public debate and rhetoric but also purported to teach them virtue and ethics and tended to be diviners and interpreters of the gods on the side. One suspects that professional rivalry may have helped swing the vote against Socrates, who prided himself on the quality of his thinking and the aristocratic standing of his clientele.

Intellectual challenge and skepticism were in the air. Athens was slowly turning away from the old Homeric deities and archaic explanation of creation, beginning to formulate dangerously abstract notions about a cosmos composed of ether and atoms, and edging its way toward a definition of the individual free from the bondage of the family and ritual dependence upon the gods. Radicals even questioned the existence of the gods, and argued that man should measure justice and truth, honor and virtue by the conventions of society. Insistence on a higher and divine authority, they said, was in reality nothing but a childish projection of man's own need to transform momentary might into enduring right. Much to the horror and disgust of an older generation, the philosophy of relativism and pragmatism was in a halting, but insidious, fashion being voiced as a rule and guide for Athenian life, especially among the young.

Although Socrates had little sympathy for the peddlers of materialism and atheism, his religious views were profoundly disturbing, for, as he confessed, he dared inquire "into things under the earth and in heaven," which exposed him to the accusation that he was "a god-maker" who disbelieved in the old deities and was bent on "producing new ones."[7] He rejected the anthropomorphic and unreliable gods of the Homeric past, believing instead in the existence of a divinely inspired and ultimately purposeful universe, in which humanity played a vital, if supremely difficult, role. Religion for Socrates was not "the art of commercial exchanges between gods and men" whereby the deities in an outrageously unbalanced transaction were expected to perform miracles on behalf of their worshipers in return for trifling sacrificial offerings which the gods could not possibly need. He rejected as unacceptable the traditional behavior of the gods, who were blind to the moral chaos that their irresponsible actions produced on both Olympus and earth. Instead, he predicated a single morality for god and man. The gods were inspired by piety and the will to do good, and the goal of humanity was to incorporate such divinity into this world and to live virtuously, doing good to others as the gods would wish.[8]

Socrates' gods were both beneficent and dependable. Throughout his adult life, he accepted as his private "divine sign" his *daimonion,* or guardian voice, which led him to stop and consider the consequences of his decisions, and he never questioned that Apollo spoke through the oracle at Delphi.[9] He was, as Plato portrayed him, a mystic and a visionary who possessed a kind of "madness that comes by divine gift."[10] He experienced periodic trances of various durations: one, during his military service, struck him outside his tent at dawn, and there he stood immobile for twenty-four hours until the next morning, when "with the return of light he offered up a prayer to the sun and went his way."[11] The divine for Socrates was omnipresent throughout the cosmos, and as he internalized that vision, he began to articulate what was already in other men's minds, a definition of the individual possessed of a conscience susceptible to good and evil and of a personality that was a reflection of the soul within, which in its turn knew itself to be answerable to the gods.

So long as Athens prospered and war brought its fair share of victory and economic gain, the city could afford to ignore novelty of thought and irreverence to the ancient gods; but in 430 B.C. the first of the ravens of war descended upon the polis and typhus fed upon its citizens, a sure sign of divine irritation. Then ensued almost two decades of military ineptitude mitigated by occasional good luck and tactical brilliance, and internal discord driven by personal greed and ambition. In the wake of both followed military humiliation and the overthrow of democracy. In defeat Athens needed an explanation, and Socrates, commanding as he always did stage center, was highly visible and available. Whether the city picked the right man was at the time—and still is—a matter of impassioned debate.

In one sense the accusation was monstrous. Socrates trained young minds; he did not corrupt them. He preached and practiced a quality of belief in the gods far more spiritual than that of his fellow Athenians, and he never overtly mocked or condemned their ritualistic worship of household and city deities. Nor did he have anything to do with Athens's defeat. On the contrary, his military career as an armed foot soldier was impeccable, and he had little to do personally with the bitter factional strife between oligarchy and democracy that tore the city to pieces as the war progressed. But in another sense, Socrates was suspect on two counts: as an arrogant man obsessed with a mission, and as a teacher and associate of two of the most disliked and dangerous political leaders in the city. These two distinguished pupils, the wealthy and talented Alcibiades and Critias, were deeply involved in the disasters that beset Athens, and it was well known that their mentor dismissed as political naiveté the argument that government entailed the participation of all free men, no matter how uneducated, and that he advocated the enlightened rule of a professional and intellectual elite. If, as the sophists so doggedly maintained, virtue was the offspring of knowledge, then Alcibiades and Critias should have been brilliant tests of the thesis; but unfortunately their actions seemed only to prove that war and defeat spawn violence, greed, and extremism.

Alcibiades, on whom his master doted, was the leader of the war party; and for reasons that had as much to do with political exhibitionism as with sound military strategy, he persuaded the Athenian council in 415 B.C. to send him as the co-leader of a brilliantly conceived but poorly executed amphibious expedition against Syracuse. Shortly before the fleet sailed, a particularly flagrant example of religious hoodlumism occurred when one morning Athens awoke to discover the busts of Hermes that adorned most doorways smashed and desecrated, the obvious consequence of impiety and religious laxity. During the ensuing investigation, reports were unearthed about midnight orgies and drunken burlesquing of the Eleusinian mysteries. Alcibiades's name was linked with these religious outrages, and just before the fleet arrived at Syracuse he was relieved of his command and ordered home to stand trial. Instead he fled and turned traitor, joining Sparta in the war against his home city, claiming that he loved his country so much that he would "go [to] all lengths to recover it."[12] Eleven years later, naked in his mistress's bed, he was murdered by assassins sent by his old student colleague Critias.

The career of Critias was equally dramatic and disastrous. He was a gifted dramatist and poet who was one of the most eloquent leaders of the oligarchical faction and the most ruthless "reformer" in the Council of Thirty that in 404 B.C., with the help of Sparta's armed presence, overthrew the democratic government, which was held responsible for Athens's defeat. Politically, Critias sought to implement Socrates' creed that only "the ones who know" should have power; he did so by systematically exiling or judicially murdering his political opponents. Critias's actions produced their predictable reactions, and along with the other leaders of the "Thirty Tyrants" he was slain in battle; and in 401 B.C. a shaky and deeply divided democracy was again restored. It was, in fact, one of the most sublime ironies of history that the man who confessed ignorance to be a virtue and knowledge to be unattainable except by the constant probing of specious arguments should have been the intellectual mentor of two men who had all the earmarks of the ideologue and who believed and practiced that the end justifies the means. Socrates may not have corrupted young minds, but as a consequence of his constant prying into false premises, he may inadvertently have helped to strip from his pupils' personalities those muddled and contradictory instincts that tend to fetter unbridled egotism and keep under control the temptation to impose self-perceived truths on others.

It is doubtless unfair to burden the pedagogue with the sins of his students three decades after they had left the classroom, but in 399 B.C. the memory of those sinners was still fresh, and public prejudice could point out that Socrates himself in the intervening years had done little to earn his city's endearment or esteem. If, as Thucydides suggested, war and civil discord foster the worst in society, in the case of Socrates they engendered the best, but in a fashion so extreme that it resulted in antagonizing almost everybody. The man who stood trial in 399 B.C. for impiety to the gods and corrupting young minds was a far different person from the sophist who some thirty years before had taught Alcibiades and Critias. Some time around his fortieth year, just as the Peloponnesian War was heating up, Socrates seems to have undergone a religious experience. Today we might describe it as a middle-aged identity crisis: Plato simply says his master found his "mission" in life. The teacher of men suddenly became the seeker after a truth for which he was willing to make any sacrifice.

The genesis of that mission is so bedeviled with the usual contradictions that envelope Socrates' career that it is impossible to tell whether his quest was inspired by honest humility or egregious arrogance. The story of the Delphic oracle's choice of Socrates as the wisest of men and of Socrates' realization that in some obscure fashion Apollo was directing him upon a personal odyssey to seek out the truth was narrated by Socrates himself at his trial, but there are two versions of what he is purported to have said. Xenophon unwittingly makes him out to be an unpleasant braggart who boasted that the oracle had proclaimed that "no man was more free, more just or more prudent" than Socrates and that he "far excelled the rest of mankind."[13] Plato's representation is different. He plays upon Socrates' marvelous sense of irony and presents the story as a riddle. What had the oracle actually meant when in answer to the question whether "there were anyone wiser" than Socrates, it had answered with a simple negative: no, "there was no man wiser"?[14] Socrates, quite rightly, was baffled by the unqualified nature of the response. He was in a sense trapped; he could not in all humility claim that the gods, who spoke only the truth, were wrong, but, as he confessed, it was hopelessly egotistical to say that they were correct. Moreover, if only the gods possessed true wisdom, it was not much of a compliment to be singled out as the single marginally wise man among a world of fools.

On reflection Socrates decided to dedicate his remaining years to testing the oracle's words; "if I could only find a man wiser than myself, then I might go to the god with a refutation in my hand."[15] The conditional structure of this sentence suggests a conceit almost as great as Xenophon's version, but Plato succeeds in blunting the effect by turning Socrates' quandary into the inspiration for his divine quest. From that moment on he spent his days seeking out all who had reputations for wisdom, only to find that in reality they were as ignorant of true knowledge as he was, but unlike Socrates they refused to admit it. Far from claiming for himself special divine knowledge or sanction, as his detractors maintained, he set about the unenviable task of showing the citizens of Athens that "god only is wise" and that "the wisdom of men is worth little or nothing."[16] He went on his pilgrimage, obedient to god's will, probing, as he said, "the wisdom of anyone, whether citizen or stranger, who appears to be wise; and if he is not wise, then in vindication of the oracle I show him that he is not wise."[17]

That mission, Socrates confessed, not only made him endless enemies but also so completely absorbed his mind that he accepted "utter poverty" as the necessary price of his commitment. His technique for testing truth and rooting out ignorance could be excruciatingly humiliating for the unlucky claimant of knowledge who dared argue with him, and at the same time it could be dangerously destructive, for Socrates, himself ignorant of real wisdom, had nothing to replace what he destroyed. All he could claim was that he had swept his opponents' minds clean of false assumptions, had made them aware of their own ignorance, and thereby had opened their souls to virtue and understanding if they chose to seek them. He sought to teach his fellow Athenians the care of their souls, not the silly acquisition of worldly knowledge. As a consequence, he left behind him a trail of ridiculed and disgruntled enemies that led directly to the accusation that he had corrupted young minds and introduced novel religious ideas.

Given Socrates' intellectual standing in the community and his willingness to speak his mind without restraint, many scholars believe that the religious attack on Athens's irritating gadfly was largely window dressing and that the real, but hidden, motive was political—Socrates as a "crypto-oligarch" was dangerous to an insecure and unstable democracy.[18] Certainly the philosopher's insistence that he was solely a "private man," never a "public man," does not ring true in a participatory democracy that defined citizenship as partaking in the public life of the polis, and Socrates himself did not hesitate to link his own efforts to lead the righteous life with politics. He was, he said, "one of the few Athenians, not to say the only one, to engage in the true political art, and of men of today, I am the only one who does politics."[19] Under the circumstances, it may not be surprising if Socrates' jurors saw him as both a spiritual and a political liability.

And so the stage was set for martyrdom, with all the props necessary for conviction: personal animosity, civic paranoia, political revenge, and a jury willing to persuade itself that the woes of the city belonged firmly at Socrates' feet. He was, as later Christian martyrs would be called, detestable to humanity, for he had outraged the gods, bringing their fury down upon the polis that had raised and protected him. Martyrdom, however, calls for more than a well-appointed stage; it requires a leading actor of great ability and determination. And Socrates, like so many martyrs after him, proved to be a superlative performer.

Some historians suspect that Socrates was never meant to stand trial, the accusation being a legal maneuver to force him into exile and thereby rid the city of one of its most unpopular citizens.[20] Unfortunately, Socrates refused to cooperate, and he insisted upon a trial, which, with Plato's skill as dramatic narrator, he transformed from a travesty of party politics and personal malice into a public forum to demonstrate that only fools and bigots could possibly believe that he was guilty of impiety or corrupting the moral and spiritual fiber of the city. On the contrary, he alone possessed the double-edged truth: the only knowledge worth knowing is the realization that wisdom belongs to the gods alone, and mankind is far better off trying to practice virtue based on humility and endeavoring to concern itself with the destiny of the soul than with silly earthly and material affairs. Indeed, he used the opinion of the Delphic oracle as the centerpiece of his defense: the gods themselves had announced that he was the wisest man alive. Apollo, he argued, had ordered him to fulfill his "mission of searching into myself and other men." He would not flee into exile, nor was he worried about the sentence of the court, for "a man who is good for anything ought not to calculate the chance of living or dying; he ought only to consider whether in doing anything he is doing right or wrong—acting the part of a good man or of a bad."[21]

Socrates knew exactly what he was doing: the gods had ordered him to fulfill his pilgrimage of searching into himself and other men, and he con-

fronted the jury with a challenge. "If you say to me . . . you [Socrates] shall
be let off, but upon one condition, that you are not to inquire and speculate
in this way any more, and if you are caught doing so again you shall
die . . . I should reply: Men of Athens, I honor and love you; but I shall obey
god rather than you. . . . Either acquit me or not; but whichever you do, understand that I shall never alter my ways, not even if I have to die many
times."[22] Defiance was followed by condescension. He informed his fellow
citizens that if they executed him, "you will injure yourselves more than
you will injure me," for he was god's gift to Athens, "a sort of gadfly, given
to the state by god" so that it could be stirred and directed to virtue and
righteousness.[23]

Socrates' "lofty words" were scarcely designed to achieve acquittal, and
when he was found guilty by a vote of 280 to 220, he was only surprised by
the closeness of the decision. Athenian justice required yet another vote: to
enforce the death penalty or to accept some lesser punishment proposed by
the condemned man himself. Instead of endeavoring to save his life by suggesting banishment or a stiff fine, Socrates indulged in mockery, calculated
to further antagonize his peers. He proposed that far from punishing him,
they should acknowledge him to be a public benefactor and reward him, a
poor man, with a lifetime of free food served in the town hall at the city's
expense. Not even Socrates had the hubris to stick to his jesting, and he
changed his proposal to a fine of one mina, all he said he could afford to
pay. This ante was almost immediately increased by his supporters'
promise to stand surety to the considerable sum of thirty minas, but the
harm had been done, and Socrates was sentenced to die by a majority
eighty votes greater than the decision to condemn.

A totally unrepentant Socrates, who had done everything in his rhetorical power to manipulate the vote, concluded the trial with words that have
become memorable throughout the ages. "The unexamined life," he announced, "is not worth living," and the real purpose of life "is not to avoid
death, but to avoid unrighteousness."[24] Momentarily he indulged in
anger—"Oh men who have condemned me . . . I prophesy to you who are
my murderers that immediately after my departure [you will suffer] punishment far heavier than you have inflicted on me"—but he quickly returned to his usual insolent reasonableness and assured his judges that he
felt no resentment, for, albeit unintentionally, they had done him a great
service.[25] Death, far from being an evil, was in fact the ultimate good; the
journey to the abode of the dead was an odyssey well worth whatever trifling pain might be involved in dying, for in the afterworld he would be able
to continue his search into "true and false knowledge" and find ultimate
wisdom. "In another world," he concluded, "they do not put a man to

death for asking questions."[26] With those words Socrates instantly became history's first martyr to free intellectual inquiry and freedom of speech; and with perfect dramatic timing, he bade his judges farewell: "I to die, and you to live. Which is better god only knows."[27]

The execution was delayed for over a month because no criminal could be put to death during the holy season when the city's sacred ship made its annual voyage to Delos, bearing gifts to the shrine of Apollo. When the vessel returned and the order was given to drink the cup of hemlock, the death scene, as described by Plato, was just as carefully orchestrated as the trial that had preceded it. The sole difference was that this time Socrates played only to his close companions, not to his enemies. The day before the execution Socrates was offered by Crito, his friend and disciple, the chance to escape. His chains would be removed, his jailors bought off, and a safe haven in Thessaly would be arranged; even his family would be able to go with him. Socrates, however, would have none of it. And rather surprisingly for a man who had preached the rule of the spiritual and professional elite, he proclaimed man, at least in his political existence, to be a herd animal, and himself to be a member of that herd. The citizen, he argued, was the creation of the state; if he had benefited throughout his life from the laws of the polis, then he was obliged to give allegiance to the city, even when that loyalty required him to die. That argument would be reiterated throughout the centuries and would eventually be directed by the modern Leviathan against the twentieth-century traitor-martyr forged in the crucible of two world wars and their aftermath.

As always, Socrates chose the high road. He enveloped his death in an ideal, but he was also aware that more than a political principle was at stake. His reputation both in the minds of his fellow Athenians and, more important, in the eyes of history was at risk. He had no intention of dying a laughingstock, the butt of endless jokes about the virtuous Socrates, the elect of the gods, creeping away disguised as a goat herder. He was determined to depart this world "in innocence, a sufferer, and not a doer of evil; a victim, not of laws, but of men." "Leave me then, Crito," he said, "to fulfill the will of god, and to follow whither he leads."[28]

The next day god—Socrates never makes it clear whether he believed in monotheism or some collective or federated divinity—willed one of the most memorable deaths in history. It became a model for the classical world on how to die well, and it established the cardinal stylistic elements essential to all later martyrdoms: perfect timing and absolute control over the circumstances. He died, as Plato's mouthpiece Phaedo put it, "so fearlessly and his words and bearing were so noble and gracious, that to me he appeared blessed."[29]

The day started with a curious episode that set the tone for what was to follow. On entering the prison in the early morning, Socrates' supporters encountered him sitting beside his wife, Xanthippe, with their infant son in her arms, and Socrates rubbing his ankles, from which his prison chains had recently been removed. Xanthippe burst into tears at the sight of his friends, and Socrates abruptly asked Crito to arrange to have her taken home. Then, still massaging his legs, he delivered a brief soliloquy on the strange relationship between pain and pleasure. The two, he said, were not opposites, as most people maintained, but necessary complements of one another. The message was clear; death for Socrates held no terror— certainly not the hemlock, which was an almost painless instrument of death. Instead it was a pleasure, for death liberated the soul from the body, allowing the spirit to pursue the greatest of all joys: the quest for pure knowledge and ultimate truth. These remarks introduced a long debate between Socrates and his companions over the soul's immortality and the care that "should be taken of her, not only in respect of the portion of time which is called life but also of eternity."[30] Eventually Socrates ended his discourse on an unequivocally optimistic note: "Wherefore, I say, let a man be of good cheer about his soul, who having cast away the pleasures and ornaments of the body as alien to him," and having imbued his life with temperance, justice, and courage, has made his soul "ready to go on her journey to the world below."[31]

"The voice of fate," Socrates said, called him, and he ordered his bath to be made ready "in order that the women may not have the trouble of washing my body after I am dead."[32] Nothing was to be left to accident, nothing allowed to interfere with his absolute monopoly of the limelight. It was as if Socrates were simultaneously writing, directing, and enacting a scene of cosmic proportions in which he was the sole actor, not even god being permitted a walk-on part. To the very human inquiry by Crito whether Socrates had any messages for his children, he answered, "Nothing in particular." To Crito's further question about where he wished his friends to bury him, he retorted with a lecture on the difference between his fleshly body and the real Socrates, which by then would have long since departed this world. After his bath, he spoke briefly with his family and then returned to his companions. At this juncture the chief jailer announced the hour of death, and with tears streaming down his face begged forgiveness for what had to be done. Socrates replied by assuring his audience that his jailor was a charming man and an excellent conversationalist. Then he requested the hemlock be brought to him and inquired whether a portion could be poured out as a libation to the gods, but he was told that there was poison enough for him alone.

Timing was Socrates' greatest concern, and he refused to allow the clock to run out. The gods, he knew, had not forgotten him, nor was his approaching death a matter of "mere chance."[33] Nevertheless, he had no intention of relinquishing control. His fate called, but he alone would choose the moment at which to die. Crito begged him not to hurry; "the sun is still upon the hill tops." Coldly Socrates answered that he had no intention of being "ridiculous in my own eyes for sparing and saving a life which is already forfeit," and he took the poison from the attendant's hand and drank it down.[34]

Saints do not lose control of their surroundings or of themselves, but mere mortals do, and in the face of the inevitable, the group of disciples burst into tears and howls of lamentation. Only Socrates kept his cool and sternly demanded: "What is this strange outcry? I sent away the women mainly in order that they might not misbehave in this way, for I have been told that a man should die in peace. Be quiet then, and have patience."[35]

As the poison began to take effect, Socrates lay down and asked that he be covered with a sheet. Death was to be totally private, concealed even from his friends. He uncovered his face only once and spoke his final words—which, as last words go, are a terrible disappointment. Nevertheless, they go to the root of the man's complex personality, for Socrates was, even to his last breath, a master of the unexpected, keeping his opponents, indeed the entire world, off balance. He offered no window into the afterlife, no prophetic message for the future. All he said was, "Crito, I owe a cock to Asclepius; will you remember to pay the debt?"[36] The man who so scornfully rejected the "commercial exchanges between gods and men" in his dying breath felt obliged to pay his ritualistic debt to the Greek god of medicine.

The triviality of Socrates' request to sacrifice a chicken to one of the minor pagan deities raises disturbing questions about his death and its place in the history of martyrdom, for his words sound very much like the amused pronouncement of someone extracting the last ounce of pleasure from his final ego trip. They are dreadfully stagey; they make one wonder how serious Socrates really was and whether his death from start to finish was not a carefully contrived suicide. Certainly those words bring into the open the question that to one degree or another underlies all martyrdoms—how much is the martyr enjoying stage center and to what extent is he deliberately seeking death?[37]

Why and how an individual chooses death is so central to any martyrdom that it is only appropriate that the issue of motivation should have dominated the story of history's first recorded martyr. Did Socrates commit suicide for reasons essentially selfish and private, or did he offer his life as the only possible means to achieve his end: to convince the world that he really did believe that "the unexamined life is not worth living" and that in condemning him of impiety to the gods and the corruption of young minds, a terrible injustice had been committed, not simply to Socrates but to all humanity? Only by giving up his life could he make the point in a fashion that would endure and strengthen that truth for generations to come. As I. F. Stone has put it, "Socrates needed the hemlock, as Jesus needed the crucifixion, to fulfill a mission."[38]

Almost from the moment Socrates asked that his debt to Asclepius be paid, the debate over society's debt to Socrates—had Athens done him a favor or an injustice?—has raged. It is difficult to avoid the suspicion that Socrates all along was manipulating the course of events, that he deliberately goaded his judges into doing what in all likelihood very few of them wanted, to vote the death sentence. Very early on Xenophon drew the conclusion that Socrates' private purpose was to depart this life as painlessly as possible and avoid the infirmities and degradations of old age. "If I am to live on," he said, "I may be forced to pay the old man's forfeit—to become sand-blind and deaf and dull of wit, slower to learn, quicker to forget, outstripped now by those who were behind me." Such a dotage Socrates could not accept: "Even were I unconscious of the change, life would be a burden to me; and if I knew, misery and bitterness would surely be my lot."[39] Not only is Xenophon's Socrates a touchy man, always aware of his reputation, but he is also disturbingly egotistical; and he informed his friend Hermogenes that "god in his kindness is taking my part and securing me the opportunity of ending my life not only in season but also in the way that is easiest . . . [and] least irksome to one's friends and one that implants in them the deepest feeling of loss for the dead." Above all else he wanted to extract the full measure of emotional drama from his death. Only by dying under his own terms and while in full command of his faculties could he guarantee that he would "be sorely missed."[40] Even Plato had to admit that his master achieved that wish: he exited in a manner designed to assure his name in the annals of history.

Later skeptics have re-emphasized the suicide theme—he "wanted to die."[41] One modern historian has argued that Socrates' death was a carefully contrived political suicide designed to embarrass the political party that had started the judicial proceedings: "He wished to place his corpse in the arms of the democrats who had condemned him." The thesis grows out of Socrates' conversation with his friend Hermogenes in which he explains why he has not really tried to defend himself during the trial, and he concludes, "But now, if I am to die unjustly, they who unjustly kill me will bear the shame of it."[42] It has even been suggested that he drank the hemlock to escape a nagging wife, whom tradition, quite unjustly, pictures as chucking chamber pots at his head because of his silly ideas and disregard for material well-being.[43] Other observers, however, regard the suicide thesis as "ludicrous."[44] He died to vindicate his mission, motivated by an "inner compulsion." His death was foreordained because a corrupt and depraved Athens could not tolerate its only honest citizen. He possessed no death wish, either for an easy way out of old age and senility or for a better life to come. He simply had to choose between denying his divine quest or death. All things considered, the choice was easy.[45]

Socrates himself never resolved the dilemma. Instead he set the stage for a debate that would engulf the early Christian era: what distinguishes suicide from martyrdom, and is it appropriate to volunteer for death? He confessed that the central purpose of philosophy was "the study of death," and he invited the sound philosopher not to tarry but to "come after me if he be a wise man."[46] But just as Socrates seems to be saying that the true philosopher, knowing that only death held the secret to ultimate truth, should "be willing to die," he backs off and appears to contradict himself, observing that it is unlawful to take one's own life because men are the possessions of the gods, who are understandably annoyed when their chattel take it into their own hands to die without their consent.[47] Permission was for Socrates the key element, as it would be half a millennium later for the early Christian martyrs: "A man should wait, and not take his own life until god summons him, as he is now summoning me."[48] Not surprisingly, Socrates' associates were in no way convinced by this argument, and tactfully suggested that he might be too eager to leave them and hinted that it was far from clear whether he had in fact been summoned or not. Socrates' answer was to claim that the gods had given intimation of their decision by means of the Athenian jury. What further evidence did his friends require? The imponderability, of course, comes full circuit when the skeptic asks: Right, but didn't Socrates arrange that verdict? To which not even Socrates' assertion that his *daimonion* would have warned him had he been in opposition to the will of the gods is a satisfactory answer.[49]

In many respects Socrates' death, its circumstances as well as its style, set a standard upon which later martyrs consciously drew.[50] The early Christians were well aware of its dramatic appeal, and as they faced their own persecutors they called upon Socrates as an ally, because his trial and execution possessed, with certain important exceptions, most of the characteristics essential to a successful martyrdom. The entire production from judgment to execution was exquisitely controlled, and Socrates in his confrontation with the powers of ignorance and bigotry managed to have not only the last word but also every word. His trial was carefully rigged, the prosecution's argument coming down in history only in terms of Socrates' own rebuttal. No later martyr could boast a more public forum from which to display his moral and, in Socrates' case, intellectual superiority, for Athens supplied—or had been tricked into supplying—a public interrogation by a jury of five hundred of his peers. Socrates, the man as well as the myth, was guaranteed not only a leading place in the evolution of martyrdom but also an equally important spot in the history of theatrics by the presence at his death of a select audience that supplied Plato with the words and images by which to transform the criminal's execution into a cosmic encounter. Heroism, idealism, serenity, and self-sacrifice were aligned against ignorance, cruelty, and malice.

Socrates was magnificent—his timing, his changes of pace, his control were perfect. Nevertheless, the total performance as a martyrdom was disappointing, for it lacked three essentials: god was absent and so, strangely enough, were pain and guilt. There was neither fear of god nor love of god, only Socrates' quest for ultimate philosophic truth. For all of his control and extraordinary sense of drama, Socrates seems to have been without passion or compassion. He stood alone and shared with no one. There was no cosmological purpose, no sense of reward or punishment, no working out of some inscrutable divine plan. There was only Socrates' personal mission, which was coming to an end here on earth. He offered the world no creed to be believed, not even a set of actions to be followed, but instead only an approach to living and dying. If the gods were in control, they were content to remain in the wings, manifest solely in the distant "voice of fate" that called him. There was no god of wrath and vengeance, let alone a god of love. There was no heaven, nor an end of suffering, because there had been no suffering. There was only Socrates' personal conviction that death, if it were not a "dreamless sleep," would be a richer experience than life and that the soul would continue to exist throughout eternity: concepts which Plato makes quite clear that few people—certainly not Socrates' fellow philosophers—considered worth testing. Some five centuries later a Christian martyr would make the obvious point: "No one trusted in Socrates so as to die for this doctrine."[51]

Possibly no death has ever been staged in such a coldly deliberate and calculated fashion, and the scene, as recorded by Plato, has a sterility and immobility about it reminiscent of a Vermeer painting—beautifully atmospheric but rigid and devoid of action: Socrates stands motionless in the limelight. The ultimate purpose of his death, its relationship to the total scheme of the universe, however, never comes through. For suffering, for passion, for God's presence, indeed for martyrdom to become an instrument of divine destiny, history would have to wait another 232 years, when Yahweh, the God of the Jews, finally taught his Chosen People how to transform their pain and persecution into an agency of divine purpose and gave to martyrdom an intensity and a horror that Socrates so obviously found distasteful and unnecessary.

A tenth-century depiction of Antiochus IV's soldiers implementing what may be history's first experiment in ideological totalitarianism

CHAPTER 3

The Maccabees and the Doctrine of Suffering

Every hero becomes a bore at last.
—Ralph Waldo Emerson,
"Uses of Great Men"

*T*HE GODS, as any Athenian could have told Socrates, are notoriously unreliable. They may have set Athens's self-designated gadfly upon his mission to persuade his fellow citizens to cast aside the desire for material wealth and concentrate on the welfare of the soul, in both this world and the next, but they did not bother to open Athenian hearts to his message. Instead, they selected as humanity's nursery in the art of curing souls an insignificant but singularly cantankerous and intractable settlement in Judea, whose citizens had, sixty-nine years before Socrates' birth, returned from two generations of exile in Babylon to rebuild in Jerusalem a temple dedicated to a deity who required His Chosen People to watch diligently after their souls and who was exceedingly harsh on sinners, individually and collectively.

The profoundly introverted, almost masochistic, and inflexible flavor of Judaism was forged during and immediately after the Babylonian exile, when the people of Zion had to confront the supreme question of human existence: how to explain pain, suffering, and agonizing adversity. Stated in religious terms, why had Yahweh, the God of their fathers, forsaken them, permitting during the terrible decade of 598–87 B.C. the destruction of His temple and sacred city by Nebuchadnezzar, sanctioning the slaughter and captivity of His followers and standing aside unmoved as the once prosperous kingdom of Judea, possibly a quarter of a million strong, was systematically reduced to a demoralized and scattered population of less than twenty thousand?[1]

When forty-nine years later, in 538 B.C., Yahweh, with the aid of the Persians, permitted His people to return to Jerusalem, they did more than rebuild the walls of their city to protect it from further invasion; they refortified their faith in their God and in themselves. The process of political and spiritual revival took almost a century to complete and involved a desperate psychological struggle as the Jews looked into their hearts and their history and reaffirmed their commitment to the heavily one-sided covenant that their forefathers had contracted with God. Yahweh had struck a hard bargain when He elected the descendants of Abraham, Isaac, and Jacob as His holy nation, demanding that they be His witnesses and His servants, "whom I have chosen that ye may know and believe me" (Isaiah 43:10).

The terms of the pact were written in time and recorded in the history of God's Chosen People. The covenant was to endure unto the thousandth generation, and, in the words of Deuteronomy, no one was to "add thereto nor diminish from it" (7:9; 12:32). As a consequence the Jews knew themselves to be a nation apart, marked by their adherence to God's Law as revealed to Moses and more visibly by their observance of stringent ritualistic regulations—circumcision, a strict dietary code, prohibitions against nudity, and observance of the Sabbath. Yahweh offered both "a blessing and a curse" (Deuteronomy 11:26). If Israel abided by the covenant and hearkened to the voice of the Lord, He contracted to set His followers "high above all nations of the earth" and "every place whereon the soles of your feet shall tread shall be yours" (Deuteronomy 28:1; 11:24). But should they forget His Law, He turned extremely nasty, threatening not only cosmological retribution—"thy heaven that is over thy head shall be brass and the earth that is under thee shall be iron" (Deuteronomy 28:23)—but also equally dire political consequences: Israel would be scattered among the nations of the world and her sons and daughters taken into slavery. Yahweh was a difficult deity to satisfy. It was not sufficient that His elect should suffer collectively as a nation for its failure to abide by His Law; His wrath fell also upon the individual, innocent and guilty alike, and with clinical delight He listed the terrible pestilences that must follow in the wake of disobedience: fever, madness, consumption, and the endless vexations of the hemorrhoids, the scab and the itch "whereof thou canst not be healed" (Deuteronomy 28:27).

Suffering was inherent in the covenant, and it became the central feature of Judaism once earthly adversity was linked with moral sin as the ultimate explanation for the disaster of the Babylonian captivity and the long struggle to rebuild Israel. The sin of disobedience, the worship of strange gods, and the refusal to walk in the path of the Lord had brought God's wrath down upon His people. However, the Lord had not forsaken them, let alone forgotten them. The dreadful events of history fell upon Israel as both a punishment and a purgation, for only suffering could wipe the slate clean of the sin of disobedience. Other tribes and peoples had suffered, often to the point of annihilation, and endured pain without relief, grief without meaning, adversity without purpose; but the people of Israel alone succeeded in transforming the horrors of the human condition on earth into the means of ultimate national and personal redemption. Mental and physical torment became for the Jews not merely a reality to be endured but a blessing to be welcomed, because suffering was a sure sign that Yahweh had not broken the terms of the covenant and that the Jewish people remained the instruments and harbingers of His ultimate design. Pain and sorrow were in a macabre way blunted, for they were imbued with a higher value and could now be seen as both the consequence and the expiation of sin. The Lord of Zion had made his method and his intent clear: "Behold, I have refined thee, but not with silver; I have chosen thee in the furnace of affliction" (Isaiah 48:3).

The God of Israel may have harbored an inflammatory and touchy personality—as Isaiah expressed it, His lips "full of indignation and His tongue as a devouring fire" (30:27)—but He possessed three other characteristics which transformed Him into something more than an irritable tribal deity who looked after His people in a perverse if effective fashion. He asserted for Himself an aggressive exclusiveness, delighted in a cosmic creativity unheard of in the Pantheon of the pagan gods, and claimed human history as the special channel through which He revealed His ultimate purpose.

Yahweh never wearied in His ceaseless reminders that He alone was God; "there is no other." Temporally and spatially He maintained absolute singularity. "Before me there was no God formed, neither shall there be after me" (Isaiah 43:19). His house was exclusively his own, and any deity brash enough to seek entry was branded a hollow idol, a graven image and "the work of men's hands" (Isaiah 37:14). Yahweh alone had "created the heavens and stretched them out," had "spread forth the earth" and given breath to all life (Isaiah 42:5). There is a problem, however, in Yahweh's exclusiveness and creativity. As the Lord of creation who, by implication at least, had shaped the cosmos out of nothing except His own sovereign will, Yahweh was a troublesome concept. In one breath He was a nameless, shapeless, incomprehensible entity that preceded all other substances and therefore had to be shared with all mankind—as Isaiah said, "Mine house shall be called an house of prayer for all people," and "I will gather all nations and tongues, and they shall come and see my glory" (56:7; 66:18). But in the next breath He was the special God of the Jews, "the Holy One of Israel" who had covenanted with His chosen clan. As Elias Bickerman has nicely put it, "the sole Lord of the Universe" paradoxically dwelt "on the hillock of Zion."[2]

The burden placed on Israel as being the permanent host to the creator of the world was heavy. But the paradox of a Janus deity who was the maker of all things and at the same time a dietary expert who, among His other commandments, had prescribed for His elected people only food that would be appropriate to their souls' welfare[3] was resolved by yet another of Yahweh's peculiarities. Unlike any of His Hellenistic rivals, Yahweh expressed His will within a temporal context; He unraveled his ultimate cosmic design in terms of human history. The God of Israel was not so much a concept as an action; He manifested Himself "in His mighty acts among the children of men." As He said, "I have declared the former things from the beginning; and they went forth out of my mouth, and I showed them; I did them suddenly and they came to pass" (Isaiah 48:3). This historical imperative was central to His goal, because the drama of earthly events was inexorably headed towards that instant when sin and inequity would reach such cosmic proportions that Yahweh would decide to roll back the heavens like a scroll, demolish the evil nations of the earth, and put an end to time itself, creating what Isaiah called "the new heaven and the new earth" (34:4; 66:22). The day of His final vengeance would take place in an apocalyptic fury; the armies of the sinful would be slaughtered, "their stink shall come up out of their carcasses, and the mountains shall be melted with their blood" (Isaiah 34:3). But out of the carnage would rise "the city of righteousness, the faithful city" (Isaiah 1:26), rebuilt by the remnant who, through their suffering and perseverance, had proven their faith. For them, the Lord would cease to be a God of indignation and terror and become, as was His ultimate intent, their final deliverer and savior. Israel's role in this historic process was clear. As the elected people of the Lord, they possessed His Law and the words of His prophets, who had been granted a window into the chasm of His mind, and Israel knew that no matter the dreadful agonies of today or the unworthiness of its people, destiny must end in the final triumph of God's holy nation and the destruction of all its enemies. There could be no uncertainty about the outcome, because the Holy One of Israel had made a promise: "Fear not, thou worm Jacob, and ye men of Israel; I will help thee" (Isaiah 41:14). With those none-too-encouraging words Yahweh revealed Himself to be an eschatologist, a diviner of the world's end, both knowing and decreeing the answer to death, judgment, heaven and hell.

Thus, just as Socrates was walking the streets of Athens commending to his fellow citizens the importance of their souls, there was evolving in Judea a people who had linked the health of their souls with the memory and destiny of their nation and had turned the tragedies of life into both a sign of God's intent and a retribution for their own spiritual failings. As the scribe Ezra said, because "our fathers had provoked the God of heaven unto wrath, He gave them into the hand of Nebuchadnezzar," who "carried the people away into Babylon" (Ezra 5:12). Here, of course, was the cruelest irony of all and the final proof that the gods could indeed not be trusted. Socrates might have felt considerable sympathy for a nation so sensitive to sin that it was ready in the midst of tribulation to pour out its soul "unto death," but it was exactly that commitment to their souls' salvation and Yahweh's glorification that provoked a clash with a culture for which Socrates and Plato were themselves in large measure responsible. Out of the ideological encounter between Hellenism and Judaism emerged the concept of martyrdom as an instrument of religious warfare. The Jews may not have invented Western martyrdom—that credit goes to Socrates and Plato—but they were certainly the first to use it as a means of national inspiration and to endow its hideous suffering with eschatological purpose.[4]

Jerusalem was located at the crossways of the ancient world, the point where three cultures met—Greek, Egyptian, and Persian. It lay close to communication lines that were to be fought over for centuries and in the midst of one of the most politically unstable areas on earth. For the first two hundred years after the return from exile, the city looked east to Persia, for it had been Cyrus, the conquering king of the Medes and the Persians, who humbled the power of Babylon and ordained in 538 B.C. the migration of the Jews back to their homeland. A century later it was another Persian king, Artaxerxes, who permitted Nehemiah to rebuild the walls of the holy city and blessed the establishment of a Jewish theocracy grounded upon the Mosaic covenant with the Lord and ruled by a high priest. Ezra, the scribe, arrived in Jerusalem in 428 B.C.[5] armed with a royal scroll ordering the people of Zion to obey Yahweh's commandments as if they were the king's own decrees, for "whosoever will not do the law of thy God and the law of the king, let judgment be executed speedily upon him" (Ezra 7:26). From the day when Ezra stood upon a wooden pulpit before the congregation of Jerusalem and recited the "Book of the Law of Moses" until "the people wept" (Nehemiah 8:1–9), acceptance of the Book became the mark of a new, militant and nationalistic Judaism and a bastion against impurity and corruption far more unyielding and enduring than the walls that Nehemiah had erected around the holy city.

The God of Israel as envisioned by Ezra and Nehemiah needed all the support that either man could muster, because during the four years between 333 and 329 B.C. the ancient world was turned upside down and the Persian empire, which had been designated by Yahweh Himself as Israel's "highway" through the desert, fell before the disciplined phalanxes of Alexander the Great. When, ten years later, in 323 B.C., Alexander died, he left a legacy of political confusion and Hellenistic cultural imperialism that came close to extinguishing Judaism forever. It took almost a generation of political murders, unstable military alliances, and wars, in which the victor's life expectancy was only marginally less short than the loser's, for the spoils of Alexander's legacy to be carved up on something resembling a permanent basis. Seleucus I, the "conqueror," and Ptolemy I, the "savior," were the eventual victors, dividing most of the territories between them. Asia Minor, Babylonia, and the eastern principalities went to Seleucus and his heirs; Egypt fell to Ptolemy and his descendants. Unfortunately for Jerusalem, Coele-Syria—of which Judea was a part—was left in dispute, to be fought over for the next hundred years, until in 198 B.C. Antiochus III, the sixth of his Seleucid line, was able to wrest the province from Egypt.

How much Judea suffered during these ceaseless wars is impossible to document but not hard to imagine as opposing armies swept across plains and valleys strategically vital to both empires. Until Antiochus's victory Jerusalem had been under the nominal rule of the Ptolemies. Now it had to adapt to a new master who, in the relaxed Hellenistic tradition of accepting all local deities as emanations of one supreme but federated being, recognized the God of Zion. Like Artaxerxes before him, Antiochus ordained that the laws of Yahweh should be strictly enforced on pagans and Jews alike.

Ironically, the cultic laws of the Jews found a stronger ally in a foreign potentate than they did among the Lord's own Chosen People, because as early as 300 B.C. a traveler was reporting that "the Jews had greatly altered the ordinances of their forefathers."[6] Throughout the Hellenistic world the walls of cultural exclusiveness, which had once distinguished the Greek city-state, were crumbling as the polis was exposed to rational criticism and its customs subjected to a cosmopolitan culture. Men were no longer judged by their birthplace but instead by their position in what was rapidly becoming a culturally and economically integrated society. Judaism, with its passionate insistence on the existence of one God to the exclusion of all others, its introverted disdain for all foreign deities and unclean things, and its obsession with ritualistic purity, resisted the Hellenistic cultural flood but eventually found, like the rest of the ancient world, enchantment with things Greek to be almost irresistible. By the time Judea was absorbed into the Seleucid empire, Jews were already beginning to succumb to Hellenism, to its religious tolerance, its rationalism, and its polytheistic approach to the universe.

A generation later there emerged in Jerusalem the anomaly of the Hellenized Jew who sought to free himself from the bondage of the Law and the narrow terms of the ancient covenant. The old barrier, the historic and sacred Law, which the Lord had erected to keep His holy people apart and pure, was systematically violated. The blood purity of the nation was polluted by marriage with pagans; more and more Jews agreed with their Greek neighbors that circumcision was a barbaric disfigurement; the athletes of Israel elected to appear naked in the cities' gymnasiums and athletic competitions, and, worse, they sacrificed to the Greek idols that presided over the games. Finally, even those prohibited foods which Yahweh Himself had pronounced as abominations to the soul's welfare were consumed in public. As one highly critical observer noted, "At that time lawless men arose in Israel and seduced many with their pleas, 'Come, let us make a covenant with the gentiles round us, because ever since we have kept ourselves separated from them we have suffered many evils.' "[7]

The ideological conditions for history's first religious war grew out of this struggle to determine whether the descendants of Abraham, Isaac, and Jacob would turn their faces against the God of their ancestors and embrace Hellenism with all its rational, cosmopolitan, and secular attractions, or whether they would maintain the covenant which their forefathers had negotiated with the Lord. The soul as well as the mind of Israel was at stake, and no one knew whether the faithful would die for the Law or live by the polytheistic rules of paganism.

Willingness to die for the faith is meaningless unless tested by the sword, and there would have been no martyrs had not the ideological clash between Judaism and Hellenism become fatally entangled with the political ambitions of the Seleucid empire to maintain its control over Coele-Syria and the city of Jerusalem. Theocracies, when exposed to internal dissension involving questions of policy and leadership, are particularly prone to mask self-interest behind ideological verities. How much the fierce rivalry among the high priests Onias, Jason, and Menelaus was fired by political conflict focusing on the control of the temple and the economic welfare of their partisans and how much it was fostered by basic religious differences between Hellenistic reformers and Law-abiding conservatives is impossible to say. To what extent the various factions within Jerusalem reflected pro-Egyptian or pro-Seleucid sympathies is equally unclear. The only statement that can be made with any sense of confidence is that Antiochus IV, when he succeeded to the Seleucid throne in 176 B.C., inaugurated a cultural

and political policy that led within nine years to a full-scale religious and
civil insurrection which ended twenty-seven years later in the independence of Judea.[8]

Antiochus IV inherited a difficult political and a desperate financial
legacy from his father, whose victories over Egypt had been all but wiped
out by his ill-starred decision to test the might of Rome. The republic's ex-
pansionistic interests, following its triumph over Carthage, were steadily
turning eastward. The result was his humiliating defeat at Magnesia in 190
B.C., where Antiochus III lost most of Asia Minor and was forced to pay
Rome the staggering indemnity of fifteen thousand talents. From that moment on the Seleucid empire was close to bankruptcy, and the heavy burden
of debt as well as the threatening presence of Rome go far to explain the
new ruler's policies toward Jerusalem. Faced with his father's financial obligations and confronted with the constant cost of defending Coele-Syria
against the Ptolemies, who were determined to win back their lost province,
Antiochus IV was willing to sanction any financial expedient offered him.
Under the circumstances it is not surprising that he became embroiled in the
religious-political struggle within Judea, for irrespective of who followed or
denied the Law, Antiochus was happy to install in the office of high priest
the man who paid him the most, and to use any pretext to get his hands on
the treasures stored within the temple. Jason, who offered 440 silver talents,
was clearly worthier in the king's eyes than Onias, but Menelaus, who was
eventually the most generous of the three with the temple treasures, was
the most acceptable of the lot.

Antiochus was a theatrically inclined, hyperactive sovereign who styled
himself "God manifest," and in selecting Jason as high priest in 175 B.C. and
shortly thereafter replacing him with Menelaus, he may have been hearkening to more than the ring of silver in his coffers. He may have been implementing history's first experiment in ideological totalitarianism, because
Menelaus even more than Jason seems to have been a Hellenizer, believing
that Judaism should adapt itself to Greek syncretistic religious ideals and
Greek fashions. Antiochus has been called the first monarch ever to claim
"the authority to issue orders even to the soul of man,"[9] and there is some
evidence to believe that in preparing his kingdom for the expected military
showdown with Rome, he sought to galvanize his territories into a single
cultural entity with the worship of Zeus as the central religious focus. As
one contemporary put it, "The king wrote to all his kingdom for all to become one people and for each to abandon his own customs," meaning that
they should worship a single preeminent deity.[10]

Whatever Antiochus's ultimate aim—financial or ideological—war with
Egypt was the ingredient that filled Israel's cup of sorrow to overflowing.

In 170 B.C. the Ptolemies played into Antiochus's hands and declared war. By the summer of 169 B.C. Seleucid armies were deep into Egypt, but the rumor circulated that Antiochus had died during the campaign. On hearing this report, Jason, the demoted high priest who had gone into exile three years before, returned to Jerusalem and staged a bloody temple coup, seeking to evict Menelaus from his priestly office. Antiochus, however, was very much alive and interpreted these events as a pro-Ptolemian uprising against his authority. On his return from Egypt he stopped off in Jerusalem, plundered the temple of eighteen hundred talents, sacked the city, and rescued Menelaus. Next summer he was again in Egypt; this time he even crowned himself king in Memphis. But his triumph was short-lived. Rome ordered him out of the land of the pharaohs, and Antiochus had no choice but to obey. In the meantime, Menelaus was again in trouble, and the king unleashed the full fury of his army on the ungrateful city and its unreliable priestly leaders. Jerusalem suffered a bloodbath and military occupation; its walls were torn down, its theocratic and governmental privileges abolished, and the process of Hellenization, which until 167 B.C. had been largely the work of the reform party within the temple, now became the king's official policy.

The exact order of events, their causal relationships, and the question of whether Antiochus was following his own policy of Hellenization or simply enforcing for self-interested reasons the will of a religious faction within Judea are issues of learned controversy.[11] His religious decrees, however, are a matter of record. The Law of Moses, which had been re-established by royal command 260 years before by Artaxerxes and rearticulated by Antiochus's father, was now abolished; circumcision, the observation of the Sabbath and the dietary code were outlawed; a high altar to Zeus was constructed in the midst of Yahweh's own sacred house;[12] and throughout Israel, Jews were ordered not only to sacrifice to Zeus with swine meat but also, as a final act of oblivion, to no longer confess themselves to be Jews.[13] Violators were not just executed; they endured death by prolonged torture.

The history of the uprising of the Jews led first by Mattathias and then by his son Judas Maccabeus, and of the complex civil war that raged between religious reformers and conservatives, is only tangential to the story of martyrdom, which deals not with those who fought and perished in war but with those who elected to be martyred. How many suffered we do not know. The records speak of two women who, having disobeyed the king's law and circumcised their baby sons, were hurled from the city walls, their strangled infants lashed to their breasts. The histories also tell of hundreds of Jews who fled the city and hid in caves in order to carry on the Law in secret; when they were tracked down, they died unresisting because they would not desecrate the Sabbath by defending themselves.[14] But legend, heavily embellished and loudly articulated by religious and political self-interest, has focused history's attention on nine individuals: Eleazar, an elderly scribe; and a mother who goes by a variety of names; and her seven sons, the youngest being a lad short on years but long on precocious heroism.

The nine heroes presumably died in 167 B.C. during the early months of the persecution, when it was still almost unthinkable to imagine armed resistance, for however detestable Antiochus's decrees may have been, he remained as much an instrument of the Lord's purpose as Artaxerxes or Cyrus had been two and a half centuries earlier.[15] As it was written, "Woe unto him that striveth with his Maker! . . . Shall the clay say to him that fashioneth it, What maketh thou?" (Isaiah 45:9).

The fate of the Maccabees has been told twice over in extensive and hideous detail. The first account was originally written down at considerable length by Jason of Cyrene at least three generations after the event, probably around 86 B.C. That narrative has not survived, but some time between 78 and 63 B.C. it was heavily abridged by an unknown author and has come down to us as Maccabees II, one of the books of the Apocrypha. The second version is a religious book of devotion entitled *On the Sovereignty of Reason*, which generally goes by the name of Maccabees IV. It was probably not composed until forty years after the birth of Christ. Scholars continue to debate where the martyrdoms took place—Jerusalem or the Seleucid capital for the western portion of the empire at Antioch—and whether they were actually performed before Antiochus himself or only in front of one of his lieutenants.[16]

Dating and placing the ordeal of the Maccabean martyrs remains highly problematical, but the amount of effort and research that has gone into establishing the provenance of the stories reflects their importance in the Jewish and especially the Christian traditions, for the agonies endured by the nine heroes added a dimension to martyrdom that was significantly lacking in the death of Socrates. The ideological aims of the two persecutions were fundamentally different. Socrates' punishment grew out of his disobedience. His offense was the crime of commission. He refused to refrain from proselytizing and preaching the truth, from teaching new doctrines and "corrupting" the youth of Athens, and he was duly executed for his actions. In contrast, the Maccabean nine died because they refused to act in a way that violated the tenets of their faith. Their sin in the eyes of the state was the crime not of commission but of omission.[17] They were ordered to prove their devotion to Zeus and thereby their loyalty to the king and their membership within the Seleucid community by eating swine flesh that had been sacrificed to the Greek gods. This they refused to do. To have done so would have been a violation of the dietary laws of the covenant and, far worse, since the pork had been already sacrificed to an alien deity, would have been tantamount to idolatry and a denial of Yahweh Himself. The king's decrees not only prohibited the Jews from practicing their ancient rites but also required them to become gentiles and to worship a strange god. Antiochus indeed had "issued orders even to the soul of man." Socrates had never been asked by his fellow Athenians to recast his soul in some alien image; he had only been required to keep his soul to himself and be quiet about it.

The aggressive and crusading aspect of the Maccabean persecutions was the element that attracted early Christian attention and earned the nine a place of particular honor in the Christian hall of martyrs.[18] They were not simply "martyrs for the sake of pork";[19] they were also victims of a law that required them to deny their faith in the one and only God. In the eyes of Saint Bernard of Clairvaux they were the equal of any Christian martyr. Of all of the pre-Christian sufferers, they stood alone, superior even to John the Baptist. John had indeed been executed by wicked and irreligious men, but Saint Bernard pointed out that those who had ordered the martyr's death had only been protecting themselves and their own beliefs. "They were not so much persecuting righteousness as defending their own wickedness." Why had Herod sent for John? "Because he preached Christ? Because he was a good and just man? No." The martyr's crime in Herod's eyes was that John had "rebuked him" about his personal life, and Bernard concluded that John suffered because he had been too zealous for the truth, not because he was being "forced [as the Maccabees had been] to deny it."[20] This distinction becomes central to the later history of martyrdom.

The element of historical authenticity in both Maccabees II and IV is even more tenuous than in the Socratic legend. That government-instigated and ideologically inspired atrocities occurred is highly probable; that some elder like Eleazar was caught up in the persecutions is quite possible; but that the mother and her seven sons died in the ecstasy of agony portrayed by the two authors stretches credulity to the breaking point. There is little doubt that the stories are legends, but as with Socrates, they are myths that have over the centuries acquired a life of their own and have for succeeding generations been treated as reality.

Eleazar, like Socrates, who was well known to the author of Maccabees IV and probably also to the author of Maccabees II,[21] is presented as a venerable and high-minded sage. But unlike his classical model, he is described as "a very handsome man," whom the tyrant had singled out because of his reputation and had ordered to eat unclean meat used in the sacrificial rites offered to Zeus. Repeatedly the king's officials tried to force him to open his mouth and eat the pork. Eleazar, however, "preferred death with glory to life with defilement." He spat out the offending substance and, well aware of the dire consequences, walked "of his own free will" to the instrument of torture, "a whipping drum."[22] According to the legend, the wisdom of Hellenism was dumbfounded by the aged hero's foolish stubbornness, and Antiochus entreated him to reconsider his decision. " 'Will you not awaken from your crazy philosophy? . . . Even if there is some power that watches over that religion of yours, it would pardon you for a transgression arising out of extreme compulsion.' "[23] Eleazar would have nothing to do with the seductive voice of secular reason and gave a response that would become the stock answer for most future religious martyrs. What was at stake was the act of believing, of faith itself, not the rightness or wrongness of what was believed or even the extent of the transgression demanded. " 'Nay,' " he answered, " 'even if our Law were in good truth, as you suppose, not divine, and we merely believed it to be divine, even so it would not be possible for us to invalidate our reputation for piety.' " As for eating unclean flesh being a trifling offense, he argued that " 'transgression is of equal weight in small matters as in large.' "[24]

Implied in Eleazar's refusal was another, equally important issue: the public nature of his ordeal and his reputation and standing in history. Like Socrates, he knew that he was on public and historic display, and he proved to be just as proud as his predecessor in martyrdom. When offered a way out, a means of saving his life, he refused. His admirers among the king's officials, for friendship's sake, wanted to save him from himself, and they offered to smuggle in clean meat and have Eleazar only pretend to consume the sacrificial offering. The old man was every bit as disdainful of escape as Socrates and just as protective of his reputation: "Shameful indeed would it be, if, having but a short shrift of life remaining," I became " 'ludicrous in the eyes of all' " for my cowardness and earned " 'the tyrant's contempt as ignoble by failing to protect our divine Law unto death.' "[25]

The link with Socrates is even more apparent in Eleazar's determination to maintain rigid control over himself and the circumstances of his death. What philosopher, wrote the author of Maccabees IV, would not want "to control his emotions"; and repeatedly the old man proved his devotion to his " 'beloved self-control,' " which neither prolonged whipping and exposure to fire nor "a noisome brew" poured down his nostrils could break.[26] Overcoming the pain by "making his mind taut like a jutting crag," he raised himself from his torments and spoke his final words, reminding both Yahweh and the audience that though he could have escaped torture and death, he endured the agony out of reverence to the Lord, and in his soul, he said, he was " 'glad to suffer it.' "[27]

The death of the seven brothers and their mother's terrible ordeal were equally gory and even more prolonged, and the macabre flavor of their fate plus the heroic quality of their encounter are established early in both narratives. The young men brought before Antiochus for their refusal to eat swine flesh that had been sacrificed to pagan gods were, in the tradition of all future Christian martyrologies, "handsome and modest and well-born and in every way charming." On seeing them "posed about their mother," the king was instantly "smitten by their comeliness and nobility," and he assured them that he had " 'compassion for your youth and your beauty.' " He entreated them to " 'share in the Greek way' " and get on with their lives, which he promised to make both comfortable and profitable.[28] The first son, speaking for the rest, immediately antagonized the monarch by his contemptuous answer: " 'Why, tyrant, do you delay? Ready are we to die, rather than transgress our forefathers' commandments.' "[29] The enraged sovereign immediately ordered the "griddles and cauldrons to be heated red-hot" and commanded that the first son's tongue be ripped out, his scalp torn off and his hands and feet amputated—all this while his brothers and mother looked on. Then, still living, the firstborn was thrown helpless onto "the fire and fried." Predictably, this appalling sight had no effect on the heroic family: "As the odor of frying began to spread widely, the brothers and their mother exhorted one another to die nobly, saying 'the Lord God is watching and in very truth will have compassion on us,' " and they called on Moses as their witness that God " 'will have compassion upon His Servants.' "[30]

The hope embodied in those words comes from Deuteronomy 32:36— "For the Lord shall judge His people and repent Himself for His servants, when He seeth that their power is gone"—and is central to the message in both Maccabees II and Maccabees IV. The sons died not for their personal sins—they were innocent—but for the collective transgressions of the Jewish nation of which they were a part and for which they had to be held responsible. In straying from the covenant and following Menelaus and his pagan ways, Israel had incurred the legitimate wrath of God. Twice over the brothers spoke of their sins and the expectation that their suffering would deflect and soften Yahweh's anger against His people. The sixth son assured the king that his brutal edicts had in reality nothing to do with bringing the brothers to torture; God's will alone had accomplished that end, and he warned Antiochus, " 'Do not indulge in vain delusions! Through our own fault we are subject to these sufferings, because we have

sinned against our God. They pass belief!' " The youngest brother expressed much the same sentiment but added that " 'if our living Lord has
for a short time become angry with us in order to chastise and teach us, He
will again become reconciled with His servants. . . . With me and my
brothers may the Almighty put an end to the rightful anger inflicted upon
our entire people.' "[31] The doctrine of suffering as a means of reconciliation is even more fully developed in Maccabees IV. Eleazar in his dying appeal to Yahweh offered his blood as expiation for the sins of God's people
and his " 'life as a ransom for theirs,' " and the seventh and youngest
brother called " 'upon the God of my fathers to prove merciful to our nation.' "[32] There is no doubt in the mind of the author that the martyrs had
"become as it were a ransom for the sin" of the Chosen People and through
their suffering Israel would be preserved and protected.[33]

As the story of the martyrdoms progresses from one brother to the next,
the "many-headed torture" reaches ever-increasing frenzies of agony and
morbid detail. The first brother had been reduced to a mutilated torso and
roasted. The sinews of the next sibling were torn with iron claws and "they
flayed all his flesh up to his chin and also the skin of his head." Brother number three had his feet, hands, and fingers systematically dislocated, and "they
pried his members asunder from their joints with levers." He was then
scalped and broken on the wheel and "when his vertebrae were being disjointed upon it, he saw his own flesh hanging in shreds and gouts of blood
dripping from his entrails." Number four offered his tongue to be cut off:
" 'Look, my tongue hangs out; cut it off.' " The fifth brother was bound and
dragged to a catapult and fastened by the knees with iron staples which
"twisted his loins back upon the circular wedge" so that he was broken open
like a "scorpion." The executioners stretched the sixth victim upon a wheel
"with care" and systematically dismembered him; then they roasted what
was left "with a slow fire," burning "away his entrails."[34] On the youngest
youth Antiochus took pity and sought to save him from the dreadful fate
of his cofrères. You, he said, see " 'how your brothers' folly has ended,' " and
he offered him power and wealth if he would only obey his king. The boy
was just as stubborn as his siblings and would "not prove renegade to the
heroism" of the others.[35] By the time the authors reached the youngest
child, however, their imaginative powers were exhausted; one simply said
he threw himself on the fire; the other left the scene to the reader's imagination and wrote that the enraged monarch "treated him still worse than
the others."[36]

The sons endured a purgation of pain so annihilating that it loses all
sense of reality, for like Eleazar they reached the neurological breaking
point where the circuits of sensation became so overloaded that they

erupted into an explosion of ecstasy. For their mother, however, no such sublimation of pain was possible. She was forced to watch each son die in agony, and behold their bodies "disintegrating in the fire; the fingers of their hands and the toes of their feet quivering on the ground; the flesh of their heads flayed down to the cheeks, exposed like masks."[37] When it came time for the youngest child to be dragged in irons to the torture, she was ordered to dissuade him from his madness. This she refused, and in words that are numbing in their cold fury, she instead begged him to " 'have pity on me who carried you in my womb for nine months and nursed you for three years and reared you and brought you to your present age. . . . Do not fear this executioner, but be worthy of your brothers and accept death, so that in His mercy I may recover you along with your brothers.' "[38]

Various fates were suggested for this terrifyingly militant yet disturbingly selfish female. Maccabees II leaves her history in studied doubt; Maccabees IV says she "flung herself into the fire, so that no one might touch her body"; other sources suggest she committed suicide by jumping off the roof of a house, or that she understandably went insane; and in the tenth-century history *Josippon* she dies surrounded by the corpses of her children by the hand of God in answer to her appeal to heaven.[39] But whatever her immediate or eventual end, her words drive home both the consuming intensity of the faith that produced these martyrdoms and the horror with which the Hellenistic world viewed their suicidal actions. Throughout both accounts Antiochus and his officials are portrayed as being totally amazed—sometimes in reluctant admiration, more often in profound disgust—by their senseless folly. There could be no reconciliation, no understanding, of mind and heart when frustrated administrators begged the fourth brother not to " 'act the mad man with that same madness your brothers have shown, but obey the king and save yourself,' " and he answered back, " 'No fire you can bring against me is so burning hot as to make a coward of me.' "[40]

They were no cowards, these seven brothers, their mother, and the sage Eleazar, and the spectacle of their ordeal quickly became the paradigm for dying "beautifully." It established most of the stereotypes that found their way into later Christian stories about heroic martyrdoms.[41] Antiochus became the symbol incarnate of rigid, senseless officialdom, bent on brutally remodeling society in its own image, the archvillain in the clash between the defenseless individual and the bloody-minded state. No future martyrdom could be without the handsome and noble countenances of the seven sons or the cheerfulness with which they rushed to their torture. Equally essential was the public nature of their heroism, displayed before a large and hostile audience, and the absolute control exercised by the martyrs in the midst of excruciating pain. Nor could the accounts be without long conversations with the tormentors, in which the martyrs invariably had the final word while the executioners were left floundering, partly in rage, partly in frustration, partly in admiration.

The Maccabean martyrs, of course, did not stand historically alone as the inspiration for later martyrdoms. Eleazar in particular owed much to Socrates for the style of his performance, especially in Maccabees IV, where he is pictured as an overly verbose philosopher, sensitive to God's good opinion and to his reputation in this world. Like his classical counterpart, he not only disdained all avenues of escape but also made it almost impossible for the state to do anything except go through with the grisly execution. Moreover, he also sought to thwart his opponents by maintaining firm control over himself and the proceedings leading up to his execution, and he was set upon demonstrating the truth of Socrates' own dictum that it is better to suffer a wrong than commit one.[42]

Eleazar and his comrades in martyrdom, however, have one overriding concern that is missing in the Socratic legend. They realized that they were not simply acting in the "public gaze" and on an historic forum; they also knew that they were part of an eschatological spectacle in which their suffering, particularly its intensity and duration, was a vital ingredient in the final outcome of God's design. Their trial was no isolated case; it was not simply a dramatic but ultimately forgettable reminder to humanity that individual dignity, whether it be called courage, pride, or stupidity, is an important weapon in the eternal war against tyranny. Instead, they perceived their martyrdom to be part of the historical process by which the Lord revealed His final intent. Neither Socrates nor Plato had any such vision of destiny determined by a single individual's death, least of all by the intensity of his suffering. Socrates had spoken vaguely about his destiny and hearkened to the imprecise directions of his "inner voice," but he had no clear historic picture of the future and was content with the philosopher's nirvana where he would continue his search for perfect knowledge. In contrast, the Maccabean martyrs sensed that they were part of a continuum, a divine and dynamic plan, which would be realized here on earth.

Equally important, the ordeal of the Maccabees was both historically and cosmologically a group endeavor.[43] The seven brothers felt far more than filial solidarity; they were conscious of having been "trained in the same Law" and "having been brought up together in a life of righteousness."[44] They were products and members of the same nation, and they knew that the reward for their suffering would be a warm reception into the company of Abraham, Isaac, and Jacob and the praise of all the patriarchs, along with everyone who had died for the sake of Israel.[45] Socrates' life may have been, as he hoped, a benefit to his city, but neither his death nor his suffering, of which there was almost none, was linked to Athens's destiny. The only person to profit from his demise was Socrates himself.

There is about the Maccabean nine a sense of battle and contest. They were described as athletes and soldiers engaged in a struggle with evil and tyranny, and in this engagement the heat of contest, the solidarity of comradeship, and above all else the contagious frenzy of martyrdom are unmistakable. Eleazar was called, despite his age, a "noble athlete," who proudly defied the king to " 'make ready your torturer's wheel, fan your fires to a fiercer heat.' "[46] The first brother in his death throes cried out to his siblings, " 'Imitate me . . . do not desert your post in my trial. . . . Fight the sacred and noble fight for religion's sake.' "[47] The sixth brother boasted that only six lads had made a mockery of the king's tyranny in a contest of suffering in which " 'we have not been vanquished.' "[48] And the author of Maccabees IV concludes his story with a metaphoric reference to the arena: "Eleazar was the prime contestant; but the mother of the seven sons entered the competition, and the brothers too vied for the prize. The tyrant was the adversary, and the world and humanity were the spectators."[49]

For the Maccabees the battle and the endurance of the pain were all-important. Plato had portrayed a serene and detached Socrates who viewed his death more as an intriguing personal experience in psychic transmogrification than as a moment of high drama. In contrast, the authors of Maccabees II and IV, by the very logic of their faith, were at pains to extract from their narrative every spasm of pain and drop of pathos, because Yahweh was a God who responded to little else but the suffering of those who adhered to His Law. Yahweh's divine logic was puzzling but nonetheless manifest: He punished His people with dreadful promptness lest their sins reach a level of enormity that could not be forgiven. The rest of mankind was allowed to wallow in its inequities because its sins were beyond redemption. The nations of the earth only seemed to prosper while Israel languished under the tyrant's rod. The day of judgment would arrive, because God did not wish to destroy His Holy People; He only wanted to teach them "by calamity."[50] Not only was the suffering of the martyrs a part of that process of benign chastisement but it actually accelerated the process. Appropriately, the mother of the seven, as the "champion of the Law, defender of religion, and victor in the contest of the heart," transformed her children's agonies into an apocalyptic vision: " 'My sons, noble is the contest; and since you are summoned to it in order to bear testimony for your nation, strive zealously on behalf of the Law of your fathers. . . . Be not dismayed, for it would be unreasonable [i.e., unthinkable] for you, who know religion, not to withstand suffering.' "[51]

In this "contest" the outcome was never in doubt, because the martyrs only appeared to stand alone. Unlike Socrates, who himself had established the terms of the debate between good and evil, keeping the limelight for himself and relegating the cosmic powers to the shadows, the Maccabean nine regarded themselves as members of a team. They were never the leaders; that position went to God, who not only captained His players but also laid down the rules by which both sides fought, refereed the game, and, somewhat unfairly, entered into the fray if the contest appeared to be going against His team. The martyrs did not hesitate to call upon such an interfering deity, " 'to hearken unto the blood that cried unto Him,' " and to assign Antiochus to " 'eternal torment by fire.' "[52] Although God did not help them in their torment—as the forces of evil invariably pointed out—the seven sons knew He would eventually answer their pleas for divine retribution, for it had been written: "He will avenge the blood of His servants, and will render vengeance to His adversaries, and will be merciful unto His land, and to His people" (Deuteronomy 32:43).

Socrates in his outrage at his fellow citizens had also threatened them with dire punishment, prophesying that they would suffer far more than he, but he never called upon Apollo for revenge. Indeed, he would not have wanted such interference, and, excellent scholar that he was, he actually thanked the jury for its stupidity which had made it possible for him to continue his studies in some research institute in the sky. Throughout his martyrdom, Socrates was largely indifferent to Athens's fate or the future in store for his enemies. Not so the Maccabees, who were passionately and personally involved in the future of Israel; they were in fact part of its inevitable historic triumph. When the fifth son thanked his royal judge for what he called the " 'kindly favor' " that his tormentors had inflicted, he did so in a very different spirit from Socrates. He informed Antiochus that the king, " 'though all unwilling,' " had "by these noble sufferings" enabled the brothers to show their "constancy toward the Law."[53]

Antiochus represented for the Maccabean nine, not stupidity or even ignorance, but a far deeper—almost demonic—evil, and the sixth son went out of his way to warn him that he would never " 'escape unpunished after having dared to contend with God.' "[54] In the unfolding drama the king was cast in an unenviable role. Like Judas Iscariot, Antiochus was both the product of divine will—the Lord's instrument on earth, by which Yahweh controlled the course of human destiny—and at the same time a mortal responsible for his own actions and consequently worthy of punishment in the everlasting fire. No appeal to realpolitik could excuse his pillaging of the temple, his policy of enforced culturalization, or his contemptuous insistence that the one and only God be worshiped at the altar of Zeus. His unpardonable crime was the sin of arrogance: he had "dared to contend with God." Satan played no obvious role in the martyrs' ordeal, and the temptations that they faced were manmade—the appeal to friendship, reason, and worldly gain—not the work of the devil. Nevertheless, Antiochus's arrogance possessed, at least by implication, demonic and cosmic qualities. As his impotent fury in the face of incomprehensible stubbornness rose to uncontrollable levels of sadism, he was told over and over again that he would endure "torments interminable" for his impious actions and that he would be branded as " 'blood thirsty and murderous and utterly abominable' " in the eyes of God and history.[55]

If Antiochus, assigned as he was the unequal part of God's challenger, found himself in an equivocal position, being at one and the same moment the Lord's sword and His opponent, the martyrs faced an equally difficult dilemma. By their nonresistance to the king's law, they displayed their loyalty to God's anointed monarch, but by their cheerful, almost greedy willingness to die, they ruined the effect and made it clear that they were in fact passive traitors to the Seleucid empire. Antiochus was undoubtedly correct in his conviction that he was confronted with rebellion of a perverse and sinister character. The martyrs might not raise a finger against him—indeed, it is never suggested that they had violated his decrees by practicing Judaism in secret. Instead, they simply drew the line at committing idolatry by publicly giving their approval to the official cult by eating pork that had already been sacrificed to Zeus. Nevertheless, their treason was manifest. Israel the nation and Judaism the faith were one and the same, and the martyrs were convinced that eventually both would triumph over all spiritual and political rivals and aggressors. It was no accident that throughout their ordeal—and in contrast to Socrates' response to the state's authority and the laws of Athens, which he always accepted as valid—the Maccabean martyrs at no time referred to Antiochus as king; he was always called "tyrant" or "fiend" in order to emphasize the underlying illegitimacy of his authority.[56]

The ordeal of the Maccabean nine made a deep impact on the imagination of later generations, especially the unyielding conviction that their death was necessary and beneficial to the fulfillment of an ideal that transcended themselves as individuals. As a weapon of final resort in the war against tyranny and as a forge in which to temper and validate their faith, the Maccabees were magnificent. Their death became "the crown and model" for all later Christian martyrdoms, and as Saint Augustine said, the church cherished their memory because of their "extreme and wonderful suffering."[57] Nevertheless, their performance was still deficient in both the quality of the acting and the staging of the production, because the actors lacked two essential qualities: they had no history or individuality and they were devoid of human sensitivity, immune to fear, uncertainty, and pain.

The Maccabees were essentially Hebraic versions of the old classical heroes who embodied in their deeds all those virtues and strengths necessary to preserve society. Eleazar, the mother, and her seven sons are hollow stereotypes empty of personality, and as Emerson wrote, "Every hero becomes a bore at last."[58] We know almost nothing about them as human beings, only as heroic models; reliable biographical data is missing, and their narrators, even had they possessed the information, are uninterested in supplying anything except an imaginative and idealized reconstruction of reality. Eleazar is sometimes called a sage or a priest; at other times a teacher or an expert in the Law.[59] Even his name is the one most often associated with Jewish heroes. He was, as were the seven brothers, handsome, courteous, and charming, and we are told that he was exceedingly ancient. Maccabees II, with Old Testament disregard for actuarial accuracy, assigned him ninety years.[60] The mother was variously called Hannah or Miriam, and she also was described as being elderly, but it was her chastity as a daughter and wife, not her age, that was the cardinal quality emphasized in her story. We are told that she was an obedient child and a dutiful wife who always remained at home in connubial bliss until her husband died.[61] Of the fatherless and nameless sons we know nothing except that they were well-born and fair to behold. Where they were born or how they came to the attention of the authorities—whether they flaunted their faith and asked to be persecuted or whether they were simply unlucky, being swept up in a general dragnet of orthodox Jews—are matters left in studied silence. In these flat, two-dimensional tabloid personalities there is no room for a death wish or for suicide. As the agents of God they had no choice except to die, and they knew that the public nature of their trial before the king and in the midst of his court demanded that they die as heroes and examples to others.[62]

Nor do the records grant these nine martyrs any individuality. Eleazar is credited with overcoming the infirmities of old age, the seventh and youngest brother the weakness of youth, and the mother the presumed frailties of her sex, but no one martyr is singled out as especially pleasing to Yahweh or particularly instrumental in achieving His final intent. They remain a group, and the seven sons speak collectively, "all together with one voice, as from a single spirit."[63] They went, not to an individualized heaven, but to a communal eternity in which they would eventually be able to participate in the new Jerusalem. Despite the insistence in Maccabees II on the resurrection of the body and the deep faith of the seven brothers that their mangled and dismembered corpses would be pieced together again by the "king of the universe,"[64] heaven remained for the Maccabean martyrs a vague concept; not a place of personal reward but a gathering of deceased national figures in whose praise they would be able to bask. Moreover, there were distinct apocalyptic overtones to their suffering and death. They died not solely to achieve personal salvation but, as the mother insisted, to testify to a new Israel. Each martyr was a bloody step along the path that would lead to the day of the Lord's vengeance when the faithful dead would rise up to join that tiny remnant of the living and create a "new heaven and a new earth." Their reward, therefore, was ultimately earthbound, and it lacked the individualized bliss of a Christian paradise. The Maccabean martyrs were offered little in reward for their suffering. Their recompense was to be measured only in terms of the admiration of mankind and the assurance that they had been "deemed worthy of a divine portion"; exactly what that portion was, they would have to wait and see.[65]

Both Socrates and the Maccabees are, of course, the product of legend, but with an important difference. In the case of Socrates his personality, as recorded by Plato, interferes with the impact of his death as a hero: we question his true motives because the complexities and perversities of his character are so transparent. He is too logical, too much the product of the philosophical mind—brittle, without love, passion, or compassion. There always remains the nagging doubt that possibly Athens was right: Socrates deserved to die. With the Maccabees, other factors operate to destroy the effect. Their martyrdoms are on such a heroic scale, the authors indulge in such lavish hyperbole, that all sense of reality dissolves. They suffer hideously, but their pain is uncommunicable. We feel for them in the abstract but do not know them as people who lived as well as died. Even the mother's agony seems stylized and stagey; she appears more a monster than a heroine. As W. H. C. Frend has noted, "Martyrdom in Judaism remained something of a *Hamlet* without the Prince."[66]

Before the martyr—Platonic or Hebraic—could break out of the prison of the faceless inhumanity and sterile unreality of a philosophic or heroic ideal, he had to be assigned narrators who possessed the literary artistry and ideological desire to portray the whole man, his history, his frailties, his frustrations as well as his purpose. And that takes the story of martyrdom ahead almost exactly two hundred years, when Jesus of Nazareth died on the cross.

Jesus' high-intensity religion generated high-intensity hatred.

CHAPTER 4

JESUS OF NAZARETH: "FOLLOW ME"

It is martyrs who create faith rather than faith
that creates martyrs.
—MIGUEL DE UNAMUNO,
Essays and Soliloquies

N O OTHER FIGURE in Western civilization has generated so
much interest or controversy as Jesus of Nazareth. Central to all
the questions surrounding the man stands the cross. Remove the
hemlock and Socrates remains a formidable figure, still Plato's spokesman
and the hero of unfettered inquiry. Remove the instruments of torture—
the mutilations and the stench of burning flesh—from the story of the
Maccabees and nothing much happens; other faceless champions of Yahweh would have been found to take their place. The outcome of Judea's
struggle to retain its spiritual and political identity in its confrontation with
Hellenistic culture and Seleucid armies would not have changed one iota.
Remove Golgotha, however, and Jesus in a sense is annihilated and history
reconstructed. Never was the style of a man's death so essential to the understanding and recounting of his life or so important to human history.

If death must be an integral part of a martyr's purpose; if suffering is the
ingredient that gives validity to his determination; if free choice is necessary to the drama of self-sacrifice; if staging, self-control, and the cooperation of the persecutor are essential to the desired end; and, finally, if
belated recognition and comprehension are the ultimate signatures that
translate an ordinary public execution into a historic—some might argue
cosmic—event, then the crucifixion of Jesus of Nazareth stands almost

alone in the annals of time. Certainly no other death has been so crucial in establishing the concept of Western martyrdom or, for that matter, in shaping the course of history. But no other death is so difficult to tie down in time, place, and circumstance. The problem goes to the root of Christology: every time the scholar reaches out for the historical Christ, Jesus dematerializes.

The basic, almost insoluble, issue in reconstructing the life of Jesus is the controversy over the use of religious sources for secular purposes. Ninety-five percent of our knowledge stems from the Gospels of Matthew, Mark, Luke, and, to a lesser degree, John. Scraps of often debated information can be gleaned from the Acts of the Apostles, certain passages from the writings of Paul, a few of the Apocryphal Gospels—especially Thomas and Peter—and from Jewish, pagan, and Islamic sources; but the central and fundamental texts remain those of the four evangelists, religious documents in which the historical Jesus is both difficult to extract and open to a broad spectrum of interpretations.[1]

At one extreme is the proposition that Jesus was the sublime figment of the evangelists' religious purpose. "The passion of Jesus," wrote Hans Lietzmann, "as it unfolds before our eyes in the Gospels, must be counted among the most tremendous creations of religious fiction."[2] Such a view turns on a two-pronged argument. The first relates to the indisputable fact that the evangelists were dependent for their information on oral tradition, and anything processed by memory, especially when that memory is second- or thirdhand, tends to become fiction. The second maintains that Jesus' life and teachings were in part or even in whole the product of a close but brilliantly imaginative reading and compilation of the many prophecies found in the Old Testament of the coming of a Messiah, a suffering but ultimately triumphant redeemer. Scarcely a particular of Jesus' life does not have its symbolic or literary genesis in the cultural and religious traditions of the Jewish people; even the hideous details of the cross, the nails of the crucifixion, and the division of the clothing are prefigured in Psalms 22, verses 16 and 18.

The early Christian church needed such a link to the authority of the past, to the Old Testament, in order to legitimize itself. Representing splinter and renegade groups of Judaism, the evangelists presumably were in the business of fabricating the historic reality out of which the new religion could emerge because the Christian Jehovah, like his close associate Yahweh, worked through history, fulfilling His purpose in time and place and conceiving His divine enterprise within a chronological framework. A specific starting point was required, and found in God's final covenant with

His people through His messenger Jesus of Nazareth. From this perspective, had Jesus not existed, he would have had to have been invented. The suspicion that he was, in fact, far more fiction than historical substance is reinforced by the manner in which the Gospel writers created not one Jesus but four different images, thereby confirming that there was little historical reality on which to draw.[3]

The physical reality of Jesus is not the only difficulty; the language of the discourse itself engenders uncertainty, because Jesus communicates as do few other human beings. Without doubt Socrates' logical but acerbic mind benefited from Plato's literary artistry; but Socrates spoke the language of mortals, albeit with a philosophical twang. In contrast, Jesus talked in parables, epigrams, paradoxes, and cosmic pronouncements. His recorded conversation often sounds less like prose and more like poetry with its cadence, parallelisms, antitheses, and repetitions. Even more than Socrates, he was a master of irony, which he used with devastating effect. Like any good debater, he invariably answered a question with another question or evaded answering by saying "if you say so" or "as you say." His meaning was often deeply obscure, because he appears to be speaking on a series of different levels—to believer and nonbeliever, to educated and uneducated, to God and man. There is the sensation that he was discoursing in a language of a higher order, fully intelligible to the deity alone. As a consequence, it is difficult to accept that such mysterious, yet evocative and provocative, words were spoken extemporaneously. Jesus the stylist, one suspects, must also have been the product of contemporary literary traditions, brilliantly shaped and improved upon by the genius of the evangelists themselves.[4]

At the opposite extreme is the school that maintains that questions about Jesus' historicity are both immaterial and inappropriate, because the issue of Christ's reality can only be discussed and understood in terms of faith. The Gospels were written by believers for the benefit of existing and future believers; they narrate the odyssey of a man so saturated in spiritual and divine meaning that in order to comprehend the historic Jesus, one must first be a believer. Only the reader who accepts that Jesus was the divine Messiah, the Christ sent by God, can fully understand the story of his life. The validity of the historical content of that divine truth does not lie in the story per se but in its meaning. Everything that is necessary to that truth has been told; there is no need to know more or to question that reservoir of historical information. Far from casting doubt upon the historicity of Jesus, the detail in which the events of his life are prefigured in the Old Testament only confirms his authenticity and reality.

In between the two poles stands a regiment of scholars who loudly debate the proportions but agree that the Gospels are a complex mix of fact and legend: tracks written in the sands of time which the winds of myth, exaggeration, interpretation, misrepresentation, wishful thinking, and deliberate editing have obscured but never obliterated. True, much of Jesus' story was prefigured in the Old Testament, but this does not turn the Gospel writers into fiction writers anxious solely to prove the predictions true. It is equally possible to postulate a Jesus who, because he knew his Torah and the works of the prophets, was determined to turn his own life into a self-fulfilling prophecy. Equally true, the Gospels were religious documents, but this does not deprive them of historical worth or strip Jesus of his historical existence any more than the Socratic legend, presented by Plato in philosophical and literary dress, destroys the reality of Socrates' life. The four evangelists recorded what was still living memory. Jesus died some time between A.D. 27 and 36, the least disputed dates being either Friday, April 7, A.D. 30 or Friday, April 3, A.D. 33, and the most authoritative guess maintains that the Gospels were composed between A.D. 65 and 100. They drew upon an oral tradition which was still fresh and reasonably accurate, and that is exactly how Luke, who is not regarded as having been the earliest of the narrators, begins his story.

> Inasmuch as many have undertaken to compile a narrative of the things which have been accomplished among us, just as they were delivered to us by those who from the beginning were eyewitnesses and ministers of the word, it seemed good to me also, having followed all things closely for some time past, to write an orderly account for you, most excellent Theophilus, that you may know the truth concerning the things of which you have been informed. (Luke 1:1–4)[5]

From the start then, the Gospels combined religious instruction with the memory of eyewitness reporters, presenting to future generations the picture of a man far too afflicted with the common flaws of humanity to have been solely the product of eschatological need. Despite the obvious scrubbing and laundering, a frighteningly human portrait emerges of a man not without anger, scorn, or violence. Jesus of the Gospels is no "painted saint," a point that speaks heavily for his reality. Even such tentative agreement, however, begins to dissolve when the degree of spiritual cleansing versus biographical accuracy is debated and the means for extracting historical truth are argued. Should the events depicted in the Gospels be accepted as true until proved otherwise, or must scholars be burdened with the infinitely more difficult task of displaying the validity of every facet of what they claim to be true in the story of Jesus?

Three lines of logical proof are open to the historian who seeks to demonstrate the historic authenticity of Jesus. Truth can be claimed on the basis of overlap; if all the Gospels confirm an event, presumably it happened. The same logic can be applied to outside confirmation. If there are pagan, Jewish, or Islamic sources that support the story, or if further verification can be gleaned elsewhere in the New Testament or in the Apocryphal Gospels, then the historian is justified in asserting an occurrence to be credible. Finally, proof can be derived from what is sometimes referred to as the principle of embarrassment: the inability of the Gospel writers to agree with one another on certain vital matters, and their failure to present an idealized picture of their hero. Inconsistencies, contradictions, and untidiness of structure, it is argued, are typical of oral memory. It would be highly suspicious if the Gospels presented an integrated and totally coherent portrait; the very existence of contradictions in the stories demonstrates the historical base from which the stories grew and were improved upon in the telling. This negative argument applies equally to the willingness of the evangelists to tolerate a Jesus who on occasion seems to run counter to their religious purpose. If an episode or remark places the life and actions of the founder of the faith in an embarrassing or equivocal position, if the Gospel writers seem to be explaining away a difficult situation by presenting it in as positive a light as possible, and if they are in effect apologizing for a story as it has come down to them, then in all likelihood it is true—otherwise, it would have been omitted or doctored. There are far too many jarring notes and unflattering descriptions of Jesus' irritability, boastfulness, prevarication, and abruptness; there is too much evidence of failure and humiliation for the picture not to be believable. Whatever else Jesus may have been, he was no fictional ideal. Instead, he was devastatingly and fatally human.

The crucifixion itself is said to be sufficient evidence that the evangelists were confronted with a difficult reality that had to be handled with exquisite care. They were forced to narrate the story of a Jewish criminal who was executed on a Roman cross without endangering their own positions within a Judaic community that was in open rebellion against that same imperial authority, and at the same time explain to a skeptical pagan audience the logic and compassion of a Godhead who could have permitted such an atrocity in the first place. As the Greek philosopher Celsus pointed out almost a century later (circa A.D. 170), Jesus was a most unlikely candidate for resurrection: "Jonah with his gourd or Daniel who escaped from wild beasts" would have been more suitable figures for deification.[6]

A variant of the embarrassment argument is the principle of discontinuity. If a statement or action by Jesus appears to be at serious odds with existing Jewish practices and theology or with early Christian beliefs, then, scholars argue, it also must be unique to Jesus and therefore true.

Appealing as the logic supporting the historical credibility of Jesus may be, it contains serious defects. Overlap proves little except that the evangelists plagiarized from one another or from a common but now lost source, referred to by biblical scholars simply as "Q." It does not demonstrate reality. Outside verification means equally little, because the Gospels contain serious gaps in their stories and lack any verifiable chronological structure. To make matters worse, the outside sources are themselves suspect; their sequence of events is often vague, and they were written after the event, often for polemical purposes. The star of Bethlehem and the census taking, as well as the massacre of the innocents by King Herod, may have all occurred. Historical and astronomical evidence has been marshaled to prove them.[7] But since we do not know the date of Jesus' birth, it is an act of faith to associate them with the nativity. It is the evangelists themselves who linked them to the story of his birth. Finally, the argument through embarrassment is a dull and double-edged sword. Merely because the Gospels tell four different tales does not prove the truth of hearsay. Nor does the existence of a flawed and inconsistent Jesus give any greater credence to the story: if the sources were drawn mostly from a multitude of references in the Old Testament, not even the evangelists could have woven them into a totally consistent and integrated tapestry.

The narrative of Jesus' life is like a three-dimensional cobweb: the intermingling of fact, fiction, and faith. Touch any part and the entire design disintegrates into an ugly tangle of discord and debate. Expose even the most immaculately documented existence to the intensity of inspection that has beset Jesus' life and it will turn into a quivering snarl of disbelief, mystification, and apologetics.

From the start the circumstances of Jesus' birth have generated a battery of queries to which no firm answers are possible. Who were his parents, and what was his ethnic and racial background—Tibetan, Hindu, Persian, African, Jewish? Was he illegitimate; did he have brothers and sisters; were they full or half-siblings, or were they simply cousins? Where was he born, Nazareth or Bethlehem? Was there in fact a star; did an imperial census or tax assessment coincide with his birth; and since there is general agreement that A.D. 1 was a sixth-century miscalculation, when exactly was he born—11, 7, 6, 5, or 4 B.C.?

The adult Jesus is also shrouded in equal uncertainty and confusion. What was his social and economic status? Was he born to poverty or some degree of substance? Was he a carpenter? Was he married, widowed, single, virginal, homosexual? What is the truth about his character? Is there any basis for the meek, mild, compassionate, and forgiving Jesus so popular a century ago, or is the more modern image of a man who could not abide fools, hypocrites, and cowards closer to reality? Was he in fact an outspoken and unyielding proponent of divine truth who called a spade a spade and on occasion could be as brusque, tactless, and sarcastic in his oral encounters as Socrates? More baffling yet, how did Jesus view himself—as a healer, an exorcist, a magician, a prophet, a teacher, the Son of Man, the Son of God, the Messiah, or the Redeemer and suffering servant—and how did he and the Jewish community define these terms?

What did he preach, and to whom? Did he include the gentiles in his message, or was this the later work of Paul? Where was the kingdom of God to be located? Was it spiritual, the heavenly abode of Jehovah and / or the spark of divine righteousness residing within each human soul, or was it temporal? If temporal, was such a kingdom limited to Palestine—the final step in the redemption of God's Chosen People—or did it include the entire world and all humanity? How did Jesus view the Hebraic Law—did he support it or violate it? And was there anything that he taught about moral behavior that any good rabbi might not have said? Indeed, exactly how revolutionary was his spiritual message? To whom did he preach? How successful was his ministry? And was he politically and socially as well as religiously dangerous?

As the story turns from the years of his ministry throughout Galilee to the crisis when he entered Jerusalem, the debate becomes even more acrimonious. Did he ostentatiously and provocatively choose his entrance to coincide with the celebration of Passover, or did he come as a simple pilgrim? Indeed, could he have entered months earlier, during the Feast of the Tabernacle, thereby extending the time from his entrance to his death from six days, as suggested by the Gospels, to six months? Did he arrive seated on an ass to associate himself with Zechariah's prophecy of a new kind of Messiah, the humble and peaceful king who conquers not with arms but with the word of God, or was this an invention of the evangelists, an artful linking of the authority of the prophets to the as yet unrevealed future Christ? More dramatic yet, how should the cleansing of the temple be read: as a symbolic act of spiritual purification, an abortive coup d'état against the leadership of the temple, or a revolutionary call for the overthrow of Roman rule in Judea?

Did Judas Iscariot actually betray Jesus, and if so, at whose instigation? Who in fact was responsible for the arrest—Jew or Roman? And how is that responsibility to be weighed and understood? Was Jesus a blasphemer against Yahweh; was he a political threat to Rome; was he a social revolutionary condemned in the eyes of both the Jewish and the Roman established order? Finally, to what extent was Jesus himself responsible for his own death: can it be said he got himself executed? What about the crucifixion? Did it take place as described? Were Jesus' fellow criminals actually thieves, simple bandits, or were they also regarded as political or religious deviants and dangerous malcontents? Was Jesus nailed or tied to the cross; how high was the structure; how was it designed; and how long did he take to die? Even the number of the disciples refuses to remain fixed: five, twelve, even seventy-two—the Gospels seem to disagree.

The study of Jesus' life is like the tar baby; touch any part of it and one immediately becomes entangled in controversy over semantics and sources, Jewish history and theology, Roman imperialism and the jurisdiction of the temple authorities, Old Testament prophecies and New Testament purposes, and the equally sticky issue of Jesus' motives and whether he actually regarded himself as the Messiah. Wherever one turns. the questions issue forth in never-ending ranks, as militantly arrayed in scholarly vestments as the mind of man can devise. Little wonder, then, that in the nineteenth century alone some sixty thousand biographies of Jesus were published.[8]

The historical substance of Jesus does not constitute the only problem. The story of his martyrdom is further confounded by the question of his divinity. Does the resurrection skew the narrative out of all human proportions and in a sense disqualify Jesus as a martyr? This, of course, is the central conundrum embedded in all christological enquiry: was Jesus a man who actually died on the cross or a god who only appeared to be human and therefore only appeared to die? If the latter, does he legitimately belong in a book on martyrdom, which, after all, is a peculiarly human action?

From start to finish, the Gospel writers composed their discourse with the benefit of divine and historic hindsight. The knowledge of the crucifixion dictated the terms of their narratives, so much so that their stories have been described as "accounts of his death with extended introductions."[9] Jesus' entire career led up to and was conditioned by what is presented as an inevitable conclusion. Once the climax had been reached, suddenly the narrative was transfigured. Almost without warning comes the resurrection, which transforms the story from a chronicle of a man's life and death into an epic about a god, changing the execution from an agonizing and demeaning conclusion to life into a triumph over death. As Paul suggests, Jesus died a man and reappeared a god.

The resurrection is much more than an unexpected happy ending to an otherwise unrelieved tragedy, turning it into a fairy tale. It is the essential denouement, revealing the true meaning of the story.[10] As a consequence, the evangelists were deeply aware that they were recounting the story of Christ, not just Jesus, and their narratives accordingly are permeated with symbolic language appropriate to God's direct and cataclysmic entrance into history. Only with the resurrection does the star of Bethlehem that shone at his birth, the heavens that tore themselves "wide open" at his baptism, or the darkness, earthquakes, and cosmic anger that accompanied his hours on the cross become fully meaningful. They all provide clear evidence that this is no normal story of a wild-eyed dreamer who scared almost everyone with a vested interest in society. Indeed, it took the resurrection to fully convince even the disciples that Jesus was in fact the child of God. Until that moment they are depicted as a singularly inept and unattractive collection of followers—quarrelsome, boastful, cowardly, rebellious, vacillating, shallow, unbelieving, and in one case traitorous. Only after Jesus' return from the tomb did they have faith even unto death and accept without reservation or hesitation his oft-repeated words "Follow me" (Matthew 16:24; Mark 8:34; John 21:19).

The contrast, structurally and psychologically, to the Socratic narrative and the Maccabean homily is startling. Death does not dominate or control the story of Socrates' life; it is simply the conclusion to it. True, he welcomed death, was in no way fearful of it, and in a sense it can be said he manufactured it, but death was never an integral part of Socrates' teachings. There is no sense of sacrifice. With the Maccabees there is no story of their lives at all, no history, simply the gruesome account of their mutilation. With Jesus, however, death controls the plot; it becomes the purpose of his life, the instrument by which God reveals His ultimate plan. The best the deity can do for Socrates is to converse with him through the riddle of the Delphic oracle and his *daimonion*. Yahweh is equally remote with the Maccabees; He appears to remain indifferent to their agonies, revealing His true colors only later, in the triumph accorded Israel in the war against the Seleucid empire.

The resurrection makes Jesus' death unique in history; without it the crucifixion would have been on a par with the Maccabees' torment, another example of human courage in the face of human cruelty. The return from the grave may have introduced a new and somewhat unfair dimension to the idea of martyrdom itself—gods do not play by the same rules as men—but the resurrection and its necessary prelude, the crucifixion, is crucial to the emerging concept of martyrdom. Not only do they add a human

and biographical factor so lacking with the Maccabees and an eschatological element so wanting in Socrates, but they also establish martyrdom as a
deliberate means to an end, and they prove it works. Jesus clearly, fiercely,
saw his death as being absolutely essential to his cause. He is the first man
to understand and to utilize the full power of martyrdom. For Socrates
death was profoundly personal; he died for private reasons, not for the ultimate and public triumph of his principles. The Maccabees died because
they would not deny their God by eating swine meat. The sacrificial and redemptive aspects of their suffering are merely spin-offs. Their agony helped
cleanse Israel of its sins and redeem the Chosen People, but the cause of
their deaths remained a matter of ritualistic purity. The seven brothers did
not actively seek martyrdom for its own sake.

The Gospels present a dramatically new and emotionally attractive concept of the role, operation, and purpose of martyrdom, whereby Jesus' entire life was directed by and concluded in a death that was essential to his
purpose. While Socrates' ordeal was cold, dispassionate, and devoid of cosmic purpose, and the Maccabees' agony was divested of human experience
and empathy, the crucifixion was loaded with emotional impact and eschatological meaning. More important, it is presented as a consciously elected
and highly advertised weapon used to achieve what words, pleas, threats,
and miracles had failed to accomplish: to convince people of the reality and
immediacy of the kingdom of God on earth. Jesus infused the Maccabean
concept of suffering as a way to expiate the sins of society and alleviate
God's wrath against His people with something new: death that validates a
message. The Maccabees did not have to prove God's word; it was there to
be read in the Law and in the words of the prophets. Jesus, on the other
hand, was peddling a very personal message that only his death and endurance of suffering could vindicate. His credentials and the truth of his
words were first proved by the agony of the cross and then overwhelmingly reinforced by his resurrection as Christ. Death in a way stripped away
the mask that concealed the Messiah. But until that point in the narrative,
the image that emerges most strongly in the Gospels is not Jesus the
prophet, the Redeemer, or the Messiah—he is hopelessly equivocal about
all three of these roles—but Jesus the martyr, a man who predicts his own
death and views it as his only means to salvage his ministry and bring God's
kingdom to earth. Only the introduction of the power of martyrdom is
sufficient to open men's hearts to God's word. No ordinary death would
have sufficed. Had Jesus died of cholera or by private vengeance, both the
man and his cause would have been lost. Death had to be the most violent,
painful, prolonged, humiliating, and public that could be devised.

Whatever else Jesus may have been in the eyes of the evangelists, the most vivid picture passed down in the Gospels for a hundred future generations to ponder is that of Christ on the cross. The historical accuracy of that image makes little difference. It was accepted as true by the Gospel writers and by those who read their works, and it inspired for the next two thousand years an endless array of imitators. From the moment of the crucifixion and the resurrection, martyrdom as an ideal became a central part of the new faith that grew up in the shadow of the cross.

To appreciate the story of Jesus as martyr, his career must be placed in its historical context, because the man who was seen by so many as the new Messiah preached in a world that was speeding toward the spiritual and political explosion of A.D. 66, when Israel would attempt to cast off the imperial yoke and thousands more Jews would end their lives nailed to Roman crosses. Palestine of Jesus' generation was undergoing political and spiritual trauma unparalleled since the days when Judea had struggled to free itself from the Hellenistic stranglehold of the Seleucid empire. The independence won by Judas Maccabeus and his brothers had been squandered away in a hundred years of bloody infighting that brought down upon Yahweh's Chosen People the heavy fist of yet another foreign power. Jewish internal discord became fatally entangled in the violent process whereby Rome transformed itself from a republic into an empire and the imperial authority was grasped by Caesar Augustus and his family. A century of precarious independence under the Hasmonean dynasty had ended in 37 B.C. when Rome established Herod the Great as puppet prince of Palestine, and then on Herod's death thirty-three years later, divided his kingdom between his three sons: Iturea and the lands northeast of the Sea of Galilee going to Herod Philip; Galilee itself and Peraea to Herod Antipas; and Samaria and Judea to Herod Archelaus, who proved to be so brutally incompetent that in A.D. 6 he was replaced by a Roman procurator. Thus, by the first decade of Jesus' life, Judea was under direct Roman rule, and a sense of betrayal, corruption, and enslavement prevailed.

Citizenship in a world empire came with a heavy price tag for those who loathed Roman legionnaires and tax collectors and who, in righteous anger, sought to rise up against the unclean and unholy foreigners in the name of the one and only God. Rome, however, proved to be a peculiarly demanding, efficient, and brutal master, and Israel came to know full well the horrors of that uniquely Roman engine of punishment—crucifixion, whereby the enemies of Caesar were left to die of shock, exposure, and slow asphyxiation.[11]

Roman rule—law, order, security, and punishment—earned Jewish respect but not love, and the high priest of the temple and his Sadducee supporters reluctantly cooperated out of necessity with the procurator to keep the peace in Judea. As a deterrent to lawlessness, however, crucifixion seems to have been a singularly ineffectual instrument in the face of desperate poverty, religious fanaticism, and a thousand years of Jewish stubbornness, carefully recorded in the suffering history of Israel and the words of the prophets. More important, to one degree or another, the entire religious leadership of the Jewish community—be it the Pharisees, who taught moral behavior in the synagogues; the scribes, who expounded the Law; the ascetic Essenes in their mountain retreats; or the conservative Sadducees, who acted as priests in the temple—was committed to a policy of bitter opposition to Rome. When that rebellious spirit did not appear in silent disapproval or outright—if abortive—rebellion, it manifested itself on all levels of Jewish society in fervent apocalyptic expectations about the imminent appearance of a warrior Messiah. A second David or Judas Maccabeus inspired by devotion to the Torah would supply the moral strength to lead Israel into political freedom and spiritual purity. Jesus' world might debate the precise form God would take when He assumed personal control of human destiny—suffering servant, Son of Man, elect one, God's anointed one, a reincarnated Elijah, or the Messiah—but Israel was agreed that the kingdom of God was near at hand. There were visionaries aplenty ready to herald its earth-shattering arrival. Small wonder, then, that Jesus of Nazareth, living in such an emotionally charged community, would have been drawn to the banks of the Jordan River to be baptized by one such dreamer and to listen to his prophecies.

The evangelists had trouble fitting John the Baptist into God's ultimate scheme of things. He preached the imminent coming of the kingdom of God, calling to all who would prepare themselves for this cataclysmic event to repent their sins, open their hearts to the presence of the Lord, and cleanse themselves of moral evil by baptism in the waters of the Jordan River. But what did the Son of God have to repent if his entire being was open to the Lord? How could the one person on earth devoid of sin be in need of spiritual purification? Nevertheless, all three synoptic Gospels are agreed that Jesus' baptism by John was the event that redirected his life. Mark actually begins his Gospel with the story, and Jesus himself gave full credit to his mentor, viewing him as the reincarnated Elijah incognito and calling him much "more than a prophet. This is he of whom it is written, 'Behold, I send my messenger . . . who shall prepare thy way before thee' " (Matthew 11:9–10; Luke 7:26–27).

Jesus owed a great deal to the Baptist both as the forerunner of his message and as the instrument through which he directly encountered God. Jesus underwent some form of conversion experience, and although he seems to have remained with John for a time as a disciple, he soon began to outgrow his spiritual teacher. Whatever Jesus may have felt his exact role and future to have been, from the moment of his baptism, he knew himself to be inspired, possibly actually filled with spiritual grace and divine wisdom. As a consequence, he departed from John in two essential ways. Jesus demonstrated the ability to perform miracles, especially the power to heal the body and, since in Jewish thought sickness was attributed to evil, to eradicate sin. The Baptist, the Gospels maintained, possessed no such power. The ritualistic act of baptism, not some transcendental force emanating from within John himself, washed away sin.

The second departure was closely connected with the first. For John the kingdom of God was something yet to come, an anticipated, ordained, but nevertheless distant and future, occurrence. John expected a successor, "the coming one," to inaugurate the new world. The evangelists were precise on this point; the Baptist was only a forecaster of good tidings, not their initiator. In contrast, Jesus insisted that God's holy community, although as yet undetected, had already arrived. He was both the heralder and the keeper of the keys. Luke had a clear sense of chronology and progress when he said, "Until John, it was the Law and the Prophet; since then, there is the good news of the kingdom of God" (Luke 16:16)[12] The covenant and the laying down of the Law had come first; then the prophets of the Lord's ultimate intent, of whom John was the last; and finally, Jesus' pronouncement that the future had become the present. God's kingdom had suddenly taken shape; Jesus was its guide and custodian.

If the Gospel narrators had difficulty with John the Baptist, modern theologians have had even greater trial with the kingdom of God itself, especially its once-and-future quality, and its psychological and geographic dimensions. Almost everything about the kingdom is unclear, and, as always, Jesus' language—indeed, his entire career—does little to dispel the mysteries. Is the kingdom a condition or an event? Is it located in each individual heart, the product of Jesus' two cardinal virtues—love of God and love of neighbor—and therefore the foundation for a new social order? Or is it a moment in time, an event initiated and orchestrated by the deity, arrived at either peacefully by degrees of enlightenment or in some apocalyptic frenzy so often predicted by the prophets? How imminent is this event? Would it come as Jesus seemed to indicate, within his own lifetime, the product of his works and ministry? Or, since the Gospel writers knew that in fact his ministry was a failure, had God's hand somehow been deflected and postponed by the forces of Satan? What, then, was the relationship of Jesus' death and resurrection to God's kingdom? Was his death central or superfluous to it?

The theological dilemmas and conundrums grow exponentially, every brooding question hatching a host of difficult offspring; but whatever Jesus may have thought or hoped as he was nailed to the cross, his message during the months of his ministry was clear. The moment of truth had arrived, and the world in which he lived would have to make a decision either to elect or to reject God's holy community. It is never absolutely clear whether he had in mind only the people of Israel or all humanity, Jew and gentile together, but a choice had to be made because the kingdom was in the process of embracing the earth. That epiphany would not be heralded, as the prophets had proclaimed, by violence and bloodshed; it would instead appear peacefully, the only apocalyptic element being the upheaval that Jesus' message would produce in the lives of those who believed and followed the narrow path that led to God's newly materialized kingdom.

If Jesus insisted that the moment of truth had descended, another kind of crisis has arrived in this narrative; any description of Jesus' ministry and subsequent life and death must be ordered and twisted to fit the procrustean bed of chronology. But as John Meir has recently warned, how can even the briefest biography be written "if one cannot discover what came before what, if the historical flow of before and after, cause and effect, remains unknowable?"[13] The chronology, then, of Jesus' life, which is so essential to any interpretation of that life, must of necessity be the invention of the narrator; the evangelists themselves were hopelessly inconsistent and contradictory about the order of events, arranging and rearranging, including or excluding vital material as it suited their individual religious priorities and purposes.

As with everything about Jesus, the circumstances under which he decided to take his message to Galilee and begin his ministry is problematic. Possibly it commenced when he was left on his own after John the Baptist was arrested as a potential troublemaker by Herod Antipas for having spoken out in religious indignation against Antipas's divorce and second marriage to his brother's wife. Equally possible, his ministry lasted for the three years between A.D. 26 and 29, but some scholars hold out for five years. The dates may be obscure, but Jesus' message is not. He delivered it in its sharpest and most revolutionary phraseology when, during the Sabbath service in the synagogue at Nazareth, he read to the startled congregation the words of the prophet Isaiah: "The Spirit of the Lord," he quoted, "is upon me, because He has anointed me to preach good news to the poor. He has sent me to proclaim release to the captives and recovering of sight to the blind, to set at liberty those who are oppressed, [and] to proclaim the acceptable year of the Lord." Then, putting aside the book of the prophets, he said in his own words, "Today this scripture has been fulfilled in your hearing" (Luke 4:18–21). Jesus spoke for all to hear that the text of Isaiah had come true in his own person and that the year of the Lord was no longer an unrealized dream but a present reality.

The kingdom had arrived, but it was difficult to describe because, as he told a group of Pharisees, it did not come "with signs to be observed; nor will they say 'Lo, here it is!' or 'There!' " because the "kingdom of God is in the midst of you" (Luke 17:20–21). On another occasion he rhetorically asked, "With what can we compare the kingdom of God, or what parable shall we use for it? It is like a grain of mustard seed, which, when sown upon the ground, is the smallest of all the seeds on the earth; yet when it is sown it grows up" into a mighty plant "so that the birds of the air can make nests in its shade" (Mark 4:30–32). Not only was the kingdom far-reaching but, equally important, it was also here and now: "The time is fulfilled, and the kingdom of God is at hand" (Mark 1:15). Jesus was its guide and messenger: "If it is by the finger of God that I cast out demons," be assured "the kingdom of God has come upon you" (Luke 11:20).

The cool shade of the Lord's creation could only be enjoyed by those who believed and acted accordingly: "Set your mind upon His Kingdom, and all the rest will come to you as well" (Luke 12:31).[14] The only key that could unlock the gate was purity of heart; "unless one is born anew, he cannot see the kingdom of God" (John 3:3). The most scrupulous observance of the Law would avail a man nothing unless his soul was open to God. Motive and intent were all-important. To be a Jew and live by the Lord's covenant and be a descendant of Abraham did not suffice. Something more was required, and Jesus sought in his ministry to supply that extra ingredient. "Think not," he said, "that I have come to abolish the law and the prophets . . . but to fulfill them" (Matthew 5:17). He offered the Jewish community a religion based on substance and action, not on form or tradition, and he was unable to conceal his contempt for the Pharisees in their synagogues, the scribes with their legal texts, the Sadducees in the temple, and, by implication, even the high priest himself, all of whom in his eyes cloaked themselves in the mantle of the Law only to conceal the hollowness of their hearts. Those who wished to pass through the gate into the kingdom of heaven on earth had to make a total commitment and experience a complete transformation of personality: "If any man would come after me, let him deny himself and take up his cross and follow me" (Mark 8:34).

High-intensity religion, which required its followers to forsake all— father, family, friends, and riches—and to leave behind the old selfish ego for a reformed and rejuvenated self that welcomed lepers and prostitutes, tax collectors and paupers as the special children of God's domain, aroused some to ecstasy, others to anger. For many, entrance into the kingdom came at too great a price; for others, the benefits and significance of that kingdom were woefully misunderstood, as was the guide himself. Too many of those who listened to his words wanted to be the beneficiaries of his cures, miracles, and promises, but offered nothing of themselves in return. More dangerous were those who were unable to see the difference between God's kingdom and a politically liberated Israel, and they acclaimed Jesus as the Messiah and new David, the king of the Jews. From the moment his ministry began to the day he died on the cross, Jesus' message of good tidings became fatally entangled with Jewish resistance to Rome; even some of the disciples themselves may in their earlier careers have been associated with the militant nationalistic movement of the Zealots.[15]

Still others—the majority—rejected his vision out of hand as preposterous; in some of its practices they found it downright blasphemous, and in all of its implications politically and socially dangerous. Herod Antipas, for one, having permitted the head of John the Baptist to be served up on a platter, regarded Jesus as a reincarnated and revolutionary Baptist returned to plague him, and he swore to have the new challenger executed. Rejection, however, was not limited to the political and religious elite. The people of Galilee were deeply divided over this newest and most miraculous prophet. Throughout the province the urban centers rejected his message and earned his anger. He upbraided "the cities where most of his mighty works had been done, because they did not repent." He singled out Chorazin and Bethsaida as the targets of his scorn: "Woe to you . . . for if the mighty works done in you had been done in Tyre and Sidon, they would have repented long ago in sackcloth and ashes." Capernaum, where he had set up his religious headquarters, earned even stronger words: "And you, Capernaum, will you be exalted to heaven? You shall be brought down to Hades. For if the mighty works done in you had been done in Sodom, it would have remained until this day. But I tell you that it shall be more tolerable on the day of judgment for the land of Sodom than for you" (Matthew 11:20–24).

At Nazareth the situation was worse; he was laughed out of town: "And on the sabbath he began to teach in the synagogue; and many who heard him were astonished, saying, 'Where did this man get all this? What is the wisdom given to him? What mighty works are wrought by his hands! Is not this the carpenter, the son of Mary and brother of James and Joses and Judas and Simon, and are not his sisters here with us?' And they took offense at him" (Mark 6:2–3). Jesus had no choice but to leave for the back country of Galilee, bitterly complaining that "a prophet is not without honor, except in his own country, and among his own kin, and in his own house," and he "marveled because of their unbelief" (Mark 6:4–6).

Not even those closest to Jesus had faith. His family and friends thought him quite mad, and Matthew placed harsh words in his mouth when Jesus bitterly complained that "a man's foes will be those of his own household. He who loves father or mother more than me is not worthy of me" (Matthew 10:36–37). Luke used even stronger language: "If any one comes to me and does not hate his own father and mother and wife and children and brothers and sisters . . . he cannot be my disciple" (Luke 14:26). Mark portrayed Jesus' relationship with his family in no better terms, claiming he refused to greet his mother and brothers, preferring the company of his followers: "Here are my mother and my brothers! Whoever does the will of God is my brother, and sister, and mother" (Mark 3:34–35).

Like his relatives, Jesus' disciples also began to fall away, exclaiming, "This is a hard saying; who can listen to it" (John 6:60). When the Pharisees and scribes criticized those same disciples for eating bread with unclean hands, he told his followers, "There is nothing outside a man which by going into him can defile him; but the things which come out of a man are what defile him." Unfortunately the disciples were unable to comprehend the meaning of the parable. In sadness and frustration Jesus exclaimed: "Are you also without understanding?" (Mark 7:15, 18) He then laboriously spelled the message out to them, but his words fell upon barren soil; they simply could not comprehend Jesus' vision or see beyond the literal meaning of his words and actions. Even when they saw him perform the miracle of the loaves and fishes and feed the five thousand, they viewed it as a kind of parlor trick and useful way to allay the hunger of the multitude. They had no comprehension of spiritual nourishment; and later, when they were without bread, they demanded a repeat performance. In despair, Jesus erupted: "Do you not yet perceive or understand? Are your hearts hardened? Having eyes do you not see, and having ears do you not hear? And do you not remember? . . . Do you not yet understand?" (Mark 8:17–18, 21).

The eyes, ears, and hearts of his own disciples remained closed; what then could be expected of the rest of society? "This people's heart has grown dull, and their ears are heavy of hearing, and their eyes they have closed" (Matthew 13:15). Only a few could be persuaded to accept Jesus' credentials as the herald of God's holy community or to understand his sense of overpowering urgency. Some other means would have to be found to convince such a "faithless generation," and Jesus cried out in disgust, "How

long am I to be with you? How long am I to bear with you?" (Mark 9:19).
Deeply disillusioned, he turned away from the magic of the charismatic
teacher and storyteller and from the miracles that so far had failed to
demonstrate the truth of the nearness of God's kingdom. He turned instead to a martyr's death as the agonizingly human means to achieve what
he still believed to be his predestined purpose. If the baptism by John was
the critical event that changed his life, the decision to leave Galilee and take
his message directly to Jerusalem was the choice that turned a prophet
without a following into a martyr who changed history.

But, as always, a question remains: did Jesus travel to the holy city deliberately seeking death, or did he go as a religious revolutionary willing to
risk, but not actually desiring, death in order to achieve his purpose? The
Gospel writers were, I think, at pains to emphasize that he was doing considerably more than just living dangerously. They insisted that his entry
into Jerusalem and subsequent challenge to the leadership of the temple
entailed far more than a calculated risk. His actions were deliberate decisions to initiate a course of events which the evangelists, because of hindsight, and Jesus, because of foresight, knew must end in death. Jesus gave
up parables, pleadings, threats, and even miracles as the means to establish
his credibility in the eyes of the Jewish community. Henceforth the truth of
God's message and Jesus' own credentials as the Lord's messenger would
be achieved by modeling himself on the suffering servant found in the
Book of Isaiah and by accepting death on the cross.

From the instant Jesus left Galilee, first to escape Herod Antipas's
bloody hand and then to journey to Jerusalem, right up to the final supper,
the Gospel writers introduce a heavy and mounting sense of foreboding,
punctuated by constant reminders of impending death. In the Gospel of
Mark the evangelist has Jesus announce that the Son of Man must "suffer
many things, and be rejected" by the religious leaders of Israel, and that he
"came not to be served but to serve, and to give his life as a ransom for
many" (Mark 8:31; 10:45). In Luke, when Jesus was warned that Herod
Antipas had ordered his execution, Jesus disparaged the threat and assured
his disciples that "it cannot be that a prophet should perish away from
Jerusalem" (Luke 13:31–33). And in that strange scene when the disciple
Peter recognized Jesus as the Messiah, Matthew says: "From that time Jesus
began to show his disciples that he must go to Jerusalem and suffer many
things from the elders and chief priests and scribes, and be killed, and on
the third day be raised." When Peter rebuked him for such a senseless decision, Jesus angrily retorted: "Get behind me, Satan! You are a hindrance to
me, for you are not on the side of God, but of men" (Matthew 16:21–23).

Once the decision to go to Jerusalem was made, the chronology of events becomes tighter, and the story reaches its crisis with shocking speed. The Gospels are clear: Jesus did everything possible to goad the authorities into action. In effect, he got himself executed. He arrived during the Passover celebration, when the city was crowded with pilgrims camped in the neighboring hills. The synoptic writers all describe him riding through the streets of Jerusalem on an ass. The symbol was transparent: this was no warrior Messiah but a new kind of king who came alone "in gentleness." Unfortunately, the message of peace and isolation was more than a little negated by the picture of the large, triumphal, and potentially dangerous crowd of enthusiastic followers who spread their garments and branches in his path (Matthew 21:5–8; Mark 11:7–9; Luke 19:35–36).

The center of Jesus' attention was the temple, controlled by the politically influential and wealthy Sadducees, from whose ranks was selected the high priest, the spiritual leader of Jewry. The high priest also had secular duties, because he was the presiding officer of the Jewish council, or Sanhedrin, composed of Pharisees and scribes as well as Sadducees, which governed, under the careful eye of the Roman procurator, the internal and religious affairs of Judea. Within the temple grounds, but outside the inner shrine, was a colonnaded area, the court of the gentiles, which contained a public market where vendors of all varieties displayed their wares and moneychangers plied their trade, largely for the benefit of the pilgrims who came to worship. Here, according to the fourth gospeler, Jesus made "a whip of cords" and drove the cattle and sheep merchants out of the temple. He poured the coins of the moneychangers upon the ground and overturned their tables, telling those who sold pigeons, "Take these things away; you shall not make my Father's house a house of trade" (John 2:15–16). However this so-called cleansing of the temple is interpreted, it was at the very least a public and violent challenge to the authority of the sacerdotal aristocracy of the city—scarcely the actions of a man seeking to avoid trouble, let alone of a prophet anxious to re-enact Zechariah's prince who conquered through words of peace alone.

To make the challenge stronger, Jesus added words suitable to his explosive actions. When he was asked by the priests of the temple by what authority he acted, Jesus refused to comment and answered with one of his most devastating parables. "A man planted a vineyard, and set a hedge around it, and dug a pit for the wine press, and built a tower, and let it out to tenants," and went himself into a distant land. In due course, he sent a servant to collect the rents and profits owed him, but the servant was sent back emptyhanded. He dispatched yet another servant, who received nothing but stones cast at him and was wounded in the head. Every servant sent was beaten, some actually murdered, by those hired to run the vineyard. Finally, the owner decided to risk his only and "beloved son," thinking, "They will respect my son." But the tenants said to themselves, "This is the heir; come, let us kill him, and the inheritance will be ours." And so "they took him and killed him, and cast him out of the vineyard." "What," Jesus pointedly asked his priestly audience, should "the owner of the vineyard do?" The answer he gave was a gauntlet thrown in their faces: "He will come and destroy the tenants, and give the vineyard unto others" (Mark 12:1–9).

When the priests of the temple had withdrawn in confusion and alarm, Jesus turned his words against the Pharisees and scribes, calling them "blind guides" and hypocrites. "Ye are like unto whited sepulchres, which indeed appear beautiful outward, but are within full of dead men's bones, and of all uncleanness. Even so ye also outwardly appear righteous unto men, but within ye are full of hypocrisy and inequity." And he dismissed them as "serpents; ye generation of vipers, how can ye escape the damnation of hell?" (Matthew 23:16–33).[16]

One final expression of defiance directed at the temple authorities and the religious elite of Judea is recorded, words that in the hands of his enemies became the foundation for the charge of blasphemy against God. Some time after the commotion in the temple, Jesus was leaving the grounds with his disciples and one of that group remarked on the massiveness and magnificence of the construction. Jesus answered, "Do you see these great buildings? There will not be left here one stone upon another, that will not be thrown down" (Mark 13:2; see also Matthew 24:2). Later these words were reported to the Sanhedrin in an even more inflammatory version: "I will destroy this temple that is made with [human] hands, and in three days I will build another, not made with [human] hands" (Mark 14:58). The threat clearly improved with the telling, but anyone who spoke of the destruction of the sacred temple, which once before had, under the most disastrous circumstances, been destroyed, was a source of the gravest concern to the temple authorities. If Jesus wanted to aggravate and alienate the religious leadership of Palestine, his actions since his arrival in Jerusalem could not have been better designed.

His entire career, while wandering about Galilee as well as his provocative actions in the temple, gave cause for alarm. He had associated himself with the dregs of society on a number of occasions, violated the Sabbath, ignored the synagogues, and preached in the open air to immense crowds. He had also encroached upon the monopoly of divine authority centered upon the one and only God by claiming for himself the power to forgive sin and open up the gates of God's holy community on earth. Worst of all, both in Jerusalem and while on the road, he had consistently failed to deny that he was the Son of God. As John summed up the situation, "The Jews sought all the more to kill him, because he not only broke the sabbath but also called God his own Father, making himself equal with God" (John 5:18).

What followed is one of the most oft-told and disputed sequence of events in recorded history: Jesus' arrest, interrogation, first before the Sanhedrin and then before Pontius Pilate, and finally his execution. The tragedy, as narrated by the evangelists, is filled with uncertainties, contradictions, and inconsistencies, and the question of ultimate responsibility—Jew or Roman—is still a matter of endless discord. There is no need to retell the tale or renew the debate, but as the story emerges, the Gospel writers make one point dramatically clear: a very human and frightened, but stubborn, Jesus, who persisted in predicting his own death, never lifted a finger to save himself, either by flight or by explanation.

For his entire stay in Jerusalem, Jesus' soul was in turmoil. From the moment he entered the holy city, saying to himself, "Father, save me from this hour," until he prayed alone on the Mount of Olives as he waited for Judas to betray him, his heart was "ready to break with grief." And he begged that God would permit "this hour" to pass him by: "Father, all things are possible to thee; remove this cup from me" (John 12:27; Mark 14:36; cf Matthew 26:42). Fearful as he was of the consequences of his actions, Jesus nevertheless continued to predict his arrest, humiliation, and crucifixion. Matthew has him say, "Ye know that after two days is the feast of the Passover, and the Son of Man is betrayed to be crucified" (Matthew 26:2).[17] He spoke often of betrayal, the Gospels intimating that he knew both the name of the traitor and the hour of arrest; "My time is at hand," he told his disciples when he ordered them to prepare the Passover feast (Matthew 26:18). Yet nothing was done to prevent or even postpone his destruction, because only death could bring Israel to a knowledge of God's kingdom on earth and validate the script of the suffering servant envisaged six centuries before by the prophet Isaiah.

Jesus' behavior at his interrogation by the high priest and the elders of the Sanhedrin was uncooperative in the extreme. To the accusation that he had threatened to destroy the temple and rebuild it in three days, he said nothing. To the question "Are you the Christ, the Son of God?" he replied, according to Matthew, "You have said so." Then he added words that condemned him in the eyes of his judges because they were tantamount to blasphemy: "But I tell you, hereafter you will see the Son of man seated at the right hand of Power, and coming on the clouds of heaven" (Matthew 26:61–64). Mark's rendering is even more incriminating. To the query "Are you the Christ, the Son of the Blessed?" he bluntly challenged, "I am; and you will see the Son of man seated at the right hand of Power" (Mark 14:61–62). In Luke's version, when the priests asked him if he were the Christ, he retreated into scornful circumlocution: "If I tell you, you will not believe." When they asked again, "Are you the Son of God, then?" he simply said, "You say that I am" (Luke 22:67–70).

In his encounter with Pontius Pilate, Jesus was equally unhelpful and even more ambiguous, despite the evangelists' suggestion that Pilate was his secret protector, searching for an excuse to find him innocent of the charges brought by the Sanhedrin. In John's account, Pilate said, "Are you the King of the Jews?" and Jesus retorted, "Do you say this of your own accord, or did others say it to you about me?" In considerable annoyance, Pilate responded, "Am I a Jew? Your own nation and the chief priests have handed you over to me; what have you done?" Instead of answering the question, Jesus pointed out that whatever he had done, his actions had not been directed against the secular power of Rome. He was no warrior king: "My kingship is not of this world; if my kingship were of this world, my servants would fight, that I might not be handed over to the Jews." Pilate again posed the crucial question: "So you are a king?" To which he received the equivocal reply: "You say that I am a king. For this I was born, and for this I have come into the world, to bear witness to the truth. Every one who is of the truth hears my voice." Wearily Pilate asked the ultimate question, to which no conclusive answer has ever been found: "What is truth?" (John 18:33–38).

Mark and Luke have more streamlined versions. Luke has the temple priests inform Pilate that they had found Jesus "perverting our nation" and calling himself "Christ a king." Pilate asked Jesus, "Are you the King of the Jews?" and received only the curt reply "You have said so" (Luke 23:2–3). Mark reported the same query by Pilate and the same unsatisfactory answer: "You have said so." Mark added, however, that the chief priests continued to accuse Jesus, who maintained his uncompromising silence, and that Pilate in desperation asked him, "Have you no answer to make? See how many charges they bring against you." Again Jesus refused to defend himself, and Pilate was amazed by what appeared to be his irrational and suicidal behavior (Mark 15:2–5).

Matthew even more than the other three evangelists enlarged upon Jesus' silence and Pilate's confusion and amazement. "Jesus stood before the governor; and the governor asked him, 'Are you the King of the Jews?'

Jesus said, 'You have said so.' But when he was accused by the chief priests and elders, he made no answer. Then Pilate said to him, 'Do you not hear how many things they testify against you?' But he gave him no answer, not even to a single charge; so that the governor wondered greatly" (Matthew 27:11–14). The picture is clear: Jesus' strange but magisterial silence confounded everyone and rose above the frenzy, confusion, and indecision that prevailed. Jesus alone was in control of the proceedings, and that quiet, almost arrogant economy of words became the standard for all future Christian trials and martyrdoms.

And so Jesus got what he had set out to achieve: public execution on the cross, as humiliating, lingering, and painful a death as has ever been devised. His death was his own self-decreed decision—even, it has been argued, a suicide.[18] But the story of the crucifixion is also portrayed as a preordained event, and the evangelists never permit their readers to forget the divine authorship of the script. No one, Jesus had warned, takes my life from me: "I lay it down of my own accord. I have power to lay it down, and I have power to take it again; this charge I have received from my Father" (John 10:18).

The contrast between Jesus and Socrates is startling and fundamental. With Socrates there was no humiliation or suffering. He died not as a common but as a most exceptional criminal. In Plato's account there is no sense of inevitability or deus ex machina. His death could not have been predicted, nor did Plato suggest that it salvaged or forwarded Socrates' cause. He died to vindicate and demonstrate his belief in a principle, not to convert society to it. His death, qua death, was not shocking. Instead it was cold and clinical. There was no smell of evil to it. True, the scene disturbs our sensibilities and notions of justice, but it does not open up the abyss. Above all, there is no betrayal, no passion, no atmosphere of overriding hatred.

As told by the Gospel writers, Jesus' trial and execution may well be the greatest piece of drama ever devised, and it is the only one of its kind where betrayal is crucial to the plot. Judas played only a secondary role in the total tragedy, because the Gospel writers were insistent that the focus of evil resided not in the actions of a simple traitor but in the betrayal of God's truth by all Israel, especially its religious leaders. The evangelists had excellent and historically compelling reasons to blacken the priests of the temple and the elders of the Sanhedrin and to portray Pontius Pilate as a well-intentioned Roman administrator maneuvered into an impossible situation. In their view, the Jewish community had displayed its evil by rejecting the true Messiah, and it was essential to their purpose that the Jewish leaders carry the full responsibility for Jesus' death. Equally important, it behooved the early Christian church to disassociate itself as completely as possible from a people who, at the time of the writing of the Gospels, had risen in defiant, if disastrous, rebellion against an empire that claimed for itself the full blessings of the gods.

Most important of all, there were pressing dramatic reasons for picturing a betrayal that involved far more than simply Judas's greed or disillusionment. The plot required villains of satanic proportions, and the priests of the temple were the prime candidates. The political opponents of Socrates were portrayed by Plato as stupid, not evil, men, goaded into an irrational act of injustice by the barbed and waspish ridicule of Socrates himself. The priests of the temple were equally driven men; but, significantly, Jesus did not laugh his enemies to scorn. He used far more powerful and painful language against those who rejected his message. He attacked not their illogic but their hearts closed to a higher level of logic. He lashed out not at their intellects but at their moral worth, and they in turn responded not with a close vote, as with Socrates, first to exile him and then reluctantly to order his execution, but with loud cries, "Let him be crucified" (Matthew 27:22–23). Simply put, Jesus' high-intensity religion generated high-intensity hatred, which was essential to the evangelists in explaining why the crucifixion was allowed to happen in the first place.

There is a final distinction between Jesus and those who preceded him in martyrdom. Jesus died alone, his enemies looking on, waiting to enjoy the agony or hoping for a last-minute surrender and recantation. Friends and sorrowers may have stood in the background, but Roman soldiers stood at the base of the cross. The scene upon the Hill of Skulls burned itself upon the minds and imaginations of all succeeding generations. The Hellenistic world knew all about death by lingering asphyxiation on a Roman cross and could associate with each agonizing breath. Jesus' death was a far more potent and vivid model for martyrdom than Socrates' execution, with its well-bred, painless hemlock, or the grisly torture of the Maccabees, with its grotesquely sterile suffering. Almost by itself the sight of the crucifixion was sufficient to prove Jesus' credentials as a martyr and validate the truth of his message.

With the resurrection added, the impact was devastating. Here was absolute proof that martyrdom really worked, visual evidence that the cause was alive and well in heaven and on earth. As a consequence, the man on the cross began to recede and the resurrected Godhead took over; so much so that whole theologies later emerged claiming that the divine Messiah could have felt no pain on the cross. For the martyrs, however, who in later generations hearkened to Jesus' words "Whosoever will come after me, let him deny himself and take up his cross, and follow me," Jesus the martyr, the man who elected to suffer and die, not the risen Christ, became the inspirational source for the philosophy of martyrdom that emerged during the next three centuries.

Vibia Perpetua and the slave girl Felicitas being gored in a Roman arena: "You can gain power when you are before the eyes of men."

CHAPTER 5

THE EARLY CHRISTIAN MARTYRS:
"MY LADY" PERPETUA

> Glory is largely a theatrical concept. There is no
> striving for glory without a vivid awareness of an
> audience. . . .
>
> —ERIC HOFFER,
> *The True Believer*

C ENTRAL TO self-immolation is the issue of motive. Even as Jesus
was exhorting his followers to deny their most basic instincts and
take up their crosses, the author of Maccabees IV felt the need to
question the bizarre behavior of his heroes. He posed for the seven brothers a problem that has resounded through the centuries and goes directly to
the core of history's fascination with martyrdom. Speaking collectively, the
brothers ask: "Why do we entertain ourselves with these vain resolutions
and make foolhardy virtue of fatal disobedience? . . . Why does such love
of contention inflame us, why does such fatal obduracy attract us, when it
is possible for us to lead an untroubled life if we obey the king?"[1] Why indeed! The Maccabees offered no answer except to place the responsibility
in God's hands; their folly had been decreed and was their fate. Such an answer, devoid as it is of any hint of choice, may be acceptable for imaginary
heroes who personify the spiritual expectations of the societies that have
created them; but flesh and blood that know pain and death require something more. History has been extravagant in assigning motives to those
who offered up their bodies to torture and execution, but the early Christians were the first to seek a direct answer to the question presented by the
seven brothers. In developing their answer, the Christians became the orig-
inators of a theory of martyrdom that transformed suffering into a matter

of free will and fashioned foolhardy disobedience and obduracy into divine necessity.

Early Christianity was obsessed with death by martyrdom to a degree that goes far beyond any normal collective effort to withstand the terror of persecution. Tertullian, one of the most controversial late-second-century church fathers, and Saint Cyprian, Origen, and Clement of Alexandria during the third century wrote at length endeavoring to formulate a spiritual and psychological rationale for martyrdom. They extolled the joys and rewards of death devised by the forces of evil and pictured them as the noblest attainments a Christian could achieve, a climax not only to be expected but also to be welcomed. Their purblind contempt for mangled and scorched flesh and obsessive insistence that Satan himself was directing the deadly onslaught against the faithful were not simply efforts to make a virtue of what they felt to be a necessity, but were reflections of a spiritual revolution that was convulsing all antiquity. For Christian and pagan alike, the traditional threads that tied humanity to the cosmos were being unraveled and rewoven into patterns that profoundly changed the Hellenistic world, and introduced to the concept of martyrdom a new attitude toward death and the afterlife.[2]

At issue was the ancient and accepted definition of self in terms of family, craft, city, and public duty. Increasingly the traditional forms that had given meaning to life seemed defective. Men and women sought a point of orientation outside and beyond the finite world. They found that focus both within themselves—the sense of possessing a tiny spark of the divine in the shape of the human soul—and within the supernatural, where power and divinity operated on a cosmic scale unencumbered by human rules and regulations. The warm coziness of pagan household and civic gods, even the historic and stern collectivism of the Chosen People of Israel, were giving way to a growing sense of the individual reaching out to find and to be found by a Godhead no longer restricted to a crowded pantheon of lesser gods or hiding itself within the wonders of an orderly universe, as the Stoic philosophers maintained. This new source of divinity now centered its creative energy in each human soul, where it produced absolute conversion and blinding revelation. The effect was like a massive electrical surge that short-circuits all systems. It made formal education superfluous, shattered family ties and civic loyalties, introduced into human existence the clash of cosmic conflict between good and evil, and completely transformed the relationship of life to death, this world to the next.

Saint Cyprian's cold comfort to the would-be martyr to remember the "defilement of life and the foulness of a polluted body" was not some cranky Christian oddity.[3] Both pagan and Christian branded the human container as "clay and gore," "a filthy bag of excrement and urine," and dismissed the ties of this world as chains that kept the soul from attaining heaven.[4] Tertullian's words of encouragement, "Though the body is shut in, though the flesh is confined, all things are open to the spirit," had impeccable pagan credentials, for Cicero had written, "Those are indeed alive who have escaped from the bondage of the body as from a prison; what you call life is in reality death."[5] Cyprian's assertion that "death makes life more complete, death rather leads to glory" spoke to all antiquity.[6]

Although the word "martyr" as a witness who suffers for the faith is essentially Christian in usage and was clearly congenial to the late-classical spirit in search of divinity, early Christian ideas about martyrdom were heavily derivative, borrowing and building upon the lessons of Judea. Like the Jews, the Christians knew that faith and tribulation were inexorably linked, that suffering was both a punishment and a purgation, and that the Messiah and Redeemer would bring judgment upon unbelievers and salvation to the faithful. The Christian Jehovah, in renegotiating the terms of the ancient Jewish covenant in order to encompass all nations, and in recasting himself as the God of all humanity, proved himself to be just as demanding and unpredictable as the Holy One of Israel. The early Christian fathers never tired of reiterating the need to forsake "brother or sister or parent or child or lands or houses" for the sake of a new life. Death had to be accepted as preferable to any denial of the Name; prolonged torture had to be endured for the sake of the Word. Christians as well as Jews were required to prove their faith both in the style of their lives and in their willingness to suffer.

Christian martyrs, however, differed from their Jewish brothers and sisters in three significant ways. They possessed in Jesus' death and resurrection historic evidence that martyrdom actually worked. They insisted that their blood cleansed only their own sins—it had no direct redemptive effect upon the sins of others. And they sensed in their struggle a desperate and deeply private encounter with Satan, who sought to bar their path to the bliss of paradise. Unlike the Maccabean model, Christians made no claim that the agonies of martyrdom could deflect God's legitimate wrath from the disobedience and evils of this world. Their torment might indeed be the necessary overture to Christ's Second Coming, but their passion could not expiate the sins of humanity. Atonement had already been made in full, sufficient for all times and all peoples, in the sacrifice of the cross. Jesus of Nazareth, according to the Gospels, had made a momentous decision. He had elected to fashion himself and his mission upon one of Judea's less-developed traditions, that of the suffering servant who, in the words of Isaiah, would be "wounded for our transgressions . . . bruised for our in-

equities" (53:5). The "Son of man" had turned his back, despite the expectations of many of his followers, upon the long-established and recurring
prophecy of the militant messiah who by force of arms would demolish
the idolatrous power of Rome. As Mark said, forsaken except for a tiny
band of believers, Jesus offered his blood as a "ransom for [the] many"
(10:45); In Saint Augustine's words, he "instituted not a form of slaying, but
of dying only."[7]

Death and dying became for the Christian a triple sign: the re-enactment
of the folly at Calvary, a bloody but potent proof of the power of the faith,
and a warranty to share with Christ in his glory within the tabernacle of the
Lord. Tertullian was absolutely certain on this last point: "The only key that
unlocks the gates of Paradise is your own blood";[8] indeed, "those whose victory is slower and with greater difficulty, these receive the more glorious
crown."[9] Martyrs first sealed their confessions of truth in the water of baptism and then in the blood of martyrdom, and in so doing they knew themselves to be "god boxes," specially ordained instruments through which the
Holy Spirit reverberated throughout the world and heralded God's ultimate
design on earth. The pain of martyrdom and the ghastly consequences of
the "love of contention" might be unspeakable, but the reward was the
prize of "life eternal,"[10] because it had been written that whosoever "shall
confess me before men, him will I confess also before my Father which is in
heaven" (Matthew 10:32).

The rewards of suffering were manifest and profoundly personal.
Those, wrote one determined advocate of martyrdom, who were "washed
in their [own] gore" were redeemed of sin—"If there is sin, it perishes; if
there is crime, it is left behind"—and they ascended to God, purified members of the elect.[11] Tertullian agreed. Do not beg, he said, "to die on bridal
beds or in miscarriages, or from gentle fevers; rather, seek to die a martyr,"
for "you are about to pass through a noble struggle, in which the living God
acts the part of superintendent, in which the Holy Ghost is your trainer, in
which the prize is an eternal crown of angelic essence, citizenship in the
heavens, glory everlasting."[12] The essence of such righteousness was made
all the more appetizing by the sweetness of revenge: "No city escaped the
punishment which had shed Christian blood."[13]

The benefits of martyrdom were not restricted to heaven; martyrs also
became posthumous heroes on earth. Very quickly—certainly by the
mid–second century—the torn and charred bits and pieces of their corpses
became relics more precious than jewels "and finer than gold," the object
of eternal veneration and assurance that their names and sacrifices would
not be forgotten.[14] The graves of the martyrs were regarded as crossroads
where heaven and earth intersected, points where the laws of man and na-

ture were confounded: places where the underprivileged could be rescued, the sick healed, and the condemned reprieved. As Tertullian was quick to note, the terrible torments were worth the bliss and power bestowed: "These sufferings are grievous, yet many have borne them patiently, nay, have even sought them on their own accord for the sake of fame and glory."[15] Martyrdom was a sure way of upgrading yourself, and such was the reputation of Christ's witnesses that one fifth-century observer could write that "the philosophers and the orators have fallen into oblivion; the masses do not even know the names of the emperors and their generals; but everyone knows the names of the martyrs better than those of their most intimate friends."[16]

If courage and perseverance earned a crown of eternal worth both in heaven and on earth, hesitation and rejection wrought their own dire consequence, for it had also been written, "Whosoever shall deny me before men, him will I also deny before my Father which is in heaven." (Matthew 10:33) No compromise was acceptable: "Surrounded as you are with the knives of the executioners, and the instruments of testing tortures," you must "stand sublime and strong, considering how great is the penalty of denial."[17]

Implicit in Matthew's record of Christ's promise and threat to those who confessed or forsook him was the vivid and impending spectacle of the Second Coming. Not only did martyrs have eyes that could behold the joys of life beyond the grave, but they could also prophesy the end of this world when the righteous would be vindicated, sinners struck down in the midst of their pride, and Satan and his legions overcome by Christ and his martyrs. The Apocalypse was certain, and both Cyprian and Tertullian were fond of plagiarizing the Gospel of Matthew, describing in detail famine, earthquake, pestilence, and the time when Christ would send "his angels with a great trumpet" and nation would "rise against nation and kingdom against kingdom" (Matthew 24:4–31).[18] For the Christian martyr the choice was clear. The persecutions of the age were a prelude to the final coming of Christ, when a cosmic battle would ensue between good and evil. The day of judgment was near; time was short, because the army of the elect was almost fully staffed, ready to march against the Antichrist. There was only one way to guarantee a place among those holy ranks, and that was enlistment through martyrdom.

Although the Christian theorists liked to hold up the Maccabees as superlative examples of martyrdom,[19] creeping into the Christian view of martyrdom were concepts alien to Eleazar and the Maccabean brothers. Those heroes of Judea had found strength in their collective struggle. They had not stood alone before a hostile mob, naked in a public arena. Nor had they been asked to test their souls against the devil; their ordeal was of the flesh alone. The seven brothers, it is true, had little doubt that Antiochus was in league with the forces of darkness, but his evil remained political and objective. It stood outside the brothers, a demonic influence to be resisted and overcome. As the sixth sibling boasted, six young men and a boy had vanquished the king's tyranny. The Christian devil, on the other hand, spent only a small portion of his time in the temples and capitals of institutional idolatry and tyranny. He had found a far vaster and more fertile domain deep within the soul of man. He was no longer simply a prince of worldly evil but was now, to use William James's phraseology, a "grisly, blood-freezing, heart-palsying sensation" that had entered into the Hellenistic world.[20] Martyrdom was no longer just a trial of bodily endurance, nor, as the Maccabees insisted, a necessary step in God's ultimate resolution for Israel. It was now a profoundly personal and individualistic encounter with Satan. The devil was a palpable and terrifying presence who operated in a world crawling with demonic fears, forces, and temptations. "The Adversary," explained Clement of Alexandria, "is not the body, as some would have it, but the devil."[21] When Sanctus, one of the Lyon martyrs of A.D. 167, despite "red-hot bronze plates against the tenderest parts of his body," refused to state his name or place of birth, confessing only that "I am a Christian," the narrator viewed the systematic mutilation of the martyr's body not as a victory over the Roman Empire but as "Christ's suffering in him [which] achieved great glory, overwhelming the Adversary."[22]

The martyrs did not regard themselves as part of some national destiny. They did not see themselves as defenders of an institution, because the church as a hierarchical organization that demanded total allegiance and obedience was only slowly taking shape. Nor did they consider themselves at war with Rome; they remained, at least in their own eyes, loyal citizens of the empire. Instead, the martyrs were men and women filled with the Holy Spirit who did immediate and violent battle with Satan and reaped the rewards of their victory. Cyprian stated the case in its bluntest, if most brutal, form; the hissing of our bodies when scorched with "red-hot plates is not for the sake of seeking our blood, but for the sake of trying us."[23] In other words, a new and demanding set of priorities was operating: "If you should gain the whole world, and lose your soul, what shall it profit you?" (Matthew 16:26).[24]

What gave to Christian martyrdom a new and desperate poignancy was the historic reality of the cross. For some of the early Christian apologists, Christ's humanity—the God who had taken on the shape of man and allowed himself to endure earthly humiliation and pain—was, in the face of pagan ridicule and incomprehension, something of an embarrassment. But for the martyrs, it was essential that the "Son of man" should have suffered, and Saint Ignatius would have no part of the Docetist doctrine that Christ was too divine to have felt the pain of martyrdom. While in prison awaiting death, Ignatius wrote in deeply troubled outrage, "If, as some that are without God, say . . . He died in appearance [only] and did not in very deed suffer, then for what reason am I now in bonds, and long to be exposed to the wild beasts? In such a case, I die in vain."[25] Earthly martyrs demanded a Jesus who could cry out in agony and feel the lash; they had no use for or need of a superhuman Christ. Nothing could be allowed to detract from the miracle or the reality of the resurrection on which they had staked their deaths, and the theorists of martyrdom repeatedly reiterated the doctrine of vicarious suffering: "Christ is in the martyr present and suffering in him." It was Saint Cyprian who spelled out the psychology involved in its starkest form. "For although the hook . . . is put back again into the wound, and with the repeated strokes of the whip the returning lash is drawn away with the rent portions of the flesh, still he stands immovable, the stronger for his suffering, resolving only this in his mind, that in that brutality of the executioners Christ Himself is suffering more in proportion to what he suffers."[26]

Quite consciously the early Christian fathers were articulating a psychology of martyrdom that suited the troubled souls and anxious minds of late antiquity. The potential for abnormal behavior is doubtless always present in any given individual, but during the second and third centuries the self-destructive and masochistic urge found a peculiarly congenial cultural setting that fostered the psychologically troubling phenomenon of voluntary martyrdom. For Tertullian and Cyprian the highest expression of the human soul and proof of the existence of the Holy Spirit was the urge for martyrdom: "We battle against all your cruelty, even rushing voluntarily to the contest."[27]

An appetite for death, however, could get out of hand, and the early church worried lest voluntarism slide into suicide.[28] The line between the two was disconcertingly thin when Saint Euphus in A.D. 304 rushed into the council chamber of the Roman prefect and shouted, "I want to die; I am a Christian"; or when the apostle in the apocryphal *Book of James* urged his disciple by saying, "No one will be saved if he is afraid of death, for the kingdom of death belongs to those who kill themselves"; or when Saint Ignatius begged his fellow Christians not to attempt the "unseasonable kindness" of rescuing him but to "suffer me to be eaten by the beasts through whom I can attain to God." At worst such cases are evidence of culturally induced death wishes; at best they are examples of dying "for the sake of fame and glory."[29] Clement of Alexandria was obviously deeply concerned lest the mindless hysteria of mass suicidal martyrdom destroy the psychological as well as the political impact of the true martyr's death. He "who does not avoid persecution, but out of daring presents himself for capture," he wrote, "becomes an accomplice in the crime of the persecution." Those, he concluded, "who are in haste to give themselves up . . . banish themselves without being martyrs, even though they are punished publicly."[30]

It was a difficult balancing act not to deny God but also not to court martyrdom, and the historian Eusebius recounted the case of three hesitant martyrs who, "burning with desire to obtain the prize," treated it lightly so that "they might not be too forward in seizing the martyr's crown."[31] Saint Cyprian, when he was being interrogated by the proconsul Paternus, tried to explain the subtle distinction: "Since our discipline forbids anyone to surrender voluntarily," Christians "may not give themselves up. But if they are sought out by you, they will be found."[32] Tertullian put the principle somewhat differently because his heroes were always more willing to die. If a Christian, he wrote, is denounced, "he glories in it; if he is accused, he offers no defense. When questioned, he confesses of his own accord. For the word of condemnation, he gives thanks."[33] Even Tertullian, however, sensed that martyrdom, if it were to have the desired effect both as a public test of faith and as a private path to paradise, had to be an act of the mind as well as of the spirit, entered into calmly and rationally. The ecstasy, the hysteria, the enthusiasm had at all costs to be controlled and curtailed.

Politics as well as psychology was implicit in Tertullian's approach to martyrdom. The early church fathers were well aware that the martyr who played his role to perfection, enduring the ordeal and defeating the devil in public combat, was one of the church's most potent weapons in its battle against paganism. "So great," wrote Saint Cyprian, "is the virtue of martyrdom, that by its means even he who has wished to slay you is constrained to believe."[34] Tertullian likewise boasted of the spectacle of Christians dying in agony for God's truth, and he assured the pagan world that "your tortures accomplish nothing, though each is more refined than the last. Rather, they are an enticement to our religion. We become more numerous every time we are hewn down by you; the blood of Christians is [the] seed [of the church]."[35] Over and over, the theorists emphasized the importance of an audience and the need for the martyr to stand in the spotlight. Origen in his *Exhortation* described "a great theater" which "is filled with spectators to watch your contests and your summons to martyrdom, just as if we were to speak of a great crowd gathered to watch the contests of athletes supposed to be champions."[36] Saint Cyprian was no less theatrical. As secular honor, he wrote, was crowned in the arena "with the people looking on and the emperor present," so spiritual grace was achieved in "a sublime and a great and a glorious contest for the reward of the heavenly crown." Such a sight was contagious when, with "all men watching, an undismayed devotion" struggled "against earthly crosses and the threats of the world. . . ."[37] Tertullian phrased it, as usual, more succinctly and in so doing went to the political root of martyrdom: "You gain power when you are before the eyes of men."[38]

Martyrdom was a matchless weapon. As much as pagans might sneer at Christians' suicidal folly and at the charnal house flavor of their religion, the sight of those who believed enough to die—not, as the Maccabees had, as part of a popular uprising, but alone before a viciously antagonistic mob—was a deeply disturbing performance to a society that was already questioning the values and tenets by which it lived. Tertullian had no doubt as to the answer to his rhetorical questions: "Who is not stirred" at the sight of such endurance to pain "to enquire what is really beneath the surface? And who, when he has enquired, does not approach us" and "join us in procuring God's grace"?[39]

Tertullian's words, written at the close of the second century, cut two ways: there were pagans who were profoundly "stirred" and wanted to know more about Christianity, but there were also those, equally stirred, who reacted very differently. Some in disgust asked: "Where is their god, and what good was their religion to them which they preferred even to their lives?"[40] Others were more vehement and wished to root out the superstition as a pernicious and corroding malaise that was spreading rapidly and destroying the moral fibers of the empire. Initially, the pagan world had difficulty differentiating Christian from Jew. During the first generation after Christ, possibly even during the second, if Christianity was noted at all, it was seen as a rather perverse Jewish splinter group which fell under the protection of the special treatment offered Judaism by Rome. Jews were permitted to practice their own national religion and, unlike other peoples of the empire, were not obliged to participate in those imperial religious and civic functions that violated their ancient covenant with Yahweh, especially the obligation on the part of imperial and local officials to sacrifice to the emperor. Jews were regarded by the empire as "licensed atheists" whose incomprehensible deity had, in the eyes of Rome, a single redeeming feature—He was at least ancestral, a part of Jewish history. This the pagan world respected and understood.

By A.D. 64, the year of Rome's destruction by fire, pagan society had awakened to the realization that Christians were not Jews and could not claim legal status as a privileged religious group. They had become sufficiently "loathsome" in the public eye to be singled out by Nero's government as useful scapegoats to deflect responsibility from the emperor for the fire that razed the imperial city. Cornelius Tacitus, writing sixty years after the event, reported in his *Annals* that an "immense multitude" of Christians were rounded up and accused of arson. As punishment the followers of Christ were tied up in skins of wild animals and fed to the dogs, nailed to crosses, or turned into human torches to light Nero's gardens. Tacitus, however, made it clear that their real crime was not incendiarism but their reputation as enemies of humanity, unfortunate but deserving victims of the emperor's cruelty. By the early years of Hadrian's reign (112–138), educated Roman response to Christianity was such that Tacitus would conclude that "their originator, Christ, had been executed . . . but in spite of this temporary setback the deadly superstition had broken out afresh, not only in Judea, where the mischief had started, but even in Rome, where all degraded and shameful practices collect and flourish."[41]

Despite upper-class repugnance, Christianity steadily gathered momentum and spread throughout the Roman world. The deeply introverted quality of the faith, combined with the absolute conviction that personal salvation awaited the believer and that the inequalities, suffering, and injustices of this world would be replaced by the bliss of paradise, attracted increasing numbers of converts who felt themselves to be a part of a new and exclusive brotherhood. Christians sensed the existence of a divine truth that had nothing to do with civic ceremonies, circuses, gladiator fights, public spectacles, or the ancient virtues and piety so praised by Roman philosophers. Above all, the new faith dispelled the sense of loneliness and abandonment experienced in the ever-growing multi-national city slums of the empire.[42]

As Christianity spread, especially within the urban population, it engendered in pagan hearts a bitterly hostile response.[43] The reason could not have been exclusively Christian refusal to burn incense to the emperor's genius or spirit or sacrifice to the local gods while asking for the emperor's good health. After all, Rome tolerated the "inexplicable monotheism" of the Hebrews. But Christianity was not Judaism; it was novel and rootless, having deserted the faith of its forefathers. The new religion appeared to be some kind of clandestine society of mixed nationality which preached millenarian nonsense about the imminent destruction of the world and the Second Coming of Christ. Christians worshiped a dangerous prophet who had been denounced by his own people and executed for his manifest religious and political crimes. Worse, Christianity was a sect devoid of piety. It lacked respect for those historic customs and religious bonds that gave structure and meaning to the Hellenistic world and preserved its three most essential features: family, city, and empire. Christians were not just disbelievers; unlike the Jews, they were also bigoted atheists who jeered at the ancient deities and denied the right of others to offer the gods thanks and praise for the security that Roman law and military legions provided to the Mediterranean world. No pagan would have questioned Cicero's warning that the "disappearance of piety towards the gods will entail the disappearance of loyalty and social union among men."[44]

The followers of Christ were seen by pagans as "a people sulking and shunning the light, silent in public but garrulous in corners," despising "the temples as dead houses," and laughing "at sacred things." Christians were accused of walling themselves off from the rest of society: "You do not go to our shows, you take no part in our processions, you are not present at our public banquets, you shrink in horror from our sacred games."[45] Who knew what abominations and evil deeds went on behind closed Christian doors and in secret meetings? It was not surprising that popular indignation created hideous stories of incestuous orgies, ritualistic infanticide and cannibalism, not to mention revolutionary plotting to unravel the bonds of social and political order.

In the eyes of the empire, Christians violated traditional Roman response to religion, which for most people was rooted, not in some inner closet of the soul, but in the physical and public observance of those rituals that linked the routine of family and business to the cosmos and that garbed the trivia of daily life with higher meaning. Christians seemed to challenge the gods by their scoffing disrespect, daring them to punish humanity for permitting such impiety, thereby bringing down upon the earth that divine retribution and apocalyptic terror of pestilence, war, and death which they expected under any circumstances. Tertullian attempted to refute with laughter the argument that Christians were the cause of all human and environmental disasters. "If the Tiber rises as high as the city walls, if the Nile does not rise to the fields, if the weather will not change, if there is earthquake, famine or plague—strait way the cry is heard, 'Toss the Christians to the lion!' "[46]

Possibly the Christian might have survived the brand of atheist, bigot, and traitor without experiencing persecution, but the final label—domestic troublemaker—struck the Roman world at its most tender and fundamental point: family and generational ties that held society together. "They get hold," wrote the Platonic philosopher Celsus, "of children in private and some stupid women with them" and "they let out some astonishing statements as, for example, that they must not pay any attention to their father[s] and school-teachers, but must obey them," claiming that Christians alone "know the right way to live."[47] Under such circumstances, Christians were undoubtedly enemies of humanity, and they deserved to die by whatever lingering vengeance society could contrive. If Christians wanted to believe that "the longer is your strife, the loftier will be your crown,"[48] Rome was perfectly willing to indulge them. Pliny the Younger, the second-century governor of Bithynia, a Roman province on the Black Sea, might have worried whether "the mere name of Christian" was sufficient reason to persecute Christians even without specific evidence of violating imperial law, but everyone agreed with him that "their stubbornness and unshakable obstinacy ought not to go unpunished."[49]

How many Christians died, at the hands of Rome and outraged public opinion that varied from province to province and decade to decade, is impossible to say. Depending on time and place, the contemporary estimates range from Origen's view that only "a few whose number could be easily enumerated, have died occasionally for the sake of the Christian religion" to Eusebius's statement that "innumerable martyrs obtained the crown."[50] Whether the historian should reckon the total count over three centuries in the thousands or in the hundreds of thousands is largely a matter of guesswork. If the scholar requires historic proof that a particular martyr ever lived and died, the numbers begin to dwindle. If eyewitness descriptions without embellishments by later hands eager to improve upon reality are required, the list dramatically shrinks even further; and finally, if one insists that the martyrs actually speak for themselves, the list all but vanishes. At one extreme we have the bloodcurdling, masterfully ludicrous, and totally imaginative account of the prolonged agonies of Saint Clement. His flesh was torn to ribbons with iron claws, his face was battered with stones, and his body broken on the wheel, slashed with knives, and beaten with wooden rods. To add to his troubles, his jaw, or what was left of it, was broken, his teeth pulled out, and his feet crushed in an iron boot. For the sake of variation, he was suspended from the ceiling and scourged with burning torches and then given to the wild beasts as a meal. Red-hot metal slivers were driven under his fingernails and his hands covered with quicklime and left for two days; afterwards he was further whipped and flayed and roasted on a red-hot griddle. The process of beating, burning, crushing, and rending went on with boring regularity for days on end until, almost as an afterthought, he was beheaded.[51] At the other extreme are a handful of heroes who cut the historical mustard; and one of these, undoubtedly the most interesting, is a young mother of twenty-two named Vibia Perpetua who died during the month of March, A.D. 203, and whose *Passion* offers a matchless glimpse into the making of a third-century martyr.

Perpetua was born in the neighborhood of Carthage in A.D. 180 or 181. Her parents belonged to a provincial elite that had enjoyed almost a century of unparalleled prosperity and splendor, a period of "deep peace" when to be a Roman citizen was "sufficient guarantee of personal safety."

By A.D. 180, however, the heyday of the empire was drawing to a close. In 192 the last of the Antonine emperors, the gladiator son of the philosopher-warrior Marcus Aurelius, was murdered by his mistress during a palace revolution. A year later, Septimius Severus, a North African general, seized Rome by force and had himself declared Caesar. Thereafter emperors sought to dress themselves in the historic robes of Roman tradition and call upon the immortal gods of the city as their allies, but the naked truth was that the army, already heavily barbarized, was the real source from which political power flowed.

Behind the urban world into which Perpetua was born, behind Carthage's impressive monuments to Roman culture and indestructibility—its temples, stadiums, baths, and forum, all modeled on the imperial city and all allegorizing in stone the semi-godlike nature of the emperor—lurked a gnawing sense of unease and nostalgia for the past and a foreboding about the future. As the second century gave way to the third and Perpetua grew to adulthood, married, and bore her child, the empire began to experience a taste of the troubles to come: inflation, plague, natural disasters, and political unrest. In Carthage the sense of malaise was reinforced by the sudden and seemingly demonic spread of Christianity. The populace reacted with angry demands that the proconsul rid the province of a cult so disloyal and ungrateful that it would not worship the gods that had given the empire over a hundred years of security or sacrifice to an emperor who was himself a North African. As Christian and pagan knew, "whatever you receive in this life you receive" from the emperor.[52]

The imperial government itself was also disturbed by the alarming presence throughout the empire of a religious sect that by its atheism and disrespect for everything that was holy seemed to dare the gods to bring upon the world a torrent of disasters. In 202 Severus gave voice to the government's willingness to listen to the demands of outraged pagan public opinion by forbidding the proselytizing of the Christian faith and ordering the punishment of those who converted to it: "For ill weeds grow apace—decay of morals grows from day to day, and throughout the wide world the abominations of this impious conspiracy multiply."[53]

Unfortunately, exactly at this moment, the well-educated, married daughter of the Vibius family, Vibia Perpetua (the classical custom was to give the family name first), was won over to the new creed. She became in the eyes of both the city magistrates and its populace an exceptionally obstinate ill weed. What emotional trauma Perpetua underwent, what induced a sudden and massive conversion, we can only surmise. If it was anything like Cyprian's blinding experience, then for Perpetua also "doubts began to clear, secrets revealed themselves, the dark grew light, seeming difficulties gave way, supposed impossibilities vanished."[54] Suddenly, inexplicably, she found it necessary, in Clement of Alexandria's words, "even at the risk of displeasing our fathers," to bend a "course towards the truth and seek after Him who is our real Father, thrusting away custom as some deadly drug."[55] The surge of her conversion—spiritual awakening, baptism, martyrdom— seems to have swept over her in less than a month, and it grew in intensity as it approached the moment of crisis. A sense of revelation—the opening of the soul to exultation and freedom so great that human ties of love and duty to father, mother, child all paled in contrast—did not come from nowhere. It had psychological roots and cultural history.

The spark that burst into a flame which "purged and purified" Per-petua's heart and split the Vibius family asunder appears to have been set by a proselytizing Christian named Saturus, her spiritual father, whose own personal quest for martyrdom was so intense that he turned himself in as a Christian so he could suffer along with his new disciples. But for his mes-sage to have had such a devastating impact, there must have been highly combustible psychological and cultural materials already existing within the recesses of Perpetua's mind. In A.D. 202 conversion and martyrdom were in the air. Perpetua lived in or near a city where a peculiarly virulent and fiercely ascetic variety of Christianity, one that glorified suffering and martyrdom, was spreading rapidly. The reading material available to an ed-ucated woman—Christian or pagan—who probably read both Greek and Latin was highly inflammatory, exciting the imagination with vivid scenes of torture and suffering. The Hellenistic romantic novel, emerging in the late second century, liked to present its heroines as defying their seducers' worst threats in order to retain their virtue. "Bring on the instruments of torture: the wheel: here, take my arms and stretch them; the whips—here is my back, lash away; the hot irons—here is my body for burning; bring the axe as well—here is my neck, sliced through! . . . A single woman com-petes with all the engines of torture and wins every round. . . . My one weapon is my freedom which cannot be shredded by lashes, dismembered by sharp blades, or burned away by fire. It is the one thing I shall never part with." It was not enough that the classical heroine should suffer; she also had, as A. D. Nock has noted, to "have the spot light" and advertise her sac-rifice. She felt compelled to let her lover know that "for your sake I left my mother and undertook a life of wanderings. For your sake I went through shipwreck and captivity at the hands of pirates. For your sake I have been a sacrificial victim . . . ; for your sake I have been sold and shackled with iron. . . ."[56]

Christian pulp literature was even more lurid. Three of the five im-mensely popular apocryphal Acts of the Apostles, produced largely for female consumption and possibly actually written by women, were composed either just before Perpetua's birth or during her lifetime. They embodied the cardinal virtues of the Christian woman—chastity, endurance of suffering, and freedom to follow her inner light. Unlike the classical novel in which the heroine invariably marries and lives happily ever after, the Christian woman found true happiness only in death. "May the remaining days of my life be cut short for me," says the heroine of the Acts of Thomas, "and may I depart from life, that I may go the more quickly and see the beautiful one whose fame I have heard."[57] Marriage for these ladies was "a device of the serpent," and the Acts of Peter claimed that many woman "fell in love with the doctrine of purity and separated from their husbands." All the Acts insist that "blessed are they who have kept the flesh pure, for they shall become a temple of God."[58] In the Acts of Paul the young virgin Thekla rejects the pleas of both her mother and her fiancé and follows the apostle Paul in order to preach the truth. Several times and in various ways she is sentenced to death, but invariably and miraculously she is saved, and as a final act of defiance and proof of her determination, she cuts her hair, dresses in male garb, and goes out on her own to proselytize for the faith and "teach the word of God."[59]

Christian imagination was excited not only by fiction, but also by morbid accounts of recent martyrdoms, and the slave girl Blandina, who died with the Lyon martyrs of A.D. 177, almost instantly became the heroic model for Christian women. The story describes Blandina's suffering in hideous detail and tells of the fears of her comrades that "bodily weakness" would make it impossible for her to hold to "a bold confession of her faith." Blandina, however, is "filled with such power that even those who were taking turns to torture her" eventually weary of their task. She receives "renewed strength with her confession of faith," and her triumphant insistence that "I am a Christian; we do nothing to be ashamed of" brings her "refreshment, rest and insensibility to her present pain."[60]

The Lyon martyrs had been heavily influenced by Montanism, a brand of early Christianity which believed that God's revelation had not ended with the cross and Christ's resurrection but was an ongoing process.[61] The Holy Spirit continued to reveal itself in the visions and inner voices of God's elect, who could sincerely say "our father which art in us." For Montanus, the mid-second-century pagan priest who had unexpectedly converted to Christianity, the divine energy did not limit itself to heaven; it was a mystical force that illuminated this world but was revealed only to a few. He claimed for himself and his two prophetic mediums—Priscilla and Maximilla—the power of prophecy. They were the vehicles through which God spoke directly to mankind, revealing His immediate goal—the destruction of the nations of this earth and their re-creation into the kingdom of God. The ecstasy of the spirit needed no institutional intermediary; it spoke directly to and for God. Those who were consumed by the fire of revelation rejected the ties and loyalties of this world, at times even its laws and obligations, as being superfluous in the light of the prophetic knowledge that spoke from within them. They longed for reunion with heaven through the path of martyrdom. They represented that intense and, in the late second century, still passionate conviction on the part of Christians that the true church lay not in brick and mortar, bishops and hierarchy, congregations and creeds. Instead it consisted of the inner faith of the individual, in God's finger as it touched each separate Christian heart and heralded the wonderful image of Christ's eternal city in heaven as well as his impending kingdom on earth.

For the Montanists there could be no uncertainty, because Christ had revealed his final coming to the prophetess Priscilla in a dream: "Christ came to me in the form of a woman clothed with a long, gleaming, flowing robe, and placed wisdom in me and revealed to me that this place is sacred and that in this place the heavenly Jerusalem shall descend."[62] That place in the mid–second century was Phrygia in Asia Minor. By the year 200 Montanism, at least in the eastern Mediterranean, was being disowned by the church; it was dangerously individualistic, and even the early church preferred that God speak discreetly and modestly through proper ecclesiastical channels and not through the embarrassing ranting and ravings of some self-ordained prophet of the Holy Spirit. Nevertheless, Montanism in the west, especially in Carthage, remained strong, the great Tertullian himself becoming a convert. This variety of fervent "New Prophecy Christianity" with its sense of expectancy, liberation, and spiritual equalitarianism caught Perpetua's imagination and led first to her conversion, then to her rejection of her family and child, and finally to her defiance of the imperial authority and her martyrdom.

Our knowledge of Perpetua's ordeal comes from her *Passion*, which consists of her prison diary, a spurious vision by Saturus, and a brief preface and longer conclusion by a third-century redactor. The diary with its grim prison description and vivid dream sequences is a compelling work of art, the authenticity of which almost no one doubts. It is far too heavily laced with pagan and erotic symbolism to have been written by some later Christian fabricator. The other two segments are less impressive. Saturus's vision of his journey with Perpetua to the abode of the angels reads more like an attack on the Carthaginian church in this world than a picture of heavenly bliss in the next. The redactor's additions are clearly contemporary to the events described and may have been written by Tertullian himself, who was a resident of Carthage. How truthful they are is another matter, for they continue the story after Perpetua's diary leaves off and give a highly contrived and imaginative account of her martyrdom.[63]

How Perpetua initially came to the attention of the authorities is never made clear.[64] She was certainly not a special case, because taken into custody with her were two slaves, Revocatus and Felicitas, who was nearly nine months pregnant, and two other converts to the faith, Saturninus and Secundulus, all presumably unbaptized novices still receiving religious instructions. The Vibius family disaster had not come without warning. Perpetua and her friends had privately been receiving religious instruction—probably from Saturus—and as a consequence had been ordered before the secular authorities for questioning. Her father was present at this interrogation and sought to dissuade his daughter from publicly confessing her Christianity. "Father," she said, "do you see this container lying here, called a water pot?" He acknowledged the name of the article, and Perpetua continued: "Can it be called by any other name than what it is?" When he admitted "No," she quickly replied with terrifying logic, "So too, I cannot call myself anything other than that I am a Christian."[65] Not without considerable justification, her father was shocked and alarmed by her words, and raised his hand in anger as if to "pluck out her eyes." But in the end he went away defeated by his daughter's consuming determination to witness Christ, and she recorded that shortly thereafter the five converts took the next step in declaring their faith—they were baptized. "I was inspired," she confessed, "by the Spirit not to ask for any other favour after the water [of baptism] but simply the perseverance of the flesh."[66] The only solace left the father was the knowledge that his two sons—one untouched by Christianity, the other a catechumen like his sister but unnoticed by the authorities and therefore, presumably, a quieter and more cautious convert—were still dutiful children. The heart-rending irony, however, was that Perpetua had been his favorite, the offspring on whom he had lavished his affection and possessions.

A number of days after the newly baptized Christians had been questioned and proved to be unyielding, Perpetua with her baby and the other believers were imprisoned, and we possess in her diary her deeply moving description of her experience in a Roman dungeon. "I was terrified as I had never before been in such a dark hole. What a difficult time it was! With the crowd the heat was stifling; then there was the extortion of the soldiers; and to crown all, I was tortured with worry for my baby there."[67]

Perpetua's narrative raises almost insolvable questions about the handling of all Christians during the early third century and in particular about why the daughter of a man of considerable local importance should have

ever been arrested in the first place. Perpetua tells us that two church dea-
cons, Tertius and Pomponius, who seemed to have been able to enter the
dungeon with impunity, were able to bribe the guards into moving the prisoners to a better location, where she was able to nurse her baby. There both
her newly converted Christian brother and her mother, whose faith is never
made clear, were able to visit her. Much tò Perpetua's grief, the prison officials insisted that she turn over her baby to them, but some days later they
reversed that decision. The prison became a nursery, and Perpetua wrote,
"At once I recovered my health, relieved as I was of my worry and anxiety
over the child. My prison had suddenly become a palace, so that I wanted
to be there rather than anywhere else."[68]

At this juncture in the diary, Perpetua introduces her first vision and offers a possible hint as to why she and not her brother or the church elders
had been singled out for arrest. Her brother, using an address of great respect, said to her, "My lady, my sister, you are now greatly blessed; so much
so that you can ask for a vision," and, he predicted, "you will be shown if it
is to be suffering unto death or a passing thing." Perpetua in no way depre-
ciated her brother's estimation of her special powers: "I, who knew I could
speak with God, whose great benefits I had experienced, promised him
faithfully, saying 'tomorrow I will tell you.' "[69] As she predicted, God was
obliging, and in her vision she saw Saturus, who had been her guide and
"builder of our strength" in this world and who had now joined her in jail,
climbing up a narrow bronze ladder of great height, reaching to the heavens. The way up was heavily and dangerously impeded by all sorts of razor-
sharp weapons—swords, spikes, spears, daggers—attached to the side of
the ladder, ready to rip open the unwary climber. At the foot of the ladder
was an enormous dragon or serpent, on whose head Perpetua had to tread
cautiously in order to reach the first step and follow Saturus up the ladder.
When she reached the top, she discovered herself in a vast pleasure garden,
where stood a stunning, white-haired shepherd who offered her "indescribably delicious" food. While she ate this divine substance, a vast array of
people dressed in snow-white gowns cried out "Amen." When she awoke,
she immediately described the vision to her brother, and they agreed that
the dream had augured death by martyrdom.

A few days later, it was rumored that their trial was about to begin, and
Perpetua had her longest and most searing meeting with her father, who
came to make a final plea before the irrevocable decision was made.
"Daughter," he said, "have pity on my grey head; have pity on me your
father, if I deserve to be called your father. . . . Do not abandon me to be
the reproach of men. Think of your brothers, think of your mother and
your aunt, think of your child, who will not be able to live once you are

gone. Give up your pride! You will destroy all of us! None of us will ever be able to speak freely again if anything happens to you."[70] Then he did an extraordinary thing: he kissed her hand, threw himself at her feet, and with tears in his eyes addressed her not as his daughter but as "mistress." The Latin is difficult, because *dominam* can mean "lady" or "woman" but it is also used as "mistress" or even "goddess."[71] In this case, he was certainly referring to his daughter as his superior, which even in a doting and hysterical parent was an unusual thing for a Roman father to do. It is almost as if Perpetua's charismatic personality—her ability to commune with divinity—was recognized within the family. Perpetua's reply is equally disturbing. She simply stated that she "was sorry for my father's sake, because he alone of all my kin would be unhappy to see me suffer."[72] That cold response has caused trouble. Some interpreters insist that here is proof that her family, except for her father, was secretly Christian and that it welcomed for her sake a martyrdom which would open up the gates of heaven for her.[73] Unfortunately for such an interpretation, the redactor makes it perfectly clear that Perpetua's second brother was a pagan. Moreover, he never refers to the mother as a Christian—and, most difficult of all, never mentions a husband. Throughout the narrative Perpetua's spouse maintains an extraordinarily invisible profile, neither the father nor his daughter ever referring to him.[74] This is strange, because the husband was clearly the injured party. Perpetua knew that, like all Roman wives, she must accept only the gods in whom her husband believed and must shut her door to all foreign religions. "No god can be pleased by stealthy and superstitious rites performed by a woman."[75]

Whatever Perpetua's opinion of her extended family—whether she was expressing appreciation for its Christian support of her actions or disdain for its cruelty in wishing to see her suffer—her efforts to console her father offered cold comfort to a pagan whose heart was overflowing with paternal love but closed to the Holy Spirit. Perpetua's sense of divine destiny was transparent: "It will all happen," she told her father, "as God wills; for you may be sure that we are not left to ourselves but are all in His power."[76]

God decreed that the summons for trial should come unexpectedly. In the midst of eating breakfast, the prisoners were hurried off to a hearing at the city forum, where they were confronted by a large and unfriendly crowd. One by one they were arrayed before Governor Hilarianus. When it came Perpetua's turn to take the stand, her father rushed up to the tribunal, his daughter's baby, who once more had been returned to the family custody, in his arms. Then he confronted his daughter and the city officials with yet another embarrassing display of his grief. Attempting to drag Perpetua from the steps, he cried out: "Perform the sacrifice and have pity on your baby." The governor also called upon her to "have pity on your father's grey head; have pity on your infant son. Offer the sacrifice for the welfare of the emperors." Perpetua's only reply was a laconic "I will not!"[77] The answer was short because the issue was simple: "Every idle word that men shall speak, they shall give account thereof in the day of judgment" (Matthew 12:26). As Origen later warned, what words could be more fatally careless than an oath denying the Lord?[78] Perpetua had no choice, and Hilarianus continued the trial with the crucial question: "Are you a Christian?" "Yes, I am," she answered; and that public confession proved her guilt and terminated her trial.

Generally such scenes in traditional Christian passions include long-winded displays of wit and repartee on the part of the hero, and the much later *Acts of Saint Perpetua* endeavored to remedy this deficiency, supplying a dialogue between Perpetua and the governor in which she punned heavily on her name.[79] But in her own diary the encounter is enriched only by a final hysterical exhibition by her father, who refused to accept his daughter's answer and had to be beaten and physically removed from the forum. Perpetua's sole reaction to this impassioned performance was to say that she grieved for her father's downfall "as if I had been beaten," and that she "felt sorry for his pathetic old age," almost as if she attributed his pagan blindness and stubborn grief to senility.[80]

Hilarianus passed sentence on the Christians and ordered them to be condemned to the beasts. They all, reports the redactor, returned to jail in high spirits. Perpetua, however, had her private troubles. She had become accustomed to nursing her son, and now that her baby had been taken away from her, her breasts began to swell and hurt. She sent Deacon Pomponius to her father to beg for the return of the child. This he refused. Perpetua's problems, however, were soon resolved by what she regarded as divine intervention: "As God willed, the baby had no further desire for the breast, nor did I suffer any inflammation; and so I was relieved of any anxiety for my child and of any discomfort in my breasts."[81] During those final days the convicts were transferred to a "military prison" where the adjutant permitted visitors. As the day of martyrdom approached, Perpetua's indomitable father again appeared, overwhelmed with sorrow and pulling the hairs from his beard, cursing his life, and saying words that would have moved "all creation." They had, however, no effect on his daughter; all she wrote in her diary was that she ached "for his unhappy old age."[82]

While waiting for martyrdom, Perpetua displayed further proof of her power to "speak with God"; she had three more visions. The first two dealt with her seven-year-old brother Dinocrates, who had died horribly years before of face cancer. Thought of Dinocrates came to her totally unexpectedly while at prayer, and she knew that she had, as a consequence, been granted the right to visit him in her dreams. That same night Perpetua saw Dinocrates and others with him crawling out of a dark hole, all hot and thirsty, dirty and pale, with the dreadful malignancy from which he had died still on his face. She watched her brother from across a vast abyss as he struggled to drink out of a large tank of water, but the sides were too high for him to reach over. When she awoke, she was convinced that her prayers could relieve her brother of his thirst and suffering, and she prayed daily until she was transferred to the military prison. There she had a second vision, in which she again saw her brother in the same place, but this time he was clean and neat and refreshed. His face was healed and the rim of the water tank had dropped to his waistline. On the edge was a golden goblet filled with water, from which Dinocrates drank, the water level never receding. When he had quenched his thirst, he turned and began to play. When Perpetua awoke, she understood that he had been delivered from his pain.[83]

On the day before she was due to face the wild animals, she experienced her final and most extraordinary vision, which clearly foretold her coming ordeal and ultimate reward. In it, she found herself alone in the center of a stadium filled to capacity with an excited crowd. To her astonishment, she was not attacked by wild beasts as she had expected, but instead a monstrously ugly Egyptian wrestler attended by his seconds entered the arena. At the same moment several handsome young men came up to her as her supporters and seconds, and they began to prepare her to fight the Egyptian. "My clothes were stripped off," she reported, "and suddenly I was a man." She was rubbed down with oil "as they are wont to do before a contest" while the Egyptian—also in the tradition of a wrestling match—rolled himself in the dust.[84] Suddenly a leviathan of a man appeared, so tall he towered above the stadium itself. He was dressed in a purple tunic with two white stripes running down the front and sandals of gold and silver. In one hand he held the baton of a *lanista,* or athletic trainer, and in the other hand he carried a green branch heavy with golden apples.[85] The giant demanded that the audience be silent and announced, "If this Egyptian throws her, he will slay her with a sword; if she throws him, she will receive this branch." He then withdrew and the match began.

The Egyptian tried to grab Perpetua by her feet, but she kicked him in the face with her heel. Suddenly she began to float in the air, hitting him with her fists from above, holding him in a hammer lock around his neck and throwing him to the ground, where in triumph she stepped on his head. The crowd roared, her supporters jubilantly sang psalms, and the giant kissed her hand and presented her with the bough of golden apples, saying, "Peace be with you, my daughter."[86] In triumph, she walked toward the "gate of life," the exit used in real life for gladiators who had triumphed or criminals who had earned a reprieve. When Perpetua awoke, she immediately understood the message, for she, like most other Romans, knew that "the greater part of mankind get their knowledge of God from dreams."[87] She had been told that it was "not with wild animals that I would fight but with the Devil," and she knew that she "would be victorious."[88]

On this triumphant note Perpetua concludes her diary: "About what happened at the contest itself, let him write of it who will." The redactor did not hesitate to take up the challenge—with how much truthfulness, it is impossible to judge. He wrote of the pregnant slave girl Felicitas and the painful delivery of her baby. Her greatest concern was not for the child but whether the birth would come in time so that she could join her comrades along the "road to hope" and eternal life. Two days before the ordeal in the arena, the imprisoned Christians joined in prayer "in one torrent of common grief," begging that she give birth in time. Their prayers were answered. It was a difficult delivery, and when a prison guard said, "You suffer so much now—what will you do when you are tossed to the beasts?" she firmly replied, "What I am suffering now, I suffer alone by myself. But then another will be inside me who will suffer for me, just as I shall be suffering for Him."[89]

The redactor narrated two other stories of prison life, in which Perpetua appeared as a highly rational and self-possessed young lady who was clearly viewed by her colleagues as the leader of the group, not even Saturus questioning her position. When the Christians were transferred to the military jail, they were initially fettered and treated with the greatest severity because the pagans feared that they were in league with demons and "would be spirited out of the prison by magical spells."[90] Perpetua dismissed these fears as being not only superstitious nonsense but also unthinkable, because she agreed with Tertullian that "we, with the crown eternal in our eyes, look upon the prison as our training ground."[91] Far from wishing to escape the chains and brutality reserved for criminals, Christians looked upon them as ways to test themselves for the final, all-important public ordeal, when it was essential to display the strength of their faith. And Perpetua scolded the adjutant in charge: "Why can you not even allow us to refresh ourselves properly? We are the most distinguished of the condemned prisoners, seeing that we belong to the emperor; we are to fight in order to celebrate his birthday. Would it not be to your credit if we ap-

peared in a healthier condition?"[92] Perpetua got her way, and, equally remarkable, her brother was again allowed to visit her and the relatives of the
condemned Christians were permitted to dine in the prison. On the final
evening, the future martyrs received their last meal—"a free banquet,"
which seems to have been watched by a large crowd. The prisoners, not un-
reasonably, were annoyed by this curiosity, and Saturus scolded the pagan
onlookers, saying, "Will not tomorrow be enough for you? Why are you so
eager to see something that you dislike?" Mark well our faces, he warned,
"so that you will recognize us again on the Day."[93] Saturus was not speaking of the courage that he expected to be on every face the next day but of
the Second Coming, when the convicted would sit in judgment on their
persecutors.

Saturus was the angry spokesman at dinner, but Perpetua was in command the next morning when at the arena she and Felicitas were ordered
to dress themselves in the idolatrous robes of the priestesses of Ceres, the
goddess of the circus and the games, and the men were told to put on the
costume of the priests of Saturn. Speaking for all the Christians, Perpetua
pointed out that "we came to this of our own free will, that our freedom
should not be violated. We agreed to pledge our lives provided that we
would do no such thing. You agreed with us to do this."[94] Her logic prevailed, and officialdom desisted from its grim humor. This did not, however, prevent Saturus and some of the others from making rude gestures
directed toward the governor, clearly indicating that "you have condemned
us, but God will condemn you."[95] This so enraged the pagan audience in
the stadium that they demanded that the criminals be promptly whipped
for their disrespect.

According to the redactor, the male martyrs were confronted with the
animal which each feared the most or which seemed most appropriate to
their position. For the women, the devil had prepared an enraged cow,
"chosen that their sex might be matched with that of the beast."[96] Stripped
of their clothing and entrapped in a rope net, they were carried into the
arena but were promptly taken back, the crowd horrified that two young
women, one fresh from childbirth and her breasts full with milk, should be
exposed naked to the public. They were returned modestly garbed in un-
buckled tunics. Perpetua was gored first by the maddened heifer; her tunic
was ripped open as she fell to the ground, where she sat endeavoring to
cover her thighs and redo her disheveled hair, from which the hair clip had
fallen. Perpetua's control was magnificent; her major concern—she was
evidently unaware of Tertullian's dictum that time wasted on hair styling
detracted from salvation[97]—was that the arrangement of her coiffure be

symbolically appropriate to the occasion. Only widows in mourning wore
their hair down. But this was Perpetua's wedding day, and she asked for,
and oddly enough received, a new pin to tie up her locks. Then she rose
from the ground, and seeing that Felicitas had been knocked down and
trampled, she helped her spiritual sister to her feet, and the two women
walked through the Gate of Life, the frenzy and anger of the mob having
been momentarily appeased.

Perpetua was in such a state of shock that she was unable to remember
what had happened and asked her fellow martyrs, "When are we going to
be thrown to that heifer or whatever it is?"[98] When she was told that she
had already been gored and trampled, she refused to believe it until her
torn dress and bruised and bleeding flesh were pointed out to her. Then, according to the redactor, not in the least daunted by her experience, she
called for her Christian brother and said to him and the other catechumens,
"You must all *stand fast in the faith* and love one another, and do not be
weakened by what we have gone through."[99] Exactly what her brother was
doing in the stadium or why the authorities continued to ignore him and
his catechumen friends is never explained.

In the meantime the men had been matched, none too successfully,
against the wild animals. A bear ignored Saturus, a boar fatally gored a
guard, and both Saturninus and Revocatus came through their ordeals with
a leopard and a bear unscathed. In the end only Saturus seems to have been
seriously mauled, by a leopard, but not so badly that he and the rest—
Felicitas and Perpetua included—could not walk back into the arena for the
final and effective execution: a sword's thrust into the throat. Saturus, the
redactor records, died first because, it will be recalled, he was first up the ladder to heaven and had to be there to greet Perpetua. Perpetua herself died
painfully, and she screamed when the young soldier, missing her throat,
struck her collarbone and shoulder. She had to hold his trembling hand and
guide the sword to her throat. The redactor drew the obvious conclusion:
"So great a woman . . . could not be dispatched unless she herself willed
it."[100] Unfortunately, his admiration reintroduces the difficult issue of voluntary martyrdom and the thorny subject of suicide. In more ways than one,
it can be argued that Perpetua cut her own throat.

Perpetua is a tantalizing figure; at one moment she seems to reveal herself completely; at the next she slams the door, leaving a crack just large
enough to excite the imagination. Her diary is the stuff from which interpretations are made. It cries out for explanation, and there has been endless
speculation as to the content of her mind during those final days, the
meaning of her dreams and the source of their images. As a consequence,

the lady and her visions have been scrutinized, analyzed, and allegorized by an army of literary scholars, psychologists, feminists, martyrologists, church fathers, and historians. Surprisingly, she has survived this second martyrdom extraordinarily well—her integrity intact—because, unlike her redactor, Perpetua wrote her story for herself, not for posterity. Hers was a private journal of the intense struggle between her inner voice and her outer loyalties. It was not a public document, and it makes a troublesome Christian morality tale because it is so personal and so steeped in pagan symbolism. On the other hand, the diary is a marvelous hunting ground for those seeking other than Christian meaning in her story and visions.

Perpetua has been presented as a study in feminine "self-awareness," as a victim of "unconscious incest," as a heroine with a social conscience, and as a protester who went to her death not so much because she was "a woman, as in order not to be a woman, with all the usual responsibilities to her family."[101] Marie-Louise von Franz, the Jungian psychologist, went even further, portraying her at war against the "spirit of Paganism," a contest between "two divine . . . suprapersonal, unconscious powers."[102]

The story of Perpetua's suffering lends itself to endless imaginative interpretations, but its genre is relatively clear. It is the record of an ongoing conversion process and of the turmoil of a soul suddenly exposed to the terrifying light of revelation. Perpetua was struggling to penetrate the mystery of ultimate truth. At no time in her narrative does she appear as a mindless, empty vessel—a mere "god box"—to be filled with the Holy Spirit and used for divine purposes, even though she accepted that she and all things in heaven and earth were subject to God's will. She was totally unlike the Maccabees who were happy, unthinking instruments of God's eschatological goal. Instead, she struggled by herself to keep her faith strong and to fortify it against overwhelming odds. She operated with little support from her colleagues or even the Holy Spirit; Saturus did not help her up the ladder, nor did the *lanista* encourage her in her duel with the Egyptian; he simply stated as an impartial umpire the consequences of success or failure. And throughout her imprisonment she had to face alone the frantic opposition of her father.

Perpetua's diary is a conversion document of a peculiar kind because it reveals not simply the intensity and exultation that accompany a revelation experience but also the rejection of social ties and the privatization of faith, as step by step she retreated into herself and repudiated her family, friends, and society. Perpetua began to display a selfishness and cruelty that is deeply disturbing. She made herself deaf to her father's cries of love and his pleas that she consider someone other than herself. She started with normal human anguish for her child's welfare but ended by dismissing the infant the moment her breasts ceased to hurt. She stated over and over again her sorrow for her father's pathetic old age, but she had no concern for his love, grief, or reputation in society. She expressed little understanding of the consequences of what she was doing to her family. Only the next world concerned her. She renounced the responsibilities of birth, marriage, and parenthood for an inner conviction and a craving for martyrdom that not only grew with each visionary experience but also makes Socrates' inner voice seem trivial in comparison. The most worrisome question of all has to do with motivation: was Perpetua's willingness to sacrifice herself and her family inspired by love of self or love of God? Her father would surely have answered the former; Saturus and Perpetua, the latter. The detached observer can only note that self and God, if they are not actually inseparable, generally interact. Nobody has ever proved that heaven is populated with humble or necessarily charitable people.

This, of course, is the core of the trouble with most martyrs; they are self-assertive, rarely self-abdicating, individuals. Perpetua was consumed with herself, every aspect of her existence being perceived solely from the perspective of herself. Her sacrifice was not made for the group or for her church or even for an ideal such as a better world or way of life. The redactor might claim that she died to reveal the truth, especially the Second Coming, but her diary never says this. Instead, she viewed death as a means to an end: her final reward and joyous existence among the saints.

The blood of the martyrs may indeed have been the seed of the church, but therein lies a baffling paradox. Martyrs such as Perpetua were filled with the Holy Spirit; they were God's elect who took literally the command to take up the cross and forsake father, mother, husband, and child for Christ's sake. But the church as an institution could not afford to forsake any of these, let alone build upon the spiritual anarchy of men and women who claimed to possess the gift of vision and prophecy. The intense individualization, the overwhelming self-interest of a Perpetua, the conviction that to her alone had been revealed the wonders of heaven, were extremely dangerous to the church, which was in the process of constructing an ecclesiastical organization modeled far more on the bureaucratic and class divisions of this world than on the equality of the next. The church blessed Perpetua and recognized her heroism and status as a saint, and during the fifth century her story was so popular that Saint Augustine had to warn that it should not be viewed as comparable to the Gospels; but it also may not be an accident that the actual manuscript of her *Passion* was lost, not to be fully recovered and printed until the seventeenth century.[103] During those intervening years the church much preferred martyrs who spoke for a socially constructed earthly ecclesia that administered the channels of salvation and grasped firmly the keys to the gates of paradise. Within two hundred years of Perpetua's death the time had passed for "god boxes," voluntary martyrs and soldiers of the spirit; the moment had come instead for the institutional martyr, the warrior who died defending the political safety of the church and the honor of God as defined by legalists and administrators, not by rebellious wives and daughters.

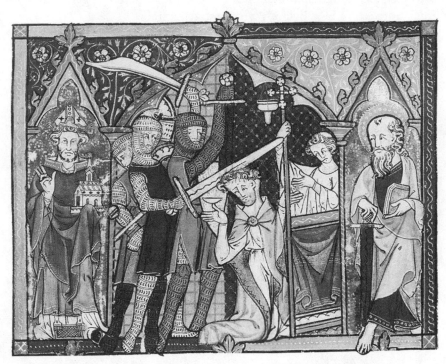

Christendom was shocked to its spiritual roots by the picture of an archbishop being murdered on the steps of God's high altar in his own cathedral church.

CHAPTER 6

THOMAS BECKET
AND THE HONOR OF GOD

Every saint, as every man, comes one day to be
superfluous.
—RALPH WALDO EMERSON,
Journals

S AINT AUGUSTINE pronounced more than once "that it is not
the penalty which makes true martyrs, but the cause."[1] By the
twelfth century, however, such a tidy and simplistic definition of
martyrdom no longer satisfied, because two new elements for assessing
martyrs were emerging. The martyr was no longer judged solely by the nobility of the goal achieved in death; instead, the quality of life lived on earth
was now of equal importance. To make matters even more confusing, the
disturbing relationship of means to ends began to change as the imperative
of the Holy Spirit waned and the honor of God, defined more and more in
terms of temporal jurisdictions, political power, and land revenues, waxed
aggressively strong.

If T. S. Eliot was correct in maintaining that a Christian martyrdom is
never an accident, then the controversy surrounding the death of Thomas
Becket, the most famous of all twelfth-century martyrs, must be argued
less as an encounter between church and state or a clash between two willful men, and more as a lesson in the paradox that pride, stubbornness, perversity, pettiness, immoderation, and a mulish thirst for retribution need
not lead straight to hell but, given a final, inexplicable twist of events, can
catapult a man directly into heaven. From start to finish, from the day in
1162 when at the insistence of Henry II he was consecrated archbishop of
Canterbury to the moment 376 years later when his bones were cast out

and burned by order of another king of England, Becket has been the center of debate, both as a man and as a saint. The desecration of his gold-and-jewel-encrusted shrine in Canterbury Cathedral and his defrocking as a martyr by order of Henry VIII in 1538 were largely political and economic, only marginally religious, in purpose; but the grounds on which the king proclaimed Becket to be a traitor, not a martyr—"There appeareth nothing in his life and exterior conversation whereby he should be called a saint"[2]—go to the root of a two-pronged controversy. History is still debating whether inner-directed spiritual ends can be well served by bellicose institutional means, and questioning the archbishop's qualifications as a saint—did they reside in his cause, his personality, the style of his death, or the multitude of miracles associated with his name and tomb?

The trouble with Becket is that we know too much about Thomas the man—his words, his 189 letters, his actions, the image he created in the eyes of friends and enemies—and too little about Thomas the martyr—the interior and hidden compulsion that systematically closed all doors except the one that led to violent death. No medieval saint, possibly no other medieval figure, is better documented than this tall, hawk-nosed, and angular son of a Norman merchant and second-generation immigrant to London. We have at least a dozen descriptions of his life and death, plus the largest collection of letters and manuscripts dealing with a single person in the twelfth century: some 678 items in all.[3] What we lack is a channel into his soul, for Thomas Becket built walls around himself just as high as those he placed about the church he so passionately defended; if he could possibly help it, Becket gave nothing away belonging either to his inner self or to the kingdom of God.

As a living actor in history as well as a dead martyr in the Christian hall of fame, Thomas of Canterbury poses difficulties; but neither his career nor his canonization can be adequately judged or appreciated without setting both within the emotional and institutional framework of his day. Becket was born, very likely on December 21, 1120 (the year is more uncertain than the day or the month), into a world that was just learning to label and define the political and religious abstractions and institutional forms that were beginning to take shape. As the fictional Becket in Jean Anouilh's play tells his king, labeling is "essential . . . otherwise we can't know what we're doing."[4] The twelfth century was taking stock of its past and planning its future, and in so doing it experienced the birth in both church and state of the bureaucratic mind with its instinctive preference for clear jurisdictional boundaries, written documentation, and systems control. The fog of custom, the babble of conflicting local traditions, and the constant appeal to private law and personal privilege were steadily capitulating to more sharply articulated political entities. Slowly the eleventh- and twelfth-century feudal kingdom was changing from an association of private geographic and historic rights and customs held together by common allegiance to and fear of the king into a public organism that operated upon fixed legal principles and demanded that all its members be subjects of and subject to the crown. The ideal, although never completely attained even in England—the most distinct and homogeneous kingdom in medieval Europe—demanded one law and one allegiance common to each territorial unit.

In the church the same categorical mentality was at work, defining and refining the confused jumble of inherited assumptions surrounding the ecclesia's central tenet governing its relationship with the state: "Render unto Caesar the things which are Caesar's and to God the things that are God's." Unfortunately, the formula left room for doubt. Where did Caesar's rule end; where did God's domain begin? What exactly was the proper role of mother church in a society beset by greed, power politics, and economic self-interest, and divided into predatory political organisms, each anxious to carve out and extend its jurisdiction? Where and how should divine law operate, and what was its proper relationship to secular authority? Saint Thomas Aquinas a hundred years in the future would write that man was called by nature to live in society so that he might not only live well but also live the "good life."[5] The state tended to view the good life as the secure life, free from riot and crime. The church, in contrast, insisted that the good life must be equated with the virtuous life, which could only be achieved through the exercise of moderation, charity, and obedience to God's law as defined and enforced by an anointed priesthood which practiced "the highest form of knowledge," the cure and salvation of souls. The world, according to the ecclesiastical persuasion, was based on the fundamental duality inherent in Christianity: the distinction between body and soul. The human carcass might be safely left to secular rulers, but the immortal soul belonged to God's church, which linked the living, the dead, and the unborn together into a universality that reached from the grandeur of heaven to the sink of hell.

Underscoring and heralding this vision of spiritual leadership and supremacy was the presence of a monastic elite which was determined to purge the world of imperfection and which called upon the papacy, as the doorkeeper of heaven and custodian of divine justice on earth, to liberate the church from temporal and carnal entanglements, free it from the self-serving interference of emperors, kings, and princes, and transform it into a separate—nay, superior—kingdom worthy of Christ and answerable only to the King of Heaven.

By the year of Becket's birth, the two swords forged by Christ to defend the truth—one given to the clergy, the other to the temporal authorities—

had been sharpened and tempered and were drawn in violent opposition. From the mid–eleventh century on, extremists on both sides were demanding immediate action. Saint Bernard advised Pope Eugenius III that "the time for action is at hand. If you start to hesitate now, it will surely be too late. . . . Put on your sword . . . and deal out vengeance on the nations and punishment on the people." On the secular front, it was asserted that "all things spiritual and temporal alike waited upon the nod of the king."[6]

The focus of the controversy was the point where church and state met and the two swords overlapped: the investiture of bishops, who were both ecclesiastical princes, responsible solely to the holy father in Rome, and feudal magnates, owing allegiance to the crown. From the spiritual perspective it was bad enough that kings should demand military service and homage from church officials for their fiefs and manors as if they were common barons; but it was infinitely more scandalous that they should claim the right to name bishops and bestow upon them their ring and staff, the sacred symbols of their pastoral authority as shepherds of Christian souls. This, in papal eyes, was an unacceptable encroachment upon the purity and privilege of the church and a violation of divine mandate, for "the Christian religion has so disposed that after God . . . the royal power shall be governed by the care and authority of the apostolic see."[7] Kings were equally intransigent, refusing to forgo their sacerdotal powers which had been sanctified by centuries of usage, and they pointed out that to renounce the homage owed by ecclesiastical barons was to forfeit a fourth or more of their kingdom and to cripple them militarily—the archdiocese of Canterbury, for example, traditionally supplied the crown with sixty armed knights.

In England a rough and ill-defined compromise evolved. Henry I in 1106 reluctantly abandoned his sacerdotal right to grant lay investitures and, in theory at least, gave up his claim to name ecclesiastical officers. In return, Christ's vicar on earth, equally reluctantly, sanctioned the practices of high church officials rendering homage to their royal overlords. Henceforth English bishops faced the delicate, often dangerous, and always thankless task of serving two masters: pope and king. The realities of political life were rather ungraciously accepted when it was recorded that although secular princes could not "attain salvation without the church," God's kingdom could not obtain peace on earth "without royal protection."[8]

In the uneasy balance between church and state, the ecclesia possessed one inestimable advantage: the medieval imagination was enthralled by the image of God's kingdom, hearkening to the voice of the Holy Spirit and obedient to "the throne and temple of justice" located in Rome. Few Christians waxed enthusiastic over the sordid, ramshackle structure of the temporal state. Saint George, at least as an ideal worth dying for, triumphed over the political dragons of the secular world. The twelfth-century feudal kingdom, with its untidy web of interacting allegiances and obligations, duties and privileges, was hard to visualize, let alone conceive, as an ideal of intrinsic value. The crown as an abstraction unrelated to the person who wore it was difficult to imagine; the realm, even under a monarch like Henry II, engendered little loyalty.

In contrast, God's kingdom could be vividly and intimately pictured in terms of those legendary figures who had suffered and died defending and extending its frontiers. The blood of the martyrs was more than the seed of the church; it was the stuff from which fantasies were spun, the substance that excited the medieval mind. "Stern saints and tortured martyrs" far more than militant barons and armored knights provided the paramount role models for Becket's generation. Their self-sacrifices, their suffering for the faith, served, if not as literal guides for daily living, as benchmarks for judging and enduring the bodily pains of this earth. Their tombs and relics became indescribably precious contact points where heaven and earth met to enact God's miracles and proclaim His truth. Red martyrs and white martyrs, men and women who had sacrificed their blood or endured a living death mortifying their flesh to prove their love of God, were immortalized in stone and made incarnate in the human imagination in every village church. All Christendom knew that God and the heavenly host ruled in high majesty and mystery in cathedral edifices far vaster and infinitely more impressive than the palaces of kings. For Becket's world, God's honor seemed vastly more tangible, more enduring, and certainly more magnificent than any honor that might attach itself to mere earthly governors.

The world of the imagination may have been populated with saints and martyrs, but the real world of the twelfth century had to make do with administrators, experts whose job it was to ministrate, adjudicate, and orchestrate the affairs of church and state. In a dual society, newly conscious of both itself and its divisions and experiencing in all of its parts a thirst for order, decorum, and self-definition, the surest avenue to worldly success lay in administration, especially for someone like Becket, who was not to the manor, let alone to the tiltyard, born.

Thomas Becket's career is one of medieval society's most spectacular success stories and gives impressive evidence that, although it was still essential to have the right connections, the highest echelons of government in both church and state were open to talent. Fortunately for young Thomas, his father had economic, social, and blood contacts on both sides of the channel. The family hailed from Normandy. The name "Becket" was a derisive nickname, possibly meaning "beak-nosed" but certainly referring to non-noble birth, which Thomas himself was far too proud to use. His father, Gilbert, seems to have been a small-time merchant-cum-landowner in the neighborhood of Rouen, who in the years before 1120 moved his operation to London, joining the commercial and educated elite of the city. His only son, Thomas, started life with three considerable advantages. He received a solid but unacademic education. Equally important, he spent time—presumably during his holidays—in the baronial residence of a close family friend, where he acquired the outward polish of aristocratic conduct, learning to hawk, to hunt, and in all likelihood to joust. And finally, at age twenty-two he was placed first in the banking household of a kinsman, where he acted as secretary and accountant for at least three years, and then in the palace of Theobald, archbishop of Canterbury, where he encountered and competed with the best minds of his generation.

Thomas served his ecclesiastical master faithfully and efficiently during years of political and military turmoil when "Christ and his saints slept" and the descendants of William the Conqueror in the third and fourth generations fought over the crown of England. Theobald threw the full weight of his ecclesiastical office behind the young contender Henry Plantagenet, count of Anjou, and helped to negotiate the final settlement in 1153 whereby the twenty-year-old Henry became the legal heir of his cousin King Stephen. Within thirteen months, on December 19, Henry II mounted the Saxon throne, won eighty-eight years before by his great-grandfather William the Bastard, duke of Normandy. During these years of high politics and international diplomacy, Theobald made constant use of his talented and adaptable clerk, and he trained him well, appointing him in the summer of 1154 archdeacon of Canterbury, a position that made Becket responsible for the entire internal administration of the archdiocese. He even sent him to Italy for a year to learn civil law, the indispensable tool of any official responsible for the secular affairs and welfare of the church.

Theobald was anxious to place a faithful friend of the church and loyal protegé close to the new king to guarantee smooth and fruitful relations between crown and miter. The new monarch owed his archbishop. Thus it was that Henry, instead of selling the position of lord chancellor to the highest bidder as was common practice, presented the best-paid office in his household—five shillings a day—to Thomas, archdeacon of Canterbury. The son of a London merchant became the foremost ecclesiastical servant of the crown.

By the time Theobald died, he may well have had second thoughts about the wisdom of his choice, because Thomas, through his inordinate drive, marvelous memory for detail, administrative expertise, and unexpected friendship with his young prince, secularized, bureaucratized, and rationalized an office of little political significance and transformed it into the crown's chief instrument of government and coercion. The first of Becket's metamorphoses had begun; the thirty-two-year-old ecclesiastical clerk became, not the moral conscience of the crown as Theobald had hoped, but the gray eminence and public voice of the sovereign of England and half of France, next to the Holy Roman Emperor the most powerful man in Europe.

These were the years when Becket "fed the winds and ran after shadows," and was "intent on securing the respect of all good men."[9] Given the characteristics that Becket later displayed—the hair shirt, self-flagellation, and unyielding insistence on punishing both himself and all others who challenged God's will—it is tempting to fantasize about these early years. Historians-turned-psychiatrists have argued that Thomas's slight stammer, the hint of homosexuality, the role playing said to be evident in those holiday months when a merchant's son learned the ways of his betters, and the postulated emotional trauma of a talented parvenu groveling before more highly born incompetents are offered as evidence of a repressed and neurotic personality, pathologically concerned with his honor and reputation.[10] But this is to project the monsters of the twentieth century back upon the twelfth. The documents reveal singularly little about the inner recesses of the new lord chancellor's mind except that he was extraordinarily efficient: "second to none in dispatch of business."[11] Consequently, most of the estimations of Thomas's psyche are largely extrapolations derived from his early political success, the salient silence on key issues maintained by even those hagiographers most anxious to transmute a fallible man into a predestined saint, and the personality traits that emerged during his later and better-recorded life.

From such slender sources there appears the stark silhouette of a man chained and shaped by convention. Quick-witted and of unbending judgment, Thomas possessed immense reserves of inner strength and outward energy locked within a high-strung, wiry body which was susceptible to what the twelfth century mysteriously called a "cold stomach" and to nervous collapse. Significantly, however, no contemporary mentions love, compassion, or humor. The new chancellor seems to have taken himself and his office with deadly, almost obsessive, seriousness, and he practiced diligently the instinctive medieval conviction that power, to be effective, must capture the imagination with ceremony and display as well as imprison the body with iron fetters. If there is a single theme running throughout Becket's life, it is his impassioned insistence on the forms and proprieties appropriate to rank and office. In an age steeped in imagery and symbolism, image building, at which Thomas excelled, was essential to po-

litical success. Symbols—especially the regalia and protocol of historic office—tended to absorb and become equated with the realities of official
power which they represented. Authority divested of its gorgeous vestments was an object of scorn.

As lord chancellor, Becket lived like a prince; indeed, he was accused of
far excelling his king in ostentatious extravagance and the trappings of
worldly power. While on diplomatic mission to Paris to arrange for the
marriage of his sovereign's three-and-a-half-year-old son to the Capetian
princess of France, he traveled with a thousand men in attendance, all
dressed in new livery. His entourage was a perambulating court replete with
250 footmen and a veritable army of armed knights, squires, pages, falcon-
ers, clerks, stewards, hunting dogs, sumpters, and war horses. At home he
maintained a magnificent table for anyone who visited the royal household.
He regularly entertained earls and barons, "his board was resplendent with
gold and silver vessels," and he kept an impressive menagerie of wild
beasts.[12] When he went off to defend his monarch's feudal rights and possessions in Europe, he campaigned with seven hundred knights who owed
him personal allegiance; and although still archdeacon of Canterbury, during a slack period in the actual fighting he jousted with and unseated a
French knight, taking the Frenchman's war horse as ransom. His revenues
were princely; unheard of sums—possibly three thousand to four thousand
pounds annually—were channeled into the lord chancellor's treasury. Much
of the money went into role playing, the enactment of a perfect lord chancellor; and Thomas with his sense of the dramatic, his ability to stage the
pageantry of pomp and circumstance, and to fit his emotions—his tears, his
anger, and his charm—to any occasion was inordinately good at enacting
the part.

The wellspring that fed this lavish display was Becket's master, the red-
haired, harsh-voiced, inflammatory, and ill-kempt sovereign, who lacked any
sense of decorum, was insatiably and unpredictably restless, and made his
court "a perfect portrait of hell" by his constant moves throughout his many
domains. Even at twenty-one, Henry II radiated an intensity of emotions
and vitality that engendered fear and respect. Thomas's biographers talk of
the close but unlikely friendship between the gaunt, stiff-necked chancellor,
who labored to sustain the honor of kingship by his over-ostentatious life
style, and the short, stocky, muscular monarch, who loathed protocol,
erupted into uncontrollable rages whenever he was thwarted, and was
"more covetous of glory than of gain."[13] Despite the thirteen-year age difference between the two men, they seem to have been boon companions, at
least during the early years, when the inexperienced prince turned to the
older cleric who was so much in his debt and who could get things done. It

is, however, important to distinguish personal friendship, flowing from emotional and intellectual rapport, and mere association based on feudal allegiance and governmental duties. Becket was Henry's vassal and liegeman, owing all, even his life, to his overlord, the king. He served his sovereign with style and effectiveness, exactly as he had served his ecclesiastical master. That is what Henry expected, because it was his right, and when Archbishop Theobald died and the king replaced him with his "friend" the lord chancellor, he demanded the same undivided service. Henry Plantagenet always believed in profiting from his friends, especially when they were also his servants and creations.

In naming his lord chancellor as primate of England, an office richer in history than the crown itself, the king faced a formidable task. The archdiocese claimed descent directly from its founder, Saint Augustine, the seventh-century missionary sent by Pope Gregory to Christianize the Anglo-Saxons. The position was regarded as a "world apart," the pope himself referring to the archbishop as "one who is almost our equal," and Henry had to overcome furious ecclesiastical opposition to his nominee.[14] Resentment against Becket had to do with his clerical status—he was not a priest, only an archdeacon in minor orders—but this was quickly remedied when, on the second of June, 1162, the day before his consecration, he was ordained a priest. Criticism also stemmed from Henry's obvious plan to unite the chancellorship and archbishopric in the person of a single royal servant; but Henry could point out that the pope had obliged other monarchs by permitting the uncanonical union of sacred and secular offices. What rankled most among Becket's detractors were the perceived defects in the archbishop's character and vocation. He had been a warlike and absentee archdeacon who had bloodied his hands in battle and a worldly lord chancellor who, sweeping aside the violent protests of the church, had extracted forced loans from the wealthier bishops and levied on the church extraordinary military taxes to pay for his master's many wars. Worse, he was neither a monk nor a biblical scholar, let alone a particularly spiritual man, and these had been the unwritten prerequisites for office since the days of the Conqueror.

Becket became primate solely because the king insisted on what he regarded as the perfect solution to the ever-present friction between church and state; his appointee would spread the mantle of royal authority over the clergy just as effectively as he had curbed baronial violence and independence. Unfortunately, Henry badly misjudged his man, and he made the cardinal error of elevating to an office that in a sense outranked his own a trained lawyer and disciplined bureaucrat who knew the exact dimensions and full potential of his new domain. Suddenly the royal clerk became the king's spiritual father, claiming authority directly from Christ's vicar in Rome. Thomas explained his position in devastatingly simple terms: "The Archbishop is subject to the judgment of the Pope alone; the Pope to that of God alone."[15] Two men so unlike in temperament but so alike in their understanding of and approach to power politics confronted one another; and within two years they were scarcely on speaking terms. The monarch was infuriated that his vassal, friend, and servant should be so faithless to his oath; the prelate was obsessed with protecting every letter of his archdiocesan rights—dotting every "i" and crossing every "t." The kingdom of England, as defined by Henry Plantagenet, was at war with the Kingdom of God, as interpreted by Thomas of Canterbury.

Conflict between the two kingdoms was nothing new. William the Conqueror had had to live with the strong-willed Archbishop Lanfranc, and Henry I had endured the censures of the saintly but formidable Anselm. But under the second Henry the ancient formula whereby the archbishop-elect just before his consecration offered his sovereign the formal feudal oath "to preserve his life, limbs and earthly honor, saving his order" broke down.[16] The stumbling point was the critical reservation "saving his order," by which was meant the historic and episcopal rights and privileges of the church. It may be, as scholars have so often warned, dangerous to personalize a struggle that was essentially institutional in nature, but the way each man responded to and structured the conflict in his own mind, not the quarrel itself, was the mainspring that drove the murder committed at Canterbury eight years later. Two inordinately immoderate men, both capable of deep, unforgiving anger, confronted one another on a stage that both admitted was not big enough for the two of them.[17]

Becket's tidy, disciplined mind, his sense of liberation from secular control, and his need to divide the world into clear-cut categories appeared the moment he received from the pope the white woolen pallium which was the symbol of his archiepiscopal authority. Within days he resigned as lord chancellor, returning the seal of office to the king. Thomas of Canterbury did not intend to serve two masters, nor would he allow his servants to do so. It was said he even dismissed anyone who had previously sworn fealty to the king.

As the premier prelate of the realm, Thomas was just as magnificent as in his chancellor years. His hospitality and generosity—especially his alms-giving—fitted the dignity of his office, and because the king could claim the firstborn sons of his barons as his pages, Becket insisted that Canterbury be served at table by the secondborn. Thomas was little interested in the morals of the clergy; he was in no way a reforming prelate. His first concern was the frontiers of his archdiocese and the recovery of those fiefs and manors, along with the ecclesiastical rights that belonged to them, which had been lost to secular personages through intimidation, negligence, or fraud. He even went so far as to excommunicate one of his feudal vassals who had forcibly evicted the prelate's appointee to the parish church of Eynsford on the grounds that the right of appointment belonged to the lord of the manor, not the archbishop. Strict legal right belonged in this instance to Canterbury, but ancient custom resided with the local magnate. Moreover, Becket ignored an even more historic tradition: no vassal who held his lands directly from the crown could be excommunicated without the king's consent, and Thomas had not bothered to consult his royal master.

The Eynsford incident did not lead to a breach between king and archbishop; Henry accepted the prelate's apology for failing to consult the crown, and Becket withdrew the anathema. Where neither man, however, was willing to back down was over the issue of criminal clerks, a point of friction that had been festering since the day the Conqueror had decreed that the church should cease bringing "to the judgment of secular men any matter which concerns the rule of souls," and had set up separate ecclesiastical courts to handle such cases.[18] From this source, heavily reinforced by papal and monastic demand for the complete separation of the church from lay interference, grew the theory of ecclesiastical immunity from royal law dispensed in the king's courts. Had the theory of privileged treatment for the clergy limited itself to those in holy orders—possibly twenty thousand to thirty thousand monks, nuns, and priests, who claimed to be members of a divinely consecrated caste set apart from the rest of society—there might have been no controversy. Unfortunately, the term "clergy" in its broadest sense included some three hundred thousand other English men and women, ranging from anyone in minor orders, as Becket had been when archdeacon of Canterbury, to the crusading knight, the cemetery gravedigger, the monastic pig-keeper, the beggar who swept the church floor, and the renegade monk. And when the secular authorities attempted to arrest a shoemaker suspected of murder, on the property of the abbey of Waverley, the cry went up from the monks that their places were as free as their altars.

The church, representing God's higher law, was unable to condone "judgments of blood" and limited the punishments delivered in ecclesiastical courts to penance, fines, and imprisonment, leaving the butchery of the human body—ear clipping, branding, blinding, castrating, hanging, burning, and flaying alive—to the secular courts. Understandably, a large, diverse, and not particularly law-abiding segment of the population was happy to seek legal sanctuary from the king's law, which believed in agonizing exemplary justice and had a nasty habit of making the punishment fit the crime. In its turn the state was outraged that college students should escape the consequences of their criminal actions because of their claim to clerical status or that a clerk should be able to rape a girl and murder her father and only be punished by imprisonment. The king's justice was clearly violated when Philip de Brois, canon of Bedford, killed a knight but was acquitted in a bishop's court in the face of overwhelming evidence. The king's honor was further violated when de Brois publicly insulted the sheriff of Bedford, who tried to reintroduce the case into the king's court. Finally, after Henry himself had intervened to save the honor of his sheriff, the worst punishment Becket, as archbishop, saw fit to pronounce was to order the canon to stand naked before the insulted royal official and be whipped.[19] Such decisions not only dishonored the king and his laws, they also ran counter to everything Henry's Norman forefathers had sought to achieve: one king, one realm, one law.

When in the fall of 1163 the king was informed by his council that over a hundred cases of homicide, all committed by clerics, had occurred since he was crowned back in 1154, he ordered his clergy before him at Westminster in October, and in words laden with sarcasm, he informed his bishops that he had "listened meekly how ye . . . are willing to dispose yourselves towards royal rights and our rule here in England." Why, he asked, had they deemed him to be "less worthy than other kings who have been before us to wear an untottering crown"? Historic custom and his royal honor, he claimed, required that all "clerks seized or convicted of great crimes should be deprived of the protection of the church and handed over to his officers."[20] Neither Becket nor any other bishop would sanction such a flagrant violation of ecclesiastical liberties, but the archbishop did not content himself with a simple rebuttal based on legal precedent. He elevated a negotiable procedural dispute into a declaration of unconditional principle and declared that "the clergy, by reason of their orders and distinctive office, have Christ alone as king. . . . And since they are not under secular kings, but under their own king, under the King of Heaven, they should be ruled by their own law . . . which has its own means of coercion."[21] Thomas overstated the case, and, worse, he affronted the king personally, denying the entire theory of Norman and Saxon kingship.

In an age that clung tenaciously to custom as the best justification for action and that was only just beginning to order, select, and rationalize ancient usage into written and codified law, both sides could legitimately claim to be in the right. Law in the twelfth century was an unpredictable mixture of historic precedent and present power, and Henry, stonewalled by his bishops, therefore appealed to the ancient tradition of his ancestors and announced that he would be satisfied if each prelate would swear to uphold the customs of England. Significantly, he did not state how far back in history those usages went; nor did he say who would interpret them. Becket, speaking for his colleagues, evaded the trap by offering a counterformula: the bishops would do as their sovereign asked "saving their order," an all-important and highly evasive phrase, meaning that they would support any custom that did not contravene the liberties and privileges of the church. Frustrated by this qualification, Henry stormed out of the meeting, announcing that "poison" lurked behind those mealy-mouthed words—"saving their order." Later, in a brief encounter with the archbishop, he gave full vent to his anger, directed at the man whom he judged to be an ingrate and betrayer: "Have I not raised you from a poor and lowly station to the pinnacle of honor and rank . . . [and] made you father of the kingdom and put you even before myself? How can it be that so many benefits, so many proofs of my love for you . . . have so soon been obliterated from your mind, that you are now not only ungrateful but oppose me in everything?"[22]

Henry was not done with his ungrateful archbishop or his disobedient prelates. In January of 1164 he again called his lords spiritual together at his hunting lodge at Clarendon, but joined with them the lords temporal of the kingdom. On the principle that if you cannot win a specific argument over criminal clergy, you broaden the debate to include the entire historic relationship between church and state, he appealed on all fronts to the customs and rights of his forefathers. In order to get around the sophistry of that difficult phrase "saving their order," he suggested that his bishops and barons write down their precise understanding of those ancient traditions governing the relations between royal and priestly authority. In the final draft of this famous document, known ever since as the Constitutions of Clarendon, four points out of the sixteen articles stuck in the bishops' maw. All four went to the root of the controversy over the crown's right to discipline the clergy, and all four were formulated—largely by laymen—so as to turn the church, at least by implication, into a department of state, making its liberties and privileges dependent upon the king's favor. With painful clarity the constitutions stated that without the crown's consent, no law case could be appealed to Rome, no vassal or servant of the king could be excommunicated, no cleric could leave the kingdom, and that all criminal clerks had to prove their right to ecclesiastical immunity in a royal court before being tried before a spiritual judge, and that after such a trial, they were to be defrocked and turned over to the secular authorities for punishment. Worse yet, Henry refused to permit his prelates to wiggle out through the loophole "saving their order." An unequivocal and public promise had to be made "on the word of truth, to the lord king and his heirs that these customs should be kept and observed in good faith without evil intent."[23]

The archbishop and his colleagues stood their ground, pointing out that merely because there was historic precedent for a claim did not make that claim right. There was good custom and bad custom, and no matter what the custom, if it violated canon law, it was illegal; the Lord had never said "I am the custom," He had said "I am the Truth" (John 14:6). Episcopal opposition seemed unbreachable until the unexpected happened: Becket broke ranks and, without consulting his associates, publicly accepted the constitutions and ordered his prelates to place their seals on the sixteen articles. In so doing and to everyone's amazement and the king's delight, he totally capitulated.

Thomas Becket's collapse of nerve has never been adequately explained. Possibly it stemmed from fear; the barons were loud in their insistence that he pledge his support. Possibly it derived from emotional exhaustion combined with residual loyalty to his sovereign. And possibly he bowed to Henry's overwhelming personality, which could make experienced soldiers cringe and throw practiced orators into incoherent confusion. Whatever the cause, the timing was crucial, for the archbishop's humiliation was the turning point of his life. Thomas never forgave himself—or, perversely, his episcopal colleagues—for his weakness at Clarendon. He stood accused by his own standard bearer: "What virtue is left to him who has betrayed his conscience and his reputation?" Almost within the hour Becket regretted his action: "I repent and am so aghast at my transgression that I judge myself unworthy as a priest to approach him whose church I have thus basely sold." He imposed on himself penance for his betrayal and weakness. He fasted—indeed, he may have started the self-flagellation that became so much a part of his later life—and he refused to celebrate the mass because he regarded himself as a self-condemned sinner. Eventually remorse reached the point where he argued himself into believing that his words at Clarendon to support the constitutions "in good faith and without evil intent" did not bind his conscience, which was still dedicated to maintaining "the honor of the church,"[24] and in violation of Clarendon he unsuccessfully attempted to leave the kingdom and secretly appealed to Rome to have the hateful constitutions annulled.

Becket earned little from either his repentance or his casuistry except possibly the easing of his conscience and a degree of self-justification. The bishops were thunderstruck that he should have abandoned them to face the king's wrath alone—"It was the general of our army," the bishop of London later complained, "who deserted, the captain of our camp who fled"—and they lost what little confidence in or respect for his leadership that remained.[25] As for Henry, he became even more convinced that Canterbury's sacred oath was worthless, and he determined to rid himself of a servant who so clearly stood on the threshold of open treason.

The king's purpose was to harass, isolate, and force the resignation of his archbishop, and in September 1164 he saw his chance to bring the prelate to heel. Becket made the mistake of ignoring his feudal obligation to his overlord and failed to respond to a summons to appear in person before the king's court to settle a land dispute between himself and one of his vassals. Peremptorily Thomas was ordered before the king's great council of bishops and barons gathered together at Northampton Castle to face the charge of contempt of court, and on October 8 he was found guilty and sentenced to forfeit all his movable possessions to the crown. Thomas was appalled that inferiors, mere bishops, had sat in judgment on the primate of England, and outraged that he, a spiritual prince, had been condemned in a secular court of law. And in contempt of his oath given at Clarendon to uphold the constitutions, he promptly appealed his case to the papal curia. Next day the king struck again. He demanded that Becket account for the enormous sums of money—thirty thousand pounds was the official royal estimate—that he had handled during his eight years as lord chancellor. This Thomas could not possibly do even had he had time to gather what few records he possessed. Most of his episcopal colleagues at this point advised him that his only escape was to humble himself and throw himself on his sovereign's mercy, or to resign his office.

The crisis, one of the most dramatic scenes in medieval history, came on Tuesday the thirteenth of November. The day began with a blatant and public act of defiance: Thomas celebrated in his lodgings a votive mass in the name of the martyr Stephen and read the dangerously provocative introit: "Princes also did sit and speak against me" (Psalms 119:23). The symbolism was transparent: Becket was announcing that his judgment before the king's council was no ordinary feudal and secular case; instead, God's holy church, for which the early martyrs had died, was on trial. Having finished the ceremony, he stepped down from the altar and informed his servants that he proposed to go barefoot but dressed in full archiepiscopal regalia to confront the king at Northampton Castle.[26] To have done so would have been an open declaration of war, and more moderate opinion prevailed. As a compromise Becket traveled in more ordinary garb, his cross of office being borne in front of him. As he entered the anteroom of the chamber where his prelates awaited him, however, he took the cross in his own hands and held up before the startled bishops the symbol of his spiritual authority. The reaction of Gilbert Foliot, bishop of London, was to warn the archbishop that if Becket brandished his cross, the king would surely unsheath his sword, and he scornfully pictured "a king bravely adorned and an archbishop likewise" engaged in armed combat. For Gilbert Foliot and many others, there was absolutely no doubt Thomas of Canterbury had always been "a fool" and always would be.[27]

As Becket waited during that long day to hear the council's decision and as messengers scuttled back and forth, rumors spread as to the king's intentions to imprison him or even turn a deaf ear to conspiracies to murder him. Thomas was of two minds: to fight back with spiritual weapons and launch the lightning bolt of anathemas at those who might dare touch his person, or to model himself on the early martyrs and pray for the souls of his persecutors.[28] As it turned out, he did neither. In a magnificent display of theatrics, he absolutely forbade his bishops, as members of the king's council, to take part in the trial against him; he refused to give account for the moneys he had dispensed as lord chancellor; he denied the competence of the council to judge him; he proclaimed his faithful obedience to his overlord the king but publicly exempted everything that touched on his duty to God and his "personal honor as archbishop"; and he placed both his "person and the church of Canterbury under the protection of God and the Lord Pope." Then, when the barons announced the council's decision, he stopped them in mid-sentence and shouted "I am your father; you are magnates of the household, lay powers, secular personages. I will not hear your judgment"; and with perfect timing he marched out of the castle.[29]

The sequence of events at the end of that dramatic day is not entirely clear, and the picture of the archbishop's grand exit is somewhat spoiled by stories of undignified verbal exchanges as the barons and the king's servants shouted "perjurer" and "traitor" and Becket responded in kind by calling Henry's illegitimate brother a "varlet and bastard," reminding Ranulf de Broc that a member of his family had been hanged as a common criminal, and telling another name-caller that "if I were a knight, I would prove thee a liar with my own hands."[30] The moment Becket reached his own lodgings, he wrote the king asking for a formal safe-conduct back to Canterbury. When Henry delayed his answer until morning, the archbishop moved rapidly and fled Northampton that night. Three weeks later he arrived in Flanders, securely outside his sovereign's jurisdiction. In Henry's eyes Becket was a forsworn and perjured priest. He had been found guilty of contempt of court, fiscal malfeasance, and now, in defiance of the Constitutions of Clarendon, had illegally fled the kingdom. At best he was a common thief; at worst a traitor—a term that in later centuries became more and more associated with martyrdom.

Even with the earliest martyrs, the scent of treason had intermingled with the stench of public execution. Ironically, however, Socrates had died because of his loyalty to the laws of Athens; Perpetua and the early Christian martyrs had loudly professed their personal loyalty to the emperor and the Roman Empire even though they could find few people to believe them; and the Maccabees had never overtly equated their refusal to eat swine meat and renounce their faith with rebellion against the Seleucid state. In contrast, Becket was the first martyr to be accused of treason and to die both a martyr and a traitor. His treason, however, was not conceived in the modern sense of aiding and abetting the enemies of the state. In the twelfth century treason was a feudal felony, a crime that severed the bond between a lord and a vassal. As such it was much more than a legal breach of contract; it was a heinous social and moral sin, rooted in viciousness and depravity of character. Any "action unbefitting a feudal gentleman," it has been said, "might be called felonious"; and for Becket's world the words "felon," "perjurer," and "traitor" were interchangeable terms.[31] In Henry II's view treason was tantamount to breach of trust and a violation of friendship, and when his archbishop went into exile, he wrote to "his Lord and friend" King Louis of France describing his faithless servant as "a wicked and perjured traitor against me." Becket was a criminal, Henry later informed his bishops, who had "disparaged my honor and the honor of the realm."[32]

In exile Thomas of Canterbury was equally bitter. He had been publicly humiliated, treated like a layman, judged and condemned by his inferiors, and driven out of the land to live as "Christ's outlaw," all because he had sought to stand against those who were seeking to subvert—nay, destroy— the historic and sacred liberties of God's church. His critics might retort that the archbishop had turned negotiable trivialities into granite principles, that no one in England questioned the inviolability of the clergy or their immunity before the secular courts, and that the only issue under debate was the occasional and extreme abuse of those privileges and the need to make the rights of the church compatible with the security of the realm.[33] To such arguments Becket answered that God's domain had to be defended like any other kingdom. When divine truth was at stake, any compromise was equivalent to defeat. At all cost those "accursed evil customs" embedded in the Constitutions of Clarendon had to be exorcised and cast down; and once safely in Flanders, Thomas headed for the papal residence at Sens to place his case and the defense of the English church at the feet of a supreme but most reluctant pontiff.

Becket arrived at Sens in state, accompanied by three hundred horsemen, to urge his political and spiritual master not to sheathe his "sword, but draw it out."[34] The exiled prelate was all for immediate and draconian action, but he reckoned without the facile mind and subtle diplomacy of Rolando Bandinelli, a trained and accomplished scholar and intellectual who, as Pope Alexander III, was an absolute master of prevarication, procrastination, and deceit. The pope's manifold talents were directed at preserving the independence of the church, but his most immediate concern was to protect himself from being replaced on the papal throne by the rival pope Paschal III, supported by Emperor Frederick Barbarossa. Alexander's golden rule was that which "cannot be cured must be endured," and he was anything but pleased to be trapped between the likes of Thomas Becket and Henry Plantagenet.[35] He supported in principle Thomas's stand, but he was short of cash, desperately needed the clerical revenues flowing from England, and felt he could not publicly censor the Constitutions of Clarendon lest the king of England join the imperial party and recognize Barbarossa's pocket antipope.

Despite the splendor in which Becket had arrived at Sens, there was a maggot eating at both the archbishop's pride and his conscience. At Clarendon and again at Northampton, he had failed to prove his mettle as either a soldier or a martyr of Christ. In one instance, he had forsaken his flock by pledging his support to a document his conscience knew to be pernicious; in the other he had fled, if not in panic, certainly to safety in exile. Equally bothersome was the knowledge that he had received his archdiocese through the blatant and uncanonical secular influence of a king who had proven to be an ungodly tyrant. Only abject penance could cleanse such an agony of evils, and in one of his most spectacular gestures he fell to his knees before the papal throne and resigned his see, confessing that the bondage of the English church was his own doing, his appointment to spiritual office had been conceived in sin, and his strength was "unequal to the burden" of defending his flock. Then he burst into such a storm of tears and "wept and sobbed" so much that everyone, even the pope, felt obliged to join in the display.[36]

Discounting the theatrics, Alexander resisted the temptation to resolve his problems by taking Becket at his word. Instead, he reinstated the embarrassing prelate but bundled him off to the remote Cistercian monastery at Pontigny and sent him an impassioned letter begging him to keep a discreet profile: "We beseech your discretion, we advise, we counsel, we urge that in your whole conduct . . . you display caution, prudence, and circumspection, doing nothing in haste or precipitately. . . ."[37]

During these years, in isolation at Pontigny and later in the more urban setting of the Benedictine abbey outside of Sens, Thomas's second metamorphosis took place: he began the process whereby he transformed himself first into a white and then into a red martyr. By and large his biographers predate Becket's choice of a hard, mattressless wooden bed, his use of a hair shirt worn next to the skin, and his masochistic need for thrice-daily, often self-inflicted, flagellations until his back ran red with blood. They associate these bodily mortifications to the divine grace that swept over the newly ordained priest and consecrated archbishop the moment he took ecclesiastical office back in 1162. This transformation, they insist, was, of course, carefully hidden; not even "his nearest friends" knew that "this saintly man had in his secret life all the tokens of sanctity and religion."[38] At least one contemporary, however, assigned the conversion to the self-imposed penance following the shattering defeat administered to his pride and conscience at Clarendon, and the first documented evidence of fleshly mortification does not emerge until his retreat to Pontigny.

Whatever the dating, everybody is agreed that a profound psychological and spiritual change took place during the years in exile.[39] Becket unrelentingly practiced the ascetic life as a means of implanting order upon a world filled with violence, duplicity, and malignancy that had fallen apart around him. Confession before Christ's vicar on earth and reappointment as primate of England had purged away the failures of the past, but there remained the gnawing need to purify the soul and seek spiritual perfection by mortifying the flesh and stamping out carnal desire and worldly ambition. "The Lord's hand," he wrote Alexander III, "has touched me and stretches over me; so leave me alone to drink the cup of my sorrow."[40]

Sorrow soon gave way to conviction; Becket found unity with Christ and at the same time total self-justification by focusing his mind on the single pervasive truth: "As faith is one, so liberty [of the church] is one." "The saintly temper," it has been written, "is a moral temper . . . a partisan temper,"[41] and Thomas of Canterbury made no distinction between his personal enemies and God's foes. In the face of such evil, he could not retreat, or compromise, even if the price were death. The only model possible was the image of Christ—not the savior but the warrior king—and in December of 1167 Becket wrote the papal legate sent to negotiate a peace between king and archbishop that "even so your master, the prince of the apostles, not by yielding to princes nor by dispensing peace to the wicked, but by resisting them, won for himself by martyrdom a name on earth and glory in the heavens."[42] The role of the martyr was the highest achievement a Christian—especially one like Becket who viewed himself as a soldier of Christ—could attain. By 1169, the year before Thomas returned to England and to martyrdom, the change in "Christ's outlaw" was so apparent that Louis of France somewhat caustically asked him: "My Lord Archbishop, do you seek to be more than a saint?"[43]

If saintdom were to be earned, Becket could not afford to hide God's light in a monastic cell. If he were destined to be "a spectacle for men and for angels," then the conflict had to be carried into the enemy's camp. It was not as if the archbishop did not have cause aplenty for personal revenge. His archdiocese had been confiscated and its nine-thousand-pound revenue turned over to Ranulf de Broc, the man who had called him traitor as he shoved his way out of Northampton Castle. The incomes of those who had believed in him and gone into exile for his sake had been cut off; and his relatives and kin, including a married sister and a number of nephews, had been banished from the realm. The final inequity was the worst: the heretical clauses of the Constitutions of Clarendon had been cruelly and godlessly enforced by a tyrant king. One unwarranted injury deserved another, and in retaliation and unbeknownst to his closest advisers or the pope, he unleashed his spiritual thunder. On June 12, 1166, he excommunicated, among others, Rannulf de Broc and "all who should in future stretch forth their hands against the possessions and goods of the church of Canterbury," and he condemned to hell all who had been involved in issuing the Constitutions of Clarendon.[44] He had intended to include Henry himself in his anathema but did not quite dare. Instead, he wrote to his fellow bishops, asking, "Wherefore do you not arise with me against my enemies? . . . Enough, and even more than enough have we put up with our Lord, the King of England. . . . We hold that it is a thing dangerous and not to be endured, to leave unpunished . . . the excessive outrages committed by him and his officials against the Church of God," and he absolved the prelates from their promise to support and enforce the Clarendon code, reminding them that "priests of Christ are appointed to be the fathers and masters of kings and princes."[45]

Predictably and accurately, the bishops retorted that Becket's harsh words had done nothing except kindle the king's anger into a flame, "provoking a lasting and inexorable hatred."[46] Gilbert Foliot of London in a private letter to Becket stated the case against the primate with devastating effect. He had always regarded the archbishop to be a fool, and with venomous forensic ability he proceeded to cut the prelate to shreds. Who had deserted his colleagues at Clarendon; who "fled by night [from Northampton] in disguise, as if plots had been laid against your life and person"; who had "escaped from the realm overseas, although no one was pursuing you or driving you into exile"; and who had chosen to reside in a foreign land and sought "to steer the ship of the church which you left without a pilot, amid the waves and storms"? Finally came the unkindest query of all— "With what face then, father, do you now invite us to meet the death from which you shrank and fled?"—and the cruelest dig: "Surely your annual revenues are not so great that you would wish to recover them by shedding the blood of your brethren!" Foliot ended his attack with the scornful, if gratuitous, comment that Becket "should have handled such matters with mature deliberation, not with the ardour of a novice."[47]

Bishop Foliot's letter was designed to draw blood, but it displays the quagmire of emotions and mutual recriminations into which a constitutional squabble had sunk. Moreover, Foliot had another complaint against his archbishop. Becket had been writing his sovereign imprudently omitting the formal and customary salutation to a king. In one letter to Henry II he abruptly began by announcing "these are the words of the Archbishop of Canterbury to the King of the English" and then had proceeded to chastise and correct him as if he had been a first-year law student. The church of God, Becket informed the king, consisted of two orders, the clergy and everybody else, including kings. Since "kings receive their authority from the church" and the ecclesia derived its from Christ, Henry had no business giving orders to the clergy, dragging clerks before secular tribunals, or forbidding bishops from dealing "with cases concerning breach of faith or oaths." This last point was particularly explosive, because Thomas was suggesting that God's kingdom, and therefore, of course, its courts and the profits thereof, included all cases of breach of contract—which meant 90 percent of the legal business of the realm. As the champion of the priestly domain, Becket concluded his lecture with the uncompromising warning that Henry would surely "incur the stern vengeance of Almighty God" unless he immediately mended his ways.[48]

Such verbal encounters, as the English bishops warned, did little except infuriate the king and make it impossible for Pope Alexander to patch up some sort of working compromise, however rickety and inadequately clothed in vague platitudes. Time and time again each side approached the threshold of a settlement only to have the door violently slammed shut by Henry's insistence that Canterbury account for all the monies spent while lord chancellor or Becket's retort that Henry should pay him all the revenues owed him as archbishop in exile. In November of 1169 the two men appeared to be on the verge of an agreement. Henry actually lifted the Constitutions of Clarendon and guaranteed the liberties of the church; Becket consented to the omission of that sacred fig leaf "saving his order" and agreed to return to England. But when Thomas insisted that the treaty be symbolically ratified with the "kiss of peace," Henry balked, claiming that years before he had sworn never to do such a thing, and Becket instantly broke off the negotiations. The next month at Montmirail much the same thing happened. Thomas in the king's presence was persuaded to agree to the carefully rehearsed formula "I now submit the whole case between us to your clemency and judgment"; but to the horror of those present and before anyone could prevent him, he demolished the effect by unexpectedly adding the explosive phrase "saving the honor of God," at which Henry stalked out of the meeting. Ten months passed, and at another encounter of the two men, the English monarch, not to be outdone by his archbishop, agreed to a papally negotiated peace but promptly ruined its chances by insisting on including the qualification "saving the dignity of his kingdom."[49] The honor of God confronted the dignity of the realm; the pride of two vengeful and stubborn men bent on humiliating one another stood rigid and unyielding to any appeal to compromise, to self-interest or even to the welfare of the two kingdoms they claimed to represent.

Both parties had been at loggerheads for so long that fear of treachery had become a conditioned response; no matter how trifling or thoughtless, every word and action took on sinister and symbolic meaning. In June of 1170 Becket's cup of suspicion ran over when Henry arranged that his young son be crowned king of England by Canterbury's personal rival and historic enemy, Roger, archbishop of York. Suddenly Thomas became an even more fervent exponent of ancient custom than Henry had been at Clarendon, for it was Canterbury's sacred right to crown the kings of England. For Becket the nature of the controversy dramatically shifted. No longer was it a question of defending ecclesiastical liberties; now it was a matter of safeguarding the privileges and jurisdiction of his own diocese. His feudal as well as spiritual rights were at stake, and he immediately wrote the pope an impassioned, if inaccurate, description of the coronation, claiming that the young king, instead of taking the traditional oath to protect God's holy church, had sworn to observe the Constitutions of Clarendon, and on these grounds he asked for authority to suspend and excommunicate the prelates who had participated in the kangaroo coronation.

Before Alexander could reply, Henry and his archbishop entered into a grudging and fragile peace. The king, under threat of papal excommunication and faced with war on the Continent, could not afford to further alienate Alexander. Becket, with Gilbert Foliot's scornful words—"With what face then, father, do you now invite us to meet the death from which you shrank?"—still gnawing at his pride, decided that the battle had to be fought at home in England and the only way he could get there was to settle with the king. A meeting was hurriedly arranged on July 22, 1170, in a field, ominously known as Traitors' Meadow, near Fréteval in Touraine, and there the two men settled their differences, largely by not talking about them. Nothing was said about Clarendon or the steady encroachment by laymen upon the properties of Canterbury that had been going on for generations. Henry, however, did guarantee the liberties of the church, but neither side insisted on specific terms, and the king promised to reinstate Thomas in full possession of his rights and lands as archbishop. In his turn Becket required neither the "kiss of peace" nor the qualification "saving his order." Henry and Thomas also spoke alone for a short time, and what they agreed upon later became a point of bitter controversy. The king without a doubt agreed to a second coronation for his son and certainly listened sympathetically to Canterbury's furious complaints directed at York and the other officiating bishops. Whether he agreed to their excommunication is anything but certain; and that confusion proved fatal, because shortly after their meeting, Thomas received discretionary papal authorization, based on the archbishop's inaccurate letter to the pope, to anathematize the clerics who had participated in the cursed ceremony.

Alexander must have realized that Becket, given his impetuous personality, and now armed with a papal bull, could not be restrained; but the pontiff had been profoundly shocked by the archbishop's description of the coronation and his claim that the boy king had omitted the traditional oath to protect the church. Thomas himself was fully aware of the truth about the coronation ceremony—the ancient formula had indeed been observed—but on November 29, just before embarking for England, he heralded his return to Canterbury by issuing the papal bull excommunicating the three men whom he regarded as his most inveterate personal enemies and the source of all his troubles in England: Roger, archbishop of York; Gilbert Foliot, bishop of London; and Jocelin, bishop of Salisbury. Twenty-five days later, he directed God's wrath at his secular enemies. On Christmas Eve, at mass in his cathedral church of Canterbury, he excommunicated all those who had during the past six years violated the rights of his archdiocese, naming among others that satanic symbol of temporal aggression Ranulf de Broc, who had held his diocese in receivership and stripped it of its revenues ever since his exile. As he pronounced the words of the anathema, he flung the flaming altar candles to the floor and announced that anyone—secular or spiritual—who had violated his rights was "damned by Jesus Christ." Vengeance may belong to the Lord, but in this case Becket was making sure that only he spoke for God.[50]

Thomas did more than strike down his enemies during that evening service; he spoke in his sermon about the martyrdom of Saint Ælfheah, whose tomb lay across the road from the cathedral, and he is reported to have predicted that "soon there will be another martyr" at Canterbury.[51] Almost without exception the archbishop's early biographers pictured their hero as having been conscious of his impending death, even striving to attain it.

Hagiographers are, of course, in the business of manufacturing martyrs, but Becket must have sensed the danger of his actions. He had returned to Canterbury inspired not by the spirit of magnanimity but by a determination to punish the guilty and to test the king's sincerity by demanding every last particle of retribution both for himself and for his church.

Thomas was probably unaware of the intensity or the extent of the dislike, consternation, and fear that his reappearance in England produced. After six years barons, commoners, even churchmen were anything but pleased to have in their midst a touchy and peremptory prelate whose obstinacy had been hardened in the fire of nearly two thousand arduous days of monastic discipline and self-mortification. The exile mentality is rarely forgiving, and Becket proved no exception: he demanded an accounting of every foot and penny of church property and revenues. Reginald, earl of Cornwall, who was no enemy of the archbishop, spoke for most of England—at least for the men of property—when he said: "The archbishop has greatly disturbed the kingdom and unless the Lord God intervenes, will drag it down to everlasting ignominy. So far but a few, soon all of us, will be sent to Hell because of him."[52]

The Lord God did not intervene; but Henry II, still on the Continent, did, and with fatal consequences. It is a moot point whether the king's wrath was sparked by the excommunication of his bishops—that all depends on what had been agreed upon at Fréteval—but the highly colored reports reaching him from across the Channel about Thomas's abrasive activities certainly produced an explosion. He felt cheated and betrayed, and he burst out with the fatal words: "What miserable drones and traitors have I nourished and promoted in my household, who let their lord be treated with such shameful contempt by a low-born clerk."[53] Whether Henry meant it or not, that outburst was Becket's death sentence, because four knights of varying age, rank, and wealth took him at his word, as indeed they had cause to do. Every knight and baron had but a single mission: their hands, their arms, even their bodies belonged "to our lord the king, and they are ready at his nod to avenge every wrong done to him and to work his will whatever it may be."[54] Those were the sentiments the barons had voiced at Clarendon; six years later they seemed even more appropriate, especially when dealing with a traitor like Thomas Becket. The archbishop may not have died by state decree in the technical sense, but in the eyes of feudal law he was certainly a felon deserving of death.

The four knights who set off, unbeknownst to the king, to uphold his honor and gain his favor arrived at Canterbury on the afternoon of December 29, 1170. They had spent the previous night at Saltwood Castle, where they joined forces with the archbishop's arch foe Ranulf de Broc, and the next day they descended on the cathedral city in impressive force. Only the four knights, however, entered the episcopal palace, and when they were shown into Becket's privy chambers, they found the archbishop sitting on his bed conversing with his servants. Thomas took no notice of his visitors. He knew most of them by name and realized that they came from the king, but it was essential for the honor of his office that they wait upon his favor to be heard. When he finally turned to recognize them, the conversation almost immediately became violent, the knights announcing that they had come in the king's name to arrest him and Becket daring them to try: "In the Lord's battle," he assured them, he would "fight hand to hand, toe to toe."[55] In this exchange of threats the intruders were at a disadvantage; they had left their arms and armor outside the palace, and they could do little else but retreat in frustration.

Becket was well aware of the gravity of the situation, and he seems to have decided to brazen it out. "My mind," he said, "is made up. I know exactly what I have to do."[56] What he had to do was to defend the dignity of his spiritual office and the honor of God, even if that meant inviting arrest or even death. He would never again capitulate as he had done at Clarendon or flee as at Northampton. Within the hour the archbishop's resolve was tested, for the knights—now fully armed with sword and axe and reinforced by de Broc's men—returned, ready if necessary to force their way into the palace.[57] Thomas was all for meeting them there, but his servants and associates threatened to subject him to the indignity of being dragged bodily to the sanctuary of the cathedral, where, they argued, armed men would be reluctant to follow. Persuaded largely by the ignominy of being carried forcibly to safety, Thomas consented to walk to the cathedral but did so with agonizing slowness, his cross borne in state before him and his associates tugging at his sleeves lest the knights catch up to them. Once the company was safely through the door of the north transept of the church, members of the group closed and began to bolt the door. Ever conscious of appearance and decorum, Thomas ordered them to stop: "It is not meet," he said, "to make a fortress of the house of prayer. . . . By suffering rather than fighting shall we triumph over the enemy."

When Thomas's procession entered the church, vespers were under way. The darkness of a winter's afternoon was closing in upon the main nave and the choir where the cathedral monks were at their prayers. The long shadows were broken only by the candlelight from the high altar. Interrupted in their services, the monks swarmed about the archbishop, urging him to take cover in the creeping darkness. Once, however, de Broc's men and the knights had forced their way first into the palace, then through the cloister that linked the episcopal residence to the cathedral, and finally to the unlocked north transept door, most of Becket's company scattered and fled, leaving only Edward Grim and Thomas's personal chaplain to protect the archbishop. Even so, there was time to escape; Thomas was dressed in a dark cloak, and he could have found endless places of concealment in the gathering darkness of night. But Becket refused flight and safety. As the four knights, accompanied now by a fifth man, a subdeacon branded ever after with the name of Mauclerk (Bad Clerk), approached, he retreated up the steps of the high altar and met his assailants with Edward Grim at his side.

Legend describes a death that would have done credit to the most immaculate soldier of Christ. Like the early martyrs, Becket retained absolute command of the situation. To the knights' summons "Where is Thomas Becket, traitor to the king and the realm?" he answered, "Lo! Here am I, no traitor to the king, but a priest. . . . Behold, I am ready to suffer in His Name who redeemed me by His Blood." To the order that he absolve all those he had excommunicated, he coldly responded, "There has been no satisfaction made, and I will not absolve them." To the threat "Then you shall die this instant," he replied, "I, too, am ready to die for my Lord, that in my blood the Church may obtain peace and liberty." Then, with perfect composure, he inclined his head "as one in prayer, and joining his hands together," he allowed his murderers to strike him down. The first blow, aimed at his head, missed and nearly severed Edward Grim's arm. The second bloodied the archbishop's face and neck. The third brought him to his knees and elbows. The fourth and fatal blow was delivered with such force that it split his head open like a soft melon and broke the sword on the stone pavement, but it did not come until Becket had a chance to speak his final words: "For the name of Jesus and the protection of the Church I am ready to embrace death." The fifth and final stroke was the most gruesome of all, if only because it was so unnecessary; Hugh, the Mauclerk, put his foot on the dead prelate's neck and used his sword point to spread the brains across the cathedral floor, intermingling the white of brain tissue with the red of blood. It was a potent mixture and an irresistible symbol of his martyrdom: Becket had "received from the Lord a stole of two-fold color—white in token of his faithful governance of his archepiscopal see, and crimson in token of the happy consecration of his martyrdom."[58]

Reality, alas, was not so perfectly staged, and far less dignified. The knights had not come to slay Thomas Becket. If they had any clear-cut plan, it was probably to arrest him—certainly not murder him on the steps of the cathedral altar. Unfortunately, they encountered a man determined to resist the humiliation of capture, especially by soldiers of no particular social standing, even if they did claim to speak for the king. One of them he knew well; Reginald Fitz Urse had once been his own vassal, and he up-braided him for violating his feudal obligations. What happened was, in all likelihood, that the knights picked up where they had left off at the first en-counter in the archbishop's privy chamber. Namecalling quickly ensued; Becket denounced Reginald as a pimp and profligate; and when one of the knights tried to hoist him onto his shoulders, Thomas fought back so fran-tically, kicking and scolding, that his would-be arrestors found themselves faced with a repeat of what had occurred in the palace. The cathedral was filling up with onlookers, the monks were beginning to return from hiding to protect their archbishop, and the only recourse was to retreat in dis-honor. This time, however, they were armed, and anger took its predictable course.

Eight hundred years after the event it is impossible to disentangle fact from fiction. Not even the eyewitnesses were certain about what hap-pened, the words actually spoken, or the exact sequence of events; and most of the accounts were written in the afterglow of a death that all the early biographers either already thought to be a martyrdom or were deter-mined to turn into an heroic death in the grand tradition. "It would be hard, we believe," wrote Benedict of Peterborough, "to find any martyr whose passion so clearly followed the Lord's."[59] Therein lies the rub: did Becket play-act at martyrdom, imitating the early martyrs, refusing escape, provoking his assailants, fearful lest delay should deprive him of his coveted crown, or was the script written for him by biographers determined to turn a man who possessed more than his share of human failings into a spiritual hero?[60] If so, they had overwhelming public backing, because Christendom was shocked to its spiritual roots by the picture of an archbishop, no mat-ter how distasteful his character, being murdered on the steps of God's high altar in his own cathedral church. No staging could have been better contrived to reach a larger audience. Even Becket's enemies granted him the right to sainthood; and as the news and circumstances of his death spread, so also did the reports of the miracles that followed in the wake of such a spectacular murder. Within the week a blind woman was restored to sight by wiping her eyes with a rag soaked in the martyr's blood. Soon the medicinal consequences of a pilgrimage to Canterbury proved to every-one's satisfaction that Thomas had indeed been received into heaven as God's martyred champion.

Canonization came with almost indecent haste; only Saint Francis of As-sisi achieved his crown with greater speed. On February 21, 1173, just over two years after he was assassinated, Becket was sainted on the triple grounds that his cause—the historic liberties of the church—had been wor-thy, the style of his death had been magnificent, and the signs of divine approval were manifest in the deluge of miracles that emanated from his grave. The thorny questions of Becket's inner saintliness, his character and life style were resolved by the unanimous opinion of his biographers that Thomas had possessed from the start an inner and secret core of holiness which had only been revealed when the corpse was undressed and made ready for burial. Only then were the hair shirt crawling with lice, the knee-length sackcloth skirt, and the scarred and lacerated back discovered. Here indeed was dramatic proof of "his twofold martyrdom, the voluntary one of his life and the violent one of his death."[61] Almost immediately it was said that the saint had throughout his entire life taken as his double model Saint Sebastian, who under cover of a warrior's armor had "conducted himself as a soldier of Christ," and Saint Cecilia, who secretly mortified her flesh but "appeared outwardly adorned with vesture of gold."[62] Only by peeling back, layer by layer, the false facades of worldliness could the true Becket, known during his life to the Lord alone, be exposed. His sanctity lay not in the multitude of miracles generated by his martyrdom but in himself, and his biographers insisted that Thomas's sacrifice could not even be compared to the suffering of the early martyrs, for his death had been offered selflessly in defense of the church universal and not selfishly to save his own soul from damnation. In death the early Christian martyrs had benefited no one except themselves, but Becket had died for the church and indirectly for all mankind.[63]

Whether Thomas Becket's death was as noble and selfless as his biographers claimed is a slippery issue. Whether a prelate who, as a few contemporaries suggested, was "haughty, rapacious, violent and cruel," and who "wanted to be more than a king" warranted a martyr's reputation raises embarrassing questions that involve the meaning of martyrdom itself.[64] Whether a self-appointed and aggressive defender of ecclesiastical liberties defined not as freedom of worship but as fiscal, judicial, and organizational privileges should be numbered among the martyrs of the faith was a debate that erupted even as Becket's corpse grew cold. In life the archbishop's militant actions had raised doubts: could such a man ever be a true candidate for sainthood? And the bishop of Hereford posed a question to which there was no satisfactory response: "If it happens (God forbid) that the archbishop should be killed in the cause of ecclesiastic freedom, shall we count him as a martyr? To be a martyr is to die for the faith."[65] Becket had surely died for an institution, but had he died for a faith? Despite the miracles and the fervent arguments of his biographers, the question remained, and it was still being debated a half-century later as a thorny theological issue at the University of Paris, where a martyr who had been born and bred in England was regarded as not being much of a saint at all.[66]

Twentieth-century judgment has shifted the debate but made it no easier. If Becket, as his twelfth-century biographers insisted, thirsted after
martyrdom, did he then, as the fourth knight in T. S. Eliot's play argues, in
effect commit "suicide while of Unsound Mind"? Or, worse, did he fall to
Eliot's fourth tempter and "do the right deed for the wrong reason"?

> Think, Thomas, think of enemies dismayed,
> Creeping in penance, frightened of a shade;
> Think of pilgrims, standing in line
> Before the glittering jewelled shrine,
> From generation to generation
> Bending the knee in supplication,
> Think of the miracles, by God's grace,
> And think of your enemies, in another place.[67]

In *Murder in the Cathedral,* Eliot suggests the debate be resolved in
Becket's favor. Thomas did not "seek the way of martyrdom . . . to be high
in heaven," but was in fact a "true martyr," God's perfect instrument, who
desired nothing for himself, "not even the glory of being a martyr."[68] In the
real world of the twelfth century, however, the archbishop may well have
found the temptation irresistible. Thomas, like everyone else, believed that
saints did in fact rule from the grave as divine mediators between heaven
and earth. He also believed equally fervently in a variety of honor belonging both to himself and to God that required the entire world, kings included, to bend the knee in supplication—which was exactly what Henry
II, three and a half years after the assassination, was obliged to do.

Becket's death meshed with a series of events that very nearly unseated
Henry as the paramount king of Europe. As a consequence, on July 12,
1174, with his empire falling apart, his sons in open rebellion, and his enemies everywhere triumphant, Henry Plantagenet came crawling to
Thomas's tomb in repentance and desperation. Barefoot and dressed only
in a hair shirt and his underwear, he knelt—doubtless to the saint's intense
satisfaction—in adoration before his old enemy. As he prayed, he was
whipped by the church he had sought to discipline: five strokes from each
attending bishop, including Gilbert Foliot of London, and three lashes
apiece from the eighty monks of Canterbury—small penance, it was argued, for the part he had played in causing the murder. Henry denied ordering or desiring the archbishop's death, but the king accepted full
responsibility for what had happened and dutifully endured a punishment
that, although largely symbolic and ceremonial, must have kept him on
his knees for several hours.[69] When the ultimate humiliation of the proud
prince had occurred, Thomas for once responded magnanimously: by the

end of the summer all of the king's enemies were defeated and ready to submit.

The problem for Becket's contemporaries was not whether the saint delighted in pilgrims creeping to his shrine or seeing his enemies in another place. Instead, it was the paradox embedded in Christian martyrdom itself: the use of immoderate means to achieve an ideal that rested on love, charity, and moderation in all things. Thomas's closest friend and admirer, John of Salisbury, was also his most persistent critic for exactly this reason: Becket's means—there is nothing quite so immoderate as martyrdom—violated Christian ends. "I have," he wrote, "reproved my Lord Archbishop more often and more sternly than any man, because from the first, with mistaken zeal, he provoked the king and his adherents to bitterness, whereas some consideration should have been given to time, to place and to persons."[70] Here was the fatal, unredeemable flaw: Becket had no sense of means commensurate to ends. The archbishop was such a self-absorbed person that he lacked the gift of empathy for others; some might say he lacked the gift of charity. He could not place himself in the shoes of Henry II, Alexander III, Gilbert Foliot, or Roger of York. He had no peripheral vision. He could see clearly enough his rights and privileges but was blinded to what lay in the shadows by his commitment to dogma and his love of bureaucratic demarcations. In such a walled-in world there was no room for face-saving platitudes behind which human weakness and ugly reality could hide. The truth for Becket was too bright a beacon for him to accept the safe, if ill-defined, features of compromise and adaptation "to time, to place and to persons." John of Salisbury might well have written his famous formula for living the Christian ideal with Thomas of Canterbury's martyrdom in mind: "Truly all enthusiasm is the foe of salvation and all excess is a fault; nothing is worse than the immoderate practice of good works."[71]

Even if Becket did the "right thing," for reasons that may not withstand the test of twentieth-century scrutiny, his own century judged him to be great: "great in the palace, great at the altar, great both at court and in the church . . . and singularly great at his journey's end."[72] He was a hero to be remembered; his tomb, as Chaucer's pilgrims all knew, was not simply a place where heaven and earth met in bejeweled and costly splendor but the spot where an unforgettable event had transpired. History, however, has not been kind to this bright "candle on God's candlestick." His light along with his memory has steadily faded. The miracles have ceased, his shrine has been demolished, and his death degraded to a minor incident in the history of a four-century-long struggle between the kingdom of God and the kingdom of men in which victory overwhelmingly went to the royal descendants of Henry II. By the sixteenth century a new definition of society was emerging that required that the realm of God and the domain of man become one. The medieval duality of body and soul was subsumed into the corpus of a divinely ordained and inspired leviathan that demanded the undivided, undisputed loyalty of all its citizens. In such a polity there was no place for a soldier-martyr who fought and died for the honor of a deity which spoke through the decretals of a pope in Rome and not through the statutes and proclamations of a king in England.

In a farcical and ironic paradox of history, Becket on the twenty-fourth of April, 1538, was cited once again to appear before the king's council to account for his actions. When after thirty days he understandably failed to materialize, he was found to be in contempt and declared to be no martyr but "a stubborn clerk" and rebel who had given aid and comfort to the enemies of his king. He had died, it was proclaimed, in an unseemly brawl before the full measure of his inequities could be revealed and justice handed down in a court of law.[73] The second Henry had been vindicated by the eighth. Never again would an English monarch kneel barefoot in penance before the saint's shrine, for history had come full cycle: Thomas Becket had been turned back into a traitor, a criminal divested of any enduring interest except to historians bent on unearthing the unappetizing facts of the case:

> When miracles cease, and the faithful desert you,
> And men shall only do their best to forget you.
> And later is worse, when men will not hate you
> Enough to defame or to execrate you,
> But pondering the qualities that you lacked
> Will only try to find the historical fact.[74]

The historian is fortunate beyond measure that Hans Holbein was commissioned to paint both the man and "the intention of his soul."

CHAPTER 7

SIR THOMAS MORE:
"A HERO OF SELFHOOD"

> One may be determined to embrace martyrdom
> gracefully, but a day of reprieve is not to be
> sneezed at.
> —ELIZABETH PETERS,
> *The Snake, the Crocodile and the Dog*

*A*N EPIGRAM of rather questionable origin declares that there is no one quite so dead as a dead priest unless it is a dead bishop; but even after 374 years Archbishop Thomas Becket could still speak from the grave. And it was a point of inestimable consolation to Sir Thomas More that he should be executed for high treason on Tuesday, July 6, 1535, the eve of Becket's translation, the official placement of a saint's body in its shrine. It was, he thought, "a day very meet and convenient for me."[1] More associated with his namesake not only spiritually—both acclaimed martyrdom as the highest goal a Christian could attain, a guaranteed highway into heaven—but also intellectually—both had a vision of the church historic, instituted and ordained by God as part of His divine plan for humanity. More's was a more subtle and complex concept, less militant and institutional and therefore more difficult to define and defend, but nonetheless grounded on the same fundamental distinction between body and soul and on the same division of society into state and church, in which the miter stood higher than the crown.

Sir Thomas's association with the saint of Canterbury involves more than a continuation of the struggle between king and pope, laity and clergy, church and state, and the growth of divergent loyalties that threat-

ened the very essence of the medieval formula regulating and balancing
the two halves of Christendom, assigning God and Caesar their proper
roles. It raises the debate over motives to a new level of intensity, because
where Becket as a man gave away nothing of his inner self and as a martyr
concealed himself from his historians, Thomas More left a multitude of
clues—over a million and a half words in English and Latin—to his mind
and soul. He tells us almost too much about his fears, his hatreds, his wild
imaginings, and the self-doubt that enveloped him. Like Socrates, he spent
a lifetime preparing for death, and every step of the way is recorded in a
maze of language—some of it magnificent, much of it contradictory, but
all of it self-revealing—that leaves the historian gasping at the multitude of
riddles to which there seem to be either no answers or too many solutions.
For four and a half centuries scholars and critics, admirers and skeptics have
been asking a double-helixed question: for what did More die—himself, his
conscience, his soul, his God, his faith, his church—and how does one distinguish the various parts from the whole?[2]

The association of the two men—so totally different in style and temperament yet so intimately bound together in their martyrdom—contains
yet another theme, the marriage of fact and fiction. If Becket's confrontation with the second Henry is steeped in impenetrable legend that historical documentation has failed either to enrich or to destroy, More's fatal
encounter with the eighth Henry is a well-recorded historical reality that
has never completely broken away from the myth that enshrines it. Despite
450 years of unrelenting research and a recent outburst of revisionism, the
More of legend persists for the excellent reason that he is a far more attractive and useful figure than the Sir Thomas of historical fact.

It is not difficult to disguise Thomas More in fictional shrouds of purity,
fortitude, and virtue, because in real life he appears as a powerful exception
to one of the golden rules of martyrdom, poignantly formulated by John
Ruskin when he wrote, "Most martyrs have been made away with less for
their faith than [for] their incivility."[3] In life More was almost always courteous; he could ponder, if not necessarily sympathize with, both sides of a
question; and he possessed what the sixteenth century admired most, the
gift of decorum. Unlike Becket, he could, up to a crucial point, adapt "to
time, to place and to persons"; he was invariably aware of his options; and
his ability to suit his words to the occasion and to use them to express the
inner reaches of his thought were unparalleled. His sense of timing, of the
dramatic—critics might say of maintaining stage center—was equaled only
by Socrates, and later possibly by Gandhi; and like his classical model, his
weapons were matchless words interlaced with irony and humor. No one

wants to give up the legendary More, especially when it is so easy to document the heroic actions and circumstances of his life.

The issue, of course, is to whom do heroes and martyrs belong? To themselves and the historical reality out of which they emerged, or to fiction as it has been preserved and used over the centuries? This question was debated in an unlikely and curious encounter between Richard Marius, one of More's most perceptive and persuasive biographers, and Mario Cuomo, then the governor of New York.[4] The governor complained that he did not "want to hear that Horatius was a secret shareholder in the bridge company, or that Lincoln was chronically constipated," or that "Thomas More was obsessed sexually." "I don't need to see his warts. I'm surrounded by people with warts; I have my own warts." Cuomo pictured his More standing eternally "a prisoner on a scaffold, joking with the sheriff, forgiving his executioners, dying the 'king's good servant but God's first.' " He wanted to preserve Sir Thomas as the most comfortable of all martyrs who could remind him "how easy it is to lose your head. And that sometimes it may be worth it."[5] In response Marius answered as any historian must: he liked and admired More "so much that I want him to appear in history as he was in life. Human beings have a right to their character."

Over the centuries, More's "character" has been recorded many times over, and it has not always been presented without its flaws; as Cuomo said in explaining why a picture of More hung in his office, "He was a good man but by no means perfect. That's made it easier to pal around with him for all these years."[6] But in the last decade, with the publication of the Yale University translations of More's vicious and heavy-fisted polemical works directed at Martin Luther and other Protestants, the More who wrote *Utopia* and *A Dialogue of Comfort Against Tribulation* has been replaced by a very unattractive and warty More indeed. He presents himself as an unyielding religious fanatic who wallows with delight in the anal symbolism of his age. More left no scatological cannon unfired in shielding his king from Luther's attack on Henry VIII's defense of the Catholic sacraments, and he announced his intention to throw back into the German's "shitty mouth, truly the shit pool of all shit, all the muck and shit which your damnable rottenness has vomited up, and to empty out all the sewers and privies onto your crown."[7]

There is not only the anal More but also the ribald More who could not resist a joke at the expense of women, even reminding his beloved daughter Meg of her close relationship to mother Eve, who offered father Adam the fatal apple. In one of his epigrams he wrote about the woman who refused to ride sidesaddle as became a proper lady: "Well, my girl, no one could deny that you are ready for a husband, since your legs can straddle so large a horse."[8] Finally there is the caustic, slashing More who left the literary as well as the religious field bloodied with his cutting witticisms. To the unfortunate author who asked him to read his work and apologized for its unfinished state, he answered, "Your book, you see, apart from any explanation from you, tells us as much," and to the writer who turned his bad prose into verse, he retorted, "Now it hath at least some rhyme, no reason."[9] These are literary canards, but they display a mind that did not abide a fool kindly. The chronicler Edward Hall, who knew his More personally, hit upon a sensitive spot when he noted that Sir Thomas was an inveterate jester who "thought nothing to be well spoken except he had ministered some mock in the communication."[10]

The secret caves of the human mind run deep, and the further we penetrate, the darker and fouler the air becomes; but the purpose of this chapter is not so much to probe More's psyche as to explore his martyrdom—martyrs, like anyone else, have warts, which only show they are human—and to note that Becket the legend, the paper martyr, was canonized in two years but More the reality, the complex and contradictory man, was denied the crown of sainthood for four hundred years. There is a mystery and a moral here that needs, if not resolution, at least discussion, because with More we can for the first time focus on martyrdom as an internal decision and not simply as a physical act. For Socrates, the Maccabees, Perpetua, Becket, and even Jesus, the internal struggle is only hinted at; with More it is laid out in agonizing detail. Revealed in every facet of his personality, Sir Thomas stands embarrassingly naked before us. In the crucible of his character we find fanaticism and pride, cruelty and obstinacy, melancholy and insecurity, self-gratification and preoccupation with death. But we also discover humor, amusement, zest for life, courage, love of friends and family, and above all else a sense of comedy, of duty, and of means appropriate to ends, which places him as the forerunner of Mahatma Gandhi. At the conclusion of this chapter, even as the axe falls, the reader will not be absolutely sure why More elected to exchange life for death. All we will know for certain is that he was deeply serious about his life and his death—both required his full and undivided attention. As a consequence, for many Sir Thomas may not be a totally satisfying martyr, but for everybody he will be a believable human being. It is well to remember that few of us are required to choose between the many personalities that are locked away within the closet of our being and to decide which is the true and lasting identity.

Thomas More is the first martyr with a portrait; there is no need to make up a face to fit the reputation. The historian is fortunate beyond measure that Hans Holbein was commissioned to paint both the man and "the intention of his soul." The More of brush and pigment appears as a tense, inner-directed, introspective man, clean-shaven, with dark brown hair, tight and unrelenting lips, strong cleft chin, prominent nose, and recessed and slightly reddened eyes that gaze steadily out upon a sorrowful world. An aura of brooding yet mocking intelligence emanates from the composed face that makes the viewer feel strangely inadequate.

There is an almost irresistible temptation to turn Sir Thomas's career into a moral and historical homily on the agonizing choice that men and women, living on the threshold of modernity but still fettered by medieval dreams, had to make. They had to choose between a secular-minded approach to a world dominated by lawyers, merchants, and courtiers, in which man was adjudged to be the measure of all things, and a religious orientation that insisted that this life was a fleeting second awarded the Christian in order to prepare for eternity. The choice for More, it is argued, took the form of three well-thought-out decisions. First, he turned down what the medieval world regarded as the spiritual high road to heaven—the monastery—and decided to marry and become a lawyer. Second, he sacrificed the reflective and philosophical life for state and crown service. And third, he defied the will of the newly articulated nation-state embodied in the startling proposition that an act of Parliament could not err, and died for the medieval fiction of a united Christendom enveloped in the historic and seamless cloak of a Catholic church which spoke with a single voice from Rome. Such a tripartite view of More's development may impose an unwarranted consistency on his intellectual and spiritual odyssey by twisting unrelated decisions into a tidy and aesthetically pleasing totality, but it has the virtue of focusing on three essential ingredients in the unfolding drama of his martyrdom: More the family man, More the statesman, and More the dissenter.

Thomas, the second child of John and Agnes More, was introduced into a solidly medieval society some time after midnight on Saturday, February 7, 1478. The momentous events that would determine the lives, capture the imaginations, and win the souls of future generations were comfortably distant: seven years until Bosworth field and the advent of the Tudor dynasty, fourteen ere Columbus sailed westward to stumble across a new continent, thirty-five before Machiavelli published *The Prince,* and almost four decades before Martin Luther would ignite the Protestant Reformation. By the time Thomas died, fifty-seven years and five English kings later, he had lived long enough to pray for the prosperity of the eighteen-month-old Princess Elizabeth and had seen, but rejected, the shape of a world profoundly different in mind and spirit from the one into which he was born.

More's father, John—four times married—was a highly successful London lawyer who eventually became a judge of the King's Bench, an authority figure before whom Thomas, even as an adult and much later as lord chancellor of England, knelt in respect, asking his blessings. There was no doubt that the son was expected to follow in the parent's powerful footsteps—the law, marriage, and worldly success. In preparation young Master Thomas was sent to a day school in the city, was boarded out at the residence of John Morton, archbishop of Canterbury, and spent two years at Oxford and another three years at the Inns of Court in London for his legal training. The final step to respectability was marriage, when, in 1504, at the age of twenty-six, he wedded Jane Colt, who promptly bore him four children in about as rapid succession as is biologically possible, dying at the age of twenty-three, two years after the birth of her last child.

The heavy hand of John More is everywhere in evidence in this sixteenth-century yuppie saga, because, given free choice, young Thomas might have rejected marriage and the law for the contemplative, celibate life of the monastery. While at the Inns of Court, he studied Saint Augustine on the side and either housed with or worshiped with the Charterhouse monks of London. What deterred him from becoming either a priest or a monk was only in part his father's threat to cut off his son's financing; More's own sexual drives also played a role. As Erasmus later rather prissily put it, "He decided to be a chaste husband rather than an unchaste priest."

In electing the secular life, however, More hedged his bets. He secretly wore a rough hair shirt and punished "his body with whips, the cords knotted," a penitential habit known only to his daughter Margaret, who regularly washed his "shirt of hair." It is customary to present the More of these early years as a "divided soul," committed in part to medieval piety and in part to Renaissance secularism. But the men and women who felt hot upon them the breath of God and dared ask the primordial question What am I doing alone in the midst of meaningless eternity? were in no way limited to the medieval past. "The sick soul" of panicky introspection and despair and "the healthy minded" approach to religion that counters the stench of the grave with the pleasing scent of church ritual and concentrates on getting on with this life can appear at any time and in any culture. Thomas More was simply a classic example of the man who knew to the very bottom of his being that existence had some greater meaning than simply living out one's allotted years on earth, but who had not been allowed, or could not allow himself, the luxury of a full-time, uninterrupted investigation into what that meaning actually was. So he compartmentalized his day between hours in his chapel assigned to God, time in his legal chambers, and leisure at home as a loving husband and father.

Once More made the decision to live in this world, he could not turn back, and within a month of Jane More's death in 1511 Thomas remarried. He needed a mother for his children and a manager for his house, a wife who belonged entirely to the material concerns of his life. In Dame Alice Middleton, More found exactly what he sought, a partner who quite unfairly has been cast, by Thomas's friends and associates, in the role of Socrates' Xanthippe—"aged, blunt and rude," with a "harpy's hooked nose." More himself was scarcely kinder and could not suppress the witticism that he had married "neither a pearl nor a girl."[11]

Many years after Jane More died and as More himself was preparing for death, he built a tomb in Chelsea Old Church large enough to contain the earthly remains of himself and his two wives, and he contributed to the monument an odd epitaph in which he revealed more of himself than he might have realized or liked. "I cannot decide whether I did love the one or do love the other more. Oh, how happily we could have lived all three together if fate and morality permitted. Well, I pray, that the grave, that heaven, will bring us together. Thus death will give what life could not."[12] Here is the courteous husband who felt obliged to be fair to both wives, but also the honest, somewhat indecisive human struggling with the possibility that he might have loved one better than the other. Here also is the imaginative, fantasizing More who could imagine a personal utopia where he could enjoy both ladies at the same time. Finally, here is the believing and deeply religious More who knew that death would "give what life could not."

So Thomas More made his first decision, to settle down, marry, and practice law. He did extremely well at both: two wives, four children, a Thames River estate at Chelsea, election to Parliament, undersheriff of London, and a legal practice that brought in the comfortable income of four hundred pounds a year. Sir Thomas, however, was more than a clone of his father—a respectable and ambitious burgher, driven by what would later be called the Calvinistic work ethic. He was also a classical scholar, humanist, and historian who moved in international literary circles and was the friend of Erasmus; and it is in this setting that biographers like to picture More working out and debating his second great decision: to give up private practice and become a public servant of the crown.

More the lawyer, the father, the scholar, and the humanist led a balanced and controlled existence; there was always a time for God, a time for books, and a time for making money. What would happen to that soul-satisfying balance if he worked for his king? What would such service achieve for either himself or the commonwealth? And what would be the ultimate spiritual price that he would have to pay? These questions are the central themes of the first book of *Utopia,* in which More and his fictional alter ego, Raphael Hythloday, debate whether the scholar-philosopher, who is by definition the upright man, should enter government and risk corruption in a vicious arena of avarice, dishonesty, and pride. In the dialogue Hythloday gets the last word—in the second book he describes the Utopia which purports to prove that truth, justice, reason, philosophy, scholarship, and courtesy can only be achieved if the state is totally reconstructed along rational and revolutionary lines. His conclusion is that "whenever you have private property" and men measure all things by cash value alone, "it is scarcely possible for a commonwealth to have justice or prosperity."[13] The real More remained unconvinced by Hythloday's utopian picture and opted for the real world. The good counselor may not be able to turn kings into philosophers or keep them from evil policies, but by "the indirect approach" he can at least prevent the bad from becoming worse; "what you cannot turn to good you must make as little bad as you can."[14] When More wrote these words, he had in fact already made his decision, for *Utopia* was conceived during the spring of 1515 and in part written while its author was on diplomatic and commercial mission to Antwerp.

Erasmus got the notion that Henry VIII dragged a reluctant More onto the royal council, but more likely the attraction was mutual. The political nation of Tudor England was small and intimate, and a man whose father was already a government official and who himself was a successful city lawyer and international literary figure was well known at court. Moreover, government service was the logical move for an ambitious and talented man who had chosen to live and thrive in the secular world. So Thomas joined the council in August of 1517, not, as some have suggested, as the king's "tame humanist" and token intellectual, but as the personal secretary to the sovereign.[15] More's qualifications were not so much his undoubted charm and ability as his status: he possessed no power base in either the church or the nobility and was therefore no threat to the man who dominated the king's government—Thomas Wolsey, lord chancellor of England, archbishop of York, and cardinal legate of England.

Political authority and state service had their rewards, and More with the support of both king and cardinal rose steadily, if not spectacularly, in the government hierarchy: knighted and appointed undertreasurer of the exchequer in 1521, selected speaker of the House of Commons in 1523, chosen chancellor of the duchy of Lancaster in 1525, assigned to endless diplomatic missions, and, rather unexpectedly, chosen lord chancellor in 1529. As a royal servant More had heavy responsibilities, but while Wolsey monopolized both the royal council and the privy chamber, Sir Thomas had little real power either to shape military or diplomatic policies, which were more often than not utterly at odds with the ideals of *Utopia,* or to make them "as little bad" as possible. Even when the great cardinal fell from power, a victim of the king's marital crisis and mounting tension with Rome, and More replaced him as lord chancellor, Sir Thomas had little influence on governmental decisions. Only as the most literate, possibly the most committed and outspoken, opponent of heresy was he allowed to display his many talents.

The middle period of More's career—judged organizationally, not chronologically, the years of government service from 1517 to his resignation as lord chancellor in May of 1532—has recently received intensive, if not always flattering, attention because this is the decade and a half during which the amused, ironic face of the author of *Utopia* recedes, and the stern, unforgiving profile of the heretic hunter who relates heresy with sedition begins to emerge. The relationship between the two personalities goes to the root of one of the most hotly debated controversies about Sir Thomas More: are we dealing with two Mores or one?

There are those who insist that the two faces are in fact the same; only the lighting of time and circumstance has changed. For them, the driving principle behind *Utopia* is not tolerance, freedom, and reason but mind control that sought to chain the source of all Christian evil: the sins of sloth and pride. *Utopia,* they argue, is a social-scientific textbook on how to suppress "possessive individualism," the unrestrained "adoration of the self," so as to achieve the intellectual and spiritual security that flows from absolute consensus. Hearts and minds in agreement, More maintained, were the threads, light as air but strong as iron, that tied the commonwealth together.[16] "A kingdom in all its parts," he wrote in one of his epigrams, "is like a man; it is held together by natural affection."[17] What gave More's Utopians their integrity and political vitality was their conditioned response to always think and feel alike. In the real world of the Tudor body politic of the sixteenth century, this agreement of mind and spirit was exactly what Martin Luther and his pernicious, soul-murdering, commonwealth-rending ideas were endangering. More sensed that the ultimate clash between God and Satan could not be long delayed, and the fury directed at heresy in his six polemical works written between 1523 and 1532 was the emotional response of a deeply worried man to the same social and spiritual dangers that a younger and more optimistic Sir Thomas had been able to treat humorously and rationally in *Utopia*.

A single unswerving conviction pervaded all of Sir Thomas's religious polemics—heresy was an evil instituted by Satan, with whom no compromise was possible. The Protestant position that the true church existed neither in a sacerdotal priesthood, sacramental rituals, and ancient customs nor in chapels constructed of bricks and cathedrals cut in stone, but solely in the hearts of believers, inspired by a deity who chose to illuminate some with His divine grace and leave others in satanic darkness, was for More dangerous nonsense. It made a mockery of fifteen hundred years of history, turned Christ into a liar, and sowed the seeds of sedition and spiritual anarchy. Only the timeless universality of an organization sanctified by history and by Christ's promise made a millennium and a half before "to be with his church all days to the world's end" contained the precious spark of divinity that God had offered mankind collectively, not individually.[18] Christ had not imprisoned God's word between the covers of a book; Scripture had been composed many years later. Instead, he had given the world the gift of understanding, which over the centuries had come to encompass both the quick and the dead. The faith of a living past continued as the recorded history of the martyrs who had died for the truth, and the knowledge of that truth was reinterpreted and reinforced in the writings of the church fathers.

In the immanent, nonhistorical church of Martin Luther, the faithful forever stood alone, cut off from the inspirational wellspring of the centuries and the institutional association of their fellow Christians, the two infallible authorities that could confirm and interpret God's truth. How could Scripture be deciphered and understood, how could the creed be taught and be passed on from generation to generation by some invisible ecclesiastical institution? More predicted that such a leaderless flock would "be borne about in doubt and uncertainty by every wind of doctrine, and you will reduce everything to doubt."[19] Here indeed was pernicious individualism at its worst. Order, security, and God's truth as revealed to humanity could, according to Sir Thomas, reside only in a visible, public organization, which was rooted in history, sanctified by custom, and led by a divinely ordained priestly order that alone could perform the miracle of the mass, which objectively testified to the truth of Christ's sacrifice for all humanity.

In the dark forest of Thomas More's highly imaginative mind, satanic beasts lay ready not only to ravish Christian souls but also to devour their bodies. Once an invisible and leaderless church, composed of a rabble of heretics claiming personal and predestined election into God's heavenly company, had unleashed the chains that held the devil at bay, social revolution was inevitable. The Protestant creed led straight to anarchy, "inciting riots, setting laymen against clergy, arming the people against magistrates, inflaming the people against princes, plotting battles, disasters, wars, massacres."[20] To defend England from such a fate, More was willing to burn the books and bodies of all diseased members of the body politic lest, like a plague of caterpillars, the infestation spread. To do so, he said, was "lawful, necessary and well done," because a single, unadulterated Catholic truth at all costs had to be preserved.[21] The Truth could never be multiple. He might countenance in his imaginary society of Utopia a variety of ritualistic approaches to God's Truth, but never a rival Truth—that would have been a contradiction in terms.

Consistency, like so much else, lies in the eye of the beholder, and there are those who present More's life as "a bundle of antitheses." He is pictured as a man who "turned his back on the ennobling enthusiasms of his youth," the "genial philosopher" who turned himself into a "merciless bigot," a living oxymoron—the "progressive reactionary." "The contradictions are stark and numerous,"[22] particularly the mystifying contrasts between *Utopia* and reality as it was actually lived by its author. The Utopians practice religious toleration, but More "fed the stake with heretics"; they permit their priests to marry, but More could not contain his disgust and outrage that Luther "being a friar" had married a nun and lived with her "under the name of wedlock in open incestuous lechery without care or shame."[23] The Utopians sanction divorce not only for adultery but also for incompatibility; but More, a layman, died because he stubbornly refused to voice his approval to the annulment of the marriage of his king to Catherine of Aragon. The Utopians permit, even praise, suicide as an escape from incurable pain and the humiliations of old age; but More agonized lest his martyrdom conceal the unforgivable pride that seeks to end one's life before God had decreed it. The list of contradictions and inconsistencies is endless, and it is probably footless to try to judge a tree by both its fruits and its roots; suffice it to say with Walt Whitman in More's defense:

> Do I contradict myself?
> Very well then I contradict myself,
> (I am large, I contain multitudes.)
> "Song of Myself"

Unlike More's earlier choices, where the initiative, at least in part, had been his own, his final and fateful decision on Sunday, April 12, 1534, to refuse to take the Oath of Succession and instead to take his stand on conscience in open defiance of the expressed will of his prince and parliamentary authority was forced upon him. Until then he had been moving with the current of history and the logic of a career lived in the shadow of Justice John More. Now he stood in opposition to events that started when Henry VIII determined to rid himself of his barren Spanish wife.

Henry's jettisoning of his wife and acquisition of another—"the King's Great Matter," as the events were called in international circles—is an oft-told tale. It has attracted historians and moralists, novelists and dramatists like bears to a particularly savory honey pot, rich in controversy and tragedy and filled with religious, historical, and moral lessons. The sovereign's matrimonial crisis has been depicted as the floodgate through which the Reformation waters poured into England, sweeping away the ancient church, spreading the Protestant faith, and establishing in its wake the new nation-state that claimed to speak for God and demanded the undivided loyalty of all its citizens. It has been presented as a study in hard-nosed Machiavellian dynastic politics on the part of Henry Tudor and his ministers, who were determined to safeguard the succession in the face of potential civil war should the king die leaving behind him a legitimate female heir, his daughter, the princess Mary, and an illegitimate son, Henry Fitzroy, duke of Richmond. And it has been portrayed as a morality play on the political, religious, and human consequences of mixing sex with politics. But for Sir Thomas More and his royal master the six-year saga of the king's effort to free himself of his Spanish wife, and the domestic and international convolutions that accompanied it, was far more than a dynastic crisis or even a cautionary tale in violating divine law; it was a matter of two consciences in open conflict.

For the king the issue from the start was crystal-clear: "All such issue males as I have received of the Queen died immediately after they were born; so that I fear the punishment of God in that behalf."[24] Set aside the presence of Mistress Anne Boleyn, a talented and vivacious lady-in-waiting at court in 1527, who may have triggered far more than the king's scruples. Disregard Catherine of Aragon's age, five and a half years her husband's senior and unable to perform her biological and dynastic wifely duties. Dismiss the concern that no woman had inherited the throne since the disastrous reign of Matilda in the early twelfth century and the presence of an illegitimate son to dispute the succession. Ignore Henry's conviction that at thirty-six he had a right to more children. All these were trifling concerns to a monarch burdened with an excessively tender conscience. What gnawed at Henry's scruples was doubt about the legality of his marriage to Catherine and fear that he had sinned against God's commandments; a long list of dead or stillborn children was sufficient proof of guilt. His soul had been touched: "Think you," he said, "that these doings do not daily and hourly trouble my conscience and vex my spirit?"[25]

The source of the trouble had been written down in Scripture for all to read—"If a man shall take his brother's wife, it is an unclean thing; he hath uncovered his brother's nakedness; they shall be childless (Leviticus 20:21)—and Catherine had been married to his older brother, Arthur. It made no difference that the queen swore that she had left her frail, short-lived, fifteen-year-old husband's marriage bed still a virgin, or that the papacy had granted a dispensation to void the biblical prohibition. "The sincerity of the truth," Henry told Pope Clement VII, "prohibited us to keep silence . . . for it toucheth not worldly things but divine."[26] The papacy had no authority to interfere with God's law, and the dispensation consequently was worthless. Henry was certain he had been living in sin for eighteen years, and any ecclesiastical court, he argued, must by divine and lawful necessity annul such an incestuous relationship. In words that would have done honor to Martin Luther, the king appealed to conscience. "Though the law of every man's conscience be but a private court, yet it is the highest and supreme court for judgment and justice."[27] He was right in his stand against the marriage, he wrote to the emperor Charles V, "not because so many sayeth it but because he, being learned, knoweth the matter to be right."[28] This was no idle bragging; even Cardinal Campeggio, who had been sent by Clement to try the marital case along with Cardinal Wolsey in London, admitted that in matters of church law the king knew "more than a great theologian or jurist." Even more impressive, Henry was a divine-right monarch whose conscience spoke directly to God, and the king confidently concluded that the truth was "so certain, so evident, so manifest, so open and approved" that it "ought to be allowed and received" by all Christians.[29]

Unfortunately, Henry's "truth" was not shared by all, and it quickly became mired down in a major international crisis, because his wife's nephew was Charles V, emperor of the Holy Roman Empire, king of Spain, ruler of the Netherlands, and the man who controlled the destiny of the papal states in Italy. Charles was a staunch supporter of his aunt's marriage rights in England, and the pope had no intention of antagonizing the titan of Europe. Henry and Wolsey tried war and diplomacy, setting France against the empire in order to persuade a vacillating and procrastinating pontiff. For a brief moment Clement wavered, and in May of 1529 he sent Cardinal Campeggio to London to hear the case. But then came news of the Treaty of Cambrai and peace between France and the empire. The pope determined "to live and die an Imperialist," and Campeggio first adjourned the marriage case and then transferred it to Rome, where a decision against Henry was guaranteed.

Denied his annulment through legal and ecclesiastical channels, Henry turned to revolutionary and secular means to achieve his ends, and the signal for the change in policy was the dismissal of Cardinal Wolsey as lord chancellor in October, his replacement by Sir Thomas, a layman, and the summoning of Parliament the following month. More's selection to the office and his acceptance are mystifying, because he was neither politically powerful nor in any way a proponent of the King's Great Matter. Actually, however, both defects proved to be assets. Having no power base, he had throughout his public career antagonized no one. He was also known as a friend of the clergy and an eloquent enemy of heresy and therefore acceptable to the queen's friends, who still hoped to persuade Henry to accept Catherine as his legal wife and Princess Mary as his heir. Finally, he was a friend and companion of the king, an excellent lawyer, and a discreet servant of the crown who had kept his mouth shut and his opinions about the annulment to himself. Certainly his conscience was not so tender in 1529 that he refused an office that symbolized the fulfillment of every ambition a royal official could hope to achieve. Moreover, it was reported—how accurately, it is difficult to say—that Henry had promised his new lord chancellor that he would never "put any man in ruffle or trouble of his conscience."[30]

The issue of the king's marriage, though it had triggered the cardinal's fall from power, was not the main concern of those who rushed to fill the power vacuum that his removal created. Clearly More was a compromise candidate in a much larger political struggle. No one could have predicted that the king's iron determination would lead the kingdom into schism and revolution, and Henry was quite sure that if it came down to a choice between his own conscience and his new lord chancellor's, his would prevail. Unfortunately, Henry and More tragically misinterpreted the future, because in 1529, for very different reasons, both men viewed the marriage crisis as just another squabble between prince and pope in which some face-saving formula would be devised; no other solution was imaginable.

In the political upheaval of the autumn of 1529 real power passed not to the lord chancellor but to an unfriendly balance of interests represented on one side by the dukes of Norfolk and Suffolk and on the other by the relatives and friends of Anne Boleyn. As the factions about the king competed to find some means by which to translate the monarch's will into reality, a third name began to emerge, that of Thomas Cromwell. He was a man who started life as the son of a brewer and blacksmith, tried soldiering in Europe, banking in Italy, marketing in the Netherlands, the practice of law in London, and eventually became Wolsey's trusted servant. He was also a highly accomplished parliamentarian, who despite his loyalty to the cardinal won the king's confidence and became the main architect of the new sovereign and theocratic state that was to emerge during the next four years.

Exactly who monopolized the king's ear during the early 1530s is not clear. Very likely he listened with increasing impatience to a babble of advice, but as the years progressed, although nobody had a clear resolution to his marital problems, almost everyone had something harsh to say against the clergy. The fall of Cardinal Wolsey, the unresolved annulment crisis, and the calling of Parliament in November of 1529 unleashed a torrent of anticlericalism and antipapalism, before which the English church retreated step by step; and when the clergy met in Convocation in January of 1531, Henry extracted from that body the unprecedented title of "singular protector, only and supreme lord, and as far as the law of Christ allows even supreme head" of the English ecclesia. In angry silence, bishops and abbots acquiesced, and Archbishop Warham, in presenting the new title, wisely decided to accept silence as the equivalent of assent.

Sir Thomas was horrified at this capitulation, but worse was to follow. A year later Convocation knuckled under to the will of its new Supreme Head and surrendered its historic independence in the face of a carefully orchestrated parliamentary attack against the church's court system and the privileged legal status of the clergy. Henry added the full weight of his royal authority when, in an explosive statement, he announced that "we thought that the clergy of our realm had been our subjects wholly; but now we have well perceived that they be but half our subjects—yea, and scarce our subjects. For all the prelates at their consecration make an oath to the Pope clear contrary to the oath they make to us, so that they seem his subjects and not ours."[31] Convocation after a brief defense of its rights surrendered completely and promised never again to promulgate a law or even meet without the king's consent and permitted all ecclesiastical laws to be reviewed by a joint panel of clergy and laymen. The spirit of the Constitutions of Clarendon had been invoked, and Henry II could not have asked for more. The independent, divinely ordained medieval church, sanctified and fortified by history and time-honored liberties, had collapsed from within. The spirit of martyrdom was dead, and the practical effect of the capitulation was not slow in appearing. On July 5, for clipping the king's coinage, a priest was hanged without being first defrocked of his sacerdotal status.

On May 16, 1532—the day after the clergy submitted—Henry graciously "allowed" his lord chancellor to resign. In a face-saving gesture, Sir Thomas assured his friends that the reason was his failing health, but most people knew that he had lost the battle to squash the annulment process and to save the church. Worse, he had compromised his conscience, because the previous year—March 30, 1531—he had been required to do his duty as lord chancellor and to present to Parliament the expert academic opinions that had been solicited from various universities throughout Europe in favor of the annulment. He concluded his address saying, "All men shall openly perceive that the King hath not attempted this matter of his will or pleasure, as some strangers report, but only for the discharge of his conscience and security of the succession of his realm."[32] More had put into words the essential nature of the struggle and the ultimate cause of his death, a clash of rival consciences, his own versus the king's; and Chapuys, the imperial ambassador, reported "that if he [More] remains in office he will be obliged to act against his conscience or incur the King's anger—as he already has done through his refusing to take part against the clergy."[33]

During the three years that More was lord chancellor, he became increasingly convinced of the existence of a three-pronged attack that Satan was conducting against the English church: the Lutheran heresy that the church militant and historic played no role in an individual's chance of salvation or in revealing God's truth on earth; the attempt to destroy the independence of a divinely ordained church and subject it to the tyrannical rule of a temporal sovereign; and finally Henry's determination to rid himself of his lawful wife and deny the authority of God's vicar in Rome. All three were interrelated in their evil design to pull down a divine mansion that history had sanctified and that rested upon the fundamental and sacred division inherent in Christianity, the separation of church and state and the superiority of the ecclesiastical office over the royal.

As lord chancellor, More had by necessity to speak on the king's behalf. He certainly told Henry that he thought patristic authority weighed against the annulment and that only a papal court could make a final decision. But at no time, even on the scaffold or when arguing with heretics, did he ever suggest that the papacy could not err or that it held infallible authority. Popes possessed the power of primacy in a divinely inspired hierarchical organization and therefore had to be obeyed, but he never suggested that such a structure necessarily endowed every one of its parts with infallibility. After all, priests could err, and did so with dreary regularity. The infallibility of the church was derived from its unity, not from the pope, who was only the organizational manifestation of that unity.[34]

More must have spoken against the annulment of the king's marriage and the attack on the clergy when they were debated in the royal council, because Emperor Charles wrote him a letter of thanks for his support of his aunt, but when Chapuys attempted to deliver the message in March of 1531, the lord chancellor begged him "to forbear," because he wanted "to abstain from everything which might provoke suspicion."[35] There are two ways of interpreting this statement: More was fearful lest public contact with the emperor weaken his position on the council to help the queen, or Thomas was endeavoring to maintain a discreet neutrality and desperately trying to keep himself the king's good servant by wrapping himself in a cloak of silence. Whichever interpretation, Thomas More was clearly no crusader or soldier of the church, except when he directed his vitriolic pen against heretics. He chose resignation in May of 1532 to opposition. There were those who wished to cast him in the role of Saint Thomas Becket, but More had no intention of emulating his namesake either as a public opponent of the crown and a militant defender of the liberties of the church or as a martyr for an institution that had, like More himself, shown little fortitude in resisting the conscience of the king.

Had conscience never been fully tested and had Thomas More died of the plague or the ill health he used as an excuse for stepping down from office, he would have found a comfortable niche in history as the author of *Utopia*, as an ardent polemicist against heresy, and as a rather ineffectual lord chancellor. There would have been no contemporary biographies, no hagiographers, and no debate over one of the most baffling saints in history. The juggernaut, however, of the King's Great Matter continued on its destined path, gathering momentum as option after option that might have resulted in a face-saving compromise for both prince and pontiff were closed out. Clement, frantic to placate both king and emperor, had offered a number of ingenious compromises—he would bless the union of the princess Mary and the king's bastard, the duke of Richmond; he would legitimize any children of Henry and Anne born out of wedlock; he even toyed with the notion of permitting Henry to enjoy two wives at once; and he tactfully suggested Catherine become the bride of Christ and retire into a nunnery, thereby allowing her spouse to remarry—but none of these doubtful schemes satisfied Henry's conscience or his needs. His future offspring had to be unimpeachably legitimate. This required a legal annulment and a legal wife, and these the pope was unable to supply. Consequently, the forces of ecclesiastical and constitutional revolution, fueled by the king's conscience and dynastic need, swept on, gathering speed in the autumn of 1532 when the timetable of events was dramatically altered. In September Anne Boleyn, freshly created marchioness of Pembroke with a lavish annual income of one thousand pounds, finally bedded down with the king. A month later she was pregnant, and on January 25 Henry and his mistress were secretly married. If the king were to save himself from bigamy and ensure the legitimacy of his heir, he had less than eight months to rid himself of Catherine of Aragon.

Since Henry knew God to be his ally and that the judgment of his own conscience could not err, he was not in the least surprised when providence came to his aid. Old Archbishop Warham died in August, and the king appointed in his place Thomas Cranmer, an unknown university don who believed in the validity of the annulment and sincerely agreed with his sovereign that kings, not popes, spoke for God. Clement, shortsighted as ever, and worried lest Henry cut off papal revenues from England, sanctioned Cranmer's appointment in March of 1533, and almost immediately the new prelate commenced plans to hear the king's matrimonial case in his archiepiscopal court. But before any decision could be final, Catherine had to be prevented from appealing to Rome. This could only be done by cutting the constitutional ties to the papacy, and therefore in April a reluctant and fearful Parliament was cajoled into enacting a statute of innocent title but of revolutionary implications: the Act in Restraint of Appeals. By a flick of the legislative wrist, Parliament declared that all spiritual cases "shall be from henceforth . . . definitely adjudged and determined within the king's jurisdiction and authority" and "not elsewhere." A month later, confident that the judgment would be final, Henry stood before his archbishop and heard pronouncement given by a prelate of his own selection. To nobody's surprise, the king's marriage was declared null and void, and Henry could now publicly present Anne as his legal wife and have her crowned queen. The coronation took place on June 1; three months and six days later, the deity failed to live up to its side of the bargain. Henry had cleansed himself of the sin of wedding his brother's wife, but to his outrage and to the confusion of physicians and astrologers but to the delight of the Catholic world, the new heir to the throne turned out to be a girl, Elizabeth Tudor. On the day the child was born, Clement VII, with ironic ineptitude, published the papal bull officially excommunicating the father.

Henry had risked his soul, endangered his throne, and defied most of Christendom for nothing; he had acquired yet another worthless daughter to further complicate the succession. The king, however, had no intention of turning back; once committed, he had little choice but to acknowledge the baby's right to inherit, commit his kingdom to all future heirs, and try a second time for a boy. And so on March 23, 1534, an obliging Parliament passed the momentous Act of Succession, which smashed forever the historic duality between body and soul, between the secular and the sacred. For the first time a purely temporal organization sat in judgment of divine law, and by act of Parliament it was stated that Catherine's marriage was "deemed and adjudged to be against the laws of Almighty God" and therefore "utterly void and annulled," and that the matrimony "solemnized between your highness and your most dear and entirely beloved queen Anne shall be established and taken for undoubtful, true, sincere and perfect ever here-after." The statute went on to decree that "all the issue had and procreated or hereafter to be had and procreated . . . shall be your lawful children," capable of inheriting "the imperial crown." In order to give teeth to these mandates, it was "adjudged high treason" on pain of death to speak, write, or act against the king's "lawful matrimony" to Queen Anne or the legality of his heirs by her body.[36]

The logical conclusion to the destruction of the old church did not come until November when the constitutional revolution was publicly recognized in the Act of Supremacy, which proclaimed Henry Tudor to be "Supreme Head of the Church of England"; the saving phrase "as far as the law of Christ allows" was quietly deleted as being contradictory to the perfect and holy union of God and Caesar. The new nation-state had already been heralded in the preamble of the Act in Restraint of Appeals, which proclaimed that "this realm of England is an empire . . . governed by one supreme head and king" who possessed "plenary, whole and entire power . . . to render and yield justice and final determination to all manner of folk."[37] In such a polity, diversity of mind or action was unthinkable, and the king's loving and dutiful subjects had to learn a "new found article of faith" that a statute made by the authority of the entire realm could not err. A unique and momentous concept had been introduced into Tudor society: it was no longer sufficient that men and women obey the law; they were now required to approve it and etch it upon their hearts—and accompanying the Act of Succession was an oath demanded of all subjects to swear "without guile, fraud or other undue means, ye shall observe, keep, maintain and defend this Act, and all the whole contents and effects thereof, *and all other Acts and Statutes made since the beginning of this present parliament.*"[38]

For the first time in Western European history, a government was reaching down into the souls of its citizens and requiring a new kind of conformity to the will of society. Here was an oath that required all honest people not simply to accept Anne as their queen but also, in the innermost reaches of their hearts, to approve without reservation the principles on which the annulment rested: the break with Rome, the subjugation of the church, the king's authority in things ecclesiastical, and the newfound definition of the divine-right state. No longer could a subject, as More wanted so desperately to do, remain a dutiful but essentially neutral observer, obedient to but disapproving of the law. Dissent was now tantamount to treason, and loyalty had to be proven by the active defense of the crown's policies. At this point Sir Thomas More drew the line, and on Sunday April 12, 1534, he refused to take what was in effect the Western world's first loyalty oath—not a medieval oath of allegiance and fealty to defend the king's person but a blank check of approval to be written on each loyal subject's heart. A year later More asked Thomas Cromwell whether it was not enough that "I do nobody harm, I say none harm, I think none harm, but wish everybody good." The answer was an unyielding no; in the new leviathan there was no place for the modern concept of a loyal opposition which More was propounding, and he sadly confessed, "If this be not enough to keep a man alive, in good faith, I long not to live."[39] Sir Thomas was to get his wish.

During the months following his resignation, More had retreated into a citadel of silence, seeking sanctuary in a private life devoid of public association. But a dismissed public official who had stood in opposition to the king's conscience could not be left alone. Step by step the government cut away the middle ground; only two options were offered; you are either for us or against us. In June of 1533 Henry made his will patently clear—Sir Thomas was expected to attend the coronation of his queen, a new gown being supplied him for the occasion. But More failed to appear. What kind of friend of the king was an ex-chancellor who refused to give public support to his prince's wife? Eleven months later, when More refused the Oath of Succession, the council began to suspect that silence indeed shielded secret treason. Sir Thomas might reiterate over and over that his "poor body" belonged totally to the king and would never speak or act against its prince, but what about his heart and soul? The government found less than satisfactory More's assurance that "except only my soul," he would willingly give up everything to avoid a single "displeasant look" from His Highness; the exception was deeply disturbing.[40] To whom did Sir Thomas's soul belong: to the king and the kingdom that had protected him and made him what he was; to the emperor and the pope, the enemies of the realm; or to himself, a single Christian who could say with just as much conviction as the king, "Though the law of every man's conscience be but a private court, yet it is the highest and supreme court for judgment and justice"?

What frustrated the government was that More declined to explain exactly how his conscience was injured by the Oath of Succession. The terms of the debate over the substance and boundaries of a man's conscience were established at Sir Thomas's first encounter with the council. His purpose, he said, was not to criticize the Act of Succession or "the oath or any man that swear it, nor to condemn the conscience of any other man." For himself, he would gladly swear to the succession—that properly belonged to Parliament to establish—but he could not take the oath without risking his "soul to perpetual damnation." More was at his forensic best and sought to trap the council by assuring it that if anyone doubted that he refused solely for "the grudge of my conscience," he was ready to satisfy the council members with an oath of his own devising, and if they should distrust his good faith, then why, he asked, did they require him to take the Oath of Succession in the first place? The council accused him of "stubbornness and obstinacy" for refusing to swear the oath or "declare the causes why." More promptly answered that he would give his reasons in writing if he were granted complete immunity from the law. This the council refused, and Sir Thomas countered that if he could not speak "without peril," no one had the right to say it was obstinacy to remain silent.

Archbishop Cranmer tried to resolve the impasse by seizing upon More's refusal to condemn the consciences of those who elected to swear, arguing that this must mean that Sir Thomas regarded such matters as the king's marriage and the constitutional break with Rome to be issues in doubt. This being the case, he should act upon what everyone accepted as a certainty: "that you be bounden to obey your sovereign lord" and leave questions of "doubt of your unsure conscience" to be decided by the higher conscience of the king. More dismissed the archbishop's sophistry out of hand. Every conscience, he said, was personal to its owner. He would not judge the consciences of others, but his own was fully informed. He had not educated it "suddenly nor slightly but by long leisure and diligent search," and he knew what was best for its health and salvation. Nothing could be more dangerous, he argued, than to say that all perplexities were best left to the "the king's commandment."

The abbot of Westminster then asked More how he could set his private conscience against "the great council of the realm." Surely the conscience of a single man must be in error when so many and wiser men thought the contrary. To this Sir Thomas asserted that the abbot had defined the problem incorrectly: More did not stand alone, nor was he bound to change his "conscience and conform it to the council of one realm" when he could appeal to "the general council of Christendom." The debate ended where it had begun, More stating his willingness to swear to the succession if he could write his own oath, refusing either to take the oath as formulated by the government or to explain his reasons, but insisting that he had nothing against those who accepted it. He had, he said, never withdrawn "any man from it, nor never advised any to refuse it," but had left "every man to his own conscience. And me thinketh in good faith, that . . . every man should leave me to mine."[41] It was a vain hope, and within the week More was in the Tower of London, where for fourteen months and two weeks he was given the chance to inspect the full meaning of conscience in the solitude of a prison cell.

If Henry's government thought it was punishing Sir Thomas by locking him away, it was in for a surprise. The hidden More, the one who had been tempted by the monastery and a philosophical life, the More who would willingly renounce wife, family, and political career for a chance to confer with God, was delighted. "I believe," he wrote his daughter Meg, "that they that have put me here think they have done me a high displeasure. But I assure you on my faith . . . if it had not been for my wife and you that be my children . . . I would not have failed, long ere this, to have closed myself in as narrow a room and narrower too." The thirst for a monk's cell was finally satisfied; God, he said, has made "me a pampered pet, and sets me on his lap and dandles me."[42] As his outer life was forcibly peeled away, the inner man became more focused, and he could concentrate on what had become the central tenet of his resistance and self-identity: his conscience.

When More entered the Tower, he was on reasonably good terms with his conscience. He thought he understood his inner self. He had long studied the matter, and so informed his conscience that it "may stand with mine own salvation."[43] More believed in "a general faith grown by the working of God universally through all Christian nations." That faith was the product of history, a pact between the living and the dead embodied in Scripture, in the church fathers, and in the collective memory of the faithful. It was grounded on historic consensus, and no act of Parliament, nor the willful conscience of a single man, even a royal one, could nullify that truth. The succession could be changed ad infinitum, but divine law could not; it was fixed and eternal. More's God was an orderly deity quite incapable of playing dice with the universe; that such a divinity could be so perverse as to deliberately leave its followers in error for fifteen hundred years was unthinkable and illogical. The essence of Sir Thomas's belief and, therefore, of his conscience was closer to instinct than to reason; it was akin to the knowledge of the bee gained from a hundred million years of membership in the colony, the historic memory of the hive. He might not judge other men's consciences because, as he said, conscience was a deeply hidden and private matter; nevertheless, he knew his own instincts to be right. He sensed the only path back to the hive was through the medieval church of his forefathers.

That definition of conscience began to change as More pondered the proximity of death and the terrible possibility of torture and barbaric execution—the traitor was bound ignominiously to a sled and drawn to the place of execution, hanged but cut down still conscious, castrated and disemboweled, and his corpse hacked into four quarters to be displayed throughout the realm.

Step by step in his devotional works written in the Tower—*On the Sadness of Christ* and the magnificent *Dialogue of Comfort Against Tribulation*—and in his letters to Meg, More turned in upon himself, and his world began to shrink. He was no longer bothered by the wrongness of other people's consciences, and the partisan passion of his polemical works receded as he concentrated on his personal encounter with Christ. He appealed to his God to aid him in his struggle to overcome his terrors: the fear of pain and, worse, the dread that John of Salisbury might be correct: "Nothing is worse than the immoderate practice of good works." Martyrdom might lead straight to hell.

Every man, More wrote, "is bounden, if he see peril, to examine his conscience,"[44] and during the long months in the Tower that is exactly what he did: he scrutinized his soul. What he found was appalling. William Roper in his biography of his father-in-law pictured More as a devout Christian surprised and delighted by his courage in refusing the oath and happily facing the consequences—"Son Roper, I thank our Lord, the field is won"[45]—but the More who appears in *A Dialogue of Comfort* is a chastened and frightened sinner, fearful for both his body and his soul. To his horror, he told Meg, "I found myself (I cry God mercy) very sensual and my flesh much more shrinking from pain and from death than methought it the part of a faithful Christian man."[46] He had to face the possibility that he would break and recant under torture, denying his conscience and forsaking his savior and "so be damned forever." He warned that should it ever be reported that he had accepted the Oath of Succession "(which I trust our Lord shall never suffer me), ye may reckon sure that it were expressed and extorted by duress and hard handling."[47] He was, he assured his daughter, "of such nature so shrinking from pain that I am almost afraid of a fillip [light blow]."[48]

Throughout his life, More, like so many others of his century, was touched by necrophilia: he was, if not obsessed by, certainly preoccupied with death, the pain, the ignominy, the uncertainty. There were but two truths in this world never to be forgotten—that "the son of God died for thee, and that thou shalt also thyself die shortly,"[49] and in *A Dialogue of Comfort* he speculated that violent, even painful, death by the axe might be preferable to a slow, lingering demise by natural causes. As death approached, More pictured "all our body in pain, all our mind in trouble, our soul in sorrow, our heart all in dread, while our life walketh away."[50] Then with clinical detail he described the act of dying: "thy throat rattling, thy flesh trembling, thy mouth gaping, thy nose sharpening, thy legs cooling . . . thy life vanishing and thy death drawing on."[51]

Had Sir Thomas known the style of his death, he might have welcomed the axe as the most painless path to heaven, except for a second dread which far outweighed the first—the fear that his martyrdom might be judged a suicide. How far could a man legitimately go in protecting conscience if in doing so he knowingly courted death? The issue in its sixteenth-century guise was the same as that voiced by Clement of Alexandria in the early third century when he wrote that whosoever "does not avoid persecution, but out of daring presents himself for capture . . . becomes an accomplice in the crime of the persecutors."[52] Too much enthusiasm for death, More knew, led straight to perdition, because only the insufferably proud man denied God's right to appoint the time of death. The gift of life and the right to end it belonged to God alone. More recognized the snake of pride hidden in his confident assertions to Meg "I have myself a respect to mine own soul" and "I can see none that lawfully may command and compel any man to change his own opinion," or "translate his own conscience from one side to the other." It was absolutely essential to his soul's salvation to keep in mind Christ's counsel "that ere I should begin to build this castle for the safeguard of mine own soul, I should sit and reckon what the charge would be."[53] The guardian of a man's soul might very well turn out to be ego masquerading as humility; in that case the charge would be damnation.

How, then, was it possible for More to passionately desire martyrdom as the highest Christian calling but at the same time escape that enthusiasm which concealed such deadly sin? His solution to this conundrum was the source of the government's frustration. More exercised the same controlled neutrality in his spiritual life as he had in his political. As interrogation after interrogation proceeded, the king's council became more and more outraged at the ex-chancellor's disloyal silence and claimed his "demeanor" to be the "occasion of much grudge and harm in the realm." His duty as a subject was patent; the king ordered him "to make a plain and terminate answer" whether he thought "the statute lawful or not" and whether he confessed "it lawful that His Highness should be Supreme Head of the Church of England," or else, as the government phrased it, to utter his "malignity" openly and plainly. With irritating regularity More replied that he was being confronted with an impossible dilemma—the law was "a two-edged sword." He was being asked to say that he approved the act "against my conscience to the loss of my soul," or to deny the statute "to the destruction of my body."[54] Neither option was possible, and therefore he chose silence. When the council claimed that this silence was the equivalent of rejection, he politely reminded them that at law silence, as when Convocation had accepted the king's title of Supreme Head, implied acceptance.

On a number of occasions, Sir Thomas told the council that he had no great desire to live—his "poor body is at the king's pleasure, would God my death might do him good"—and that his health was so bad (most historians suspect he had heart disease) that he did not expect to worry the council for many months longer. In mounting annoyance, the government asked him the central question that had been plaguing More for over a year in prison: why, if he expected soon to die, even wanted to die, not play the hero to his conscience and speak out against the statute? His pusillanimous, hole-in-the-wall silence was clear evidence that he was afraid to die for his conscience. More's answer embodied the heart of the problem, his ultimate estimation of himself, and his determination to avoid the delusive, paradoxical temptation to seek heaven through deliberate, self-centered martyrdom. "I have not," he said, "been a man of such holy living as I might be bold to offer myself to death, lest God for my presumption might suffer me to fall, and therefore I put not myself forward, but draw back. Howbeit if God draws me to it Himself, then trust I in His great mercy that He shall not fail to give me grace and strength."[55] These words were spoken scarcely a month before his execution. The formula, however, had been worked out during More's long meditation on Christ's agony, during which he had vividly fantasized "the treacherous betrayer . . . binding ropes . . . blows, thorns, nails, the cross, and horrible tortures stretched out over many hours."[56] The sense of support he derived from these meditations is best expressed in a passage from his final work in the Tower, *On the Sadness of Christ*, where he imagines Christ saying to those in fear of death by terrible and agonizing means: "Let the brave man have his high-spirited martyrs, let him rejoice in imitating a thousand of them. But you, my timorous and feeble little sheep, be content to have me alone as your shepherd, follow me as leadership; if you do not trust yourself, place your trust in me. See, I am walking ahead of you along this fearful road."[57]

Sir Thomas More's calling for martyrdom lacked Socrates' cold, intellectual detachment, the Maccabean brothers' sterile, two-dimensional superhuman heroism, Perpetua's overwhelming, self-consuming sense of divine grace, and Becket's militant defense of a church built of bricks and mortar, decretals and lawyers' briefs. His appeal lay in his quivering, qualifying humanity, beset by fear, doubt, and confusion. He had no desire either in life or in death to be a hero, let alone be the leader of the opposition. He became a hero almost despite himself, and that is what makes him among martyrs so attractive: he is absolutely believable but profoundly mystifying at the same time.

There was something oddly controlled about Sir Thomas More. He was an extraordinarily self-contained man who was able to manipulate his passions and his words for any occasion—a man for all seasons. He was invariably on stage, an actor possessed of a marvelous sense of timing and theatrics, always playing to a variety of audiences. He could converse in the reasoned language of the humanist and lawyer as well as the strident idiom of the polemicist, but the one role he would not accept was the Becket model, the soldier-martyr. He was not a cleric or a church official, and he insisted that he was not a warrior. He had elected the secular life over the ecclesiastical, and it was not the function of a layman to assume the responsibilities of a priest. From first to last, he viewed himself as a loyal subject of his prince.

In refusing, however, to defend the church as his namesake had done, to speak out against the king's supremacy and the violent rendering of Christ's seamless cloak that embodied and protected the unity of all Christendom, he was forced step by step to change the terms of the controversy and the nature of his opposition to the encroachment of the crown upon the church. It now became the trespass by the state upon something uniquely precious to himself, his conscience. The moment More left office, his public life turned in upon his private person. He believed without reservation in the Roman Catholic Church of his forefathers, but with each passing year he deinstitutionalized that organization, declining to defend its political, economic, and jurisdictional liberties or to justify the supremacy of the papacy. He sought instead to protect his soul in a church of his own imagination, the historic church which from the start was always more a vision than a reality and which on inspection tended to dissolve. Historic consensus, about which More loved to speak, turned out to be a singularly unreliable sword with which to defend the castle of one's soul. Sir Thomas rested his case on the single indisputable fact that after fifteen hundred rather disreputable years Mother Church, shabby and battered as she was, was still around to offer solace to tender consciences; he asked no greater proof that God was still alive and caring. Unfortunately such an image of the church was difficult to defend—longevity in itself did little to justify institutional authority—and so he retreated into the final citadel of self, his own private conscience, which he could ferociously protect. No matter how deeply he tried to wrap himself and his conscience in the consensus of all Christendom and shielded both with the voice of history, the "I," the self, was clearly evident.

With each step—his resignation and retreat to his estate at Chelsea; his refusal, like Socrates, to escape through exile; his imprisonment; and finally the removal of all of his books and writing materials, leaving only four stone walls to contemplate—the private part of More grew and flourished. There was, as with so many other saints, a steady renunciation of contact with the outer world. Family, friends, office, and even the church were interfering distractions, and in one of the most famous encounters between a husband and wife, reported by his son-in-law, More made his priorities cruelly clear to Dame Alice when she came to plead with him in the Tower. Bluntly she saluted her husband and launched into a scolding attack. "I marvel that you, that have always hitherto [been] taken for so wise a man, will now so play the fool as to lie here in this close and filthy prison and be content to be shut up among mice and rats, when you might be abroad at your liberty, and with the favor and good will both of the King and his Council." All Sir Thomas had to do was what every other learned man had already done, swear the oath. What about, she asked, his "right fair house, your library, your books, your gallery, your garden," and what about "me your wife, your children and household"? What in God's name did he "mean still thus foolishly to tarry here?"

Uncharacteristically More answered with a cliché—"Is not this house as nigh heaven as mine own?"—which Dame Alice dismissed out of hand. Sir Thomas then gave the matter further thought and finally said, "I see no great cause why I should much rejoice in my gay house, or anything belonging thereunto, when if I should but seven years lie buried under ground, and then arise and come thither again, I should not fail to find some therein that would bid me get out of the door, and tell me it were none of mine. What cause have I then to like such a house as would so soon forget its master?"[58] It was an excruciatingly cruel retort but an honest one; More in the Tower was shutting himself off, which was an inescapable process when conscience, soul, salvation, and the nearness of death were so closely associated in his mind. When confronted with eternity, More's self, his identity, could not be bothered with worldly trifles.

Dame Alice, his son-in-law Roper, his favorite fool, his entire household, even Margaret, the daughter closest to him, all took the oath. Sir Thomas spoke no word against them. He refused to judge anyone except himself. He was discovering that all-consuming egotism which had been a disturbing part of martyrdom from the very beginning and was praised by Tertullian when he wrote: "My only business is with myself. . . . None is born for another, being destined to die for himself."[59] In the Tower More was without care except for his soul. He did not, he said, "intend to pin my soul at another man's back, not even the best man that I know this day living," and he offered Margaret rather cold comfort when he told her "as concerning mine own self . . . mine own conscience in this matter (I damn none other man's) is such as may well stand with mine own salvation." He was as sure of that truth as he was that "God is in heaven."[60]

The ultimate irony, of course, is that the man who called Martin Luther a monster set loose by Satan found his final solace and comprehension of God's ultimate purpose in a personal faith bereft of images, Scripture, history, or consensus; his church was just as invisible as Luther's and his justification based on his faith alone. More never experienced Perpetua's blinding light of God's cosmic design; instead he had to make do with his own conscience. Call it what you may—unreasoning conviction, a point of irrefutable reference, Socrates' *daimonion,* or just plain pride—Sir Thomas More knew with Saint Paul that "every man stands or falls before his own Lord," alone and by himself.[61]

More did not have to wait long to put conscience to the final test. The end came with unexpected swiftness once Henry's government found a way to break through the shield of silence that had encased and protected him during his retirement and months in the Tower. For over a year the government had been using grimly modern psychological techniques to grind down Sir Thomas's resistance, alternating good news with bad, hope with despair, relative physical comfort with total isolation. The final step came on June 12, 1535, when Sir Richard Riche arrived to confiscate his books and writing materials. He stayed long enough to trap More into what proved to be a fatal conversation.

By the terms of the Act of Succession More had, by refusing the oath, committed the crime of misprision of treason—technically, the conscious concealment of treason. On these grounds he had been imprisoned without trial, his punishment a year later being regularized by a parliamentary act of attainder. Misprision, however, was not treason, because More had neither spoken nor acted treasonously. Matters changed in November of 1534 with the passage of the famous Treason Statute, making it high treason to "maliciously wish, will or desire, by word or writing, or by craft imagine, invent, practice or attempt" the bodily harm of the sovereign or his queen, deprive them of their "dignity, title or name of their royal estates," or claim that the king was a "heretic, schismatic, tyrant, infidel or usurper of the crown."[62] In this sweeping reconstruction and redefinition of treason the crucial and mitigating word was "maliciously." The government had to show the evil thought that accompanied any criticism of the monarch, and although the council was convinced that Sir Thomas's silence did indeed harbor malice, it could not prove it at law until More spoke words to Sir Richard Riche that could be construed as treason.

Endless and partisan controversy rages over what transpired between the two men; whether Riche, a government flunky, lied and perjured himself at More's trial in order to ensure a conviction, or whether Sir Thomas did in fact make a fatal slip. To make matters more difficult, the existing evidence is contradictory, and one crucial document is badly mutilated.[63] While waiting for More's books to be carted away, Riche, being "charitably moved," urged Sir Thomas to cease his obstinacy and take the oath. More cautiously replied, "Your conscience shall save you and my conscience shall save me." Then Sir Richard, assuring the prisoner that their talk was private, and phrasing his question in the hypothetical language of legal debate, asked: "Admit there were, sir, an Act of Parliament that all the realm should take me for King. Would not you, Master More, take me for King?" Sir Thomas had no hesitation in saying yes, he would do so, but he countered with an even more improbable theory: "Suppose the Parliament should make a law that God should not be God, would you then, Mr. Riche, say God were not God?" Sir Richard correctly complained that his opponent had changed the terms of the debate. Of course Parliament could not legislate God out of existence, but what about a halfway question—could not Parliament create the king Supreme Head of the Church, and if so, "why should you not, Master More, affirm and accept him to be so in just the way you would be obligated to take me and affirm me as king?" Then came More's fateful rejoinder as reported by Riche: "The cases are not alike." Parliament could legally make or break a king, and subjects were obligated to obey, but in the case of the supremacy, "the subject cannot be obligated to give his consent to such a thing in Parliament. And though the king is so accepted in England, most foreign lands do not accept the same." If More actually spoke these words, then here indeed was evidence of a malicious heart.

Many historians happily insist that Sir Richard played Judas to More's Christ, because at his trial Sir Thomas is reported to have turned on Riche point-blank when he swore he spoke nothing but the truth, and said, "If this oath of yours . . . be true, then I pray I may never see God in the face, which I would not say were it otherwise, to win the whole world." Unfortunately, More's powerful outcry comes from son-in-law Roper, who was not at the trial and who undermined any sense of verisimilitude by claiming that Sir Thomas, having branded Riche an inveterate liar, tried to argue that if he had indeed spoken any such words they could not be construed as being malicious because they were "spoken but in familiar secret talk, nothing affirming, and only imagining cases."[64] Consequently, other scholars prefer to weasel; More did speak words that, when taken selectively out of context or slightly rephrased, could be said to have constituted treason.[65] If Riche did in fact commit perjury, his conscience would not have bothered him for long; after all, everyone knew that More was hiding behind a legal technicality and that his silence was aggravated secrecy that concealed treasonous dissent.

Sir Richard's conversation took place on June 12; on July 1 More was brought by boat from the Tower of London to Westminster Hall for trial. He was indicted on four counts: he had refused to acknowledge the royal supremacy; he had corresponded while in the Tower with Bishop John Fisher, a convicted traitor and the only prelate to deny the supremacy and the principles on which it rested; he had in refusing the Oath of Succession referred to the authorizing act as a "two-edged sword" which would kill his soul if he accepted and his body if he refused; and he had spoken malicious treason in the presence of Sir Richard Riche. An ill, unkempt, gray-bearded More, who was so emaciated and weak he could not stand during the proceedings and who like all other accused traitors had neither legal counsel nor a chance to review the evidence against him, turned his trial into a public stage where, like Socrates, he was the chief actor, speaking in part with an eye to the law but mostly to history. The first three counts collapsed with disconcerting speed. More's silence about the supremacy could not be twisted into treason; no one could show evidence that his letters to Fisher contained treason; and his reference to the Act of Succession as a double-edged blade had only been meant hypothetically. The government's case therefore stood or fell on Sir Richard Riche's testimony, and perjured or not, it was enough to find him guilty. The jury required fifteen minutes to make its decision.

The verdict having been given, Lord Chancellor Thomas Audley, More's successor on the wool sack, rose to give sentence but was stopped by Sir Thomas's quiet words: "My lord, when I was engaged in the law, the custom in such a case was to ask the prisoner before judgment, why judgment should not be given against him."[66] More had a multitude of reasons for stopping the judgment, and in voicing them he combined rhetoric directed at posterity with a final legal device to save his neck. He broke silence in an effort to undercut the legal basis of the court's decision, and for the first time spoke against the supremacy as "grounded upon an Act of Parliament directly repugnant to the laws of God in His holy Church." The supremacy, he said, was in violation of "that sacred oath" which the king had taken at his coronation to protect the liberties of the church, and it denied the historic words preserved in Magna Charta that "the English church should be free and have all its rights untouched and its liberties unimpaired." England, he argued, "being but one member and a small part of the Church," could not "make a particular law different from the general law of Christ's holy Catholic Church" any more than the city of London could pass "a law against an Act of Parliament to bind the whole realm." He was not, he reiterated, bound "to conform my conscience to the council of one realm against the General Council of Christendom."[67]

It was a powerful and moving speech, and son-in-law Roper reported that it shook the lord chancellor's confidence so totally that he turned to the lord chief justice for advice and received what must be the most convoluted quadruple negative ever devised in a court of law: "I must needs confess, that if the Act of Parliament is not unlawful, then by my conscience the indictment is not insufficient."[68] Audley interpreted these words as sustaining the legality of the decision and immediately gave judgment.

As was customary, More was granted the final word: did he have anything further to say in his own defense? Sir Thomas said no but proceeded to deliver a farewell message that not only bristled with double meaning but also embodied the many sides of his multiple personality: the biblical scholar, the ironic humorist, and the passionate avenger who, like Becket, enjoyed (at least in the quiet of his mind's eye) to think of his enemies in another place. He spoke of Saint Paul, who before his conversion to Christianity "was present and consented" to the death of the martyr Stephen, and he reminded his judges that the two men were "now both holy saints in heaven, and shall continue there friends forever." "So I verily trust," he slyly concluded, "and shall therefore right heartily pray, that though your lordships have now on earth been judges to my condemnation, we may yet hereafter in heaven all merrily meet together to our everlasting salvation."[69] With exquisite irony that only More could devise or phrase, he sent his judges straight to hell unless, of course, they, like Paul, joined the man condemned to die for maintaining God's truth.

We do not know when More learned that his greatest fear—the terrible physical agony of death by hanging, castration, and disemboweling—would not be inflicted on his poor body. He would die by the axe, and as he made ready for his final exit, he must have felt close to Socrates; Sir Thomas also could now cheat sickness, old age, and the degradation of a slow and debilitating death or, worse, senility. As a Renaissance man and a future martyr, it was important to die well, in absolute control of himself and of the stage upon which his last act would take place. The hair shirt could now be made public, and it was collected by Margaret Roper's maid Dorothy Colly along with his last letter to his daughter, "written with a coal." Biographers customarily quote Sir Thomas's famous farewell to his "dear Meg"—"Pray for me and I shall for you and all your friends that we may merrily meet in heaven"—as if it were the conclusion to his letter, his final thought. Actually, More's last written words were far more practical and prosaic and a little reminiscent of Socrates' final request: Sir Thomas warned his son John that in the unlikelihood of his being allowed to inherit land from a condemned traitor, he should not break "my will concerning his sister Daunce."[70]

As with Socrates and Becket, the staging of death was all-important, and on the last day he dressed himself in "his best apparel" until the lieutenant of the Tower warned him that the axeman, "a worthless fellow," by tradition claimed the clothing of the corpse. At first More was not persuaded; he wanted to imitate Saint Cyprian, who had given his executioner thirty pieces of gold. But in the end he compromised and donned the plain clothing of his servant John Wood and sent a gold angel to the headsman.[71]

The scene of the execution is well known in film and stage, almost as treasured in history as Christ's, which must have been uppermost in More's mind as he walked to the scaffold. On the way he was offered a cup of wine but turned it away, saying, "Christ in his passion was given not wine but vinegar to drink."[72] A woman called out that when he was chancellor he had done her wrong, and he answered: "Thou hast no injury, so content thee and trouble me not."[73] A Winchester man cried out that he was "ill troubled" and asked for help. Sir Thomas replied, "Go thy way in peace, and pray for me, and I will not fail to pray for thee."[74] In mounting the scaffold he cracked the most famous sick joke in history: "I pray you, I pray you, Mr. Lieutenant, see me safe up, and for my coming down let me shift for myself."[75] To the executioner, he urged him to "pluck up thy spirits," and "be not afraid to do thine office. My neck is very short. Take heed therefore thou strike not awry for saving thine honor."[76] He had been ordered to be brief, and so he spoke little as he stood before the block: he asked only that his audience "pray for him in this world," and with supreme confidence he assured them "he would pray for them elsewhere."[77] Then he coined the theater's best exit line: "He died," he said, "the king's good servant but God's first."[78] And so, insisting that he tie the blindfold around his own head, he knelt, stretched himself out on the block, prayed, and, like Socrates, waited for eternity to close in upon him.

More had been expertly dispatched, his noisy and dangerous silence terminated; and although the humanist world of the Continent was horrified, at home his death was greeted with cold indifference—a traitor of "malicious mind" had "condignly suffered execution" according to his "demerits."[79] For Henry VIII, an embarrassing problem had been resolved. For history, however, two questions essential to martyrdom remain: What exactly did Thomas More die for? And did his death do any good? Death by martyrdom, Sir Thomas knew, must never be a means to a personal end. It was vitally important to yearn for heaven and to safeguard conscience, but not to want to die for the sake of salvation or reputation on earth. Death had to be a decision that was essential to the cause; it had to embody, symbolize, dramatize, and further that cause. Socrates' death was necessary to his goal. So was the agony of the Maccabees, the cause being God's purpose on earth. In a sense Jesus had elected to die in order to establish his credentials and the truth of his ministry. The same was true of Perpetua; the blood of the martyrs was the seed of the faith on which the church's victory rested. With Becket his cause was the church militant, and his death, at least for a time, destroyed the Constitutions of Clarendon. His biographers were clear: he died not to save his soul or assure himself salvation; these were not his ends but simply the known rewards for winning the battle.

What, then, of Sir Thomas More? Here nothing is clear and all is astigmatic and out of focus. There is little evidence that Sir Thomas viewed his death as a glorious example to be emulated, a public act of defiance. Instead, he wrapped himself in the darkness of privacy. He may have died for a complex set of ideas—of the church historic, the sacerdotal priesthood, the apostolic succession, the papal primacy—but he showed no great desire to share those concepts with anyone, not even with Meg. Unlike Becket, he was never the outspoken champion of his church.

The Becket controversy can be told as a straightforward narrative involving an institutional clash in which the protagonists had deeply vested emotional and material interests, and their motives, as far as they are documented, were clear and convincing. Violent passions accorded with violent

actions. The situation is totally different with More and Henry. Many scholars have sought to discover the driving force behind the tragedy in Henry's
fury directed at a friend who failed him, the infantile emotions of a vengeful monarch who could not purge himself of doubt except by physically destroying those who rejected his friendship and denied his authority.[80] But
the eighth Henry's fury was not matched by the proud and unyielding, but
understandable, militancy of a Becket; it was instead smothered by the
conceit of a man who hid himself in a tangled thicket of inconsistency, ambiguity, contradiction, compromise, and mixed emotions, and spoke endlessly about conscience.

Sir Thomas can be cast in many roles: as a martyr "for the faith of the
Catholic Church"; as a hero of civil and religious liberty; as a man who died
for the "irreducible freedom of the individual conscience in the face of an
authoritarian state"; as a witness that a man, according to More, may indeed "lose his head and have no harm"; and as historic evidence that if you
scratch a medieval man deeply enough, you will find an "adamantine sense
of his own self."[81] These, of course, are twentieth-century judgments made
in retrospect; and in retrospect the Roman Catholic Church first declared
More to be blessed in 1886 and conferred full martyr's honor in 1935, the occasion of the four hundredth anniversary of his death. The delay remains
controversial but understandable; More was never a comfortable saint or,
like Becket, an establishment hero. Other saints have had to await their
crowns even longer than More—Joan of Arc 489 years and Bishop John
Fisher a fortnight longer than Sir Thomas. But as a hero of the Counter Reformation or a soldier of papal authority and later papal infallibility, Sir
Thomas does not bear close scrutiny. Politically he died, of course, a traitor
to his kingdom; spiritually he died for a very personal definition of his
faith; psychologically he died for conscience, by which he ultimately meant
his sense of his own identity and his soul's salvation. The twentieth century
tends to divide conscience and soul. For More, however, they were one and
the same; for him the question was not so much believing in his conscience
as it was defining immortality and life after death. On that subject Erasmus
reported very early in Thomas's life that "when he talks with friends about
life after death, you recognize that he is speaking from conviction and not
without good hope."[82] In his last week on earth, as a condemned traitor,
More wrote a prayer in charcoal.

> Give me thy grace, good Lord
> To set the world at nought
> To set my mind fast upon thee.
>
> . . . .

> To be content to be solitary
> Not to long for worldly company;
>
> .   .   .   .
>
> To walk the narrow way that leadeth to life,
> To bear the cross with Christ.[83]

More was always content to be solitary—it made very little difference to him whether his death did anybody else any good, so long as it satisfied his own God.

Hugh Latimer and Nicholas Ridley burning at the stake: A battle of wills between Catholic resolve to light the faggots and Protestant determination to endure the flames.

CHAPTER 8

THE MARIAN MARTYRS:
GROUP IDENTITY THROUGH
SELF-DESTRUCTION

Persecution does not prove either side to be
right: it proves that both sides are in desperate
earnest.
—GILBERT CHESTERTON

SIR THOMAS MORE had written that he was content to be solitary, "not to long for worldly company" but to walk alone "the narrow way that leadeth to life." He asked that no one accompany him
on his final encounter with his deity, and he declined to speak for or defend
either the church militant or the church historic. Two decades later, when
fortune's wheel had come full circle—when the persecuted had become
the persecutor, and Henry VIII's daughter earned the bitter epithet of
"Bloody Mary" by her efforts to set time back to a golden age when the
kingdom had stood firm in its Catholic faith and obedient to its papal
father—a new set of martyrs sought and attained group and self-credibility
in martyrdom. Instead of dying as isolated criminals, each struggling to
come to terms with himself and his God, they enacted an extraordinary
paradox: they found self-identity through collective self-destruction. This
chapter, then, is a study in two aspects of martyrdom that so far have only
been hinted at: the interaction between persecutor and persecuted—it
takes two sides to create a martyr—and the operation of group dynamics,
of how ten martyrs consciously prepared themselves for death and developed the means to transform their executions from a demonstration of

defeat, futility, and demoralization into a spectacle of individual and community triumph and rehabilitation.[1]

Between July 19, 1553, the day that Princess Mary was officially acclaimed lawful queen of England, and March 21, 1556, when Archbishop Thomas Cranmer died at the stake—a period of thirty-two months—a nation of God's elect was first conceived in the minds of ten imprisoned Protestant leaders and then tested in the fires of persecution. It was forged in a battle of wills between Catholic resolve to light the faggots and Protestant determination to endure the flames, thereby proving the personal worth of the members and the truth of their faith. For all its imaginary frontiers and visionary boundaries, this chosen community of the elect proved to be aggressively resilient. From its conception the bonding was more than simply a state of mind sharpened by theological debate and a tenaciously held body of beliefs; it was a state of being, a religious commune held together by ties of spiritual kinship, pride of election, and a sense of drama in which every member was on public display, being tested before the eyes of God and man. To use the phraseology of Benedict Anderson, "imagined reality" and loyalty to an "imagined community" proved stronger than the physical and emotional reality of prison, the dread of death by slow fire, or the instinct to survive.[2]

Numbers are deceptive, meaning different things to different generations. At least 288 men and women, possibly more, were burned to death during the last four years of Mary Tudor's reign. To contemporaries that number may not have seemed either large or unreasonable, but it was hard to ignore, because on average six public executions took place every month for forty-five months. Moreover, two-thirds of these burnings were located either in the immediate environs of London or within fifty miles of the capital. To later Protestant generations, brought up on John Foxe's spectacular and vivid "Book of Martyrs," the figures seemed appalling, absolute and incontrovertible evidence that the horror of the Inquisition was indeed the true and frightening face of Catholicism. To modern historians intent on placing the statistics in their broader European perspective, the count seems modest in the extreme when compared with the six thousand heretics executed by Emperor Charles V in the Lowlands or the holocaust of similar proportions conducted by Francis I of France. Finally, to observers of a more analytical and sociological bent, the full significance of the numbers resides not in their total but in their components. Most of the victims were young people, under thirty; fifty-one, or 17.8 percent, were women; twenty-one, or 7.3 percent, were clergymen; and only nine of the lay martyrs could call themselves ladies or gentlemen, the overwhelming majority being cloth workers, tradesmen, and agricultural laborers.[3]

The clerical minority was shockingly small. Six years of government-enforced Protestantism under Henry VIII's son, that godly imp Edward VI, had produced only twenty-one clergymen courageous enough to face the flames. On the surface the real heroes of the English Reformation seemed to be the humble followers of Christ, not the clean-fingered clergy. Tiny as the ecclesiastical representation was, however, it was crucial to the decision on the part of the lay majority to die for the faith. Even Christ's flock needed shepherds to establish the terms of membership, strengthen its nerve, and guide it through the straight and narrow gate to heaven. That leadership was supplied by ten of the martyred ministers: one archbishop,[4] four other prelates,[5] two canons of Saint Paul's Cathedral, two rectors, and an archdeacon, all but one of whom had been closely associated with one another before the ordeal of Mary's reign began.[6] These ten men were intensely, almost obsessively, aware of the magnitude of the struggle they faced. They sensed that upon them alone had fallen the double challenge of choosing life or death for themselves and setting an example for others to follow, and of delivering Protestantism from the moral and spiritual morass into which it had sunk during the six fat and sinful years of Edward's reign.

On the evening of July 6, 1553, their world had disintegrated around them. The unimaginable had occurred; their deity had allowed their sixteen-year-old king, the acclaimed Protestant David who would cleanse his land of papist corruption, to die miserably, "his sputum livid, black and fetid" and his body smelling "beyond measure." When God's purpose was clear and Edward's death a certainty, the dying boy and his Protestant advisers made a desperate attempt to defeat the Antichrist and subvert the last will and testament of his father, who had decreed that should his son die the realm would pass to his elder daughter, the Catholic princess Mary. By a document known as Edward's Device, drawn up by the young sovereign and his chief minister, John Dudley, duke of Northumberland, and possibly improved upon by the duke, the crown was conveyed to Henry's grandniece, the pious and Protestant Lady Jane Grey, cousin to Edward and coincidentally Northumberland's daughter-in-law. This experiment in monarch-making was short-lived. Depending on the reckoning, Queen Jane ruled for nine, at the most thirteen, days—and ended in disaster for its chief architect and those who associated with him in treason, especially the two leading ecclesiastics of Edward's reign: Thomas Cranmer, archbishop of Canterbury, and Nicholas Ridley, bishop of London.

Both men were highly vulnerable to the charge of treason. Cranmer had reluctantly signed both the device and the council's proclamation declaring Jane to be queen, and Ridley not only subscribed to the device but also further compounded his treason by publicly preaching that the princesses

Mary and Elizabeth were bastards, incapable of inheriting their father's throne. Both ecclesiastics soon paid the price of unsuccessful sedition. Ridley was promptly clapped in the Tower of London on July 26, and Cranmer, largely because he had important friends at court, remained at liberty until the fourteenth of September, when he joined his fellow prelate in the Tower.

The remaining eight future clerical martyrs were gathered up, not as overt traitors or even as legal heretics—until Parliament passed the necessary legislation, Protestantism was still the official faith of the kingdom—but as disturbers of the peace who were judged by the government to be men of "suspicious demeanor" and potential traitors. Rowland Taylor, the flamboyant and provocative rector of Hadleigh in Suffolk, was briefly arrested a week after the reign began, but did not suffer permanent imprisonment until late March of 1554, when he was placed in the King's Bench prison in Southwark. The two canons of Saint Paul's Cathedral, John Bradford and John Rogers, were brought before the council on August 16. Bradford was incarcerated first in the Tower, then in King's Bench and the Counter and briefly in Newgate prison. Rogers suffered only house arrest until January of the following year, when he was jailed in Newgate. Troublesome John Hooper, bishop of Gloucester, and the elderly patriarch Hugh Latimer, onetime bishop of Worcester, were swept up in early September, Hooper being sent to the Fleet, Latimer joining Ridley, Cranmer, and Bradford in the Tower. Lawrence Saunders, rector of All Hollows in Bread Street, London, was apprehended in October and remained in the Marshalsea for the next fifteen months. Robert Ferrar, bishop of Saint David's—a hot gospeler like Hooper—had already run afoul of the government under Edward and by March of 1554 had sufficiently outraged Mary's government that he was placed in King's Bench. The same was true of John Philpot, archdeacon of Winchester; he spoke loudly and impolitically in defense of the Protestant faith during the October meetings of Convocation and was in King's Bench at least as early as March of 1554.

The ten ecclesiastics whom Mary's government incarcerated at various times in six different London jails were at the nadir of their lives, publicly disgraced and forsaken. Their church had collapsed both institutionally and spiritually. The overwhelming majority of onetime Protestants either fell into confused conformity—after all, God had brought about the new Catholic succession—or remained silent. The backbone of the Protestant faith appeared broken, its moral and political leadership spineless. Of the 472 Protestants who with their wives and children fled the country, 119 were clergymen or theological students, 49 were merchants, lawyers, physicians, or yeomen, and only 52 could be described as artisans, laborers, or servants.[7]

Even the episcopal leaders failed to stand firm. Eighteen—all except for the five already imprisoned—cheerfully returned to the Catholicism of their youths or resigned their sees to live in quiet retirement or sought safety across the Channel.[8] Protestantism was devoid of the spirit of martyrdom, a point John Bradford was keenly aware of when he wrote Richard Hopkins, sheriff of Coventry and a prisoner in the Fleet, saying that "not many noble, not many rich, not many wise in the world hath the Lord chosen."[9]

The duke of Northumberland himself betrayed the cause. The man whom John Hooper proudly described as the "faithful and intrepid soldier of Christ" and "a most holy and fearless instrument of the word of God" proved to be in reality the spokesman of Satan. At his execution he sealed his pact with the papal Antichrist by publicly recanting his heresy. Speaking "unfeignedly from the bottom" of his heart, he announced that "through false and seditious preachers" he had "erred from the Catholic faith and true doctrine of Christ."[10] Those words were a body blow to the Protestant church, and it was quickly noted that the recanting duke had "edified the people more than if all the Catholics in the land had preached for ten years."[11] It seemed indisputable to all that "the doctrine taught in King Edward's day was heresy." No scriptural proof was needed to prove the assertion: the reign had ended in Northumberland's attempted "treason and rebellion." That was sufficient evidence that the doctrine was "naught."[12]

Not only was the Protestant doctrine naught in the eyes of most of their countrymen, but the very rock on which the ten champions had built their lives, their faith, and their ecclesiastical home—the royal supremacy—had also crumbled beneath them, or, more accurately, been turned against them. For twenty years they had preached that the deity spoke through the crown, not the papacy: "The word of God is to obey the king and not the bishop of Rome." Now God's voice in the person of Catholic Mary was ordering all English men and women in the name of social unity and divine ordinance to once again accept the authority of Rome. The Protestants were hoisted on their own petard.

Nineteen years before, in April of 1534, Thomas Cranmer had brought the full logic of the royal supremacy to bear on Sir Thomas More, who had wrapped himself in the unyielding armor of personal conscience and stubbornly refused to sign the Oath of Succession. "You know for a certainty," the archbishop had told More, "that you be bounden to obey your sovereign lord your king," and therefore had no choice but to put aside "the doubt of your unsure conscience in refusing the oath, and take the sure way in obeying your prince."[13] Unfortunately, "the sure way" applied to Cranmer just as logically as to More, and the archbishop struggled for thirty-two months, canting and recanting in the battle to decide between his "unsure conscience" and his bounden duty to obey his sovereign. Of the ten prisoners, only Cranmer agonized for months, but the other nine in their prison cells to one degree or another had to debate with themselves the answer to a conundrum: if the new queen "had been an Adversary of His truth and His holy word," God "would never had so aided her."[14] In the midst of their shattered lives, they, as did Protestants of all walks of life, had to find an answer to that riddle.

The smell of treason that clung to the new faith was as strong as the stench of open latrines that befouled their prison cells, but the odor the prisoners found hardest to ignore rose from the knowledge that they and all their clerical colleagues under King Edward had unwittingly supped with Satan and "played the wanton gospelers, the proud Protestants, hypocritical and false Christians."[15] They had been given six years in which to win the kingdom over to Protestantism, but had proved unequal to the task. Instead of laboring in the Lord's vineyard, the Protestant leaders had indulged in unseemly squabbles over theological trifles and, for political reasons, had compromised the purity of their religious principles by cooperating with the secular majority on the young king's council that sought to satisfy its own economic greed and the government's fiscal crisis by plundering episcopal revenues and properties. As Ridley later sadly admitted, "Many of us were too cold" and too involved "with the wicked world; our magistrates did abuse, to their own worldly gain, both God's gospel and the ministers of the same."[16]

Their guilt in having failed the Lord was manifest, and retribution had come from on high. Each had drunk of "the cup of the Lord's wrath," and John Hooper spoke for them all when he wrote to Henry Bullinger in Germany in early September that "our king has been removed from us by reason of our sins."[17] John Bradford may have had his own personal sense of guilt, but he knew that the "heavy plague of God . . . in taking away our good king and true religion" and in imprisoning "God's true prophets and ministers" was not his punishment alone. It belonged to all who had failed to warn their flock that "the way to heaven is not the wide way of the world which windeth to the devil."[18]

Weighed down by the terrible knowledge of their past failures, seeking an answer to why their God, even by way of punishment for their sins, had replaced Protestant Edward with Catholic Mary and exposed England once again to the papal Antichrist, and endeavoring to voice their opposition to a divinely ordained queen without falling into the sin of sedition, the ten dispersed and incarcerated prisoners faced almost alone a formidable threefold task. They had to turn their private despair into the voice of public optimism, re-establish their credibility in the eyes of the entire Protestant community, and confront Catholicism with a challenge that, in their own opinion at least, was free of treason. In the midst of their tribulations, they eventually discovered that their Lord had not entirely forsaken them. He permitted them sixteen months in which to construct the sense of unity and fellowship that would purge their minds of doubt and fear and prepare them for the flames, and to generate a collective voice that could reach out not only to their fellow prisoners but also to all beleaguered and hesitant Protestants. John Bradford described the miracle best: time was given them to rebuild so that God's "people may both better know themselves, and be known."[19]

The sixteen months that were granted them were the offspring of legalism and greed. Purgation by fire could not begin until Mary's Parliament had dismantled the Protestant state church of Edward's reign, petitioned for reunification with Rome, and reinstated the old Catholic heresy laws of the previous century. These last two steps the cautious legislators refused to take until the holy father in Rome made clear that he would not require, as the price of absolution for schism, the return of the monastic properties confiscated by Henry VIII and in part sold to the landed interests heavily represented in Parliament. A return to the days of the queen's father—Catholicism without the pope—was completed before the end of the year, but a return to Rome took another twelve months of hard negotiation and careful wording before a determined and suspicious House of Commons was satisfied. Only then, in late December of 1554, was the necessary heresy legislation passed in time for the new year and the first execution on February 4, 1555.

The incarcerated Protestants made excellent use of the interlude, communicating by epistles, messenger, and personal contact. A hundred and eighty-six letters have come down to us, and there is impressive evidence that many more were written.[20] Industrious Bradford was responsible for eighty-two, and Saunders, Philpot, Hooper, and Ridley were a poor collective second with eighty-six. The letters ranged from private notes to wives and family to public exhortations to the faithful and challenges to the queen and her council; but the most revealing epistles were the twenty-two exchanges among the prisoners themselves, Ridley writing Bradford ten times and Bradford responding twice.[21] Letters, unfortunately, could be dangerous if they fell into the wrong hands and were often difficult to write. Bradford warned his mother, "If it were known that I have pen and ink, and did write, then should I . . . be cast into some dungeon in fetters of iron."[22] Ridley counseled Augustine Bernhere not to carry correspondence signed by the prisoners lest retribution fall on him and "on all the rest," and he told Hooper not to be hasty to set forth anything, "especially under the title of your own name."[23] Philpot had the most difficult time of all; he had to carry on his correspondence much of the time in a coal cellar, pinioned in "a painful pair of stocks." Written words may have been relatively infrequent, but when they did arrive, they were eagerly read by all. Saunders shared Bradford's letters with other prisoners in the Marshalsea, and Philpot and Bradford did the same for those who sought their spiritual support in the King's Bench.

"Letters," Cranmer explained, were "wont to occasion so much danger and mischief" that he preferred the security of a reliable and knowledgeable messenger, and William Punt and Augustine Bernhere along with his wife ran a highly efficient, if dangerous, messenger service between the various prisons.[24] Punt was Saunders's link with Bradford, and the Bernheres were regular visitors to King's Bench, carrying back and forth information, encouragement, and various theological tracts composed by Ridley and Bradford. Even when Bradford was moved, a few days before his death, to the Newgate prison, Bernhere maintained contact, and Bradford wrote him that he had "good hope that if you come at night about nine of the clock, I shall speak with you, but come as secretly as you can."[25]

The most satisfying means of communication was, of course, direct contact, and full advantage was taken of the government's extraordinary laxity in handling its heretic criminals. They often shared the same cell, could visit one another in prison, and on occasion actually met colleagues in other jails—Saunders in the Marshalsea wrote Bradford in King's Bench that he would meet him "on the backside about an eleven of the clock," when the guards were "at dinner."[26] The extent to which Mary's council knew what was going on is something of a mystery. Most of the prominent martyrs had either friends in high places or secret sympathizers in the prisons themselves—and most of them were neither totally isolated nor closely confined, an oversight that the queen's government soon learned to regret.

The construction of a new edifice now that their previous home, built upon the sands of Edward's reign, lay in shambles, was a team enterprise; but two of the ten martyrs stand out as the central architects. Cranmer, because of his rank, should have been the leader, but the archbishop was kept under strict surveillance and was theologically and psychologically paralyzed by his struggle between duty to God and to queen. Hugh Latimer possessed a highly developed social conscience and a rich and provocative pen, but he disliked philosophical debate, was in poor health, and was content to let others offer the determination needed to organize God's people into a unified and resilient brotherhood of the elect. The two prelates Ferrar and Hooper were outspoken religious radicals, but the bishop of Saint

David's in the face of the fire almost failed the test, and Hooper of Gloucester spent much of his energy in angry outbursts and outraged complaints about the harsh treatment he endured in jail. It fell to John Bradford and Nicholas Ridley to supply the cerebral and emotional drive that could take all that remained of the Protestant church—the fire of individual and inner faith—and galvanize it into a coherent body aware of its own existence and proud of its destiny. Bradford stated the achievement in its most succinct and colorful form: in writing to two of the chosen band he said, "I trust . . . you are of these few, my dearly beloved; I trust you be of the 'little flock, which shall inherit the kingdom of heaven.' "[27]

The two men could not have been less alike, and each offered different talents. Tall, introverted, auburn-haired Bradford, who slept only four hours a night and could not rid himself of the agonizing conviction that the guilt of all mankind was somehow focused within himself—he was a highly proficient spiritual hypochondriac who bared his soul to all who would listen—poured forth a torrent of words that reached out and touched everyone around him. As God's self-avowed herald angel he gave to the community its sense of theatrics and evangelical commitment. More than any of the others he wove the emotional ties that held the brotherhood together.

In contrast, precise, organized, and witty Ridley was an intellectual and academician whose clarity and logic of mind, as well as his position as bishop of London, allowed him to act both as the theological moderator of the group and as its emotional ballast. Ridley more than any of the others understood that the theological core of the community had to be reestablished and redefined, and that group solidarity rested on clear-cut and basic principles to which all could subscribe. It was Ridley who delineated the boundaries, the territorial lines, that differentiated Protestant from Catholic, defined what it meant to be a Protestant, and established exactly what the community, collectively and individually, was willing to die for.

Although Bradford's and Ridley's aims and methods overlapped, Ridley's work had to come first, and in April of 1554 the bishop wrote to the brethren in captivity about the need for "agreeing together in one faith" so that they could all "take comfort one of another, and be the more confirmed and strengthened thereby." It was not, he warned, "any ceremony for the which we contend" but "the very substance of our whole religion."[28] Later he spelled out to Bradford, whom he suspected of making "an elephant of a fly," exactly what that substance was. Two things, he said, were the "mighty pillars" upon which Lucifer built his "satanical synagogue": the "wicked and abominable usurpation" of the leadership of God's church by the see of Rome, and the "false doctrine and idolatrous use of the Lord's supper."

With scant regard for a mixed metaphor, he assured Bradford that these "two poisonful rotten posts" supported the diabolical but, alas, growing structure in which the "wily serpent" concealed his "falsehood, craft and treachery." Against this fortress of evil, he said, "I have bended mine artillery," spending "a good part of my powder" in scribbling and distributing treatises and letters to prove Satan wrong. The devil, not God, spoke through the papacy—"The see is the seat of Satan." The Lord's Supper was not, as Lucifer would have the world believe, a carnal and bloody reenactment of Christ's death performed by priests claiming divine powers, but a ceremonial commemoration of his sacrifice in which the power of the miraculous lay solely in the hearts of the communicants.[29] All else was inconsequential, and he diplomatically wrote prickly Hooper that they did indeed agree on the "substantial points of our religion," suggesting that under the present circumstances they should not indulge, as "in time past," in debate over those "smaller matters and circumstances of religion, when your wisdom and my simplicity (I confess) have in some points varied."[30]

Bradford was equally concerned with unity, but he understood it in terms, not of creed, but of fellowship, and he wrote his "own good brother Philpot" that "if once we come into an unity and love, then shall we not suspect one another, neither take things into the worse part."[31] The sense of identity that Bradford preached entailed far more than theology. Definitional beliefs served as useful party badges, but his conception of unity centered on a community held together by two common denominators: present suffering and future death. Both, of course, were the traditional pathways to heaven, but hope of paradise in and by itself was not the cement that gave the group its sense of collegiality and union; collective adversity and the constant support system that the group developed created the bonds that gave meaning to their suffering and held their lives together.

The martyrs constantly reminded one another that their present agony was a dress rehearsal for the final event, a test of their faith and proof in the eyes of each of them that they were indeed members of the elect. Bradford and the others reiterated endlessly in their letters to one another and to those outside the prison walls a single refrain—pride of place in God's nursery. As the Lord's children, they told each other, they stood among the select, for the winds of adversity had divided the wheat from the chaff; they were "faithful fellow-soldiers," "most constant companions in bonds," "sweet saints of the Lord," God's "elect darlings before the world was made," and "citizens of heaven." "Though the weather be foul and storms grow apace," Bradford wrote one fellow sufferer, "yet go not ye alone, but other your brothers and sisters pad the same path,"[32] and he assured another that their mutual faith in Christ united them, "I to you and you to me, we to all the children of God, and all the children of God to us. . . ."[33]

In almost every letter Bradford penned from King's Bench, he sought to encourage, reinforce, and generate a sense of community and election among his "stakefellows." Death by fire, he told his friends, was not only "the port of paradise" but also the surest way "to judge of our election and salvation."[34] For those imprisoned in Kent he set himself up as a model: "Now am I going before you. . . . I go before; but you shall come after, sooner or later. . . . Ah! dear hearts, be not faint-hearted for these evil days, which are come to try us and purify us, that we may the more 'be partners of God's holiness'; as to ourselves, so to the world we shall be better known." His final words to his fellow martyr John Leaf, as they were bound to the stake, reiterated that message of sublime confidence and elitism: "Straight is the way, and narrow is the gate, that leadeth to eternal salvation, and few there be that find it."[35]

The stake then became the signature that set God's elect apart from Satan's corrupt and crooked world, and Bradford did not hesitate to use the prospect of his own death to beat down the fear and hesitancy that welled up even among the chosen few. "My blood," he told them, will "cry for vengeance against you, my dearly beloved in the Lord, if ye repent not, amend not and turn not unto the Lord."[36] Their tiny band, Ridley said, were the "people of God," and they had an obligation to quit themselves "like men, and be strong" both in their suffering behind bars and in their final test of strength at the stake. Only the strong and the elect could answer the bishop's call to martyrdom: "If thou, O man of God, dost purpose to abide in this realm, prepare and arm thyself to die."[37] Bradford turned the call into a challenge: "What can God the Father do more unto us than to call us into camp with his Son? What may Christ our Saviour do more for us, than to make us his warriors? What can the Holy Ghost do to us above this, to mark us with the cognizance of 'the Lord of Hosts'?" That cognizance "standeth not in forked caps, tippets, shaven crowns, beads or such other [Catholic] baggage and anti-Christian pelf, but in suffering for the Lord's sake."[38]

Suffering became the hallmark of the citizens of heaven, but the job of reconstruction did not end simply with establishing group identity by preparing the members, as Ridley wrote Hooper, for "the day of our dissolution."[39] Even imaginary nations require a past and a future. Unfortunately, the immediate past was tarnished and corrupt; at all cost the resurrected church had to disassociate itself from those days when the purity of God's word was corrupted and used to justify the plundering of ec-

clesiastical wealth by voracious courtiers. With self-conscious pride the
new ecclesia found its heroes and historical sanction in the early martyrs to
Christ. Exactly when the Lord would call the new martyrs "by prison, fire,
[or] halter" could not be known, but they should never be dismayed, because, said Bradford, "no small number of God's children are gone that
way, and we are a good company here together, which are ready to follow
the same way through God's grace, if God so will."[40]

The same problem beclouded the immediate future: all predictions had
to avoid mention of the queen's death. Any hope of a rejuvenated church,
all anticipation of the fall of the papal Antichrist and the defeat of Satan,
had to be free of the taint of treason. Over and over Bradford and the
others repeated the warning "Never for anything resist, or rise against the
magistrates." God, reiterated Hooper, "biddeth us be patient, and in no
case violently nor seditiously to resist our persecutors"; and seven of the
ten Protestant leaders circulated among themselves and signed a declaration to the queen that ended by promising "to behave themselves as obedient subjects to the queen's highness and 'the superior powers which are
ordained of God' under her." They offered their heads upon the block
rather "than in any point to rebel, or once to mutter against 'the Lord's
anointed'; we mean our sovereign lady queen Mary."[41]

The public image that the community of the elect desired above all else
to present was one of dignity, patience, and loyalty. Their community was
populated not with ranters and ravers, members of some lunatic and seditious religious fringe, but with loyal and obedient subjects of the crown. It
preached no Second Coming of Christ that would pull down the papal
Babylon and introduce a "gathered church" of God's saints. Unlike their
early Christian models, the Marian martyrs disassociated themselves from
any hint of eschatology whereby they became the instruments of the
Lord's wrath and an apocalyptical punishment for the sins of humanity.
Their nation was neither the church militant nor the church triumphant.
Unlike the old corrupt edifice of Edward's reign, the new mansion was an
invisible structure sans brick and mortar, sans supreme head, sans hierarchy. It was a gathering of souls, not of bodies—what Ridley described as
"an unspotted church of Christ." "The congregation of the faithful" was
bound to no "one place" but was "spread throughout all the world . . .
where Christ's sacraments are duly ministered, his gospel truly preached."
Only there could be found Christ's church shining "as a city upon a hill."
This was the picture of the ultimate future, to be achieved without violence or sedition.[42]

Step by step Sir Thomas More had retreated into himself; so now, in a
sense, did the Marian martyrs, but with a double difference. They did so

collectively, and they refused to cut their ties to the world, because they firmly believed that their "dissolution" would make a difference, not simply for themselves but for their imagined and invisible church here on earth. Lawrence Saunders was absolutely certain on that point and assured Cranmer, Latimer, and Ridley, those three heroes "under Christ's cross," that their suffering was "a spectacle unto the world, both to the angels and unto men . . . insomuch that many of the brethren in the Lord, being encouraged through our bonds, dare more boldly speak the word without fear."[43]

The new church of the elect may have been invisible and imaginary, but it was not without teeth. It could and did fight back, not, as Ridley phrased it, "with carnal, but with spiritual weapons."[44] When Bradford in the late fall of 1554 penned his challenge to Philip and Mary and their council, demanding that they repent and return to the true church, he brandished for all to view the spiritual weapon in its sharpest form. If, he said, he and his brothers could not prove in public debate the truth of the doctrine "set forth in the most innocent King Edward's day" and disprove the creed now practiced in the queen's church, then "we offer our bodies, either to be immediately burned, or else to suffer any other painful and shameful death, whatsoever it shall please the king and queen's majesties to appoint."[45] Bradford knew full well that should such an encounter ever take place, Mary's government would never accord his side the victory. The challenge was, in effect, not an offer to debate but an invitation to burn him and his colleagues at the stake. That was the untried weapon by which the new nation of the elect sought to defend itself and overcome the enemy.

In forging an instrument which could only be tested in the fire, the letters sent to the prisoners and distributed among them proved crucial. Rowland Taylor sent the three prelates imprisoned in Oxford words of high praise for their "constant suffering." "I cannot utter with pen," he wrote, "how I rejoice in my heart for you three such captains in the foreward under Christ's cross."[46] In a deeply worried letter, Bradford informed Saunders that he had heard that the government planned to tempt Saunders to "subscribe" to the Catholic creed by offering him the saving caveat "so far as the thing subscribed to repugneth not against God's word." He begged his dear brother Saunders, with whom he wished "to live and die," to resist any such deadly hypocrisy, because he was sure that the Lord would "make perfect the good he hath begun in us."[47]

What the martyrs craved most was news, the assurance that the ramparts still held and that reports of their defeat, spread by the enemy, lied. Ridley informed Bradford that he had heard all sorts of stories about his being pardoned, having managed to escape, or actually having been pro-

moted by Mary's government.[48] In a collective letter from the Oxford martyrs, he told Bradford and his "prison-fellows" that they had heard how
valiantly Rowland Taylor had withstood the interrogation of his judges:
"how joyful it was to us" to hear such news "is hard for me to express."[49]
And John Hooper, writing only two days before the first fire was lit, angrily
told "his brethren and sisters" and fellow sufferers that he was horrified to
hear that reports were being circulated in Europe among the exiles "that I,
John Hooper, a condemned man for the cause of Christ, now after sentence of death (being a Newgate prisoner, looking daily for execution)
should recant and abjure that heretofore I have preached." He begged them
to refute such false rumors and promised that he was "as gladly to suffer
death for the truth I have preached as a mortal man may be. . . . Pray for
me, gentle brethren, and have no mistrust."[50]

Words are brave, but they are also cheap: until February of 1555 no one
knew whether the spiritual weapon would prevail. There had been suffering aplenty—cold and deprivation, long confinement in coal cellars, and
the painful "pinching seat" of the stocks—but as the ease and frequency
with which the prisoners communicated with one another within prisons
and between prisons attested, their lives had not been intolerable. Now,
however, on February 4, 1555, the ultimate trial came: John Rogers was chosen as the first to try the mettle of the newly founded citadel of the Lord.

The burning of John Rogers served as a test for both sides: Protestant determination to endure the flames and prove the truth of its convictions,
and Catholic certainty that heresy was a spineless jackal, a vicious scav-
enger that had feasted under Edward on the prostrate body of the old
church but now had crept back into the darkness of Satan's forest. Sir
Robert Southwell contemptuously told Rogers during his first interrogation for heresy that he would never have the courage to endure the flames,
and Dr. Weston scornfully informed Hugh Latimer that his stubbornness
came "of a vain glory, which is to no purpose, for it will do you no good
when a faggot is in your beard."[51]

In retrospect, Catholic confidence raises a query; why bother with an insignificant band of religious lunatics; why not simply ignore them and let
them rot in jail? The total number imprisoned during 1554 and early 1555
probably did not exceed eighty.[52] So why should the government concern
itself with the spiritual fate of such a tiny cluster of religious outcasts when
God was so openly lavishing his blessings on the queen and her restored religion? Mary stood at the apogee of her reign. She was certain she was
pregnant by her husband, Prince Philip, the son of Emperor Charles V who
had stood by her and her mother during the long and bitter years of heresy
and schism. Her kingdom had rallied to her defense the year before during

the dangerous but abortive rebellion of Thomas Wyatt and his Kentish rebels, and her church had been absolved of its sins and welcomed back into the Catholic fold by its papal shepherd.

The order to send Rogers to the stake was the product of two considerations: expectation of a spectacular propaganda victory over a demoralized and disgraced Protestant church and the argument that heresy struck at the spiritual, political, and moral sinews of the kingdom and deserved the severest and most public punishment possible, a foretaste and confirmation of the agony awaiting the heretic in hell. At the same time the existence on the statute books after December 1554 of the legislative means—the re-enactment of the old heresy laws decreeing that religious criminals be burnt so "that such punishment may strike fear to the minds of others"—made it possible to achieve both these desired ends.[53] The boastful challenge by the Protestant leaders to either burn them or acknowledge the verity of their beliefs had gone on long enough; the time had come to call their bluff. Mary's council may have been divided over the timing of the policy and the vigor with which it should be enforced, but few members would have questioned the opinion of the queen's closest religious adviser that "there cannot be a greater work of cruelty against the commonwealth, than to nourish or favor" heretics. No kind of treason could be compared with theirs, for they undermined the religious foundation of the kingdom.[54]

Mary's lord chancellor, Stephen Gardiner, who tended to view the Protestant menace more as a political and a party threat than as a spiritual movement and who had learned under Henry VIII the efficacy of laws written in blood, is usually held responsible for the decision to light the faggots. Bishop Gilbert Burnet, for one, did not hesitate to write in his seventeenth-century history of the English Reformation that Gardiner "was confident the preachers then in prison were men of such tempers, that, if they saw they were to be burnt, they would comply; or if they stood out, and were burnt, that would so terrify the rest, that the whole nation would soon change."[55] If this indeed was Gardiner's premise, he did not stand alone; he had wide support, and four and a half months after the first execution and twenty-three burnings later, Dr. John Storye, professor of civil law, was still of the mind "that by discreet severity we have good hope of universal unity in religion."[56] A few years later the martyrologist John Foxe was quite certain that the initial victims, drawn from the ranks of the Protestant leadership, had been selected and executed on the elitist principle "that all the rest would soon be quailed by their example."[57]

Whatever the outcome—"turn or burn," as Nicholas Ridley jocularly described the choice[58]—Gardiner and his cohorts anticipated an immediate propaganda triumph. "Turning" was much to be preferred to "burning," and the government expended endless hours and extraordinary patience examining, cajoling, beseeching, threatening the Protestant leaders to recant. John Philpot endured thirteen examinations between October 2 and December 16, 1555, a process that must have extended the government's resources to the limit, involving as it did eleven different bishops, twenty other high ecclesiastics, seven noblemen plus other court personages, and endless chaplains, scribes, and clerks—a gigantic effort to recapture the soul of a single heretic.[59] Burning, however—the cutting off and consuming of "the rotten and hurtful members" of the body politic—was expected to have equally desirable effects. The stake was the ultimate psychological as well as physical weapon.

Why John Rogers was elected for the first demonstration of Protestant weakness baffled and alarmed both Ridley and Bradford. When Rogers was taken from Newgate prison and carted off for incineration at Smithfield, Bradford reported to Cranmer, Latimer, and Ridley that he had expected that the three prelates, as the symbolic chiefs of the faith, would be given the place of honor.[60] Ridley responded in kind, confessing that "when the state of religion was once altered and persecution began to wax whole, no man doubted but Cranmer, Latimer and Ridley should have been the first to have been called to the stake," and with considerable pride of office he told Bradford that he suspected Gardiner of the "subtle purpose" of assaulting first those "whom the world esteemed weakest" in the expectation of an easier victory. If that was the government's objective, it was badly mistaken.[61] To use Bradford's own disturbing metaphor, brother Rogers broke "the ice valiantly."[62] Ridley could not conceal his relief that the first warrior of Christ had met the challenge: "My heart," he wrote Bradford, "so rejoiced of it, that since that time, I say, I never felt any lumpish heaviness in my heart, as I grant I have felt sometimes before."[63] Whether that lumpishness stemmed from fear of weakness within the ranks of the saints or from faintness of his own heart is difficult to say, but clearly on February 4 the first test of the spiritual weapon had succeeded. Far from striking terror into their souls, Rogers's death renewed and hardened every soldier's determination to die. The flames could be endured. In reporting to Ridley on Rogers's performance at the stake, Bradford said: "This day [February 8], I think, or tomorrow at the uttermost, hearty Hooper, sincere Saunders, and trusty Taylor end their course and receive their crowns. The next am I, which hourly look for the porter to open me the gates after them, to enter into the desired rest." He urged his spiritual captain to "make you ready, for we are but your gentlemen-ushers . . . trusting shortly to see you, where we shall never be separated."[64]

Bradford's prediction, except for himself, was dead on the mark: Saunders died on the eighth, Hooper and Taylor on the ninth. Bishop Ferrar's martyrdom was delayed until March 30, largely because he was sent back to his old diocese to be tried and executed. Bradford himself, for reasons still unclear, did not suffer until July 1.[65] Latimer and Ridley went to the stake on October 16; and Philpot endured his ordeal on December 18. Of the original ten only Cranmer remained. In his case the spiritual weapon prevailed only because Mary's government overplayed its hand and mixed politics with vengeance. In the face of psychological and intellectual annihilation, reinforced by fear of the flames, Cranmer collapsed, renounced his faith, and signed a series of recantations, which, according to ecclesiastical procedure, should have saved him from the fire, but Mary insisted that the archbishop's reconversion was a sham and that he must die a heretic's death. When on March 21, 1556, he learned he must go to the stake, that there was no choice, Cranmer publicly returned to the Protestant fold even as the fire engulfed him, thereby depriving the government of its most spectacular propaganda victory and preserving the community of the elect intact.[66] In the end even its weakest link held firm. The technical captain of God's nation may not have died exactly in the style Bradford and Ridley would have wished, but at least the community's purpose was achieved— every last one of its citizens met the test. As a result the initiative suddenly and invisibly passed into the hands of the Protestants, even before the Catholics were aware of it.

The spiritual weapon would have remained an empty cannon had it involved merely the death of ten heretics. As Perpetua—who had worried so much about the state of her coiffure—and the other early Christian martyrs had sought to exercise absolute control over the process of their martyrdoms, so the Protestant chiefs tried to turn their deaths into a theatrical and symbolic spectacle, playing to an audience that reached far beyond the hundreds who had gathered to watch them die.

The sixteenth century was deeply concerned with the art of dying well; the Marian martyrs took this concern a step further, copying the early Christian martyrs and laying down the style for dying in the flames. Denied the traditional scaffold confession-address offered secular criminals, they were reduced to prayers and gestures to communicate the intensity and absolute conviction of the faith that dwelt within them and which could only be verified and proclaimed by death.[67]

The stake was the last and most public chance to re-establish the credibility of their leadership and their religion. The martyrs had, of course, no way of knowing that years later the vivid picture of their deaths would be immortalized in print by John Foxe in a work that, next to the Bible, would become the single most important influence in shaping Elizabethan religious sentiment, but they lived in a world steeped in pageantry and ritual that gave to every action significance far beyond its earthly meaning. As Sir Francis Bacon said, "Nothing can be found in the material globe which has not its correspondence in the crystalline."[68] In the interconnected universe of the sixteenth century, every event was a potential parable possessed of hidden significance; it was the job of the martyrs to extract and publicize that meaning. Sensory impacts—encounters of sight, sound, and smell—served as the vehicles by which political and religious concepts were communicated and public opinion shaped in a semiliterate society; and Ridley, Bradford, and the rest were fully aware of the importance of the sight and smell of their burning in communicating their message to the kingdom at large and in achieving their purpose both in heaven and on earth.

Rogers set the standard for dying well, but he did not supply the symbolic style for those who followed. His death was filled with pathos. He was met on his way to Smithfield by his wife and eleven children, who watched as first he refused the queen's pardon and then, as Foxe so vividly phrased it, "washed his hands in the flame, as though it had been in cold water." The crowd, reported the French ambassador, made "him many exclamations to strengthen his courage" and his sons and daughters comforted "him in such a manner that it seemed as if he had been led to a wedding." The Spanish ambassador added the macabre touch that the audience "gathered the ashes and bones and wrapped them up in paper to preserve them."[69]

Rogers, by the standards of any age, died splendidly, but it was Lawrence Saunders and Rowland Taylor who developed the symbolic theatrics that became customary form for most future martyrdoms. Both men independently embraced and kissed the stake before allowing themselves to be bound to it. Lest the language of symbolism be obscure, Saunders made its meaning dramatically clear: he cried out as he clutched the post, "Welcome the cross of Christ! Welcome everlasting life."[70] No one could mistake that he was a member of God's elect, one of the legion of Christ's holy martyrs, his ashes destined to be the seed of his church. By the time Bradford died, kissing the faggots that would fuel the flames, as well as embracing the stake, had become standard procedure.[71] Central to the performance, both as evidence that they rejoiced in the prospect of "everlasting life" and as a grisly reminder of the villainy of the Antichrist, was the need to demonstrate that the martyrs themselves had chosen to die: there was no compulsion; the decision was theirs. With great pride John Foxe boasted that "no murmuring, no repining was ever heard amongst them"; they "joked and danced their way to the stake."[72] To have complained would have cast doubt on the single truth that counted: by dying in the fire they were proving themselves to be of the nation of the elect.

The words these martyrs spoke in the midst of the flames—always so brilliantly to the point—and their final conversations with their persecutors, in which they invariably come out best, may well have been contrived or doctored by Foxe. But the staging of their martyrdoms has the ring of verisimilitude to it. Without exception the ten spoke to the kingdom symbolically, and they were acutely aware of the dramatic effect of their smallest actions. Even the clothes they wore—Bradford put on a newly cut shirt especially made for his burning—and the manner in which they disrobed and made ready for the flames were carefully orchestrated symbolic acts that would have been difficult to falsify.[73] If we are ready to accept Sir Thomas More's final joke about asking to be helped up the steps to the scaffold and his willingness to make the return journey on his own, we should accept John Philpot's quip to the two officers who offered, because the ground around the execution place was so foul, to carry him up to the stake. "What! Will ye make me a pope? I am content to go to my journey's end on foot."[74]

Of all the executions, stylistically and symbolically, the deaths of Latimer and Ridley in Oxford on October 16, 1555, had the greatest dramatic impact and, one suspects, were the most carefully staged by the protagonists.[75] Nicholas Ridley appeared as befit an ecclesiastical prince and bishop of London, dressed in a black fur gown faced with foin and a sable scarf around his neck. On his head he wore a velvet nightcap surmounted by a corner-cap, the traditional headgear of a divine and academic, and on his feet a pair of slippers to take him to the stake. In contrast Hugh Latimer wore a shabby wool "frock" and a "buttoned cap" and a kerchief on his head; a long "shroud" hung to the ground, covering his hose. The symbolism was perfectly clear: the costume of the one stood for "the honor they sometimes had," that of the other for "the calamity whereunto they were fallen."

As they entered the execution ground, the two men rushed to embrace and kiss one another, Ridley urging the older churchman to "be of good heart, brother, for God will either assuage the fury of the flame, or else strengthen us to abide it." Then Ridley moved to the stake, knelt in prayer, and kissed it, Latimer kneeling directly behind him. The government momentarily regained the initiative when Dr. Richard Smith gave a brief sermon insisting that "the goodness of the cause, not the order of death maketh the holiness of the person," and urging them to save their lives and souls and recant. Ridley then turned to Lord Williams of Thame, the ranking nobleman and presiding government official, to ask permission to

speak in rebuttal "but two or three words." Before Lord Williams could answer, the vice-chancellor of Oxford clapped his hands over Ridley's mouth
and informed him he could only speak if he recanted, offering him in return life, liberty, and reward. The bishop refused, and in a loud voice announced, "Well then, I commit our cause to Almighty God, which shall
indifferently judge all," to which Latimer added, "There is nothing hid but
it shall be opened." Technically their words were free of treason, but their
message was patently clear.

Both men were ordered to undress. Ridley gave his gown and scarf to his
brother-in-law George Shipside, presenting other pieces of apparel and an
extraordinary number of small possessions which he carried on his person
to those around him. To Sir Henry Lea he offered a new silver groat; to another he presented his "dial"; and to "divers of my Lord Williams's gentlemen some napkins, some nutmegs and rases [measures] of ginger." Even
his truss, or inner jacket, was given away, leaving the bishop in his shirt. As
for Latimer, he gave nothing because he had nothing of worth to give, and
stripped himself down to his shroud. So garbed, the two walked to the
stake, Ridley calling out, "Oh, heavenly Father, I give unto thee most
hearty thanks, for that thou hast called me to be a professor of thee, even
unto death. . . . I beseech thee, Lord God, take mercy upon this realm of
England, and deliver the same from all her enemies."

As the iron chain that manacled them to the stake was wrapped around
their waists, Ridley shook it, ordering the blacksmith, "Good fellow, knock
it in hard, for the flesh will have his course." When his brother-in-law offered him the customary gunpowder, placed in a bag and tied to the victim's neck, to speed his death and curtail his suffering, Ridley accepted but
insisted he share it with Latimer, and he begged Lord Williams to look after
his sister and "divers poor men" to whom as bishop of London he had
promised grants of land. He feared, he explained, that his successor would
not honor his gifts and would deprive them of their livings. "I beseech, my
lord, be a mean for them: you shall do a good deed, and God will reward
you." The climax finally arrived, and as the faggots were "kindled with
fire," Latimer turned to his fellow martyr and put into words the full theatrical and historical impact of the spiritual weapon that Ridley, Bradford,
and the others had forged; "Be of good comfort, Master Ridley, and play
the man. We shall this day light such a candle, by God's grace, in England,
as I trust shall never be put out." Whether such words and images flowed
from Latimer's fertile imagination or John Foxe's magic pen makes little
difference. That is how the drama of their deaths has come down in history,
and it highlights the impending defeat that Mary's church and government

sustained at the hands of a group of spiritual nation-builders who con-structed an invisible but invincible commonwealth of the elect of God.

The first deaths infused the remaining champions of God's kingdom with extraordinary confidence and pride of association. They sensed that not only was the spiritual weapon working, but it was also giving them the upper hand against their enemies and the means to consolidate and expand their own position. Bradford in an open letter to the University and town of Cambridge pulled out all the stops. "Let the imprisonment of thy dear sons, Cranmer, Ridley, and Latimer, move thee. Consider the martyrdom of thy chickens, Rogers, Saunders, Taylor. And now cast not away the poor admonition of me, going to be burned also, and to receive the like crown of glory with my fellows."[76] John Careless, a fellow prisoner with Bradford in King's Bench, used the successful suffering of his spiritual captains as models for all the other prisoners, and he wrote six captives readying them-selves for martyrdom that Christ had prepared "your place under the holy altar with Cranmer, Latimer, Ridley, Rogers, Hooper, Saunders, Ferrar, Taylor, Bradford, Philpot. . . ."[77]

The re-establishment of the credibility of the Protestant leadership and the faith for which they were willing to die was complete—expiation for the failures of Edward's reign had been made in full—when Matthew Plaise, a weaver in the diocese of Canterbury, frustrated his examiners by saying, "When Cranmer, which was here my bishop, was in authority, he said, that he did hold the truth, and commanded us to believe him; and he hath given his life for his opinion. And would you [now] have me to believe you, because you say that you hold the truth?"[78] Nothing verified the truth so dramatically as burning at the stake. It is doubtful whether Plaise knew of his bishop's recantation; it was enough that the defrocked and disgraced ecclesiastic had died for his faith, thrusting the hand that had signed the confession into the fire so that it might be symbolically as well as physically punished first.

Latimer's and Ridley's deaths were sensational events, but it was John Philpot's burning two months later that drew the sharpest protest, in the form of a long epistolary diatribe sent to Edmund Bonner, the Marian bishop of London, who next to Stephen Gardiner drew the sharpest Protes-tant ire. The letter, as recorded by Foxe, is a set piece of religious polemics, blasting bloody Bonner for his cruelty and warning him of the futility of his policies, but it revealed the grisly optimism that martyrdom engendered. "I will give you to understand," the outraged writer said, "that the death of this constant martyr . . . hath given a greater shake towards the overthrow-ing of your papistical kingdom, than you shall ever be able to recover again these seven years. . . . You have broken a pot indeed, but the precious nard contained therein is so notably . . . shed abroad that the sweet savour thereof hath wonderfully well refreshed all the true household or congregation of Christ. . . ."[79]

It is a troublesome question whether the Marian government, given another seven years, could have exterminated heresy. After one year of persecution all the Protestant leaders were dead, leaving only Cranmer, who was being spiritually prepared for the government's most spectacular propaganda victory. History was filled with evidence that the blood of martyrs was not necessarily the seed of the faith. Few would have questioned that "the unity of the state exists not merely in its houses or its streets but . . . in the agreement of its minds."[80] Nevertheless, the government was clearly worried by the impact of the burnings. The customary last-minute pardon granted martyrs on condition of their recantation was rescinded: it was bad public relations to have the queen's mercy so consistently scorned. Barriers had to be placed around the burnt-out graves of the martyrs lest their ashes and remaining bones be taken off as holy relics, and orders were sent out to apprehend John Bernard and John Walsh, who were trucking the remains of the martyr John Pygot about the kingdom.[81] There is evidence that Gardiner himself before he died in November of 1555—only six months after the fires were lit—began to back away from the policy of terror. A year later the desperation of officialdom and its willingness to make concessions in the face of men and women whose behavior gave the government little choice except to burn them was dramatized by its bargaining with Julian Palmer. An Oxford fellow and onetime vehement Catholic, Palmer was converted to an equally vehement Protestant position by the sight of Ridley's and Latimer's executions. According to Foxe, Dr. Jeffrey, chancellor of Salisbury, attempted to lure Palmer back into the fold by the offer of "a good living," the only condition being that "he would outwardly show himself conformable, keeping his conscience secret to himself, or at least declare that he doubted which was the truest doctrine."[82] Palmer refused even this fig leaf to conceal the government's embarrassment, and Bishop Bonner himself heralded the government's sense of defeat in the propaganda war against the heretics when in July of 1558 he wrote that he thought all future burnings should be done as speedily and quietly as possible so as not to attract so many people.[83]

In the battle of wills and reputations the martyrs were the victors; their imaginary commonwealth, which in order to survive had like the Cheshire Cat to lose its body, leaving only a smile, was proving to be more resilient than the kingdom of reality. Whether such a victory would have endured as a lasting memory had Mary lived a further decade is another matter, but on

November 17, 1558, fortune's wheel did to the Catholics what five and a quarter years before it had done to the Protestants: it removed divine support, permitting Catholic Mary to die. For the Protestants the timing was much more than a fortunate fortuity; they saw the hand of God vindicating the champions of His precious nation. In 1558 the memory of their deaths was still strong enough to shape the future, and John Jewel, one of the returning exiles, when he became bishop of Salisbury in the new reign, gave voice to the sixteenth-century certainty that the martyred chiefs had not died in vain. He assured his flock that the heroes were "yet so fresh in your eyes and spoken of in your hearing and witnessed in your hearts and consciences that you cannot deny that the kingdom of God is come amongst us."[84]

Charles I (portrait by Anthony Van Dyck): That a divine-right king could be publicly executed or that he would be required to play the role of the martyr were unthinkable eventualities.

CHAPTER 9

CHARLES I:
MARTYR BY ACT OF PARLIAMENT

The tyrant dies, and his rule ends; the martyr
dies, and his rule begins.
—SØREN KIERKEGAARD

He that dies a martyr proves that he was not a
knave, but by no means that he was not a fool.
—C.C.COLTON,
Lacon

MARTYRS MUST HAVE a stage on which to display their self-control and superiority. They thrive on publicity; it is essential to the process whereby common criminals, the disagreeable caterpillars of society, transform themselves into butterflies that capture the imagination and attract the attention of history. So why didn't the state learn to stamp on such insects before they took wing, squash them underfoot effectively, quietly, and ignobly, and deprive them of public exposure? One might have thought that by the seventeenth century the mistakes of the past would have been recognized, and society would have learned how to protect itself. Handled differently—left to rot in prison, silently done away with by hired assassins, or simply ignored—all of the central protagonists of this book might have vanished into the shadows of the past, never to become dangerous symbols of resistance to authority and conformity.

In each case, of course, the state was not a free agent. Athens was a victim of its own laws and of the need to find a scapegoat for military humiliation. The Seleucid empire faced the novelty of ideological war on the part of a theocratic community that fitted no previous pattern and seemed to thrive on pain and adversity. Judea was unable to disassociate the warrior from the spiritual Messiah, and in a religious society dominated by a foreign power both were dangerous to the established order. Roman officialdom was swept along by a fatal combination of mob hatred for and state misunderstanding of Christianity. Henry Plantagenet never planned the accidental and emotionally charged events that led to the murder of an archbishop on the altar of his own cathedral; Henry Tudor's society was too conditioned to statutes written in blood to permit an ex–lord chancellor to live out the remainder of his life in the Tower of London; and his daughter Mary could only see heretics as murderers of the soul and subverters of the commonweal deserving of the stake. In each circumstance, social and moral reflexes were at work. In contrast, the decision by an English Parliament to try and publicly execute its legal king was an unprecedented act made with deliberation and forethought. The members of the revolutionary government that determined and orchestrated the death of Charles I debated at length the wisdom of quiet assassination—there was precedent aplenty for doing away with an unwanted sovereign—as opposed to dramatic condemnation and execution in full public view. They opted for the latter with profound consequences for themselves and for history, because with the exception of Jesus of Nazareth, never did the style of a man's death so redeem the cause for which he stood. Charles's performance at his trial in the last week of January 1649 and the manner of his final exit from this world on the thirtieth of the month saved his crown, which a lifetime of ineptitude, obstinacy, and obtuseness nearly destroyed. Indeed, nothing became Charles Stuart so perfectly as the fashion of his death.[1]

The execution of a divine-right sovereign was not something that could be done in secret, because Oliver Cromwell and the other grandees of the army had decided not simply to decapitate a king—they were no mere regicides—but to execute monarchy itself.[2] For the first time in English history, a reigning sovereign was to be put to death in the name of law. As Cromwell curtly told an unhappy and uncertain colleague who questioned the justice and legality of judging a king, "I tell you we will cut off his head with the crown on it."[3] It was, in fact, crucial to the destruction of kingship that the crown remain firmly upon the sovereign's severed head. At his trial the English monarch was no deposed king, a private citizen, as Louis XVI of France would be 144 years later. Nor was the problem of the English royal succession—Prince Charles's right to succeed his father the moment the king's head hit the scaffold—to be resolved by mass murder in the fashion of the Bolsheviks, who rounded up and shot as much of the Romanov royal family as they could get their hands on. Instead, the military junta was determined to demystify and desanctify a divine-right monarch by turning him into a royal war criminal to be impeached as "a tyrant, traitor, murderer and a public and implacable enemy to the commonwealth of England."[4]

The republicans in Parliament and the military could have legislated the overthrow of the monarchy long before Charles died on the scaffold, but they waited to pronounce kingship "unnecessary, burdensome and dangerous" until a week after the king's death because they wanted much more than the abolition of an ancient institution. They sensed correctly that they had to symbolically defrock and degrade monarchy, to hold the divine-right king up to public scorn, and to cleanse the commonwealth of royal evil by focusing attention upon the bloody hands of the man who believed to his dying breath that "a subject and a sovereign are clean different things," and claimed he spoke directly for God.[5] Almost everyone in England agreed with Charles when he said at his trial that he was no "ordinary prisoner."[6] This was the root of the army's difficulty in first warring against and then judging the king: he was legitimate and historic, and it was not. Although parliamentary forces eventually defeated Charles during the Civil War, the moral advantage always rested with the monarchy, and late in the fighting the earl of Manchester voiced the fear of all rebels against the throne: "If we beat the king ninety-nine times yet he is king still . . . but if he beats us but once we should be hanged and our posterity be undone."[7]

As a king, Charles possessed two bodies: his corporal person, which could suffer and die, and his mystical presence, which was immortal and inspired the body politic of which, as God's deputy on earth, he was the "head and soul." Only by smashing the divinity and mystery of kingship could the revolutionaries destroy the hold that monarchy exercised over the minds of its subjects. The war crimes—evidence that Charles as a king as well as a man was a tyrant, traitor, and bloody murderer—had to be openly and firmly placed on his shoulders. To simply murder the king by stealth or purchase achieved no purpose except to cleanse the throne of guilt and pave the way for Charles II; but to try Charles I and then to execute him in public was to attack the concept of monarchy itself.

That challenge could never succeed unless kingship was transformed, stripped of its divinity and redefined as a "thing men made for their own sakes, for quietness' sake, just as in a family one man is appointed to buy the meat."[8] But before Charles could be judged and tried as a mere purveyor of meat to be accepted or dismissed on the basis of the efficiency of his service to the community, a new metaphor had to be devised. Sovereignty and divinity, which in the seventeenth century could not yet be separated from one another, had to be vested not in the king's body, corporal and mystical, but in a new agency: "the good people of England."[9] In a wave of the metaphorical wand, Charles suddenly became the "grand administrator" of the realm who had entered into "a contract and bargain made between the king and his people." The contract was held together solely by "the bond of protection that is due from the sovereign" and "the bond of subjection that is due from the subject." Once that tie was broken, "farewell sovereignty." Kings were limited, not by conscience and their personal obligations to God, but by contract, and during his trial Charles was subjected to a cannonade of admonitions on the obligations and nature of his kingship. It was "an office of the highest trust lodged in any single person" and it was "seizable and forfeitable as if you had it but for a year or for your life."[10]

In presenting Charles as a "defaulting functionary and criminal magistrate" who had brutally and heedlessly broken the terms of his royal contract, the trial court, established to expose and judge the king's heinous and manifold crimes, was voicing a revolutionary concept of treason. Thomas Becket had been a feudal felon, a faithless vassal and traitor to his prince's friendship and service. His treason was directed against the king as a man and an overlord. In More's day the monarch's person had come to personify the kingdom, and Sir Thomas died as a criminal to that unity of mind which was becoming the hallmark of nationhood. By the seventeenth century the king's two bodies began to separate, and when Charles's archbishop William Laud was impeached and eventually executed by order of Parliament, the ominous assertion was made that treason might be against the realm as well as against the monarch.[11] By 1649 the division was complete. King and kingdom had parted company. Sovereignty no longer resided in the monarch or even in his historic crown but in "the good people of England" who claimed to be both state and sovereign at the same time. The realm in a sense had become disembodied, an organic monstrosity and social phantom without a head, hard to define and impossible to represent in clear and certain institutional form. Without a king, who spoke for such a fiction—Parliament or the army or some self-professed moral minority?

Who rightfully voiced the will of society might be a matter of debate, but Charles's jailers and judges agreed unanimously on two points. The criminal charges brought against the king entailed "the highest treason that ever was brought upon the theatre of England," for he was the "occasioner, author and continuer" of the bloody wars and therefore guilty of "all the treasons, murders, rapines, burnings, spoils, desolations, damages and mischiefs to this nation";[12] and God had removed His divinity from the king and given it to the saints who ruled in Parliament and the military.

When Parliament and the army spoke of "the good people" of England so cruelly butchered, by inescapable logic they also acknowledged the existence of bad people of whom the king was the satanic head. In striking down such manifest evil, the parliamentary and military saints were quite certain they were doing the bidding of a God who had "no respect of person" and was "the avenger of innocent blood."[13] The legal machinery that was set up to pronounce justice and condemn Charles constituted "the great Day of Judgment, when the Saints shall judge all earthly powers."[14] Retribution was "the design of heaven," and in cutting off the head of a tyrant, in obliterating the very idea of monarchy, the judges of the high court knew they had "done well: undoubtedly it is the best action they ever did in all their lives." John Cook, the solicitor of the commonwealth, spoke for the entire company of the elect when he said that he went about the trial of the royal tyrant as "cheerfully . . . as to a wedding," certain that "the glory of this administration" belonged wholly to God.[15]

The revolutionaries in their ideological zeal miscalculated: neither the army nor Parliament could get along without kingship; and even after they had cut off the king's head, they discovered that the prince's other body, the mystical monarchy, refused to die. Charles reiterated the central importance of his office many times over, first to the army ("You cannot do without me. You will fall to ruin if I do not sustain you") and then to Parliament ("My Lords, you cannot but know that, in my fall and ruin, you see your own").[16] Such words were more than the fatuous bravado of a man desperately trying to salvage an untenable position. Charles voiced two truths that his executioners ignored at their peril: old habits die hard, and a king's position in a divinely ordained political hierarchy kept the "giddy, hot-headed, bloody multitude" in its proper place and sanctioned the rule of men of property and social position.

A time would come, a decade after the king's death, when the revolutionary saints would decide that the second of Charles's dictums—they could not manage without a legitimate king—was correct; but for the present it was Charles's first truism that concerned them, because they discovered that even an imprisoned king, stripped of his sovereignty, remained a king. During most of his imprisonment, the ancient respect and ritual of kingship held sway. Charles dined regularly in state; he seems to have enjoyed endless credit to buy new clothes; and even as he was being brought from Windsor Castle to London in preparation for his trial and execution, a lone horseman spotted the cavalcade and doffed his hat in respect to monarchy. It made no difference that the rider and his horse were thrown into the ditch by the soldiers escorting the king. As the radicals in the military complained, even their own officers seemed to be kowtowing to the king: why, they asked in outrage, did they "kneel and kiss and fawn upon him? . . . Oh, shame of men! Oh sin against God!" This was no way to treat a man who was a traitor to "the good people of England."[17] To the very end the habits of centuries held firm, and the executioner could think of nothing else to say in response to the king's final order to swing the axe only when he gave the signal except "Yes, I will and it please your Majesty."[18]

Soldier-saints were clearly no more successful than Antiochus IV or Mary Tudor in handling ideological conflict. Although they thought they were demoting a king into a common criminal, they were in fact promoting a monarch, who already claimed divinity and a special place in heaven, into a martyr. Later, when Colonel Axtell escorted Sir Purback Temple to view Charles's corpse in its coffin, the colonel raised the lid and said, "If thou thinkest there is any sanctity or holiness in it, look here"; what Sir Purback reported he saw, however, was not a dead monarch, let alone a demystified body, but "the head of the blessed martyr'd King" lying "in a coffin with his body, which smiled as perfectly as if it had been alive."[19]

A few strong-willed souls, working within the limits of historic circumstance, can achieve martyrdom as acts of volition; others, like Charles, have the decision thrust upon them. The possibility that he might die by the blade of the public executioner in full sight of his people did not penetrate the king's mind until almost the last moment. He had always accepted as an attribute of his office the risk that he might die in battle or by the assassin's knife, and he acknowledged that his enemies might seek to depose and replace him or that he might have to escape into exile once he lost the war. But that a divine-right king could be publicly executed or that he would be required to play the role of the martyr were unthinkable eventualities.

In retrospect, it is difficult to deny that the roots of the tragedy went far back in time to that fatal moment when chance, heredity, and environment conspired to place upon the throne a sovereign whose personality was almost guaranteed to exacerbate the already existing irritations that were eroding the bonds which tied the monarch and his people together in a mystical union known as "King in Parliament." Long-term economic, social, and ideological forces helped produce the growing political tension between king and Parliament and the conflict that exploded in August of 1642. But in the ultimate recipe for the war and the revolution that followed, obtuseness, well-meaningness, and mental rigidity may have been the essential ingredients, and Charles I had more than his fair share of all three. No matter what the long- or short-term causes may have been, the second Stuart indisputably made a far better martyr than ruler and was venerated far more sincerely in death than in life.

Archbishop William Laud delivered the most barbed indictment of his master when he said that Charles was "a mild and gracious prince who knew not how to be or be made great." Taciturn, secretive, and reserved,

Charles never achieved the dignity of inscrutable silence; instead, his quietness concealed a stammer in speech and a lack of confidence in himself. For all his good intentions and the deadly seriousness with which he took his office, he was coldly impersonal in his human contacts and rigidly narrow in his moral and spiritual approach to life. He made a virtue of inflexibility and proudly proclaimed that he could not "defend a bad or yield on a good cause." As a Christian king he was ready to sacrifice all—even his kingdom—for his conscience, which proved in action to be an extraordinarily devious set of moral principles based on the assertion that he, as a divine-right sovereign, could do no wrong but everybody else could. Behind a face that shone with an incandescent mixture of sadness and serenity lay concealed the ruthless will of a monarch who lived, prayed, and thought by a single, irrevocable creed—God's will be done.[20]

The root of the emerging crisis between king and Parliament lay less in constitutional principles (Did the taxing power reside solely in Parliament, or could the king legally raise forced loans and extra-parliamentary taxes on his own, and to what extent did a king have to listen to the wishes of Lords and Commons in the formation and exercise of foreign or domestic policy?) than in psychology and matters of trust. Lack of trust created the atmosphere for civil war. It was fostered by Parliament's fear that because Charles had surrounded himself with papists at court and had married a Catholic wife, he was soft on religion. Distrust, heightened by religious hysteria, exploded in October of 1641, when the kingdom was confronted by rebellion in Ireland and highly exaggerated stories of Catholic atrocities across the Irish Sea. Parliament could not risk financing an avenging army which an untrustworthy king might use not in Ireland but at home against God-fearing Protestants. And finally, fear and doubt sprang from the conviction that the king did not feel himself in conscience bound by the political concessions he made to Parliament the year before fighting broke out; he had signed the Triennial Act of May 1641, ensuring the calling of Parliament every three years, had accepted the dismantling of the machinery of his prerogative powers, and had acknowledged all nonparliamentary taxation to be illegal; but would he live up to his word? All these fears led to a "bloody and unnatural war," a war fueled more by unspecified dread of the future than by specific political goals.

When in August of 1642 the country slipped into a conflict that nobody had planned and few wanted, neither side was clear as to who or what constituted the enemy. The mental reservation that the king can do no wrong, although cracked and tarnished, still deflected criticism from the crown. Four years of war, however, smashed that shield forever. When Charles commenced his reign, he had been the good father of his kingdom; when the war began, he was viewed as a gullible and misled parent; when the war ended in 1646, he had become an evil stepfather; within two more years, the possibility of having no father at all was being accepted as God's will. The final step whereby Charles was stripped of his crown and all trust in him both as a man and as a sovereign was destroyed resulted from the fatal interaction of the king's own actions during the concluding months of his life and the forces of revolutionary change that gave political power to the military. The place to start the story of Charles's martyrdom is on May 5, 1646, when, after four years of war and a shattering defeat at the Battle of Naseby, he surrendered to the Scots, reminding himself that he was, after all, born in Scotland and a Scottish sovereign.

The king's defeat in war had been the work of three distinct and not overly friendly groups. Parliament, cleansed of its royalist and Anglican members and dominated by a large Presbyterian majority, who represented the economic interests of the city of London and the mercantile elements throughout the kingdom, served as the paymaster of the rebel forces. The Scots, whose aid in battle had been purchased by Parliament with the promise to reform religion in England "according to the Word of God"—a deity who presumably spoke only the language of Scottish Presbyterianism—had entered the conflict in the fall of 1643. Finally, the New Model Army, commanded by Thomas, Lord Fairfax, and his far more vigorous and committed lieutenant Oliver Cromwell, was created during the concluding years of the war when Parliament recognized that not even with Scottish help could it win the struggle. The rebels needed an instrument that could not only outfight the king's troops but also outmatch Charles's claims to speak for God. The new army of saints was no mere mercenary force but a dangerous and highly effective military weapon, shorn of its political and aristocratic leadership and led by "plain russet-coated" captains who knew what they were fighting for. Once the military fell into the hands of men of lesser social standing but greater desire to win the war, the conservatives in both Lords and Commons, who favored constitutional monarchy and a Presbyterian state church, discovered they had a tiger by the tail, one with strong Congregationalist and republican markings.

The core of the problem, politically and religiously, was that no one knew exactly what to do with a divine-right king who had been worsted in battle but adamantly maintained that God was still on his side. All three parties sought to make use of him, because Charles was absolutely correct in his assertion that "a king cannot be so low" that he did not add great "weight to that party where he appears."[21] For his part, Charles sought to sow the seeds of dissension among the victors and, as he said, to "really be king again."[22] His purpose was made easier by the growing rift between the military and its civilian paymasters. Once peace arrived, Parliament attempted to do away with its own creations. It paid off the Scots with 400,000 pounds and sent them home, but voted to disband most of the New Model Army without paying the arrears owed to the rank and file or making arrangements for the widows and orphans of the fallen heroes. Such parsimony proved to be a shortsighted and dangerous policy, because it drove the military leaders to make common cause with the religious and political radicals within the rank and file. In its turn fear of the army and of government by coup d'état led Parliament to look to the king and the Scots to sustain its authority. Charles saw his chance to regain his ancient authority, and spinning a tangle of duplicity and intrigue, he played on mounting Presbyterian and parliamentary fear of the army, promised the Scots to reform the Church of England along Presbyterian lines, and sparked a second round of fighting known as the second Civil War. It lasted less than six months.

The so-called second Civil War changed the rules of the game. Until then, royalist Cavaliers and parliamentary Roundheads had treated one another with considerable restraint, and with the king's surrender in 1646 few war crimes charges had been pressed or punishments inflicted. Now in 1648 with the resumption of fighting, Cromwell's army viewed Parliament as a citadel of the Antichrist and executed royalist and Scottish commanders as war criminals who had obstructed God's purpose. The renewal of civil war in the teeth of Charles's avowals that he would never again "engage our people in another war" not only convinced the military that a divine-right monarch could not be trusted but also called into question the very foundations of monarchy itself. Even before the second round of fighting ended, the military council of war resolved that "it was our duty, if ever the Lord brought us back again in peace, to call Charles Stuart, that man of blood, to an account for that blood he had shed, and mischief he had done to his utmost against the Lord's cause and people."[23]

Defeat in war sealed the fate of both king and Parliament, for the military had come to see no difference between them; they were both rotten relics of a godless past. The army moved first against the monarch. On November 30, Lieutenant Colonel Cobbett seized Charles and on the second of December imprisoned him in Hurst Castle, a dark and friendless fortification surrounded on three sides by water. Four days later it was Parliament's turn: Colonel Thomas Pride posted his troops at the door to the House of Commons, arrested forty-seven members, and turned away ninety-six others. Twenty other legislators, outraged by this military coup, refused to take their seats, leaving only a "Rump" of some fifty-six godly men, a tiny remnant purged of all conservative and Presbyterian corruption, who heeded the word of God and the will of the army. The ancient and historic constitution had been reduced to a travesty of fifty-six members out of an original total of over five hundred.

Legality had been reduced to a fig leaf, but one that was willing and eager, with Cromwell's legions to sustain it, to claim full sovereignty and cooperate with the military in dethroning monarchy. On December 17 Colonels Harrison and Cobbett escorted Charles in a carefully guarded six-day journey to Windsor Castle. Between January 1 and 6 the purged House of Commons passed legislation establishing a high court of 135 commissioners to try the king for treason against "the good people" of England, and pronounced the revolutionary statement that "the good people under God" were "the original of all just power" and that "the Commons of England in Parliament assembled" possessed "the supreme power of this nation." Only then did it finally and fully dawn upon Charles that he might "die a King, by the hands of my own subjects, a violent, sudden, and barbarous death."[24]

Precisely who made the decision to try and execute Charles Stuart is far from clear, but the real initiative seems to have resided with the military, established in its headquarters at Whitehall Palace. Even here, however, there was no unanimity. Thomas, Lord Fairfax, the commander-in-chief, never took his seat on the high court during the actual trial and persisted to the very end in believing that the entire performance was a scare tactic designed by Cromwell either to frighten the king into further concessions—possibly to abdicate in favor of one of his sons—or to reinstate the monarchy with himself as king. Cromwell expressed everyone's unease when, in the debate in Commons, he warned that killing the king had to be done out of principle, not profit; otherwise God would never sanction the act. He added, however, that he was not sufficiently certain of the Lord's purpose to tell them how to vote. All he could do was to pray God to bless their decision.[25]

The trial took place on Saturday, January 20, in Westminster Hall. The 240-by-67-foot chamber had been cleared of its vendors' stalls to make room for the spectacle—half of London clamored to attend—and extreme security measures had to be taken. The Gothic hall with its immense wooden arches was decorated with the military banners captured from Charles at the Battle of Naseby—colorful but blatant evidence as to who was the victor, who the vanquished—and troops were stationed in such a way as to cut the king off from the view of his poorer subjects, who were crowded into the north end of the building by a wooden divider that obscured everything except the top of the king's hat. The galleries around the hall, however, were crammed with well-to-do spectators who had either the influence or the wealth to obtain an advantageous position to watch the drama. At the south end the commissioners, appropriately garbed in somber clothing, sat on a tiered platform, John Bradshaw, the lord president, presiding from a raised chair in the front row. The prisoner's dock consisted of a red velvet armchair located in front of the commissioners. Between the two, on a table covered with a Turkish carpet, rested the sword and mace of state, the traditional symbols of royal authority, now claimed by Parliament.

The first official action of the lord president was to record the act of Commons that had erected the court and on whose authority it operated. The session, however, got off to an embarrassing start when the names of the commissioners were read aloud. Bradshaw's came first, and he rose to acknowledge his presence, but when General Fairfax's name was announced, there was no answer. The clerk read the name a second time, and in the ensuing silence a voice from the spectators' gallery—later discovered to be Lady Fairfax's—was heard to say, "He has too much wit than to be here." This caused an instantaneous uproar; but when order had finally been re-established, it was discovered that only 68 of the 135 commissioners attended that first day.[26]

The court having officially opened, the prisoner was conducted to the dock. He arrived dressed from hat to shoes in black, except for the white of his collar and cuffs and a brilliant embroidered silver star of the Order of the Garter on the left shoulder of his cloak. Around his neck he wore the blue ribbon of the Garter; from it hung a diamond George in the form of a locket in which he kept a miniature of his wife. Once he was seated, the charges, a two-page, closely printed document, were read out. He was indicted on the grounds of "High Treason and other High Crimes." "Being admitted king of England and therein trusted with a limited power to govern by and according to the laws of the land and not otherwise," he had criminally sought "out of a wicked design to erect and uphold in himself an unlimited and tyrannical power" and to "overthrow the rights and liberties of the people." Then followed a long list of Charles's personal involvement in the "unnatural, cruel and bloody wars" and the demand that he be impeached as "a tyrant, traitor, murderer and a public and implacable enemy of the commonwealth of England." Charles's only recorded reaction was to burst into laughter when he was branded a tyrant, traitor, and murderer.[27]

The charges having been read, Bradshaw began the judicial proceedings. "Sir," he said, "you have now heard your charge. . . . The court expects your answer whether you plead innocent or guilty." Charles rose and replied, "I would know by what power I am called hither. . . . Remember I am your King, your lawful King, and what sin you bring upon your heads. . . . Think well upon it. . . . Let me know by what lawful authority I am seated here and I shall not be unwilling to answer."[28]

The king's response had been anticipated, and Bradshaw sternly informed him that he stood before the high court "by the authority of the Commons of England, assembled in Parliament, in the behalf of the people of England, by which people you are elected King." Charles, excellent historian that he was, would accept no such misrepresentation of history: "Nay, I deny that; England was never an elective kingdom; it was a hereditary kingdom for near this thousand years." He insisted the court's authority was "raised by an usurped power" and that he, not Parliament, was entrusted with "the liberty of my people." "I do stand more," he said, "for the liberties of my people than any one that is seated here as a judge." In a debate punctuated by interruptions from both the king and the lord president, Charles pounded away at the obvious. He had come here by force; "I do not come here as submitting to the court." Then he shifted the terms of the argument, asserting that a king could only come before a full Parliament. Where, he asked, was the House of Lords "that might constitute a Parliament," and where was their true king? How could this illegal court claim to represent "King in Parliament"? "Let me see," he concluded, "a legal authority . . . warranted either by the Word of God, by Scripture, or warranted by the ancient laws and constitutions of this realm, and I will answer."[29]

Charles was in excellent voice—even his stammer had left him—and for once he did the right thing. Instead of grounding his case solely on the divinity of kings in splendid isolation from all else, he wrapped that divinity in the security of history, associating his rights as king and the authority of his throne with the historic laws of his kingdom and the ancient liberties of his people. In so doing he saved, if not his own life, the sanctity of his throne. As never before or since, history was at a premium, both sides appealing to the past. Charles, at least in the eyes of most of his subjects, had the stronger case, and when for a third time he said, "I stand more for the liberty of my people than any here that seateth to be a judge," and avowed "that it is as great a sin to withstand lawful authority as to submit to a tyrannical . . . authority," there were loud cries of "God save Your Majesty!" from the audience.[30]

In the exchange between the king and Bradshaw, the lord president was reduced to the ineffectual assertion that a criminal had no right to question the authority of the court—"The interpretation doth not belong to you"—and in order to stop Charles's discourse, he adjourned the meeting until Monday. He ordered the guards to "withdraw the prisoner," but Charles managed the final words of the session: not "the prisoner," he retorted, but "the king."[31]

Since the next day was Sunday, the commissioners had time to consider the situation. Charles's refusal to plead innocent or guilty to the charges laid against him had spiked the commissioners' guns, because by law, if the accused failed to plead one way or the other, the court could not do what its creators had planned: publicly demonstrate the king's full guilt as a war criminal. The court had anticipated that Charles would attempt to deny its authority, but it had expected him to argue his innocence. Instead, Charles had spent his time during the first day in a highly effective onslaught, attacking the court's authority without bothering to defend or justify his own. As a consequence, Bradshaw was maneuvered into the awkward position of having to construe the king's silence as guilt and condemn him to death without a full hearing of the evidence.

The second and third meetings of the court, on Monday and Tuesday, were anticlimactic repeats of the first, Charles hammering away at the weakest point of the prosecution's argument. His rights as a king, he insisted, were enshrined in the Common Law, that precious resource of the kingdom, and he astutely associated those rights with the property rights so important to the ruling elite of society. "It is not my case alone, it is the freedom and liberty of the people of England. For if power without law may make law, may alter the fundamental laws of the kingdom, I do not know what subject he is in England, that can be assured of his life or anything that he can call his own."[32]

What Charles wanted was equal time to debate; "I do require that I may give . . . my reasons why I do not [answer], and give me time for that." "It is not for prisoners to require," Bradshaw retorted, and Charles shot back the obvious: "Sir, I am not an ordinary prisoner." To disprove the point, Colonel John Hewson stepped up and spat in the king's face, his troops calling out, "Justice! justice!! upon the traitor." Charles, with disdainful but infuriating calm, drew out his handkerchief, wiped his face, and said, "Well, sir! God hath justice in store, both for you and me." Throughout the entire spectacle, it was clear to all that the moral initiative had passed from court to king; Charles had never put on such a brilliant performance.[33]

Each day the charade followed the same formula. Bradshaw would enjoin: "Sir, in plain terms (for justice knows no respect of persons) you are charged with high treason, you are to give your answer, your positive and final answer (in plain English), whether you be guilty or not guilty of these treasons laid in your charge." And the king would launch into a lecture on "the liberties of the people of England that I stand for." Each day the lord president would adjourn the court warning the king that he stood before a "court of justice," and Charles would answer, "Well, sir, I find I am before a power," or, as another observer reported, he more characteristically replied, "Pish! I care not a straw for you."[34]

For the next three days—Wednesday to Friday—the court gave up interrogating the king and concentrated on hearing thirty-two witnesses to prove Charles's bloody participation in the war and his intrigues to continue the fighting—a point that at law was superfluous, since the prisoner had failed to plead one way or the other. By Saturday there was nothing left to be done except sentence the sovereign, and Bradshaw prepared a long eight-page statement systematically arguing the case against the king as a traitor, tyrant, and murderer. It was scarcely the propaganda triumph the military and Commons had hoped to achieve during the trial, but was better than nothing, and to dramatize the finality of the occasion, the lord president divested himself of his black lawyer's gown and donned a scarlet robe.

Bradshaw stood to address the court and prisoner, but got no further than "Gentlemen" when he was interrupted by the king, who asked leave to speak. A verbal struggle ensued, both men seeking to give the opening lecture. Eventually Charles retreated on the promise that he would be heard before any sentence was pronounced. For a second time the lord president commenced his address, only to be again interrupted when he referred to the king's high crimes against "the people of England." The unrepentant Lady Fairfax, far more strong-willed than her husband, and now joined by a Mrs. Nelson, shouted from the gallery, "It is a lie; where are the people or their consent" and "Oliver Cromwell is a traitor." Tension was running high, and Colonel Axtell was reported to have shouted back "down with the whores" and to have ordered his soldiers to "shoot them if they say one word more."[35]

Eventually Bradshaw finished his introductory remarks and permitted Charles to speak so long as he did not question the jurisdiction of the court. As usual the king ignored the reservation, but before he could be silenced, he got to the request he wanted to make: "I desire before sentence be given, that I may be heard in the Painted Chamber [an adjoining hall] before the Lords and Commons. . . . If I cannot get this liberty, I do protest that these fair shows of liberty and peace, are rather specious shows than otherwise, and that you will not hear your king."[36]

Charles never got his wish, and we do not know what proposals he might have made to achieve what he claimed would be "the kingdom's peace." Possibly he was getting ready to abdicate in favor of his son. More likely, he was continuing to throw dust in his opponents' eyes, hoping to delay sentence and divide his enemies. Whatever his reasons, his words were a tactical success. Not only did they once again highlight the illegality of the court—the only forum that could hear a king was a full Parliament of Lords and Commons—but they also so demoralized the commissioners that Bradshaw was forced to call a temporary halt in order to debate the king's request. A combination of Cromwell's unswerving determination to see the business through without postponement—he called Charles "the hardest hearted man upon the earth"—and fear that equivocation would lead to a military takeover prevailed, and the commissioners decided to continue with the sentencing.[37]

When the court reconvened, the monarch was bluntly told that no further delays would be permitted and that judgment must be given. Then Bradshaw launched into a long oration on the age-old debate over the source of ultimate authority. Did it reside in the individual or in society, in the divine monarch or in a godly minority, in the conscience of the martyr-heretic or in the institutional voice of a church or state that spoke for some higher power? Bradshaw was clear as to the proper answer. He informed the king: "Sir, as the law is your superior, so truly, Sir, there is something that is superior to the law, and which is indeed the parent or author of the law, and that is the people of England." Forty minutes later, he finally concluded his exposition with a lengthy explanation of why Charles in the eyes of all good and rational men and women should be executed as a war criminal, deserving death many times over.[38]

The verdict had now in effect been given; the court had found its king guilty, although he had never pleaded innocent or guilty or spoken in his own defense. By legal tradition, however, before actual sentence could be pronounced, the prisoner was offered the chance to state "why judgment should not be given against him," and Charles now tried to exert that right.[39] While Bradshaw was offering some rather gratuitous prayers, pleading that "God would give you a sense of your sins, that you might see wherein you have done amiss," the king interrupted. "I would desire," he said, "only one word before you give sentence . . . concerning those great imputations that you have laid to my charge." The lord president pointed out the illogic of this request: "You disavow us as a court and therefore for you to address yourself to us . . . is not to be permitted"; and he ordered the clerk to read the formal death sentence: "that the said Charles Stuart, as a tyrant, traitor, murderer and a public enemy to the good people of this nation, shall be put to death by the severing of his head from his body."[40] As a group the commissioners rose to acknowledge their assent; but significantly, attendance had now dropped to sixty-seven.

The legal process concluded with the death sentence, but the king and the lord president had one final exchange of words. Charles still expected to be heard. He might already be dead in the eyes of the law, but custom allowed the criminal a final word: Sir Thomas More had been given that chance. "Will you hear me a word, sir," the king called out. "Sir," replied Bradshaw, "you are not to be heard after the sentence. . . . Guard, withdraw your prisoner." In the face of this unexpected rebuff, Charles's composure left him: "I may speak after the sentence—by your favor, sir—by your favor—" (he began for the first time to stammer). When Bradshaw interrupted and repeated the command to withdraw the prisoner, Charles regained control of his emotions and speech. As he was leaving the court, he succeeded in getting in the final words, which encapsulated the message that for a week he had been propounding: "I am not suffered for to speak. Expect what Justice other people will have."[41]

Charles had been denied the chance to speak on that last day of his trial, but he got his wish at his execution three days later. Had there been bookie offices available, the odds in favor of executing even a condemned sovereign would not have been great. It was an unprecedented act, and even the military retreated from regicide or worse sacrilege. Lord General Fairfax was obviously extremely reluctant, and to the very end he was privately urging a postponement, but he was unwilling to speak out in public for fear of splitting the army and precipitating yet another civil war. Judging from the difficulty that Cromwell and the hard core of the military had in getting the commissioners to sign the death warrant, few people wanted to take the responsibility for executing a king. In the end only fifty-nine signatures appeared on the document, and it took three days to gather that number, Colonel Ingoldsby later claiming that Cromwell held his trembling and reluctant hand while he signed his name. Even the state executioner, it was rumored, had declined to do his grisly task upon a divine-right monarch, and another report claimed that on the day before the execution the "prime leaders" came to the king with a proposal to save the army from cutting off his head. He was to be permitted his life and the shadow of his throne if he would accept a standing military force of forty thousand men ruled by a council of war with the power to recruit new officers and enlisted men, raise taxes to pay the troops, and to govern the kingdom without resort to what was left of Parliament—to wit, a military dictatorship. Wisely Charles declined the offer, allegedly saying "he would rather become a sacrifice for his people" than endure the intolerable bondage of an "armed faction."[42]

The only person who does not seem to have been searching his soul or looking for a way out of the business was Charles himself. He closeted himself with his confessor, Bishop William Juxon, refusing to accept visitors and preparing "to meet that great God to whom ere long I am to give an account of myself." He spoke briefly to his two youngest children, Elizabeth and Henry, distributed his remaining jewelry, burnt his private papers, and spent his time devising an anagram from his title "Carolus Rex," rearranging the letters into "Cras ero lux": tomorrow I shall be light.[43]

On the morning of the execution—Tuesday, January 30—he rose early, telling his valet, Thomas Herbert, that he had "a great work to do this day," and ordering him to take special care of his hair and beard: "This is my second marriage day; I would be as trim today as may be, for before tonight I hope to be espoused to my blessed Jesus." The weather was bitter, and he told Herbert to dress him warmly. He wore an extra shirt so that when he removed his cloak and doublet on the scaffold, he would not shake with cold and be accused of fear. "I fear not Death," he said. "Death is not terrible to me. I bless my God I am prepared." Indeed, he was so prepared that he brought to his execution a satin nightcap to hold up his long, graying locks so that the axeman would have an unobstructed view of his neck.[44]

Execution was scheduled for ten a.m., but Charles was forced to endure four agonizing hours of waiting in one of the antechambers in the palace of Whitehall. The delay has never been adequately explained. Possibly Commons had not finished last-minute legislation making it illegal to proclaim Charles II sovereign the moment his father died on the block, an embarrassing oversight on the part of those set upon exterminating kingship. Possibly the scaffold had not been completed or there was trouble finding an axeman willing to do the job. Possibly dissension still smoldered in the ranks of the ideologues; there is a story that General Fairfax arrived at Whitehall, asked how the monarch was doing, and was stunned to hear that he had already been executed.

Just before two, Colonel Hacker knocked on the door of the antechamber where Charles had been waiting. He conducted the king through the second-story banqueting hall of the palace, which was lined with soldiers on both walls, and escorted him through an enlarged window on the west side of the building and onto the scaffold. The structure was large enough to hold fifteen people, and the courtyard below was filled with horse troops. Those who had made the local arrangements and were so determined to decapitate kingship as well as the king were peculiarly concerned with the decorum and propriety appropriate to executing a reigning sovereign. A century and more later, across the Channel, another set of ideologues would execute their king but do so on an unadorned and functional wooden structure with a public guillotine used for all enemies of the French Republic. After another hundred and twenty-four years the czar of Russia would not even be accorded a public execution; he and his family would simply be gathered up and shot. Seventeenth-century English kingship, however, deserved better, and Charles's specially constructed scaffold was draped in expensive black fabric, and the wooden coffin that rested by the block was covered in black velvet. Almost despite themselves, Cromwell and the military seemed to be mourning the execution of the king and the ancient constitution. The result of this funereal splendor was that although Charles was publicly executed, his death was strangely private, because the black cloth which hung along the railing concealed his body from view. All that could be seen, except by those agile spectators who had crawled to the roofs of nearby buildings, was the flash of the axe and the king's head as it was lifted by the executioner.

There was another significant contrast between the demise of the English and French monarchies: Charles was expected to have the final word, and two shorthand experts were supplied on the scaffold to take down and preserve his message. For Louis Capet, alias Louis XVI, the roll of military drums gave him no chance to address his onetime subjects or even those who stood close to him.

Charles had prepared a short speech, and he carried with him a slip of paper with an outline to refresh his memory. He realized that his voice would never carry to the immense crowd that was clinging to every rooftop, but he was determined to "speak a word unto you here." It was, he said, "my duty to God first and to my country for to clear myself as an honest man, a good King and a good Christian." After smiling at the grim sight of ropes and staples driven into the scaffold floor to tie him to the block should he resist and warning a soldier who by accident touched the axe— "Hurt not the axe that may hurt me"—he spoke his final public words and eloquently summed up the principles for which he felt he was dying. He had, he said, lived all his life by the ancient constitution of the kingdom. "Sirs, it was for this that now I am come here. If I would have given way to an arbitrary way, for to have all laws changed according to the power of the sword, I need not to have come here. And, therefore, I tell you, and I pray God it be not laid to your charge, that I am the martyr of my people."[45]

Charles was at his theatrical best, and his words rang true because he had finally found the role for which he was perfectly suited: martyr, not king. Still holding stage center, Charles turned to Bishop Juxon and said: "I go from a corruptible to an incorruptible crown where no disturbance can be, no disturbance in the world." He gave the bishop his George with its miniature of his queen to hold; took off his doublet and cloak; and warned Colonel Hacker to "take heed of the axe, pray take heed of the axe." He complained that the block, which was only eighteen inches high and required him to lie on his stomach to place his head on it, was far too low; and he put on his nightcap, stuffing his abundant hair inside and inquiring of the executioner, "Does my hair trouble you?" Then he awkwardly stretched himself out and placed his neck on the block, offered a final prayer, and gave the signal for the axe to fall. As it did and as the severed head was raised high by the masked executioner, who shouted, "Behold the head of a traitor," a young observer reported that "such a groan" rose from the crowd "as I never heard before, and desire I may never hear again."[46]

In seeking to do away with the satanic and corrupt past and to desanctify kingship, the military unwittingly created a specter that refused to die. Within six months of the king's execution, a report circulated of "a Miracle of Miracles, wrought by the blood of King Charles the First of happy memory." A young girl of fourteen had been given back her eyesight by the touch of a "handkerchief dipped in the king's blood."[47] The year 1649, of course, was not 1170, and no saintly rebel came crawling to worship at the tomb of the martyred king. Nevertheless, Charles's death was not in vain. Just before he died, he told his daughter Elizabeth she need not "grieve for him, for he should die a martyr, and he doubted not but the Lord would settle his throne upon his son," and the kingdom would "be happier than . . . if he had lived."[48] The king got his wish. Eleven years later the crown was restored and in 1660 his son succeeded his father to the throne of England. Parliament signaled the country's grateful recognition of the sacrifice made by its martyred king by decreeing that the anniversary of Charles's death should be observed as a day of "fasting and humiliation" in every church of England, and the form of service was officially incorporated into the Book of Common Prayer two years later. The celebration was not removed from the church calendar until 1858, nor the service deleted from the prayer book until 1928. Charles's official status as a martyr within the Church of England fell short of Becket's by a century, but 268 years of recognition is not a bad record for a sovereign who through the magnificent style of his death not only wiped clean a lifetime of political blunders, deceptions, and broken promises but also re-established the credibility of monarchy and ensured his son, if not a divine-right throne, at least one that was regarded as being fundamental to the ancient constitution and essential to the future welfare of the realm.

Charles's "martyrdom" was profoundly schizoid. As a man he died for a deeply religious perception of society, divinely ordained and justified, which he adamantly refused to renounce. But as a king he was executed in the name of treason to a state defined as a collective human entity endowed with sovereignty. Both king and military saints continued to argue their cases in terms of God's will; but as society began to divest itself of its religious orientation, martyrdom likewise came to be defined in more secular terms: the heretic and the spiritual warrior gave way to the traitor and the ideologue.

John Brown's photograph reveals the image of a martyr; the face of the saint seems to be indistinguishable from that of the devil.

CHAPTER 10

JOHN BROWN:
"LET THEM HANG ME"

Saint: A dead Sinner revised and edited.
—AMBROSE BIERCE,
The Devil's Dictionary

This thing of being a hero, about the
main thing to it is to know when to die.
—WILL ROGERS,
Autobiography

OW DID a singularly unsuccessful fifty-nine-year-old, Connecticut-born tanner turned surveyor, sheep raiser, and land speculator, who twice married and sired twenty children, become one of history's most successful martyrs? A less propitious set of circumstances can scarcely be imagined. If there is any explanation for such an unlikely outcome of events, it lies in three questions which so far in the evolving story of martyrdom have been touched upon only by implication and suggestion. First, can there be a martyr personality? "Unusual talents," as one historian has noted, "are required to make a success of being hanged."[1] Second, what is the relationship between the martyr and his cause—does one depend upon the other in creating the conditions out of which martyrdom emerges and thrives? And finally, do martyrs in effect get themselves executed; are they in reality aggressors against, not victims of, society?

In the twenty-four-hundred-year march of martyrs through Western history, one factor stands out as a constant: the geometric accumulation of the evidence documenting their careers. From Socrates, the Maccabees, Jesus, and the early Christian martyrs, where the balance between fact and legend tends in varying degrees toward the mythological, to Becket, More, the sixteenth-century Protestant martyrs, and Charles I, the physical features and inner persona of the martyr have grown steadily sharper. With John Brown, the historian has both an unprecedented volume of private correspondence—he was a prolific and revealing letter-writer, and despite the ravages of fire and the deliberate destruction of incriminating evidence, close to seven hundred intimate specimens are still extant—and a rich and varied record by those who witnessed his actions and experienced the full weight of his granitelike magnetism.[2] More important, the nineteenth century produced two new and revolutionary instruments of historical evidence and insight: the mass-circulation newspaper, which records while events are still unfolding, shaping public opinion even as it is being generated, and the photograph, which preserves with grim and undoctored accuracy the faces of both the privileged few and the forgotten many. Available for the first time are the features not only of John Brown the celebrity but also of those who believed in him, financed him, and died for him.

It used to be said that the physiognomy and coloring of the face displayed the humors locked within the body and exposed the inner intentions of the soul. Today we are less sanguine that the polished walls guarding the inner secrets of the mind and heart can be breached simply by studying the topography of the skull. Nevertheless, in photography as well as painting the artist, sometimes by conscious interpretation, other times by lucky accident, may capture the fullness and complexity of personality. John Brown's photographs reveal the image of a martyr, and we turn away deeply shaken, because the face of the saint seems to be indistinguishable from that of the devil. The high, supercilious, and arrogant eyebrows; the abnormally wide, humorless, and unbending mouth, perfectly bisected by the long, straight nose; the eyes, intense, unrelenting, and unblinking, staring out upon an evil world; and the strong cleft chin: the viewer can't decide which feature is the most striking and domineering. They all convey strength of character, but the total effect is disquieting. The photographs capture the inescapable aura of the fanatic; his enemies might go further and say "of the maniac." "The angel wings," wrote George Gill, who at twenty-six had been swept up by Brown's extraordinary presence and had briefly joined his crusade against slavery, "were so dim and shadowy as to be almost unseen," because they were overwhelmed by his selfishness, intolerance, and "great self-esteem."[3]

The picture frames the man and communicates the tensions and contradictions of a personality that would be a psychiatrist's dream as well as his nightmare. Born on May 9, 1800, to an upwardly mobile and rigidly Puritan Connecticut Yankee family, John Brown imbibed both the capitalistic work ethic and the Calvinist fear of God, reinforced in equal measures by an intense belief in "the divine authority of the Bible" and the knowledge that the world was composed of saints and sinners, who would receive their just deserts when the Lord in His absolute sovereignty saw fit to exercise His terrible justice. Brown survived the discipline of parents who rarely spared the rod, let alone ever spoiled the child; the migration of his family westward to the log-cabin hardships of Hudson, Ohio; his mother's death when he was eight; and the remarriage of his father a year later. He emerged a vulnerable—Brown in later life liked to talk about "his extreme bashfulness"—yet aggressively ambitious and inflexible overgrown adolescent, who at fifteen did a man's job, gave orders to his peers as if he were "a king against whom there is no rising up," and possessed a highly developed gift for rationalization which united self-deception with prevarication and deliberate deceit.[4]

In a curious document—part factual autobiography, part wishful thinking, part calculated propaganda—written many years later for the edification of a small boy from whose parents Brown was seeking money for the war against slavery, John confessed that as a youth he had been addicted to "telling lies: generally to screen himself from blame or from punishment."[5] Deflecting blame and rearranging the truth to protect himself were habits he never outgrew, and eventually they became central to his personality, the armor in which he encased his righteousness and the wall that kept reality at bay. John Brown the legend was the offspring of John Brown the consummate spin doctor, who viewed all his motives and actions through the distorted moral lens of self-justification, twisting events into a travesty of reality and transforming turpitude, lawlessness, and murder into instruments of divine justice and historic necessity. John Brown the young adult, however, had not yet developed such accomplished defense mechanisms. He had to face the trials and tribulations of marriage and the ruthless competition of American unregulated economic growth with two lesser, if related, weapons: the oddly contradictory but obstinately held convictions that his own judgment was infallible and that God's providence was inescapable and could be relied upon to rectify any calamity inflicted upon him by a society crawling with rogues and sinners.

Trained in his father's craft as a tanner, John set himself up in business, determined to be "head of the heap" and enact the American frontier success story. Fulfillment of that dream demanded a wife, and on June 22, 1820, aged twenty, he married Dianthe Lusk—a girl who, he confessed, had "a most powerful and good influence over him," but who, he added in his starkly honest fashion, was "remarkably plain."[6] He joined briefly the Masonic order, taught Sunday school, required his employees join him and his

family every morning in his cabin in communal prayer, and begat of Dianthe seven children in twelve years.

In business and in marriage, he assumed the role of the Christian patriarch, vigilantly holding his workers and children to an unrelenting moral
standard and punishing any lapses with a style of punishment that would
have put Old Testament justice to shame. Instead of firing an employee
caught in petty thievery, he sentenced him to social ostracism, ordering the
man's fellow workers to punish him with total silence. The miscreant endured his sentence for two months and then fled. Brown applied the same
unrelenting discipline to his children and kept a tally of his eldest son's mis-
demeanors, assigning a fixed number of lashes according to the seriousness
of the fault—eight lashes for telling a lie, three for "unfaithfulness at work."
On one occasion, when the total had reached the maximum and punishment with a "blue-beech switch" was being administered, Brown completed only about one-third of the strokes, then removed his own shirt and
ordered his son to deliver the remaining two-thirds on his father's back
until the elder Brown had "received the balance of the account." The experience, John Brown Jr. later noted, was a startling and unforgettable lesson
in the principle of biblical atonement—"how justice could be satisfied by
inflicting the penalty upon the back of the innocent instead of the guilty."[7]

The decade of the 1820s was a time of plenty and prosperity for the
Browns; thereafter the Lord tested the mettle of his servant until the cup of
his afflictions ran over. Dianthe and their three-day-old son died in August
1832; and eleven years later, four of his children by his second wife, Mary
Day, died of dysentery during the terrible month of September 1843. No
matter how fervently he prayed, how uncontrollable his tears, of his
twenty children, two of Dianthe's seven and eight of Mary's thirteen died
in childhood, five never making it through their first year. The boom-or-
bust nature of unregulated economic growth was no kinder, and Brown
was caught up in a series of disastrous enterprises that left him either bankrupt or nearly destitute. No amount of faith in God's providence could save
him from the consequences of a vision of life that rigidly divided the world
into absolute categories of right and wrong, good and bad, in which he was
always in the right and possessed a divinely inspired clairvoyance into the
economic system while everyone else was wrong.

His tanning business went under during the financial panic of 1837; his
excursion in 1844 into sheep raising and the export of wool led to the mis-
appropriation of funds and bankruptcy; and his efforts to protect sheep
farmers against the greed of big eastern wool manufacturers was a noble
but total failure. One creditor understandably described Brown as an in-
curably stubborn man with "a propensity to business failure in whatever he

attempted" which "nothing short of a mental rebirth" could alter.[8] Another, who had been mesmerized by the aura of absolute integrity that Brown always radiated, summed up his disastrous business experiences with the Ohioan with admirable restraint: he "had little judgment, always followed his own will and lost much money."[9] Brown's response was invariably the same: though he suffered innumerable setbacks, divine providence would eventually rescue him and allow him to pay back his many debts.

Brown never did pay his business debts (although he did leave one creditor fifty dollars in his will), but providence did not entirely forsake him. Just when his faith was being tested to Jobian limits, he met the philanthropist Gerrit Smith, who sold him for a dollar an acre 244 acres of wilderness in the Adirondack Mountains. Smith, who hoped to populate the area with freed blacks, thereby giving them economic status and New York voting rights, was, like many men before and after him, profoundly impressed by Brown's magnetism and sincerity. The Ohioan had assured Smith that he wanted to help his black neighbors by teaching them the fear of God and how to farm the obstinate soil of such a rugged and unfriendly part of New York State.

Geographically John Brown had come home—he was captivated by the magnificent mountain views "where every thing you see reminds one of Omnipotence"[10]—and after a number of false starts, in June of 1855 he finally scraped together enough money to settle his family permanently at North Elba, New York. Not even the explosion that was taking place across the Mississippi in the Nebraska Territory or the decision of five of his sons—John, Jason, Frederick, Owen, and Salmon—to settle in Kansas and defend the territory from slavery could deflect him. At fifty-five he was old, discouraged, and exhausted, and he wanted only the serenity and majesty of mountains that seemed to place all things—even slavery and the devil's legions which supported it—in proper perspective. In retreating, however, to upstate New York and turning his back on the evils of the world, John Brown reckoned without the hand of destiny. On the very day of his arrival at North Elba, he received an impassioned appeal from John Junior to join him and his brothers in saving Kansas from Satan and slavery, which kindled the crusading fire, turning it into a consuming beacon.[11]

All conversion experiences are more implosive than explosive; they infuse emotions with action and focus the hot heat of conviction upon ideas and impulses long held but never translated into deeds. Hatred of slavery was part of Brown's background and mentality.[12] Human bondage violated every tenet of his education and faith, especially his sense of equity. He had been born into a militantly antislavery family, where he had taken to heart the terrible contradiction that was eating away at the soul and sinews of the Republic. The new nation, conceived in liberty, had proclaimed to the world the self-evident truth that all men are created equal, yet in 1800 close to 16 percent of its inhabitants lived in legalized bondage. Calvinism and abolitionism merged in a family who believed that slave owners were unregenerate sinners and that slavery was a satanic organization in open defiance of God's Higher Law.[13]

Family values were reinforced by community values; the area around Hudson, Ohio, was abolitionist country, a key staging area for the Underground Railroad, which transported fugitive slaves north to Canada. As Brown grew to manhood, he absorbed the moral outrage that was sweeping Ohio and the East, distilling it down to the saber-sharp faith and unyielding conviction of a Calvinist fundamentalist who viewed the world around him as the preordained battleground between God and Satan.

Brown never actually joined William Lloyd Garrison's Boston-based pacifist and deeply religious abolitionist crusade and the National Anti-Slavery Society founded in 1833—he had early sensed the limitations of seeking to defeat the devil simply "by pricking the slave holders' consciences" and overcoming evil by moral force alone. But he subscribed to Garrison's *Liberator,* and he was profoundly shocked by the murder in 1837 of the antislavery journalist and printer Elijah Lovejoy. Lovejoy had been lynched by a proslavery mob that had crossed the Mississippi from St. Louis into the small Illinois town of Alton, where his press was located. Both Brown and his father attended a memorial prayer service in Hudson, where they listened to a declaration of war by the abolitionist speaker: "The crisis has come. The question now before the American citizens is no longer alone, 'Can the slaves be made free?' but 'Are we free, or are we slaves under Southern mob law?' " The possibility of a war between the states had become a viable option. Garrison's nonviolent means no longer sufficed, and it was reported that Brown took a public oath saying, "Here, before God, in the presence of these witnesses, from this time, I consecrate my life to the destruction of slavery." In doing so, he received the fervent blessings of his father, who closed the emotionally charged meeting with a passionate and tear-stained prayer.[14]

The deity John Brown worshiped was a God of iron and wrath, who never hesitated to punish the wicked with fire, brimstone, and the sword. There was not the slightest doubt in Brown's mind that his country was rushing insanely toward perdition and deserved whatever punishment the Lord might inflict: "Should God send famine, pestilence and war upon this guilty, hypocritical nation to destroy it," he wrote in January of 1855, "we need not be surprised. Never before did a people so mock and despise Him.

There seems to be no sign of repentance amongst us."[15] In that spirit, Brown knew that the horrors and human degradation which followed in the wake of slavery could only be destroyed by violence that was equal to the violence slavery itself did to God's law and man's dignity. On that point he was adamant, and John Junior reported that his father told his children in 1839 he was determined "to make war on slavery—not such war as Mr. Garrison informs us . . . but war by force and arms," and he "asked who of us were willing to make common cause with him in doing all in our power to 'break the jaws of the wicked and pluck the spoil out of his teeth.' "[16] Since his sons in 1839 ranged in age from three to eighteen, the question was largely rhetorical. In 1855, however, they were strapping young men already committed to the war against slavery.

To tender abolitionist senses, the stench of slavery during the 1850s seemed to be on the increase. The Fugitive Slave Act—part of the political bargain in 1850 to let California into the Union as a free state—compelled Northerners to assist federal agents in hunting down runaway slaves. Emerson called the act a "detestable law," which he refused to obey, and he wrote in his journal: "Slavery, we eat it, we drink it, we breathe it. . . . We are all poisoned with it."[17] Worse, in February of 1854 the Missouri Compromise, which was regarded by all antislavery supporters as the sacred bulwark, containing all future slave expansion south of 36°30′ north latitude was swept away by the principle of popular sovereignty when Congress passed the Kansas-Nebraska Act, allowing the inhabitants of the vast western territory to decide for themselves whether they would go slave or free. In outrage the abolitionists branded the decision a Southern plot and evidence that the nation's government had collapsed before the "audacious villainy of the slave power." In New York City the cry went up: "This crime shall not be consummated; . . . despite corruption, bribery and treachery, Nebraska, the heart of our continent, shall forever continue free."[18]

The Kansas-Nebraska Act with its principle of popular sovereignty openly invited an armed and bloody free-for-all, a mini–civil war where each side could display its ardor in a conflict in which both North and South claimed God as an ally. Slave states and free states immediately marshaled their propaganda campaigns and sent men and guns to defend the territory from the "malignant spirits" and fiends who sought to defeat the moral right. Senator William Seward of New York inaugurated the contest with splendid political rhetoric: "Come on, then, gentlemen of the slave states; since there is no escaping your challenge, I accept it in behalf of the cause of freedom. We will engage in competition for the virgin soil of Kansas, and God give the victory to the side that is stronger in numbers as it is in right."[19]

Emigrant Aid Societies sprang up throughout the North and the East; the black abolitionist Frederick Douglass appealed for "companies of emigrants from the free states . . . to possess the godly land"; and by the summer of 1855 some twelve hundred free-soil settlers had migrated to Kansas, ready to build "a piece of New England set down in the prairies," and pit Yankee virtues against "the blighting mildew of slavery." In response, armed border bands from Missouri poured into Kansas to support Missouri farmers already settled in the area. Senator David Atchison of Missouri announced that Kansas must become the slave gateway to the Pacific and urged the new emigrants and pro-slave settlers to defend their property with "bayonet and with blood," and if necessary "kill every God-damned abolitionist in the district."[20]

During the summer of 1854 the four oldest of the Brown boys came down with acute cases of "Kansas fever," caused in part by the frontier dream of starting over with virgin land, and in part by missionary zeal to "defeat Satan and his legions." With their father's fervent blessings, they decided to sell their farms, herd their stock west, and establish their claims in culture-torn and "bleeding Kansas." By May of the following year they and the free-soil advocates were in deep trouble. Bands of Missourians, sometimes several thousand strong, were crossing the border, intimidating the free-soil settlers, packing the ballot boxes and voting in a territorial legislature that could be depended upon to safeguard slave property and bring Kansas into the Union as a slave state. In desperation John Brown Jr. wrote to his father, and this was the letter the parent received on his first day at North Elba.

John reported that the brothers, now joined by Owen, had made five separate claims of rich prairie land, stretching in every direction "in vast, gently rounded waves as though the ocean once were here." All but Jason and his wife were well pleased, having never before encountered land so ripe in potential for "health, wealth and usefulness." "I know of no country where a poor man endowed with a share of commonsense and with health can get a start so easy." Then John added the crucial proviso: "if we can succeed in making this a free state." Thousands, he said, of "the meanest and most desperate men, armed to the teeth with revolvers, bowie knives, rifles and cannons" and "under pay from slave holders," were terrorizing the land. "Every slave holding state from Virginia to Texas is furnishing men and money to fasten slavery upon this glorious land by means no matter how foul." The situation could only be retrieved if "the anti-slavery portion of the inhabitants should immediately, thoroughly arm and organize themselves in military companies." Then came the punch lines: "Some persons must begin and lead off in the matter"; the five brothers were "thoroughly determined to fight," for " 'it is no longer a question of Negro slavery, but it is the enslavement of ourselves' "; what they needed from their father were arms: "We need them more than we do bread."[21]

Those words transformed John Brown and rewrote his history. Suddenly, inexplicably, the burdens, the failures, the depressions, the preoccupation with business that for the past fifteen years had blinded him to his true calling, all evaporated. He knew himself to be the Lord's instrument. Before that sudden revelation he had felt "a steady, strong desire to die"; now he saw himself as a " 'reaper' in the great harvest" and was ready not only to live but also to enjoy life.[22] He had things to do, and he resolved at that instant to join his children at Brown's Station, Kansas, located thirty miles south of Lawrence and twelve miles west of Osawatomie, near Pottawatomie Creek. He arrived on October 7, 1855, with only sixty cents in his pocket but with a wagonload of armaments.[23]

The arctic cold of the winter of 1855–56 kept the extremists on both sides huddled close to their fires. As spring broke out in Kansas, so did civil war. Both sides armed, the East sending in a steady stream of free-soilers, the supporters of slavery determined "to tar and feather, drown, lynch and hang every white-livered abolitionist who dares to pollute our soil."[24] Panic, hysteria, hatred, and violence took their predictable course. Border ruffians and proslave rifle companies, incited by Senator Atchison's inflammatory words—"If any man or woman stand in your way, blow them to hell with a chunk of cold lead"[25]—attacked the Free-state Hotel in Lawrence on the grounds that it was being used as an abolitionist arsenal. The building was cannonaded and torched, and by the time the rampage was over, the headquarters of two free-soil newspapers had been destroyed, the town pillaged, and its taverns drunk dry.

When the frantic call went out to save Lawrence, local free-soil vigilante groups, including the Pottawatomie Rifles, to which the Brown clan belonged, marched on Lawrence only to discover that they had arrived too late; the marauders had left and federal troops were keeping the peace throughout the region with orders to send the armed companies of both sides back from whence they came. Frustrated and disheartened, the Pottawatomie Rifles trudged back home. Only John Brown thought that God and man required vengeance for such an atrocity. "Something," he said, "is going to be done now. We must show by actual work that there are two sides to this thing and that they cannot go on with impunity."[26]

What occurred was the cold, calculated retaliatory murder of five proslavery settlers (not one of whom owned a slave) who lived down the road from Brown's Station. On the night of May 24, 1856, Alan Wilkinson, William Sherman, and James Doyle and his two sons were called out of their beds in the dark of the night by old man Brown, and hacked to pieces by three of his boys (Frederick, Salmon, and Owen), his son-in-law Henry Thompson, and two others of the Pottawatomie Rifles. The raid was a prolonged and grisly action which took all Saturday night and into the early hours of the Sabbath to complete. Brown supplied the granite will to do murder; but when his son Jason asked him point-blank whether he had had "a hand in the killing," he categorically answered, "I did not." He lied, but technically he spoke the truth: others wielded the swords that lopped off one young Doyle's arm and fingers, impaled the father, smashed the jaw of the other son, cut Wilkinson's throat, and split open Sherman's skull until the brains ran out. Brown had hammered on the cabin doors and ordered the victims out into the night to their deaths, but his single contribution to the actual slaughter was to shoot the dead body of the elder Doyle in the forehead, an act of incredible redundancy. In the literal sense he was not the instrument of vengeance, but he did not deny he "stood by and saw it" and approved what happened. "God is my judge," he told Jason. "We were justified under the circumstances."[27]

Neither the federal government nor the South thought that Brown was justified, and each did its best to capture him, but the story of the old man in Kansas soon became an epic bordering on the miraculous. Little wonder Brown thought God had reserved him for some future and greater deed in behalf of His ultimate purpose. "We feel assured," he wrote his wife and children back in North Elba, "that He who sees not as men see does not lay the guilt of innocent blood to our charge."[28] Proslavery forces bent on lynching never caught up with him; he constantly avoided federal troops and never stood trial for murder; and free-soil partisans, despite their horror at the massacre and fear that their own homes and families were now at risk, did not turn him in. Most extraordinary of all, the national press failed to dramatize the murders or associate Brown's name with them.

John Brown escaped the consequences of his actions, but his two eldest sons suffered horribly. John Junior went into hiding, only to be discovered by a company of Missourians, turned over to federal troops, forced to walk the eight miles to Osawatomie with his arms pinioned and his hands tied behind his back, and then beaten senseless. Jason Brown was caught by another band of Southerners, almost shot on sight, and nearly lynched by an irate mob. Eventually both brothers, along with other prisoners accused of treason, were chained together and "like a gang of slaves" driven on foot the sixty-five miles to Tecumseh (just east of Topeka), "dragging their chains after them."[29] Once Jason was interrogated by federal officials, the charge of treason was dropped and he was released, but John Junior remained in jail for another three months.

While the sons were being dragged off in chains, accused of treason, the father became one of the heroes of the Kansas freedom fighters. Proslavery forces and federal troops could never get their hands on him and his men, but free-soil volunteers had no trouble joining the group, and other free-state guerrilla captains were in constant touch with the old man. On June 2, he won a splendid victory over eighty militiamen at Black Jack Spring, taking twenty-nine prisoners and a mountain of provisions; and three months later, against all odds, he survived the hopelessly unequal Battle of Osawatomie, when his thirty newly organized "Kansas regulars" sought unsuccessfully to prevent a 250-strong contingent of Missouri troopers from burning the town to the ground. Captain Brown escaped, only slightly wounded from a six-gun cannonade, but his son Frederick was not so fortunate. He was one of the first fatalities, deliberately shot because he was recognized for what he was— a member of the notorious Brown clan. Even in defeat, Brown was proud to be known as "Osawatomie Brown," and as he stood and watched the town go up in flames, he turned to Jason and swore, "I will die fighting for this cause. There will be no more peace in this land until slavery is done for. I will give them something else to do than to extend slave territory. I will carry the war into Africa."[30] John Brown had declared war on the South and had determined to take that conflict into the very heartland of Satan's domain.

No one knows exactly when Osawatomie Brown determined that stemming the expansion of slavery into Kansas was not enough, that abolitionists would have to go on the offensive. Certainly by late September, when he decided to leave Kansas where public opinion was steadily turning against lawlessness, some form of plan for a direct attack on the South and the citadel of slavery had taken shape in his mind. The Brown clan left Kansas in stages, and it was not until January 4, 1857, that its patriarch reached Boston. He arrived with a carefully edited version of the events of Bleeding Kansas that excluded all mention of the Pottawatomie massacre, and he carried with him the chains that had fettered his freeborn sons to a chain gang guarded by federal troops. Osawatomie Brown was already a national celebrity; Northerners had read his highly colored account of his actions at Black Jack Spring in the *New York Tribune;* and they knew all about his heroism while defending Osawatomie. His mission now was to persuade the intellectual and financial elite of the East to open their souls and pocketbooks to the cause of freedom and God's service. War, especially holy war, required money as well as moral outrage, and he sought to generate both through the magnetism of his personality and his equally magnificent flair for public relations.

He would reveal what he had sensed ever since June of 1855, that "God had created him to be the deliverer of the slaves as Moses had delivered the children of Israel,"[31] and he would preach the truth of the two pillars upon which he had built his faith and was willing to stake his life: the Declaration of Independence and the Golden Rule. "Better," he informed Ralph Waldo Emerson, "that a whole generation of men, women and children should pass away by a violent death than that a word of either should be violated in this country."[32]

His reception was electrifying. Emerson and Thoreau opened up their houses and spoke of him as "the rarest of heroes," "a pure idealist," "a true hero."[33] He spoke before a joint session of the Massachusetts legislature, demanding that the state appropriate a hundred thousand dollars to make Kansas free. He approached first the Massachusetts and then the National Kansas Committee to appoint him their official agent and assign him the funds and arms to organize the defense of Kansas on a massive scale; he was voted by the Massachusetts organization two hundred Sharp's rifles; and the national body gave him supplies for one hundred men and the promise of five thousand dollars (which was never fulfilled).

He traveled incessantly—Massachusetts, Connecticut, New York— spreading the gospel according to John Brown. The federal government and all its agencies, he proclaimed, were in the hands of slaveholders and had spent millions "to harass poor Free-State settlers in Kansas."[34] The territory had been "watered by the tears and blood" of his children. The terrible ordeal of his two eldest sons, who had been "most barbarously" dragged in chains by federal troops, and the cruel execution of Frederick proved that there was indeed a concerted plot to bleed Kansas of every freedom-loving settler and enslave the territory. Surely proslavery murderers deserved "to be hung" and their property confiscated. A crusade was needed to negate the forces of evil, and only the arms and money of the North could guarantee the soldiers of justice and freedom with success. The tide was running heavily in favor of Brown's vision of God's purpose when the chaplain of the Massachusetts legislature could write that he expected to "serve in Capt. John Brown's company in the next Kansas war," which he hoped was "inevitable and near at hand."[35]

Wherever the old man spoke, the force of his charismatic personality, his voice so "masculine, deep and metallic," drew men of all walks of life to him like iron to a magnet. Young romantic Franklin Sanborn, a Harvard graduate and Concord schoolteacher, thought him a second Oliver Cromwell, a blend of "the old soldier and the deacon." Fire-breathing Unitarian preacher Theodore Parker, who, like Brown, knew that "the Father is with me," relished his prophecy that Kansas would soon run red in the blood of civil war. Samuel Howe, peripatetic adventurer, freedom fighter in the Greek war of liberation against the Turks, and crusader against all brands of social injustice, compared him to Christ. The Reverend Thomas Wentworth Higginson, rabble rouser, campaigner for temperance and women's rights, and an outspoken advocate of disobedience against the Fugitive Slave Law of 1850, proudly referred to "old Captain Brown" as a "belated Covenanter" "who swallows a Missourian whole, and says grace after the meat." George Stearns, wealthy self-made businessman and chairman of the Massachusetts Kansas Committee, was profoundly impressed by Brown's "sagacity, courage and stern integrity" and became one of his most faithful and consistent financial supporters. As for philanthropist Gerrit Smith, the wealthiest of all Brown's backers, he remembered the old man before he became famous in Kansas and highly esteemed his "unswerving bravery," "self-sacrificing benevolence," and "devotion to the cause of freedom."[36] These six—"the secret six" as they liked to refer to themselves—became John Brown's most dedicated allies, supplying him with the financial sinew to launch his attack on "Africa"—first a dress rehearsal in Missouri and then an all-out war against the leader of Satan's army, the sovereign Commonwealth of Virginia.

Northern abolitionists were lavish in their praise but disappointingly close with their pocketbooks. Their hesitation stemmed in part from the financial panic and depression of 1857–58—the East was short of capital and the National Kansas Committee nearly bankrupt—and in part from an underlying distrust as to exactly how and where Brown planned to spend their money and use their weapons. He refused absolutely to disclose his plans and abruptly told the National Kansas Committee in January of 1857, "I am no adventurer. You all know me. . . . I will not be interrogated; if you wish to give me anything I want you to give it freely. I have no other purpose but to serve the cause of liberty."[37] Brown elected to stand on his honor, and there were skeptics, as there are today, who suspected his campaign to raise arms and money for the defense of Kansas was from the start a cover for what he knew public opinion in the East was not ready to finance: an offensive military attack on the entire slave system throughout the South. Those doubts were warranted; as the months went by, Brown slowly began to disclose his real purpose to the secret six, playing them like a consummate fisherman, luring them in until they were fatally enmeshed.

Brown's plan was based on the argument that no amount of moral persuasion could induce the South to forgo slavery and that short of a civil war in which the North would crush the South, slaves had no hope of freedom except insurrection, in which "only slave self-help would be effective."[38] True, certain slaveholders might be murdered in such an uprising, but they had "no rights more than any other thief or pirate." They had "forfeited even the right to live." Slaves throughout Dixie were straining at their chains, their hearts filled with hatred for their white overlords. What was needed was a spark—or better, a series of sparks—to ignite the fire that would make slavery untenable. He proposed the creation of a small guerrilla band of twenty-five highly trained, principled, and dedicated men who would cross into Virginia at the town of Harpers Ferry and operate as an independent and mobile unit in the Allegheny Mountains, making excursions into the plantation lands to induce the slaves to join them. The more militant blacks would swell the ranks of the guerrilla combatants, and the more peaceful-minded would be escorted north into Pennsylvania and Ohio and then on to Canada via the Underground Railroad. Brown assured the secret six that such armed bands could survive for months in the ravines and crags of the Blue Ridge Mountains, avoiding state militia and federal troops, attacking or retreating, moving or hiding as they chose. "God had given the strength of the hills to freedom." The ultimate aim was to destabilize the entire slave structure, "to destroy the money-value of slave property . . . by rendering such property insecure." Landowners, he argued, were not going to invest in property "likely to take legs and walk off with itself." In time the campaign could be pushed further and further south as guerrilla bands began to penetrate into the Carolina mountains and the swampland of the Deep South.[39]

As proof of how serious he was and how feasible he thought his plan, Brown revealed to the secret six that he already had recruited a nucleus of "principled" men, mostly hardened in the crucible of Bleeding Kansas and all pledged to "stand by the work" and ready to follow him into the mountains of northwestern Virginia. At first the secret six were appalled by the sheer audacity of the proposal; then they became ecstatic. They recognized the risks and the high probability of violence as the South responded to the invasion and called upon a Southern-dominated federal government and President to protect slave property; but here was a way to show their faith in the Higher Law, a method of expressing moral outrage. Almost despite themselves they were convinced by Brown's calm assurance that "if God be for us, who can be against us," and they accepted his promise that the "experiment" was nothing more than running the Underground Railroad "on a somewhat extended scale." Even if, as young Sanborn admitted, the scheme was tainted with treason, they felt that with God as their support, "treason will not be treason much longer but patriotism."[40]

In their enthusiasm Brown's supporters opened their purses wide and urged him to implement his strategy immediately. Unfortunately, one of Captain Brown's men, a "Colonel" Hugh Forbes, after first trying to blackmail the secret six into giving him money to ensure his silence, divulged the conspiracy to the government in Washington. Forbes had originally been recruited because of his military experience, but he immediately began to quarrel with Brown over the leadership of the enterprise—he regarded his commander as hopelessly incompetent—and over the strategic concept of the plan. The slaves, he said, would not rebel, and even if they did, the insurrection would get out of control, the slaves would panic and the rebellion be suppressed.[41] Predictably, Brown dismissed him from the inner circle of his advisers. The six were badly divided as to what to do; Stearns and Smith wanted to postpone the operation, fearful of a federal investigation and arrest; Higginson urged the group to action despite Forbes's treachery. In the end they compromised. Brown was promised at least two thousand dollars for the Virginia enterprise if he conducted a diversionary operation in Kansas, thereby undermining Forbes's credibility when he claimed that Kansas money and arms were being used against Virginia. To safeguard themselves further, Captain Brown was told not to keep the six informed of "his plans in detail, nor burden them with knowledge that would be to them both needless and inconvenient."[42]

In early June, Brown headed west once again, and by the end of the month he was back in Kansas determined to pick up where he had left off, anxious to organize an armed posse and carry the war into enemy territory. He ignored talk of peace and getting on with business-as-usual. He dismissed as inconsequential the fact that Kansas voters by a margin of 11,300 to 1,788 had defeated the proslavery constitution, thereby ensuring the territory's eventual entrance into the union as a free state. Instead, he told the *New York Tribune*'s correspondent, William Phillips, "The war is not over. It is a treacherous lull before the storm. We are on the eve of the greatest war in history, and I fear slavery will triumph." He had drawn his sword and would "never sheathe it until this war is over."[43] True to his word, he organized just before Christmas of 1858 a two-pronged excursion into Missouri, during which two slave homesteads were burned, one of the owners shot dead, eleven slaves "kidnapped" and taken back to Kansas and freedom, and a number of wagons, horses, mules, and saddles "liberated." Brown, as he boasted on his return, had "carried the war into Africa." The raid, as Brown probably wished, nearly restarted the civil war in Kansas. The governor of Missouri put a $3,000 bounty price tag on his head, and President Buchanan added another $250 for his capture; the Missouri legislature threatened invasion; the proslavery press went out of its mind; and Kansans found themselves deeply divided: Brown "could strike a blow and leave," but retaliation would fall on those who had homes and families in Kansas.[44]

Back East, Gerrit Smith was delighted at the news from Kansas—"Our dear Brown is . . . pursuing the policy which he intended to pursue elsewhere"—but in Kansas the old man suddenly found that he had scarcely a friend.[45] The era of armed, marauding gangs was over; and with sadness and dignity he announced that "it was no pleasure to him, an old man, to be living in the saddle. . . . If the Free-State men of Kansas felt that they no longer needed him, he would be glad to go." He would, he added, "draw the scene of the excitement to some other part of the country."[46] But before he left Kansas, he did what he did best: justify his actions. In a letter to the *New York Tribune,* he set forth "Old Brown's Parallels," comparing the forcible roundup of eleven free-staters the year before—who were shot "without trial or opportunity to speak" and left for dead (five died) by proslavery thugs whom no government agency, federal or territorial, lifted a finger "to ferret and punish"—to the present restoration of eleven Missouri slaves "to their natural and inalienable rights," an act that stirred up "all Hell." It was a masterful piece of editing. Brown transformed the unnecessary murder of a slave owner into an act of self-defense, since the victim had "fought against the liberation." He made it appear that his men had returned most of the loot (which was untrue), and spuriously compared two episodes that had nothing in common except the number eleven.[47]

As usual, Brown's luck held to divine form. Miraculously, he transported himself, his men, all of the confiscated loot, and his eleven freed slaves out of Kansas and succeeded in avoiding all efforts to catch him. As he said, "The Lord has marked out a path for me, and I intend to follow it."[48] By the time he reached Ohio he felt confident enough to quip that if President Buchanan could place a price of $250 on his head, he could put a price of $2.50 on the President's.[49]

The path the Lord had marked out for John Brown led straight back to Boston and the secret six; and true to their orders not to "burden them with knowledge," he failed to mention that his grand experiment in purging the nation of slavery had fundamentally changed. Whether the old man had a hidden agenda from the moment he encountered the secret six two years before is difficult to say. Certainly by the time he arrived in Boston in May 1859, his whole conception of the Virginia invasion had changed. No longer did he see Harpers Ferry as the jump-off point for a prolonged guerrilla campaign on the part of a tiny band of idealistic desperados operating in the mountain fastness of the Alleghenies, bent on making slavery economically unfeasible. He now planned to occupy the town, seize its federal armory and rifle works, round up hostages, and rally blacks to the cause of freedom in the expectation that such actions would either immediately set in motion an irresistible tidal wave of slave insurrections throughout the South or act as the violent psychological shock that would stampede the North and the South into war. The specter of slave rebellion instigated by the North would induce the South to secede; then the North could "whip the South back into the Union without slavery." Certainly Salmon Brown thought this was his father's purpose in selecting Harpers Ferry as the focus of his attack on the entire structure of Southern slavery.[50] The underlying principle, never fully voiced but always unspoken at the back of his mind, was that violence would produce an apocalyptic transformation of North and South so that each side could fulfill the roles that God had ordained: Brown's last written words were, "The crimes of this guilty land will never be purged away but with blood."[51]

A half-century later the Frenchman Georges Sorel would transform what for Brown was a tenet of Old Testament conviction into a secular philosophy of violence which twentieth-century terrorists would later apply with a vengeance. Calculated atrocities could incite an enemy to forgo the protection of peaceful negotiation and indulge in open war that in the end would result in its destruction; at the same time it would restore to the forces of revolution, long stupefied by a policy of concession and compromise, the will to fight.[52] Brown's version of the Sorelian doctrine was considerably more biblical in tone. "God," he wrote to Sanborn in February 1858, "has honored but comparatively a very small part of mankind with any possible chance for such mighty and soul-satisfying rewards. . . . I expect nothing but to 'endure hardness'; but I expect to effect a mighty conquest, even though it be like the last victory of Samson."[53] Even though the pillars of the temple of the Antichrist might come tumbling down and crush him in the process, he knew that in the destruction Satan and his institution of slavery would be demolished.

Still not fully aware of Captain Brown's true purpose, the secret six—except for Parker, who was in Italy dying of consumption, and Howe, who didn't want to know what was being planned—greeted Brown enthusiastically on his return from Kansas.[54] They were particularly pleased with his invasion of Missouri. Slave owners on the border had panicked and sent their slaves off to Texas and Arkansas for safekeeping, and this seemed to be proof that Brown's design to make slavery economically unfeasible was working. They now gave him two thousand dollars more to "raise the mill" in Virginia. With the money, Brown set off to purchase 950 pikes as weapons for liberated slaves; to collect the arms the Massachusetts Kansas Committee had originally given him for the defense of the territory and which he had squirreled away for this occasion; to persuade his sons to join him in this greatest of all ventures; and to organize and recruit his troops. By early June of 1859, with two of his sons—Watson Brown arrived later—he set up his headquarters seven miles from Harpers Ferry in a rented farmhouse belonging to the widow of Dr. Booth Kennedy.

Twenty-one volunteers joined him at the Kennedy farm. Three were his sons; seven were hardened campaigners from Kansas; two, the brothers Edwin and Barclay Coppoc, were Quakers; one was a Canadian; another was a one-eyed last-minute recruit who arrived with six hundred dollars in gold in his pocket; two were Brown's neighbors in North Elba, New York; and five were blacks of varying complexions. Of the leaders, John Henry Kagi, who "had more the appearance of a divinity student than a warrior," was a deeply principled ex-schoolteacher and newspaper correspondent; John Cook, an impulsive young man of twenty-nine, had attended Yale University and had clerked for a New York law firm; and Aaron Stevens stood six-foot-two-inches tall, a "young Greek gladiator" with a glorious voice, who had run away from home at sixteen, enlisted in the United States cavalry, and eventually become an abolitionist gang captain in Kansas. Only two of the group were over twenty-nine—Owen Brown was thirty-five, and Dangerfield Newby, born a slave, was forty-four—and their average age was twenty-five. John Brown had created for himself a contingent of young idealists—only one of their number, Albert Hazlett, could be called a mercenary—who were filled with the irrational optimism of youth. William Leeman, only twenty, caught the tone when he wrote his mother, "I am in a Southern slave state and before I leave it, it will be a free state, and so will every other one in the South."[55] Ten of these young men would die in battle; six others would be executed by the state of Virginia; and only five would escape.

"Madness" is a word steeped in ambiguity. It was madness for an army of twenty-two men to think that it could overthrow the sovereign Commonwealth of Virginia. It was equal madness to follow a crazed old man on a hare-brained expedition to seize and hold a triangular-shaped town surrounded by the Potomac on one side and the Shenandoah on the other and populated by 1,251 free blacks, 88 slaves, and 1,212 skilled white workers from the North employed by the federal government.[56] Frederick Douglass warned Brown that he was "going into a steel-trap and once in he would never get out alive."[57] But what appears in retrospect to be suicidal seemed a thrilling adventure at the time. Edwin Coppoc and the youthful Kansas campaigner Charles Tidd had their doubts; even Owen Brown questioned his father's wisdom. But in the end they followed him to Harpers Ferry. As Coppoc said in answer to his captors' query why had he followed, he answered, "Ah, gentlemen, you don't know Captain Brown. When he wants a man to do a thing, a man does it."[58]

As for the captain, he had no second thoughts whatsoever. He was on a divine mission, and, like Nietzsche, he believed that "one good, believing, strong-minded man is worth a hundred, nay, twenty thousand men without character."[59] It made no difference that Frederick Douglass had told him only two months before he launched the attack on Harpers Ferry that the basic concept of his plan was flawed: no slave would hear his trumpet call to arms and freedom. Practical men, like Abraham Lincoln, realized that "the indispensable concert of action cannot be attained. The slaves have no means of rapid communication; nor can incendiary freemen, black or white, supply it."[60] It made even less difference that Brown had failed to send out messengers of good tidings to alert the slaves or that no one had reconnoitered the area for an escape route. Demographically, he had picked the worst possible spot to start his avalanche of slave insurrections, because the area around Harpers Ferry contained only 18,048 slaves in a total white population of 125,449, and the vast majority were relatively well-off household servants. These were all trifling matters, because, as he told Henry Thoreau, "the reason why such greatly superior numbers quailed before him was . . . because they lacked a cause."[61] God would be his buckle and his sword; "He shall direct thy path" and turn "the most il-logical movements into a grand success."[62] So, on the evening of Sunday, October 16, with a "fervent prayer to God" and 200 Sharp's rifles, 200 re-volvers (with the wrong size ammunition) 15 sabers, 52 bayonets, and 950 pikes, a small cannon, and ten kegs of gunpowder, twenty-two men set off to do war on slavery and the Commonwealth of Virginia.

At first all went as scheduled. The arms and ammunition were stored at a nearby schoolhouse, with three men left on guard, waiting to greet and arm the battalions of slaves that were expected to flock to Brown's crusade. The bridges over the rivers were seized; the United States armory and arse-nal with over a million dollars' worth of arms and munitions were overrun; the Hall's Rifle Works were occupied; the 1:15 a.m. Baltimore and Ohio train from Cincinnati was stopped; and by dawn forty freed slaves and hostages, including Colonel Lewis W. Washington, the first President's great-grandnephew, were rounded up and ensconced in the armory. Brown pictured himself as a heroic liberator: he had come, he told one of the prisoners, "to free the Negroes of Virginia" and "by twelve o'clock would have fifteen hundred men with him, ready armed."[63] The trumpet call had been sounded, the blow had been struck; all he had to do now, as the word of his triumph spread, was to sit and wait for the great upsurge of liberated black humanity to take place. He was so confident it would occur that he had brought with him to the Kennedy farm a constitutional manifesto, composed the year before, to greet the slaves and organize them into a con-structive military and political nation.

The word indeed spread and a vast upsurge took place, but not as the captain predicted. The event that the South feared most had occurred:

"Negro Insurrection . . . Fire and Rapine on the Virginia Border!"[64] All over northwest Virginia the local militia responded with extraordinary speed and streamed into Harpers Ferry to do battle with slave rebellion. By noon Brown's men, badly scattered and tied down in small groups defending their strategic positions and finding it increasingly difficult to communicate, were engulfed in a full-scale battle. And not a single slave appeared, either at Harpers Ferry or at the schoolhouse. John Henry Kagi begged his commander to retreat across the Shenandoah to the safety of the Blue Ridge Mountains, using their hostages as shields. But the old man seemed paralyzed; he did nothing, waiting for God to act and the slaves to pour in. By evening, the bridges across the Potomac and Shenandoah had fallen; escape was now impossible and defeat certain. Long before Colonel Robert E. Lee and Lieutenant J. E. B. (Jeb) Stuart arrived with ninety United States Marines to demand Brown's surrender and order the final charge against the engine house of the armory, the steel trap had sprung.

Surrender was unthinkable. Brown was a man of "iron," and as George Gill said, he "had neither sympathy [n]or feeling for the timid and weak of will."[65] To his son Oliver, who lay on the floor of the engine house dying in agony and begging his father to put him out of his pain, his only reply was, "Be quiet, son. If you must die, die like a man."[66] Even if Brown's God seemed to have deserted him, as He so often appeared to do, the captain would make no concessions to human frailty: he would fight on for the right until the absolute end.

Oddly enough, in a backhanded sort of way, John Brown's deity did not forsake him, and his incredible luck continued to hold. When Jeb Stuart's demand to surrender was ignored, Colonel Lee gave the order to storm the engine house. Lieutenant Israel Green was the first to reach Brown. As he raised his saber to dispatch the captain once and for all, a miracle occurred. Instead of piercing the old warrior's body, the sword hit his belt buckle and bent double. Green had accidentally gone into battle with his thin dress sword, and the lieutenant had to try to finish his opponent off by clubbing him senseless with the hilt.[67] So John Brown miraculously lived to become a martyr—the single successful role of his entire life.

Twenty-four men died as a consequence of the Harpers Ferry debacle. Seventeen fell in battle—two "liberated" slaves; a slave-owning country gentleman who had come into town to see what had happened to his friend Colonel Washington; a marine; three townsmen (including Hayward Shepard, a highly respected free black, shot, it was said, by Oliver Brown for refusing to join the insurrection),[68] and ten of Brown's army of liberation, including two of his sons. Six other raiders, plus their captain, were hanged by the state of Virginia. By any standard the venture was a fiasco of epic proportions. Yet less than a month after the raid Brown was writing his wife that "the sacrifices you and I have been called to make in behalf of the *cause we love,* the *cause of God* and of *humanity,* do not seem to me as at all too great. I have been *whipped* as the saying is; but am sure I can recover all the lost capital occasioned by that disaster by only hanging a few moments by the neck; and I feel quite determined to make the utmost possible out of a defeat."[69] Brown commenced making the "utmost possible out of a defeat" within hours of his capture; and during the six weeks left him, he transformed himself from a disowned criminal and "mad man," dismissed at first by the Northern press as an insane crank, into not merely a martyr but a new kind of martyr. As he insisted, his cause was not "the cause of God" alone, it was also "the cause of humanity."

Even though John Brown did not die to guarantee himself a place in paradise—he was far too good a Calvinist to think that he necessarily merited a seat among God's elect—the religious motive was immensely strong. Almost every letter he wrote was steeped in the imagery of the Old Testament; he knew himself to be a holy soldier in a cause dear to the Lord. For Brown, the cause of God and man was indistinguishable, the two dissolving into a single ideological truth. The extermination of slavery was not simply a political and moral necessity; it was also a divine injunction. His deity was an avid social reformer who viewed the liberation of humanity from political bondage to be part of the larger and never-ending struggle against the hordes of hell. Brown was the first martyr to die for a concept that concerned man's body, his political and social well-being, as well as his soul's welfare. The early Christian martyrs had said nothing about slavery as a political, social, and economic condition; they spoke only about the freedom and equality of the soul as it ascended to heaven.[70]

Implicit, of course, in all martyrdoms is the taint of treason. Becket, More, and Charles I were all branded as traitors; Jesus, Socrates, and the Protestant martyrs died as political criminals, dangerous to the state's security. But only with John Brown does treason take center stage. He was absolutely frank about what he was doing. When a badly frightened Dauphin Thompson, who had come to Harpers Ferry "only to free the slaves," asked him "whether this constituted treason," the old man answered, "Yes, this is treason."

In committing overt treason—Virginia tried him for murder, treason, robbery, and insurrection—John Brown introduced a new element into martyrdom. He was a political and revolutionary martyr and the aggressor. He sought not to defend an ideal but to overthrow society. Socrates was an intellectual maverick but not a revolutionary; he upheld the laws of Athens. The Maccabees sought not to reconstitute society but to defend the old ways; the Seleucid empire was the revolutionary offender. The early Christian martyrs constantly proclaimed their loyalty to the Roman Empire; all they desired, they said, was to worship in peace. Becket fought to defend the church, not to destroy the state. Thomas More fell victim to a new structuring of society and a changed view of the relationship of the individual to the whole—the revolutionary concept of the nation-state. The Protestant martyrs and Charles I were both put on the defensive against the power of the government of the day.

Brown was different: he was a political as well as a spiritual revolutionary, and in the eyes of the state he was a felon and a traitor. He struck at the moral sinews of society, but, unlike his predecessors in martyrdom, he also endangered property. That is why at first everyone in the North, except Thomas Higginson, disowned him after Harpers Ferry. The destruction of slave property might be condoned in terms of a higher law, but no law, not even God's law, could excuse the seizure of government property—its armory and its arsenal. That constituted an act of brigandage. Yet that action was nothing more than the logical extension of Brown's oft-stated argument about a government controlled by slave interests—slave owners were pirates who had no rights. Society might brand him a murderer, but Brown knew that his kind of mayhem was justified in the eyes of the Lord. The punishment of unrepentant slaveholders and the destruction of all they possessed, more than the relief of suffering for the slaves, propelled him to action; he was, after all, the earthly instrument of Jehovah, the God of wrath and vengeance.

Brown's ultimate purpose in going to Harpers Ferry, the one he voiced only to his God, remains unfathomable. On the face of it, he came to Virginia as a warrior, invader, liberator, terrorist, not as a martyr. His model was Samson: he was willing to risk, even sacrifice, his life to bring down the pillars of slavery; his death would simply be the price of success. But why did he allow himself to be trapped?

Why did he ignore Kagi's frantic pleas to escape while he could? Why did he stand firm in the engine house with a puzzled expression on his face, waiting for a sign that never came? Why did he oppose all efforts of his Northern friends to organize his escape from prison?[71] Throughout his life Brown had sensed that all along God had been preserving him for some special occasion. "For many years," he wrote his kinsman Dr. Heman Humphrey from jail, "I have felt a strong impression that God had given me powers and faculties, unworthy as I was, that He intended to use. . . ." At first, he had thought he was being saved to deliver the slaves out of bondage; now, he realized that the Lord had granted him "many times deliverances" from death, "so miraculous that I can scarce realize their truth," for the sole purpose of dying on a Virginia gallows. "He intends to use me in a different way. . . . I humbly trust that He will not forsake me 'till I have showed His favor to this generation and His strength to everyone that is to come' "[72]

When Brown revived after his pummeling by Lieutenant Green, he began the metamorphosis from the soldier into the martyr. That transformation was not his work alone; he had the indispensable cooperation of the Commonwealth of Virginia, which over and over again supplied him with the necessary public stage on which to play his role and focused the spotlight on his spectacular performance. "No theatrical manager," noted Henry Thoreau, "could have arranged things so wisely to give effect to his behavior and words."[73] And in the North the abolitionists were busily creating the emotional atmosphere that would blind men's eyes to the reality of the old man's new clothes—he was dressed solely in the fervent imaginative power of political need and the potency of an ideological cause. Twenty-three years before, William Channing had written, "One kidnapped, murdered Abolitionist would do more for the violent destruction of slavery than a thousand [Abolitionist] societies."[74] In that spirit Henry Ward Beecher advised: "Let no man pray that Brown be spared! Let Virginia make him a martyr. Now, he has only blundered. His soul was noble; his work miserable. But a cord and a gibbet would redeem all that, and round up Brown's failure with a heroic success." When Brown read these words in the *New York Herald,* he wrote beside the passage the single word "good."[75] But it was Brown himself who made the metamorphosis possible. The very qualities that had caused him to fail as a businessman and as a warrior—his absolute, unyielding faith in his own righteousness and his highly developed powers of self-justification and self-deception—now made him a magnificent martyr. On the afternoon of October 19 he proved his worth and found his true calling, thereby redeeming a lifetime of obstinate blunders and deadly failures.

Ninety United States Marines and the militia of seven neighboring communities, including three companies from Frederick, Maryland, and five more from Baltimore, were brought to Harpers Ferry to crush an armed rebellion that turned out to number twenty-two men. Understandably, Brown's captors were anxious to interrogate this extraordinary commander who almost singlehandedly had declared war on Virginia and the entire South. They discovered in Brown a shrewd, composed, courteous, and highly articulate public-relations expert who instantly recognized that here was his chance to speak out to the entire nation, because among his interviewers and the spectators were not only Governor Henry Wise and Senator James Mason of Virginia but also, and far more important, reporters from the *New York Herald* and the *Baltimore American.* John Brown was fully aware of the power of the press and intended to use it. He lay on a "shake-down" on the floor and for three hours fielded questions. The picture of himself, his motives and actions, painted in heroic and tragic colors for the benefit of public consumption, bore little relationship to reality but made splendid copy, which was read throughout the land. John Brown the ideal-ist, the man who could change sordid reality into a magnificent myth and make himself and much of the world believe that he was giving his life to that fiction, was in the making.

Query—Can you tell us who furnished money for your expedition?

Answer—I furnished most of it myself; I cannot implicate others. [Brown's nobility in remaining silent to protect his friends scarcely corresponds with his incredible carelessness in leaving behind at the Kennedy farm much of his correspondence with the secret six for his captors to find.] It is by my own folly that I have been taken. I could easily have saved my-self from it, had I exercised my own better judgment rather than yielded to my feelings.

Query—You mean if you had escaped immediately?

Answer—No. I had the means to make myself secure without any escape; but I allowed myself to be surrounded by a force by being too tardy. I should have gone away; but I had 30 odd prisoners, whose wives and daughters were in tears for their safety, and I felt for them. Besides, I wanted to allay the fears of those who believed we came here to burn and kill. . . .

Comment—But you killed some people passing along the streets quietly.

Answer—Well, sir, if there was anything of that kind done, it was without my knowledge. Your own citizens who were my prisoners will tell you that every possible means was taken to prevent it. [As at Pottawatomie, he was skirting the truth.]

Query—Mr. Brown, who sent you here?

Answer—No man sent me here; it was my own prompting and that of my Maker, or that of the Devil—which ever you please to ascribe to it. I ac-knowledge no master in human form.

. . . .

Query—What was your object in coming?

Answer—We came to free the slaves, and only that.

Query—How many men, in all, had you?

Answer—I came to Virginia with eighteen men only, besides myself. [Brown may have deliberately given a wrong number in the hope of safeguarding the men left back at the schoolhouse, who he hoped had escaped.]

Query—What in the world did you suppose you could do here in Virginia with that amount of men?

Answer—Young man, I do not wish to discuss that question here.

. . . .

Query—How do you justify your acts?

Answer—I think, my friend, you are guilty of a great wrong against God and humanity—I say it without wishing to be offensive—and it would be perfectly right for any one to interfere with you so far as to free those you willfully and wickedly hold in bondage. I do not say this insultingly. . . . I think I did right, and that others will do right who interfere with you at any time and at all times. . . .

. . . .

Query—Do you consider this a religious movement?

Answer—It is, in my opinion, the greatest service man can render to God.

Query—Do you consider yourself an instrument in the hands of providence?

Answer—I do.

Query—Upon what principle do you justify your acts?

Answer—Upon the Golden Rule. I pity the poor in bondage that have none to help them: that is why I am here; not to gratify any personal animosity, revenge, or vindictive spirit. It is my sympathy with the oppressed and the wronged, that are as good as you and as precious in the sight of the Lord.

. . . .

Query—Did you expect a general rising of the slaves in case of your success?

Answer—No, sir; nor did I wish it. I expected to gather them up from time to time and set them free. [He ignored all those rifles, revolvers, bayonets, and pikes that had been amassed to arm the slaves, not to mention his constitutional proclamation organizing the slaves of the South into a free political nation and his maps of seven Southern states with their most densely slave-populated regions and the location of their federal arsenals carefully marked.]

Query—Did you expect to hold your position here till then?

Answer—. . . I do not know that I ought to reveal my plans. . . . You overrate your strength in supposing I could have been taken if I had not allowed it. . . .

. . . .

Comment (by a reporter)—I do not wish to annoy you; but if you have anything further you would like to say, I will report it. . . .

Answer—. . . You may dispose of me very easily—I am nearly disposed of now; but this question is still to be settled—this Negro question I mean;

the end of that is not yet. These wounds were inflicted upon me—both sabre cuts on my head and bayonet stabs in different parts of my body—some minutes after I had ceased fighting and had consented to a surrender, for the benefit of others, not for my own. [This statement was vehemently denied by everyone.] I believe the Major [meaning Lieutenant Jeb Stuart] would not have been alive; I could have killed him just as easy as a mosquito when he came in, but I supposed he came in only to receive our surrender. There had been loud and long calls of "surrender" from us—as loud as men could yell—but in the confusion and excitement I suppose we were not heard. I do not think the Major, or anyone, meant to butcher us after we had surrendered. [Again, this was denied by the marines, who insisted they fired only after being fired upon. The prisoners agreed.]

. . . .

Query—Brown, suppose you had every nigger in the United States, what would you do with them?
Answer—Set them free.

. . . .

Comment—To set them free would sacrifice the life of every man in this community.
Answer—I do not think so.
Comment—I know it. I think you are fanatical.
Answer—And I think you are fanatical. "Whom the gods would destroy they first make mad," and you are mad.[76]

It was a brilliant performance. Defeated, wounded, and in pain, his life's work in shambles, and, as the *New York Herald* reported, "the gallows staring him full in the face," he emerged a humane and self-sacrificing hero, who, unresisting, had been mercilessly struck down by federal troops. Even the enemy was impressed, and Governor Wise announced, "He is the gamest man I ever saw."[77]

"Whom the gods would destroy they first make mad": the South in its frenzy played directly into Brown's hands. The *Mobile Register* shouted, "The ark of the covenant has been desecrated. For the first time the soil of the South has been invaded and its blood has been shed upon its own soil by armed abolitionists" invoking "our slaves to rebellion."[78] The cry for revenge spread throughout the South. "Hang these villainous wretches," cried the *Fredericksburg Herald*, "the wheel and the rack are not a whit too hard for them. . . . Hemp, do your duty!"[79] In such an atmosphere Southern states vied with one another for the honor of supplying the rope to hang him. There was no ear for the admonitions voiced on both sides of the

Mason-Dixon line that the South was responding exactly as Brown hoped. The proslavery *New York Journal of Commerce* advised Virginia that "to hang a fanatic is to make a martyr of him. . . . Better send these creatures to the penitentiary" and turn them into "miserable felons," because the martyr was "hydra-headed, and decapitation only quickens vitality and power of reproduction."[80] *Harper's Weekly* argued that as "the hanging of Brown would strengthen" so "the pardon of Brown would discredit the Northern Abolitionists," and the *New York Times* wrote, "We can tell the South that Brown on the scaffold will do more damage and involve them in far more peril than a hundred Browns at large in the Northern states."[81] The *Frankfort* (Kentucky) *Yeoman* agreed, and said that "if Old John Brown is executed, there will be thousands to dip their handkerchiefs in his blood, relics of the martyr will be paraded throughout the North, pilgrimages will be made to his grave and we shall not be surprised to hear of miracles wrought there as at the tomb of Thomas à Becket."[82]

Fortunately for Brown, no one listened to this excellent advice. "The miserable old traitor and murderer," wrote the *Richmond Whig,* "belongs to the gallows, and the gallows will have its own."[83] The only advice the South was willing to take was not to create a shrine to treason. Brown's scaffold was placed out in the middle of a field where there were no landmarks to identify it; the structure was immediately taken down and the timbers mixed with other lumber in a nearby lumberyard; and the hemp rope was burned. On one point the overwhelming majority was agreed: Brown and his colleagues should be tried "in double quick time," lest any of them die before justice could be rendered; Virginia and the South were "ready to face all the consequences of the execution."[84]

Only a plea of insanity could have saved the old man, and he firmly slammed the door on that escape route. When, during the course of his trial, his counsel tried to introduce evidence that he was mad, he rose from his portable cot and announced to the court, "I look upon it as a miserable artifice and pretext of those who ought to make a different course in regard to me . . . and I view it with contempt. . . . I am perfectly unconscious of insanity, and I reject, so far as I am capable, any attempt to interfere in my behalf on that score."[85] The presiding judge agreed, and no plea was ever made; both John Brown and the Commonwealth of Virginia infinitely preferred the gallows to an insane asylum.

The trial of the five raiders taken at Harpers Ferry (John Cook and Albert Hazlett were not taken into custody until later) was organized with extraordinary dispatch. Brown, John Copeland, Edwin Coppoc, Aaron Stevens, and Shields Green were captured on October 18, and the legal system commenced on October 25 in the form of a preliminary hearing before eight magistrates. The five men were held over for trial by the circuit court and the prisoners asked whether they had counsel. Brown immediately took advantage of the question, and, speaking to a courtroom packed with five hundred spectators and pressmen from every major newspaper in the country, he called out, "Virginians, I did not ask for any quarter at the time I was taken. I did not ask to have my life spared. . . . If you seek my blood, you can have it at any moment, without this mockery of a trial. I have no counsel. . . . There are mitigating circumstances that I would urge in our favor, if a fair trial is to be allowed us; but if we are to be forced with a mere form—a trial of execution—you might spare yourselves that trouble. I am ready for my fate. . . . I beg for no mockery of a trial—no insult."[86] The press listened avidly and reported every word of what was clearly the opening shot in a dramatic and politically loaded encounter.

Having been assigned counsel by the magistrates, the defendants appeared that same afternoon before a grand jury and the next morning were indicted. The prisoners chose to be tried separately, and Brown's jury was selected first. No plea for a change of venue was made; and his request that his trial be postponed because of his wounds was denied. During the week the prosecution and defense argued their cases. The state produced massive evidence that Brown had committed murder, inspired a slave rebellion, and perpetrated treason. The defense pointed out that Brown could scarcely be guilty of treason, since he owed no allegiance to the Commonwealth of Virginia. It insisted that since no slave had voluntarily joined the insurrection, his alleged incitement of slaves had hardly constituted a threat to Virginia, and that if there had been any insurrection, it took place on federal property, and therefore the defendant should be tried by the national government. Finally, the defense argued that Brown had acted humanely and generously to his prisoners, Colonel Washington testifying that "at no time did he threaten to massacre us or place us in front in case of assault."[87] To no one's surprise, nothing the defense could say was able to persuade the jury of John Brown's innocence, and it took only forty-five minutes to find him guilty. Formal sentencing, however, was delayed until November 2 so as not to prejudice the trial of Edwin Coppoc, which was still going on.

Those extra days were crucial, because they allowed Osawatomie Brown to compose one of the most remarkable courtroom speeches ever delivered, a message clearly designed for the Northern press. He started, like any effective debater, by establishing his motives, which, he maintained, were pure and above reproach. His only purpose had been "to free slaves. I intended certainly to have made a clean thing of that matter, as I did last winter, when I went into Missouri and there took slaves without the snapping of a gun on either side"—this was, of course, a boldfaced lie—

"moving them through the country, and finally leaving them in Canada. I designed to have done the same thing again on a larger scale. That was all I intended. I never intended murder, or treason, or the destruction of property, or to excite or incite slaves to rebellion, or to make insurrection."

Then in a brilliant change of pace he introduced the principle of equity. "Had I interfered . . . in behalf of the rich, the powerful, the intelligent, the so-called great . . . it would have been all right. Every man in this Court would have deemed it an act worthy of reward rather than punishment." Appeal to equity was only the start. He attained what the *Lawrence* (Kansas) *Republican* described as a "sublimity and solemn appeal"[88] when he called upon the deity to testify on his behalf. "I see a book kissed, which I suppose to be the Bible or at least the New Testament which teaches me . . . to remember them that are in bonds. . . . I endeavored to act up to that instruction. . . . I believe that to have interfered as I have done . . . in behalf of His despised poor, I did no wrong, but right. Now, if it is deemed necessary that I should forfeit my life for the furtherance of the ends of justice, and mingle my blood further with the blood of my children and with the blood of millions in this slave country whose rights are disregarded by wicked, cruel, and unjust enactments, I say, let it be done."[89] His conclusion was a graceful bow to Virginia justice: "Considering all the circumstances, it has been more generous than I expected."

The oration was Brown at his best and worst. What he said was delivered with overwhelming sincerity and conviction. The *New York Times* called him "the stuff of which the great heroes of mankind are made"; but his words were a tissue of fabrications and half-truths that should not, as Robert Penn Warren harshly noted, have "deceived a child."[90] Nevertheless, the speech had an electrifying impact on the North—Emerson later compared it to Lincoln's Gettysburg Address.[91] In Virginia, however, it fell on alien and unbelieving ears, and John Brown was sentenced to hang by the neck until dead in exactly one month's time.

Brown was dead right on one point: given the circumstances, justice had been "more generous" than he had any reason to expect. In a narrow legal sense his trial was fair. He had organized, if not personally committed, murder, and he had no legitimate defense that was acceptable in a court of law, despite all the mitigating circumstances which he sought to introduce. Nevertheless, the appearance of a kangaroo court prevailed. The refusal to delay the trial to give Brown time to recover from his wounds (they were never as bad as he claimed, but they permitted him to pose as a victim of cruelty as he conducted his defense from a cot in full view of the courtroom), and to prepare his case, as well as consult with counsel of his own choosing was a serious blunder, creating, as the *New York Times* commented, "an unwholesome reaction in the prisoner's favor."[92] Equally serious was the failure of Virginia to recognize the paramount right of the federal government to try Brown. Not only had the Virginia Court of Appeals refused to review a case riddled with flaws, but Brown's counsel had also failed to attempt to appeal his case to a federal court. Henceforth, Brown, who rarely missed a trick, could with considerable legitimacy refer to his trial as a "public murder."[93]

The Commonwealth of Virginia and Governor Wise blundered somewhat differently but even more seriously when, in an act of charity and human decency, they allowed John Brown pen and paper and permitted him to correspond from his prison cell. He made magnificent use of that equipment. James Redpath, Brown's first hagiographer, described the consequences best: the old man "could afford the loss of his Sharp's rifles while he retained the faculty of speech." With the pen, not the sword, he set about to fulfill the prediction of the *New York Independent* that "not John Brown but Slavery will be gibbeted when he hangs upon the gallows."[94]

The letters averaged, despite his wounds, better than one a day for the next month, and they supply an extraordinary probe into the disturbed recesses of a martyr's mind. Part a self-congratulation, part a debate with himself, part a dialogue with his deity, part both a gesture of comfort to and plea for forgiveness by his family, and always written with an eye to public consumption, they picture the turmoil, anguish, and self-satisfaction of a man determined to be a successful martyr. He set about making a well-advertised virtue out of a peculiarly disagreeable necessity.

He wrote to his wife, children, siblings, old friends, and well-wishers reiterating the themes of his final courtroom speech and asking that his letters be copied and passed on. He assured one and all that he was "quite cheerful," in no way felt degraded by his chains, and had "no consciousness of guilt."[95] He was ready, he said, to "go joyfully [to the scaffold] in behalf of millions that 'have no rights' " and was "content to die for God's eternal truth and for suffering humanity."[96] Over and over he repeated—almost as if he had to reassure himself as well as his readers—that his death had a meaning far greater than his life. Death would be in a sense the act that wiped clean the sorry failures of the past: "My death will not be in vain." To his wife and children he wrote, "For me at this time to seal my testimony for God and humanity with my blood will do vastly more toward advancing the cause I have earnestly endeavored to promote than all I have done in my life before." To his brother he said that he was totally persuaded that he was "worth inconceivably more to hang than for any other purpose." His "seeming disaster," he told his family, "will ultimately result in the most glorious success," and he informed his old friend Daniel Tilden,

"It is a great comfort to feel assured that I am permitted to die for a cause [and] not merely to pay the debt of nature as all must."[97]

Like so many martyrs before him, he was concerned with both this world and the next, his future reputation on earth and his chances for heaven. He was fearful that his family might "blush" for having a father who died on the scaffold. Although he was cheered that so many friends were writing him that "posterity at least will do me justice," he was worried by the thought of being labeled insane. He was, he claimed, "neither conscious of being infatuated nor mad," but if he were insane it was "like a very pleasant dream," and he hoped to continue in his insanity till "I come to know of those realities which 'eyes have not seen, and which ears have not heard.' "[98] The religious motif became stronger as the day of execution advanced. He more and more associated his views on slavery with his faith in God. He was certain his deity would not forsake him in his moment of need, because he was "a faithful soldier" of Christ, who was "the great Captain of Liberty as well as of salvation." On that "rock" he had set his foot and taken his stand. The image of Christ on the cross, dying the death of a felon, was constantly before his eyes, and in his last letter to his family he said that "eternal life" is what "my soul is 'panting after' [at] this moment."[99]

The scaffold had no terrors for him, and he assured his children he did not say this simply to "brave it out."[100] He was determined to die well, not only because he had faith but also because he had staked his death upon creating a legend. With the full expectation that his letter would be widely read and quoted, he wrote Mrs. George Stearns, the wife of his most generous Boston patron, that he was determined not to be mocked at death by "hypocritical prayers made over me when I am publicly murdered." Instead, conjuring up a picture filled with pathos, he asked that "my only religious attendants be poor little, dirty, ragged, bare headed and barefooted Slave boys and girls, led by some old grey headed Slave Mother."[101] His final words to his wife and offspring were even more stagey. Modeling himself on John Rogers, who had set the standards for the sixteenth-century Protestant martyrs, he announced: "John Rogers wrote to his children, 'abhor that arrant whore of Rome.' John Brown writes to his children to abhor with undying hatred also that 'sum of all villainies'—Slavery."[102]

John Brown corresponded with Mrs. Stearns because Mr. Stearns, like others of the secret six, had panicked at the news of Harpers Ferry and taken refuge in foreign parts. They were ready to finance treason but not to go to prison or die for it. The redoubtable Reverend Thomas Higginson alone was made of sterner stuff. He applauded the action, defied Virginia and the federal government to arrest him, sought to extract the fullest public-relations impact from Brown's imprisonment, and made elaborate plans for his hero's escape, even suggesting that Governor Wise be kidnapped and Brown's pardon be his ransom. But old Osawatomie Brown categorically rejected any escape plan. "Let them hang me," he told the Reverend James McFarland; "I forgive them, and may God forgive them, for they know not what they do." Though he had obeyed the law of God, he had gone "against the laws of men" and was willing, even anxious, to pay the price.[103]

Punishment was scheduled for 11 a.m. on December 2, 1859. Dressed in a black cashmere suit and red-embroidered slippers, Brown rode to his execution, in an open wagon, sitting on his coffin, his arms "pinioned at the elbows." In proper martyr style, when he saw the hundreds of troops that had been marshaled to guard his passage, he quipped, "I had no idea that Governor Wise considered my execution so important."[104] When his escort reached the execution field, he was led up the steps of the scaffold, a white hood was placed over his head to prevent him from making any public oration, a halter was fitted around his neck and his ankles bound together. His only request was that his executioners "be quick" and not keep him "waiting any longer than necessary."[105] Necessity, unfortunately, took close to fifteen minutes; fifteen hundred militiamen and cavalry had to be drawn up in review to ensure that Virginia justice be properly done. For an eternity the prisoner waited in the darkness of his hood, hanging by a thread between heaven and earth, for the trap door to be sprung. Once the abyss had opened up, the body hung for thirty-five minutes before doctors were convinced that the pulse had ceased.[106]

Two years later, Julia Ward Howe, the wife of Dr. Samuel Howe of the secret six, was watching Union troops on the border of Virginia marching back from inspection; they were singing, "John Brown's body lies a-mouldering in the grave, / His soul goes marching on," to the tune of a popular Methodist hymn. She was asked whether she could not write "better words" to the music. Thus was born "The Battle Hymn of the Republic."[107] Captain Brown could have asked for no better proof that he was indeed "an instrument in the hands of providence": his death had brought about "the glory of the coming of the Lord."

Greatness rarely stands in splendid isolation. It is accompanied by its ugly associates—self-delusion, pride, obsession that borders on insanity, and a willingness to sacrifice everything, friends, family, followers, nation, even the truth itself, for the sake of the cause. At his interrogation after Harpers Ferry, Brown was called fanatical; he rejoined that not he but the South was mad. Possibly he should have included the North as well, where "madness" was also on the increase. As Wendell Phillips said in the old man's funeral eulogy at North Elba, "How vast the change in men's hearts!

Insurrection was a harsh, horrid word to millions a month ago."[108] The transformation was not the work of Osawatomie Brown working in a vacuum, impelled by a fanatical vision of his own making. The times were ready for a "new saint" who, in Emerson's words, could make "the gallows glorious like the cross."[109] Without the guilt and passion that slavery generated, John Brown would have died a hollow bigot, a self-deluded failure, who would have gone to an empty grave without the public esteem his sense of self-importance so desperately desired. Yet the cause of abolition needed its red martyr as much as Brown needed a cause. Abolition required someone who was willing to witness his faith in God and his sense of moral and social outrage with death. Whenever beliefs, even a belief in oneself, are in question, "the greatest testimony and the most efficacious demonstration is to die for them."[110]

Gandhi advocated a school for martyrs: "Just as one must learn the art of killing in training for violence, so one must learn the art of dying in the training for nonviolence."

CHAPTER II

MAHATMA GANDHI:
SCHOOL FOR MARTYRS

Rebellion is the common ground on which
every man bases his first values. I *rebel*—therefore
we exist.

—ALBERT CAMUS,
The Rebel

$\mathcal{J}$F JOHN BROWN, the failed Yankee entrepreneur and twice-married father of twenty children, makes a strange and disturbingly unattractive martyr, Mohandas K. Gandhi, the bespectacled, self-proclaimed "God's eunuch" and—to use Winston Churchill's unflattering terminology—half-naked "seditious fakir," raises questions that go to the root of the concept of martyrdom itself.[1] Few men have ever offered so wide a vista into the temple of their souls; few have ever allowed the outside world so close a look at the arena of their minds. We possess ninety volumes of Gandhi's letters, speeches, telegrams, petitions, appeals, conversations, pronouncements, newspaper editorials, and political, religious, philosophical and autobiographical discourses. We also have a veritable library of reflections, memoirs, and biographies penned by those who knew Gandhi or whose private and public lives touched upon his career. Mercifully, the purpose of this chapter is not to distill this mountain of documentation down into a capsulated molehill of his life. Instead it seeks the difficult but far simpler goal of justifying the inclusion of a man who was not a Westerner and did not die by the legal actions of the state in a book on the concept of Western martyrdom.[2]

Culturally Gandhi may not have been a Westerner, but he was not totally an Easterner either; instead he was the extraordinary product of the two worlds. He was a Janus phenomenon that could only have emerged in a multicultural environment—Hindu, Jain, Buddhist, Christian, Muslim, Parsi—and could only have blossomed in a society that had already had prolonged contact with Western standards, ideals, and aspirations presented to it in the governmental and regimental dress of the British Raj. Gandhi started life as a Gujarati-speaking subject of the British crown, and for his first fifty years he regarded himself to be a loyal, if highly maverick, citizen of the British Empire. His entire life, except for the final two years, was spent trying first to make that empire live up to its own ideals of liberty, equality, and the rights and dignity of man and then to overthrow the same empire in the name of the equally Western concepts of nationalism and national self-determination. "In schools established by the British Government in India," he proudly asserted, he had learned to recite (not quite accurately) Lord Byron's words: " 'Freedom's battle once begun' is 'bequeathed from bleeding sire to son.' "[3]

The stage on which Gandhi performed in both South Africa and India was impressively imperial, but the seed from whence he sprang, although constantly watered by Western thought, remained deeply buried in an ancient Hindu soil, which derived its cultural potency from family, caste, and religion. He was born on October 2, 1869, into a bania, or trading caste, family—the name "Gandhi" means grocer. The initial expectation for a Gandhi son was to emulate his father and grandfather, who had risen by dint of hard work and loyalty to become senior administrative servants to local maharajas on the Kathiawar peninsula, 250 miles northwest of Bombay. A mischievous but sensitive boy, married at thirteen to an illiterate bride of the same age, and devoted to a deeply religious mother, who fasted regularly and went daily to temple to worship the lord Vishnu, Gandhi displayed nothing unusual in his progress through adolescence into adulthood, except possibly an overly developed sense of duty and guilt. He never forgot or forgave himself for his failure after months of nursing his father to be at his parent's bedside at the moment of his death in 1886. Instead he was across the corridor in the bedroom of his pregnant wife, a "double shame" and irredeemable "blot" upon his character, as Gandhi called it, which has made him an irresistible target for psychoanalytical speculation.[4]

The lockstep of a young caste Indian's predictable career was changed when Gandhi's father decided to make his youngest and brightest son the family's conduit into modern times. By the last third of the nineteenth century, even an isolated and provincial bania family, like the Gandhis, had come to recognize that its collective welfare required greater contact with the British Raj. Accordingly, young Mohandas was first sent to an English-speaking high school where Western pedagogy and English cricket were esteemed, then given a further year at a local community college, and finally, in defiance of caste regulations, shipped off to London to become a proper English barrister and "brown Briton." His legal studies at the Inner Temple—Justinian's Code and the Roman law, Blackstone and the English common law—were, judging from Gandhi's autobiography, not topics that either interested or influenced him, nor did they occupy his full time. More important to him during his three years in London were his efforts to become an Englishman—enrollment in London University, classes in Latin, French, physics, and elocution, and lessons in bridge and the violin—and his discovery of religion, his own included, all in English translation. He was deeply moved by the New Testament, especially the Sermon on the Mount; he was introduced to the teachings of Buddha through Sir Edwin Arnold's *The Light of Asia;* and he encountered for the first time in Arnold's *The Song Celestial* one of the most sacred Hindu texts, the Bhagavad-Gita, or Song of God, a work that eventually became his "infallible guide of conduct" and "dictionary . . . for a ready solution of all my troubles and trials."[5]

The desire to absorb the wisdom of the West, first acquired in London, continued on into Gandhi's South African years. By the time he had turned forty he had absorbed Bacon, Carlyle, Emerson, Huxley, and Thoreau's "The Duty of Civil Disobedience"; had translated Plato's Dialogues on the trial of Socrates into Gujarati; had been "overwhelmed" by Tolstoy's *The Kingdom of God Is Within You* and had corresponded with the Russian novelist; and had avidly absorbed John Ruskin's *Unto This Last: Four Essays on the First Principles of Political Economy*—a book, he said, that "brought about an instantaneous and practical transformation in my life." Ruskin's book spoke to Gandhi as few others did because it preached three doctrines that by 1904 Gandhi was ready to put into practice: in his own words, "the good of the individual is contained in the good of all," "a lawyer's work has the same value as the barber's," and "a life of labor, i.e. the life of the tiller of the soil and the handicraftsman, is the life worth living." Ruskin's message struck another sympathetic chord in his disciple; it confirmed Gandhi's growing distaste for Western materialism and acquisitive-competitive civilization: a society devoid of moral principles, which had lost touch with God and had forgotten, as Ruskin put it, how to seek "not greater wealth but simpler pleasure, not higher fortune but deeper felicity."[6] If nothing else, Western thought and doubts about its own civilization unlocked in Gandhi what in all likelihood was already there in nascent form: an abiding need to comprehend the divine, a compulsive desire to immerse himself in his own cultural and religious roots, and a passion to serve his fellow man, politically and spiritually, the two being for him one and the same: "For me there is no distinction between politics and religion."[7]

Except for an obsession for punctuality and meticulously kept account books (Gandhi became a kind of bania Benjamin Franklin, always careful of time and money), the union of East and West bore little fruit until M. K. Gandhi, attorney-at-law, encountered for the first time in May of 1893 the physical and psychological trauma of virulent racism. While traveling by rail between Durban and Pretoria, he was thrown off the train and left stranded in the bitter cold because he was an Indian who dared sit in a first-class compartment. That humiliation was the catalyst that refashioned a shy, introverted, and family-oriented young man into a popular hero and revealed to him a calling that demanded the sacrifice of all privacy for the higher good of humanity. Henceforth, every act and thought had to be open to public inspection; nothing could be held back for the sake of friend, kin, wife, children, or self. And it is here in South Africa that the second and far more difficult question emerges: how a man who practiced martyrdom without dying fits into a book that claims as its central definition of martyrdom death by the legal action of the state.

Phyllis McGinley's harsh words about the early Christian martyrs quoted in chapter 1—"It is easy to be a martyr. You only have to be it once"— unerringly go to the core of martyrdom's fatal flaw as a political weapon: it is an unrepeatable, once-in-a-lifetime act. It may project its practitioner into heaven, but it leaves the battlefield empty, and rarely does it have prolonged or practical consequences. For nearly two and a half millennia Socrates' death has remained a topic of intense intellectual interest, but it did nothing to further the cause of free inquiry in Athens. Jesus' crucifixion had no immediate impact that can be documented; his message of God's kingdom remained mute, and it took another three hundred years plus the magic of Matthew, Mark, Luke, and John and the reinterpretation of Paul to launch it as a world religion. By any but divine standards, three centuries is a long time to wait for a cause to be fulfilled. The political effect of Becket's martyrdom was spectacular but not enduring; the encroachment of state upon church continued unabated, and the archbishop's bones eventually ended on the rubbish heap. Arguably, what saved England for Protestantism was not the public incineration of its martyrs but the natural demise of Mary Tudor; and it is anybody's guess whether John Brown's execution forwarded the cause of abolition or hastened the coming of the Civil War. As a means to a political end, martyrdom rarely has staying power, if only because the ideal for which a martyr dies is often not the one that triumphs after his death. Moreover, public memory is a slender reed on which to base one's reputation, let alone further a cause.

Mahatma Gandhi resolved most of these difficulties by adding a new dimension to martyrdom. He insisted that ends and means had to be interchangeable; the worth and therefore the contribution of martyrs were inseparably linked to the quality of the life they lived; style and control over oneself and the circumstances under which life was being sacrificed were as important to the success of the cause as death itself. Death for Gandhi was the easy part. The real test of the martyr lay in the protracted training and self-discipline that transformed a mere willingness to die, a sensibility often tainted by the hint of suicide, into a positive act of heroism that improved and reinvigorated all people. He devised a spiritual as well as social and political weapon, known as satyagraha, that not only accepted brutal police beatings, prolonged imprisonment, and violent death as the necessary and ultimate means for reinvigorating society and teaching government officials the error of their ways, but also offered the promise that in a conflict of wills the state, not the individual, would back down. Protected by the impenetrable armor of Truth, a single individual could successfully "defy the whole might of an unjust empire to save his honour, his religion, his soul. . . ."[8]

Until Gandhi, aged twenty-three, arrived in South Africa in the spring of 1893, he was a man without clear cultural identity, neither Christian nor Hindu, British nor Indian; and worse, he was a professional failure. Returning to India in the summer of 1891 with his newly minted law degree and textbook knowledge of Blackstone and Justinian, but sorely deficient in Indian law and legal practices, he pleased his family by undergoing ritualistic purification for having violated his caste purity by residing overseas, but insisted on wearing English dress and sought to persuade his family to adopt those symbols of Western gentility, the knife and fork. For two depressing years he experienced, as a consequence of ineptitude, inflexibility, and lack of training, one professional humiliation and setback after the other. There were so many that Erik Erikson in his analysis of Gandhi postulated, at least by implication, a thesis about all potential saints and martyrs: "A soul that sensitive, proud and self-centered can find vocation only by *not* succeeding in ordinary ways, even if that means to perish."[9] (Shades of John Brown.) Presumably, then, because it afforded not a new challenge but an escape from old failures, Gandhi grabbed at the offer of the Muslim import-export firm of Dada Abdullah and Co. to be its legal representative in Durban, the major port of the British crown colony of Natal.

On arriving in South Africa, Gandhi found himself even more of a maverick than in India. As an English-speaking and -educated Indian lawyer who almost overnight became a professional and economic success, he stood out as a cosmopolitan citizen in a part of the British Empire where "white" Englishmen and Boers, "black" Africans, and "brown" Indians confronted one another in an atmosphere of uncontrolled economic growth, acute political tension and open racism. In one sense Gandhi had greatness thrust upon him—only he had the social and educational status to lead. In another sense he manufactured that leadership by fashioning himself into a secular saint and giving to political conflict a spiritual dimension that transformed self-interest into self-understanding. He went, he said, "to South Africa for travel, for finding an escape from Kathiawar intrigues and for gaining my own livelihood. But . . . I found myself in search of God and striving for self-realization."[10] He came, he thought, for one year; he stayed for twenty-one.

Gandhi's eviction from the train between Durban and Pretoria awakened him to the mounting plight of the Indian in South Africa. For thirty years before his arrival, impoverished low-caste and untouchable Indians had been imported into South Africa as indentured laborers to work on the sugar plantations and in the coal mines of Natal. By 1886, 51,000 Indian workers, some still indentured, others technically free and electing not to return to India, had settled in the colony, where some 50,000 whites and 400,000 blacks also resided. Elsewhere the presence of "Asian dirt," as Indians were termed, was less threatening—only slightly over 11,000 in 1904 in the Transvaal and almost the same number in the Cape Colony. But throughout South Africa, English immigrants and Boer farmers alike perceived a growing "Asian peril," especially since Indians were turning to domestic trade and monopolizing the mercantile needs of the black population. Racism found expression in legal and commercial restrictions, disenfranchisement, and systematic humiliation—curfews were imposed, first- and second-class tickets denied, European hotels restricted, residential ghettos established, and discriminatory trade practices countenanced. As a "coolie barrister" and victim himself of racism, but also as an imperial citizen who had read and believed Queen Victoria's proclamation of November 1858 promising equality before the law for all subjects of her empire, Gandhi was almost immediately swept up in the battle to preserve and defend Indian legal and commercial rights. He soon became convinced that "South Africa was no country for a self-respecting Indian."[11] It was, however, not until September 11, 1906, that he offered the Indian community his own peculiar and inspirational brand of political action and formula for restoring self-respect, because not until then had he successfully transformed the British-trained lawyer and bania-caste Hindu into a Gandhian-defined seeker after truth.

The occasion was Gandhi's address to a mass meeting at the Empire Theatre in Johannesburg protesting the Transvaal government's proposed "Black Act" requiring all Indians, men and women, not only to register but also to be fingerprinted and carry passes with them at all times. The humiliation was heightened by the right of the police to stop Indian women in the street and enter their houses demanding proof of registration. Indian outrage was witnessed by the response of one incensed husband: "If anyone came forward to demand a certificate from my wife, I would shoot him on that spot and take the consequences."[12]

During the course of the meeting a resolution was offered that, "with God as [their] witness," Indians would swear never to comply with the new law. Gandhi picked up on the reference to the deity. "We all believe in one and the same God," he said, and for Muslim or Hindu to vow "to take an oath in the name" of that God was "not something to be trifled with. If, having taken such an oath, we violate our pledge, we are guilty before God and man. . . . A man who deliberately and intelligently takes a pledge and then breaks it forfeits his manhood." Having introduced divine authority into the conflict against the forces of evil, and having committed Indian manhood to it, Gandhi spelled out the consequences of such a vow: police reprisals, jail sentences, loss of jobs, deportations, and years of suffering. Some, he admonished, would even be asked to become martyrs and offer up their lives, because the struggle was no longer simply a political campaign; now a moral principle was at stake. He asked that the leaders, those standing with him on the stage, be on their guard: the resolution might pass as a unanimous group enterprise, but the whole was only as good as the moral fortitude and worth of its individual parts, especially its leaders. Each had to be "true to his pledge even unto death, no matter what others do." The prospects might be grim, but of one thing Gandhi was certain: "So long as there is even a handful of men true to their pledge, there can only be one end to the struggle, and that is victory."[13]

Although the term "satyagraha" had not yet been coined, many of the principles it encompassed were present in embryonic form in Gandhi's speech linking politics and morality in the Indian defiance of the "Black Act." But to understand the shape that satyagraha was taking in its author's mind and its relationship to martyrdom, the focus must be turned inward on the man himself. The political agitator who reminded his audience of the sacred nature of a pledge before God and warned that each Indian alone would have to wrestle with the strength of his conviction was no longer the secular young attorney with starched collar, black tie, and polished boots who had docked at Durban thirteen years before. During the intervening years Gandhi had redefined his deity, discovered the meaning of existence, refashioned himself into an Indian sadhu, or holy man, and confronted head-on Saint Augustine's dictum that the cause, not the penalty, sanctifies the martyr, coming up with a very different conclusion.

Satyagraha—literally *satya,* or truth that engenders love, plus *graha,* or firmness that contains conviction—is, to use Gandhi's definition, the political "force which is born of Truth and Love or nonviolence."[14] It rests on twin but inseparable pillars: that God must be reintroduced into political life and that the individual, before qualifying as a servant of that deity, must demonstrate in his private life absolute self-control and self-denial. Together as interlocking principles the two concepts, Gandhi insisted, would elevate politics out of the muck and discord of self-interest and group conflict, turning it into a revolutionary moral force for which men and women would be willing to die, and would reshape the individual into a crusader worthy of practicing satyagraha.[15]

How, why, or when Gandhi rediscovered and redefined his deity is not clear; the presence of the divine in his life simply grew over the years, reaching towering and all-encompassing proportions by 1906. His friend and earliest biographer wrote three years later that Gandhi was "too closely allied to Christianity to be entirely Hindu, and too deeply saturated with Hinduism to be called Christian."[16] Being neither, he brought to religion a deeply private and nonsectarian approach whereby he took God out of the brick and mortar of church and temple. He dismissed as hollow acts the ritualistic worship of stone figures and the mindless recitation of holy words in song and prayer, and placed his deity in the midst of humanity—a living, active, and highly demanding immanence that pervaded all aspects of life and refused to be compartmentalized or constrained by institutional religions and warring creeds. God was "the sum total of life," and he quoted the words of an Islamic poet: "I did not find God on the cross. I went to find Him in the temple, but in vain. . . . He could be found neither on the hill nor in the cave. At last I looked into my heart and found Him there, only there and nowhere else." Gandhi himself phrased the sentiment more prosaically: "Religion is not really what is grasped by the brain, but a heart grasp."[17] The sole way to find God was "to see Him in His creation," and this could only be achieved through the "service of all." If, Gandhi confessed, "I could persuade myself that I should find Him in a Himalayan cave, I would proceed there immediately. But I know that I cannot find Him apart from humanity."[18]

Such a deity, formless and faultless but at the same time the embodiment of ultimate truth, reality, and unity, could only be comprehended in diversity. Drawing upon Jain beliefs in the interchangeability and sanctity of all life and the "many-sidedness" of truth, and reshaping ideas mined from

Ruskin, Tolstoy, and a highly idiosyncratic reading of the Gita, Gandhi formulated his three most politically explosive doctrines: tolerance and understanding for all peoples and creeds; nonviolence and love (Gandhi's definition of his oft-used term "ahimsa") in all behavior, both public and private, collective and individual; and the importance of action, not contemplation, in achieving self-improvement and salvation. If truth were multiple, "the golden rule of conduct" must be "mutual toleration, seeing we will never all think alike and . . . always see Truth in fragment and from different angles of vision." Conscience, Gandhi warned, "is not the same thing for all."[19] If all life is the gift of God, nonviolence must prevail in all human conduct. Ahimsa for the Mahatma meant much more than simply nonkilling or even not offending anyone or not harboring an uncharitable thought; it meant respecting your opponent's concept of truth and his right to hold his own ideas. The aim of ahimsa was to establish, not to destroy, links among people and to find a common denominator. Finally, if "the truth requires constant and extensive demonstration," and our "thoughts, however good in themselves, are like fallen pearls unless they are translated into action," then cerebral activity had to lead to deeds. A change of heart was meaningless unless it resulted in a change in the social and political structure. There could be no "escape from social service"— that was the only way God could be found and worshiped.[20] Exactly this "active spirituality" had attracted him to Jesus and Buddha in the first place.

Believers who sought to find God in the service of humanity had to prepare and train themselves and become "celibates for the sake of God," and in 1906 Gandhi took the oath of brahmacharya, or celibacy. Let "no one believe," he warned, "that it was an easy thing for me." Let no one believe, he should have added, that it was an easy thing for his family, who discovered that merging the public and private spheres into a single spiritual totality could only be achieved at a terrible cost—theirs. Brahmacharya involved not simply renouncing sex; celibacy had to be without any sense of regret. It entailed the total sublimation of all appetites—food, lust, possessions, greed—and absolute freedom from "the opposing currents of love and hate, attachment and repulsion." The true devotee treated "friend and foe alike," was "jealous of none," "without egotism," "ever forgiving," "not puffed up by praise," and "free from exultation, sorrow and fear."[21] Eventually Gandhi divested himself of all possessions, all fleshly attractions, all love that might distract him from his goal of modeling himself into "a fit instrument" to serve his fellow man, because "he who serves mankind serves God."[22] In the end he reduced the links with this world to the irreducible essentials: a loincloth, shawl, and sandals; a typewriter with which to spread the truth; false teeth, worn only for eating; metal-framed circular glasses; and a "dollar" pocket watch to keep track of God's precious commodity: time.

Only the disciplined man who was in absolute control of himself could successfully wield the newly emerging weapon of satyagraha, because "soul force" was as much a state of mind as a means to a political end. Only the practitioner who realized that "true humility requires us to dedicate ourselves to the service of all living creatures" could fulfill the meaning of love embodied in ahimsa and practice nonviolence as an ideal based on strength, not weakness. Only the perfectly conditioned soldier could conquer the "adversary by suffering in one's own person."[23] Such a totally spiritualized individual possessed extraordinarily explosive political potential. Gilbert Murray had Gandhi as his model when he wrote that modern governments should be exceedingly careful of the potential martyr "who cares nothing for sensual pleasure, nothing for riches, nothing for comfort or praise or promotion but is simply determined to do what he believes to be right. He is a dangerous and uncomfortable enemy because his body which you can always conquer gives you so little purchase upon his soul."[24]

Until 1906 satyagraha was largely a product of Gandhi's private encounter with his deity. If he were to translate his personal commitment into public policy, he needed not just believers in soul force and the principles on which it rested but also trained soldiers who understood exactly what sacrifices were required and who possessed the fortitude to endure them. "I have not known," Gandhi was to write many years later while preparing to do battle with the British in India, "of a war gained by a rabble, but I have known of wars gained by disciplined armies. . . . We must train ourselves in discipline and self-sacrifice."[25] In South Africa he had to transform a rabble of conflicting interests and prejudices—Hindu, Muslim, rich Indian, poor Indian, indentured Indian, and untouchables—into a solid phalanx of people determined to act in unison, a group that placed Indianness above religious, regional, and economic divisions, and into a body sufficiently aware of its own identity and the principles for which it was fighting to supply the necessary dedicated troopers—satyagrahis—ready to defy the unjust laws of the land.

Over and over Gandhi reiterated that satyagraha was not passive resistance, the policy of the weak and desperate who, weaponless, had nothing but hatred in their hearts to strengthen them, and who would unhesitatingly take up arms should they be offered. Instead, satyagraha was the weapon of the strong and the brave who were willing to "observe perfect chastity, adopt poverty, follow truth and cultivate fearlessness" as well as practice ahimsa and nonviolence.[26] "Wherein is courage required?" Gandhi asked. "In blowing others to pieces from behind a cannon, or with a smiling face to approach the cannon and be blown to pieces? Who is the true warrior—he who keeps death always as a bosom friend, or he who controls the death of others?"[27] A man devoid of courage and manhood could never wield the sword of soul force. Gandhi had more than a touch of the early Christian martyr in him. He would have understood Tertullian's exhortation: "We battle against all your cruelty, ever rushing voluntarily to the contest."

Gandhi called nonviolent resistance by many names—noncooperation, civil resistance, civil disobedience—but "civilized disobedience" captures its essential flavor better than any other title, because "truth force" was the opposite of brute force in attaining one's end and was based on humanity's two cardinal and, according to Gandhi, divinely inspired qualities: love and reason. Each act of disobedience was a calculated response to injustice but was always committed with love in the heart. "One who is free from hatred requires no sword."[28] Unlike John Brown, Gandhi maintained that he never hated the perpetrators of injustice. He had no desire to wreak vengeance on wrongdoers in the name of God's retribution; there was no word of God to be enforced by sword and terror. His sole concern, he said, was for those who suffered injustice.[29]

The trained satyagrahi possessed one paramount virtue, self-control, be-cause the nonviolent warrior filled with ahimsa was expected to do battle with a twofold enemy—the beast within and injustice without. The evils of this world could not be confronted, let alone conquered, unless the soldier had mastered himself: "Without Brahmacharya," Gandhi insisted, "the satyagrahi will have no luster, no inner strength to stand unarmed against the whole world."[30] The danger was "only from within; if there was depar-ture from truth and non-violence, whatever the provocation, the movement would be damned."[31] Only those who had themselves, their appetites, their thoughts and actions under absolute control and were inspired by their faith to serve God in this world could attain the standards Gandhi set for his troops.[32] "What I shall expect of you is that, even if someone subjects you to the most inhumane tortures, you will joyfully face the ordeal and make the supreme sacrifice with God's name on your lips and without a trace of fear or anger or thoughts of revenge in your hearts. That will be heroism of the highest type."[33]

What gave muscle to soul force as opposed to brute force was the satya-grahi's willingness to die. The highest goal of the satyagrahi, Gandhi wrote, was "to lay down his life performing his duty whatever it may be."[34] In a sense, Gandhi was advocating a school for martyrs. "To fight with the sword does call for bravery of a sort," he admitted, "but to die is braver by far than to kill. He alone is truly brave, he alone is a martyr in the true sense who dies without fear in his heart and without wishing hurt to his

enemy. . . ."[35] As with all martyrs, the election of death as a conscious decision, not to have it thrust upon you in battle, was the mark of greatness and
the quality that enhanced the cause. Here was the early Christian martyr's
ideal of love-thine-enemy adapted to the political needs of the twentieth
century and used not as a key to the kingdom of heaven, although this was
always implied, but as a revolutionary weapon to change the political structure of society. Martyrdom was to be endured as much for the sake of humanity as for God.

Death for the Mahatma was an instrument which, to be effective, had to
be used with calculation, artistry, and control. "Just as one must learn the art
of killing in training for violence, so one must learn the art of dying in the
training for nonviolence. . . ."[36] There could be no nobler or more dramatic
way of proving oneself and the credibility of the cause than to die for it. The
early Christian martyrs had sensed this: "So great is the virtue of martyrdom that by its means even he who wished to slay you is constrained to believe." Gandhi, however, added a crucial proviso to the believer's willingness
to die. In order to prevent it from becoming a death wish and suicide, he insisted on a series of conditions: the sufferer had to have undergone the discipline of self-purification, practiced nonviolence in mind, deed, and word,
and be ready to give his life for the welfare of humanity, not simply for the
sake of salvation. There was for Gandhi a vast distinction between wanting
to die and a willingness to die. "I am not aching," he confessed, "for martyrdom, but if it comes in my way in the prosecution of what I consider to be
the supreme duty in defense of the faith . . . I shall have well earned it."[37]
Unlike any other theorist about martyrdom, the key for the Mahatma lay in
the earning, not in the act, of dying.

In South Africa satyagraha was still adolescent, its disciples only just
learning how to earn their martyrdom and to make death and suffering
count; but in India on May 21, 1930, Gandhi's soldiers proved their training
and their mettle in one of the most extraordinary examples of nonviolent
resistance ever recorded—the attack by some twenty-five hundred satyagrahis on the government's monopoly of the salt works at Dharasana, 150
miles north of Bombay. Gandhi himself was in jail, and his troops, "dressed
in the regulation uniform of rough homespun cotton dhotis and triangular
Gandhi caps," were under the leadership of the English-educated Indian
poet Sarojini Naidu. The offensive began in the early morning with a
prayer and Mrs. Naidu's words: "You will be beaten but you must not resist;
you must not even raise a hand to ward off the blows." The defenders, con-
sisting of a half-dozen English officers and four hundred police in khaki
shorts and brown turbans, armed with lathis—long clubs with steel tips—
were protected by a barbed-wire stockade. In complete silence the "Gandhi

men" advanced in waves, each contingent being met by a rain of blows as the police rushed out upon them. They went down in a flood of blood only to be replaced by the next wave. "From where I stood," reported Webb Miller of the United Press, "I heard the sickening whacks of the clubs on unprotected skulls. The waiting crowd of watchers groaned and sucked in their breaths in sympathetic pain at every blow. Those struck down fell sprawling, unconscious or writhing in pain with fractured skulls or broken shoulders. In two or three minutes the ground was quilted with bodies. Great patches of blood widened on their white clothes." When the first wave had been eliminated and the stretcher bearers had carried off the bodies, the second wave marched slowly forward with "heads up, without the encouragement of music or cheering or any possibility that they might escape serious injury or death." They too were systematically beaten to the ground; "there were no outcries, only groans after they fell."[38]

Toward the end the satyagrahis varied their tactics; they sat on the ground in groups of twenty-five near the salt pans, where they also were beaten by the police with lathis. "Bodies toppled over in threes and fours, bleeding from great gashes on their scalp." Group after group endured the same torment "without raising an arm to fend off the blows." Finally, the police lost control of themselves and began "kicking the seated men in the abdomen and testicles" and dragging them by the arms and legs and throwing them into a nearby ditch, all the while hitting them with their clubs. "Hour after hour stretcher bearers carried back a stream of inert, bleeding bodies." By eleven, the heat had reached 116 in the shade, and both sides, exhausted, fell quiet. "I counted 320 injured," Miller concluded his report, laid out "in the shade of an open palm-thatched shed."[39] Eventually at least two died of their injuries. Even more remarkable than the self-control of the satyagrahis who allowed themselves to be clubbed senseless was the control of the watching crowd. Mrs. Naidu's most difficult problem was not urging her troops forward but restraining the anger of those who stayed behind. At one point it looked as if the crowd would overrun the salt works and encounter the twenty-five riflemen the British had held in reserve. Instigating a blood bath, however, and driving the opponent to extreme actions was not a proclaimed part of satyagraha. Its aim was to reform and convert the enemy, not to destroy him. The sharp edge of soul force was the moral and ethical superiority and self-control of the satyagrahis, which helped to allay the fear that resided in the hearts of the opponents. Unlike Brown, Gandhi ruled out the destruction of government property and sought to cultivate in the mind of the enemy the expectation that there was no fear of reprisal. You cannot, as Louis Fischer has wisely noted, "inject new ideas into a man's head by chopping it off."[40] There was to be no hatred of policemen qua policemen, only opposition to the unjust laws that they enforced. An attempt to take over the salt works by mob action would simply have invited greater violence and confirmed British reliance on force. The suspicion that all would-be martyrs are people like John Brown, who believed in doing unto others exactly what others had done unto them, had to be dispelled. The cardinal principle of satyagraha was to "attack measures and systems. We may not, we must not, attack men."[41] The purpose was twofold: to create conflict between principles of good and evil so that evil would be forced by moral pressure to give way to righteousness, and always to save the opponent's dignity by offering him an honorable retreat.

The satyagrahi was no common soldier, and there is in satyagraha an elitism about which Gandhi was avowedly proud. "Strength in numbers is the delight of the timid; the valiant of spirit glory in fighting alone"; and it was "ungodly to believe that an act of a majority binds a minority."[42] Only the few, the fearless and the dedicated, could sharpen the sword of soul force into an effective fighting weapon. All satyagrahis were leaders, all were followers, "so that the death of a fighter intensifies rather than slackens the struggle."[43] Quality, not quantity, counted, and as he said in his speech at Johannesburg, "so long as there is even a handful of men true to their pledge, there can only be one end to the struggle, and that is victory."

Underlying satyagraha were three interconnected principles dealing with the relationship between means and ends. For Gandhi there was "just the same inviolable connection between the means and the end as there is between the seed and the tree. . . . We reap exactly as we sow."[44] Jawaharlal Nehru, the Mahatma's most famous disciple, phrased the relationship differently—"A worthy end should have worthy means leading up to it"—but Gandhi would have countered that when nonviolence is the core of a policy, "means and ends are convertible terms" and become one "in my philosophy of life." Means are simply "the end in process and the ideal in the making."[45] For this reason the point of departure was always the means, because no end, no matter how noble, could justify an ignoble means. "I have often said that if one takes care of the means, the end will take care of itself. Nonviolence is the means."[46] He might have added that it was also the end.

It was Gandhi's insistence on means that led him to maintain the second underlying principle—the union of public and private morality and the danger of compartmentalizing conduct. "If a person has violated a moral principle in any one sphere of his life, his action will certainly have an effect in the other spheres. . . . The belief generally held that an immoral man may do no harm in the political sphere is quite wrong."[47] No matter how high-minded their purpose, immoral men tarnish their ends. Gandhi would have had a difficult time condoning Martin Luther King's extramarital activities—"A man cannot do right in one department of life whilst he is doing wrong in any other department. Life is one indivisible whole."[48] Nor would he have set aside Thomas Becket's anger, pride, and militancy in the name of a higher good, and he would have agreed with the twelfth-century critic of the archbishop who pointed out that suffering that lacks charity "is of no avail." Gandhi sensed that credibility was central to soul force. "There must be power in the word of a Satyagraha general—not the power that possession of limitless arms gives, but the power that purity of life, strict vigilance and ceaseless application produce." The Mahatma was adamant: "This is impossible without the observance of Brahmacharya. . . . An impure thought is a breach of Brahmacharya, so is anger."[49] For Gandhi Saint Augustine was surely wrong: the impure martyr soiled and discredited the cause for which he died just as any ill means corrupted the end. The cause alone could never sanctify the martyr, for the cause was only as good as the men and women willing to die for it.

In the Mahatma's tapestry of interwoven moral principles, the third canon had to do with the importance of the individual: only the individual supplied the thread that held the picture together, because Gandhi started and ended his conception of satyagraha not with the collective force of group activity but with the actions of indivisible human beings. The whole was no more than the sum of its parts; and as each member at the Johannesburg meeting was told to confront his own conscience and seal his pledge with his own manhood, so also he was warned not to think that he could be released from that pledge simply because the whole reneged. "There is no such thing . . . as mass conscience as distinguished from the consciences of individuals"; there was no mystique similar to Rousseau's public conscience that might justify the use of force to achieve the greater collective good. Conscience was individual, "the ripe fruit of strictest discipline." "The only tyrant," Gandhi confessed, "I accept in this world is the still voice within."[50]

Extolling the restraining powers of conscience, Gandhi liked to quote "conscience makes cowards of us all."[51] Oscar Wilde rather more astutely put it differently: he quipped, "Conscience makes egotists of us all."[52] There resides in all martyrs a conceit noted by Lord Acton when he pointed out that Socrates in boasting that he would obey God rather than man really meant "God manifest within—with no oracle, no sacred book, no appointed minister—with no organ but within" himself.[53] Like Socrates, the Mahatma had his *daimonion*, "the voice of God, of truth, or the inner voice or 'the still small voice'" which, Gandhi said, had to be obeyed "even though such obedience may cost . . . all that you have held as dear as life itself."[54] When Professor Edward Thompson met Gandhi in Oxford in 1930, his reaction was also to compare him to the Greek sophist: "Not since Socrates has the world seen his equal for absolute self-control and composure; . . . I understood why the Athenians made the martyr-sophist drink the hemlock. Like Socrates, he has a 'daimonion.' And when the 'daimonion' has spoken, he is as unmoved by argument as by danger."[55] Conscience, for Gandhi, was profoundly private, "a quality or state acquired by laborious training," and it was available only to the few who recognized it for what it was: an inner determination to act in a way that seemed morally right, practically attainable and in accord with the dictates of truth. Raghavan Iyer may well be correct: "It is at the fire of exceptional and spiritually subtle egotism that many of the saints and mystics . . . have warmed their hands." It was that heat that gave to Gandhi "the marvelous spiritual power to turn ordinary men around him into heroes and martyrs."[56]

Men and women who know the truth and communicate even indirectly with the deity can be dangerous fanatics, but Gandhi possessed two attributes that tended to keep both fanaticism and egotism at bay: self-criticism and practicality. The Mahatma knew his own foibles and limitations better than any other man, and he was descended from a long line of highly opportunistic bania ancestors who dealt with the politics of the possible. Lord Willingdon, viceroy of India, thought the Mahatma was a most pragmatic visionary: "He may be a saint; he may be a holy man. . . . But of this I am perfectly certain, that he is one of the most astute politically-minded and bargaining little gentlemen I ever came across."[57] Gandhi softened but did not deny the description. "Men say," he confessed, "I am a saint losing myself in politics. The fact is I am a politician trying my hardest to be a saint."[58]

Gandhi disapproved of waste—waste of time, money, resources—and he believed that ends had to be commensurate to means. As a politician, he realized that civil disobedience, propelled by soul force, was a delicate and dangerous political instrument, to be used with care and precision—so much depended on the spiritual vigor and determination of the satyagrahi and upon the vulnerability of the enemy. Organized nonviolent civil resistance, therefore, was always the weapon of last resort: "Satyagraha does not begin and end with civil disobedience," because "an able general always gives battle in his own time on the ground of his choice." Nor did he believe in wasting the lives of his satyagrahis. Death must be made to count: "We must be prepared to lay down our lives, but there should be an occasion for it." He sought always to wean the enemy "from error by patience and sympathy" and attempted to persuade and to negotiate before risking his troops.[59] No government ever received such an extraordinary declaration of war as did the British viceroy in India when Gandhi wrote him a long letter announcing the campaign against the salt tax which culminated in the clash of warring styles at Dharasana. The letter politely began: "Dear friend, Before embarking on civil disobedience and taking the risk I have dreaded to take all these years, I would fain approach you and find a way out. . . . Whilst . . . I hold the British rule to be a curse, I do not intend harm to a single Englishman or to any legitimate interest he may have in India." And it ended:

> I respectfully invite you to pave the way for the immediate removal of those evils [i.e., the consequences of British rule], and thus open a way for a real conference between equals. . . . But if you cannot see your way to deal with these evils and if my letter makes no appeal to your heart, on the 11th day of this month [March 1930] I shall proceed . . . to disregard the provisions of the salt laws. . . . It is, I know, open to you to frustrate my design by arresting me. I hope that there will be tens of thousands ready, in a disciplined manner, to take up the work after me. . . . If you care to discuss matters with me . . . I shall gladly refrain on receipt of a telegram. . . . I remain,
>
> Your sincere friend,
M. K. GANDHI[60]

Alerting the government of his intentions seems on the face of it strange military tactics, but Gandhi believed that his politics should be as open as his private life. Secrecy had "no place in a movement where one could do no wrong, where there was no scope for duplicity or cunning."[61] More important, satyagraha had two objectives: to confront injustice and right political wrongs and to heighten and shape public opinion. Not since Tertullian wrote that the martyrs of the church "gain power when you are before the eyes of man" had a theorist understood the power of publicity and propaganda as well as Gandhi; he knew it solidified the ranks, generated domestic support, and molded world opinion. If his soldiers had to die, it was essential that every gasp of their agony be heard and recorded by the press—that is why Webb Miller was informed about the planned encounter at Dharasana. John Brown may have sensed the importance of the mass media, both for his own reputation and self-esteem and for the cause of abolition and his own violent solution to slavery; but Gandhi went much further: he established and controlled four newspapers, one in South Africa and three in India. Even when a satyagraha campaign missed or only partially achieved its political objectives, as it often did in both South Africa and India, victory was still achieved in the sense that the cause for which men and women suffered and died was advertised and dramatized to an ever-widening audience. Gandhi knew as well as the early church fathers that the blood of the martyrs was the seed of the movement, especially if the spotlight of public attention was kept on the spectacle of unresisting satyagrahis being clubbed to death by policemen. "It is not because I value life low," Gandhi said, "that I can countenance with joy thousands voluntarily losing their lives for Satyagraha, but because I know that it results in the long run in the least loss of life, and, what is more, it ennobles those who lose their lives and morally enriches the world for their sacrifices."[62] Put in less moralistic and idealistic terms, martyrdom made splendid propaganda and put the enemy in the wrong.

Satyagraha was a self-perpetuating force, but the growing number of its disciples had to be taught that soul force was not just a political weapon but a way of life that involved moral uplift and the reconstruction of society along Ruskinian ideals of social harmony and equality. In South Africa Gandhi established first the Phoenix Settlement in 1904 and then the Tolstoy Farm in 1910; in India he formed a series of communal hermitages or ashrams, homes "where men and women may have scope for free and unfettered development of character, in keeping with the national genius."[63] These utopian settlements were more than test-tube experiments in a new kind of social engineering based on religion and ahimsa, not on conflict or enforced social control from above. They were models of what Gandhi hoped Indian society as a whole would become, spawning grounds of future satyagrahis and retreats for the families of his soldier-martyrs. Like any good general, Gandhi knew how to recruit his troops and look after them.

Satyagraha in South Africa was only marginally successful. What he achieved by nonviolent disobedience between 1906 and 1913—mass strikes, mass violation of the law, mass arrests, and his own imprisonment for 249 days as a consequence of his seven arrests—was a compromise: the repeal of the Black Act and other specific discriminatory measures but not the end of discrimination. His actions, however, were sufficient to earn from Jan Christian Smuts, when he learned in late 1914 that Gandhi had sailed for India, the delighted comment: "The saint has left our shores, I sincerely hope forever."[64]

In South Africa Gandhi was up against a government just as committed to principle as he was, and it refused, except on the periphery, to give way on the principle of white supremacy and racism. The prime minister of the newly formed Union of South Africa, Louis Botha, made the point painfully clear in 1913; the government, he said, was "not prompted by a desire to get rid of the Asians, but was prompted by principle. In this country they had colored races to deal with, and they did not want to have the position complicated any further" by enfranchising the Indian population.[65] Not until Gandhi encountered a far more vulnerable and morally less intransigent opponent—the British Raj in India—and not until he developed a new and ultimate weapon in the arsenal of satyagraha—the fast—did the blood of the satyagrahi become the seeds of a revolution that eventually coerced, unnerved, and shamed the British out of India.

The image of a free India took shape in Gandhi's imagination long before he left South Africa. It first appeared in written form—*Hind Swaraj or Indian Home Rule*—as he was returning from London to Capetown in 1908, a fortnight's voyage. Like so many Gandhian mental pictures, the treatise's conceptual starting point was the individual and the spiritual regeneration of men and women as separate entities filled with divine potential. A free India had to do with a metamorphosis of a people into a nation fit to be free. No amount of speechifying, grandstanding, constitution scribbling, demagoguery, or armed resistance could make India worthy of self-government; the message had to touch each Indian heart, move each Indian hand and foot. "Nobility of soul," he told his cousin Maganlal Gandhi, "consists in realizing that you are yourself India. In your emancipation is the emancipation of India. All else is make-believe."[66]

Gandhi transposed the political and explosive issue of independence from British rule onto a higher moral and historic plane, thereby turning hatred of the English and the violence which that implied into a philosophical principle devoid of particular human faces. India, he argued, was not being ground down "under the English heel but under that of modern civilization."[67] Hatred of the British should be "transferred to their civilization," which was satanic because Western civilization was founded on, propelled by, and fostered violence, greed, and aggression.[68] India had to be twice purged: sterilized of its modern industrialized corruption and cleansed of an attitude of mind that perceived only Indian inferiority, cowardice, and helplessness in the face of presumed white superiority. "Ours is a religious movement," he wrote the British viceroy in 1921, "designed to purge Indian political life of corruption, deceit, terrorism and the incubus of white supremacy."[69] That incubus, he insisted, was in fact a myth, the invention of British political strategy and historians who had rewritten Indian history to prove that India was the creation of the Raj and could not get along without British rule. The English, the Mahatma said, had "not taken India" because of the superiority of their culture or race, but because "we have given it to them," and they continue in India not "because of their strength but because we keep them."[70]

India had to be awakened to its own greatness and to the quality of its historic past, and Gandhi painted a magnificent picture of an ancient Hindu culture devoid of the destructive rapaciousness of lawyers, the moral turpitude of modern doctors, and the brutalizing effect of railroads. He described a civilization based on harmony and nonviolence and an educational system that taught duties, not rights. A truly civilized society was one where "performance of duty and observance of morality" were "convertible terms," and with considerable pride he noted that in Gujarati the word "civilization" meant "good conduct."[71]

For Gandhi the past and the future were inseparably linked—what India would become after independence was a reflection of what it had once been before Western civilization and industrialization had engulfed and corrupted it. Both his vision of a future society and his myth of a past India rejected the hierarchical model of social organization. He denied the need for a vertex of privilege, monopolizing economic and military power and enforcing its will in the name of law and order on the rest of society. His paradigm was an ocean of harmoniously interacting and highly self-controlled individuals, each reacting to the ebb and flow of tradition and each fulfilling those collective and historic duties assigned them by family, caste, and community: in microcosm, a romanticized version of the Indian village. The dynamism, the creative force within such a body politic, rested with the individual, not with the state or the system. Gandhi was emphatic: "That government is the best that governs the least."[72] As a saint who was also a revolutionary, he repudiated the premise that humanity is both a victim and a product of its social environment and that society has to be restructured before people can be reformed. For the Mahatma the path to the kingdom of God on earth lay in inspiring the hearts of individuals and nourishing the desire within them to change themselves. Only then could society be improved.

"I cannot conceive," Gandhi once said, "a greater loss to a man than the loss of self-respect."[73] The trick, of course, was to make Indians both in South Africa and on the subcontinent aware of self-respect so that they could be conscious of its loss. That meant cultivating and reviving pride of culture, rediscovering an Indian identity. Nehru had an inspired sense of his mentor's purpose when he pointed out that the Mahatma achieved for India the equivalent of "a psychological change": he probed deeply into the subconscious of the Indian mind, disclosed the origins of its complex, and rid the patient of the nightmare of misconception and inferiority.[74]

"To command respect is the first step to *swaraj*"—literally *swa*, meaning self, and *raj*, meaning rule. But for Gandhi neither respect nor the self-rule of independence could be achieved by merely outdoing the English and their civilization: hoisting the Indian flag, possessing an army and a navy, and standing tall in the world community of aggressive nations. Such a victory was simply to evict the British tiger from Indian soil but to keep the "tiger's nature," to "make India English," and replace "Hindustan" with "Englistan," the substitution of one kind of tyranny for another. "This is not the *swaraj* that I want."[75] His "scheme for the country's freedom" was very different: "The instant India is purified India becomes free and not a moment earlier."[76] Like the phoenix (for which Gandhi had named his first utopian community in South Africa), India was to rise anew out of the ashes of Western civilization and foreign domination. The secret to such a miracle lay, not in the "mere withdrawal of the English," but in the true meaning of *swaraj*—"real home-rule is self-rule or self-control" on a national level.[77]

Gandhi never desired Indian freedom in the sense that John Brown aimed at the abolition of slavery by force of arms. The Mahatma claimed—not too convincingly—that he was willing to retain the British Raj if it would only function "as the servant of the people"; "if the English become Indianized we can accommodate them."[78] Gandhi's dream was Indian self-dignity and fearlessness. "If we trust and fear God, we shall have to fear no one, not Maharajas, not Viceroys, not the detectives, not even King George."[79] And in 1930 he proved his words. Dressed only in loincloth, shawl, and sandals, he visited George V and Queen Mary. When asked whether he thought he had enough clothes on for the occasion, he retorted, "The King has enough on for both of us."[80] For Gandhi the awe and magic that sustained majesty and authority had gone out of the Raj.

The Mahatma was a dealer in symbols and spells. No one knew better than he how to smash the hypnotic paralysis which had allowed India, a country of 300 million, to be subjugated by 168,000 white foreigners for decades. He had an unerring instinct for the dramatic and the symbolic, for what caught and held the eye and the imagination, for what best expressed the core of India's debasement yet at the same time supplied a release to anger and a means by which rich and poor alike could unite to answer and defy the Raj. The famous salt march of 1930 and the calculated violation of the salt law were such symbolic acts, signs of both defiance and contempt. So were the wearing of homespun Indian cloth—khadi—and the spinning wheel. Khadi, claimed Nehru, was "the livery of our freedom." The spinning wheel, as the emblem of India's freedom from industrialization and Western civilization, was for Gandhi the symbol of "national consciousness."[81] In a sense the Mahatma himself—his asceticism, his self-control and self-inflicted suffering—was a living symbol of the new India that would replace the old India of the Raj. The governor of Madras spoke political truth when he said, "There is no doubt that Gandhi has got a tremendous hold on the public imagination."[82]

Gandhi arrived in Bombay in January of 1915 already a Very Important Person. For the next decade and a half he perfected satyagraha, suiting it to the peculiar needs of India and placing it at the service of *swaraj;* and he introduced into the satyagrahi's arsenal the fast, the Mahatma's most symbolic yet devastating weapon and his most potent spell in the battle to control the heart and soul of India. During those early years the magician learned four fundamental truths—two about his homeland and two about satyagraha—that set him apart from the rest of India's political leaders, turning him, as one British official bitterly complained, into "a religion" where "ordinary standards of logic and reason cannot be applied" except with "grave risk."[83]

The first truth about India was revealed almost the moment Gandhi returned: the British Raj was a paper tiger. Its backbone was the one thousand or so top administrators who ran the civil service and the British officers in charge of an Indian-recruited army supported by a few British regiments. Its strength lay in the fragmented nature of Indian society and in the support and loyalty given by the English-speaking and educated elements of the population. Lord Lamington, the governor of Bombay in 1906—two years before Gandhi wrote *Hind Swaraj*—had no doubts about the future of English rule: "The real guarantees of our stay in India remain as strong as ever, viz. the caste system, the diversity of nationalities and creeds, and the lack of confidence and trust of one native for another."[84] He might have also added the leaden apathy of India's toiling millions. By 1920 Gandhi sensed that these guarantees could not be relied on and that the Raj was "running on the momentum" of its previous prestige.[85] Equally important, the will to rule was dying. More and more "the empire was a daily grind,"[86] while the authoritarianism of the Raj was becoming a source of increasing embarrassment to the British themselves. As Gandhi put it: "I have found Englishmen amenable to reason and persuasion, and, as they always wish to appear just, it is easier to shame them than others into doing the right thing."[87] The Mahatma was certain that he could rely on British "moral sensibilities," so that he could convert, instead of coerce, them into submission. The campaign for self-rule did not have to evict the British; so long as it created Indian identity, a sense of national cohesion and self-control, independence would inevitably follow, because the moral credibility of the Raj and the self-confidence of the men who ran it would have been destroyed.

The Raj may have been fatally vulnerable, but Gandhi soon learned another truth about power: human nature being what it is, men do not give up authority willingly. During and after the First World War, the British spoke temptingly about devolution, sharing power with the Indians and working toward future independence and dominion status. The Mahatma soon came to the conclusion that these fair-sounding words were simply wartime palaver and fig leaves placed over actual tyranny. The British—both the imperial government in London and the viceroy in Delhi—would never give up India unless forced to do so. In February of 1920 Gandhi sought to supply that force by inviting the Indian National Congress to participate in an all-India satyagraha to evict the British bag and baggage. He called upon India to boycott the educational and judicial systems and foreign- and British-made goods and to cease paying taxes. He also appealed to Indian civil servants to resign their positions and return their imperial honors and decorations. In doing so, he not only learned that the Raj was far from moribund and its physical and psychological hold on India impressive but also discovered two other important truths about satyagraha itself: civil disobedience possessed within it the seeds of anarchy, and it had little chance of success unless based on Hindu-Muslim cooperation.

In calling for nationwide noncooperation, Gandhi made what he described as a "Himalayan miscalculation." He placed the cause of independence in the hands of untrained satyagrahi unable to sustain nonviolence—the very essence of satyagraha. As a consequence, civil disobedience became entangled with local hatreds, vendettas, and passions. The ensuing violence "stunk" in the Mahatma's nostrils, and after two years he canceled the campaign: "Our swaraj has got to be won, worked and maintained through truth and ahimsa alone."[88] Ahimsa demanded absolute discipline, but it also required focus, a symbolic purpose with which all India could associate yet which was politically attainable. Civil disobedience that simply aimed at evicting the British was difficult to control, invited violence, and required such a fundamental change of heart on the part of the Raj as to be politically unimaginable. Noncooperation had to be organized and staffed by trained and dedicated satyagrahis—potential martyrs who would rather die than defend themselves or commit violence. Only leaders who believed in ahimsa and had calculated beforehand every tactical and strategic aspect of the campaign could control the weapon of civil resistance and prevent its violent misuse.

The realization that satyagraha would lead to mass bloodshed unless sternly harnessed was only one of the truths learned during the early 1920s. The other was that any moral confrontation with the Raj was doomed unless Indians of all creeds, castes, and tongues acted in unison and worked together for swaraj through satyagraha. What little success noncooperation had attained in the past was largely the result of Hindu-Muslim cooperation, and religious rivalry between the two faiths had at all cost to be averted. Almost from the start Gandhi sensed that "before they dare think of freedom" Hindu and Muslim had to be "brave enough to love one another, to tolerate one another's religion, even prejudices and superstitions, and to trust one another."[89] Equally important, the Indian National Congress Party had to be viewed as the sole organ for all India and an acceptable governmental option to the Raj. "My ambition," Gandhi said, "is to see the Congress recognized as the one and only party that can successfully resist the Government and deliver the goods. It is the only party which, from its inception, has represented all minorities."[90] This meant Congress had to speak for Muslims as well as Hindus, for untouchables as well as caste Indians, for Dravidian-Tamil southern India as well as Aryan-Hindi-speaking northern India. At all costs the specter of a Hindu, caste-dominated Congress replacing a British Raj had to be dispelled. Most of the Mahatma's energies during the 1920s went into the extraordinarily difficult act of heightening Indian awareness of its Hindu historic and cultural greatness, in reintroducing the spirit of religion into national politics, and in advertising the essential spiritual unity of all India without alienating the Muslims and the untouchables and generating in their minds the image of orthodox Hindu domination.

Evidence that the Raj still possessed teeth and was ready to use them came a month after Gandhi ended his all-India disobedience campaign: the government arrested, tried, and sentenced him to jail. But if the government thought it could dispel the "old zealot's" magic by imprisonment, it was sadly mistaken. Since mass satyagraha had failed, Gandhi simply carried on the campaign as a one-man enterprise, and he promptly turned his arrest and trial into a highly advertised media spectacle of politeness, sweet reason, and perfect ahimsa confronted by the naked force of the Raj. He never denied the government's case that he was a rebel and a threat to authority. He had indeed preached "disaffection towards the existing system of government"; it was his "passion" to do so. And in words reminiscent of John Brown, he proclaimed, "I do not ask for mercy. I do not ask for any extenuating act of clemency. I am here, therefore, to invite and cheerfully submit to the highest penalty that can be inflicted upon me for what in law is a deliberate crime." Then, in a marvelously typical Gandhian maneuver, he turned the tables on the presiding judge and placed him in the moral wrong: "The only course open to you" is "either to resign your post, or inflict on me the severest penalty, if you believe that the system and the law you are assisting to administer are good for the people of this country." Gandhi was in no way repentant, and he took the occasion to outline the enormity of the British crime against India, a "crime against humanity which is perhaps unequaled in history." British rule had "emasculated" an entire nation. When an unhappy and highly embarrassed judge sentenced him to six years in prison but expressed the hope the sentence would be set aside or reduced by a higher authority, the Mahatma rose, said he thought the judgment mild, and congratulated the judge—"I could not have ex-

pected greater courtesy."[91] As the criminal was escorted out of the court-
house, the spectators wept and tried to kiss the floor where he walked on
his way to prison.

The performance was not only a magnificent gesture in defiance of the
Raj but also a central part of satyagraha, a way of turning jail into "a gateway of liberty" and a temple of honor. "We must widen the gates of
prison" and "enter them as a bridegroom enters the bride's chamber. Freedom is to be wooed only inside prison walls and sometimes on the gallows,
never in the council chambers, courts or the school room."[92] Gandhi knew
exactly how frustrating it was to the law-and-order mentality to be confronted with a prisoner who regarded going to prison a favor and a positive
aid to his criminal purpose, especially when that authority suspected that
he might be correct: jail did not remove the Mahatma or the cause of independence from the public mind; it simply publicized both.

Off and on during the next two decades, Gandhi spent over five and a
half years in Indian jails, where he thrived largely because the Raj treated
him as a very special kind of criminal, and it permitted him visitors and
communication with the outside world. Jail also had the added advantage
of focusing and personalizing the cause of swaraj on the Mahatma himself.
But the soul-force weapon that proved to be Gandhi's special hallmark,
maintaining the limelight on him, permitting him to carry on a form of private satyagraha, and bringing him to the brink of martyrdom, was the
fast—"an infallible weapon in the armoury of satyagraha."[93]

Fasting, as Gandhi himself observed, is as old as Adam.[94] As a method of
self-purification and chastisement of the flesh in preparation for a closer association with the deity, it is admired by Christians, Buddhists, Hindus, and
Muslims alike. Fasting is central to the self-control and self-focusing that
unite man and God. Medieval Irish saints and kings regularly warred against
one another by fasting. Modern Irish political prisoners go on hunger strikes
to embarrass and coerce the British government. An American doctor has
taken up fasting as a way of dramatizing the injustice of laws prohibiting the
medical profession from assisting terminally ill patients to a painless death.
And Indian beggars at one time fasted as a way of protesting and advertising
the failure of the rich to satisfy them. Fasting for the Mahatma became the
most potent, far-reaching, and theatrical way of publicizing and symboliz-
ing the plight of India; the perfect example of his extraordinary instinct for
tapping and manipulating the popular imagination and concentrating it
upon himself and his cause. In his hands it became a new kind of political
weapon, against which there was no real defense. It possessed all of the psychological and dramatic impact of actual martyrdom but none of martyrdom's defects. It was, he bluntly put it, "a very strong measure."[95]

Fasting "had its own science" and was "a fiery weapon" which had to be handled with care and discretion. It was only to be wielded by an expert long practiced in self-control. "He who has no inner strength," Gandhi said, "should not dream" of employing it. "No one who has not earned the right to do so should . . . use this weapon."[96] Fasting was the culminating action of the experienced and inspired brahmachari, the application of asceticism to politics and the badge of his right to lead and instruct. Asceticism runs through the lives of many of the martyrs—Socrates, Becket, More—but only Gandhi was able to use it as a political force. The Mahatma was secure in his faith that all those years living "a life of truth and nonviolence" had given him "the right to speak through his fast." He regarded the weapon as being uniquely his own, to be shared with no one. Fasting was his "special gift from God to appeal to the heart and soul of the people."[97] After enduring the physical agony and spiritual exhilaration of ten public fasts since his arrival in India, he did not hesitate to claim in 1946 "that no one was to undertake a fast without my permission."[98]

Of one thing Gandhi was certain: the fast was a means to an end. He was inflicting desperate suffering upon himself and playing brinkmanship with his most precious commodity—his life—and he had no intention of squandering that commodity on the unattainable. No fast was ever conditional upon the British retreat from India; that would have been suicidal. He made this point manifestly clear in 1932 when he wrote that "if Gandhi took up his stand at the Viceregal gateway and threatened to fast even for one day unless the British Government withdrew from the country, the Government would be justly entitled to arrest him and imprison him till he came to his senses."[99] Eight years later, in 1940, he was contemplating a fast that would have "significance not only for the whole of India but for the whole world," but he was careful not to require of the Raj what it could not give: "Seeing the present situation [World War II] and the present attitude of the British, it is not likely that the Government will change their policy to save my life. Saving their own lives has become so important to them that they will not hesitate to sacrifice fifty Gandhis for it."[100]

Only once did the Mahatma tangle directly with the Raj; this was when he felt that his personal honor was in jeopardy. Lord Linlithgow, the viceroy, accused Gandhi and the Congress Party in 1943 of having caused the appalling violence of 1942–43 (208 police stations and 749 other government buildings destroyed, sabotage to the cost of 2,735,125 rupees, over 2,500 killed or injured and some 66,000 jailed) as a consequence of the nationwide satyagraha called by Gandhi to force the British to quit India. Gandhi in his turn blamed the violence on the government's excessive repressive measures and its shortsighted and panic-generated imprisonment of all the Congress leaders, including the Mahatma, thereby leaving the campaign leaderless and throwing it into mob hands. The seventy-four-year-old Gandhi set about a twenty-one-day fast to prove his integrity and to appeal to a higher tribunal than the Raj's so-called justice. He was determined to place the government in the wrong: if he did "not survive the ordeal . . . posterity will judge between you [the viceroy] as representative of an all-powerful Government and me a humble man who tried to serve his country and humanity through it."[101] The viceroy, urged on by an adamant Churchill in London, allowed him to achieve his purpose and took the appalling risk of his dying while in jail. To this day the purpose of the fast remains obscure, and for many the encounter seemed to be the performance of two stubborn men, neither of whom could afford to back down. Since the fast resolved nothing, had no definable purpose, and neither side could retreat, Gandhi did not risk a "fast unto death." As with two previous efforts to achieve unmeasurable ends—fostering Hindu-Muslim unity in 1924 and purifying Hinduism of the spiritual bigotry of untouchability in 1933—he carefully limited the fast to the precise length of time that would not be fatal: twenty-one days.

Gandhi had no intention of dying. As he said, he hoped to live to be 125, and he was extremely careful, especially when committed to fasts unto death, either to leave himself a way out by maintaining easily redefinable ends or by staking his life on issues that were politically resolvable. His most famous fast, the epic ordeal of September 1932, was a fast unto death announced and concluded with immense public fanfare while he was a prisoner of the Raj in Yeravda jail, and it lasted six days. Its spiritual aim was to "sting the conscience of caste Hindus into right action,"[102] but its political purpose was more pragmatic and obtainable: to force the untouchables, under the leadership of Dr. B. R. Ambedkar, and the British government in London to give up plans for a separate electoral system for the untouchables. The establishment of a dual electorate whereby the depressed classes, as the untouchables were called, would receive a double vote—one as Hindus, the other as untouchables—was part of a larger constitutional scheme to increase the electorate and to safeguard the rights of minorities, Muslims and untouchables, within an overwhelming Hindu majority. For Gandhi this plan cruelly publicized and aggravated the cancer of untouchability, constitutionalizing a moral monstrosity and vivisecting and corrupting Hinduism forever. "I have to resist," he wrote the British prime minister, "your decision with my life. The only way I can do it is by declaring a perpetual fast unto death from food of any kind save water with or without salt and soda."[103]

For a week all of India was held captive to a single overriding concern: how to save the Mahatma's life and prevent him from becoming a martyr. If Rome worked to supply the early Christians with a public stage on which they were so anxious to die, the British Empire, stuck with the Mahatma in its jail, worked even more vigorously to remove such a forum from its most important potential martyr. Dr. Ambedkar, crying foul and describing the fast as a "political stunt," but confronted with an opponent who was clearly using the threat of his own death as a bargaining weapon at each step of the negotiations, finally backed down. Gandhi in his turn accepted a partial compromise whereby untouchables lost their double vote—a symbolic anathema to the Mahatma—but received an increased number of reserved seats in the new assembly. Having achieved this victory, Gandhi went on to beard the British lion—the prime minister's acceptance of the new formula or the Mahatma's life. It was a safe call. The prime minister and the Raj were delighted to adopt the new political solution—it did not touch upon the realities of British power in India.

Gandhi used a somewhat similar approach in his fast unto death in 1939. This time his life was staked against the thakur of Rajkot's refusal to live up to his promise to introduce political reforms into his princely state. The Mahatma regarded the issue to be a spiritual one—a breach of faith—and threatened a death fast until the thakur did as he had promised; but just in case he shouldn't, and to break a potential impasse, Gandhi let it be known that he would accept the intervention of the viceroy on behalf of the people of Rajkot. Lord Linlithgow, far more agitated by the thought of the Indian-wide consequences of the Mahatma's starving to death than by any reforming zeal, promptly placed the issue in the hands of the chief justice of India, thereby affording Gandhi grounds for ending his fast after four days.

Gandhi's two final fasts were also without a life-saving time limit. They took place after independence, when an India torn by religious violence had emerged that was in the Mahatma's eyes a hideous and bisected distortion of the unified and nonviolent vision which he had hoped would replace the British Raj. He no longer wished to live to be 125. Death, he said, would be "a glorious deliverance rather than that I should be a helpless witness of the destruction of India, Hinduism, Sikhism and Islam."[104] But even so, he carefully left the door ajar and tied his suffering to realistic ends. On the last day of August 1947, only a fortnight after independence, Calcutta erupted into religious rioting and Gandhi himself was almost hit by a brick. His physical presence in the city seemed to have no effect; so he turned to the satyagrahi's weapon of last resort, the fast, to "touch the hearts of all the warring factions in the Punjab." He anchored the fast, however, to a more reasonable and attainable conclusion: he would end it "when sanity returned to Calcutta," which it did in seventy-three hours.[105] Four months later, in January of 1948, he faced an even more serious Hindu-Muslim confrontation, which seemed to be escalating into a spiral of never-ending atrocities. After brooding over the renewal of violence in Delhi, he announced that "No man, if he is pure, has anything more precious to give than his life." He would offer his life in an all-in fast to soften hearts hardened to compassion and tolerance, and he would conclude that slow death only when he was "satisfied that there is a reunion of hearts of all communities brought about . . . from an awakened sense of duty." The out, however, was clear: "If the whole of India responds or at least Delhi does, the fast might be soon ended." Delhi took longer than Calcutta, but it responded to the Mahatma's threat in six days.[106]

Gandhi fasted for all sorts of reasons and for varying lengths of time—three, five, six, seven, twenty-one days. His first recorded fast in response to pressures outside himself and his personal spiritual odyssey was in 1913, when he fasted as penance for a perceived moral breach within his Phoenix community. He endured a seven-day fast for another case of moral lapse—the sexual transgressions of a group of young boys—in his Satyagraha Ashram in 1925, saying that corporal chastisement did not purify children, it only hardened them: "If I am to identify myself with the grief of the least in India . . . let me identify myself with the sins of the little ones under my care."[107] (Again, shades of John Brown.) Fasting was employed many times over to do penance for the sins of humanity and to "strengthen the weak, to energize the sluggards and to give faith to the skeptics."[108] He applied it to prick Hindu conscience and rid Hinduism of untouchability, and he used it again to insist on his right while in prison to do the menial and polluting work of an untouchable. But despite its many lengths and occasions, the generic purpose of the fast for Gandhi was threefold: personal, symbolic, and political.

Fasting was always a private concern, a question between the Mahatma and his Maker. It was a form of prayer: "Fasting which is not an integral part of prayer is mere torture of the flesh doing no good to anyone." It could only be undertaken at God's instigation and with divine help. "I am not responsible for these fasts," he said, and, as if he were addressing Tertullian, he added, "I would not torture the flesh for the love of fame." His fasts were "bearable only because they were imposed upon me by a higher power." They were the product of an "intense agony of the soul," and when "God bids me [fast], no one can prevent me." The fast was a form of high-intensity prayer and self-purification which put him in direct contact with God and filled him, despite the pain, with "indescribable peace."[109]

Gandhi was, in psychiatric parlance, the perfect approval seeker. He blamed himself when others disappointed him or failed to maintain his high moral standards. The fault lay in his own failure to purify himself, not in the sins of others. In a sense he practiced a sort of social Christian Science: the evils of this world, its violence, falsehood, wars, and other social diseases, were in some inexplicable way associated with his own inability to eradicate sin within himself. He took upon himself the burden and responsibility of all humanity's guilt; only by spiritual self-cleansing could he help the world and atone for its misdeeds. "Real fasting puts the soul in tune with the Maker. It puts life into one's prayer." Even more important, the "true fast generates a silent, unseen force which may, if it is of requisite strength and purity, pervade all mankind."[110]

Fasting, Gandhi explained, could only be directed at "lovers" who might sense that "silent, unseen force."[111] Two cardinal limitations were attached to a satyagrahi's fast: "It should be against the lover and for his reform," never "for extorting rights from him." The satyagrahi could fast against his father "to cure him of a vice," such as drinking, because the desire to abstain from alcohol already existed and there was love between the father and son. Thus the son's own purification and supplication to God would give the father the strength to reform himself. The son, however, should never fast "in order to get from him an inheritance": that would be a misuse of fasting, rather like the beggar fasting against the rich man.[112]

Faith, self-purification, and the atonement for sin in others was the underlying core of a fast, but it was also a sign of the Mahatma's own commitment. Like living up to a principle by dying for it—an interesting oxymoron—his self-inflicted suffering was proof he was in earnest. He had devised a means of establishing his own credibility in the eyes of society, and at the commencement of his first public fast at Ahmedabad to strengthen mill workers and keep them true to their pledge, he fasted in order to prove he was not "out to have fun at your cost or to act a play." In part he was punishing himself for the workers' weakness; in part he was driving home to them the anguish he felt for their having broken a "vow so solemnly taken"; and in part he was giving them new determination to carry on the strike.[113]

The fast, however, was more than a personal pledge; it was also a magnificent public-relations ploy, a gripping symbol with which all India could empathize. Gandhi was extraordinarily astute about what the fast could achieve politically, and he was perfectly frank about why he used it. He needed, he said in 1931, "some definite, drastic action which even millions could understand" in order to make all of India believe him when he said that the country "must take him literally in all he spoke," and "that there was no conscious mental reservation." When he said he believed in nonviolence, he spoke the absolute truth; there were no possible exceptions. "Hence I deliberately adopted the method of public expiation by open fasting."[114] Three years later he was even more explicit: "You can influence the mass mind not through speeches or writings but only by something which is most well understood by the masses; that is suffering, and the most acceptable method is that of fasting." Only by fasting could he shake India out of its complacency. It was a spectacular moral weapon, and the man who wielded it was totally credible: "How can I speak to these millions, or identify myself with them, without . . . knowing myself what pangs of hunger mean?"[115]

Symbolically the fast exercised the same devastating shock that the cross had achieved, but in this case the messiah did not have to die to achieve his purpose. Both fast and Calvary relied on the spectacle of suffering freely elected; both reached out to humanity, and both established the spiritual credentials of the holy man. Indeed, it could be argued that the fast was an even more forceful symbol than the cross, because all of suffering India knew what it meant to starve; the agony of death impaled on the cross was beyond imagination. Moreover, the fast had a double impact; its conclusion, the rejoicing when the Mahatma took his first nourishment, as well as the agony of starvation possessed tremendous emotional effect and publicity value. On the final day of the 1924 twenty-one-day religious-unity fast, crowds, which wanted to be present at the climax, gathered at the home of Mahomed Ali, where Gandhi had elected to carry out his ordeal. At the bedside as he took his first sip of orange juice, verses from the Koran and the Upanishads were read, and the hymn "When I Survey the Wondrous Cross"—Gandhi's favorite—was sung. The theatrics could not have been better staged. The same planning was applied to the epic fast of 1932. It ended on September 26 in the presence of 203 people and a large number of journalists.

Such a weapon, although always advertised as an instrument of moral improvement, had immense political clout.[116] Gandhi argued that its strength lay in the force of persuasion to do the right thing. Others said that the persuasion, since the Mahatma's life was at stake, of necessity spilled over into coercion. Still others openly claimed that Gandhi's fasting was blatant political blackmail. The debate emerged the very first time the Mahatma took his fasting public in the mill strike at Ahmedabad in 1918. Gandhi was a close friend of Ambalal Sarabhai, the leading mill owner, who understandably felt that his friend was not playing fair when he in-

troduced his life into the confrontation between the owners and the workers. Gandhi was capitalizing on friendship and Sarabhai's reluctance to see
a friend suffer. The Mahatma recognized the strength of the argument and
did not like it. His pledge to fast, he admitted, carried "a taint." "It is likely
that, because of my vow [to fast], the mill owners may be moved by consideration for me and come to grant the workers' thirty-five percent increase [in pay]. . . . They would do so out of charity, and to that extent this
pledge is one which cannot but fill me with shame." He comforted himself, however, by noting that "in doing public work, a man must be prepared to put up even with such loss of face."[117] Gandhi was nothing if not
a pragmatist.

For Dr. Ambedkar, "there was nothing noble" about the Mahatma's epic
fast of September 1932. "It was a foul and filthy stunt," which by a single
adroit political move, carefully disguised as high principle, cut the ground
from under his leadership of the untouchables and turned him into a vil-
lain.[118] The Raj felt rather the same way in its name-calling dispute with
Gandhi in 1943: in its estimation the "naked fakir" had confronted them
with an "utterly illegitimate method of political controversy, levying blackmail on the best of human emotions—pity and sympathy—by his fast."[119]

Gandhi never quite extricated himself from the logic that fasting was in
fact a form of threatening and coercion. He admitted his epic fast did "unfortunately coerce some people into action which they would not have en-
dorsed without my fast," and he confessed his fast of August 16–23, 1933, to
persuade his jailers to let him work with untouchables was instrumental in
their decision to release him from prison.[120] He was set free for exactly the
same reasons he had been liberated three months earlier for the duration of
his twenty-one-day self-and-all-India purification fast: the government did
not want him dying in one of its jails. During the August fast he was so
weak he had to be hospitalized on August 20, and consequently was unconditionally released on the twenty-third. With considerable sophistry
Gandhi maintained that any coercion inherent in fasting in no way detracted from the purity of the nonviolence that fasting as a weapon represented. "In any examination of moral conduct," he argued, "the intention
is the chief ingredient." He had not intended to pressure anyone. His purpose in the epic fast "was most decidedly not to induce, irrespective of mer-
its, the decision I desired." Instead, "it was to stir the Hindus to action on
my submission." That it went beyond this and coerced people was "unfortunate," but such was life. As for the August fast, his intent was not to pressure the superintendent of the prison. "I wanted the Government to take
me at my word and let me die in peace, if they could not see the justice" of
allowing him to work with untouchables.[121]

The Mahatma was quite prepared to practice what he preached. It was, he stated, theoretically possible for two people to fast against one another and both be wrong. If so, "let both of them die."[122] When General M. R. Awari fasted in February of 1946 on an issue Gandhi felt to be invalid and disruptive of society, Gandhi was absolutely ruthless. He dismissed the fast as a mere "hunger strike" and wrote that it was regrettable that the general "should persist in committing suicide by fasting. . . . If he refuses to listen, I fear, he must be allowed to die without evoking the slightest sympathy. I say this as the author of Satyagraha including fasts. . . . Public sympathy with capricious fasting can disrupt society."[123]

Over the years Gandhi's position on the fast changed. Originally he had argued that fasting to express one's displeasure or to pressure someone by the sight of your suffering was "the worst form of compulsion."[124] By 1944, however, he was asserting not only that fasting was "the last resort of the satyagrahi" but also that it could be undertaken for "protest" as well as for "penance" and "purification." "When people cannot be made to do anything, it is the right of the lone satyagrahi to resort to this final measure."[125] To the argument that a fast might be disguised blackmail, he insisted on a redefinition of the meaning of coercion: "If I fast in order to awaken the conscience of an erring friend whose error is beyond question, I am not coercing him in the ordinary sense of the word."[126] To the Raj's charge of blackmail, he had a slightly different answer. Wasn't it better to openly credit the enemy with sensitivity and nobility and to evoke these virtues by fasting than to take the opponent's life secretly by force? Wasn't it better "to trifle with one's own life by fasting or some other way of self-immolation" than "to trifle with it" by attempting to kill the "opponent and his dependents"?[127]

Blackmail, Gandhi argued, implied both a selfish purpose and a bluff. If one's opponent regarded "the end of a fast to be selfish or otherwise base," he "should resolutely refuse to yield to it, even though the refusal may result in the death of the fasting person."[128] If, as did Dr. Ambedkar, he thought a fast unto death to be a political trick, he should call that bluff, because on one issue the Mahatma was adamant: a satyagrahi should never go into a fast expecting or even thinking about the political consequences. The fast was an end in itself, a testing of the body, and it should only be entered into with the firmest willingness to die: fasting "must come from the depths of one's soul." The last words the Mahatma ever spoke about fasting, only days before his own death, stressed this point: "A pure fast, like duty, is its own reward. I do not embark upon it for the sake of the result it may bring. I do so because I must. Hence I urge everybody dispassionately to examine the purpose and let me die, if I must, in peace which I hope is ensured."[129]

The fast unto death may have been "the last seal" upon the satyagrahi's faith, and the Mahatma may have been absolutely sincere in his insistence that no one should "look upon the possibility of a fast by me as the sword of Damocles," but there was inherent in all his fasts a built-in paradox.[130] The fast was a means to an end, and its political teeth relied in large measure on the threat of death and its violent consequences. But if the faster died, he destroyed his means, and, worse, in dying he generated ends that could change, possibly ruin, the original purpose for which the fast was intended. Despite all of Gandhi's assurances to let him die, he was generally very careful not to do so. One feels considerable sympathy for Viceroy Lord Irwin, who threw up his hands in bafflement and confessed that the Mahatma was "as hard to pin down on a point of logic as a butterfly on the plains of his native Gujarat."[131]

The Mahatma's logic was as unpredictable as a butterfly, because Gandhi could never decide how to handle the presence of death in fasting. Its existence was irrefutable, but he always denied its coercive potential and adamantly maintained that a proper fast must never be associated with suicide, which was the philosophical negation of ahimsa and nonviolence, because suicide was the ultimate violent violation of the body. The great weakness of the cross as a symbol had been its brutality: Calvary was suffering steeped in violence. Fasting, in contrast, was nonviolent suffering and therefore more appealing. When asked whether fasting unto death did not imply loss of faith in nonviolence, Gandhi vigorously denounced the implication and asserted that the death fast served as "the final weapon in the hands of a nonviolent person."[132] He distinguished the fast from suicide just as strenuously and for much the same reason as did the early church fathers when they differentiated martyrdom from self-annihilation. Any suggestion of suicide undercut the principles upon which both martyrdom and fasting rested, and it destroyed their psychological impact. He admitted that there was danger that fasting might stem from despair—that was "rank suicide"[133]—but even after independence, when his voice cried in the wilderness of religious hatred and national disunity, and when his final two fasts might well be interpreted as having been motivated in part by desperation, he insisted that penance and purification, never hopelessness, inspired his actions. "Fasting unto death," he said, was a "corrupt expression"; far better to say he was "fasting unto a new life," rather in the style of the early Christian martyrs except that his "new life" could be attained, at least in theory, in this world.[134]

The presence of death, however, could not be denied; it hovered over the fast like a brooding omnipresence, and Gandhi was forced to admit "any fast must require some risk, otherwise it has no meaning."[135] Fasting involved torture of the flesh that could kill, and most of India waited in fear for exactly that to happen. The world press covered Gandhi's 1943 fast in day-by-day detail; but what concerned the media was not the saint's cause but the primordial question whether he would live or die. That gave the kick to the drama. Gandhi stated the reality which underlay the fast when he justified the presence of a regiment of doctors attending his May 1933 twenty-one-day fast to purify Hinduism of untouchability. "I was battling against death. I accepted all the help that came to me as Godsend."[136]

Fasting was clearly a "business" and a special calling as real and demanding as martyrdom, and it had the immense advantage of being repeatable (but not too repeatable). The Mahatma had no use or sympathy for the many abuses of the fast that were springing up all over India, and he complained bitterly that an epidemic of fasting was afflicting the subcontinent. He himself was threatened with fasts if he did not send his worshipers his autograph or if he did not stop off at their villages. Workers, erroneously believing they were modeling themselves on his mill workers' pledge fast, fasted for higher wages. Imprisoned satyagrahi fasted against unjust floggings while in prison (when they should have been welcoming such suffering).[137] All these abuses he scornfully dismissed as mere "hunger strikes," conducted "without previous preparation and adequate thought," and he warned that if "the process is repeated too often," such so-called fasts would "lose what little efficacy they may possess and become objects of ridicule." Even the legitimate fast, his own fasts, had to be "undertaken on very rare occasions" and only under "exceptional circumstances."[138]

Gandhi sensed, especially toward the end of his life, that the fast as a political weapon had severe limitations and contained within itself an unresolvable dilemma for the committed satyagrahi. It might, as with the Mahatma's final two fasts, have immense and immediate psychological impact, but, like martyrdom, it had little long-term staying power. Hindu-Muslim hatred, fanned by economic forces and new borders that left large religious minorities on each side of the frontier, could not be held in check for long by a holy man who refused to eat. The epic fast of 1932 coerced Dr. Ambedkar into accepting what he bitterly opposed, and the Mahatma was successful in pressuring the Raj into action where it had little at stake, but he wisely never tested the weapon against political issues that involved the government's survival. The fast by itself could never force the Raj to quit India; only Gandhi's death might have achieved that end. And therein lay the dilemma.

"What should I do?" Gandhi argued the case with himself in 1944. "Should I start mass Satyagraha? Or a revolution? That is possible. I can bring it about. But I do not want to do it. Nonviolence cannot remain in it. I will not take that risk. . . . Therefore the satyagrahi has only one weapon left and it is the fast. If I can move my forces thereby, I would do so. But nothing is certain yet."[139] The uncertainty revealed itself in two questions posed by the Mahatma's critics. "What guarantee was there that, if anything happened to him as a result [of a fast], it would not let loose a storm with none left to control it?" Gandhi's answer was an unhappy but honest one: "That may happen. I do not want it. But I would face that risk if the upshot of living a conscious life of truth and nonviolence for over half a century is that India, too, has to go through a blood-bath." His answer to the second question was considerably less honest, because the query contained a dilemma that he refused to confront. "Why should you not in that case invite the risk of chaos in pursuit of nonviolence while you are there in the flesh to control it?" Gandhi was faced with the lady-or-the-tiger situation. Behind one door stood his nonviolent means—the fast—and his survival, which would not generate sufficient social passion to force the British out of India but would maintain the sacred union of means and ends. Behind the other door also stood his nonviolent means, but this time in the company of his death, which would produce a sufficiently violent revolution to force the withdrawal of the British and lead to independence, the achievement of twenty-five years of struggle. In the second case, however, means and ends were no longer one; they had been parted not in the usual sense of the means corrupting the ends but of the violent ends invalidating the nonviolent means. In such a crisis, the very essence of satyagraha and soul force would be destroyed. Which was he to choose? Gandhi found no solution and avoided the dilemma by tying himself up in illogical knots. He would neither abandon the fast with its underlying threat of death and anarchy, nor would he accept the leadership of a revolution so as to control its violence, "because I do not want anarchy or chaos. I must work for orderliness, not anarchy. But if in that attempt anarchy comes in my way, I must not be deterred by it."[140] Nehru knew his Gandhi when he rather sourly wrote in his prison diary that the politics of fasting was "sheer revivalism, and clear thinking has not a ghost of a chance against it."[141]

Mercifully, the Mahatma never had to make a choice between means and ends. As World War II drew to its conclusion, it became apparent that the British, especially after the election of a Labor government, this time really did mean what they said: they would voluntarily quit India. Gandhi had been correct; their will to rule was dead.

By one count Gandhi spent 2,089 days in the Raj's prisons,[142] and he endured ten fasts related in one way or another to satyagraha aimed at swaraj; but ironically, he survived independence by only 168 days. On January 30,

1948, at a five o'clock open-air prayer meeting, for which he was ten minutes late, he was shot three times by an orthodox Hindu who saw in the 109-pound Mahatma the symbolic cause of India's woes after independence. Death resolved the paradox of a live martyr, especially one whom history, circumstance, and political style were passing by and who longed for the protection that martyrdom affords its heroes: they do not have to live with the consequences of their actions. For Gandhi, thirty-two years of labor had come on August 15, 1947, to "an inglorious end" as the imperial flag of the Raj was pulled down and replaced by the tricolors of a free India. There was no place for him in an independent India, and he did not like the independence he saw; this was not his definition of swaraj: the consciousness of "strength that comes from right doing."[143] The final sentence of his life—"I hate being late. I like to be at the prayer punctually at the stroke of five"[144]—was sadly inappropriate: he would have been a happier man, a sadhu who had fulfilled his calling, had he arrived to his execution two years early instead of ten minutes late.

M. K. Gandhi's death by the assassin's hand parallels the fate of Martin Luther King and calls into question the possibility of any valid definition of martyrdom. Both men died victims of private violence spawned by their public words and actions and for causes deeply entangled with state policy and religious morality. Technically, neither qualified as a martyr; but the Mahatma—like Tertullian, who also did not die a martyr—might be said to have mastered martyrdom. He understood its appeal and devastating psychological impact on society, and in a sense he found in fasting a device that allowed him to approximate martyrdom and to challenge death in a situation where the state declined to be the executioner. As he said, "We serve as well by dying as by living."[145]

"Why don't you make us all feel better and just *admit* that you're a deeply flawed
human being?"

Drawing by D. Reilly; © 1993 The New Yorker Magazine, Inc.

CHAPTER 12

THE TWENTIETH-CENTURY MARTYR:
AN ENDANGERED SPECIES?

MARTYRDOM AS a political instrument in the arsenal of satyagraha had worked reasonably well in India because the Raj was spiritually and structurally a relic of the past, far closer to the Austro-Hungarian Empire of the eighteenth and nineteenth centuries than to a twentieth-century nation-state. It was a political accident, held together partly by self-interest and force of arms, partly by force of habit and allegiance to the crown. Highly authoritarian, but not in the least totalitarian, the Raj was a ramshackle political conglomerate, possessing little ideological purpose except to keep the peace and interfering as little as possible in local government. For better or for worse, the viceroy and his cabinet exercised a minimum of directive planning and control as the subcontinent slowly acquired the economic infrastructure that could transform it from a geographic expression into a self-conscious modern state.

Gandhi himself was equally anachronistic. As a moral reformer trained in a nineteenth-century liberal tradition, he clung tenaciously to a spiritual and individualistic view of society and man. Except in India, he was a holy man out of place in a world exposed to virulent social ideologies, centripetal government forces, and secular justifications for action which had been set loose by the industrial revolution and World War I. Ironically, he won the battle of independence only to lose, in his own estimation, the war to make India a society worthy of political freedom. Almost from the start he sensed that "everyone was trying to fall at my feet, but no one was willing to listen to me."[1] He branded himself a failure because the India that emerged in 1948 rejected as nineteenth-century romantic nonsense his two cardinal principles for human progress: the state governs best that governs least, and the moral and spiritual regeneration of the individual must precede social and economic reorganization in order to achieve lasting reform in society. Even before Gandhi's death, the kind of martyrdom he preached and that had been practiced throughout Western society was being questioned. What possible place did the self-sacrifice of the martyr have in a world where the centralized, bureaucratic power of the state had grown into a juggernaut, where the totalitarian leviathan loudly proclaimed as its goal the merging of the individual into some idealized myth of racial or structural totality, and where God had been removed from the formula of what constitutes the good on earth?

Gandhi had sensed that martyrdom possessed two fatal weaknesses: it lost much of its effectiveness when overtly associated with political treason and violent social revolution, and it lost most of its meaning when secularized and stripped of its religious component. Both elements, the treasonous and the secular, were inherent in martyrdom from the start, but they grew exponentially as the martyr moved into the nineteenth and twentieth centuries. Socrates had opened up Pandora's box and undermined the moral fiber of Athenian society by teaching his fellow citizens to question historic and religious authority, but he never sought to reconstruct his city's society or to deny its laws. The Maccabees had refused to be Hellenized and were part of a violent Judaic insurrection against Seleucid rule; but as the story of their martyrdom is told, had Antiochus refrained from reshaping their Jewish souls, they would have granted him authority over their bodies. Only by implication are the Maccabees depicted as political rebels.

The career of Jesus had inescapable political overtones—existing Judaic-Roman reality fitted ill with God's kingdom—but Jesus made his political position clear. He assured Pontius Pilate, "My kingdom is not of this world"; had it been, "my soldiers would fight that I might not be handed over to the Jews."[2] Rome approached the early Christian martyrs as Antiochus had viewed the Jews: they were political-cum-religious deviants whose refusal to sacrifice to the emperor and participate in the accepted symbolic act of loyalty to Rome were tantamount to treason. But the martyrs themselves vigorously proclaimed their loyalty to the empire. They were far more concerned with the health of their souls and their chances of attaining heaven than in changing the social-political system, which Christianity, when it eventually prevailed, left unchanged. Thomas Becket was called a traitor to his feudal overlord, Henry II, and the archbishop achieved martyrdom as a consequence of a power struggle between two very human institutions—church and state—but he was no revolutionist, only a single-minded soldier of the Lord. His namesake Sir Thomas More was executed as a traitor to his king and as a criminal to an emerging national ideal that demanded not only the obedience of all citizens but also their active approval and support, and that united love of state with love of God. But More was such a passive and self-contained traitor that it took the institution for which he presumably sacrificed his life four centuries to honor him as one of its saintly heroes. As for Charles I, he may have been the luckless victim of power politics, economic change, and constitutional conflict, but in his own estimation at least, he died a martyr to a deeply religious approach to authority and society which assured him a warm welcome in heaven.

Only with John Brown do treason and martyrdom meld into a single explosive force and the cause of God and man join together into a revolutionary truth that aggressively demanded man's political and social well-being as well as his soul's salvation. Until old Osawatomie Brown entered the picture, martyrdom had been essentially a defensive act—defending the faith, the crown, the church, or the self. Brown took martyrdom on the offensive; he sought not to defend freedom but to destroy slavery. But even though Brown's goals were secular, the religious element remained dominant. He was driven by the overwhelming presence of divine wrath directed at the existence of human slavery. He saw himself as the Lord's revolutionary instrument on earth, the crusader for God's justice, not man's. Brown died to make the black man free; he stole government property and sought to abolish slave property; and he was executed by the Commonwealth of Virginia for a combination of theft, murder, and treason. But his actions were inspired by a messianic, not a secular, revolutionary zeal. He was committed to the knowledge that he was fulfilling God's purpose for mankind; he served as the catalyst that would bring about an apocalyptic fury sufficiently terrible to purge the nation of the sin of slavery. His was, he said, "the greatest service man can render God."

The deeply religious gloss that John Brown placed on the distasteful pill of treason and murder made violence and revolution palatable to many Northern abolitionists, but his violation of and attack on government property and the murder and kidnapping of Virginian citizens at Harpers Ferry shocked them deeply. For the first time the public was being asked to judge between the martyr and the terrorist. Were they one and the same? Did the term "martyr" have any meaning when linked to treason and the violent disruption and overthrow of government? Was there actually all that much difference between the idealistic rebel, who violated man's law in the name of God or human betterment, and the common criminal who did so for private gain? The results proved much the same. And most disturbing of all, how should society judge martyrdom motivated by hatred? Today we face the same dilemma: wherein lies the distinction between the hate-filled martyr bent on destruction and the revenge-filled terrorist who happily, if suicidally, drives a car bomb into the ranks of his enemies, killing hundreds to satisfy an obsession?

Gandhi was also an aggressive and self-proclaimed rebel, and, like Brown, he wrapped his revolutionary actions in the mantle of religion— but with a profound difference. For Brown, God and man were separate entities; for Gandhi they were one—the deity could not be found or worshiped apart from His creation, humanity itself. While Brown had equated love of God with the deity's hatred of slavery and slave owners, Gandhi had equated service to God with service to mankind, free of hatred, even of the perpetrators of injustice. Satyagraha—"the force that is born of truth and love or nonviolence"—was for Gandhi an ideology that sought not merely political independence but also attempted to achieve that end by spiritually revitalizing and morally reforming India, thereby making British rule both irrelevant and morally reprehensible. He always maintained the fiction that his purpose was to overthrow the government solely by love, never by force. Such means—soul force—required soldier-martyrs who, through absolute self-control, could conquer their adversaries "by suffering in one's own person." Gandhi insisted that no satyagrahi should ever lose sight of his means and the relationship of those means to self-improvement. Even fasting had to be entered into for the purification and strengthening of the satyagrahi, not for the political consequences of his suffering.

Gandhi and his disciples achieved an extraordinary level of heroic self-discipline, but it is well to remember that the Mahatma was operating in an environment unique to the twentieth century. Between the two world wars, even up to the moment of the Japanese entry into the Second World War, the Raj treated its political criminals, especially Gandhi, with respect and restraint in the style of the nineteenth century—no traitor was executed in Britain between 1820 and 1914, and after 1877 political prisoners were segregated from common criminals.[3] Equally important, it did not systematically deprive Gandhi and his fellow revolutionists access to the media or cut off the Mahatma from the rest of the world, even when in jail. As the commissioner of police in Bombay complained in 1931, Gandhi and the Congress Party relied on "the traditional humanity of the British combined with their fear of international criticism to protect them from any really drastic action." As a result the Raj had been maneuvered into a position of fighting the rebellion in a gentlemanly fashion on Congress's own terms "and with methods chosen by them." This kind of warfare, instead of generating fear, "which is the root of all decent government," begat only contempt.[4] Gandhi's "methods" succeeded largely because they were being applied by an increasingly self-conscious majority on the offensive against an already self-critical Raj. The experience of South Africa, however, was sufficient evidence that satyagraha was far less effective in the hands of a beleaguered minority on the defensive against an aggressive government determined to encroach upon, even abolish, civil rights.

British India was one of the last major states, democratic or authoritarian, to concern itself with world opinion or to view its rebels as uncommon and high-minded criminals. Elsewhere the nation-state was learning how to cope with its ideological traitors and would-be martyrs in a more ruthless and effective manner. At the same time, the concept of martyrdom itself was beginning to flounder on the judgmental rocks of definition. More and more the modern world was being forced to respond to martyrdom and suffering that had been stripped of their religious base, and asked to judge actions that were hopelessly enmeshed with the violent overthrow of governments and the activities of "seditious" minorities.

What follows is a brief excursion into four areas where twentieth-century martyrdom has begun to come apart at the joints: the modern state's determination to degrade the martyr; the impact of the Nazi holocaust on the concept of Judaic martyrdom; and two case studies—Dietrich Bonhoeffer and Julius and Ethel Rosenberg—in which the traitor and martyr are so confounded as to place in question any meaning to the term "martyrdom."

I. RECONDITIONING THE MARTYR

Essential to martyrdom, both as it emerged in the West and as Gandhi articulated it, was the stress placed on the individual and the heroic. The hallmark of the martyr was his exceptionality; he stood out from the herd, and his inner drive and conviction gave credence and strength to his cause. In the twentieth century the state has learned to strike directly at those qualities, denying the martyr his individuality and treating him simply as a type. It has systematically sought to deprive him of the internal heroism born of private self-control and the external heroism engendered by public exposure.

Gandhi never fully comprehended the magnitude of the change in the twentieth-century state's handling of dissent. He could not believe that Hitler and Mussolini were "beyond redemption."[5] His answer to the Italian invasion of Abyssinia was to urge its people to say, " 'You are welcome to reduce us to dust and ashes, but you will not find one Abyssinian ready to cooperate with you.' What could Mussolini have done? He did not want a desert."[6] The plight of Czechoslovakia moved Gandhi deeply, but again his advice was "to refuse to obey Hitler's will and perish unarmed in the attempt. In so doing, though I lose the body, I save my soul, that is, my honour."[7] Gandhi had even greater sympathy for the Jews, calling them "the untouchables of Christianity." He was convinced "that if someone of courage and vision can arise among them to lead them in nonviolent action, the winter of their despair can in the twinkling of an eye be turned into the summer of hope." What has now, he said, "become a degrading man-hunt can be turned into a calm and determined stand offered by unarmed men and women possessing the strength of suffering given to them by Jehovah." The result would be "a truly religious resistance . . . against the godless fury of dehumanized man," and a lasting victory by the German Jews; they would convert all Germans "to an appreciation of human dignity."[8] What Gandhi could not fathom was that honor and human dignity were exactly the elements the dictators were bent on destroying.

The modern totalitarian state's urge to obliterate all forms of deviation from the prescribed truth is nothing new. From the moment the Seleucid empire entered into the business of mind control, the state has portrayed those who disturb the mental peace of society as madmen, fools, and perverts. The common offender—the murderer of the body, the thief, and the destroyer of property—could be summarily executed and forgotten; but the spreader of criminal ideas—the murderer of men's souls, and those who attacked the cherished ideals that give life meaning and society cohesion—proved far more difficult to handle, because their reputations, their good names, and the validity of their ideas had to be destroyed as well as their bodies. Antiochus had appealed to the youngest Maccabee son not to follow his brothers into madness. The proconsul of Pergamum ordered Bishop Carpus and Deacon Papylus to "sacrifice to the gods, both of you, and do not play the fools."[9] In the eyes of Rome, early Christian martyrs were not simply lunatics; all Christians by definition were moral degenerates. They were sodomites, cannibals, incestuous perverts, and enemies of the human race, whose denial of the gods would surely bring down upon all humanity the fury of the heavenly hierarchy. Christians deserved whatever punishment the state could devise, and their public torture and dismemberment were manifest proof of the folly as well as the evilness of their beliefs: what sane person would pick a deity who would not or could not save his followers from the agony and humiliation of death in the arena?

Torture in the Roman Empire was judicial in purpose. It sought to extract information and to inflict punishment upon those guilty of violating imperial law or denying legal and divine authority, a ritualistic and effective display of public authority. Its purpose was neither purgative, a catharsis to bring about the spiritual purification of the victim, nor reformative, an attempt to reshape the criminal into some travesty of his former self. Those refinements were developed in medieval and early modern society and perfected in the twentieth century.[10] Modern torture aims not so much at punishment as at betrayal and submission. As Jean-Paul Sartre has grimly noted, the purpose of state-inflicted pain is to turn a person "by his screams and by his submission into a lower animal, in the eyes of all and in his own eyes. His betrayal must destroy him and take away his human dignity. He who gives way under questioning is not only constrained from talking again, but is given a new status, that of a sub-man."[11]

In recent years the modern leviathan has learned to deflate and degrade the would-be martyr in more ingenious sociological and clinical ways than simply by inflicting physical pain, and possibly this is why in our century the martyr appears to be such an endangered species. We have, in Kai Erikson's words, learned to regard the political criminal "as 'sick' rather than 'reprobate,' " thereby pulling his fangs and depriving him of any claim to superiority, satanic or divine.[12] He has become simply a deviant, to be explained in terms of either a diseased mind, which can be cured by therapy, or a traumatic experience—broken home, child abuse, ghetto environment—which can be rectified by rehabilitation and re-education. Rebecca West's verdict on Great Britain's twentieth-century traitors is symbolic and symptomatic. In *The New Meaning of Treason* her devils are psychopathic personalities driven by inner demons or alienated, frustrated, and muddle-headed intellectuals greedy for power, victims of their environment and their own intellectual limitations. They are never men and women worthy of our admiration, struggling with the slippery meaning of loyalty to self, to law, to community, to a moral or political principle. She has only pity for the Irish-American expatriate William Joyce, better known as Lord Haw-Haw in World War II, who preached treason and defeatism over the radio waves and in 1945 paid for his words with his life: "It seems to me that he lived in a true hell." He was so much "a damn fool" that he could only come forth with "a peculiarly idiotic variety of anti-semitism," and was fated throughout life "to be puny and plain."[13] Certainly this is not the stuff of which martyrs are meant to be made.

Today the twentieth-century state, like some vast epicene enterprise, no longer demonstrates its power by public spectacles of corporal punishment inflicted upon the body, using pain as the official instrument of social vengeance. Instead it reaches out for the criminal's soul, seeking to remodel and reform it. The tearing, stretching, and mutilation of the human carcass upon rack, wheel, and scaffold has been replaced by the even more persuasive styles of the doctor, the psychoanalyst, and the educator who hope to renovate the criminal's mind and reshape his personality. "I believe," wrote one ruthlessly optimistic student of social pathology in 1970, with only a passing reference to the potential dangers of a Brave New World, "that the day has come when we can combine sensory deprivation with drugs, hypnosis, and astute manipulation of reward and punishment to gain almost absolute control over an individual's behavior. It should be possible then to achieve a very rapid and highly effective type of positive brainwashing that would allow us to make dramatic changes in a person's behavior and personality. I foresee the day when we could convert the worst criminal into a decent, respectable citizen in a matter of a few months—or perhaps even less time than that. . . . We should reshape our society so that we all could be trained from birth to want what society wants us to do. We have the techniques now to do it."[14] O'Brien in George Orwell's 1984 would have agreed: "Power is in tearing minds to pieces and putting them together again in new shapes of your own choosing."[15]

Any sixteenth-century educator would have jumped at the chance to train his pupil "from birth to want what society wants." Moreover, the medieval inquisitor searching for signs of Satan and the early modern official turning the rack or lighting the fire under Lutheran, Catholic, and Anabaptist "heretics" and "traitors" were probing for their victims' souls just as doggedly as any modern purveyor of mental and physical pain. What is new—"the new techniques"—is the discreetness of the process and the technological improvement of the means by which governments neutralize what they define as a "dangerous state of mind." The modern martyr, unlike his predecessors, faces a world that has learned that retributive justice is best handled secretly behind barbed wire and stone walls, not in public trials and executions, and that the mental hygiene clinic serves as a far more effective weapon against political and ideological deviancy than the Roman arena or the Spanish auto-da-fé. The martyr, as history has shown, can thrive on pain—indeed, for the Christian it constituted the surest path to salvation—but even faith of steel can be shattered by today's technicians trained in neurology and anatomy and armed with electric probes and "truth"-inducing drugs. Prolonged exposure to psychiatric hospitals can reshape the strongest personality. As Alexander Solzhenitsyn cried out in fury in 1970, "The incarceration of free-thinking healthy people in madhouses is SPIRITUAL MURDER; it is a variation on the GAS CHAMBER, but is even more cruel: the torture of the people being killed is more malicious and more prolonged."[16]

The agonizing history of intellectual dissent and the struggle for civil and human rights in post-Stalinist Russia stands as sufficient evidence that sane men and women can endure corrective labor camps "designed to humiliate the prisoner, to ruin his health, to break his spirit." They can challenge the camps' "education officers" and can withstand years of enforced brainwashing.[17] The political activist and writer Anatoly Marchenko survived six years in labor camps where a political dissenter was "reformed" by carefully calculated starvation—he worked "like an elephant" but got "fed like a rabbit." Every effort to coerce Anatoly elicited an ever stronger desire to protest what was happening to him, until he reached a point where he could not tell when his "refusal to submit voluntarily stopped being a protest and became simply asinine stubbornness." But even Marchenko, as he looked about him and saw what was happening to his fellow prisoners, had to admit that "it isn't too difficult, it seems, to reduce a man to the condition of a beast, to force him to forget his own human dignity, to forget honor and morality."[18] Moreover, Marchenko's heroism was possible only in a Marxist society that was already beginning to disintegrate. The Soviet Union of the 1960s and -70s, determined as it was to view any form of dissent as insanity or treason, was not Stalinist Russia, when there was no recorded voice to political opposition, because dissenters "simply disappeared" and "no one protested their fate."[19]

The Soviet Union, as Harrison Salisbury observed, viewed even a single dissenter as "an affront to the state ideology."[20] Nazi Germany went further, not only branding any opposition to its fascist paradise as the product of insanity or degeneracy or treason but also introducing into its definition of absolute orthodoxy the need to exterminate all defective genes. As the state was justified in protecting itself from traitors, so the national community, the *Volk,* in its preordained drive to achieve a homogeneous civilization of "higher human culture," was obliged to defend itself against spiritual and racial impurities.[21] In so doing the state, which was but the servant of the *Volk,* systematically eradicated all sense of individual worth. People were gassed not because as human beings they were evil, dangerous, or could not be reconditioned into good citizens but because they belonged to certain corrupt categories in society. The Nazis called upon the efficiency of the modern factory system of mass production to organize the mass destruction of millions of undesirables—Jews, Gypsies and the mentally ill or retarded.[22]

Hitler's threat to treat would-be martyrs as "ordinary criminals" and, if that were not enough, to "make them appear ridiculous and contemptible" became reality.[23] In the concentration camp as well as the death camp individuality was brutalized and dehumanized in a paroxysm of calculated violence and degradation aimed at changing prisoners from separate-thinking entities into a spiritless mass from which all individual or group resistance had been expunged. Even torture became impersonal. In past tyrannies the infliction of pain had as its purpose the reformation, interrogation, or punishment of the individual—the victim's soul, mind, or information. In the concentration camp torture had nothing to do with the individual. It was simply an instrument by which to terrorize the group, and it made no difference which prisoner screamed, only that the rest heard him.[24] At all times camp officials were on the watch for potential martyrs and heroes. "If," as Bruno Bettelheim, who spent a year at Dachau and Buchenwald, has written, "a prisoner tried to protect others and it came to a guard's attention, the prisoner was usually killed. But if his action came to the knowledge of the camp administration, the whole group was always punished severely." The aim was to make the group resent its benefactor and prevent him from becoming a "hero or a leader (if he survived) or a martyr (if he died) around whom group resistance might have formed."[25] Even the suicide, if he failed, was punished, because it was the final "act of self-determination" and individuality.[26]

II. THE HOLOCAUST AND THE MURDER OF JEWISH MARTYRDOM

The German concentration camp sought to defeat the martyr's actions and individuality, but the death camp struck at the very concept of martyrdom itself. Hitler's success in committing the Nazi regime to a policy of genocide did more than nearly liquidate European Jewry. It had terrifying theological implications for a providential God who claimed to reveal His purpose in terms of human history: what conceivable divine plan could require the death of over five million of Yahweh's specially chosen people? It left in shambles the ancient Judaic belief in martyrdom—dying "al kiddush ha-Shem" to witness God's reality and the sanctity of His name. Such a death was a voluntary act of suffering to purge Israel of its sins, thereby deflecting divine wrath and reminding the Lord of His promise to set Judea "in fame and renown and glory, high above all the nations that He has made."[27] In the words of Emil Fackenheim, "Hitler murdered Jewish martyrdom itself."[28]

For many Jewish thinkers the Holocaust hopelessly compromised Yahweh, placing His divine justice in doubt and changing forever the relationship between man and God and man and man. For theologians like Fackenheim, the Holocaust was unlike any previous catastrophe. In the past Jews had been carted off to the slaughterhouse for what they had allegedly done or actually had not done: poisoned Christian wells, kidnapped and ritualistically murdered Christian babies, or refused to eat swine meat, kiss the cross, or pay tribute to Rome. Now they died simply because they were Jewish, not in a theological but in a genetic sense. They died not for their religion but for their existence. Past governments had offered the Jews a choice: change your ways, deny your God, convert or die. Hitler offered the Jews only the gas chamber. It made no difference whether they were professing Jews, Christian Jews, atheist Jews. Blood, not faith, became the mark of Cain, because the Nazi state cared not whether Yahweh lived or died, only that Jews died.[29]

The German death camps had as their purpose a "final solution" extending far beyond the simple, sanitary, and efficient extermination of all undesirables as if they were fleas and cockroaches. "We don't argue with bacilli or with thread-worms; we don't try to re-educate them; we render them harmless as speedily as possible."[30] The principle applied to Jews as well as threadworms. The Nazi regime sought to convince the troops who operated the death machines and, more important, the victims themselves that those being made ready for the gas chamber were in fact vermin. It was not enough to deprive the prisoners of their ethnic, religious, and family identity. Their humanity had to be destroyed as well as their bodies. For the Jews the struggle was no longer to sanctify Yahweh's name but to retain faith in humanity and to remain human.

What made the Holocaust so terrible was that it was a man-willed horror, not a disaster like the Black Death or the Lisbon Earthquake of 1755 which could readily be pushed off onto the shoulders of a wrathful deity. Such inhumanity to man more directly even than two world wars shattered any belief in scientific progress, rationally organized society, and the perfectibility of man, and it struck at the very concept of a caring God. By a mind-rendering act of faith, one might still continue to believe in a deity that allowed such systematic and clinically processed genocide to happen, but how could Jew or Christian speak to such a God, let alone enter into a dialogue with Him?[31] The Holocaust constituted an enterprise of such monstrous human and cosmic absurdity and demonic evil that it placed Yahweh's purpose in question and cast doubt upon the validity of the covenant itself. Who, wrote Irving Greenberg, dares "talk about [a] God who loves and cares without making a mockery of those who suffered"?[32] The Holocaust made the covenant by which five million Jews had sought to live "an illusion and their death a gigantic travesty."[33] How could any divine force be "present in history," let alone be satisfied by the death of a million Jewish children? It might be possible to view Antiochus IV as God's preordained instrument to administer divine justice if only because twenty-one hundred years had dulled the pain, but to accept Hitler as the Lord's agent was unconscionable.[34] All that remained of the covenant was a hideous perversion of "biblical chosenness": the Nazi regime had chosen the inmates to die. Those in Auschwitz and the other death camps had no more to say about their death than cockroaches. In an absurd world where men and women stripped themselves naked and walked passively into the gas chambers, there was no place for, no meaning to, the freely given sacrifice of the Maccabees, who had died because "God needs man to manifest Himself."[35] In such a hell both God and man seemed totally worthless, historically and morally superfluous. Long before the twentieth century revealed its savage technological proficiency for mass slaughter, the warning had been given: "The man who sees and suffers death seems to have his belief engulfed by meaninglessness."[36]

For some Jewish thinkers, not only did the traditional concept of Hebraic martyrdom have no role in the twentieth century but, more serious, it also contributed to the horrors of the century. The Holocaust seemed to offer evidence that martyrdom generated that fatalistic acceptance of suffering which led millions to "walk quietly, without resistance, to their death" with no thought of turning on their murderers, even as a suicidal gesture.[37] The dreadful possibility that a God who required martyrdom as proof of His reality could have produced the Jewish response to the Nazi death machines stands at the heart of Elie Wiesel's novel *The Oath,* in which he offers a radical solution to Jewish suffering. "The people of history," argues Moshe, Wiesel's chief protagonist in the novel, should cease to record and glorify the martyrs of their past and "testify no more." For centuries they had given themselves to Yahweh by permitting themselves to be led to the slaughter chamber. "We think that we are pleasing Him by becoming the illustrations of our own tales of martyrdom." Moshe insists that the endless agony of the Jews will never end—not even with the coming of a Messiah—unless the storytelling itself ends. History when recorded repeats itself; the glorification of past martyrs only breeds more martyrs and more death. "Whether or not our enemies scoff at us, trample us, mutilate us, we shall not speak of it. Whether the mob massacres or humiliates us, we shall tell neither God nor man."[38]

When God is removed from life, or when He conceals Himself so totally that man is forced to accept the paradox "If there is a God, He doesn't exist"[39]—then death is radically altered. It becomes the sterile conclusion to life, an organic decomposition of the body. It is no longer a unique human event, but a tiny particle in the senseless flux of universal destruction and creation. How, then, does the martyr survive in an environment that dehumanizes him and at the same time deprives him of any sense of spiritual apotheosis, creative theatrics, and religious purpose?

In any martyrdom there are two players—man and a cause. If the deity is unavailable, some secular ideology must substitute; but no matter the players, the key to martyrdom is the link between life and death. To make sense out of death, to make the sacrifice of life worthwhile and to make death count for something, life must have some meaning. To deny value to one is to negate the worth of the other. Martyrdom links life and death together as no other concept does, and it seeks to make sense out of both. The martyr is never a simple victim but always a participant and organizer of his life and death. He looks to the future and seeks to influence it either in this world or in another. The Holocaust seemed to deny any meaning to either life or death. It seemed impossible to restore value to either in a nightmare of purposeless suffering in which both existence and nonexistence had become absurd.

Almost without exception the liberal Jewish theological response has been to renegotiate the relationship between God and man, replacing a deity who could only manifest Himself through a cruelly rigid contractual interpretation of the covenant with divinely inspired but existentially interpreted actions on the part of man. The cardinal need was to reintroduce choice, without which Jewish martyrdom was impossible, and to reestablish the link between life and death. The signature of humanity, of being individuals—the ultimate freedom—is the right to determine whether we live or die and whether we choose to die with dignity and compassion. The essential first step was to replace the model of the Maccabees, dying to sanctify God's name by refusing to violate His covenant, with "an imperative to sanctify not death but life."[40] It was ridiculous to die for swine meat when every heartbeat of the body had to be concentrated on remaining alive and human after weeks, months, years of dehumanization. The sanctification of life meant far more than sheer survival. It meant courage that testified not only to Yahweh's existence but also to humanity's determination to retain its individuality. Therein lay the crucial choice and the challenge: to choose to be human.

Auschwitz, according to Elie Wiesel, signified "death—total, absolute death—of man and of mankind, of reason and of heart, of language and of the senses."[41] A terrible numbness, without hope, beyond terror, and lacking any sense of individuality, prevailed. As Bruno Bettelheim has said, "A few screams evoke in us deep anxiety and a desire to help. Hours of screaming without end lead us only to wish that the screamer would shut up."[42] Humanity is an empty concept, void of meaning, without individual reference points. Mass suffering engenders only incomprehension and disinterest. When sixty-eight thousand prisoners were crushed into an area designed for eight thousand, they were transformed from people into digits, as Leo Baeck became at Theresienstadt—number 187,984.[43] The only way to defeat such physical, mental, and moral annihilation was to re-create the individual

by act of faith and will power. For Emil Fackenheim, the paradigm for heroism was no longer the Maccabees but Pelagia Lewinska, a Polish woman
who left a testimony of her struggle to retain her humanity at Auschwitz:

> They had condemned us to die in sour own filth, to drown in mud, in our own
> excrement. They wished to [de]base us, to destroy our human dignity, to ef-
> face every vestige of humanity . . . to fill us with horror and contempt to-
> wards ourselves and our fellows. . . . From the instant when I grasped the
> motivating principle . . . it was as if I had been awakened from a dream. . . . I
> felt under orders to live. . . . And if I did die in Auschwitz, it would be as a
> human being; I would hold on to my dignity. I was not going to become the
> contemptible, disgusting brute my enemy wished me to be. . . . And a terrible
> struggle began which went on day and night.[44]

Elie Wiesel gave the same courage and refusal to submit to Shaike in *The Oath*
when the young firebrand exclaimed, "If die we must, let us die standing, in
the open air, not in cellars with the rats. With dignity, not resignation."[45]

Choice and individuality, the two essential ingredients of martyrdom,
were restored. Death was still inevitable, there was no choice except to die;
but style had now returned, and the numbness, the namelessness of being
number 187,984, was transformed into a sense of self, understanding, and
pride. "I had this one thought," wrote Leo Baeck, "never to resign before
rudeness, never to become a mere number, and always to keep my self-
respect."[46]

Leo Baeck, leading liberal rabbi in Berlin, international scholar, highly
controversial leader of German Jewry, and five-times-arrested septuagenar-
ian who stubbornly refused to leave Germany and join his family in Britain,
spent the final two years of the Hitler nightmare in Theresienstadt, a
prison city—not an extermination camp—where elderly and prominent
Jews and their families were sent in the false expectation of privileged treatment. In all, 200,000 men, women, and children were caged in Theresienstadt, but the fear voiced by one inmate—"You never know whether you
are really going to be staying"—was terrifyingly real: of those 200,000,
120,000 were moved on to death factories, and between 33,000 and 40,000 of
those who remained died of malnutrition, disease, or exhaustion.[47] During
this struggle to remain alive and human, Baeck was able to draw on a redefinition of Jewish martyrdom which he first formulated as early as 1905.[48]

Baeck shifted the emphasis from the need for God to reveal Himself to
the need for man to manifest his individuality and prove his humanity. "The
choice of death" was transformed into what one of Baeck's more recent interpreters has described as "the choice of *meaning in death* given by the individual in his personal struggle for self-understanding."[49] For Baeck the

Hebrew prophets were not so much harbingers of God's purpose as prototypes of "heroic individualism"—models to be followed by later generations. The strength to endure suffering and the will to overcome the temptation to give up the fight and conform became the elements out of which the martyr constructed his sense of selfhood and uniqueness. How the martyr used life's opportunities, limited as they might be, not blind devotion to the covenant, was the mark of true heroism. Since there could be no lasting consequence to actions performed in a death camp, the style in which those deeds were performed and the motive standing behind them became all-important in judging the "human value of existence."[50] "In the area of martyrdom," Baeck argued, "there is fulfilled the commandment that our intention must unconditionally become our action and must find its clear and constant expression in our life. . . . 'Speak truth in the heart' and testify of it through life itself."[51]

Speaking the truth—the ultimate test of personality—was for Baeck, as for Gandhi, based not on hate but on love. Eleazar ben Judah of Worms, whose wife and child had been killed by crusaders and who yet in retrospect could write "not one word of hatred against his enemies," became for Baeck the paradigm for living in this world.[52] The heroic individual chose to rise above his isolated and often hideous environment and defy the meaninglessness and absurdity of the immediate existence which the tyrant was hell-bent on imposing. He proclaimed a love of humanity and found order and purpose in life, because life demanded more of a human being than simple survival. "Only by choosing meaning," S. Daniel Breslauer has written of Baeck's theology, "rather than meaninglessness, does an individual become a personality."[53] The nature of that defiance of chaos will vary from circumstance to circumstance, individual to individual, because, in Baeck's estimation, every person must create his own religion, "establish its significance," and perform his own unique style of martyrdom. Unlike the Maccabees, who did not have to seek meaning in their decision to defy Antiochus—it was already written down in the Law—Baeck's martyrs impose their own meaning on their actions and their choice. Only then is life given purpose and the individual's own personality awakened and inspired; only then can life be sacrificed, not simply terminated. Such a view made martyrdom possible even when choice did not exist for those who confronted death, because each individual could achieve his own spiritual transformation—what Elie Wiesel would later call an act of "mystical madness," whereby one believes in God and man despite God and man.[54] In the harsh words of Richard Rubinstein, men are called upon "to create with lucidity their own private meanings and purposes in the knowledge that no power in the cosmos will ultimately sustain or validate them."[55]

The martyr in the secularized and existentialistic environment of the twentieth century has been placed in an equivocal position. There is no higher seat of judgment than the value that the martyr or his associates place on his sacrifice. Bruno Bettelheim recorded that vulnerability when in his description of death and human sacrifice at Dachau, he felt obliged to divide the martyr from the hero: "Since all prisoners were exposed to severe treatment, those who died because of it, though perhaps martyrs to political or religious convictions, were not considered heroes by other prisoners. Only those who suffered for their efforts to protect other prisoners were accepted as heroes."[56] To Saint Augustine's definition of martyrdom—the cause, not the punishment, qualifies a "true martyr"—had now been added another element: the human act of heroism that precedes death. When human courage and purpose are seen as the essential ingredient, then martyrdom as both an action and a concept had become thoroughly humanized and individualized. "The sum of all men is not God," Elie Wiesel has written, "whereas my innermost self is."[57]

III. Dietrich Bonhoeffer and German Efforts to Assassinate Hitler

Not only has the purpose for which martyrs die been redefined to include the style by which they display their humanity, but the cause itself has also been placed in doubt as martyrdom has become more and more entangled with treason. No longer can we uncritically accept William Kuhns' confident statement that Dietrich Bonhoeffer died on April 9, 1945, in a Nazi extermination camp at Flossenbürg "a martyr to the cause for which he had so long struggled."[58] The assertion that Bonhoeffer died a martyr has been voiced many times over;[59] but exactly what was that cause, and did the thirty-nine-year-old German pastor actually die for it?

Can it be said Bonhoeffer was a witness to a passionate but highly provocative and idiosyncratic belief in Christ struggling in a hostile world? Not exactly. The Nazis never required him to deny his faith or forced him to sacrifice to Hitler or wrap his altar in the swastika. They simply ordered him to remain quiet, stay in one place, and report regularly to the Gestapo, all of which he did up to a point.

Did Bonhoeffer offer his life as testimony to human resilience in the face of unparalleled evil and as a sacrificial gesture to prove humanity's worth by speaking out against the violation of human rights, ethnic cleansing, and aggression that his church, his country, and in a sense the entire world had refused to repudiate? Possibly, but he was not arrested because he was a fearless critic of Nazism; like any other patriotic German, Bonhoeffer was

always careful to raise his arm in the Nazi salute. He was imprisoned as a consequence of a power struggle between the Schutzstaffel, or SS, which included the intelligence organ of the Gestapo, and the Abwehr, the army's intelligence agency. The Gestapo was determined to prove the criminal, possibly treasonous, negligence of the Abwehr. Its immediate target was Hans von Dohnanyi, the civilian second-in-command of the Abwehr's central administration and Bonhoeffer's brother-in-law. Bonhoeffer's initial crime as a part-time member of the Abwehr was largely guilt by family association. The worst the Gestapo could charge him with was unpatriotic and antimilitary activity by avoiding and helping others to avoid military service. Not until Dohnanyi's secret papers were discovered seventeen months later did the Gestapo learn that both men had been involved in an ongoing plot to assassinate the Führer. When that was revealed, the conspirators were executed as traitors to their country.

Did Bonhoeffer then sacrifice his life for a better Germany? That is a matter of interpretation. He died because he was a member of a resistance group which unsuccessfully plotted to kill the head of state. It planned to stage a coup d'état in order to extract the country from a disastrous war and create a Germany more to its economic and educational liking. There is always a fine line between noble self-sacrifice and personal self-interest.

Even if the cause for which Bonhoeffer died could be agreed upon, further questions swarm to mind. Did he choose death, and did that death in any measurable way further his cause? Again the evidence is unclear. "All who take the sword will perish by the sword" was, Bonhoeffer told his brother-in-law, as valid for them as for anyone.[60] The conspirators all knew the risks involved in treason. They were brave men willing to die if they failed, but equally willing to live if they succeeded and to profit from their treason. Even in jail Bonhoeffer struggled to remain alive, living on the hope of escaping death. When, however, after the disclosure of his brother-in-law's papers, his fate became certain, he refused the offer of escape from prison under cover of an Allied air attack because he did not want to endanger his family, especially his eighteen-year-old fiancée and his brother Klaus, arrested only days before the escape was scheduled. From this perspective it might be argued that Dietrich chose death. Whether that death did anybody or any cause a modicum of good is more problematical: four days after his execution, American troops seized Flossenbürg, and in another twenty days, Hitler was dead by his own hand.

Two further questions need to be asked. Can it be said that Bonhoeffer died by the authority of a state protecting itself from the virus of dissent? Not really. By April of 1945 the German state had in effect ceased to exist. His death was the decision of Hitler and a cadre of condemned Nazi leaders determined to extract the last measure of private vengeance. Finally, is there any basis at all for ranking Dietrich Bonhoeffer among the true martyrs? Not according to the Lutheran bishop Hans Meiser, who refused to attend a memorial service for him because, the prelate said, Bonhoeffer was a political rebel, not a proper Christian martyr. Even the leaders of his own Confessing Church denied him the martyr's crown; they could not sanction the murder, "whatever the intention behind it," of a legal head of state, even if he were a tyrant. As the pastors of Bielefeld said in an appeal to members of the Bonhoeffer family, pleading with them not to permit a street to be named after their son, "We don't want the names of our colleagues, who were killed for their faith, lumped together with political martyrs."[61]

Clearly the "political martyr" is a hero, a questionable asset, or a terrorist depending on who is making the judgment. The boundaries are difficult to discern, and even the definition of a martyr proposed in the first chapter of this book grows exceedingly murky when martyrdom becomes entangled in treason. Ironically, Dietrich Bonhoeffer himself, quite unwittingly, forecast the confusion in which his life would end. In a sermon given in Berlin on June 19, 1932, he predicted a time "when the blood of martyrs will be called for. But this blood, if we really have the courage and the fidelity to shed it, will not be so innocent and clear as that of the first who testified."[62]

"Martyr," "traitor," "terrorist," "would-be assassin," and "spiritual maverick"—these terms could be associated with Dietrich Bonhoeffer only under the extraordinary conditions existing in Nazi Germany between 1933 and 1945. In appearance and ancestry, he in no way fitted the stereotype of a violator of law, order, and respectability. Born into the cultural and professional elite of twentieth-century Germany, Dietrich started life on the fourth of February, 1906, the fourth and youngest son among the eight children of Paula and Karl Bonhoeffer. His father was a professor of psychiatry and neurology and Berlin's most prestigious psychiatrist. One grandfather was president of the high court of Tübingen, the other a member of the Lutheran Supreme Church Council. His maternal grandmother was Countess Klara von Kalckreuth, whose father and brother were both distinguished nineteenth-century painters. As in any well-connected German family, there were close links to the military, and his mother's brother, Paul von Hase, rose to be a general and commandant of Berlin. The house in which Dietrich grew up was solidly upper-middle-class, replete with governess, nurse, housemaid, parlor maid, cook, and chauffeur. As a child he appeared impishly angelic with his cherubic face, blond hair, and ruffled dress to his knees; as a young man, despite his square face and chunky build, he was extraordinarily handsome—almost the perfect picture of the Nazi ideal, the fair-haired, blue-eyed Aryan paragon. In later life, with glasses and balding head, he looked more like a congenial and generous publican. The intense scholar, revolutionary, and radical theologian were well concealed behind an extroverted personality.

Members of the Bonhoeffer family were deeply ethical—regular family prayers, hymns, and scripture readings—but they rarely went to church, even on Christmas or Easter, and their interests were almost totally secular. Brother Karl-Friedrich became a nuclear physicist, and Klaus a lawyer, while Walter, killed in World War I, had hoped to be an environmentalist, writer, and linguist. Dietrich was the exception: he set his heart on entering the ministry and becoming a theologian; and as proof of that commitment, he began the study of Hebrew at fifteen. His father, a scientist, physician, and skeptic, did not try to dissuade his son; but in 1934, looking back on his son's decision, he confessed he had thought "a quiet, uneventful, minister's life" would "be a pity" for young Dietrich.[63] How terrifyingly wrong the prediction of an uneventful life was became apparent almost the moment it was made.

The path to ordination in the Lutheran church of Berlin-Brandenburg, an affiliate of the Prussian Union of Protestant Churches, was long and steep. By the time the ceremony took place, on November 15, 1931, Bonhoeffer had graduated in theology, first from Tübingen University and then from Berlin with a published doctoral thesis; spent a year in Barcelona as assistant pastor to the German Lutheran church; produced a second thesis, published as *Act and Being;* spent a year as an exchange student at the Union Theological Seminary in New York; and been appointed lecturer in the theological faculty at Berlin. When his religious education was complete, Bonhoeffer fitted neatly the archbishop of Canterbury's caustic description of German theological thinking: "The Germans can never discuss what to do tomorrow without showing how their view depends on the divine purpose in creation—the existence of which must therefore be first established."[64] A decade of unimaginable evil was required before the young theological student could entirely overcome the ethical paralysis implied in the archbishop's criticism.

The German Protestant church, for which Bonhoeffer had spent eight hard years training, was a clumsy association of twenty-eight highly bureaucratized provincial "landed," or territorial, churches, some Reformed, some Lutheran, some a union of the two; a number of "free" churches (Moravian, Methodist, Baptist, etc.); and various sects—all of which cherished their confessional and governmental independence from state and central control. Yet these same ecclesiastical entities were strident in their cries that the government support religious education in the schools, champion Christian services on Sundays and holy days, safeguard church property, cooperate in raising ecclesiastical taxes, and grant financial subsidies from public funds. As a product of a peculiarly complex and rich past in which both the Reformed and Lutheran faiths started as state religions and local princes regarded themselves as the administrative heads of their provincial churches, German Protestantism could never entirely divest itself of strong emotional ties and a sense of duty to the state or refrain from demanding closer involvement in state and national policy. As a consequence, it was ill prepared to withstand the National Socialist onslaught and the Nazi gospel of "positive Christianity."[65]

In October of 1931, the year after the Nazi party first emerged as a major force in German politics, Bonhoeffer wrote a friend, "I sometimes simply cannot see what is the right thing to do . . . in the unprecedented situation of our public life in Germany."[66] Eleven years later, he confessed that "evil approaches . . . in so many respectable and seductive disguises" that "the man with a conscience" becomes "nervous and vacillating, till at last he contents himself with a salved, instead of a clear, conscience."[67] The German Protestant church found it easy to salve its conscience, and indeed the times were unprecedented. For many, Hitler seemed to be the nation's savior, the heroic messenger of Germany's destiny, the crusader who would slay the triple dragons of national humiliation, economic chaos, and moral degeneracy which had beset the fatherland ever since the ignominy of defeat in 1918. Theological students proudly displayed their Nazi badges during lectures, and it was reported that over half of the candidates for ordination in 1930 were "followers of Hitler." So was almost a third of the country at large, which saw in National Socialism a creed of action and inspired leadership capable of defending the country against an atheist-Communist takeover and of dispelling the stagnation, political gridlock, and sense of betrayal that had pervaded the Weimar Republic and postwar years. As the dean of Magdeburg Cathedral exclaimed, "The swastika flags round the altar radiate hope—hope that the day is at last about to dawn."[68]

As the leader of the largest, but still minority, party, Adolf Hitler was appointed chancellor on January 30, 1933. His ability to parlay a political organization which had never attracted more than 38 percent of the popular vote into a dictatorship in less than three months was a piece of alchemy that defied all known laws of political science. It took place under an atmosphere of near political panic in which decisions were made that could never be undone and expectations were formed that were never realized. The event that most helped the process was the spectacular burning of the Reichstag building on the night of February 27–28. The timing was diabolically perfect, for it seemed to confirm what the Nazis had been preaching: the Communists were the enemies of the fatherland, representing everything debased, un-German, and dangerous, and their "terrorist acts and attacks must be met with all severity." The next day, Hitler went to the eighty-six-year-old Reich president, Field Marshal Paul von Hindenburg, with a freshly drafted emergency presidential decree "to ward off Communist acts of violence which endangered the state."[69] The new proclamation swept away all civil rights safeguarded by the constitution. It abolished free speech, freedom of the press, and the right of public assembly; it granted the government authority to intervene "in the privacy of the post, telegraph and telephone"; to arrest and search without warrant or stated reason; and to confiscate property at will.

Five days later, in a political environment bordering on chaos and hysteria, which the Nazis both fostered and capitalized upon, the German public went to the polls for the last time under the Weimar Republic. Although the National Socialists won only 43.9 percent of the vote in a heavily manipulated election, they were able to manufacture a working majority in the Reichstag; and on March 24, Hitler succeeded in conjuring a two-thirds majority into passing the Enabling Act, or the "Law to Relieve the Need of the People and the State," whereby the Reichstag divested itself of all legislative power and conferred upon the chancellor unlimited executive authority. Having already persuaded Hindenburg to issue a presidential decree ordering that all government critics who impaired "the welfare of the Reich" be jailed for a minimum of three years—in serious cases of insidious attacks on the state, be executed—and having set up the necessary special courts to try such cases, Hitler was now in a position to exercise full dictatorial powers.[70] With all opposition terrified or legally paralyzed, he set about reorganizing and rejuvenating the state into a totalitarian polity in which all interests— political parties, trade unions, business organizations, professional groups, even the army, and certainly the church—were required to sacrifice themselves to the principle of a spiritually, politically, and racially pure and united fatherland that marched to the chancellor's orders. The realities of power and the ceremonial trappings were finally brought together the following year when Hindenburg died and Hitler combined the offices of chancellor and president. The Führer had risen fully armed from the dead body of the old republic.

The test of the church's will to make the required sacrifices for the sake of "folk and fatherland" came with unexpected speed. In early April of 1933, in accordance with a new law for the "reconstruction of the professional Civil Service," the government commenced dismissing all Jews and left-wing sympathizers from public office. Clergymen were civil servants, and the status of the thirty-seven non-Aryan Protestant pastors soon became a test of the church's loyalty.

The church's immediate and instinctive reaction was to ignore the Jewish question, especially the explosive debate over what constituted Jewishness— blood, in which case the non-Aryan pastors were Jews, or faith, in which case they were Christians. Unfortunately for the vast majority of pastors, who wanted the energies of the church to go into the creation of a unified national Protestant church, neither the state nor the Nazi sympathizers within the church—the "German Christians"—would drop the subject of "racial conformity." The seductive argument prevailed that the status of a mere thirty-seven non-Aryan pastors out of a total pastorate of eighteen thousand was not a matter of sufficient worth to risk tearing the church apart or antagonizing the state at a time when unity and cooperation were at a premium. Moreover, the theological issues involved were confusing, and the church was scarcely in a position to reprimand the government which had every legal and historic right to regulate its own civil servants. Accordingly, the General Synod of the Prussian Churches voted that only those who gave "unconditional support to the National Socialist State" and were of Aryan descent could become ministers. Conscience was partly salved by retaining in office already ordained non-Aryan clergymen.[71]

Bonhoeffer's own position on the Jewish question, given his Lutheran respect for state authority, his conventional family background, and his early absorption in theology, emerged with surprising suddenness and radicalism. Matters of principle strike hardest when they touch the people we know best; Bonhoeffer's twin sister had recently married a Jew, and one of his closest friends was a Jewish Lutheran pastor. His published reaction to the government's decree was lucky to have escaped the Nazi censor. In an article entitled "The Church and the Jews" he refused to limit the debate to the theological standing of the non-Aryan clergy and bluntly stated that his church had "an unconditional obligation towards the victims of any social order, even where those victims do not belong to the Christian community." If the state proved to be a demonic juggernaut and rode roughshod over human decency and morality, it was, he argued, the church's duty "not only to bind up [the wounds of] the victims beneath the wheel, but also to put a spoke in that wheel."[72] In April of 1933 Bonhoeffer placed the burden for action on the church; ten years later he accepted the individual's responsibility to make that decision for himself and to act alone.

The Jewish issue—the fate of German Jews, especially after the Nuremberg Laws of 1935, depriving them of German citizenship and declaring them to be second-class nationals, soon to be relegated to third-class aliens—and the theological absurdity of a purely Aryan Christian church transformed Bonhoeffer from a theological scholar into a "political churchman." It also placed him in the van of those who were willing to split the church wide open and to defy the dictatorial actions of the state. The transformation began in early September of 1933, when the Prussian Union of Protestant Churches accepted the Aryan decree of the government. Bonhoeffer and Pastor Martin Niemöller, an ex–submarine commander, immediately penned a protest that led first to the formation of the Pastors' Emergency League, then to a formal break with the union, and finally to the formation of the free Confessing Church. On September 7, they declared that the entire Protestant church—Lutheran and Reformed—by adopting the Aryan clause had in effect separated itself "from the Church of Christ," and they asked the Protestant clergy of Germany to join the Emergency League to demand its repeal. By the end of the year they had six thousand members in defense of the Christian faith and rejection of the Aryan clause;[73] by May of 1934 a schismatic church had been formed.

During much of the time that the Emergency League was turning itself into an independent church, Bonhoeffer was in London, where he was appointed pastor to a suburban Lutheran parish. In Britain he was able to continue his passionate interest in ecumenical religion and the World Alliance of Churches, and he became a close friend of George Bell, the bishop of Chichester and president of the alliance. Although Bonhoeffer was away for eighteen months, he kept in close touch as the Protestant church fell more and more under the control of German Christians who claimed to wear the swastika on their breasts and the cross in their hearts and who said that "Christ had come to us through Adolf Hitler." The newly installed Reich bishop, Ludwig Müller, and his loyal henchmen called for the full implementation of the Jewish clause and for the liberation of the church from "the Old Testament with its Jewish money morality and from these stories of cattle-dealers and pimps."[74] Step by step the dissenters moved toward schism until at the Synod of Barmen in Prussia the Confessing, or Opposition, Church was born on the twenty-ninth of May, 1934, when Karl Barth, Martin Niemöller, and others declared against "the false doctrine" that the mission of the German Protestant church could be left to the "ideological and political views that happen to prevail" or to "special leaders [such as Bishop Müller] with sovereign powers."[75]

The Confessing Church was a misalliance of Lutheran and Reformed ecclesiastical entities. From the start it lacked the courage of its convictions, and in August it failed the test when the National Protestant Church under Müller, in recognition of the new office of Führer, resolved that all ministers "swear before God" that they would be "true and obedient to the Führer of the German people and state" and pledge themselves to "every sacrifice and every service on behalf of the German people." Most of the Confessing ministers took the oath in the hope that in doing so they would display their loyalty and patriotism. They were even unwilling to accept Karl Barth's conditional phraseology—so reminiscent of the Becket–Henry II controversy—that he was ready to swear to the oath only "in so far as I can responsibly do so as a Christian."[76] When Barth refused to take the oath without the condition and was dismissed from his professorship at Bonn and the Confessing Church failed to support him, he wrote an open letter noting that the church which he had helped to establish had "as yet shown no sympathy for the millions who are suffering injustice. She has not once spoken out on the most simple matters of public integrity. And if and when she does speak, it is always on her own behalf."[77] Hitler was not far off the mark when he cynically observed that "the pastors will be made to dig their own graves. . . . They will betray anything for the sake of their miserable little jobs and incomes."[78] The issue at stake, as Bonhoeffer wrote to George Bell, was now "no longer a national issue but the question of the continued existence of Christianity in Europe."[79]

Bonhoeffer's alarm was at the heart of his decision in May of 1935 to return to Germany and accept the invitation of the Prussian branch of the Confessing Church to become a director of one of its newly established seminaries, set up to train its own ministers now that the break with the National Church was complete. In doing so, he gave up plans to visit

Gandhi in India, participate in the Mahatma's ashram, and learn the lessons of satyagraha and passive civil disobedience. The logical conclusion, Bonhoeffer argued, of being a practicing Christian was the moral and religious imperative of pacifism. He had little confidence left in his church's moral strength to oppose Hitler, and as the Führer commenced the rearmament of Germany and introduced universal conscription, Bonhoeffer felt the need to learn techniques that could challenge Hitler without violence. There was, he said, more Christianity in Gandhi's " 'paganism' than in the whole of our Reich Church."[80]

Bonhoeffer never sailed for India, but he saw in the new Confessing seminaries a chance to duplicate in Western-Christian style Gandhi's success in training satyagrahis in his ashrams. He jumped at the opportunity to forge a new caliber of ministers, Christian satyagrahis who would put the Sermon on the Mount into practice. Through communal living, constant prayer and confession, and spiritual self-discipline, he expected to create a Christian elite who would be able to sense what it meant to be disciples of Christ and would speak out against what Hitler called his "positive Christianity," which in effect was turning out to be a great deal more German than Christian: "We don't want," as the Führer phrased it, "people who keep one eye on the life in the hereafter. We need free men who feel and know that God is in themselves."[81] To the considerable horror of many in the Confessing Church, the new seminary director created at Finkenwalde, in what was then Pomerania, something alarmingly akin to a monastery, or more accurately an ashram, in which he overwhelmed "the young men by his religious ardor—one might even say passion."[82]

In his growing disgust with the German Protestant churches, Bonhoeffer turned to high-intensity, noninstitutional religion, but he never became a religious fanatic. During his directorship he wrote what is arguably his most influential treatise, *The Cost of Discipleship,* in which he struggled to define the church not as a congregation of souls or as a pulpit from which to declaim the truth, but as a society of individuals committed to concrete Christian acts of faith. There could be, he argued, no safety in collective action, in formulas, or in retreat into meditation and contemplation. Salvation could be won only by personal, individual, and painful commitment to being a disciple of Christ in this world. His approach was surprisingly close to Gandhi's concept of truth as God and God as truth and the Mahatma's belief that the deity could not be separated from his own creation and could be worshiped only through service to all humanity.

Bonhoeffer was director of Finkenwalde for two and a half years; during that time his Confessing Church retreated and finally dissolved under the onslaught of the Nazi state. By 1937, 804 of its pastors had been placed in jail for varying lengths of time; Confessing services and congregations held anywhere except in a state-recognized church were declared illegal; Confessing seminary students were randomly questioned at local police stations; church proclamations, letters, and publications were banned; church collections were prohibited; and on the twenty-eighth of September, by order of Himmler, the chief of the Gestapo, Finkenwalde was seized and boarded up and the entire Confessing Church's machinery for the education and examination of its ordinands was outlawed. The final blow came in April of 1938 when the president of the Supreme Church Council of Prussia, by way of celebrating the Führer's fiftieth birthday and the Anschluss with Austria, ordered all pastors to swear personal allegiance to Hitler or be dismissed. The full implication of this oath was carefully spelled out in detail: it meant "the most intimate solidarity with the Third Reich . . . and with the man who . . . embodied it" and a "personal commitment to the Führer under the solemn summons of God"—in other words, a blatant violation of their ordination vows.[83] The Confessing Church knuckled under. Barth wrote from Switzerland that the church had lost all credibility. Bonhoeffer found himself in the unenviable position of having nothing to lose. As a seminary director he was not technically a pastor, and his denunciation of the oath was consequently dismissed as something easy for him to proclaim. "Will the Confessing Church," he wrote in bitter disillusionment, "be willing to confess publicly its guilt and disunion?"[84] The guilt was doubly severe in Bonhoeffer's eyes since his church already knew of the impending order for all non-Ayran identity cards to be stamped with the letter J.

In November came Kristallnacht, the Night of Broken Glass, when in retaliation for the assassination of a Nazi diplomatic official in Paris by a Polish Jew, Hitler ordained the mass destruction of Jewish homes, shops, and synagogues. Bonhoeffer's response was to underline in his Bible "they burned all the meeting places of God" (Psalms 74) and "there is no longer any prophet, and there is none among us who knows how long" (Psalms 75). It had taken a respectable, God-fearing, heel-clicking clergyman who believed in law and order a long time, but he now confessed that "when I pray, 'deliver us from evil,' it is Hitler whom I mean."[85]

As war came closer, Bonhoeffer had to make a grave decision. He could remain in Germany, declare himself a conscientious objector, and not only decline to serve in a war that he regarded to be the product of evil and a violation of everything the Sermon on the Mount stood for, but also refuse to take the required military oath of allegiance to Hitler—"unconditional obedience . . . before God." If he followed such a course, however, he placed his church in jeopardy; the Nazi regime would see his defiance as evidence of the hostility of the entire Confessing Church.[86] His other choice was to flee his homeland and go into exile. When he was called for active duty and ordered to report on May 22, 1939, he postponed a final decision by wrangling permission from both his church and the state to leave the country for one year. After a three-month stay in Britain, he landed in New York on June 9 with an invitation from the Union Theological Seminary to lecture and another offer from the Federal Council of Churches to remain permanently in the United States and do refugee work.

The moment Pastor Bonhoeffer arrived in the United States, he began to agonize over the moral implications of permanent exile. He was, he admitted, "never quite clear about the motives that underlie my decision."[87] Was he retreating before evil, simply saving his own skin and indulging in the luxury of high-minded Christian virtue by wrapping himself in the egotistical sanctity of claiming to be a conscientious objector? Or was he in fact forsaking his country in the moment of its greatest anguish and guilt as it stood on the threshold of world war? To be safe in New York, he wrote in his diary, "during a catastrophe is simply unthinkable."[88] He could not separate himself from what he felt to be his "destiny." The closest Bonhoeffer ever got to analyzing his motives for returning was in a letter to Reinhold Niebuhr. He had made a terrible mistake in coming to America. He had to share Germany's trials, otherwise "I have no right to participate in the reconstruction of Christian life" after the war. Then he revealed his underlying purpose in returning. "Christians in Germany," he explained, "will face the terrible alternative of either willing the defeat of their nation in order that Christian civilization may survive, or willing the victory of their nation and thereby destroying our civilization. I know which of these alternatives I must choose; but I cannot make that choice in security."[89] He was deliberately re-entering the devil's domain to become a traitor at home, not a critic operating from the safety of a foreign and neutral country.

How a devout Christian, a confirmed pacifist who believed fervently in "peace on earth," and an ardent admirer of Gandhi's nonviolent resistance through love, not war, became the ethical leader of a den of carefully camouflaged political assassins is the story of how a man of immense integrity and self-honesty reluctantly concluded that ethics were not a matter of high-minded principle but of "earth and blood" that had meaning only in terms of concrete circumstances.[90]

The simple, straightforward justification for soldiers who broke their oaths and committed treason was that, as General Ludwig Beck put it, "exceptional times demand exceptional actions."[91] Old definitions of patriotism, duty, and honor had to be put aside in the face of an enemy that itself had discarded honor and was endangering the reputation of the army by ordering it to commit actions that violated every military code. For Bonhoeffer, however, the problem was more complex; he was not a soldier but a clergyman asked to sanction treason and conspire to commit murder. "The great masquerade of evil," he told his brother-in-law Hans von Dohnanyi, had "played havoc with all our ethical concepts." In the end he concluded that "only the man whose final standard is not his reason, his principles, his conscience, his freedom, or his virtue, but who is ready to sacrifice all this when he is called" to act on behalf of his faith, can be said to be truly responsible. "The ultimate question" for such a man was "not how he is to extricate himself heroically from the affair, but how the coming generation is to live." Bonhoeffer owed a "responsibility towards history."[92]

The devil had been set loose upon the land. The responsibility for doing so rested not merely with a few wicked men but with all of Germany. Bishop Bell reported that Bonhoeffer once called Hitler "the anti-Christ" who must be exterminated, but on another occasion Bonhoeffer thought the Führer not big enough to be credited with such a title. "The anti-Christ uses him, but he is not as stupid as that man!"[93] There was only one way to exorcise evil; that was to assume the collective guilt of his country, especially of his church, for not having branded National Socialism for what it was— the creed of Satan—and for having failed to put a spoke in the wheel of the juggernaut: "The dark and evil world must not be abandoned to the devil."[94] "Our action," he told the bishop of Chichester in 1942, "must be such that the world will understand it as an act of repentance."[95] He was perfectly willing to admit that he prayed "for the defeat of my country, for I think that is the only possibility of paying for all the suffering that my country has caused in the world."[96] In committing treason he was, in an almost Maccabean style, seeking to expiate the sins of Germany and in a way of all humanity: "If any man tries to escape guilt in responsibility, he detaches himself from the ultimate reality of human existence, and what is more, he cuts himself off from the redeeming mystery of Christ's bearing guilt without sin."[97] In a novel begun but never finished in prison, Bonhoeffer argued that if all our alternatives are equally unacceptable, the individual must then act on conviction alone, because "anyone who avoids the issues will be a traitor to himself, his past, his calling, and his people."[98] When the inescapable reality was forced upon him that a coup d'état was impossible without first eliminating Hitler, he was ready to accept the responsibility of calculated murder. As early as September 1941 he was saying that he was ready to do the job personally. First, however, he would have to resign from his church; its guilt was heavy enough without adding assassination.[99]

In actuality Bonhoeffer was tainted with treason before he left New York City. By 1938 he had been informed by Dohnanyi of the existence of a political underground with its nerve center in the top echelons of the military and the Abwehr. Through his brother-in-law he met with all the key figures: the German chief of staff, Ludwig Beck, who was dismissed in 1938 for his open opposition to all but a defensive war but who even in retirement remained the military chief of the opposition; Carl Goerdeler, onetime mayor of Leipzig and price commissioner during the early Nazi government, who became the political organizer of the conspiracy; General Hans Oster, Dohnanyi's immediate head in the Abwehr and the man who on his own authority gave the Dutch advance warning of the scheduled day of the German invasion of the Netherlands; Ulrich von Hassell, one-time German ambassador to Rome; and World War I submarine hero Admiral William Canaris, the head of the Abwehr. In Nazi Germany to think sedition was tantamount to committing treason, and as an accessory to treason, Bonhoeffer placed himself in grave danger.

From the moment that cells of resistance began to form against Hitler during the late 1930s, it became quickly apparent that only a military coup could unseat the Führer because only the army, the Wehrmacht, had immunity from the Gestapo and the SS and could successfully hide a resistance group, and only the military had the power to stage a revolution. During the early months of the opposition there were enough high-ranking officers who considered Hitler's diplomatic-military policies—the Anschluss with Austria and the takeover of the Sudeten territory of Czechoslovakia—so recklessly dangerous and so likely to produce a European war, which Germany could not possibly win, that there was considerable expectation of a military takeover and the forced resignation of the Führer. Any hope that Hitler could be declared certifiably insane and forcibly removed from office by a spontaneous revolt within the government collapsed at Munich when England and France backed down and permitted the dismemberment of Czechoslovakia. Less than a month before Munich, General Beck had told one German diplomat en route to London, "Bring me certain proof that Britain will fight if Czechoslovakia is attacked, and I will make an end of this regime."[100] After Munich Hitler's diplomatic and military infallibility was unassailable. When the Führer invaded Poland in September of 1939, and within a year France had surrendered, it began to dawn on all the conspirators that no revolution could possibly remove the man who had the devil's own luck and had led the Wehrmacht to unparalleled victory. Hitler would have to first be destroyed, then the coup d'état staged. Worse, now that war had been declared, the plotters could no longer think of themselves as men seeking to save their country from a madman, but were cast as Judases seeking to betray the fatherland by murdering its savior.

Not until the invasion of Russia in the summer of 1941 and Hitler's orders to the army to execute without trial all civil and military commissars who fell into German hands—criminal activities heretofore committed only by SS troops—did the situation change. The command to the military to conduct itself as SS murder squads touched the honor of the Wehrmacht and made some high-ranking officers, trained in the tradition of the old imperial army, willing once again to consider treason. They began to suspect that Hitler's "fanatical will for a new order" might also entail their own liquidation. But only after the military debacle at Stalingrad, when Germany's total defeat became merely a matter of time, did Beck in retirement and the conspirators within the Abwehr begin to discover friends courageous and desperate enough to join the conspiracy. Still, however, the conspirators found themselves in an almost impossible position. Instead of appearing to rescue Europe as well as Germany from the Nazi destruction of all civilized values, now that the tide of battle had turned, they seemed to be seeking to salvage acceptable peace terms and attempting to save Germany from certain defeat.

The conspirators all had to assume a double life and live a constant lie. As Bonhoeffer said, "We have learnt the arts of equivocation and pretence; experience has made us suspicious of others and kept us from being truthful and open."[101] Timing was all-important. It was not enough simply to kill Hitler; elaborate plans had to be laid for a military and political takeover once he was dead. Senior military officers had to be found with the will and courage to act; experienced leaders approached who could govern the country. The price of failure was too awful to contemplate. Their own lives were the smallest part of the cost, for Hitler was devastatingly precise as to the revenge he would exact. Should any kind of revolt occur, he said at a dinner on April 7, 1942, "all the leaders of the opposition, including the leaders of the Catholic Party, would be arrested and executed; all the occupants of the concentration camps would be shot within three days; all the criminals on our lists—and it would make little difference whether they were in prison or at liberty—would be shot within the same period."[102]

Bonhoeffer's usefulness to the resistance became obvious the moment war was declared and the borders of Germany sealed from the rest of Europe. He was a clergyman with close links to the World Alliance of Churches and therefore to religious leaders who had the ear of the British Foreign Office—specifically, Bishop Bell of Chichester. Bonhoeffer sensed the conflict of interests and the danger of spiritual corruption in placing his ecclesiastical connections at the service of treason, so much so that he even thought his double life might force him to give up his ministry after the war. Since the rationale of the proposed assassination and coup was to end the war, General Beck and the Abwehr conspirators were desperate to get the Allies to commit themselves to a negotiated peace with a new, denazified government. Equally important, they needed peace terms that would strengthen the conspirators' hands when urging strategically placed commanders to break their personal oaths of allegiance to Hitler and commit treason. Bonhoeffer was one of the essential players in reaching out to the enemy and probing the possibility of a negotiated peace.

Dietrich Bonhoeffer's introduction into the Abwehr resistance cell was the logical extension of shared conversations that had already taken place in his brother-in-law's house with Beck, Oster, and others.[103] His appointment to the Abwehr also prevented him from being conscripted and got the Gestapo, which had him marked as a religious troublemaker, off his back. Having been granted leave of absence by the Confessing Church, and now protected by Admiral Canaris and the military secret service, Bonhoeffer could be sent under cover of legitimate Abwehr business to Switzerland and Sweden to meet in secret with foreign church officials and help organize the resistance's efforts to smuggle Jews out of Germany. Bonhoeffer's most important assignment was his meeting with Bishop Bell on May 30, 1942, in Stockholm. There he informed the bishop of the existence of the opposition inside Germany, describing its membership—ex–trade union officials, Catholic and Protestant church leaders, high-ranking officers in the army, important men in broadcasting, business, and politics. He was actually authorized to name the chief organizers. He outlined the aspirations of the new government: renunciation of aggression, repeal of the Nuremberg Laws, "withdrawal by stages of German forces from occupied and invaded countries," and cooperation with the Allies in rebuilding the devastation of Europe. Then he posed the crucial question. Would the Allies "announce now publicly to the world in the clearest terms that, once Hitler and the whole regime were overthrown, they would be prepared to negotiate with a new German government"? The only incentive Bonhoeffer could offer was the threat that the resistance had "full confidence in the strength of the German army and is ready to go on with the war to the bitter end if the Allies were to refuse to treat with a new government."[104]

Timing was crucial. The only hope of success was to negotiate through strength, but as each month went by, the Wehrmacht grew weaker and the Allies grew stronger, and any possibility of a negotiated peace receded. In fact, almost from the start the conspirators were operating in a fantasy world in which they had convinced themselves that a new government would not be a "liquidation commission" responsible for and presiding over Germany's total defeat and occupation.

Unfortunately, speed was the one element denied the resistance. Even if the conspirators successfully convinced strategically placed senior officers to participate in treason, those commanders might be transferred, dismissed, or offered sizable monetary gifts by the Führer, who astutely reinforced the loyalty of his commanders with large bribes. Moreover, Hitler's own life style was so unpredictable that it was impossible to foretell where he was going to be and to plan accordingly. "Vain are all our efforts," Ulrich von Hassell complained in his diary, "to pour iron into the bloodstream of the people who are supporting a half-insane, half-criminal policy with all their might."[105]

Finally, after a series of false starts, unlucky accidents, and endless hesitation on the part of indispensable army officers, all was ready on March 13, 1943, nine and a half months after Bonhoeffer's talk with Bell in Stockholm. A bomb had been successfully spirited aboard Hitler's plane as it returned from the Russian front, and in Berlin everything was set for a full-scale uprising. But the British acid-operated time-delay fuse, which the Allies used for acts of sabotage in German-occupied territories and which the Abwehr had captured, failed to work. Immediately the resistance organized a second attempt, and eight days later Major Rudolf von Gersdorff of the Abwehr attempted a suicide delivery of a bomb. This also failed when Hitler unexpectedly cut short his visit to an exhibition of captured Russian war machines. Less than a month later, on April 5, Dohnanyi and Bonhoeffer were arrested and General Oster placed under house surveillance by the Gestapo. Except for Canaris, the coordinating and directing nerve center of the resistance had quite inadvertently been smashed.

Even though the brothers-in-law had been arrested as political criminals, not traitors, and the Gestapo was unaware that it had wiped out a nest of assassins, the conspirators had in fact lost a three-way race against time: to act before any hope of a negotiated peace perished on the battlefield; to launch a successful attack on Hitler and plan a well-coordinated revolution against his government; and to stem the Gestapo's growing suspicions about the Abwehr and thwart its desire to destroy the army's intelligence agency. Murphy's Law had from the start operated overtime: everything imaginable had gone wrong. With the arrest of Dohnanyi it was only a matter of time before the Gestapo would get rid of Canaris himself, and it was already questioning Bonhoeffer about "Operation 7"—a successful plan to whisk a small group of Jews, many of them personal friends of Canaris, out of Germany and into Switzerland under the guise of Abwehr business. The Abwehr fell to Reichsführer Himmler in February of 1944, and Canaris was dismissed and forced to retire in April. Even Beck was useless; he was desperately ill with stomach cancer. The race to assassinate Hitler and seize the government went on, but it now had little to do with the Abwehr cell and was organized by a younger group of officers led by Colonel Claus Schenk, Count von Stauffenberg, and was not ready until July 20, 1944, when Allied armies on both the eastern and western fronts were on the verge of penetrating the borders of the fatherland itself. In the end, even that attempt failed. The bomb went off, but seconds before it did an officer accidentally moved the bomb, concealed in a briefcase, out of range of the Führer, and he miraculously escaped with only a few bruises. "A handful of infamous officers," as the only still-licensed church newspaper described the assassination attempt, "driven by their own ambition," had been thwarted in their frightful attempt to defile the fatherland.[106]

The devil looked after his own; and in so doing he sealed the fate of the Abwehr conspirators. As soon as the Gestapo realized that Stauffenberg was not a lone assassin but involved in a far-reaching revolutionary plot, Hitler, true to his promise, took his revenge. Canaris, Oster, Hassell, Goerdeler, and dozens of army officers were arrested and either promptly shot or summarily tried and executed; the Abwehr's records were searched and Dohnanyi's papers eventually discovered; and Bonhoeffer, his brother-in-law, plus others originally imprisoned in military detention centers, were moved to the basement prison of the Gestapo headquarters in the Prinz Albrecht Strasse.

During the early months of his confinement and endless interrogation as to the Abwehr's activities, prison life for Bonhoeffer was not too dreadful. Fear of torture always lurked in the shadows, and the prisoners constantly worried that the Gestapo would persuade, trick, or force one or another of them into revealing their collective treason. For a brief moment Bonhoeffer even contemplated suicide, "not from a sense of guilt, but because I am basically already dead"; but he soon recovered from the shock of arrest and close confinement.[107] It helped that he was the nephew of the commandant of Berlin, and he soon obtained from the outside world pipe, tobacco, hair brush, slippers, writing paper, ink, and books. Most important of all, he was able to maintain through the cooperation of friendly guards an illicit and coded correspondence which kept him abreast of Stauffenberg's progress and eventual failure. Suffering, Bonhoeffer knew, was relative, and he refused to consider himself a martyr: "Suffering must be something quite different, and have a quite different dimension from what I have so far experienced."[108]

Eighteen months in a military prison and almost another six in a Gestapo cell, living with the certain knowledge he would eventually be executed, focused Bonhoeffer's mind on the nature of faith and the role of the deity in a fashion he had never experienced when writing *The Cost of Discipleship* at Finkenwalde or working on his *Ethics* during the years before his arrest. The prison months were his most creative period; it was, as he said, a kind of "good spiritual Turkish bath" that liberated his thinking from a lifetime of conventional and formal theology.[109] There is, of course, nothing like the title of martyr to lend verisimilitude to religious ponderings; but even had Bonhoeffer not died in a Nazi prison camp, the question he posed—how do we speak to God in a world that has rejected the religious vocabulary of its past?—and the answers he suggested, although opaque and tentative, would have been sufficient in themselves to sustain his reputation as one of the most seminal religious thinkers of the twentieth century. The letters he wrote from prison are little more than fragmentary and enigmatic thoughts—Karl Barth dismissed them as a peep "around some corner" to a profound but obscure truth—and they in no way constitute a sustained theological discourse.[110] Nevertheless, they have spawned religious debate far beyond what Bonhoeffer himself could have imagined.

During those months of close confinement, Bonhoeffer outlined a view of religion and God divested of the sterile religious formulas and "liturgical monkery" of the past. His sense of the deity had nothing to do with a "God of the gaps," a deus ex machina, who stood at the periphery of human experience and whose existence was necessary to fill in the missing segments and explain the mysteries created by the inadequacies of human knowledge and understanding. His God was a paradoxical divinity that insisted that "we must live as men who can get along very well without Him" because He exists within, not outside of, each human being. "Only by living completely in this world," never by retreating from it, could God be fully comprehended and worshiped. His faith grew and prospered, Bonhoeffer said, "only along the road that I have traveled," and "so I am grateful for the past and the present, and content with them."[111]

Bonhoeffer was grateful for the past and the present even though he already knew that Hitler had survived Stauffenberg's bomb; it had exploded the day before he wrote of his gratitude and contentment. The past failures of the resistance had gone undetected; the Stauffenberg fiasco was different and could only end in vengeance. In September the Abwehr's secret files were discovered; by October Bonhoeffer and Dohnanyi had been transferred to Gestapo cells and Klaus Bonhoeffer and another brother-in-law had been arrested; and on April 9, 1945, Dohnanyi was executed at

Sachsenhausen, and Bonhoeffer along with Canaris and Oster were hanged at Flossenbürg, all by direct orders from the Führer. It is difficult to retain any vestige of humanity, let alone dignity, when required to remove one's clothes and climb naked to the gallows, but Dietrich Bonhoeffer seems to have achieved the impossible; the camp physician wrote ten years later that "in the almost fifty years that I worked as a doctor, I have hardly ever seen a man die so entirely submissive to the will of God."[112] As Allied heavy artillery sounded in the distance, all the bodies were immediately carted off to the crematorium; even Bonhoeffer's Bible and his volume of Goethe were burned along with the corpses.

During the Christmas season of 1942, by way of reassuring his fellow conspirators, Bonhoeffer had written that he believed as an absolute article of faith that "God can and will bring good out of evil, even out of the greatest evil."[113] Whether that evil resided in their own treason or in the Nazi regime is not clear, but Bonhoeffer was a believer who had confidence in his deity. He was, according to a British prisoner of war who met him during those final days at Flossenbürg, "one of the very few men I have ever met to whom his God was real and ever close to him."[114] The reality of such a God may have given Bonhoeffer confidence in salvation, but, more important, it assured him that his life on earth had meaning: "As I see it, I am here for some purpose, and I only hope I may fulfill it."[115] He had no regrets and wrote his close friend Eberhard Bethge on April 11, 1944: "If I were to end my life in these conditions . . . that would have a meaning that I think I could understand; on the other hand, everything might be a thorough preparation for a new start and a new task when peace comes."[116] In April of 1944 Bonhoeffer did not know which way his career would end. Either way his life had meaning, and he said he never regretted "my decision in the summer of 1939" to return to Germany and commit treason; his life had "been an uninterrupted enrichment of experience" for which he was thankful.[117]

Whether the fulfillment of a deeply internalized concept of divine purpose, which made both life and death worthwhile, is a cause sufficient to qualify Bonhoeffer as a martyr can never be resolved. For Pastor Bonhoeffer, if not necessarily in the eyes of history, his life had not been wasted and his death had a purpose. Whether he belongs in the company of the martyrs is equally difficult to say. Like the Maccabees, he bore the burden of his country's guilt and sought to expiate it. Like Thomas Becket, he violated his allegiance to the state; but unlike the archbishop, his treason was fundamental; it sought the total destruction of a regime dedicated to evil. Like Sir Thomas More, he was conscious of cosmic direction and had a profound sense of historic necessity; but his vision was focused not on political meaning but upon himself and his personal destiny. As he said, when a man "acts because the will of God seems to bid him to . . . no one but himself and God can know whether he has acted well or badly."[118]

The courage of the Abwehr conspirators, Count von Stauffenberg, and others has not been forgotten in today's Germany, but no statues stand in praise of their treason.[119] Nor is there any particular reason that they should; society is generally loath to commemorate its failures. Traitors carry with them the stigma of failure, the price paid—sometimes willingly, sometimes not—for not having been successful. Martyrdom, in contrast, is lifted up by the aura of success. It gives comfort to the living by assigning meaning to death, which is immediately transformed into an act of choice, pride, and purpose to be remembered and celebrated by all. That, Bonhoeffer confessed in one of his most revealing prison letters, was what he wanted most: to be remembered. "There comes over me a longing (unlike any other that I experience) not to vanish without a trace." Then he added with amused candor: "An Old Testament rather than a New Testament wish, I suppose."[120] As long as the debate over the true color of the political martyr continues, Dietrich Bonhoeffer will have his wish.

Dietrich Bonhoeffer was a political martyr, a nomenclature that has bedeviled martyrdom from the start. The moment society began to classify and define its martyrs, the dilemma emerged: how to differentiate within a Christian context between religion and politics, faith and social justice. Becket, More, Charles I, John Brown, and Bonhoeffer were all convinced in their various ways that they were defending their faith against the Antichrist, but the moment the devil dressed himself in secular garb and began playing politics, the trouble began. All five men died as a consequence of their "treason." In each case faith was the motivating force, but when doing battle with the Antichrist, that faith quickly became synonymous with their private definitions of what constituted the true structure of God's kingdom on earth.

To preserve the essential element of faith from political misinterpretation and corruption and to prevent an avalanche of political martyrs from overwhelming the Catholic Church, Pope Benedict XIV in the eighteenth century established guidelines for determining martyr status, which have remained to this day.[121] Clear evidence had to exist that the victim died for the faith as laid down by the church, that those who committed the murder or execution did so out of "hatred for the faith," and that the martyr's motives were essentially spiritual and religious. These are the central reasons why Archbishop Oscar Romero, "the people's saint" of El Salvador, who was shot and killed on March 24, 1980, while saying mass in the hospital chapel of the Carmelite sisters, has never been recognized by the Catholic Church as a proper martyr; Romero had entered politics and was a victim of his own impolitic attacks on the existing right-wing government. He may have, in his own words, offered his "blood to God for the redemption and for the resurrection of El Salvador" and willingly given his life "for the liberation of my people," but Rome required more than a "people's saint." He had to be "a martyr of the church."[122] Romero, like Bonhoeffer and Martin Luther King Jr., might be categorized as "a martyr for justice," an all-encompassing term that includes a multitude of worthy warriors who have died combatting evil and injustice in the name of God's kingdom, but the archbishop did not die for the Roman Catholic faith as defined by Rome. And when a small delegation of Lutherans, after Vatican II in the early 1960s, urged the Catholic Church to consider the canonization of Bonhoeffer as a dramatic ecumenical act, the Vatican politely but firmly declined, suggesting that it was up to the German Lutheran Church to define its own martyrs.[123]

The sentiment today is to blunt the distinction between politics and faith and to include Bonhoeffer as a legitimate martyr, and he has been added to the informal list of those whom Lutherans hold in special remembrance. But what happens when the political martyr who remains in the eyes of society a political traitor and pariah qualifies as a legitimate martyr for faith, and what happens when that faith is anathema to the great majority of citizens? This issue leads directly to the complex and confused case of Julius and Ethel Rosenberg, who by the definition of martyrdom proposed in this book may both be acceptable candidates as martyrs.

IV. JULIUS AND ETHEL ROSENBERG AND THE ATOM BOMB

At eight o'clock on the evening of June 19, 1953, Julius Rosenberg, his pant legs slit and his head partially shaven to receive the electrodes, was seated in the electric chair at Sing Sing prison. At 8:03, he received the standard three high-voltage shocks. In two and a half minutes he was declared dead. Five minutes later, after the chair had been washed clean of his urine, his wife, Ethel Rosenberg, was similarly executed, but for her it took five bolts of electricity and five minutes to pronounce her dead, thereby confirming President Eisenhower's opinion that she "is the strong and recalcitrant character, the man is the weak one" in a crime that involved "the deliberate betrayal of the entire nation and could very well result in the death of many, many thousands of innocent citizens."[124]

Three months after their deaths, the Communist Party announced that the Rosenbergs would be enshrined "in the ranks of innocent martyrs who died in the cause of truth."[125] The juxtaposition of the adjective "innocent" with the noun "martyr" poses a philosophical conundrum: can martyrs for truth be innocent and continue to be martyrs, or do they become victims? Must true martyrs know exactly what they are doing and work so that their actions and deaths further the cause in which they believe? Gandhi would have unhesitatingly argued that the innocent martyr, when truth was introduced into the equation, was a contradiction in terms. If there were "no other God than truth" and all properly trained satyagrahi knew that truth and were willing to die for it, then martyrs might be innocent of wrongdoing but never ignorant of what they were doing. Knowledge, deliberation, and choice, not innocence, were the hallmarks of true martyrdom. "I have no sense of repentance," the Mahatma said, "for I have no sense of having done any wrong to any person. . . . I have no consciousness of guilt."[126]

The introduction of the term "innocent" goes to the root of the Rosenberg tragedy—or to use J. Edgar Hoover's terminology, the "crime of the century"—because in their case the word has a double meaning. Were this undistinguished, economically struggling Jewish couple guiltless of the crime for which they were executed and therefore victims of either a deliberate government frame-up or an appalling miscarriage of justice? And did they or did they not knowingly elect to become martyrs by frantically maintaining and systematically publicizing their innocence and deliberately sacrificing themselves and their two young sons to a cause that was more real and precious to them than life itself? In brief, were they in control of their fate?

"Guilt" and "innocence" are flexible terms. Gandhi had "no consciousness of guilt," but he would have been the first to admit that he was the "leader of an open rebellion" which sought to overthrow the British Raj. The Rosenbergs proclaimed themselves innocent; but innocence and guiltlessness are not necessarily the same things, and the debate over what to call the Rosenbergs—innocent victims, guiltless martyrs, ruthless criminals, self-righteous ideologues, or diabolical traitors worthy of being hanged, drawn, and quartered—continues to rage, because labeling tends to be more the offspring of conviction than the child of proven evidence. Their "crime of the century" in an era when, as I. F. Stone has observed, "fanaticism had the same momentum on both sides"[127] is encased in one of the most inflamed periods of American history, and any determination as to guilt or innocence rests on the debater's response to and handling of three emotionally charged events: their trial, their punishment, and the publication of their *Death House Letters*.[128]

Ethel and Julius Rosenberg were the children of Jewish emigrant families living in the crowded slums of the Lower East Side of New York City, where at the turn of the century some 350,000 Jews were packed into jerry-built cold-water flats. They worked long hours in the garment industry and mostly spoke Yiddish. Ethel Greenglass's father, Barnet, repaired sewing machines in his shop in front of the Greenglasses' three-room sunless ground-floor apartment, which until they later managed to rent two rooms in the flat above them, housed his wife, Tessie; Ethel; her older half-brother, Sam; and her two younger full brothers, Bernard and Davy. Julius was no better off. He was the youngest of five children, and the family was so poor that they had to hard-boil their eggs so as to divide one among the family. His father, after giving up business on his own, was a cutter and sample maker in a clothing factory. Unlike Barnet Greenglass, Harry Rosenberg had a steady salary, eventually moved into a heated apartment, and could afford to have his elder son, David, attend Columbia University on a scholarship and later send Julius to tuition-free City College of New York.

Ethel and Julius met in December of 1936 at an International Seamen's Union benefit for its striking members. He was an eighteen-year-old engineering student far less committed to his studies than to left-wing student politics, and an ardent member of the Young Communist League, where he spoke of "the new world, the future, [and] Socialism," not as if they were abstractions or far-off matters of speculation, but "in immediate terms, living and vital." "His humaneness, his devotion and his singleness of purpose" were, according to a fellow student, the attributes that "marked him."[129] Ethel was twenty-one. She worked recording clothing shipments for the National New York Packing and Shipping Company and had successfully sued her employer to get her job back when she was fired as a consequence of her actions as a union organizer and strike leader. As one fellow worker said, "You couldn't forget Ethel. . . . She put her heart and soul in all she did."[130] She also possessed a fine soprano voice and sang often and passionately for the Communist-influenced Workers' Alliance of America, especially during its rallies on behalf of Loyalist Spain. It was, in fact, Ethel's voice that brought her to the Seamen's Union benefit, where she sang Pestalozza's "Ciribiribin" and won Julius's heart.

Julius graduated in electrical engineering in February 1939; he married Ethel in June; and on December 12, 1939, he joined the Communist Party as a card-carrying member—an action that he vehemently denied to his dying day but is on record in the FBI files. His participation in the Party is also confirmed by an associate who was a member of branch 16-B, which met often in the Rosenberg apartment since Julius was its chairman. There is no evidence that Ethel ever officially joined the Party; but along with Julius, she sold copies of the *Daily Worker,* and she sang at party functions.[131]

For the Rosenbergs, 1939 to 1943 were the halcyon years. The optimism of the political left still prevailed; once the fascist beast had been destroyed, the future could be shaped to the noblest dreams of the human mind by those who were "attuned to the inner rhythms of History." World War II for all its horrors ended almost a decade of depression, and Julius—always called Julie—found his first job in August of 1940 in the Army Signal Corps as a civilian inspector of electronic equipment supplied to the military. Ethel could now afford to give up her job, and when the Soviet Union was invaded in June 1941, she became a full-time volunteer secretary for the East Side Conference to Defend America and Crush Hitler, a Communist-sponsored organization to raise money, medical supplies, food, and clothing for the peoples of the USSR. Julie's only concerns on the horizon were the Signal Corps loyalty check in January of 1941, a danger he easily averted by assuring his interrogators that "at no time in my life have I ever had anything to do with [the] distribution of Communist literature,"[132] and mounting political tension within the Greenglass family. Sam Greenglass was adamantly opposed to communism and resented young Davy's hero-worship of his brother-in-law Julius, and he disapproved of the radical political views the Rosenbergs were feeding his brother. He even "offered to pay" Julie and

Ethel's "transportation to Russia if they would agree to stay there."[133] His efforts to decontaminate David Greenglass were of little avail, for Davy became a vigorous member of the Young Communist League; and when he was drafted in early 1943, he wrote to his newly married wife that he was busy proselytizing and would "raise the red flag yet." She agreed: "Dearest, remember what Julie told you, as a Communist it's up to you to set an example to the other soldiers."[134]

These relatively affluent and harmonious years came to an end when Michael Allen Rosenberg was born on March 10, 1943, an event that transformed Ethel's life and sent her to a social therapist and eventually to a psychiatrist because Michael turned out to be an extraordinarily difficult child. He was defiant, demanding, constantly sick and crying, and totally unmanageable, while Ethel was a doctrinaire mother who, because the authorities said it was right, refused to cross or discipline him in any way. The Rosenbergs even went so far as to move out of their only bedroom and sleep on the living-room sofa so that Michael could have his own room and living space. The addition of Robert in May 1947, although he was a model infant, simply made matters worse. Domestically, life had become a living hell for the Rosenbergs.

In 1945 Julie's world also collapsed. As a consequence of information supplied by the FBI, he was summarily dismissed from the Signal Corps as a security risk on the grounds of his membership in the Communist Party. Again he indignantly denied the charge, writing, "I am not now, and never have been a Communist. . . . I know nothing about Communist branches, divisions, clubs, or transfers."[135] The Signal Corps, however, ignored his protestation and placed him on "indefinite suspension." After brief employment with a war-related company, which came to an end after the surrender of Japan, Julius tried business for himself, teaming up with his brothers-in-law Bernard and David, both freshly demobilized from the army. Despite three reorganizations of the enterprise to purchase, sell, and manufacture nuts, bolts, and screws, the venture began to flounder. As the profits failed to materialize and the debts mounted, acrimony between the partners increased. Davy, who had briefly attended Brooklyn Polytechnic Institute and had been trained by the army as a machinist when stationed at Los Alamos, accused Julius of failing to give his full attention to the business. Davy's wife, Ruth, was considerably more outspoken. Julius simply "handed out orders" instead of generating new orders through his Signal Corps contacts. Moreover, he wanted to be "King Tut or nothing." Her husband, she said, not Julie, was doing all the work, but being paid a pittance. Julius in his turn complained that Davy was henpecked, lazy, slovenly, stupid, and a "slob."[136]

Then, during the summer of 1950, the Rosenbergs' life fell apart completely. Suddenly Julius and Ethel were indicted for conspiracy to commit espionage on the basis of information supplied by Ruth and David Greenglass.

The trail that led the FBI to the Rosenbergs' apartment, G.E. 11 in Knickerbocker Village on the Lower East Side of New York City, started when the Soviet Union exploded its first atomic bomb in August of 1949. A month later, on September 23, President Truman announced the event to an American public that was already dangerously close to hysteria, convinced that red spies and traitors lay curled within the body politic like so many tapeworms eating at the nation's lifeblood. Communists were seen as "masters of deceit," "bottled spiders" weaving a black web of conspiracy; and Senator Joseph McCarthy claimed that "men high in this government" were plotting treason "on a scale so immense as to dwarf any previous such venture in the history of man."[137] The country jumped to the conclusion that the secret of the bomb had been stolen by an infamous "espionage ring," which in Congressman Richard Nixon's opinion "was responsible for turning over information on the atomic bomb to agents of the Russian government."[138] Nobody wanted to listen to the advice of the atomic physicists themselves, who warned that there was in reality no secret to steal—the theory of the bomb was common scientific knowledge, and any industrial power could develop the technological means to explode one. No, the country had been betrayed; and FBI director J. Edgar Hoover ordered his organization to go out and "find the thieves."

As it turned out, the British found the "thief" first.[139] On February 2, 1950, they arrested Klaus Fuchs, a Communist refugee from Nazi Germany who had become a British subject and atomic scientist. Fuchs had extensive knowledge of atomic research under way in England, Canada, and the United States. He had worked for over a year at Los Alamos and confessed that between 1943 and 1946 he had supplied an American courier, code name "Raymond," with information on "the design of the plutonium bomb." The FBI immediately began the hunt for "Raymond." This unknown man, said Hoover, "simply had to be found"—and to the satisfaction of most people he was.[140] On the twenty-third of May a soft, retiring little thirty-nine-year-old chemist from Philadelphia by the name of Harry Gold, who looked as if he might be scared of his own shadow and who indulged in a fantasy world of daydreams as a substitute for a social life, was arrested. A week later he told government agents that he was indeed the mysterious "Raymond." He also said that he had another source of atomic information—a solidly built, snub-nosed, dark-curly-haired soldier with a New York accent who was married, lived in Albuquerque, New Mexico, and worked at Los Alamos as a machinist. He had paid five hundred dollars to this man on the instructions of his Soviet espionage superior Anatoli Yakovlev for what Gold described as "general information" on the Los Alamos installations. Within two days the FBI had located David Greenglass, partly because he fitted the description, partly because Davy was already on record: he was suspected (correctly so) of having been one of a number of soldiers who had liberated small, walnut-sized containers for uranium as souvenirs.

Davy and Ruth proved to be model witnesses—some critics would argue, far too model—and they preceded to recount a damning story implicating the Rosenbergs. When Davy was stationed at Los Alamos, Ruth in November 1944 went out to visit him, carrying with her Julie's urgent appeal that her husband "share" his knowledge about the bomb. Davy agreed and gave his wife a verbal description of the Los Alamos operation and the names of the most prominent people working on the project. On her return to New York Ruth dutifully reported this information to Julius. Davy himself visited the city in January on furlough and prepared for Julius a handwritten report on the Los Alamos layout and supplied him sketches of an experimental detonating device called a "lens mold," which presumably provided the important information that research was moving in the direction of an implosion-detonated plutonium bomb. The Greenglasses also met the Rosenbergs in their apartment, and Julius presented his brother-in-law with one-half of a side panel of a Jell-O box, saying that he would be contacted later on by a courier with the other half. After Ruth had moved to Albuquerque, where she found a secretarial position and lived in a small apartment, Davy on the weekends commuting the forty miles from Los Alamos, the man who appeared at her door on June 3 with the second half of the Jell-O panel was Harry Gold, to whom Davy gave a six- or seven-page account of the lens mold in return for five hundred dollars.

Ethel's involvement in espionage, according to her brother and sister-in-law, had been as deliberate as her husband's: she had been a willing collaborator to all his activities and had in fact typed out and copyedited Davy's report on the lens mold and the Los Alamos operation. Their story did not emerge fully developed from the Greenglasses' memory; it came out over a period of almost nine months, and the government hammered in the final nails of both their coffins when Harry Gold asserted that he had indeed gone to Albuquerque armed with the side panel from the Jell-O box and moreover had used the recognition signal "I come from Julius." Finally, just to be sure the nail stayed in place, Davy said that Julius, immediately after the news that Fuchs had been arrested, had told him that the British spy's courier was the same man as Davy's, that it was only a matter of time before Gold would be found and forced to confess, and he had offered the

Greenglasses five thousand dollars (in the end he only came up with four thousand dollars) to help them flee the country.

The government was delighted; it had found the master spy, his Lady Macbeth wife, and an elaborate espionage ring. All that was now required to rid the land of this nest of traitors was for Ethel and Julius to confess their sins and name their fellow conspirators. Unfortunately, the Rosenbergs refused to do so; and on March 29, 1951, still clinging to their innocence, they were found guilty, in the prosecutor's words, of a conspiracy to deliver to the enemy "the information and the weapons which the Soviet Union could use to destroy us."[141]

A book about martyrdom is no place to debate at length the question of guilt or innocence; two immensely convincing books—*Invitation to an Inquest* by Walter and Miriam Schneir and *The Rosenberg File* by Ronald Radosh and Joyce Milton—have done so, reaching quite opposite conclusions. If the verdict is a matter of disagreement, the trial itself is not. Almost no one argues that the Rosenbergs received anything resembling legal justice. The proceedings were conducted in an atmosphere of monumental international tension. Throughout the trial, March 6–29, 1951, Chinese troops were overrunning Tibet and putting American troops to flight in Korea, and the *New York Times* was carrying headlines about the danger of atomic war and the cost of bomb shelters for the city. Under such conditions an impartial trial of a couple accused of giving the A-bomb to the Soviet Union was impossible. Worse, the verdict was based almost entirely on evidence that was not only disturbingly circumstantial but also supplied by three admitted spies: the self-confessed fantasizer Harry Gold, who had already received a thirty-year sentence; David Greenglass, who had been found guilty and was awaiting sentence and knew his cooperation as a government witness would affect both his punishment (which turned out to be fifteen years) and the government's handling of his wife; and Ruth Greenglass, who, as a consequence of David's willingness to confess and her own corroboration of that confession, got off scot-free, even though her proven involvement in espionage was considerably greater than Ethel Rosenberg's. The Greenglasses were out to save their own skins, and Davy was brutally candid when he said that the Rosenbergs "gotta take care of themselves."[142] Equally disquieting, Harry Gold and David Greenglass were housed together on the eleventh floor of the Tombs prison in New York, thereby opening the prosecution to the accusation that it was permitting the two men to rig their evidence. Added to this, Judge Irving Kaufman's bias throughout the trial was transparent; evidence was allowed that today would be inadmissible; the case may well have been tried under the wrong law—the Espionage Act of 1917 should probably have been superseded by the Atomic Energy Act of 1946—and the actions of the attorney general, the Supreme Court and the President of the United States are open to heavy criticism. Finally, the behavior of the defense lawyer during the trial and throughout the appeal process was sufficiently bizarre to raise the issue of outright malpractice and the possibility that, as a convinced Communist, he was more interested in the welfare of the Communist Party than his clients' innocence. Certainly Supreme Court Justice William O. Douglas thought that "the Communist consensus" felt that "it was best for the cause that the Rosenbergs pay the extreme price."[143]

Justice Douglas's suggestion raises a difficult but related point: throughout the trial the Rosenbergs made a terrible impression on the judge, the jury, and the news media. Neither did anything to help their case, and their posturing went a long way to create the impression that they were saying, We are innocent but have so little faith in or love for the existing social system in the United States that we would have been delighted to give the bomb away to the USSR if we ever had the chance. Both used the Fifth Amendment so often that it was difficult not to suspect that in fact they had a great deal to hide; and Julius, knowing full well the mood of the country, lectured the court on the advantages of the Communist system and the sacrifices that the Soviet Union had made during the war. The Soviet government, he said, "has improved the lot of the underdog there, has made a lot of progress in eliminating illiteracy," and "contributed a major share in destroying the Hitler beast who killed six million of my co-religionists, and I feel emotional about that thing."[144] Even their close friend Morton Sobell, who was being tried for espionage along with the Rosenbergs, observed that "one would have hardly thought" that Julius and his wife "were on trial for their lives."[145] They seemed to go out of their way to appear unconcerned and contemptuous, as if they never expected anything else except a guilty verdict, and they erected about themselves a wall of pride and defiance that stopped dead any sympathy the outside world might have felt for two people whom their lawyer was trying to depict as hapless victims of intrafamily animosity and a ruthless government frame-up. Such a picture simply did not fit a couple who, after sentence of death had been pronounced, returned to their cells, where Ethel burst into an aria from Puccini's *Madama Butterfly* and Julius sang "The Battle Hymn of the Republic."

Until very recently the balance of judgment as to guilt or innocence, given the unfairness of the trial and their death-chair avowals of innocence, has been to give the Rosenbergs the benefit of the doubt. Who could deny innocence to a husband and wife who in their last letter to their children categorically stated, "Always remember that we were innocent and could not wrong our conscience"?[146] It was monstrous to believe that they could have lived and died a lie. That is, until 1990 and the publication of the Khrushchev tapes, in which he says, "I cannot specifically say what kind of help the Rosenbergs provided us, but both Stalin and Molotov were informed. . . . I heard from both Stalin and Molotov that the Rosenbergs provided very significant help in accelerating the production of our atomic bomb." Khrushchev's memory may not be proof of guilt, but it has altered the balance against the Rosenbergs. The balance has tipped even further with the revelation in 1995 that during the final years of World War II the United States had broken the Soviet Union's secret code and had evidence of a spy ring that included Julius Rosenberg, whose cover identity in Russian communiques was "Liberal." [147]

Innocence or guilt, however, is not the central issue. It may help to know that the Rosenbergs were guilty in fact as well as in law, but that knowledge does nothing to lessen the furor surrounding their punishment once Judge Kaufman gave sentence: "I consider your crime worse than murder. . . . Your conduct in putting into the hands of the Russians the A-bomb . . . has already caused, in my opinion, the Communist aggression in Korea with the resultant casualties exceeding 50,000 and who knows but that millions more of innocent people may pay the price of your treason. Indeed, by your betrayal you undoubtedly have altered the course of history to the disadvantage of our country. . . . The sentence of the court . . . is . . . you are hereby sentenced to the punishment of death."[148]

Why were two confessed spies given a minimal sentence or allowed off free, but a couple who staunchly maintained their innocence sent to the electric chair? One answer—that passionately held by the Rosenbergs— maintains the existence of a vicious frame-up whereby the Rosenbergs were deliberately sacrificed in order to create the necessary war hysteria that would permit the country to rearm and a diabolical plot to suppress all "progressives" in the country. A considerably less hysterical, but only marginally less ugly, explanation is that the FBI and the prosecution were convinced of the existence of a spy ring that had to be smashed even at the cost of due process. Their ruthlessness was so great that they were willing to inflict the death penalty on two spies who at worst had only given information to an ally fighting alongside of the United States against a common enemy and who in England would only have received a maximum of fifteen years—the sentence of Klaus Fuchs.

The government's justification was the need to force a confession. Myles Lane, one of the assistant prosecutors, stated the argument in its starkest form. "The only thing that will break this man Rosenberg is the prospect of a death penalty or getting the chair, plus that if we can convict his wife too, and give her a stiff sentence of 25 or 30 years, that combination may serve to make this fellow disgorge." It was, he concluded, "about the only thing you can use as a lever on these people."[149] Judge Kaufman's willingness to include Ethel in the death sentence, though Hoover was hesitant for fear of the public reaction, was seen simply as a bonus lever, and the FBI was so certain that Julius would eventually break that it set up a hot-line telephone in the death house and wrote down a set of questions should the Rosenbergs desire "to talk after they go into the execution chamber and even after they are strapped into the chair."[150] What took place was a battle of wills which the government eventually lost.

The death penalty changed the Rosenberg case from a sordid matter of espionage into an issue of universal principle, giving Julius and Ethel the opportunity to reach out to a worldwide audience. Instead of languishing silently in jail as dirty Communist traitors—out of sight, out of mind—they were suddenly metamorphosed into heroes representing everything decent, honest, and just while the United States government became the symbol of vengefulness, hysteria, and tyranny. The transformation was in large measure due to the savagery of the punishment, but in smaller part it was also the consequence of an important victory Julius Rosenberg himself had won. "I don't want to die," he told a fellow prison inmate immediately after hearing Judge Kaufman's sentence of death. "I want to live. . . . But I'll tell you one thing now and I'll never change: They'll never use the name Julie Rosenberg to make the word 'Communist' mean 'spy' and 'spy' mean 'Communist.' " He repeated the same resolution by way of consolation for his lawyer. The verdict, he explained, was inevitable, "part of the government's plan to intensify hatred against the Soviet Union and terrorize left-progressives and those for peace in this country." The government "hoped to sell the people finally the concept that an espionage agent must be a Communist, and a Communist an espionage agent."[151]

As best he could, Julius attempted to thwart this purpose. He denied association with the Communist Party, he claimed protection under the Fifth Amendment to prevent the prosecution from proving his Communist sympathies, and he maintained his own and his wife's absolute innocence of any espionage activity, Communist or otherwise. No one was going to link communism to spying through Julius. The prosecution might assume the association and base its case on that premise, but that was simply further evidence of its kangaroo-court tactics. To the day they died the Rosenbergs rarely mentioned the Communist Party; if they did so, they usually put "Communist" and "communism" in quotation marks; and they invariably referred to themselves as "progressives" free of any taint of treason or espionage. The Communist Party itself clearly agreed with Julie's strategy, because it never said a word to defend the Rosenbergs or even to protest the guilty verdict. Only after the backlash of the death sentence became apparent, and when it was clear that in the test of wills the Rosenbergs would win, did the Party publicly claim them as heroes and martyrs. Miriam Moscowitz, a left-wing sympathizer and jailhouse friend of Ethel's, could not understand why the Communist Party was not "immediately screaming" about "frame-ups," and Ethel had to quietly explain to her that the Party "shouldn't get contaminated by these [atom spy] cases."[152]

There was a price to pay for protecting the Party and the Communist ideal from the smell of treason: the Rosenbergs could never change their story even to save their lives. But in maintaining their innocence of both spying and membership in the Party, they achieved, certainly in their own eyes and in the eyes of many throughout the world, a new and heroic stature. They were threefold heroes: for many they were innocent victims of injustice; for a few they were good soldiers of the Party; and for all radicals they were martyrs to a faith in social and economic justice that would endure long after their deaths.

The Rosenbergs took every advantage of their newfound heroism, and their story became one of the great media events of the decade. As the hours ticked away, bringing them ever closer to the electric chair, the world went into a frenzy of moral outrage and protest. Supporters gathered outside of Sing Sing prison on the Sunday before Christmas 1952 to sing carols, which, of course, the Rosenbergs, inurned behind stone and concrete, could not hear. Mass rallies took place in Paris, Rome, and throughout Europe. News bulletins on the radio and television kept the public up to date, and on the eve of their deaths, when reporters were ordered to gather at Sing Sing, the news was sufficiently momentous to interrupt the television broadcast of the afternoon baseball game. When the execution finally took place, some thirty-eight news reporters—only three were allowed to actually view the deaths—were on hand to supply an avid public with the gory details: Julius, ashen-faced, being helped to the death chair; Ethel, dressed in a green dress and cloth slippers, going to her death with a faint smile and almost "triumphant" expression; the convulsions of their muscles and the smoke that rose from their heads as the electricity passed through their bodies. Passions erupted on both sides of the political spectrum at the news. Anti-Rosenberg pickets in front of the White House carried signs demanding "Death to the Communist Rats," drivers honked their horns in celebration, and in Los Angeles counterdemonstrators cheered. Elsewhere, in New York City nearly seven thousand people joined to publicly mourn the deaths; in Italy government workers staged a fifteen-minute sympathy strike; and in Rome, Paris, and Tel Aviv the American embassies were besieged. On June 21, eight thousand supporters attended the funeral, but not Ethel's mother, Tessie Greenglass.[153]

The media quality of the Rosenberg execution was captured a generation later by Robert Coover, who wrote the best-selling postmodernist novel *The Public Burning* in 1976, a scathing satire of Cold War mentality and a tasteless parody of Julie's and Ethel's ordeal. In it, they are turned into carnival figures, their deaths a celebration of the absurd in which the execution takes place in Times Square at the conclusion of an all-day public spectacle organized by Cecil B. DeMille with the assistance of Walt Disney, Ed Sullivan, and Betty Crocker, who plays hostess to the invited VIPs. A Texas high-school marching band performs; Bob Hope, Bing Crosby, and Dorothy Lamour entertain; Fred Astaire and Ginger Rogers dance; Abbott and Costello crack jokes; and President Eisenhower addresses the expectant multitude. Almost as an afterthought, Julie and Ethel are the last on stage, and their performance is rather second-rate. Coover describes the occasion as "a Roman Scandal of Roaring Spectacle."[154]

The Rosenberg execution is indeed reminiscent of Roman days. Like Pliny the Younger searching out Christians but not knowing what to do with them once he has arrested them, the United States government was never quite sure whether Julius and Ethel were to die for their ideology or their espionage. Certainly Pliny's words "Whatever the nature of their admission, I am convinced that their stubbornness and unshakeable obstinacy ought not to go unpunished" could have been spoken by almost any official connected with the Rosenberg case.[155] Moreover, like Rome, the United States in its war on an alien and what it regarded as a seditious ideology was willing to conduct the conflict in a blaze of publicity. In returning to an older, more traditional style of handling martyrdom, the federal government was trying to emphasize the difference between its own and totalitarian techniques; but the cost was to supply Julius and Ethel with what they desired most—a public stage on which to display, like early Christians in a Roman arena, their courage, their faith, and the truth of their convictions.

The dramatization—some would say, the fictionalization—of their cause was for the Rosenbergs a moral obligation they owed their fellow Americans. Duty was realized in the *Death House Letters,* a series of epistles to their

children, their lawyer Emanuel (Manny) Block, and to one another in which
they addressed each other as "sweetest bunny," "honey wife," "precious
heart of mine," "loving nightingale," "adorable Ethel" and "sweetest Julie,"
"darling husband," "my very own dear love." Unlike Dietrich Bonhoeffer's
prison letters, the Rosenberg correspondence did not have to be smuggled
out; it only had to be inspected by prison officials, and the Rosenbergs were
delighted to have as many people as possible read their words.

Everything about the Rosenbergs is controversial, and the *Death House
Letters* are no exception; even their authorship has been disputed. That
they were at times heavily and astutely edited to achieve the maximum
propaganda effect when they first appeared in excerpted form in the *National Guardian* and were published in pamphlet and book forms by the
Committee to Secure Justice for the Rosenbergs is undeniable.[156] Mostly
penned during their twenty-six-month imprisonment in Sing Sing and depicting their most private thoughts and feelings, the letters, like John
Brown's epistles from prison, were in fact designed for public consumption. They are in fact a little like the Synoptic Gospels: it is difficult to tell
where reality ends and fiction begins or to be sure that the authors are
fully aware of the distinction between truth and falsehood. As with Deacon Papylus and his Roman interrogators, a lie can be a form of truth. Papylus, asked whether he had any children, answered in the affirmative.
When the proconsul pointed out that this was patently untrue, the deacon replied, "I do not lie . . . I am telling the truth. I have children in the
Lord in every province and city."[157] With the *Death House Letters,* the
reader encounters the same Alice in Wonderland confusion between prevarication, equivocation, and misrepresentation on one side and telling
the truth on the other, especially when it comes to the question of innocence or guilt. The letters are deeply unsettling, because they ring of conviction and fakery, truth and propaganda. As Ilene Philipson has
observed, they present the Rosenbergs as both superhuman and subhuman,[158] and they are not easy to dissect without destroying their full emotional impact. The pieces are shrill and easily ridiculed, but the totality
possesses an awkward dignity that is hard to ignore. They are a strange,
jarring, and at times embarrassing mixture of the intimate, the banal, the
political and the polemical which pull at our hearts but worry us that we
are being manipulated.

The letters pose yet another problem, because they are living documents that still arouse passion and debate. Michael Meeropol, the Rosenbergs' elder son, has published them in their entirety to reveal his parents in
the full richness and complexity of their thought and purpose, but beware
the scholar who seeks permission to quote brief excerpts from them; any

use that does not meet the sons' approval is denied. And so the letters remain a double minefield: difficult to interpret without raising ire and dangerous for anyone seeking to keep within the laws of copyright and fair use. And this is a pity because any understanding of the Rosenbergs depends on an appreciation of the intensity with which they believed in themselves and their cause.

The correspondence develops two themes: one, the moral torture that as honorable people they are being forced to undergo; the other, the suffering they are enduring in defense of true democracy, peace, and social justice.

The Rosenberg tragedy is presented in epic style: two unassuming but highly principled and wholesome people are, through no fault of their own, suddenly confronted with the ultimate human dilemma, the horrifying choice between betraying their honor—denying the basic standards that shaped their personalities and formed the very core of their existence—or dying in the electric chair. They are being told that the price of life was to lie, to disown the truth of their innocence and not only to confess to what they had not done but also, and far worse, to fabricate the untrue story of their espionage and name other people in a nonexistent plot, thereby destroying lives just as innocent as their own.

Both Julius and Ethel narrated at length the unbearable pressure being placed on them to "cooperate." The Greenglasses thought that Ethel had disgraced the family, and her brother Sam ordered her to quit playing the martyr and act like a responsible human being. Her mother, Tessie, begged her to confess, "even if it was a lie"; better a live liar than a dead hero.[159] Julius reported to his lawyer that the government was telling him to save himself and Ethel by cutting a deal.[160] As the day of execution neared, the pressure grew apace. After Eisenhower refused to consider a pardon, *Time* magazine speculated that "the only real opportunity of escape" now lay with the Rosenbergs themselves. "If they broke their long silence—if they confessed the secrets of their spy ring—then the President might consider a new appeal for clemency."[161] With only seventeen days to go the government took an unprecedented step; on the second of June it sent John Bennett, the federal director of prisons, to make a last-minute appeal to cooperate. In retrospect the actions of the government are understandable. If the United States had indeed broken the Russian secret code and knew that Julius was a member of a Soviet spy ring but could not admit such knowledge without revealing to the Russians that their code had in fact been breached, then the pressure on the Rosenbergs to divulge whatever they knew makes cruel, if politic, sense. Certainly, Washington continued to hope for the best and maintained its FBI hot line ready as Julius walked to the electric chair, but no one was surprised when the presiding rabbi, moments before Ethel went into the death chamber, tried but failed to persuade her "to talk for her children's sake."[162] As Gandhi wrote of his fasts, "In the last resort a satyagrahi vindicates his honor by laying down his life."[163]

Throughout their ordeal, Ethel and Julius present themselves as being speechless at the disgraceful behavior of the Greenglass family, and outraged by the immoral actions of their government. This was the tyranny of a police state. How could a government that claimed it believed in and practiced due process of law ask anyone to manufacture a fabricated confession blackening forever the names of their children and destroying perfectly innocent people by including them in an imaginary spy ring? Even if it meant going to their deaths, they would not lie or violate their standards.

In depicting themselves as "two insignificant little people" faced with an appalling moral choice—a decision that but for the grace of God and the accident of fate might confront any American citizen—the Rosenbergs were at pains to allude to their second theme: they were victims of a police state, simple but sincere patriots of democracy and defenders of the American tradition who were being punished for the sole purpose of silencing the voice of all true "progressives" who believed in patriotism, democracy, morality, and family values. Imprisonment, disgrace, and mental torture beset them for a single reason—they had clung to the truth. The declaration of their innocence to the world, even the courage to face electrocution, were necessary to save the country from tyranny at home and war abroad. They had, they said, embarked on a "history-making journey," and if necessary, they were ready to die for what they constantly referred to as "peace and bread and roses." Throughout their suffering, their oft-reiterated private motto was "courage, confidence and perspective." These qualities would see them through their ordeal; they were also the attributes that would eventually save the country from tyranny.[164]

Every means was used to heighten the message and win support. Julius told how he struggled to explain death and electrocution to Michael, not yet nine; and Ethel described the happy faces of the children in the photographs on her prison wall.[165] These are compassion-wrenching images, and had they stood alone, spoken solely in anguish and love, their impact would have been devastating. Unfortunately the Rosenbergs could not resist bending their private agony to the service of their public cause. Their love for one another and for their children was unmercifully linked to a broader—one senses, more important—political purpose.

The Rosenbergs rarely missed a chance to use their children to soften public opinion and further their cause. Julius mixed strident political outrage at the establishment of U.S. air bases in Franco's Spain with tender references to his sons. His parental pride in his children's achievements was commingled with appeals not only to insist on justice for Ethel and himself but also to curb the growing fascist beast endangering the country. Ethel could be equally ruthless in the way she used her love for her children, linking her passionate devotion to her boys with an admonition to all American mothers to speak out against the injustice being done to the Rosenbergs.[166]

Ethel and Julius seemed to live in a polemical world where even the most banal event had political significance. When in October 1951 the Dodgers won a World Series game 10 to 1, Ethel gloated over the victory of her favorite baseball team, but could not refrain from adding that their real triumph lay in having treated blacks and whites equally. On the previous Fourth of July Julius reported that he had cut from the *New York Times* a copy of the Declaration of Independence, to which he had added his own name to those of the signers. Unfortunately this picture of simple patriotism is ruined by his supplying a political lecture in which he associates freedom of speech, press, and religion with the Declaration and bewails that all three are under attack throughout the land. The Declaration of Independence says nothing about these freedoms, but such inaccuracies made little difference. Historical truth had to bow to a higher ideology.[167]

The ideological undertow of the *Death House Letters* is often more powerful than the steady waves of innocent suffering that beat upon the reader. Hidden away under the crush of progressive patriotism, love of children, defense of democracy, and justice for all is a concealed agenda: a strident clarion call to action and a pride and militancy that ill fits the picture of violated innocence and simple unassuming lives caught up in a nightmare of politics and bigotry. Apparent throughout the correspondence one senses not so much the victim as the crusader, unrelenting, unforgiving and willingly dying for the one and only truth. Tessie Greenglass's description of her daughter and son-in-law as "soldiers of Stalin" may be overly harsh, but every time Julius and Ethel put pen to paper their ideological bias erupts and the Communist orientation of their thinking emerges.

In an ongoing letter to Manny Block Julius brought out all the Communist heavy artillery to attack the society that had put him behind bars. Wisely the editors of the *Death House Letters* only used a small portion of this diatribe. At every turn, Julius asserted, the will of the American people was being thwarted by capitalistic special-interest groups—the "fraternity brothers." The so-called free press had hired itself out to the

interests of big business, and news slanting was controlled by the pluto-
crats. Proof of this assertion was self-apparent. What major newspaper
was opposed to the Eisenhower policy of remilitarization or to alliances
with fascist regimes? Was the press supporting the common people? No,
under the guise of patriotism it was harassing labor unions and all "progressive" elements in the country. The truth, Julius concluded, was that
the entire press was being controlled by the industrial-military complex
that spoke through Washington.[168]

Ethel was even more flamboyant in her application of Communist dogma
and jargon, and no less militant. The revolution of the oppressed against a
privileged plutocracy was coming and it was inevitable. The injustices of the
past would soon be avenged. Who knew, the Rosenberg case might even be
the spark that set off the revolution. Vengeance and retribution might have to
wait, but a future generation would someday triumph. This was their final
message of hope to their sons.[169]

In a very real sense the Rosenbergs, throughout their prison years, were
fighting to create and maintain their historic identity. Like Dietrich Bonhoeffer, they longed above all else "not to vanish without a trace." They
sought to salvage meaning in life and to reach out for a form of immortality within a fully secular belief system.[188] Their relationship with the deity
was distant and academic. They attended Jewish services because they
found them "intellectually stimulating" and comforting, but they clearly
placed their commitment to social amelioration and justice well before
their concern for an omnipotent deity. Salvation was here on earth in a
human paradise, not some future and spiritual existence.[170] The rabbi who
intoned the Psalms as they walked to the electric chair was there more for
the benefit of the executioners' sense of decorum than for the consolation
of the accused.

Significantly, neither Julius nor Ethel called upon the prophets of their
faith or the martyrs of Judaism to support them in their time of need.
Theirs was a secular creed, and nothing sets the Rosenbergs off from
Gandhi and the other practitioners of martyrdom more than their refusal
to introduce the deity into the equation of life and death or to associate
Yahweh with the truth for which they were willing to die. There was no reward in heaven for their suffering on earth, only the safeguarding of their
identities and reputations in this world. Martyrs, least of all those who forgave their persecutors, were never their role models. On this point Ethel in
her plea to President Eisenhower for executive clemency was dramatically
clear. "We are not martyrs or heroes, nor do we wish to be. We do not want
to die. . . . We desire someday to be restored to society where we can con-

tribute our energies toward building a world where all shall have peace, bread and roses."[171]

The only martyr Ethel ever mentioned was Joan of Arc, but her interest in the Maid of Orléans was not as a role model but as a lesson—the terrible fate awaiting those who warred against the truth. In prison Ethel read Shaw's *Saint Joan,* and liked to think of herself as a new and more dangerous Saint Joan and to picture her enemies along with the English chaplain who attended Joan at her death in hell forever.[172]

If the Rosenbergs did not regard themselves as martyrs, what were they? Were they a new breed, or the same old species under a new label? It is at this point that the debate over the Rosenbergs slides into the quagmire of semantics and ideology, because the opponents of communism are just as loath to call Julius and Ethel martyrs as the Rosenbergs themselves.

For Ethel and Julius the role of martyr was unbecoming on three counts. First, the faith to which they adhered so tenaciously was secular; it had no admiration for traditional martyrs passively going to their deaths while seeking heavenly reward and forgiving their enemies. The Rosenbergs had no place in their hearts for forgiveness or passive resistance. They believed in confronting the capitalistic evil head-on with every available means. Second, they were entrapped by their own acclaimed innocence; they could never admit to choosing death or deliberately closing the door to reprieve or clemency. Their elected role was that of the victim, helpless and innocent before the fascist tyrant. Finally, and most important of all, they could never confess themselves to be martyrs to a particular creed or faith, least of all to the Communist Party. That was the stigma placed upon them by their archenemy Judge Kaufman, who said, "They prefer the glory which they believe will be theirs by the martyrdom which will be bestowed upon them by those who enlisted them in this diabolical conspiracy (and who, indeed, desire them to remain silent)."[173] Any association with the Party, any hint of treason, had to be vehemently denied if they were to play the role most useful to the Party: innocent patriotism and inoffensive, well-meaning progressivism crushed by capitalistic brutality. Ideologically and strategically, the Rosenbergs could not claim the status of martyr, and the best the Party could do for them was to use the "double speak" of placing them in the ranks of "innocent martyrs" to "the cause of truth."

Julie and Ethel had been asked in a sense to make a double sacrifice—to become martyrs but to renounce the title—for by almost any definition of martyrdom they should have qualified. Quite deliberately, they closed the door on saving their lives, and they willingly offered themselves on the altar of complex and deeply interwoven causes which, one suspects, became in-

separable in their minds. They died for their avowed innocence, however
that may be defined. They viewed themselves as valiant and last-ditch defenders of an ideal that embodied "peace, bread and roses" for all mankind,
which seemed to be in the process of being overwhelmed by the satanic legions of evil; they were eager participants in that vast surge of history
which through sacrifice and suffering they knew would end in a new kind
of kingdom of God on earth; they may even have thought of themselves as
soldiers in the army of the Soviet Union, which they regarded as the harbinger of future social justice and equality; and most basic of all, they
found in their own sacrifice and suffering a sense of pride and identity that
gave meaning to their lives and deaths. What meant most to them was the
knowledge that they possessed the power of choice. And they chose death
because they were convinced that the termination of their lives on a public
forum before the entire world would help to bring about the fulfillment of
their dream of a different and better world. True, they did not want to die;
they had no hope of a life after death, only of a human record here on earth
that would be enshrined in history; and in a news release issued to the *National Guardian* on October 16, 1952, they said they yearned for "a long life
of accomplishment." But they also added a crucial proviso: "If the only alternative to death is the purchase of life at the cost of standards, there is no
future for us or any legacy we can leave our children or those who survived
to follow us. . . . Death holds no horror as great as the horror of a sterile existence devoid of social responsibility and the courage of one's convictions."[174] The words may be stagey, but the message is clear: if death were
the only way to leave a "legacy," to prove "the courage of one's convictions," then so be it.

Within a year of their executions, two critics—Leslie Fiedler and Robert
Warshow—set about defrocking the Rosenbergs of their claim to martyrdom. They did so by resurrecting a specter raised by the Indian poet Ra-
bindranath Tagore when he voiced the fear that a moral crusade in the
name of absolute truth, conducted by anyone except Gandhi, would end in
mindless violence uncontrolled by moral judgment or restraint. "Martyrdom for the cause of truth [might] degenerate into fanaticism for mere verbal forms, descending into self-deception that hides itself behind sacred
names."[175] The Rosenbergs, Fiedler and Warshow said, had become such
fanatics. In their letters and actions they were nothing more than two-
dimensional cardboard figures with no substance to them except a fiction
that they had assumed and endeavored to enact in their lives. "They filled
their lives," wrote Warshow, "with the secondhand."[176] Their careers were
in fact counterfeit: their identity was not their own but belonged to the

Communist Party. They were for Fiedler automatons, thoughtless believers who had absolute faith in hollow political prescriptions, and they did exactly what they were ordered without the slightest regard for morality. They were in fact subhumans, and Fiedler was aghast that two people should "deny their *own* humanity in the face of death." This was surely "the ultimate horror, the final revelation of a universal moral calamity." Where, he asked, had the frank, honest "old style radical" gone? What had happened to the American tradition of individualism whereby a man stood up in public and declared that he had "acted in the teeth of accepted morality and law for the sake of certain higher principles"? In contrast, the Rosenbergs sulked behind their innocence, took orders from Moscow, and salved their moral accountability with meaningless social formulas. There is no room for sympathy in Fiedler's picture for traitors who do not see themselves as "real," responsible people with the power of choosing good or evil, but who instead view themselves solely as "cases." "The very possibilities of any heroism and martyrdom," he argued, had been "blasphemed." Their "case" was "a parody of martyrdom . . . too absurd to be truly tragic, too grim to be the joke it is always threatening to become." His final verdict is both severe and gender-biased: they had lived a blatant lie for the sake of a foreign power and therefore had "failed in the end to become martyrs or heroes, or even men."[177]

Had Fiedler and Warshow been able to divest themselves of the ideological paranoia that darkened their thinking, they might have been able to make a more convincing case. Julius and Ethel were indeed documented believers, people who craved the support system of authority. They accepted as demonstrable, scientifically validated truth the laws by which Marxist social evolution operated, and they never doubted the word of those social-scientific experts who claimed to understand the process. At one time, as a young teenager, Julie had given equal faith to the Torah and the word of the Prophets. He had believed without reservation; so much so that his Hebrew teacher said that he "believed everything we taught him—literally. He took it very seriously. I felt he was becoming over-religious, more than I liked."[178] The same attitude of mind was true of Ethel. According to her prison friend Miriam Moscowitz, she was a "doctrinaire" Communist, always a "good soldier." She followed "the party line uncritically, unquestionably, and aggressively. It wasn't only that she followed the line, but she argued for it and justified it with a lot of voluminous verbosity. She was totally uncritical."[179]

It is a strange definition of martyrdom to exclude the "uncritical" and the "overly religious" believer. To do so would be to cast out Saint Perpetua and her fellow early Christian martyrs. Death in a Roman arena or in a modern electric chair, when willingly chosen, by definition takes a liberal dose of fanaticism. But what disturbed Fiedler and Warshow was not so much the strength or fanaticism of the Rosenbergs' belief system but its location. Robert Bolt's Thomas More in *A Man for All Seasons* poses the conundrum in its most baffling form. When accused of risking his life for a mere belief—the theory of the apostolic succession and the primacy of the papacy—More answers, "What matters to me is not whether it's true or not but that I believe it to be true, or rather, not that I *believe* it but, that *I* believe it." He then characteristically adds, "I trust I make myself obscure."[180] The obscurity lies in the location of the belief. Does it lie outside the individual—a script to be imposed on the human personality and therefore something to be accepted uncritically—or does it reside within the self, an expression and proof of one's individuality? The ideology that has been subsumed into the ego and therefore has become the inward hallmark of individuality was the belief process that Fiedler and Warshow demanded of the Rosenbergs. They required proof that Julius's and Ethel's strength was generated from within and did not stem from some mindless brainwashing imposed upon them by the Communist creed. Of course, they are quite sure that had the "I" really spoken, treason would never have occurred.

Whether the distinction Bolt's More seeks to elucidate is valid or not is anybody's guess. Certainly Julius and Ethel would have maintained that their own identities, their very selves, were at stake when making the choice to die rather than to live. Elizabeth Phillips, Ethel's psychotherapist, who visited her in prison, may have come closest to the truth when she speculated years afterwards: "Who knows what happens in prison to people who begin to perceive themselves as maybe [of] some use to the world forever as martyrs? . . . Who knows what changes psychologically" for inmates imprisoned for thirty-four months who think they are "making a mark"?[181] Henrik Ibsen wrote that "to die in agony on a cross" does not create a martyr; you must first will your own execution.[182] Sometimes martyrs themselves supply the wood and the nails to construct their own crosses; sometimes the structure is erected for them by order of the state; but always the cross is a symbol. For the state it represents just retribution upon criminals who seek to strike at the very sinews of society; for the martyr it stands for humanity's hope for the future, either in this world or in the next; but whatever its function, the cross takes immense courage to mount. The Communist Party may have approved; the Rosenbergs may even have thought the "cause" required their decision to die as a duty "to mankind." But Julius and Ethel alone supplied the fortitude to face physical annihilation in order to satisfy some inner drive that craved ideological approval. No matter what society may think of the ideology that bolstered their self-esteem and justified in their minds the sacrifices they were willing to demand of themselves and their children—their cruelty and fanaticism were far less than that displayed by the mother of the Maccabee brothers or even by Vibia Perpetua—no one can deny them their courage and their faith; and these, after all, are the common badges of all martyrs.

SS Lieutenant Kurt Gerstein in 1941 after enlisting with
the Black Shirts: He was desperate because no one, neither
the Germans nor the French, would take him seriously.
As it were, a discredited Joan of Arc deprived of her
funeral pyre.

CHAPTER 13

EPILOGUE:
THE DISINTERESTED MARTYR

> As his reward for having helped the heroic Rama,
> one of the Lord Visnu's many incarnations, in his
> epic victory over Ravana, the demon king of
> Lanka, Hanumàn, the monkey God, asks only
> that he "live so long as your story and your glory
> are sung in this world." Rama grants his request
> and Hanumàn achieves immortality.
>
> —RAMAYANA,
> Book 7

JULIUS ROSENBERG with his steel-rimmed glasses and curious charcoal mustache, which made him look like an underdone Groucho Marx, and Ethel with her rosebud lips and Mona Lisa smile violate our image of the martyr. A more pedestrian, inoffensive, and unfanatical looking couple is difficult to imagine. But except for Gandhi, sitting cross-legged and fitting our Western stereotype of a holy man capable of any oddity, and John Brown, with his ravaged face radiating the burning obsession that consumed him, who does look the part of a proper martyr? Certainly not the robust ex-soldier Socrates or the efficient chancellor-archbishop Becket or the urbane humanist Thomas More or the well-groomed Nicholas Ridley, bishop of London, or the dapper, aesthetic Charles I or the well-fed Dietrich Bonhoeffer. Yet all possessed a hidden energy and rigidity—call it what you will: determination, faith, stubbornness, fanaticism—that would have done credit to any early Christian martyr. So once again we are confronted with the question posed by the Maccabee brothers: "Why does such fatal obduracy attract us?" But this time a new complexity has been added. Did the inspiration that led

Socrates, Jesus, Becket, Brown, and Gandhi to conceive the challenge and sacrifice their lives to it lie hidden in the core of their personalities—a spark ready to burst into flame when offered the necessary emotional and environmental fuel—or was it a form of spontaneous combustion, a new life form that emerged from the shock of cultural conflict and political crisis and reshaped perfectly normal human beings into something exceptional, both monstrous and divine?

Most of the martyrs recorded in this book were asked to violate what Julius Rosenberg called "standards." They were required by word or action to deny a sacred belief, to commit acts that conscience forbade and to refrain from following their own definition of the truth. In the face of overwhelming family, community, and state pressure, they refused to do what so many of us would have done—salve their consciences, yield to authority and save their skins.

In a sense Tessie Greenglass and Ethel Rosenberg stand at opposite poles. Tessie was a ruthless pragmatist blind to any standard except immediate family gratification and sheer survival, urging Ethel to lie, even if innocent people suffered, so long as the family benefited. At the other extreme, Ethel was an equally ruthless idealist, driven by who knows what. We may be repelled by Tessie, but secretly we understand her—but not Ethel and Julius or any of the other martyrs, and we wonder exactly how altruistic their sacrifices actually were. Was there a certain kind of pleasure or profit to be gained by martyrdom? Can it be that martyrs are in fact not instruments of ideology, selfless soldiers joyfully terminating their lives for some greater good, but instead victims of their own overdeveloped self-esteem, which sets them apart from and above the herd? Their thunderous faith and lightning consciences not only reveal insights denied the rest of humanity but also fuse sense of self with pride of revelation. Martyrs know the stakes are high and therefore worth the cost, because they cannot permit consciousness of self to vanish even in death. The martyr's message may belong to God or history or Satan, but it is always the "I" that is gratified by fulfilling the mission, even by dying for it. Martyrs are obsessed with securing a place in heaven or with maintaining their reputations on earth because they are incapable of comprehending a state of being in which their inner selves, even after death, have no influence on the course of history or no place in the cosmic design of things. In this sense martyrs die not so much for a cause as for themselves. T. S. Eliot confronted this issue head-on when he asked whether Thomas Becket had done "the right deed for the wrong reason." To phrase the problem slightly differently, is there such a thing as a totally disinterested martyr?

It is difficult to deny that martyrs are men and women driven by ego presented to the world in the more palatable and pleasing guise of conscience. Ultimately, as Bolt's More admits, the "I" prevails, an attribute insisted upon by More's real-life opponent Martin Luther, who wrote that he believed so tenaciously in "the word revealed by the Gospel that were I to see all the angels of heaven coming down to me to tell me something different, not only would I not be tempted to doubt a single syllable, but I would shut my eyes and stop my ears, for they would not deserve to be either seen or heard."[1] Self-confidence reinforced by deadly self-seriousness is the common property of all martyrs, scarred only by the cry of dereliction from the cross. But even in the Gospels the "I" predominates. Jesus was no self-effacing messenger—that would have been a contradiction in terms—and he repeatedly replaced the Old Testament formula "thus saith the Lord" with "I say unto you."[2] Little wonder he was so often asked, "Are you the Christ, the Son of the Blessed?"

The same sense of self-defining destiny exercised Gandhi. Despite his insistence that man is zero and can expect no salvation except by putting "himself last among his fellow creatures," the Mahatma had a highly developed concept of his own uniqueness, what he sometimes referred to as his "honor."[3] He knew that he was exceptional if only because God had made him that way. He was "gifted with the eye to see myself as others see me and *vice versa*"; he possessed "God-given opportunities" to train himself; he was certain his fasts were "a special gift from God to appeal to the heart and soul of the people" and that his divinely inspired inner voices were reserved for "one among tens of millions."[4] The "I" never ceased to dominate Gandhi, and he explained in startling terms of self-identity his need to do social work for India: "I am here to serve no one else but myself, to find my own self-realization through the service of these village folk."[5]

The Mahatma may have been God's puppet, his strings firmly grasped by the deity; nevertheless, God's will is hard to disentangle from Gandhi's own when he announced, "There come to us moments in life when about some things we need no proof from without. A little voice within us tells us, 'you are on the right track.' "[6] As a holy man his avowed ideal was that of the perfect karma yogi "who is without egotism, who is selfless," but his earthly model remained Socrates—the man, he wrote, who "made his best speech holding a cup of poison in his hand and, by his death, won immortality for himself and his ideas."[7] The reality of immortality, the preservation of self, was rarely out of the Mahatma's mind as the desire for salvation was never out of John Brown's thoughts whose soul was constantly "panting after" eternal life.[8] As a devout believer in reincarnation, Gandhi was never quite clear whether he sought moksha, the kingdom of heaven where the soul was liberated from the endless cycle of birth and death, or whether as an act of continued earthly sacrifice and human service he wished to be reborn an untouchable "so that I may share their sorrows, sufferings and the affronts levelled at them."[9] Certainly of all the figures discussed in this martyrology of very human martyrs, Gandhi is the one who comes closest to the Indian concept of absolute sacrifice, bodhisattva, or the renunciation of heaven for the sake of others, because he alone prayed to have the strength to desire "neither earthly kingdom nor paradise, no, not even release from birth and death," but "only the release of afflicted life from misery."[10]

In *Murder in the Cathedral* Eliot brings the debate over disinterestedness in through the backdoor. The assassins of Thomas Becket justify their actions on the grounds that they gained nothing by their heroism in ridding the kingdom of "a monster of egotism." The third knight is an eloquent speaker on the subject. "There is one thing I should like to say. . . . Whatever you may think of it, we have been perfectly disinterested. . . . *We* are not getting a penny out of this. We know perfectly well how things will turn out. King Henry—God bless him—will have to say, for reasons of state, that he never meant this to happen; and there is going to be an awful row; and at the best we shall have to spend the rest of our lives abroad. And even when reasonable people come to see that the archbishop *had* to be put out of the way . . . they won't give *us* any glory."[11] The implication here is an uncomfortable one: the knights, not Becket, are the real martyrs. The archbishop sacrifices nothing except his life—"It's easy to be a martyr. You only have to be it once"—and gains in return something far more precious: eternal life and recognition. In contrast, the murderers out of loyalty to their king and a sense of duty to their country sacrifice their good names; they get no "glory" in either this world or the next.

The martyr is generally extremely solicitous of his reputation, be it in God's eyes or man's. The predicament is manifest. In giving up life the martyr, far from destroying the self, reinvigorates it; but in giving up his good name he annihilates not only the story of his heroism but also his very self. This is the dilemma faced by Lieutenant Kurt Gerstein in Rolf Hochhuth's play *The Deputy*. In order to do battle with the Nazi scourge, the lieutenant joins the devil's team. He deliberately enlists in the SS, that kind of hated Praetorian Guard which incorporated police work (the Gestapo), intelligence services, and the management of the death houses and concentration camps. Trained in medicine and engineering, he is employed in the SS Public Health Department and is responsible for bacterial and insect decontamination of state and military barracks and prisons. As a consequence, he knows all about the Final Solution and that poison gas designed for killing fleas is actually being used to exterminate that other kind of "vermin," undesirable human beings. In order to function Gerstein must operate behind an absolute shield of secrecy, thereby suppressing the cardinal instinct of most martyrs: the urge to publicize their actions. More fundamental, not only must he conceal his true beliefs, indeed his very soul, and pretend to sanction genocide in the name of Aryan racial purity, but he must also do something far more costly—sacrifice his good name and go down in eternity as one of the villains, forever loathed as the devil's minion. He does not even have the secret agent's comfort of knowing that a record of his true identity is hidden somewhere and that someday the truth will be revealed.

In a conversation with a Jesuit priest the SS lieutenant pours out his indecision in the face of an excruciating choice. Should he instruct the chemical manufacturers to bill the poison gas directly to him and send the cannisters to his address, thereby gaining better control of their use and preventing the gas from reaching the death chambers but also leaving behind a paper trail that might eventually hang him? Or should he cleanse his hands of evil and escape to Sweden, leaving the slaughter to others? The priest answers, "What does your conscience say?" Gerstein does not seek justification from within; he desires the voice of authority from without—to be told what is right—and he explodes: "Conscience? Who could trust that! Conscience or God: men never have wreaked such havoc as when invoking God—or an idea. Conscience is a treacherous guide. I am convinced that Hitler acts according to his conscience." After a pause the priest starts to say, "To lend your name to something monstrous—" but the lieutenant interrupts, "My name! What is a name? Is it my *name* that matters?" and he scornfully dismisses name savers as "scarcely better than the murderers," lukewarm people who seek to keep their reputations as "immaculate as . . . the Pope's white vestments."[12] In the end all of Gerstein's sacrifices are in vain, and the play concludes with Satan triumphant. The lieutenant's disguise is torn away; he is arrested and led offstage, his fate perfectly apparent—he will die in his SS uniform, forever branded a war criminal.

There is a second dilemma that looms large in Hochhuth's play: martyrdom for a cause or simply to save lives. The priest with whom Gerstein debates his decision to sacrifice his good name is Father Riccardo Fontana, a Jesuit assigned to the papal secretariat of state, who takes upon himself the guilt of the Catholic Church for its institutional failure to speak out against the Nazi extermination of the Jews. The pope, as Christ's deputy on earth, has raised no public cry against unmitigated evil, and for worldly and political reasons has refrained from confronting Satan. As an act of redemption and expiation to preserve the concept of the papacy pure "for all eternity,"

Riccardo seeks to wipe clean the sins of his superior. To the horror of the pope, he pins the star of David upon his cassock, joins a death train to Auschwitz, and is predictably and unheroically shot while unsuccessfully helping a Jewish prisoner escape in his priest's clothing. Riccardo's death— suicide or martyrdom—is embraced in the style of the Maccabees deflecting divine wrath against Israel, of Gandhi assuming in his frail person the sins of all humanity, and of Bonhoeffer shouldering responsibility for the criminal blindness of his Confessing Church. Riccardo would have understood the decision of a young Polish historian in 1984 who was told if he signed a statement supporting the Communist regime he could go free, possibly even leave the country. If he didn't sell his soul, however, he would be imprisoned for a very long time. He elected jail and wrote the minister of interior: "For me the value of our struggle does not lie in the expectation of victory, but in the value of the cause for which we have undertaken this struggle. Let my gesture of refusal be a tiny contribution to the sense of honour and dignity of this country, which every day is being plunged into ever deeper misery."[13]

Kurt Gerstein has no sympathy for such valiant gestures. He will have no truck with what he regards as senseless symbolic martyrdom; redeeming the church in the eyes of God has no earthly purpose. "Forget the salvation of the Church," he tells Riccardo. "You would no longer have it in your power to aid a single human being. Riccardo, you'd only take on greater guilt yourself."[14] Gerstein is a most unorthodox martyr-hero. He is a Protestant and a Christian but has no respect for creed or dogma or ideal. He is instead the quintessential moral man, unconcerned with heaven or hell or even conscience, but irrevocably committed to saving lives. He is not a Jew and ideologically owes nothing to Judaism. He does not risk his life to defend Jewry; nor is he, like Bonhoeffer, working to overthrow the Third Reich. He simply seeks to save his fellow human beings from the slaughterhouse. He operates as if the twentieth century in creating a new kind of culprit—the criminal against humanity—is in need of a new kind of martyr, the martyr for humanity. Death for the SS lieutenant is a price to be paid for saving lives. Death is not an end in itself either in the sense of personal reward or helping a cause, and he rejects his friend's desire for expiating martyrdom as a criminal waste of time, life, and blood. Indeed, Gerstein's downfall is brought about by attempting to arrange for Riccardo's escape from Auschwitz. His death is neither planned nor an integral part of his purpose. It is simply a hazard inherent in his actions. Gerstein is a hero, but whether he can be called a martyr remains one of the many mysteries to which there are no clear answers as the depths of martyrdom are probed.

Hochhuth does not have his Kurt Gerstein shot on stage, because there is yet another, even more baffling, dimension to the man. He is both fictional and real, and the flesh-and-blood SS Obersturmführer Gerstein is a far greater mystery than the stage protagonist, for in real life he appears to have led two lives—the Nazi war criminal and the crusading Christian—surviving the war only to die in a French prison.

An immense effort has been made to rescue Kurt Gerstein from his historical oblivion. The skeleton upon which reality has been molded is the lieutenant's own appalling report of his career as an SS officer, written during the final months of the war.[15] This autobiographical account has been in part verified and enlarged upon by official documents, by letters the lieutenant wrote to his father, wife, and friends, and by the memories of those who encountered this "strange fish," as his SS colleagues described him. There are, however, serious gaps and contradictions in the report, which was designed as a statement of accusation and revelation to be used against Nazi war criminals when they stood trial; and it places Gerstein's own actions and motives in as favorable a light as possible. A number of writers have tried to give historical substance to this elusive and shadowy man. *A Spy for God* by the French novelist Pierre Joffroy is the richest of these, but Joffroy's reconstruction is only that: an imaginative portrait, far more complex, tragic, and human than Hochhuth's stage character, but possibly no more real.[16]

The story is a Greek tragedy; the tale of a man trapped by a combination of volition and fate into an impossible situation from which there is no escape. Kurt Gerstein chose to join the SS to confront evil; this was the only way to discover for himself and to reveal to the public the truth about the Nazi "witch-pot" euthanasia program. His posting to the Institute of Hygiene in Berlin seemed doubly ideal. It placed him in a position to learn about the handling of the "biologically useless," a savagery that had touched his family closely; and it permitted him to use his medical and engineering skills in a constructive, life-saving way. Ironically, these same skills and the successes he achieved in hygienic methods destroyed him, because they enmeshed him in the Final Solution, a course of events that Gerstein always felt to be somehow providential. God for this SS lieutenant was "the Creator and the prop who controls all and dominates all, and without whose knowledge and will not even a grain of sand on the ocean bed can approach another."[17]

Kurt Gerstein is reminiscent of Dietrich Bonhoeffer, a maverick born into a well-to-do German family of ancient and exceedingly self-satisfied lineage. His father was a judge—president of the Court of Justice at Hagen in Westphalia—and an ardent monarchist who organized his world hierar-chically with Kaiser Wilhelm II at the top, the household servants at the bottom, and, as Pierre Joffroy has suggested, God somewhere in between.[18] The family gave three of its six sons to the fatherland: one in World War I and two in the second carnage. Kurt was born on August 11, 1905, and al-most from the start he "went his own way." He did poorly in school, was a loner, and grew into a deeply religious and introverted young man in a fam-ily that was only conventionally devout. As his brother Karl wrote, he "did not make it easy to get close to him."[19] He grew into a blond scarecrow of a man, neither handsome nor ugly but always striking-looking, and too tall for the standard French coffin in which his body was carried to an un-marked grave. He took his degree in mining engineering in 1931; joined the Nazi Party in May of 1933 as number 2,136,174; and, like Bonhoeffer, was an active participant in the Confessing Church and a longtime friend of the Martin Niemöller family. He was also a diabetic, which may have con-tributed to the despondency and emotional instability he suffered in later life.[20]

In 1936, when the Gestapo discovered that he was distributing on his own initiative anti-Nazi religious tracts, Gerstein was arrested and impris-oned. After six weeks the Confessing Church had brought enough pressure to get him released, but he was drummed out of the party, dismissed from the Ministry of Mines, and forbidden to accept professional employment in Germany. As a branded troublemaker, his life for the next four years was a close race between a suspicious government, anxious to jail him for good, and his own efforts plus those of influential family and personal friends to reinstate him in the regime's good graces. He penned an abject letter of apology vehemently denying he had ever lacked "fidelity to the National Socialist movement" or had ever joined with "those who seek to sabotage the work of the Führer." He swore that his "most ardent desire" was to serve the movement and to "further the work of Adolf Hitler, with all my strength and by all the means in my power, even at the cost of my life."[21] It took the party considerable time to forgive its errant member, and not be-fore it launched one last, abortive charge of treason, which landed him in a concentration camp for another six weeks; but eventually he was condi-tionally reinstated and was able to get a job in private industry and take courses in medicine at the Institute for Tropical Medicine in Tübingen. Then, on March 10, 1941, to the absolute horror of his Confessing Church friends but to the pleasure of his father, he enlisted in the SS.

The decision to join the SS, Gerstein says, was triggered by the death of his sister-in-law Berta Gerstein, who had been institutionalized in a mental hospital and unexpectedly died of what the officials said was a cerebral thrombosis. Owing to "the danger of an epidemic in the clinic," her body was cremated and her ashes sent to her family with the appropriate official regrets. Kurt, but no one else, was convinced she had been murdered, a victim of the Nazi policy of ridding the fatherland of defective genes; the so-called mental clinic—Hadamar Hospital—was in fact a slaughterhouse. Only by entering "the lion's mouth" could he discover the truth.[22]

Gerstein was as maverick an SS trooper as he had been a son. He could never learn to march in step; his uniform was always disheveled; he carried a clothes brush in his pistol holster instead of a pistol; and very likely he was the only member of the entire SS who had spent time in a police jail and a concentration camp and who regularly smuggled food, cigarettes, and medicine to the inmates of the death camps he visited. Fortunately, the Institute for Hygiene was, as Kurt acknowledged, an extraordinarily "broad-minded establishment."[23] More important, its head, Professor Joachim Murgowsky, who was eventually hanged as a war criminal, was willing to overlook Gerstein's past because he was so useful to him. The young engineer with a medical background helped bring a serious outbreak of typhus on the eastern front under control; he developed new and highly effective delousing methods and a mobile water-filtering unit for the use of the army and the prisoner-of-war and concentration camps; and he became known as "a technical genius" in sanitation, disinfection, and decontamination. In gratitude the SS promoted him to second and then to first lieutenant.

June 8, 1942, was the day that turned a rewarding and successful career into a living hell. Because of his reputation and success in using poison gas to exterminate vermin, Gerstein was approached by Major Rolf Günther of the Gestapo and ordered to procure 260 kilos (572 pounds) of prussic (hydrocyanic) acid and deliver it to the Lublin area of Poland, where three death camps were operating—Belzec, Sobibor, and Treblinka—which among them had the capacity of exterminating fifty-six thousand people daily. A fourth camp, at Maidanek, was in the process of being fired up.

Prussic acid emits a deadly poison that had been used ever since its discovery in 1782 as a fumigating gas. Gerstein knew the purpose to which it would now be put by the Nazis and why he was being involved. It was reported that he was so upset that he contemplated suicide, but in the end he did as he was ordered. As an expert on pest control, he was expected to help make the death factories more efficient; they were currently dependent on exhaust gases from internal combustion engines, which took at least thirty-two minutes to produce death. Hitler himself had ordered the speed-up. When Gerstein arrived in Lublin and visited the death camps, he was told by the area commandant that his job was twofold, "to disinfect the immense quantity of woolen stuff, linen clothes and shoes produced by our factories," and "to modify the way our death institutes work. At present, we have rooms which are run by gases exhausted from an old Russian Diesel motor. This should be improved and work much faster. There must be something to do with the prussic acid."[24]

Gerstein has left one of the most horrifying descriptions of an extermination "institute" ever written.[25] At Belzec trains forty-five cars long would arrive with Jews twice daily; the victims were ordered to strip naked and give up their glasses, false teeth, and artificial arms and legs; the women were taken off to the "hairdresser" to be shorn of their hair for the sake of the war effort; and men, women, and children were crammed seven hundred to eight hundred at a time into sealed gas chambers approximately 82 feet by 148 feet—as Gerstein estimated, somewhere around 55,550 pounds of humanity per room. The corpses when they were removed were like marble statues, entire families entwined together in a death grip. The bodies before they were disposed of were inspected down to their "genitals and anus" for concealed coins and jewels, and the jaws broken open to extract the gold teeth. Gerstein wrote that he would have gladly died along with the victims, but "if my corpse in SS Officer uniform had been found in the gassing room, nobody would have believed that I was dead in protestation against these murders. . . . My death would have been regarded as an accident and my epithet would have been: 'Dead for his dearest Führer while on duty.' "[26]

Unlike his stage counterpart, the real Gerstein was not ready to sacrifice his name to a protest that none but God would have recognized. Indeed, his good name was the most precious thing he possessed in the midst of the hell in which he lived; and when the BBC in its German broadcast named him as one of the operators of the death factories and as someone who was involved with medical experiments on human guinea pigs who would someday be made to pay for his crimes, Gerstein was "horribly upset." It seemed to be yet one more plank to the coffin of his despair. Nobody—not the Swedish embassy, the Swiss embassy, the papal nuncio in Berlin, or even the Dutch underground—would accept his description of Belzec; such atrocities had to be gross exaggerations. Now that he was branded by the Allies as "an object of execration and abhorrence," who would ever believe him?[27] He even attempted, according to a close friend, to fly to Sweden to contact people who could let the British know the truth about him. During Christmas of 1942 his depression reached suicidal proportions, and he broke open the institute's poison cupboard. A vial of cyanide as well as his pistol had to be forcibly taken from him. In the end he became a man demented, all gaiety and every vestige of youth gone. By the time the war was over, Gerstein at thirty-nine was not the cool, collected hero of Hochhuth's play but a haggard, white-haired, twitching victim of despondency. "I am," he told a friend, "one of the most unhappy men on God's earth."[28]

In the fall of 1944 Gerstein tried to approach his father, who had little respect for or understanding of his son and had but one unbending criterion by which to judge him: "You are a soldier and a servant of the State, and it is your business to obey your superiors. The responsibility lies with those who give the orders, not with those who execute them."[29] Kurt thought otherwise, and earlier that year had informed his friend and mentor the Confessing pastor Kurt Rehling that the atrocities at Belzec had to be made "known and judged. And they will be, even if I have to be crucified for it."[30] To his father he wrote he had never lent his hand to evil; "when I have received orders of that kind, I have never carried them out and I have diverted their execution. Where I am concerned I come out of this business with clean hands and a clear conscience. . . . What does death matter, after all? It is principles and conduct that matter."[31]

Lieutenant Gerstein may have come out of his nightmare with a clear conscience, but he did not do so with a clean reputation. At the death factory at Oranienburg he was a familiar visitor known as "gas man no. 1," and when after the war he surrendered to the French forces and was shipped to Paris, his interrogators refused to accept his story. They could not believe he could have stood by for over two years and watched the slaughter camps in operation without ever participating in the carnage. Nor could they accept that he was nothing except a pest-control and pure-water expert or that he had successfully diverted, misplaced, buried, or "accidentally" car-wrecked the steady flow of prussic acid he had been ordered to send to Poland. It was a most improbable story and made no sense.[32] Moreover, they pointed out, his efforts were to no avail, and even Gerstein had had to admit that "the SS think I'm too slow in delivery. . . . They're using another channel."[33] More disturbing, why even make the effort? He knew that the Jews were dying at a rate of fifty-six thousand or more a day from exhaust fumes; hydrocyanic gas would at least cut the death time by half. Understandably the French became more and more suspicious as they interrogated him during July of 1945. They even thought he might have been the inventor of the gas chamber, and in the end they formally charged him "with war crimes, murder and complicity."[34] Five years later the "denazification court" of Tübingen was still thinking along the same lines; his efforts all seemed suspiciously useless, and the court turned down Gerstein's wife's application for a war widow's pension on the grounds that, though he might not have been a war criminal, he was clearly "tainted" with the crime.[35]

Having surrendered to the French in the expectation that he would be the key witness against a brand of evil which, in Gerstein's words, had been done "less with sadism than with a complete indifference," the man who was so determined that the truth be made "known and judged" that he was willing to be "crucified for it," was indeed crucified, not by the SS but by the liberators of Germany.[36] His evidence was never seriously used during the Nuremberg war-criminal trials; instead it was directed against him and those he named as having given him help and whom he hoped to exonerate. Based on Gerstein's testimony, a list of war criminals was forwarded to the United Nations Commission in London. It started with Hitler and Himmler and included Kurt Gerstein; they were all designated "organizers of the system of extermination."[37] Everything he had risked and worked for was in vain. The previous March, as the war ground to an end, he had expected that "as a direct witness of the worst crimes of the Nazis, the important role of informing the German people" would devolve upon him; "he was on the threshold of a vital stage in his life, with many positive tasks to perform." Now that optimism dissolved into total despair.[38] And on the night of July 25–26, 1945, locked away in a cell in the Cherche-Midi military prison in Paris, he hanged himself. It was three years before his widow learned what had happened, and not until 1949 did she receive his effects, including an unmailed letter to a Dutch friend: "I thank God that I did everything in my power to lance that abscess in the body of mankind. Will you do me a service? Write what you know about me. . . . After all, mine is a unique case."[39]

There was another letter by Gerstein, to the presiding magistrates of the French war crimes tribunal; but this later disappeared. So did his dossier; it was "mislaid" and never reached the central repository of archives. So also did Gerstein's body. It had been mislabeled "Garstein." By the time anybody came looking for it and the bureaucratic mistake had been unraveled, the coffin and its remains had long since gone to the "bone pit."[40]

The first reaction to Lieutenant Gerstein's suicide was one of outrage; he had cheated the French gallows. He did the deed himself. "He went off," complained one French intelligence officer, "with all those crimes on his conscience! More than sixty thousand murders. He wouldn't confess. And you let him do away with himself."[41] In retrospect, Lieutenant Colonel Gilbert Mantout, the head of the French War Crimes Research Office, was kinder; years later he said, "My impression of the man was that he was a mystic in a state of traumatic shock, and desperate because no one, neither the Germans nor the French, would take him seriously. As it were, a discredited Joan of Arc deprived of her funeral pyre."[42] Pastor Otto Wehr, who knew him as an ardent Confessing Protestant and supplied much of the material for his biography, was the most dispassionate of all. "A personality like Kurt Gerstein's is necessarily a twilight figure. Or rather, viewed by the standards of the average man, he must seem absolutely incredible. . . . All attempts to do justice to this man's innermost nature and aims from the moralistic and politico-psychological angle are bound to remain inadequate."[43] The odds were heavily stacked against Gerstein. Had he lived, he very likely would have been hanged. As it is, his name stands in limbo—officially neither damned nor blessed. The jury remains out, uncertain how to judge an actor who, as Pastor Wehr noted, possessed an "uncanny mastery" in camouflaging "his inward Christian being by the outward demeanor of the perfect SS man."[44] Hochhuth's Gerstein had dismissed his name as if it were a senseless tag, something easily discarded. SS Obersturmführer Gerstein discovered otherwise; a reputation is not all that easy to lose or to retrieve.

Reputation stands at the heart of martyrdom. To some degree all martyrs are products of and victims of both the role models they seek to fulfill and the judgment placed upon them by those who record and interpret their actions and motives. History swarms with martyrs of every stripe and hue. There are introverted martyrs who were tortured with doubt and oppressed with guilt and sought to test themselves and their faith upon the cross of martyrdom. There are extroverted martyrs, those athletes of faith and warriors of truth, who regarded themselves as instruments of God's ultimate design. There are conceited and ambitious martyrs who did the right thing for the wrong reason, seeking power, paradise, and self-esteem through martyrdom. There are accidental martyrs who through chance and circumstance stumbled upon death, and useless and silly martyrs who squandered their lives for a chimera. There are false martyrs and fabricated martyrs, products of society's need for heroic symbols, and there are traitor-martyrs who may be any or all of the above. And finally on the dark frontiers of time, there are the unrecorded martyrs, unknown men and women whose mark on history is like the air we breathe—there but unobserved.

They were led into martyrdom for a host of reasons: some from spiritual hypochondria and exceedingly tender consciences; some from egotism and pride; some from a perverted desire to display their worth to themselves and to the world; some from simplistic and monocausal thinking; some from a distorted sense of proportions and priorities; some from recklessness or lack of adaptability; some from paranoia and oversensitivity; some from weakness of character and others from strength of character; and some from the absolute conviction that they could "serve as well by dying as by living."[45] The final pronouncement on their success or failure must of necessity remain open, because who can say whether the martyrs' actions were good or bad in themselves or done for the right or wrong reasons? Their sacrifices may seem pure and noble to contemporaries but may survive neither the test of human time nor the judgment of God. But it is comforting to believe with Mahatma Gandhi that for the deity "life and death are one," and that "all that is pure and good in the world persists because of the silent death of thousands of unknown heroes and heroines."[46]

NOTES

Chapter 1
The Debate over Definition

1. Erik Erikson, *Gandhi's Truth* (New York, 1969), p. 197.

2. Timothy J. McNulty, "The American Hero," *Chicago Tribune*, January 12, 1986, sec. 5, pp. 1–6.

3. William Purcell, *Martyrs of Our Time* (St. Louis, Mo., 1983), pp. 1–2; "Saints and Martyrs," *Encyclopedia of Religion and Ethics,* ed. James Hastings (Edinburgh, 1920) vol. 11, pp. 49–82.

4. *Times* (London), January 21, 1970, p. 6. Gerekens's suicide was not an isolated case; see also January 26, p. 4, and January 27, p. 4.

5. St. Augustine, *The City of God*, bk. 1, ch. 25; trans. Marcus Dods, 2 vols. (New York, 1948), vol. 1, p. 37.

6. Sir John Harington, *Epigrams*, ed. Norman E. McClure (Philadelphia, 1926), p. 164.

7. The sources for the life and death of Joan of Arc were originally collected by Jules Quicherat in *Procès de condamnation et de réhabilitation de Jeanne d'Arc, dite la Pucelle,* 5 vols. (Paris, 1841–49), and more recently by Pierre Tisset and Yvonne Lanhers, *Procès de condamnation de Jeanne d'Arc,* 3 vols. (Paris, 1960). The bibliography on Joan is enormous and highly partisan, but the reader is referred to two reasonably balanced accounts: Frances Gies, *Joan of Arc: The Legend and the Reality* (New York, 1981), and Marina Warner, *Joan of Arc: The Image of Female Heroism* (New York, 1982).

8. Warner, *Joan of Arc*, pp. 269–70.

9. Quicherat, *Procès de condemnation*, vol. 2, p. 5.

10. Ibid., pp. 3–4; vol. 1, pp. 477–85.

11. Warner, *Joan of Arc*, p. 270, and p. 332 n. 55. From Paul Claudel, *Théâtre*, ed. J. Madaule (Paris, 1964–65), p. 1520.

12. T. S. Eliot, *Murder in the Cathedral* (London, 1947), p. 49.

13. Francis A. Allen, *The Crimes of Politics: Political Dimensions of Criminal Justice* (Cambridge, Mass., 1974), p. 29. See also Barton L. Ingraham, *Political Crime in Europe: A Comparative Study of France, Germany, and England* (Berkeley, 1979), pp. 41–44.

14. L. B. Smith, *Elizabeth Tudor: Portrait of a Queen* (Boston, 1975), pp. 186–90.

15. There are endless variations of this story, and the words have been attributed to a number of people. Possibly the most authentic are the sentiments assigned to Jean Tressard, secretary to the king of England: "We are all lost, for we have burnt a good and holy person" (Régine Pernoud, *Joan of Arc by Herself and Her Witnesses*, trans. Edward Hyams [New York, 1982], p. 233).

16. Sylvia Plath, "Lady Lazarus," in *Ariel* (London, 1965), p. 17.

17. Eusebius Pamphili, *Ecclesiastical History*, trans. Roy J. Deferrari, bk. 8, chap. 10, in *The Fathers of the Church*, vol. 29, ed. R. J. Deferrari (New York, 1955), p. 181.

18. This story comes from William James, *The Varieties of Religious Experience*, Modern Library ed. (New York, 1939), p. 278 n. 2.

19. Richard Challoner, *Memoirs of Missionary Priests* (London, 1924), pp. 176–77.

20. James, *Varieties*, p. 292. See also Richard Kieckhefer, *Unquiet Souls: Fourteenth-Century Saints and Their Religious Milieu* (Chicago, 1984), pp. 50ff.

21. See for example Donald Attwater, *Martyrs from St. Stephen to John Tung* (London, 1958), p. 139.

22. L. Mariotti, *A Historical Memoir of Frà Dolcino and His Times* (London, 1853), pp. 290–91, 296.

23. Virginia Woolf, "On Being Ill," in *The Moment and Other Essays* (New York, 1948), p. 11.

24. Ronald Melzack and Patrick D. Wall, *The Challenge of Pain*, revised ed. (New York, 1983), p. 27; see also pp. 19–44. Melzack and Wall remains the classic text; for a more recent and argumentative treatment, see David B. Morris, *The Culture of Pain* (Berkeley, 1991), esp. pp. 1–78.

25. Quoted in James, *Varieties*, p. 283, from Claparède and Goty, *Deux Héroines de la foi* (Paris, 1880), p. 112.

26. James, *Varieties*, p. 18, quoting J. F. Nisbet, *The Insanity of Genius* (London, 1893), pp. xvi, xxiv.

27. James, *Varieties*, pp. 23–24.

28. M. K. Gandhi, *An Autobiography: The Story of My Experiments with Truth*, trans. Mahadev Desai (Boston, 1957), p. 19.

29. John M. Mecklin, *The Passing of the Saints: A Study of a Cultural Type* (Chicago, 1941), p. 72.

30. See Donald W. Riddle, *The Martyrs: A Study in Social Control* (Chicago, 1931).

31. Zachary Cawdry, *A Preparation for Martyrdom: A Discourse About the Cause, the Temper, the Assistances and Rewards of a Martyr of Jesus Christ* (London, 1682), p. 48.

32. Phyllis McGinley, *Saint-Watching* (London, 1970), p. 38.

33. See for example Riddle, *Martyrs*, pp. 60–69, 99.

34. John Foxe, *Acts and Monuments*, ed. George Townsend, 8 vols. (London, 1845–49), vol. 7, pp. 688, 705.

35. Nicholas Ridley, *Works*, ed. Henry Christmas, (Cambridge, 1841), p. 384.

36. Ernest Becker, *The Denial of Death*, (New York, 1973), p. 197.

37. Alfred Alvarez's *The Savage God: A Study of Suicide* (New York, 1970), is a sensitive treatment of the subject.

38. Marcus Aurelius Antoninus, *Thoughts*, trans. George Long (London, 1901), bk. 11, 3, p. 186; Eliot, *Murder in the Cathedral*, p. 84.

39. British Library, Harleian Mss., 425, fol. 63.

40. Foxe, *Acts and Monuments,* vol. 7, p. 385.

41. *The Writings of Cyprian, Bishop of Carthage,* vol. 1, trans. Robert E. Wallis (Ante-Nicene Christian Library, ed. Roberts and Donaldson, vol. 8) (Edinburgh, 1870), letter 25 (3), pp. 72–73.

42. Riddle, *Martyrs,* pp. 60–69.

43. Samuel S. Klausner, "Martyrdom," in *The Encyclopedia of Religion,* 15 vols., ed. M. Eliade (New York, 1987), vol. 9, pp. 230–38.

44. The 280 or so English Protestant martyrs burned at the stake by Catholic Mary between 1555 and 1558 contained fewer than a dozen individuals who were politically or socially important. The vast majority were tradesmen and artisans, with a significantly high percentage of women and an equally significant low percentage of clergymen. The opposite, however, appears to have been the case with Catholics executed under Elizabeth later in the century. The majority came from the wealthier elements of Tudor society, and they were predominantly male and clerical. See Philip Hughes, *The Reformation in England,* 3 vols (London, 1954), vol. 2, pp. 259–60; vol. 3, pp. 338–39.

45. Becker, *Denial of Death,* p. 196.

46. C. S. Lewis, *The Screwtape Letters* and *Screwtape Proposes a Toast* (London, 1961), pp. 8–9.

47. The most successful analytical treatment of martyrdom is Eugene and Anita Weiner, *The Martyr's Conviction* (Atlanta, 1990), a slim little volume of which parts 1 and 2 are more successful than part 3.

Chapter 2
Socrates: The Genesis of Martyrdom

1. The Socratic literature is immense and growing; "more work on Socrates is appearing now in a single year than in a decade during the thirties, forties or fifties." These words come from *Socrates, Ironist and Moral Philosopher* (Ithaca, N.Y., 1991), p. 19 n. 71) by Gregory Vlastos, who has become the dean of modern Socratic studies. Despite its age and heavy liberal bias, A. E. Taylor's *Socrates* (New York, 1932) is still the best short biography. I. F. Stone's *The Trial of Socrates* (Boston, 1988) is the most recent biographical excursion into the Socratic quagmire, and predictably he becomes badly entangled in Socrates the intellectual and political elitist who condemned democracy and Socrates who died a martyr to free inquiry and freedom of speech. E. R. Dodds's *The Greeks and the Irrational* (Berkeley, 1951) makes Socrates out to be the victim of the black side of the classical mind: the irrational; and Karl Popper's *The Open Society and Its Enemies,* 2 vols. (London, 1945), endeavors with only partial success to divide the historic Socrates from Platonic fiction so as to disassociate Socrates the liberal equalitarian from the authoritarian (vol. 1, pp. 157–69, 189–94). The Socratic sources are investigated at length in the works of Mario Montuori: *Socrates, Man and Myth: The Two Socratic Apologies of Xenophon* (London, 1957); *Socrates: Physiology of a Myth* (Amsterdam, 1981); and *Socrates: An Approach* (Amsterdam, 1988). Possibly the clearest analysis of Socrates' ideas can be found in Luis E. Navia, *Socrates: The Man and His Philosophy* (New York, 1985). An important recent work to which this chapter is indebted is Thomas C. Brickhouse and Nicholas D. Smith, *Plato's Socrates* (New York, 1994).

2. Plato remains the pre-eminent source for the historic Socrates. The *Euthyphro, Apology, Crito,* and *Phaedo* are central to Socrates' trial and death, but other dialogues, especially *Symposium* and *Gorgias* and the *Republic,* give a broader, more complex and often contradictory picture of the man. All quotations from the Platonic dialogues come from B. Jowett's translations in *Plato* (New York, 1942). The references in parentheses are to the 1578 *Plato* by Henri Estienne, which is the customary method of citation. Xenophon's "Socratica" (in particular, *Memorabilia* [or *Memoirs*] *of Socrates; The Apology of Socrates,* or *Socrates' Defense;* and *The Banquet,* or *Symposium*) can be read in a host of translations. I have used volume 4 of the Loeb Classic Library, trans. E. C. Marchant (London, 1967). Aristophanes had the most to say about Socrates in *Clouds.* Anton-Hermann Chroust, in *Socrates, Man and Myth* (South Bend, Ind., 1957), has attempted to reconstruct much of the lost literature about Socrates, especially Polycrates' pamphlet *Xarnvogla Euxgarous,* which purported to be a speech delivered by the prosecution during Socrates' trial; see chapter 4 and particularly pp. 99–100. Diogenes Laertius's "Socrates" can be read in *Diogenes Laertius: Lives of Eminent Philosophers,* trans. R. H. Hicks, 2 vols. Loeb Classical Library (London, 1865–66), pp. 149–77.

3. Thucydides, *The History of the Peloponnesian War,* trans. R. W. Livingston (Oxford, 1943), pp. 189–91.

4. Diogenes Laertius, "Socrates," p. 171. See also Taylor, *Socrates,* p. 106, and Chroust, *Socrates,* pp. 16–29.

5. A. D. Lindsay, *The Historical Socrates and the Platonic Form of the Good* (Calcutta, 1932), p. 7.

6. Plato, *Apology,* pp. 48–50 (30D–31E).

7. Ibid., p. 35 (18BC); *Euthyphro,* 26.

8. Vlastos, *Socrates,* pp. 165–66, 173–76.

9. Having written this, I must confess that the authority for the statement is Plato, and that Montuori, *Socrates: Physiology of a Myth,* ch. 8 and 9, has endeavored to prove that Socrates' encounter with the oracle is a Platonic fabrication. See, however, Diogenes Laertius, "Socrates," p. 163, and Dodds, *Greeks and the Irrational,* pp. 185–86, 217.

10. Plato, *Apology* (21B, 33C); *Crito* (44A); *Phaedo* (60E).

11. Plato, *Symposium,* pp. 212–13 (220D).

12. Thucydides, *Peloponnesian War,* pp. 287–88, 304–05, 306, 327.

13. Xenophon, *Apology of Socrates,* 14–15.

14. Plato, *Apology,* p. 37 (21A).

15. Ibid., p. 37 (21C).

16. Ibid., p. 39 (22A).

17. Ibid., p. 39 (22B).

18. Stone, *The Trial of Socrates,* pp. 138–39, is the most outspoken: in the trial it "was the political, not the philosophical or theological, views of Socrates which finally got him into trouble. The discussion of his religious views diverts attention from the real issues." For the opposite view—the trial was motivated solely by religious concerns—see Brickhouse and Smith, *Plato's Socrates,* chap. 5.

19. For two key discussions of this important quotation (*Gorgias,* 521D) see Vlastos, *Socrates,* pp. 240–42, and Brickhouse and Smith, *Plato's Socrates,* pp. 137–141.

20. Chroust, *Socrates,* p. 24; Taylor, *Socrates,* p. 102; Montuori, *Socrates: Physiology of a Myth,* p. 197.

21. Plato, *Apology,* pp. 46–47 (28B).

22. Ibid., pp. 47–48 (29C).

23. Ibid., pp. 48–49 (30D–E).

24. Ibid., pp. 56, 57 (38A, 39A).

25. Ibid., pp. 58, 60 (39C, 41D).

26. Ibid., pp. 59–60 (41A–C).

27. Ibid., p. 60 (42A).

28. Plato, *Crito,* p. 79 (54E).

29. Plato, *Phaedo,* p. 86 (58E).

30. Ibid., p. 146 (107C).

31. Ibid., p. 149 (114DE). See Brickhouse and Smith, *Socrates,* pp. 201–11, for Socrates' ambivalent views on death and the immortality of the soul.

32. Ibid., p. 149 (115A).

33. Plato, *Apology,* p. 60 (41D).

34. Plato, *Phaedo,* pp. 151–52 (116E–117A).

35. Ibid., p. 152 (117D).

36. Ibid., p. 153 (118A).

37. See Arthur J. Droge and James D. Tabor, *A Noble Death: Suicide and Martyrdom Among Christians and Jews in Antiquity* (San Francisco, 1992), for a discussion of Socrates' decision to take his own life and the classical view of voluntary death, esp. chap. 2.

38. Stone, *Trial of Socrates,* p. 230.

39. Xenophon, *Memorabilia,* 4, 8, 8. See also *Apology of Socrates,* 8–9.

40. Xenophon, *Apology of Socrates,* 5–8.

41. Stone, *Trial of Socrates,* p. 183.

42. Montuori, *Socrates: Physiology of a Myth,* p. 200; Xenophon, *Memorabilia,* 4, 8, 9.

43. See for example Diogenes Laertius, "Socrates," p. 167.

44. Taylor, *Socrates,* p. 116 n. 1.

45. Chroust, *Socrates, Man and Myth,* p. 42, has the best general discussion of motivation.

46. Plato, *Phaedo,* pp. 89, 115 (61B, 80–81E).

47. Ibid., pp. 90–91 (62BC).

48. Ibid., p. 91 (62C).

49. Ibid., p. 91 (62DE); Plato, *Apology,* p. 59 (40B); Xenophon, *Apology of Socrates,* p. 5; *Memorabilia,* 4, 8, 5.

50. For example, see Herbert Musurillo, *The Acts of the Christian Martyrs* (Oxford, 1972), pp. 159 (Pionius), 95 (Apollonius), 349 (Phileas). Also T. W. Manson, "Martyrs and Martyrdom," *Bulletin* of the John Ryland Library 39 (1957), pp. 478–80; *II Maccabees,* trans. Jonathan A. Goldstein (New York, 1983), p. 285; and *The Third and Fourth Books of Maccabees,* ed. and trans. Moses Hadas (New York, 1953), pp. 116–17.

51. Justin, *Second Apology,* chap. 10 in *The Writings of Justin Martyr and Athenagoras,* trans. Marcus Dods and George Reith, Ante-Nicene Christian Library, vol. 2 (Edinburgh, 1874), p. 80.

Chapter 3
The Maccabees and the Doctrine of Suffering

1. The bibliography on the development of Judaism and the history of the Jews from the Babylonian captivity in 597 B.C. to the restoration of Jerusalem in 539 B.C. and the revival of Judaism during the 3rd and 4th centuries B.C. are especially rich. John Bright, *A History of Israel* (Philadelphia: 4th ed., 1981) is the most up to date (see especially chapters 8–12), and Victor Tcherikover, *Hellenistic Civilization and the Jews* (New York, 1979), is essential reading, as is also Elias Bickerman, *From Ezra to the Last of the Maccabees* (New York, 1962). See also the introductions to *The Second Book of Maccabees*, ed. Solomon Zeitlin (New York, 1954); *II Maccabees*, trans. and ed. Jonathan A. Goldstein, *The Anchor Bible*, vol. 41A (New York: 1983); and *The Third and Fourth Books of Maccabees*, ed. and trans. Moses Hadas (New York, 1953). Moshe Pearlman, *The Maccabees* (New York, 1973), is a good popular account. Somewhat more idiosyncratic is John M. Allegro, *The Chosen People* (New York: 1972). All references to Maccabees II and IV except where indicated are from Goldstein and Hadas.

2. Bickerman, *From Ezra*, p. 8.

3. Maccabees IV 5:25–26.

4. W. H. C. Frend, *Martyrdom and Persecutions in the Early Church* (Oxford, 1965), pp. 31–33. See also H. A. Fischel, "Martyr and Prophet," *Jewish Quarterly Review*, 37 (July 1946), pp. 265–80 and 363–86, and A. R. C. Leaney, "The Eschatological Significance of Human Suffering in the Old Testament and the Dead Sea Scrolls," *Scottish Journal of Theology* 16, no. 2 (June 1963), pp. 286–96.

5. The date of Ezra's arrival in Jerusalem is in doubt. See Bright, *History of Israel*, pp. 279–86, 391–402.

6. Quoted in Frend, *Martyrdom and Persecutions*, p. 37; E. R. Dodds, *The Greeks and the Irrational* (Berkeley, 1951), p. 237.

7. I Maccabees, trans. Jonathan Goldstein, *The Anchor Bible*, vol. 41 (New York, 1976), 1:11. See Tcherikover, *Hellenistic Civilization*, chaps. 3 and 4, and Elias Bickerman, *The God of the Maccabees*, trans. H. R. Moehring (Leiden, 1979), pp. 83–88.

8. The far-from-clear interrelationship between internal Jewish policy and Antiochus's policies is debated in Bickerman, *God of the Maccabees*, passim, and Tcherikover, *Hellenistic Civilization*, pp. 183–200. See also Goldstein, *II Maccabees*, Introduction, pp. 84–105.

9. Quoted in Bickerman, *God of the Maccabees*, p. 76, from Jean Bodin, *De Republica* bk. 4, chap. 5.

10. Maccabees I 1:4.

11. See note 8; for the order and dating of events I have followed Bickerman, *God of the Maccabees*, chap. 3, secs. 3–6, and Goldstein, *II Maccabees*, Introduction, pp. 89–96.

12. Maccabees I 1:55.

13. Maccabees II 6:6.

14. Ibid., 6:10–11.

15. Goldstein, *II Maccabees*, notes, pp. 292–93.

16. The dating of Maccabees II and IV is extremely uncertain. I have followed Goldstein, *II Maccabees*, Introduction, pp. 71–83, and Hadas, *Books of Maccabees*, Introduction, pp. 95–99; but also see Zeitlin, Introduction, pp. 27–29, and John Downing, "Jesus and Martyrdom," *Journal of Theological Studies*, new series vol. 14 (1963), p. 280. For the de-

bate over location, see Margaret Schatkin, "The Maccabean Martyrs," *Vigilae Christianae* 28 (1974), pp. 97–113.

17. Bickerman, *God of the Maccabees,* chap. 5.

18. For the importance of the Maccabees in Jewish literature, see Gerson D. Cohen, "The Story of Hanna and Her Seven Sons in Hebrew Literature," in *Mordecai M. Kaplan Jubilee Volume,* ed. Moshe Davis, vol. 2 (New York, 1953), pp. 109–22.

19. Bickerman, *God of the Maccabees,* p. 88.

20. *The Letters of St. Bernard of Clairvaux,* trans. Scott James (London: 1953), pp. 144–47.

21. Goldstein, *II Maccabees,* p. 285 note; Hadas, *Books of Maccabees,* Introduction, pp. 101, 116–17.

22. Maccabees II 6:19–20.

23. Maccabees IV 5:8–13.

24. Ibid., 5:18–20.

25. Ibid., 6:20–21.

26. Ibid., 5:35, 6:25, 7:21.

27. Ibid., 7:5; Maccabees II 6:30.

28. Maccabees IV 8:3–10.

29. Ibid., 9:1.

30. Maccabees II 7:3–6, and *The Second Book of Maccabees,* ed. Solomon Zeitlin, p. 161.

31. Maccabees II 7:18, 7:33–38. Goldstein *II Maccabees* argues (pp. 315–16 note) that Maccabees II does not contain the doctrine of vicarious atonement for the sins of Israel as found in Maccabees IV. The martyrs do not "substitute for the rest of suffering Israel." They are simply part of the punishment demanded by Yahweh.

32. Maccabees IV 6:29, 12:17.

33. Ibid., 17:21.

34. Ibid., 9:28, 10:5–8, 10:19, 11:10, 11:18.

35. Ibid., 12:3, 12:16.

36. Ibid., 12:18; Maccabees II, 7:39.

37. Maccabees IV, 15:15.

38. Maccabees II, 7:27–29.

39. Ibid., 7:41; Maccabees IV, 17:1; *The Second Book of Maccabees,* ed. Zeitlin, pp. 168–69 n. 41.

40. Maccabees IV, 10:12–15.

41. Frend, *Martyrdom and Persecution,* p. 20; Frend, "The Persecutions: Some Links Between Judaism and the Early Church," *Journal of Ecclesiastical History* 9 (1958), p. 151; Hadas, *Books of Maccabees,* Introduction, pp. 125–27.

42. Hadas, *Books of Maccabees,* Introduction, p. 116; Plato, *Gorgias* (Loeb Classical Library), p. 335 (469C).

43. For the importance of the group as opposed to the individual in the Judaic understanding of martyrdom, see Robert L. Cohn, "Sainthood on the Periphery: The Case of Judaism" in *Sainthood: Its Manifestations in World Religions,* eds. Richard Kieckhefer and George D. Bond (Berkeley, 1988), pp. 43–53.

44. Maccabees IV 13:23–24.

45. Ibid., 13:17.

46. Ibid., 5:32, 6:10.

47. Ibid., 9:22–24.

48. Ibid., 11:20–25.

49. Ibid., 17:13–14.

50. Maccabees II 6:16.

51. Maccabees IV 15:29, 16:16–23.

52. Maccabees II 8:3; Maccabees IV 9:9.

53. Maccabees IV 11:12.

54. Maccabees II 7:19–35.

55. Ibid., 7:34–36; Maccabees IV 10:11.

56. Goldstein, *II Maccabees*, p. 305 notes.

57. St. Augustine, *City of God*, 18:36; Hadas, *Books of Maccabees*, Introduction, pp. 125–27; Frend, *Martyrdom and Persecution*, pp. 20–22; Margaret Schatkin, "The Maccabean Martyrs," *Vigilae Christianae* 28 (1974), pp. 97–113.

58. Ralph Waldo Emerson, "Uses of Great Men," *The Complete Works*, 12 vols. (Boston, 1903), vol. 4, p. 27.

59. Maccabees IV 5:4; Maccabees II 6:18.

60. Maccabees II 6:18.

61. Hadas, *Books of Maccabees* pp. 147 notes; Maccabees IV 18:6–15.

62. J. H. Greenstone, "Martyrdom," *Jewish Encyclopedia* (New York, 1904), vol. 8, pp. 353–54.

63. Maccabees IV 8:29.

64. Maccabees II 7:9.

65. Maccabees IV 18:3.

66. Frend, *Martyrdom and Persecution*, p. 67.

Chapter 4
Jesus of Nazareth: "Follow Me"

1. There is nothing that can be said about Jesus that has not been stated a hundred times before in a dozen different languages. My own reading on the subject, inadequate as it is, is still too long to profitably reproduce and of no particular value to the uninitiated. A number of excellent recent works, however, are worth noting: John Meir, *A Marginal Jew: Rethinking the Historical Jesus* (New York, 1991); John Crossan, *The Essential Jesus: Original Sayings and Earliest Images* (San Francisco, 1994); Geza Vermes's trilogy, *Jesus the Jew: A Historian's Reading of the Gospels* (London, 1973), *Jesus and the World of Judaism* (Philadelphia, 1983), and *The Religion of Jesus the Jew* (Minneapolis, 1993); and Raymond E. Brown, *The Death of the Messiah*, 2 vols. (New York, 1994). Equally important is the earlier image of the historical Jesus found in Albert Schweitzer, *The Quest of the Historical Jesus* (London, 1922). The two books to which this chapter owes a great deal are Michael Grant, *Jesus: An Historian's Review of the Gospels* (New York, 1977), and C. H. Dodd, *The Founder of Christianity* (New York, 1970). *The Dictionary of Jesus and the Gospels*, ed. J. B. Green, S. McKnight, and I. Howard Marshall (Downers

Grove, Ill., 1992), is not always as useful as it sounds, but it gives excellent coverage of the scholarly debate which still continues over most aspects of Jesus' life, teaching, and theological meaning.

2. Hans Lietzmann, "Der Prozess Jesu," *Sitzungsbericht der Preussischen Akademie der Wissenschaften, Philosophische-historische Klasse,* 23–24 (Berlin, 1931), p. 313, quoted in Ethelbert Stauffer, *Jesus and His Story* (New York, 1967), p. vii.

3. The argument that Jesus literally never existed is rather different from admitting that his story has been fictionalized largely as a result of oral history. Ever since the eighteenth century the nonexistence thesis has had a small but vocal and generally polemical following. The most scholarly of these works is G. A. Wells, *Did Jesus Exist?* (Pemberton, 1975). Wells has not been able to breach the academic-theological academy of modern scholarship on Jesus, and John Meir's words speak for the entire establishment; referring to Wells, Meir writes that he is "representative of a whole type of popular Jesus book that I do not bother to consider in detail" (*Marginal Jew*, p. 87 n. 59). See also James M. Robinson, *A New Quest of the Historical Jesus* (London, 1959), p. 88, especially note 2.

4. For Jesus's style of expression, especially its uniqueness, see Joachim Jeremias, *New Testament Theology* (New York, 1971), pp. 1–37.

5. Luke 1:1–4. Unless indicated, all biblical quotations for this chapter come from the Revised Standard Version of the Bible (1946–52), except for occasional lapses back into the King James rendering for reasons of nostalgia.

6. Origen, *Contra Celsum* VII, 53, trans. Henry Chadwick (Cambridge, England, 1953), p. 440.

7. Of all the authors who have attempted to demonstrate the historical reality of the events of Jesus' life, Ethelbert Stauffer in *Jesus and His Story* (New York, 1967) is the most aggressive. For the census and the star, see pp. 21–34.

8. This figure comes from Grant, *Jesus*, p. 197.

9. Ibid.; Robinson, *A New Quest*, p. 55 and note 3.

10. See Dodd, *Founder*, p. 29.

11. See Pierre Barbet, *A Doctor at Calvary* (New York, 1953), for a grim but clinical medical analysis of crucifixion.

12. This is the rendering in Dodd, *Founder*, p. 55.

13. Meir, *Marginal Jew*, p. 409.

14. This is the rendering in Grant, *Jesus*, p. 15.

15. Jesus as a political (nationalist) revolutionary can be studied in Hyan Maccoby, *Revolution in Judea, Jesus, and the Jewish Resistance* (London, 1973).

16. This is the King James rendering.

17. Ibid.

18. Arthur J. Droge and James D. Tabor, *A Noble Death: Suicide and Martyrdom Among Christians and Jews in Antiquity* (San Francisco, 1992).

Chapter 5
The Early Christian Martyrs: "My Lady" Perpetua

1. *The Third and Fourth Books of Maccabees,* ed. and trans. by Moses Hadas (New York, 1953), 8:18–26.

2. A brief listing of books on the classical Christian setting is difficult to devise, but this chapter owes much to Peter Brown, *The World of Late Antiquity, A.D. 150–750* (New York, 1971) and *The Body and Society: Men, Women and Sexual Renunciation in Early Christianity* (New York, 1988); E. R. Dodds, *The Greeks and the Irrational* (Berkeley, 1951) and *Pagan and Christian in an Age of Anxiety: Some Aspects of Religious Experience from Marcus Aurelius to Constantine* (Cambridge, 1965); Ramsay MacMullen, *Christianizing the Roman Empire (A.D. 100–400)* (New Haven, 1984); Robin Lane Fox, *Pagan and Christian* (New York, 1967); and A. D. Nock, *Conversion: The Old and the New in Religion from Alexander the Great to Augustine of Hippo* (Oxford, 1933). The two indispensable books on early Christian martyrdom are W. H. C. Frend, *Martyrdom and Persecution in the Early Church: A Study of a Conflict from the Maccabees to Donatus* (Oxford, 1965), and Donald W. Riddle, *The Martyrs: A Study in Social Control* (Chicago, 1931).

3. *The Writings of Cyprian, Bishop of Carthage,* vol. 2, trans. Robert E. Wallis (Ante-Nicene Christian Library, vol. 13) (Edinburgh, 1869), p. 233.

4. Dodds, *Pagan and Christian,* p. 29.

5. Tertullian, "To the Martyrs," in *Writings,* vol. 1 (Ante-Nicene Christian Library, vol. 11) (Edinburgh, 1869), p. 3; Cicero, *Republic* (Loeb Classical Library edition) 6:14.

6. *Writings of Cyprian,* vol. 2, p. 235.

7. Augustine, *Contra Litteras Petiliani,* ii. 88–192 in *A Select Library of the Nicene and Post-Nicene Fathers,* vol. 4 (New York, 1909). See also John Downing, "Jesus and Martyrdom," *Journal of Theological Studies* n.s. 14 (1963), pp. 276–93.

8. Tertullian, "To Scapula," in *Apologetical Works,* trans. Rudolph Arbesmann et al. (The Fathers of the Church, vol. 10) (New York, 1950), p. 300.

9. Herbert Musurillo, *The Acts of the Christian Martyrs* (Oxford, 1972), "The Martyrdom of Saints Marian and James," p. 207.

10. Tertullian, "Apologeticus," in *Writings,* vol. 1 (Ante-Nicene Christian Library, vol. 11), p. 138.

11. Cyprian, "On the Glory of Martyrdom," in *Writings of Cyprian,* vol. 2, p. 247.

12. Tertullian, "Apology," in *Apologetical Works,* p. 126; "Flight in Time of Persecution," in *Disciplinary, Moral and Ascetical Works,* trans. E. A. Quain (The Fathers of the Church, vol. 40) (New York, 1959), pp. 294–95; "To the Martyrs," p. 4.

13. Tertullian, quoted in Alfred Alvarez, *The Savage God: A Study of Suicide* (New York, 1970), p. 59.

14. Musurillo, *Christian Martyrs,* "The Martyrdom of St. Polycarp," p. 17.

15. Tertullian, "To the Martyrs," in *Disciplinary, Moral and Ascetical Works,* p. 24.

16. Quoted in Peter Brown, *The Cult of the Saints* (Chicago, 1981), p. 50, from Theodoret, Bishop of Cyrrhus.

17. Cyprian, "On the Glory of Martyrdom," p. 240.

18. For example, see Cyprian, "Exhortation to Martyrdom," in *Treatises,* trans. Roy J. Deferrari (The Fathers of the Church, vol. 36) (New York, 1958), pp. 332–33.

19. *Origen: Exhortation to Martyrdom,* trans. Rowan A. Greer (New York, 1979), pp. 56–59.

20. William James, *The Varieties of Religious Experience,* Modern Library edition (New York, 1936), p. 159.

21. Clement of Alexandria, "Miscellanies," in *The Writings,* vol. 2, trans. William Wilson (Ante-Nicene Christian Library, vol. 12) (Edinburgh, 1872), p. 182. See also Tertullian, "Flight in Time of Persecution," p. 278.

22. Musurillo, *Christian Martyrs*, p. 69.

23. Cyprian, "On the Glory of Martyrdom," p. 240.

24. Ibid., p. 242.

25. Ignatius, "Trallians," x. 1 (Ante-Nicene Christian Library, vol. 1) (Edinburgh, 1873), p. 201. See also Frend, *Martyrdom and Persecution*, p. 244.

26. Cyprian, "On the Glory of Martyrdom," p. 233.

27. Tertullian, "To Scapula," p. 151.

28. See Arthur J. Droge and James D. Tabor, *A Noble Death: Suicide and Martyrdom Among Christians and Jews in Antiquity,* especially chapters 5 and 6. Droge and Tabor argue the early church encouraged voluntary martyrdom. For an opposite view, see G. E. M. de Ste Croix, "Why Were the Early Christians Persecuted?" *Past and Present* no. 26, (Nov. 1963), pp. 6–38.

29. Musurillo, *Christian Martyrs*, "Acts of Euplus," p. 311; *Apocryphon of James* CGI 5, 31–36, 20, quoted in Pheme Perkins, *The Gnostic Dialogue* (New York, 1980), p. 146; Ignatius, "Epistle to the Romans," in *The Writings of the Apostolic Fathers*, trans. Alexander Roberts et al. (Ante-Nicene Christian Library, vol. 1) (Edinburgh, 1873), p. 212.

30. Clement of Alexandria, "Miscellanies," pp. 147, 173.

31. Eusebius, *Ecclesiastical History,* bk. 7, chap. 12, trans. C. F. Crusé (Philadelphia, 1937), p. 285.

32. Musurillo, *Christian Martyrs,* "The Acts of St. Cyprian," pp. 169–71.

33. Tertullian, "Apology," p. 10.

34. Cyprian, "On the Glory of Martyrdom," p. 241.

35. Tertullian, "Apology," p. 125.

36. *Origen: Exhortation to Martyrdom,* p. 53.

37. Cyprian, *Letters,* trans. R. B. Donner (The Fathers of the Church, vol. 51), p. 169; "On the Glory of Martyrdom," p. 248.

38. Tertullian, "Flight in Time of Persecution," p. 294.

39. Tertullian, "Apology," p. 126.

40. Musurillo, *Christian Martyrs,* "The Martyrs of Lyons," p. 81.

41. Tacitus, *Annals* 15.44, trans. Michael Grant (London, 1963), p. 354.

42. The best work on conversion is Nock's *Conversion,* esp. pp. 187–89.

43. For the relationship of Christianity to the Roman Empire, see, besides the works listed in note 2, Stephen Benko, "Pagan Criticism of Christianity During the First Two Centuries A.D.," *Aufstieg und Niedergang der Römischen Welt* (Berlin and New York, 1980), vol. 2, pt. 23.2, pp. 1055–1112; R. M. Grant, *Early Christianity and Society: Seven Studies* (New York, 1977); Paul Keresztes, "The Imperial Roman Government and the Christian Church," *Aufstieg und Niedergang der Römischen Welt,* (Berlin and New York, 1980), vol. 2, pts. 23.1 and 2, pp. 247–315 and 373–86; Marta Sordi, *The Christians and the Roman Empire,* trans. Annabel Bedini (Norman, Okla., 1986); Robert L. Wilken, *The Christians as the Romans Saw Them* (New Haven, 1984). See also A.N. Sherwin-White, "The Early Persecutions and Roman Law Again," *Journal of Theological Studies,* m.s. vol 3 (1952), pp. 199–213; J. Moreau, *La Persécution du Christianisme dans l'Empire romain* (Paris, 1956); and the debate between G. E. M. de Ste Croix and Sherwin-White in *Past and Present* no. 26 (Nov. 1963), pp. 6–38, and no. 27 (April 1964), pp. 23–33.

44. Wilken, *The Christians*, p. 58.

45. Origen, *Contra Celsum*, VIII 2, trans. Henry Chadwick (Cambridge, England, 1953), p. 454; Wilken, *The Christians*, p. 66; Benko, "Pagan Criticism of Christianity," p. 1082.

46. Tertullian, "Apology," p. 102.

47. Origen, *Contra Celsum*, III 55, p. 165.

48. Cyprian, *Writings*, I, letter XV (3), vol. 8, p. 53.

49. *Pliny: A Self-Portrait in Letters*, trans. Betty Radice (London, 1978), no. 96, pp. 241–42. Compare Benko, "Pagan Criticism of Christianity," pp. 1068–69; Keresztes, "The Imperial Roman Government," pp. 273–87; and Sordi, *The Christians*, pp. 56–66.

50. Origen, *Contra Celsum*, III 8, p. 133; Eusebius, *Ecclesiastical History*, bk. 5, Preliminary, p. 168. See Frend, *Martyrdom and Persecution*, p. 537, for a modern estimate.

51. Hippolyte Delehaye, *The Legends of the Saints*, trans. Donald Attwater (New York, 1962), pp. 71–72.

52. Origen, *Contra Celsum*, VIII. 67, p. 503.

53. Minucius Felix, *Octavius*, 9. 1, ed. G. H. Rendall, Loeb Library edition (London, 1931). For the debate over Septimius Severus's edict and his responsibility for the persecutions, see Sordi, *The Christians*, pp. 79–86. See also Paul Keresztes, "The Emperor Septimius Severus: A Precursor of Decius," *Historia* 19 (1970), pp. 565–78.

54. E. W. Benson, *Cyprian: His Life, His Times, His Work* (London, 1987), p. 16.

55. Clement of Alexandria, *Exhortation to the Greeks*, x. 73, trans. G. W. Butterworth (Cambridge, Mass., 1960), p. 197.

56. *Leukippe and Kleitophon*, in *Collected Ancient Greek Novels*, ed. B. P. Reardon (Berkeley, 1989), pp. 241, 259; Nock, *Conversion*, pp. 199–200.

57. Judith Perkins, "The Apocryphal Acts of the Apostles and the Early Christian Martyrdom," *Arethusa* 19, no. 2 (Fall 1985), p. 214; Stevan L. Davies, *The Revolt of the Widows: The Social World of the Apocryphal Acts*, (Carbondale, Ill., 1980) pp. 32–37.

58. Perkins, "The Apocryphal Acts," p. 215.

59. Ibid., p. 218.

60. Musurillo, p. 67.

61. Frederick C. Klawiter, "Study of Montanism," *Church History* 49, no. 3 (1980), pp. 251–61; Dodds, *Pagan and Christian*, pp. 63–68, 77–80; W. H. C. Frend, *The Donatist Church: A Movement of Protest in Roman North Africa* (Oxford, 1952), pp. 112–20; Sordi, *The Christians*, pp. 72–74.

62. Klawiter, "Study of Montanism," p. 253.

63. For the scholarly debate on the diary and Passion as a whole, see Hippolyte Delehaye, *Les Passions des Martyrs et Les Genres Littéraires* (Brussels, 1921); Dodds, *Pagan and Christian*, pp. 47–52; J. Armitage Robinson, ed., "The Passion of S. Perpetua," *Texts and Studies: Contributions to Biblical and Patristic Literature*, vol. 1 (Cambridge, 1891), pp. 1–57; W. H. C. Frend, "Blandina and Perpetua: Two Early Christian Heroines," *Les Martyrs de Lyon* (177), (Paris, 1978), p. 170; C.J.M.J. van Beek, *Passio Sanctarum Perpetuae et Felicitatis* (Bonn, 1938), pp. 17–65; Mary Ann Rossi, "The Passion of Perpetua, Everywoman of Late Antiquity," *Pagan and Christian Anxiety: A Response to E. R. Dodds*, Robert C. Smith and John Lounibos, eds. (New York, 1984), pp. 71–76; and Brent D. Shaw's wide-ranging and eclectic article "The Passion of Perpetua," *Past and Present* no. 139 (May 1993), pp. 3–45. There are endless translations of the Passion. I have used throughout Herbert Musurillo, *The Acts of the Christian Martyrs*

(Oxford, 1972), where the Latin and English renditions are given side by side. All references appear as "Musurillo."

64. See note 56.

65. Musurillo, p. 109.

66. Ibid.

67. Ibid.

68. Ibid., p. 111.

69. Ibid. This is a modification of Musurillo.

70. Ibid., p. 112.

71. Musurillo translates *dominam* simply as "woman," p. 113, but Jan den Boeft and Jan Bremmer, "Notiunculae Martyrologiae: Passio Perpetuae," *Vigiliae Christianae* 36, no. 4, pp. 387–89, point out its other usages.

72. Musurillo, p. 113.

73. Peter Dronke, *Women Writers of the Middle Ages* (Cambridge, 1984), pp. 10 and 284 n. 36, calls the family not Christian but "Christian sympathizers." See also W. H. C. Frend, *The Rise of Christianity* (Philadelphia, 1984) p. 291, and Shaw, "The Passion of Perpetua," pp. 24–25.

74. The best discussion of the husband is in Dronke, *Women Writers of the Middle Ages*, pp. 281–83 n. 3, but see also Shaw, "The Passion of Perpetua," pp. 24–25.

75. Mary Lefkowitz and Maureen Fant, eds., *Women's Life in Greece and Rome* (London, 1982), no. 227, p. 240.

76. Musurillo, p. 113.

77. Ibid., pp. 113–15.

78. Origen, *Exhortation to Martyrdom,* "Apostasy," trans. John J. O'Meara (Westminster, Md., 1954), pp. 147–48.

79. Van Beek, *Passio Sanctarum Perpetuae at Felicitatis,* pp. 58–73. See also Robinson, "The Passion of S. Perpetua," p. 15, and Shaw, "The Passion of Perpetua," pp. 33–35.

80. Musurillo, p. 115.

81. Ibid.

82. Ibid., p. 117.

83. Ibid., pp. 115, 117.

84. Ibid., pp. 117, 119.

85. Ibid., p. 119. Musurillo translates *lanista* as "athletic trainer," but Jan den Boeft and Jan Bremmer in "Notiunculae Martyrologiae: Passio Perpetuae," p. 391, argue for "the President of the Games." Marie-Louise von Franz, *The Passion of Perpetua* (Irving, Texas, 1980), pp. 62–66, associates the giant with Saturn, since he seems to be wearing the costume of the priests of Saturn.

86. Musurillo, p. 119.

87. Tertullian, "Da Anima," 47.2 in *Writings* (Ante-Nicene Christian Library, vol. 15), p. 518.

88. Musurillo, p. 119.

89. Ibid., pp. 119, 123, 125.

90. Ibid., p. 125.

91. Tertullian, "To the Martyrs," p. 4.

92. Musurillo, p. 125.

93. Ibid.

94. Ibid., p. 127.

95. Ibid.

96. Ibid., p. 129.

97. Tertullian, "The Apparel of Women," 2.7, in *Disciplinary, Moral and Ascetical Works*, p. 138.

98. Musurillo, p. 129.

99. Ibid.

100. Ibid., p. 131. This is a slight modification of Musurillo.

101. Dronke, *Women Writers*, pp. 1–17, esp. p. 1; Mary R. Lefkowitz, *Heroines and Hysterics* (New York, 1981), pp. 53–58, esp. p. 56, and *Women in Greek Myth* (Baltimore, 1986), p. 105; and P. Wilson-Kastner, G. R. Kastner, Ann Millin, Rosemary Rader, and Jeremiah Reedy, *A Lost Tradition: Women Writers of the Early Church* (Washington, D.C., 1981), pp. 1–32, esp. p. 9.

102. Von Franz, *The Passion of Perpetua*, pp. 52, 75.

103. Robinson, "The Passion of S. Perpetua," pp. 1–22.

Chapter 6
Thomas Becket and the Honor of God

1. St. Augustine, *Letters*, vol. 2 (The Fathers of the Church, vol. 18), trans. Wilfrid Parsons (New York, 1953), no. 89, p. 35; Jacques-Paul Migne, *Patrologiae Cursus Completus, Series Latina* (Paris, 1844–82), vol. 28, col. 310; *Sermons*, in *The Works of Saint Augustine: A Translation for the 21st Century*, trans. Edmund Hill (Hyde Park, N.Y., 1994), vol. III/8, no. 275, p. 26.

2. *Tudor Royal Proclamations*, 3 vols., ed. Paul L. Hughes and James F. Larkin (New Haven 1964), vol. 1, p. 276.

3. The sources on Becket are manageable and compact. The overwhelming majority are in *Materials for the History of Thomas Becket, Archbishop of Canterbury*, ed. J. C. Robertson (vols. 1–6) and J. B. Sheppard (vol. 7), (all of which constitute volume 67 of *Rerum Britannicarum Medii Aevi Scriptores* [Rolls Series, 1875–85]). Volumes 1 to 4 include the biographies by William of Canterbury (1), John of Salisbury (2), Edward Grim (2), Benedict of Peterborough (2), Alan of Tewkesbury (2), Herbert of Bosham (3), and William Fitzstephen (3) as well as three anonymous works (4). Volumes 5–7 cover the archbishop's correspondence; see also Anne Duggan, *Thomas Becket: A Textual History of His Letters* (Oxford, 1980). Two other descriptions are useful: Guernes de Pont-Sainte-Maxence, *La Vie de Saint Thomas le Martyr*, ed. E. Wallberg (London, 1922), and *Thómas Saga Erkibyskups (A Life of Thomas Becket)*, 2 vols., ed. E. Magnússon (Rolls Series, London, 1875–83). Translations of the Becket *Materials* can be found in G. W. Greenaway, *The Life and Death of Thomas Becket* (London, 1961); *English Historical Documents*, vol. 2, 1042–1189, ed. D. C. Douglas and G. W. Greenaway, 2nd ed. (London, 1981) (hereafter cited as EHD); and E. A. Abbott, *St. Thomas of Canterbury: His Death and Miracles*, 2 vols. (London, 1898). Three other sources contain material about Becket: A. Morey and C. N. L. Brooke, eds., *Gilbert Foliot and His Letters* (Cambridge,

1965); John of Salisbury, *Later Letters,* eds. W. J. Millor and C. N. L. Brooke (Oxford, 1979); and William of Newburgh, *History of England,* trans. J. Stevenson, vol. 4, pt. 2 of *The Church Historians of England,* (London, 1856). The best biography of Becket is Frank Barlow, *Thomas Becket* (Berkeley, 1986), but useful are three excellent older works: W. H. Hutton, *Thomas Becket* (Cambridge, 1926); David Knowles, *Thomas Becket* (London, 1975); and *Archbishop Thomas Becket: A Character Study* (London, 1949). See also R. Foreville, *Thomas Becket dans la Tradition historique et hagiographique* (Variorum Reprints, London, 1981), and Beryl Smalley, *The Becket Conflict and the Schools: A Study of Intellectuals in Politics* (Oxford, 1973). For Henry II, see W. L. Warren's monumental *Henry II* (Berkeley, 1973). An excellent review article is James W. Alexander, "The Becket Controversy," *Journal of British Studies* 9, no. 2 (May 1970), pp. 1–26.

4. Jean Anouilh, *Becket* trans. Lucienne Hill, (New York, 1960), p. 27.

5. Thomas Aquinas, *On Kingship: To the King of Cyprus,* trans. Gerald B. Phalan (Toronto, 1949), pp. 59–60.

6. St. Bernard of Clairvaux, *Five Books on Consideration,* trans. J. D. Anderson and E. T. Kennan, (Kalamazoo, Mich., 1976), pp. 61–62; Eadmer, *Historia Novorum,* ed. M. Rule, Rolls Series (London, 1884), p. 9, from Warren, *Henry II,* p. 404.

7. EHD, no. 100, Pope Gregory VII to William I, 8 May 1180, pp. 692–93.

8. *Materials* 7, Epistola VLXV, pp. 86–87.

9. *Materials* 3, p. 167 (Herbert of Bosham); EHD, no. 119, p. 705.

10. See, for example, Barlow, *Thomas Becket,* chap. 2.

11. William of Newburgh, *History of England,* p. 465.

12. *Materials* 3, pp. 20–21 (William Fitzstephen).

13. EHD, no. 135, p. 791.

14. Warren, *Henry II,* quoting Eadmer, *Vita Sancti Anselmi,* ed. R. W. Southern (London, 1963), p. 105 and n. 2.

15. *Materials* 3, p. 60 (William Fitzstephen).

16. Quoted in Barlow, *Thomas Becket,* p. 71, from Gervase of Canterbury, *Chronica,* in *Historical Works,* vol. 1, ed. W. Stubbs, Rolls Series (London, 1880), p. 168.

17. *Materials* 3, p. 55 (William Fitzstephen).

18. EHD, no. 379, pp. 647–48.

19. EHD, no. 123, pp. 761–62 (Edward Grim).

20. *Thómas Saga Erkibyskups,* vol. 1, p. 14; *Materials* 3, p. 266 (Herbert of Bosham).

21. *Materials* 3, pp. 266–69 (Herbert of Bosham).

22. EHD, no. 125; *Materials* 4, pp. 27–28 (Anonymous I).

23. W. Stubbs, *Select Charters and Other Illustrations of English History,* 9th ed., rev. H. W. C. Davis (Oxford, 1921), pp. 163–64.

24. EHD, no. 128, pp. 771–72 (Alan of Tewkesbury); *Materials* 3, p. 66 (William Fitzstephen).

25. Gilbert Foliot, *Letters and Charters,* no. 170, pp. 233–34, quoted in Greenaway, *Life and Death of Thomas Becket,* pp. 112–16.

26. Most of this story comes from William Fitzstephen, EHD, no. 129, pp. 772–83; *Materials* 3, pp. 56–68.

27. Ibid.; *Materials,* pp. 56–57.

28. Ibid.; *Materials*, p. 58.

29. Ibid.; *Materials*, pp. 63–66.

30. Ibid.; p. 782 n. 3; *Materials*, p. 68.

31. W. R. J. Barron, "The Penalties for Treason in Medieval Life and Literature," *Journal of Medieval History* 6, no. 2 (June 1980), pp. 187–89.

32. EHD, no. 130, pp. 783–84; no. 133, pp. 790–91.

33. H. G. Richardson and G. O. Sayles, *Law and Legislation from Aethelbert to Magna Carta* (Edinburgh, 1966), pp. 61–63; and Leona Gabel, *Benefit of Clergy in England in the Later Middle Ages* (Northampton, 1928–29), p. 8.

34. *Materials* 5, Epistola CLVI, p. 291 (Herbert of Bosham writing for Becket).

35. Smalley, *The Becket Conflict and the Schools,* chap. 6, "Alexander III."

36. EHD, no. 132, pp. 786–70 (Alan of Tewkesbury); *Materials* 2, p. 343.

37. *Materials* 5, Epistola XCV, p. 179; EHD, no. 137, p. 792.

38. Jennifer L. O'Reilly, "The Double Martyrdom of Thomas Becket: Hagiography or History?" *Studies in Medieval and Renaissance History,* n.s. vol. 1 (o.s. 17) (1985), pp. 200–202.

39. Barlow, *Thomas Becket,* pp. 75–76, 159.

40. *Materials* 5, Epistola XCV p. 290 (Herbert of Bosham writing for Becket).

41. William James, *Varieties of Religious Experience,* Modern Library, ed. (New York, 1936), p. 335.

42. EHD, no. 142, pp. 799–800.

43. *Materials* 3, p. 425 (Herbert of Bosham).

44. EHD, no. 139, pp. 794–95.

45. *The Annals of Roger de Hoveden,* trans. and ed. Henry T. Riley, 2 vols (London, 1853), vol. 1, pp. 275–78.

46. EHD, no. 140, pp. 795–98.

47. Foliot, *Letters and Charters,* no. 170, pp. 229–43, quoted in Greenaway, *Life and Death of Thomas Becket,* pp. 113–16.

48. EHD, no. 138, pp. 793–94.

49. EHD, no. 144, pp. 801–803; Barlow, *Thomas Becket,* pp. 180–81, 190.

50. EHD, no. 150, pp. 809–10; *Materials* 2, p. 428 (Edward Grim); *Materials* 3, p. 130 (William Fitzstephen); *Materials* 4, pp. 484–85 (Herbert of Bosham); Barlow, *Thomas Becket,* pp. 232–33.

51. EHD, no. 151, pp. 811–12; *Materials* 2, p. 434 (Edward Grim).

52. *Materials* 1, p. 114 (William of Canterbury).

53. Barlow, *Thomas Becket,* p. 235; p. 809 n. 4; *Materials* 2, p. 429 (Edward Grim).

54. William Fitzstephen, *The Life and Death of Thomas Becket,* ed. G. W. Greenaway (London, 1961), p. 113.

55. Barlow, *Thomas Becket,* p. 242; EHD, no. 152, p. 763.

56. Barlow, *Thomas Becket,* p. 242.

57. The various versions of what transpired after the knights left, their return fully armed, Becket's retreat into the cathedral, and the murder in the north transept near the step going up to the high altar are analyzed by Edwin A. Abbott, *St. Thomas of*

Canterbury: His Death and Miracles, vol. 1 (London, 1898). (Vol. 2 deals with the accounts of the miracles following his death.) Edward Grim, William Fitzstephen, and
John of Salisbury are probably the most reliable accounts, but John had taken refuge
before the actual assassination occurred.

58. Fitzstephen, *The Life and Death of Thomas Becket*, pp. 157–58; Abbott, *St. Thomas of Canterbury*, p. 150 and n. 4. (William Fitzstephen is speaking.)

59. *Materials* 2, pp. 18–19 (Benedict of Peterborough).

60. See O'Reilly, "Double Martyrdom of Thomas Becket," for a discussion of how his biographers turned his life and death into a "perfect" martyrdom.

61. EHD, no. 153, p. 821 n. 3.

62. EHD, no. 119, p. 753.

63. O'Reilly, "Double Martyrdom of Thomas Becket," pp. 189, 198, 201–202; Smalley, *Becket Conflict*, p. 194.

64. *Materials* 4, pp. 135–36 (Anonymous II).

65. *Materials* 3, p. 60 (William Fitzstephen). See also *Materials* 4, 129, 135 (Anonymous II).

66. Smalley, *Becket Conflict*, p. 201.

67. T. S. Eliot, *Murder in the Cathedral* (New York, 1935; rep. 1963), pp. 44, 37–38.

68. Ibid., pp. 39, 49.

69. EHD, no. 156, pp. 825–27; no. 158, p. 828 (Barlow says July 12, 1174).

70. *Materials* 5, Epistola CCXXVI, p. 545 (John of Salisbury to Bartholoaeum, Bishop of Exeter).

71. John of Salisbury, *The Statesman's Book*, trans. John Dickenson (New York, 1927), pp. 43–44.

72. *Materials* III, p. 471 (Herbert of Bosham).

73. Hughes and Larkin, *Tudor Royal Proclamations I*, vol. 1, 275–76.

74. Eliot, *Murder in the Cathedral*, p. 38.

Chapter 7
Thomas More: "A Hero of Selfhood"

1. Thomas More, *The Correspondence of Sir Thomas More*, ed. Elizabeth F. Rogers (Princeton, 1947), p. 564.

2. There are three sixteenth-century biographers (or, more accurately, hagiographers) of More on whom all scholars depend: William Roper (More's son-in-law), *The Life of Sir Thomas More*, penned about 1567; Nicholas Harpsfield, *The Life and Death of Sir Thomas More*, written in 1558; and Thomas Stapleton, *The Life and Illustrious Martyrdom of Sir Thomas More*, written in Latin in 1588. More's nephew William Rastall preserved and published More's *English Works* in 1557. Biographies are legion; the four on which this chapter is most heavily dependent are T. E. Bridgett, *The Life of Blessed Thomas More* (London, 1891); R. W. Chambers, *Thomas More* (Ann Arbor, 1958); Richard Marius, *Thomas More* (New York, 1984); and L. L. Martz, *Thomas More: The Search for the Inner Man* (New Haven, 1990). Over the past three decades the *Complete Works of St. Thomas More* (hereafter cited as CW) have been published by the Yale University Press. Interest in More has been consistent. There is an entire journal devoted to him—*Moreana*—and in recent years there has been an outbreak of articles and

monographs dealing with the political and religious activities of the martyr. For a start see A. Fox, *Thomas More: History and Providence* (New Haven, 1983); J. A. Guy, *The Public Career of Sir Thomas More* (New Haven, 1980); *St. Thomas More: Action and Contemplation,* ed. R. S. Sylvester (New Haven, 1972) (especially G. R. Elton, "Thomas More, Councillor 1517–1529"); P. D. Green, "Suicide, Martyrdom, and Thomas More," *Studies in the Renaissance* 19 (1972), pp. 135–55; B. Bradshaw, "The Controversial Sir Thomas More," *Journal of Ecclesiastical History* 30, no. 4 (Oct. 1985), pp. 536–69; *Essential Articles for the Study of Thomas More,* ed. R. S. Sylvester and G. P. Marchadour (Hamden, Conn., 1977); and the supplement of *Albion* (vol. 10, 1978), "Quincentennial Essays on St. Thomas More."

3. John Ruskin, *Fors Clavigera, Letters to the Workmen and Labourers of Great Britain,* 8 vols. in 4 (New York, n.d.), vol. 3, letter XXVI, p. 29.

4. *Commonweal* 112 (1985), pp. 320, 418.

5. Mario Cuomo, letter to his son, 22 November 1985.

6. Ibid.

7. Thomas More, *Responsio ad Lutherum,* ed. John M. Headley, CW 5:1 (New Haven, 1969), p. 311.

8. *The Latin Epigrams of Thomas More,* ed. L. Bradner and C. A. Lynch (Chicago, 1953), no. 219, p. 216.

9. Ibid., no. 224, p. 217.

10. Edward Hall, *The Triumphant Reigne of Kyng Henry the VIII,* fol. ccxxvii in *The Union of the Two Noble and Illustre Fameries of Lancastra and York* (London, 1550).

11. Nicholas Harpsfield, *The Life and Death of Sir Thomas More,* ed. E. V. Hitchcock, Early English Text Society, vol. 186 (London, 1932), pp. 93–94.

12. Thomas More, *Selected Letters,* ed. Elizabeth F. Rogers (New Haven, 1961), pp. 182–83.

13. Thomas More, *Utopia,* ed. Edwart Surtz and J. H. Hexter, CW 4 (New Haven, 1965), p. 103.

14. Ibid., p. 101.

15. Elton, "Thomas More, Councillor," p. 109.

16. See Marius, *Thomas More,* chaps. 10–12; and Stephen Greenblatt, *Renaissance Self-Fashioning: From More to Shakespeare* (Chicago, 1980), chap. 1.

17. *Latin Epigrams,* no. 94, p. 172.

18. Thomas More, *The Second Parte of the Confutation of Tyndale's Answers,* ed. Louis A. Schuster et al., CW 8:1 (New Haven, 1973), p. 159.

19. More, *Responsio ad Lutherum,* p. 599.

20. Thomas More, *Letter to Bugenkagen,* ed. Frank Manley et al., CW 7 (New Haven, 1990), p. 17.

21. Thomas More, *A Dialogue Concerning Heresies,* ed. Thomas Lawler et al., CW 6:1 (New Haven, 1981), pp. 405–406.

22. Chambers, *Thomas More,* pp. 352–55; Marius, *More,* p. 518.

23. More, *Dialogue Concerning Heresies,* p. 375. For more contrasts and contradictions see Anthony Kenny, *Thomas More* (New York, 1983), pp. 98–99.

24. George Cavendish, *Thomas Wolsey, Late Cardinal: His Life and Death,* ed. R. Lockyer (London, 1962), p. 117.

25. Hall, *Triumphant Reigne of Kyng Henry VIII,* fol. clxxx.

26. British Library, Cotton mss. vol. B XIII, ff. 171–72.

27. *Letters of King Henry VIII*, ed. M. St. Clare Byrne (London, 1968), p. 86.

28. Public Record Office, State Papers I, vol. 77, fols. 175–76. (*Letters and Papers of Henry VIII*, VI, no. 775..)

29. Ibid.

30. More, *Correspondence*, p. 496.

31. Hall, *Triumphant Reigne of Kyng Henry VIII*, fol. ccv.

32. Quoted in Kenny, *Thomas More*, pp. 64–65.

33. *Calendar of Letters, Despatches and State Papers Relating to the Negotiations Between England and Spain*, ed. Pascual De Gayangos (London, 1882), vol. 4, pt. 2 (1531–33), no. 952, p. 449.

34. More, *The Confutation of Tyndale's Answer*, CW 8:2, p. 577.

35. *Letters and Papers of Henry VIII*, V, no. 171, p. 85.

36. *Documents Illustrative of English Church History*, ed. Henry Gee and W. J. Hardy (London, 1896), no. LIV, esp. pp. 234, 235, 237, 239.

37. Ibid., no. L, p. 187.

38. Philip Hughes, *The Reformation in England* (London, 1954), vol. 1, pp. 270–77, esp. p. 270 n. 1. Italics added.

39. More, *Correspondence*, p. 553.

40. Ibid., p. 500.

41. Ibid., pp. 501–507.

42. William Roper, *The Life of Sir Thomas More*, ed. Mildred Campbell (New York, 1947), pp. 260–61.

43. More, *Correspondence*, p. 559.

44. More, *Selected Letters*, p. 242.

45. Roper, *More*, p. 259.

46. More, *Selected Letters*, p. 237.

47. Ibid., p. 243.

48. Ibid., p. 242.

49. Thomas More, *The English Works*, reproduced in facsimile from William Rastell's edition of 1557, ed. W. E. Campbell, 2 vols. (London, 1931), vol. 1, p. 13.

50. Thomas More, *A Dialogue of Comfort, Against Tribulation*, ed. L. L. Martz and F. Manley, C.W. 12 (New Haven, 1976), pp. 301–302.

51. More, *English Works*, vol. 1, p. 77.

52. Clement of Alexandria, "Miscellanies," in *The Writings*, vol. 2, trans. William Wilson (Ante-Nicene Christian Library, vol. 12) (Edinburgh, 1872), p. 147.

53. More, *Correspondence*, pp. 524, 525, 530.

54. Ibid., pp. 556–57.

55. Ibid., p. 559.

56. Thomas More, *De tristitia Christi*, CW 14:1, ed. Clarence H. Miller (New Haven, 1976), p. 47.

57. Ibid., pp. 103–05.

58. Roper, *More*, pp. 265–66.

59. Tertullian, *De Pallio* 5.4–5.5, quoted in W. H. C. Frend, *Martyrdom and Persecution in the Early Church* (Oxford, 1965), pp. 372–73.

60. More, *Correspondence*, pp. 521, 528.

61. Ibid., p. 559; Romans 14:4.

62. *Documents*, no. LVII, p. 248.

63. Marius, *More*, pp. 501–508, is the best analysis; Roper, *More*, pp. 267–68; Thomas Stapleton, *The Life and Illustrious Martyrdom of Sir Thomas More*, trans. Philip E. Hallett (London, 1966), pp. 160–61; *Letters and Papers of Henry VIII*, vol. VIII, p. 974.

64. Roper, *More*, p. 270.

65. Marius, *More*, pp. 506–507.

66. Roper, *More*, pp. 272–73.

67. Ibid., pp. 273–74.

68. Ibid., p. 274.

69. Ibid., p. 275.

70. More, *Correspondence*, pp. 564–65.

71. Roper, *More*, p. 279.

72. Stapleton, *More*, p. 188.

73. Chambers, *More*, p. 348.

74. Ibid.

75. Roper, *More*, p. 279.

76. Ibid., p. 280.

77. Chambers, *More*, p. 349.

78. Marius, *More*, p. 514; Chambers, *More*, p. 349.

79. John Strype, *Ecclesiastical Memorials*, 3 vols. in 6 (Oxford, 1822), vol. 1, ii, 211.

80. The best example can be found in G. R. Elton, *Policy and Police* (Cambridge, 1972), pp. 388–417.

81. R. W. Chambers, "Martyr of the Reformation: Thomas More," in *Essential Articles for the Study of Thomas More*, p. 500; Chambers, *Thomas More*, p. 400; C. H. Miller, "The Heart of the Final Struggle: More's Commentary on the Agony in the Garden," *Albion* 10, supplement (1978), p. 123; More, *Correspondence*, p. 530; Robert Bolt, *A Man for All Seasons* (London, 1961), p. xii.

82. *The Correspondence of Erasmus*, trans. R. A. B. Mynors, 86 vols. (Toronto, 1974–93), vol. 7, no. 999, p. 24.

83. The complete prayer is given in Marius, *More*, pp. 487–89.

Chapter 8
The Marian Martyrs: Group Identity Through Self-Destruction

1. The last three volumes of John Foxe's *Acts and Monuments*, ed. George Townsend, 8 vols. (London, 1846–49) (often called Foxe's "Book of Martyrs"), are the primary source for all research on the Marian martyrs; I hereafter will refer to Townsend's edition as "Foxe." Foxe's information should be supplemented by Miles Coverdale, *Let-*

ters of the Martyrs (London, 1564); *The Writings of John Bradford,* ed. Aubrey Townsend, 2 vols. (Cambridge, 1848); *The Works of Bishop Ridley,* ed. Henry Christmas, (Cambridge, 1843); and *Later Writings of Bishop Hooper,* ed. Charles Nevinson, (Cambridge, 1852). The best general surveys of the Reformation are A. G. Dickens, *The English Reformation,* 2nd ed. (London, 1989), which has a Protestant slant to it; and Philip Hughes, *The Reformation in England,* 3 vols. (London, 1954), which has a Catholic bias. D. M. Loades, *The Oxford Martyrs* (London, 1970), is a fine, detailed study of the martyrs, especially Cranmer, Latimer, and Ridley, and his *The Reign of Mary Tudor* (New York, 1979) is the best political coverage of the period. For a discussion of "Truth and Legend: The Veracity of John Foxe's Book of Martyrs," see Patrick Collinson in *Clio's Mirror: Historiography in Britain and the Netherlands,* ed. A. C. Duke and C. A. Tamse (Zutphen, 1985), chap. 2.

2. Benedict Anderson, *Imagined Communities: Reflections on the Origin and Spread of Nationalism,* (London, 1983), pp. 14–16.

3. The final count on the total number of martyrs varies slightly. See Dickens, *English Reformation,* pp. 293–301; Hughes, *Reformation,* vol. 2, pp. 254–304; John Strype, *Ecclesiastical Memorials,* 3 vols. in 6 (Oxford, 1822), vol. 3, pt. ii, no. LXXV, pp. 554–56; and John H. Blunt, *The Reformation of the Church of England,* 2 vols. (New York, 1882), vol. 2, pp. 214–332.

4. Technically, Cranmer does not qualify as a martyr as defined in this book: he had no choice. But because he was archbishop of Canterbury, he remained the symbolic leader of the Protestant party.

5. Possibly the number should be given as three prelates, because Hugh Latimer in 1553 was no longer bishop of Worcester, having resigned that see back in 1539. He was, however, still regarded as one of the principal figures of the Protestant church.

6. Of the ten martyrs, six have found biographers. Cranmer has at least twenty. G. W. Bromsley, *Thomas Cranmer, Archbishop and Martyr* (London, 1955) is among the best. Bromsley also wrote a *Nicholas Ridley* (London, 1953), but see too Jasper Ridley, *Nicholas Ridley* (Oxford, 1962). Latimer has two recent studies: A. G. Chester, *Hugh Latimer, Apostle to the English* (Philadelphia, 1954), and H. S. Darby, *Hugh Latimer* (London, 1953). There is a eulogistic life of Rowland Taylor by William J. Brown (London, 1859), and an equally biased account of John Rogers by Joseph L. Chester (London, 1861). See also a psychological article on Bradford: Seymour Byman, "Guilt and Martyrdom: The Case of John Bradford," *Harvard Theological Review* 63 (1975), pp. 305–31. The remaining eleven clerical martyrs either left no record of their thoughts and actions or, because they were imprisoned outside of London and were isolated from the rest, were unable to participate in rebuilding the moral and spiritual strength of English Protestantism. Three other Protestant leaders—Bishop Barlow of St. David's; Edwin Sandys, the future archbishop of York; and the polemical and volatile Thomas Becon—were more fortunate and escaped from prison.

7. C. H. Garrett, *The Marian Exiles: A Study in the Origins of Elizabethan Puritanism* (Cambridge, 1938), p. 41.

8. Gilbert Burnet, *The History of the Reformation,* ed. E. Nares, 4 vols. (London, 1839).

9. *Writings of John Bradford,* vol. 2, letter XCVIII, p. 246.

10. Dickens, *English Reformation,* p. 255; Patrick F. Tytler, *England Under the Reigns of Edward V and Mary,* vol. 2 (London, 1839), pp. 230–31.

11. Dickens, *English Reformation,* p. 287; *Calendar of State Papers, Spanish,* 17 vols., ed. Royall Tyler (London, 1862–1954), vol. 11, p. 186.

12. Foxe, vol. 7, p. 152.

13. Thomas More, *The Correspondence of Sir Thomas More*, ed. Elizabeth F. Rogers (Princeton, 1947), p. 152.

14. John Christopherson, *An Exhortation to alle menne to take hede and beware of Rebellion* (London, 1554), fol. Qiiii.

15. Foxe, vol. 7, p. 207.

16. *Works of Bishop Ridley*, letter XXXI, p. 393. See also Foxe, vol. 7, p. 435.

17. *Original Letters Relative to the English Reformation*, ed. Hastings Robinson (Cambridge, 1846), letter XLIV, p. 100.

18. *Writings of John Bradford*, vol. 2, letter XV, p. 37; Foxe, vol. 7, pp. 197, 206.

19. Foxe, vol. 7, p. 206.

20. The sources are filled with references to letters sent or received that have now been lost. See, for instance, Foxe, vol. 6, p. 630; Foxe, vol. 7, p. 426; *Works of Bishop Ridley*, letters VIII, p. 349; IX, p. 355; XII, p. 365; *Writings of John Bradford*, vol. 2, letters XXXI, p. 83; XXXVIII, pp. 100–101; LXII, p. 170; LXXXIV, p. 207; XCIV, p. 237; XCV, p. 239.

21. These figures are based on Miles Coverdale, *Letters of the Martyrs*, collated with those found in Foxe; *Writings of John Bradford*, vol. 2; *Works of Bishop Ridley*; *Later Writings of Bishop Hooper*; *Miscellaneous Writings and Letters of Thomas Cranmer*, ed. John Cox (Cambridge, 1886); and *Sermons and Remains of Hugh Latimer*, ed. George Corrie (Cambridge, 1845).

22. Foxe, vol. 7, p. 265.

23. *Works of Bishop Ridley*, letter IX, p. 365.

24. *Miscellaneous Writings of Thomas Cramner*, letter CCXVII, p. 457; *Writings of John Bradford*, vol. 2, letter LXVII, p. 179 (Foxe, vol. 6, p. 630).

25. *Writings of John Bradford*, vol. 2, letter CI, p. 251. See also letter LXXIV, p. 187.

26. Ibid., letter LXVII, p. 179 (Foxe, vol. 6, p. 630).

27. *Writings of John Bradford*, vol. 2, letter XV, p. 37.

28. *Works of Bishop Ridley*, letter VII, pp. 343–44.

29. Ibid., "supplement," p. 539; Foxe, vol. 7, pp. 425–26.

30. *Works of Bishop Ridley*, letter IX, p. 355.

31. *Writings of John Bradford*, vol. 2, letter XCVII, pp. 243–44.

32. Ibid., letter XIX, p. 46.

33. Ibid., letter XCVI, pp. 242–43.

34. Ibid., letters LXXXV, p. 210; XLIV, p. 126; XCIV, p. 249; LXXI, p. 182.

35. Ibid., letter LXXX, p. 197; Foxe, vol. 7, p. 194.

36. Foxe, vol. 7, p. 207.

37. Ibid., p. 431.

38. *Writings of John Bradford*, vol. 2, letter XC, pp. 221–26.

39. *Works of Bishop Ridley*, letter IX, p. 355.

40. *Writings of John Bradford* vol. 2, letter XXIII, p. 62.

41. Foxe, vol. 7, p. 200; *Later Writings of Bishop Hooper*, letter XXVI, p. 580; *Writings of John Bradford*, vol. 1, I, "A Certain Declaration," p. 370.

42. Foxe, vol. 7, p. 524.

43. Foxe, vol. 6, p. 620.

44. *Works of Bishop Ridley,* letter IX, p. 355.

45. *Writings of John Bradford,* vol. 1, "Declaration Concerning King Edward His Reformation," p. 400. See also Foxe, vol. 6, pp. 589–90.

46. Foxe, vol. 8, pp. 100–101.

47. *Writings of John Bradford,* vol. 1, letter LXV, p. 176; Ibid., letter LXVI, p. 178.

48. *Works of Bishop Ridley,* letter XVI, p. 370.

49. Foxe, vol. 7, p. 424.

50. *Later Writings of Bishop Hooper,* letter XLIX, pp. 621–22.

51. Foxe, vol. 6, pp. 596, 510.

52. *Original Letters Relative to the English Reformation,* letter LXXVIII, p. 171.

53. *Statutes of the Realm,* vol. 2 (London, 1816) (reprint, 1963) 2 Henry IV. C. 15 (1401), p. 128.

54. Strype, *Ecclesiastical Memorials,* vol. 3, pt. ii, p. 487.

55. Burnet, *History of the Reformation,* vol. 2, pp. 464–65.

56. *Calendar of State Papers, Venetian,* ed. Rawdon Brown et al. (London, 1864–98), vol. 6, pt. i, p. 111.

57. Foxe, vol. 6, pp. 703–04.

58. *Works of Bishop Ridley,* p. 363.

59. Foxe, vol. 7, pp. 606–81.

60. *Writings of John Bradford,* vol. 1, letter LXXVII, p. 190.

61. *Works of Bishop Ridley,* letter XVI, p. 190.

62. *Writings of John Bradford,* vol. 2, letter LXXVII, p. 190.

63. *Works of Bishop Ridley,* letter XXI, p. 378.

64. *Writings of John Bradford,* vol. 2, letter LXXVII, pp. 190–91.

65. Bradford clearly had powerful friends who sought to save him. See *Writings,* vol. 1, pp. 515–18.

66. The best discussion of Cranmer's ordeal can be found in Loades, *Oxford Martyrs,* pp. 221–33.

67. The behavior of the martyrs at the stake can be studied in Seymour Byman, "Ritualistic Acts and Compulsive Behavior: The Pattern of Tudor Martyrdom," *American Historical Review* 83 (June 1978), pp. 623–43; and in an unpublished paper by Terrance Murphy delivered at the Conference of British Studies in Philadelphia, Nov. 4, 1988.

68. Francis Bacon, *Advancement of Learning and Novum Organum,* ed. James Creighton (New York, 1889), p. 258.

69. Foxe, vol. 6, pp. 611–12; *Dictionary of National Biography,* "John Rogers," quoting *Ambassades des Messieurs de Noailles, Ambassades en Angleterre,* ed. R. A. de Vertot (Leyden, 1743), vol. 4; *Calendar of State Papers, Spanish,* vol. 13, p. 138.

70. Foxe, vol. 6, pp. 699, 628.

71. Foxe, vol. 7, p. 194.

72. Foxe, vol. 8, pp. 668–69.

73. Foxe, vol. 7, p. 147.

74. Ibid., p. 685.

75. The full story of their deaths is in Foxe, vol. 7, pp. 547–50.

76. Foxe, vol. 7, p. 203.

77. Foxe, vol. 8, p. 178.

78. Ibid., p. 332.

79. Foxe, vol. 7, p. 712.

80. British Library, Harleian MSS 4894 "Robert Rypon Sermonum Liber," fol. 182; William Baldwin, *A Treatise of Morall Philosophie* (1547), ed. Robert H. Bowers (Gainesville, Fla., 1967), p. 164.

81. Foxe, vol. 7, p. 76; Loades, *Oxford Martyrs*, p. 161.

82. Foxe, vol. 8, p. 217.

83. *Second Report of the Historical Manuscript Commission* (Abingdon Mss), app. p. 152; D. M. Loades, *The Reign of Mary Tudor* (New York, 1979), pp. 447–48 and p. 456 n. 104.

84. John Jewel, *Works*, (Cambridge, 1844–45), vol. 2, p. 1034.

Chapter 9
Charles I: Martyr by Act of Parliament

1. There are over fifty biographies of Charles I, most of them in the hagiographical tradition, but some of them systematic character assassinations. The five best modern treatments are John Bowle, *Charles I: A Biography* (London, 1975); Pauline Gregg, *King Charles I* (London, 1981); Charles Carlton, *Charles I, the Personal Monarch* (London, 1983); Kevin Sharpe, *The Personal Rule of Charles I* (New Haven, 1992); and an important article by Martin J. Havran, "The Character and Personality of an English King: The Case of Charles I," *Catholic Historical Review* 69 (April 1983). C. V. Wedgwood's remains the classic and still the best account of Charles's final year: *The Trial of Charles I* (London, 1964). The record of the trial and Charles's performance at his execution can be found in a number of places. The sources I have used are J. G. Muddiman, *Trial of King Charles the First* (Toronto, 1928); the Folio Society's *Trial of Charles I*, ed. R. Lockyer (London, 1959); and *The Letters, Speeches and Proclamations of King Charles I*, ed. Charles Petrie (London, 1968). The chapter draws heavily on the introduction to Michael Walzer, *Regicide and Revolution: Speeches at the Trial of Louis XVI* (Cambridge, 1974), which is as much about Charles as about Louis. Most of the historical background and some of the phraseology comes from my own text *This Realm of England* (Lexington, Mass., 1992), esp. chaps. 12 and 13.

2. Most of what follows is dependent on Walzer, *Regicide and Revolution*, pp. 1–89.

3. Muddiman, *Trial of King Charles*, p. 70.

4. Ibid., p. 79.

5. Ibid., p. 262.

6. Ibid., p. 93.

7. *Manchester's Quarrell: Documents Relating to the Quarrel Between the Earl of Manchester and Oliver Cromwell*, Camden Society, n.s. XII (London, 1875), p. 93.

8. John Selden, *Table Talk*, ed. Frederick Pollock (London, 1927), p. 61.

9. Muddiman, *Trial of King Charles*, p. 129.

10. Ibid., p. 121.

11. Walzer, *Regicide and Revolution*, p. 48.

12. Muddiman, *Trial of King Charles*, pp. 97, 79.

13. Ibid., p. 124.

14. Ibid., p. 258.

15. Ibid., pp. 257, 259.

16. Gregg, *Charles I*, p. 415; Wedgwood, *Trial of Charles I*, p. 33.

17. Gregg, *Charles I*, p. 415.

18. Muddiman, *Trial of King Charles*, p. 263.

19. Ibid., pp. 157–58.

20. The best brief description of Charles's character and the political consequences of his personality can be found in four vignettes, by C. V. Wedgwood, Mary Coate, Mark A. Thomson, and David Piper, published as *King Charles I, 1649–1949* (London, 1949). A more psychological approach is Havran, "Character and Principles," esp. pp. 183–208.

21. *Eikōn Basilike, or The King's Book*, ed. Edward Almack (London, 1904), p. 153.

22. *Letters, Speeches and Proclamations*, p. 176.

23. William Allen, *A Faithful Memorial*, in *Somers Tracts*, ed. Walter Scott (London, 1809–15), VI, p. 501.

24. Quoted in Gregg, *Charles I*, p. 431.

25. Wilbur Abbott, *Writings and Speeches of Oliver Cromwell* (Cambridge, Mass., 1937), vol. I, p. 719.

26. Muddiman, *Trial of King Charles*, pp. 71–131, esp. p. 74.

27. Ibid., p. 78.

28. Ibid., pp. 81–82.

29. Ibid., pp. 82–83.

30. Ibid., pp. 83–84.

31. Ibid.

32. Ibid., p. 90.

33. Ibid., pp. 92–94.

34. Ibid., pp. 98–100.

35. Ibid., p. 106.

36. Ibid., p. 108.

37. Ibid., p. 111.

38. Ibid., pp. 114–24.

39. Richard Marius, *Thomas More* (New York, 1984), p. 508.

40. Muddiman, *Trial of King Charles*, pp. 125–29.

41. Ibid., p. 129.

42. Wedgwood, *Trial of Charles I*, pp. 169, 185; Muddiman, *Trial of King Charles*, p. 135.

43. Muddiman, *Trial of King Charles*, pp. 133, 136–38.

44. Lockyer, *Trial of Charles I*, p. 126.

45. Muddiman, *Trial of King Charles*, pp. 261–62.

46. Ibid., pp. 154, 263; Wedgwood, *Trial of Charles I*, p. 193.

47. Muddiman, *Trial*, p. 189.

48. Ibid., p. 138.

Chapter 10
John Brown: "Let Them Hang Me"

1. Richard O. Boyer, *The Legend of John Brown: A Biography and a History* (New York, 1973), p. 4.

2. Three quite different but excellent biographies of Brown appeared in the early 1970s, and this chapter owes much to all three: Stephen B. Oates's *To Purge This Land with Blood: A Biography of John Brown* (New York, 1970); Jules Abels's *Man on Fire: John Brown and the Cause of Liberty* (New York, 1971); and Boyer's *Legend of John Brown*. Two older works are indispensable since they include letters and recollections not available elsewhere or difficult to find in manuscript form: F. B. Sanborn, *The Life and Letters of John Brown* (originally published 1885; New York, 1969); and Oswald Garrison Villard, *John Brown, 1800–1859: A Biography Fifty Years After* (Boston, 1910). *Public Life of Capt. John Brown* (Boston, 1860), by James Redpath, who knew Brown, is the first Brown eulogy (hagiography), and Redpath made a journalistic killing with it. H. P. Wilson's *John Brown, Soldier of Fortune: A Critique* (Lawrence, Kans., 1913), is an unrelenting attack on the old man, and James C. Malin's *John Brown and the Legend of 1856* (Philadelphia, 1942) is a scholarly but highly critical interpretation of Brown's Kansas days. Allan Nevins has an interesting psychoanalytical study of Brown in his *Emergence of Lincoln*, 2 vols. (New York, 1950), vol. 2, pp. 5–27, 70–97. Louis Ruchames has composed a useful and fairly thorough anthology of Brown letters and documents—*A John Brown Reader* (New York, 1959)—but see also Richard Warch and Jonathan F. Fanton, *John Brown* (Englewood Cliffs, N.J., 1973). For the emotional atmosphere of the 1850s as the nation headed for civil war, see David Brion Davis's slim volume *The Slave Power Conspiracy and the Paranoid Style* (Baton Rouge, 1970). Allan Nevins's *Ordeal of the Union*, 2 vols. (New York, 1947), remains a rich narrative account of the years immediately preceding the Civil War.

3. Ruchames, *Reader*, p. 232.

4. The information and quotes in the paragraph come from Brown's so-called autobiography, which can be read in its entirety in either Villard, *Brown*, pp. 1–7, or Ruchames, *Reader*, pp. 35–41.

5. Ruchames, *Reader*, p. 37.

6. Oates, *To Purge This Land*, p. 16.

7. Sanborn, *Life and Letters*, pp. 91–93.

8. Villard, *Brown*, p. 28.

9. Abels, *Man on Fire*, p. 27.

10. Oates, *To Purge This Land*, p. 66.

11. There are different ways of interpreting Brown's decision to go to Kansas. I have followed Boyer, *Legend of John Brown*, pp. 456–60, 524–27. See also Abels, *Man on Fire*, pp. 38–42, and Oates, *To Purge This Land*, pp. 84–90.

12. Ruchames, *Reader*, p. 183.

13. Sanborn, *Life and Letters*, pp. 40–41.

14. Ruchames, *Reader*, pp. 180–81.

15. Boyer, *Legend of John Brown*, p. 557, quoting a letter dated Jan. 23, 1855, Chicago Historical Society.

16. Villard, *Brown*, pp. 45–46.

17. Ralph Waldo Emerson, *Journals*, 10 vols. (Boston, 1912), vol. 8, pp. 190, 201.

18. Nevins, *Ordeal of the Union*, vol. 2, p. 127.

19. Ibid., p. 301.

20. Oates, *To Purge This Land*, pp. 83–84; Nevins, *Ordeal of the Union*, vol. 2, pp. 306–10.

21. Together Villard, *Brown*, pp. 83–84 and Boyer, *Legend of John Brown*, pp. 524–26, give the entire letter.

22. Sanborn, *Life and Letters*, pp. 444–45.

23. Ibid., pp. 200–202; Villard, *Brown*, p. 93.

24. Villard, *Brown*, p. 93.

25. Ibid., p. 145.

26. Ibid., p. 151.

27. Sanborn, *Life and Letters*, pp. 272–73; Villard, *Brown*, p. 165. The best discussion of Brown's responsibility for the murders and the public reaction to them is in Abels, *Man on Fire*, pp. 62–80.

28. Ruchames, *Reader*, p. 97.

29. Villard, *Brown*, pp. 194–97; Oates, *To Purge This Land*, p. 145.

30. Villard, *Brown*, p. 275.

31. Oates, *To Purge This Land*, p. 222.

32. Ralph Waldo Emerson, *Complete Writings*, 2 vols. (New York, 1929), vol. 2, p. 1203.

33. Gilman M. Ostrander, "Notes and Documents, Emerson, Thoreau, and John Brown," *Mississippi Valley Historical Review* 39 (March 1953), pp. 720, 723.

34. Sanborn, *Life and Letters*, p. 333.

35. Oates, *To Purge This Land*, p. 191.

36. Abels, *Man on Fire*, pp. 128, 129, 131, 143; Oates, *To Purge This Land*, pp. 183, 185, 189, 227.

37. Villard, *Brown*, p. 275.

38. Jeffery Rossback, *Ambivalent Conspirators: John Brown, the Secret Six, and a Theory of Slave Violence* (Philadelphia, 1982); p. 155.

39. Sanborn, *Life and Letters*, p. 419; Ruchames, *Reader*, p. 327; Abels, *Man on Fire*, p. 167.

40. Rossback, *Ambivalent Conspirators*, p. 268; Sanborn, *Life and Letters*, pp. 436, 439.

41. Oates, *To Purge This Land*, pp. 210–12.

42. Sanborn, *Life and Letters*, p. 466.

43. Ruchames, *Reader*, p. 217.

44. Villard, *Brown*, p. 371; Oates, *To Purge This Land*, p. 263.

45. Oates, *To Purge This Land*, o, 262.

46. Villard, *Brown*, pp. 374–75; Oates, *To Purge This Land*, p. 264.

47. Villard, *Brown*, pp. 375–76.

48. Ibid., p. 382.

49. Oates, *To Purge This Land*, p. 267.

50. Villard, *Brown*, p. 56; Sanborn, *Life and Letters*, p. 545.

51. Ruchames, *Reader*, p. 159.

52. Georges Sorel, *Reflections on Violence*, trans. T. E. Hulme and J. Roth (New York, 1961), pp. 80–92.

53. Sanborn, *Life and Letters*, pp. 444–45.

54. Oates, *To Purge This Land*, p. 270; Villard, *Brown*, pp. 531–32.

55. Oates, *To Purge This Land*, p. 281; Villard, *Brown*, pp. 678–87.

56. These figures come from Oates, *To Purge This Land*, p. 274.

57. Ibid., p. 283; Ruchames, *Reader*, p. 330.

58. Abels, *Man on Fire*, pp. 161–62.

59. Emerson, *Journals*, vol. 9, p. 82; see also Abels, *Man on Fire*, p. 213.

60. Warch and Fanton, *John Brown*, pp. 132–34; *Abraham Lincoln: His Speeches and Writings*, ed. Royal P. Basler (New York, 1969), p. 530.

61. Thoreau, *Writings*, vol. 4, p. 413.

62. Ruchames, *Reader*, p. 232.

63. Warch and Fanton, *John Brown*, p. 63; Sanborn, *Life and Letters*, p. 557.

64. Oates, *To Purge This Land*, p. 293.

65. Ruchames, *Reader*, p. 232.

66. Abels, *Man on Fire*, p. 294; Villard, *Brown*, p. 448.

67. Sanborn, *Life and Letters*, p. 559.

68. Abels, *Man on Fire*, pp. 278–80.

69. Villard, *Brown*, p. 540. The letter was dated Nov. 10, 1859.

70. Abels, *Man on Fire*, p. 294; Sanborn, *Life and Letters*, p. 559; Warch and Fanton, *John Brown*, p. 65.

71. Oates, *To Purge This Land*, p. 335; Villard, *Brown*, p. 512.

72. Ruchames, *Reader*, pp. 149–50.

73. Ibid., p. 304.

74. Abels, *Man on Fire*, p. 177.

75. Villard, *Brown*, p. 519 n.

76. Villard, *Brown*, pp. 456–63; Ruchames, *Reader*, pp. 118–25, from *New York Herald*, Oct. 21, 1859.

77. Villard, *Brown*, p. 456.

78. Oates, *To Purge This Land*, p. 320.

79. Abels, *Man on Fire*, p. 319.

80. Villard, *Brown*, p. 501.

81. Abels, *Man on Fire*, p. 343.

82. Villard, *Brown*, p. 502; Abels, *Man on Fire*, p. 344.

83. Villard, *Brown*, p. 500.

84. Oates, *To Purge This Land*, p. 308; Villard, *Brown*, p. 500.

85. Villard, *Brown*, p. 507.

86. Ibid., p. 487.

87. Abels, *Man on Fire*, p. 325.

88. Ibid., p. 331.

89. Villard, *Brown*, pp. 498–99.

90. Abels, *Man on Fire*, p. 331; Robert Penn Warren, *John Brown: The Making of a Martyr* (New York, 1929), p. 414.

91. Emerson, *Complete Writings*, vol. 2, p. 1219.

92. Abels, *Man on Fire*, p. 334.

93. Ruchames, *Reader*, pp. 155, 156.

94. Abels, *Man on Fire*, pp. 313–14.

95. Brown's prison letters can be read in Sanborn, *Life and Letters*, pp. 578–620, or Ruchames, *Reader*, pp. 127–59. I have used Ruchames; see pp. 129–30, 132, 139.

96. Ruchames, *Reader*, pp. 139, 142.

97. Ibid., pp. 143, 132, 134, 156, 154.

98. Ibid., pp. 128, 149, 154.

99. Ibid., pp. 151, 135, 143, 156, 132, 158.

100. Ibid., pp. 153, 142.

101. Ibid., p. 155.

102. Ibid., p. 158.

103. Ibid., p. 146.

104. Villard, *Brown*, p. 554.

105. Abels, *Man on Fire*, p. 366; Villard, *Brown*, p. 556; Oates, *To Purge This Land*, p. 352.

106. Robert W. Dewitt, *The Life, Trial, and Execution of John Brown* (New York, 1859), p. 101.

107. Abels, *Man on Fire*, pp. 129–30, 390–92.

108. Ruchames, *Reader*, p. 283.

109. James Elliot Cabot, *A Memoir of Ralph Waldo Emerson*, 2 vols. (Boston, 1887), vol. 2, p. 597.

110. Ernest Renan, *L'Église chrétienne*, vol. 6 in *Histoire des Origines du Christianisme* (Paris, 1906), pp. 317–18.

Chapter 11
Mahatma Gandhi: School for Martyrs

1. Nirmal K. Bose, *My Days with Gandhi* (Calcutta, 1953), p. 154.

2. The literature on Gandhi is immense—well over four hundred biographies—but all draw from a single foundation, the Mahatma's own works, which have been compiled and published by the Publications Division of the Government of India as *The Collected Works of Mahatma Gandhi* in 90 volumes (Ahmedabad, 1958–84). Of special importance are Gandhi's *An Autobiography: The Story of My Experiments with Truth*, trans. Mahadev Desai, Beacon paperback (Boston, 1953); *Hind Swaraj, or Indian Home Rule* (Madras, 1921); *Satyagraha in South Africa*, trans. V. G. Desai (Ahmedabad, 1928); and *Non-Violence in Peace and War*, 2 vols. (Ahmedabad; vol. 1, 3rd ed., 1948; vol. 2, 1949), which is a rich assortment of Gandhi's essays. The best political biography is Judith M. Brown, *Gandhi, Prisoner of Hope* (New Haven and London, 1989),

but Louis Fischer (who knew and vastly admired Gandhi), *The Life of Mahatma Gandhi* (1950; Harper paperback, New York, 1983), is a flawed but highly readable classic. Immensely valuable is Nayar Pyarelal, *Mahatma Gandhi: The Early Phase* (Ahmedabad, 1965) and *The Last Phase*, 2 vols. (Ahmedabad, 1956–58). Erik H. Erikson, *Gandhi's Truth* (New York, 1969), is a controversial but important psychoanalytical study. Antony Copley, *Gandhi Against the Tide* (Oxford, 1987) is a brief (104-page) but thoughtful account. Joan V. Bondurant, *Conquest of Violence: The Gandhian Philosophy of Conflict* (Berkeley, 1965); Margaret Chatterjee, *Gandhi's Religious Thought* (Notre Dame, 1983); Susanne H. and Lloyd I. Rudolph, *Gandhi: The Traditional Roots of Charisma* (Chicago and London, 1983); Raghavan Iyer, *The Moral and Political Thought of Mahatma Gandhi*, Oxford paperback (Oxford, 1978); and B. R. Nanda, *Gandhi and His Critics* (Delhi, 1985) are indispensable special studies. Useful also are three anthologies: *The Essential Gandhi: An Anthology of His Writings on His Life, Work and Ideas*, ed. Louis Fischer (Vintage Books, 1986); *The Gandhi Reader: A Source Book of His Life and Writings*, ed. Homer A. Jack (Bloomington, 1956); and the most substantial of all, *The Essential Writings of Mahatma Gandhi*, ed. Raghavan Iyer (Delhi, 1991).

3. Gandhi, *Works*, vol. 77, no. 27, p. 87.

4. Gandhi, *An Autobiography*, pp. 20, 31.

5. Ibid., p. 265.

6. Ibid., p. 299; John Ruskin, *Unto This Last: Four Essays on the First Principles of Political Economy* (New York, 1901), p. 163.

7. Gandhi, *Works*, vol. 22, no. 172, p. 404; vol. 23, no. 101, p. 196.

8. Ibid., vol. 18, no. 91, p. 133.

9. Erikson, *Gandhi's Truth*, p. 153.

10. Gandhi, *An Autobiography*, p. 258.

11. Ibid., pp. 131, 139.

12. Gandhi, *Satyagraha*, p. 101.

13. Ibid., pp. 104–107.

14. Ibid., p. 109.

15. Gandhi, *Works*, vol. 15, no. 141, p. 135.

16. Joseph Doke, *M. K. Gandhi: An Indian Patriot in South Africa* (Madras, 1919), p. 93.

17. *Essential Writings*, p. 156; Gandhi, *Works*, vol. 7, no. 27, p. 44; *Gandhi Reader*, p. 137.

18. *Essential Writings*, p. 156; Gandhi, *Works*, vol. 63, no. 297, p. 240.

19. Gandhi, *Works*, vol. 63, no. 297, p. 211.

20. Ibid., pp. 159, 183; Gandhi, *Non-Violence in Peace and War*, vol. 2, p. 265.

21. Gandhi, *An Autobiography*, pp. 209–11, 504; *Essential Gandhi*, pp. 70–71.

22. Gandhi, *Works*, vol. 88, no. 25, p. 36; no. 88, p. 116.

23. *Essential Writings*, p. 219; Gandhi, *Satyagraha*, p. 114.

24. Gilbert Murray, "The Soul as It Is, and How to Deal with It," *Hibbert Journal* 16, no. 2 (January 1918), p. 201.

25. Gandhi, *Swaraj in Our Year* (Madras, 1921), p. 5.

26. Gandhi, *Hind Swaraj*, p. 61.

27. Ibid., pp. 59–60.

28. Ibid., p. 63.

29. Gandhi, *Works*, vol. 64, no. 101, p. 85.

30. Ibid., vol. 73, no. 48, p. 69.

31. Ibid., vol. 15, no. 191, p. 204.

32. Chatterjee, *Gandhi's Religious Thought*, p. 95.

33. *Essential Writings*, p. 221.

34. Ibid., p. 325.

35. Ibid., pp. 221–22.

36. Gandhi, *Works*, vol. 72, no. 462, p. 416.

37. Ibid., vol. 58, no. 129, p. 108.

38. *Gandhi Reader*, pp. 249–51.

39. Ibid., pp. 252–53.

40. Fischer, *Gandhi*, p. 77.

41. Quoted in Ibid., p. 195; see also *Essential Gandhi*, p. 93.

42. *Essential Gandhi*, p. 205; *Gandhi Reader*, p. 113.

43. Iyer, *Moral and Political Thought*, p. 341.

44. Gandhi, *Hind Swaraj*, pp. 51–52.

45. Bondurant, *Conquest of Violence*, pp. 34, 127; *Essential Gandhi*, p. 190.

46. Gandhi, *Works*, vol. 68, no. 430, p. 390.

47. *Essential Writings*, p. 182.

48. *Essential Gandhi*, p. 190.

49. Gandhi, *Works*, vol. 67, no. 267, p. 195.

50. *Essential Writings*, pp. 210–11; Iyer, *Moral and Political Thought*, p. 120.

51. *Essential Writings*, p. 211.

52. Oscar Wilde, *The Picture of Dorian Gray* (London, 1945), p. 133.

53. Iyer, *Moral and Political Thought*, p. 125.

54. Quoted in Ibid., p. 120; see also Gandhi, *Works*, vol. 55, no. 305, p. 255.

55. Quoted in Fischer, *Gandhi*, p. 284.

56. Iyer, *Moral and Political Thought*, p. 126; Fischer, *Gandhi*, p. 108; H. S. L. Polak et al., *Mahatma Gandhi* (London, 1949), p. 76.

57. Quoted in Brown, *Gandhi*, p. 255.

58. Quoted in Fischer, *Gandhi*, p. 103.

59. *Essential Writings*, p. 325; Gandhi, *Works*, vol. 55, no. 465, p. 396.

60. Gandhi, *Works*, vol. 43, no. 3, pp. 2–8.

61. *Essential Gandhi*, p. 67.

62. Gandhi, *Non-Violence in War and Peace*, vol. 1, pp. 43–44.

63. Gandhi, *Works*, vol. 13, no. 405, p. 534.

64. Quoted in Brown, *Gandhi*, p. 74.

65. Quoted in Nanda, *Gandhi and His Critics*, p. 30.

66. Gandhi, *Works*, vol. 10, no. 136, p. 207.

67. Gandhi, *Hind Swaraj*, p. 30.

68. Ibid., pp. 27, 48.

69. Quoted in Fischer, *Gandhi*, p. 196.

70. Gandhi, *Hind Swaraj*, p. 27.

71. Ibid., p. 44.

72. Gandhi, *Works*, vol. 13, no. 49, p. 45; no. 59, p. 60.

73. Quoted in Fischer, *Gandhi*, p. 110.

74. Jawaharlal Nehru, *Discovery of India* (New York, 1946), pp. 361–362.

75. Gandhi, *Hind Swaraj*, p. 21.

76. Quoted in Fischer, *Gandhi*, p. 218.

77. M. K. Gandhi, *The India of My Dreams,* compiled by R. K. Prabhu (Bombay, 1949), p. 16; Gandhi, *Hind Swaraj*, p. 76.

78. Gandhi, *Hind Swaraj*, pp. 47, 72.

79. Gandhi, *Works*, vol. 13, no. 166, p. 214.

80. Polak et al., *Mahatma Gandhi*, p. 191.

81. *Essential Gandhi*, pp. 223, 299.

82. Quoted in Brown, *Gandhi*, p. 168.

83. Quoted in Ibid., p. 342.

84. Quoted in Nanda, *Gandhi and His Critics*, p. 51.

85. *Wavell: The Viceroy's Journal,* ed. Penderel Moon (London, 1973), p. 402.

86. Fischer, *Gandhi*, pp. 364–65.

87. Quoted in Nanda, *Gandhi and His Critics*, p. 68; *Works*, vol. 13, no. 361, p. 465.

88. Gandhi, *Works*, vol. 69, no. 38, p. 50.

89. Ibid., vol. 25, no. 166, p. 217.

90. Ibid., vol. 66, no. 431, p. 344.

91. Ibid., vol. 23, no. 57, pp. 114–20.

92. Ibid., vol. 22, no. 1, p. 10.

93. Ibid., vol. 83, no. 470, p. 401.

94. Ibid., vol. 69, no. 61, p. 51.

95. Ibid., vol. 55, no. 465, p. 396.

96. Ibid., vol. 73, no. 72, pp. 91, 83; no. 470, p. 401.

97. Ibid., vol. 78, no. 277, p. 223.

98. Ibid., vol. 83, no. 260, p. 225. He would endure two more fasts after independence in August of 1947.

99. Ibid., vol. 52, no. 283, p. 219.

100. Ibid., vol. 73, no. 187, p. 175.

101. Ibid., vol. 77, no. 7, p. 60.

102. Brown, *Gandhi*, p. 266.

103. Gandhi, *Works*, vol. 50, no. 396, p. 383.

104. Ibid., vol. 90, no. 388, p. 410.

105. Ibid., vol. 89, no. 160, p. 132.

106. Ibid., vol. 90, no. 388, p. 409.

107. Ibid., vol. 29, no. 21, p. 291.

108. Ibid., vol. 52, no. 1, p. 1.

109. Ibid., vol. 52, no. 503, p. 376; vol. 58, no. 389, p. 357; vol. 69, no. 61, p. 51; vol. 78, no. 368, p. 281.

110. Ibid., vol. 78, no. 278, p. 225; vol. 52, no. 503, p. 376.

111. Ibid., vol. 67, Appendix I, p. 447.

112. Ibid., vol. 23, no. 382, p. 517.

113. Ibid., vol. 14, no. 175, p. 257; see also no. 194, pp. 283–86.

114. Ibid., vol. 45, no. 283, p. 213.

115. Ibid., vol. 58, no. 192, p. 171; vol. 78, no. 277, p. 223.

116. Ibid., vol. 55, no. 305, p. 257.

117. Ibid., vol. 14, no. 178, p. 263.

118. B. R. Ambedkar, *What Congress and Gandhi Have Done to the Untouchables* (Bombay, 1945), p. 270.

119. Gandhi, *Works,* vol. 77, no. 25, p. 83.

120. Ibid., vol. 55, no. 481, p. 410.

121. Ibid., p. 411.

122. Ibid., vol. 52, no. 85, p. 62.

123. Ibid., vol. 83, no. 198, pp. 177–78; no. 209, p. 186.

124. Ibid., vol. 24, no. 50, p. 91.

125. Ibid., vol. 78, no. 278, p. 225; no. 293, p. 233.

126. Ibid., vol. 55, no. 481, p. 412.

127. Ibid., vol. 77, no. 27, p. 91.

128. Ibid., vol. 55, no. 481, p. 412.

129. Ibid., vol. 69, no. 61, p. 51; vol. 90, no. 388, pp. 409–10.

130. Ibid., vol. 73, no. 627, p. 440.

131. Quoted in Copley, *Gandhi*, p. 47.

132. Gandhi, *Works,* vol. 53, no. 618, p. 460.

133. Ibid., vol. 52, no. 359, p. 269.

134. Ibid., vol. 49, no. 337, p. 275.

135. Ibid., vol. 58, no. 192, p. 171.

136. Ibid., vol. 55, no. 305, p. 256.

137. Ibid., vol. 56, no. 394, p. 369.

138. Ibid., vol. 69, no. 61, p. 52; vol. 55, no. 465, p. 396.

139. Ibid., vol. 78, no. 293, p. 235.

140. Ibid., vol. 78, no. 277, p. 224.

141. *Selected Works of Jawaharlal Nehru,* 15 vols. (New Delhi, 1972–82), vol. 5, p. 478 (prison diary, June 4, 1933).

142. Fischer, *Gandhi*, p. 394.

143. Gandhi, *India of My Dreams*, p. 18.

144. Pyarelal, *Gandhi: The Last Phase,* vol. 2, p. 772.

145. Gandhi, *Works,* vol. 52, no. 359, p. 269.

Chapter 12
The Twentieth-Century Martyr: An Endangered Species?

1. Penderel Moon, *Gandhi and Modern India* (London, 1968), p. 105.

2. John 18:33–38.

3. Barton L. Ingraham, *Political Crime in Europe: A Comparative Study of France, Germany and England* (Berkeley, 1979), pp. 25, 34, 201, 304–305.

4. Quoted in B. R. Nanda, *Gandhi and His Critics* (Delhi, 1985), p. 64.

5. M. K. Gandhi, *The Collected Works,* 90 vols. (Ahmedabad, 1958–84), vol. 68, p. 205.

6. Louis Fischer, *The Life of Mahatma Gandhi* (New York, 1950, 1983), p. 344.

7. Gandhi, *Collected Works,* vol. 67, no. 597, p. 405.

8. Ibid., vol. 68, no. 157, pp. 137–41, esp. p. 140.

9. Herbert Musurillo, *The Acts of the Christian Martyrs* (Oxford, 1972), p. 23.

10. Edward Peters, *Torture* (Oxford, 1978), is the best history of torture; see especially pp. 162–66. See also Michel Foucault, *Discipline and Punishment: The Birth of the Prison,* trans. Alan Sheridan, (New York, 1979), and Malise Ruthven, *Torture: The Grand Conspiracy* (London, 1978).

11. Quoted in Ruthven, *Torture,* p. 284 n. 6.

12. Kai T. Erikson, *Wayward Puritan: A Study in the Sociology of Deviants* (New York, 1966), p. 205. See also F. A. Allen, *The Crimes of Politics: Political Dimensions of Criminal Justice* (Cambridge, Mass., 1974), esp. pp. 6–7.

13. Quoted in *Sunday Telegraph* (London), April 5, 1987.

14. James V. McConnell, "Criminals Can Be Brainwashed—Now," *Psychology Today* 3 (April 1970), pp. 14–18, 74.

15. George Orwell, *Nineteen Eighty-four* (New York, 1949), p. 270.

16. Quoted in Joshua Rubenstein, *Soviet Dissidents: Their Struggle for Human Rights,* 2nd ed. (Boston, 1985), p. 137, from Solzhenitsyn's "This Is How We Live."

17. Rubenstein, *Soviet Dissidents,* pp. 52–53.

18. Anatoly Marchenko, *My Testimony* (New York, 1969), pp. 3, 87; and *From Tarusa to Siberia* (Royal Oak, Mich., 1980), p. 35.

19. Rubenstein, *Soviet Dissidents,* p. 31.

20. Quoted in Ibid., p. vii.

21. Adolf Hitler, *Mein Kampf,* trans. Ralph Manheim (Boston, 1943), vol. 2, chap. 2, pp. 391, 393; Peters, *Torture,* pp. 106–107, 121.

22. Bruno Bettelheim, *The Informed Heart: Autonomy in a Mass Age* (New York, 1960), p. 243.

23. Hermann Rauschning, *Hitler Speaks* (London, 1939), p. 60.

24. Bettelheim, *The Informed Heart,* pp. 109, 240.

25. Ibid., p. 139.

26. Ibid., p. 151.

27. Deuteronomy 26:19.

28. Emil L. Fackenheim, *The Jewish Return into History: Reflections in the Age of Auschwitz and a New Jerusalem* (New York, 1978), p. 247.

29. Steven T. Katz (ed.), *Interpreters of Judaism in the Late Twentieth Century* (Washington, D.C., 1993), pp. 45–53.

30. Bruno Bettelheim, *Surviving and Other Essays* (New York, 1979), p. 93; Pierre Joffroy, *A Spy for God* (New York, 1971), p. 141, quoting Paul Anton De Lagarde (1827–91), the German political and religious thinker and one of the spiritual godfathers of National Socialism.

31. William E. Kaufman, *Contemporary Jewish Philosophies* (New York, 1985), p. 72.

32. Katz, *Interpreters of Judaism*, pp. 62–63.

33. Ibid., p. 65; cf. Irving Greenburg, *The Jewish Way: Living the Holiday* (New York, 1988), pp. 314–20.

34. Katz, *Interpreters of Judaism*, pp. 46–47; Richard L. Rubenstein, *After Auschwitz: Radical Theology and Contemporary Judaism* (Indianapolis, 1966), pp. 3–4, 8–9, 171.

35. Elie Wiesel, *The Oath* (New York, 1973), p. 93.

36. Leo Baeck, *The Essence of Judaism*, trans. Victor Grubenwieser and Leonard Pearl (New York, 1948), p. 137.

37. Bettelheim, *Informed Heart*, p. 264.

38. Wiesel, *Oath*, pp. 237; 239–40.

39. Rubenstein, *After Auschwitz*, p. 230.

40. Michael L. Morgan, *Dilemmas in Modern Jewish Thought* (Bloomington, 1992), p. 87.

41. Elie Wiesel, "For Some Measure of Humility," *Sh'ma, A Journal of Jewish Responsibility*, vol. 5 (Oct. 31, 1975), p. 314.

42. Bettelheim, *Surviving*, p. 260.

43. Leonard Baker, *Days of Sorrow and Pain: Leo Baeck and the Berlin Jews* (New York, 1978), pp. 3, 285.

44. Fackenheim, *Jewish Return into History*, pp. 249–50.

45. Wiesel, *Oath*, p. 183.

46. Baker, *Days of Sorrow*, p. 3.

47. Ibid., p. 285. Albert H. Friedlander, *Leo Baeck, Teacher of Theresienstadt* (New York, 1968), gives somewhat different but even more terrifying figures, p. 45.

48. Leo Baeck, *Das Wesen des Judentums* (Berlin, 1905; 2nd rev. ed., Frankfurt am Main, 1923). Cf. Baeck's later work, *The People Israel: The Meaning of Jewish Existence*, trans. A. H. Friedlander (New York, 1965).

49. S. Daniel Breslauer, "Martyrdom and Charisma: Leo Baeck and a New Jewish Theology," *Encounter: Creative Theological Scholarship* 42, no. 2 (Spring 1981), p. 138. Much of what follows depends heavily on this article, pp. 133–42.

50. Quoted in Friedlander, *Leo Baeck*, p. 256.

51. Ibid., p. 88. This is Friedlander's own rendering of Baeck's *Essence of Judaism*, which is rather different in flavor from the 1948 translation. See above, n. 36.

52. Baeck, *Essence of Judaism*, p. 216.

53. Breslauer, "Martyrdom and Charisma," p. 139.

54. Alan L. Berger, "Elie Wiesel," in Katz, *Interpreters of Judaism*, p. 381.

55. Rubenstein, *After Auschwitz*, p. 205.

56. Bettelheim, *Informed Heart*, p. 139.

57. Wiesel, *Oath*, p. 79.

58. William Kuhns, *In Pursuit of Dietrich Bonhoeffer* (London, 1967), p. 264.

59. Bonhoeffer has attracted a sizable assortment of biographers and commentators on his theological works, most of which have been translated into English. The best and most authoritative biography is *Dietrich Bonhoeffer: Man of Vision, Man of Courage* (New York, 1970), an 841-page opus by Eberhard Bethge, who was Bonhoeffer's close friend, student, and disciple and who only just managed to survive the Nazi regime. Far more manageable are Mary Bosanquet, *The Life and Death of Dietrich Bonhoeffer* (London, 1968), and E. H. Robertson's much shorter *Dietrich Bonhoeffer* (London, 1966). Selections from Bonhoeffer's collected works, *Gesammelte Schriften*, 6 vols. (Munich, 1958–74), have been translated as *No Rusty Swords* (New York, 1965), *The Way to Freedom* (New York, 1967), and *True Patriotism* (New York, 1973). His famous letters from prison are best read in Dietrich Bonhoeffer, *Letters and Papers from Prison*, ed. and trans. Eberhard Bethge, rev. ed. (London, 1967). Bonhoeffer's major theological works include *Act and Being*, trans. Bernard Noble (New York, 1962); *The Cost of Discipleship*, trans. R. H. Fuller (New York, 1959); *Ethics*, trans. Eberhard Bethge (London, 1955); and *Life Together*, trans. John W. Doberstein (New York, 1954).

60. Bethge, *Bonhoeffer*, p. 530.

61. Eberhard Bethge, *Bonhoeffer: Exile and Martyr* (London, 1975), pp. 159–60; Bethge, *Dietrich Bonhoeffer*, p. 834.

62. Bethge, *Dietrich Bonhoeffer*, p. 176.

63. Ibid., p. 23.

64. Frederic A. Iremonger, *William Temple, Archbishop of Canterbury: His Life and Letters* (London, 1949), p. 403.

65. The best works on the German churches and Hitler are Ernst Helmreich, *The German Churches Under Hitler* (Detroit, 1979), and Klaus Scholder, *The Churches and the Third Reich*, 2 vols., trans. John Bowden (Philadelphia, 1988).

66. Bethge, *Dietrich Bonhoeffer*, p. 129.

67. Bonhoeffer, *Letters and Papers*, p. 27.

68. Bethge, *Dietrich Bonhoeffer*, pp. 157, 191.

69. Helmreich, *German Churches*, p. 130.

70. Bethge, *Dietrich Bonhoeffer*, p. 201.

71. Ibid., pp. 236–37.

72. Ibid., p. 208.

73. Helmreich, *German Churches*, pp. 146–51; Bethge, *Dietrich Bonhoeffer*, pp. 240–41.

74. Bethge, *Dietrich Bonhoeffer*, p. 263.

75. Ibid., p. 297.

76. Ibid., pp. 299, 353.

77. Ibid., p. 354.

78. Rauschning, *Hitler Speaks*, p. 58.

79. Mary Craig, *Candles in the Dark* (London, 1984), p. 28.

80. Bethge, *Dietrich Bonhoeffer*, p. 330.

81. Rauschning, *Hitler Speaks*, pp. 57–58.

82. Ibid., p. 379.

83. Ibid., p. 505.

84. Ibid., p. 507.

85. Ibid., p. 511; Craig, *Candles in the Dark*, p. 26.

86. Bonhoeffer, *Gesammelte Schriften*, vol. 1, pp. 281, 400.

87. Ibid., p. 303.

88. Bethge, *Dietrich Bonhoeffer*, p. 559.

89. Ibid.

90. Bonhoeffer, *No Rusty Swords*, p. 47.

91. Bethge, *Dietrich Bonhoeffer*, p. 533; Peter Hoffmann, *German Resistance to Hitler* (Cambridge, Mass., 1988), pp. 81–83.

92. Bonhoeffer, *Letters and Papers*, pp. 26, 28; Bethge, *Bonhoeffer: Exile and Martyr*, p. 129.

93. Bethge, *Dietrich Bonhoeffer*, p. 627; Bonhoeffer, *Gesammelte Schriften*, vol. 1, p. 398.

94. Bonhoeffer, *Ethics*, p. 70.

95. Kuhns, *In Pursuit of Dietrich Bonhoeffer*, p. 231.

96. Bethge, *Dietrich Bonhoeffer*, p. 648.

97. Bethge, *Bonhoeffer: Exile and Martyr*, p. 135.

98. Bonhoeffer, *True Patriotism*, p. 232.

99. Bethge, *Dietrich Bonhoeffer*, p. 656.

100. Hoffmann, *German Resistance*, p. 85.

101. Bonhoeffer, *Letters and Papers*, p. 40.

102. *Hitler's Table Talk, 1941–1944*, trans. Norman Cameron and R. H. Stevens (London, 1953), p. 409.

103. The best works on the German resistance and the Abwehr plots are Hoffmann, *German Resistance to Hitler*; Michael Balfour, *Withstanding Hitler in Germany* (London, 1988); and Roger Manvell and Heinrich Fraenkel, *The Canaris Conspiracy* (New York, 1969).

104. Bonhoeffer, *True Patriotism*, pp. 170–79.

105. Manvell and Fraenkel, *Canaris Conspiracy*, p. 140.

106. Bethge, *Dietrich Bonhoeffer*, p. 730.

107. Ibid., p. 41.

108. Bonhoeffer, *Letters and Papers*, p. 140.

109. Ibid., p. 41.

110. Bethge, *Dietrich Bonhoeffer*, p. 792.

111. Bonhoeffer, *Letters and Papers*, pp. 153, 156, 172, 174–75, 178–82, 196, 199, 201–202, 208–11; Bethge, *Dietrich Bonhoeffer*, p. 767.

112. Bethge, *Dietrich Bonhoeffer*, p. 831.

113. Bonhoeffer, *Letters and Papers*, p. 34.

114. Bethge, *Dietrich Bonhoeffer*, p. 823.

115. Bonhoeffer, *Letters and Papers*, p. 159.

116. Ibid., p. 149.

117. Ibid.

118. Bonhoeffer, *No Rusty Swords,* p. 44.

119. A possible exception to this generalization may be the nude statue that stands on the spot in Berlin where Count von Stauffenberg and two others were shot. It is said the face was modeled on that of Stauffenberg. My thanks to my colleague Peter Hayes for this information. The German Lutheran Church accepted Bonhoeffer as a legitimate martyr in the 1960s, but the Federal Republic of Germany did not get around to fully exonerating him of treason until August of 1996. *Chicago Tribune,* August 18, 1996, sec. 1, p. 13.

120. Bonhoeffer, *Letters and Papers,* p. 107.

121. Kenneth L. Woodward, *Making Saints* (New York, 1970), pp. 76, 130.

122. Ibid., pp. 45–46.

123. Ibid., pp. 400–401.

124. Stephen E. Ambrose with Richard H. Immerman, *Ike's Spies* (New York, 1981), p. 183; *New York Times,* Feb. 12, 1953.

125. *The Worker,* Sept. 20, 1953, quoted in Ilene Philipson, *Ethel Rosenberg: Beyond the Myths* (New Brunswick, N.J., 1993), p. 2.

126. Gandhi, *Works,* vol. 77, no. 27, p. 97.

127. I. F. Stone, *I.F. Stone's Bi-Weekly,* July 2, 1956.

128. Almost everything written about the Rosenbergs is partisan. The three best books are Walter and Miriam Schneir, *Invitation to an Inquest* (New York, 1965) (they were totally innocent); Ronald Radosh and Joyce Milton, *The Rosenberg File: A Search for the Truth* (New York, 1983) (they were guilty); and Ilene Philipson, *Ethel Rosenberg: Beyond the Myths* (New Brunswick, N.J., 1993) (a fascinating if controversial psychological study). Virginia Gardner's short (126-page) essay, *The Rosenberg Story* (New York, 1954), despite its left-wing journalist style, is valuable for its personal interviews. Still useful are John Wexley, *The Judgment of Julius and Ethel Rosenberg* (New York, 1977); Malcolm P. Sharp, *Was Justice Done? The Rosenberg-Sobell Case* (New York, 1956); Jonathan Root, *The Betrayers: The Rosenberg Case—A Reappraisal of an American Crisis* (New York, 1963); and Louis Nizer's best-selling *The Implosion Conspiracy* (New York, 1973). The Rosenberg correspondence can be read in *Death House Letters of Ethel and Julius Rosenberg* (New York, 1953), which ends on March 19, 1953; *The Testament of Ethel and Julius Rosenberg* (New York, 1954), which includes letters up to the day of execution, June 19, 1953; the additional and relatively unexpurgated letters in Robert and Michael Meeropol (the adopted name of the Rosenberg children), *We Are Your Sons* (Boston, 1975); and Michael Meeropol (ed.), *The Rosenberg Letters: A Complete Edition of the Prison Correspondence of Julius and Ethel Rosenberg* (New York, 1994). This volume comprises some 560 letters, the great majority of the Rosenberg correspondence, and contains an excellent, if understandably biased, analysis of the most recent literature dealing with the Rosenberg controversy. Throughout the footnotes this volume is referred to as *Rosenberg Letters.* The two-volume, continuously paginated transcript *Julius Rosenberg and Ethel Rosenberg, Petitioners, vs. The United States of America* (United States Supreme Court, October term, 1951, no. 111) was reprinted by the National Committee to Secure Justice for the Rosenbergs in 1952, and hereafter is referred to as Rosenberg Trial.

129. Gardner, *Rosenberg Story,* pp. 54–55.

130. Ibid., p. 31.

131. For a discussion of the Rosenbergs' involvement in the Communist Party, see Radosh and Milton, *Rosenberg File*, pp. 495–99 n. 52.

132. Philipson, *Ethel Rosenberg*, p. 132.

133. Ibid., p. 103.

134. Radosh and Milton, *Rosenberg File*, p. 59.

135. Ibid., p. 498 n. 56.

136. Ibid., p. 71; Wexley, *Judgment*, p. 109; Rosenberg Trial, p. 664; Schneir, *Invitation*, pp. 132–33.

137. Richard Hofstadter, *The Paranoid Style in American Politics and Other Essays* (New York, 1965), pp. 7–8, quoting *Congressional Record*, 82nd Congress, 1st session (June 14, 1951) p. 6602.

138. Philipson, *Ethel Rosenberg*, p. 215.

139. See Alan Moorehead, *The Traitors* (London, 1952), and Robert C. Williams, *Klaus Fuchs, Atom Spy* (Cambridge, Mass., 1987).

140. J. Edgar Hoover, "The Crime of the Century," *Reader's Digest* (May 1951), p. 159. Walter and Miriam Schneir are deeply suspicious of Gold's confession. See *Invitation*, esp. pp. 406–16.

141. Rosenberg Trial, p. 181.

142. Radosh and Milton, *Rosenberg File*, p. 88.

143. William O. Douglas, *The Court Years, 1939–1975* (New York, 1980), p. 79. The fullest discussion of the defense attorney's handling of the case is Radosh and Milton, *Rosenberg File*, esp. chap. 26, and Joseph H. Sharlitt, *Fatal Error: The Miscarriage of Justice That Sealed the Rosenbergs' Fate* (New York, 1989).

144. Rosenberg Trial, p. 1079.

145. Morton Sobell, *On Doing Time* (New York, 1974, p. 213).

146. *National Guardian*, July 13, 1953, and also Rosenberg, *Letters*, p. 703.

147. *Khrushchev Remembers: The Glasnost Tapes*, trans. and ed. Jerrold L. Schecter and Vyacheslav V. Luchkev (Boston, 1990), pp. 193–94; *New York Times*, July 12, 1995, p. A10; see also the long report in the *Washington Post*, pp. 1 and A18, March 16, 1997.

148. Rosenberg Trial, pp. 1614–16.

149. Philipson, *Ethel Rosenberg*, pp. 265–66.

150. Radosh and Milton, *The Rosenberg File*, p. 416.

151. Gardner, *Rosenberg Story*, pp. 94, 96–97.

152. Philipson, *Ethel Rosenberg*, pp. 315–16.

153. Gardner, *Rosenberg Story*, p. 125; Philipson, *Ethel Rosenberg*, pp. 351–52; Radosh and Milton, *Rosenberg File*, pp. 418–19.

154. Robert Coover, *The Public Burning* (New York, 1976), pp. 211, 215. For a literary critique of the extensive drama, art, and fiction the Rosenberg case generated, see Virginia Carmichael, *Framing History: The Rosenberg Story and the Cold War* (Minneapolis, 1993).

155. *Pliny: A Self-Portrait in Letters*, trans. and ed. Betty Radice (New York, 1978), bk. 10, no. 96, p. 241.

156. Exactly how much editing is apparent when the *Death House Letters* is compared to Michael Meeropol's edition of *Rosenberg Letters*.

157. Musurillo, *Christian Martyrs*, p. 27.

158. Philipson, *Ethel Rosenberg*, p. 7.

159. *Rosenberg Letters*, pp. 25–26 n. 27, 561.

160. Ibid., p. 524.

161. Philipson, *Ethel Rosenberg*, p. 346, quoting *Time*, Feb. 23, 1953.

162. Philipson, *Ethel Rosenberg*, p. 351.

163. Gandhi, *Works*, vol. 73, no. 627, p. 440.

164. *Death House Letters*, pp. 29, 39, 47, 74, 90, 150; Petition of Ethel Rosenberg for Executive Clemency, International Association of Democratic Lawyers, Brussels, 1953, p. 11.

165. *Death House Letters*, pp. 29, 61–62.

166. Ibid., pp. 49, 56; *Rosenberg Letters*, pp. 649–50.

167. *Death House Letters*, pp. 46, 67.

168. *Rosenberg Letters*, pp. 488–89.

169. Ibid., p. 412, 703.

170. *Death House Letters*, pp. 42, 67, 140–41.

171. Ibid., pp. 42, 67, 140–41; Petition of Ethel Rosenberg for Executive Clemency, p. 11.

172. *Rosenberg Letters*, pp. 550–51, 592.

173. Philipson, *Ethel Rosenberg*, p. 343.

174. Ibid., p. 340.

175. Penderal Moon, *Gandhi and Modern India* (London, 1968), p. 288.

176. Robert Warshow, "The 'Idealism' of Julius and Ethel Rosenberg" (1953), in *The Immediate Experience: Movies, Comics, Theatre and Other Aspects of Popular Culture* (New York, 1971), p. 76.

177. Leslie Fiedler, "Afterthoughts on the Rosenbergs," in *A Fiedler Reader* (New York, 1977), pp. 56–64. See Andrew Ross, "Reading the Rosenberg Letters," in *No Respect: Intellectuals and Popular Culture* (New York, 1989), for an attempt to rehabilitate the Rosenbergs and their letters.

178. Gardner, *Rosenberg Story*, p. 50.

179. Philipson, *Ethel Rosenberg*, p. 318.

180. Robert Bolt, *A Man for All Seasons* (London, 1961), p. 53.

181. Philipson, *Ethel Rosenberg*, p. 312.

182. Henrik Ibsen, *Brand*, Trans. Michael Meyer (London, 1960), act III, p. 54.

Chapter 13
Epilogue: The Disinterested Martyr

1. Martin Luther, Table Talk no. 1687, in Frantz Funck-Bretano, *Luther*, trans. E. F. Buckley (London, 1939), p. 246.

2. Michael Grant, *Jesus: An Historian's Review of the Gospels* (New York, 1977), p. 89.

3. M. K. Gandhi, *An Autobiography* (Boston, 1957), pp. 505, 248.

4. Margaret Chatterjee, *Gandhi's Religious Thought* (Notre Dame, 1983), p. 34; M. K. Gandhi, *The Collected Works* (Ahmedabad, 1958–84), vol. 55, no. 305, p. 255; vol. 73, no. 159, p. 156; vol. 78, no. 277, p. 223.

5. Gandhi, *Works*, vol. 63, no. 297, p. 240.

6. Ibid., vol. 13, no. 226, p. 311.

7. Louis Fischer, *The Life of Mahatma Gandhi* (New York, 1983), p. 35; Gandhi, *Works*, vol. 23, no. 2, p. 6.

8. Oswald G. Villard, *John Brown, 1800–1859: A Biography Fifty Years After* (Boston, 1910), p. 552.

9. Chatterjee, *Gandhi's Religious Thought*, pp. 27, 156, 168; Gandhi, *Works*, vol. 20, no. 27, pp. 53–54; B. R. Ambedker, *Gandhi and Gandhism* (Jullundur, 1970), p. 152.

10. Chatterjee, *Gandhi's Religious Thought*, p. 27.

11. T. S. Eliot, *Murder in the Cathedral* (London, 1937), pp. 8, 79.

12. Rolf Hochhuth, *The Deputy*, trans. Richard and Clara Winston (New York, 1964), Act I, scene 3, p. 83.

13. J. M. M. de Valk, "More: A Man of Our Times," *Moreana* 25, no. 97 (March 1988), p. 46.

14. Hochhuth, *Deputy*, Act III, scene 2, p. 157.

15. This document is printed as a postscript to Pierre Joffroy's *A Spy for God*, pp. 275–99. See note 16 below.

16. Pierre Joffroy, *A Spy for God: The Ordeal of Kurt Gerstein* (New York, 1971) (*L'Espion de Dieu*, Paris, 1969), is the most recent account of Gerstein, and Joffroy's many interviews with those who remembered the German SS lieutenant add depth to the story. Saul Friedländer, *Kurt Gerstein: The Ambiguity of Good* (New York, 1969) (*Kurt Gerstein, ou L'Ambiguité du bien*, Paris, 1967), remains the basic historical account. Helmut Franz, *Kurt Gerstein: Aussenseiter des Wilderstandes der Kirche gegen Hitler* (Zurich, 1964), is the only published account by a close friend. Hochhuth's *Deputy* has a brief but useful appendix (pp. 289–95) on the historical Gerstein in which Pastor Otto Wehr's letter is given almost in its entirety. Much of the material for Gerstein's life has been collected at the Kurt-Gerstein-Haus (Museum) at Berchum.

17. Friedländer, *Gerstein*, p. 7.

18. Joffroy, *Spy for God*, p. 22.

19. Ibid., p. 24.

20. Friedländer, *Gerstein*, pp. 173–74.

21. Joffroy, *Spy for God*, p. 59; cf. Friedländer, *Gerstein*, pp. 48–50.

22. Joffroy, *Spy for God*, pp. 84–85. Friedländer speculates that Gerstein's decision to enlist in the SS was part of his attempts to re-establish himself in the Nazi Party, p. 83.

23. Ibid., pp. 112, 281.

24. Ibid., pp. 283–84. Friedländer has a careful analysis of Gerstein's report and what he has to say about his efforts to dispose of the prussic acid in *Gerstein*, chap. 8, pp. 182–200.

25. Joffroy, *Spy for God*, pp. 285–89.

26. Ibid., p. 287.

27. Ibid., pp. 193–94.

28. Ibid., p. 213.

29. Ibid., p. 220; Friedländer, *Gerstein*, p. 4. In the end Ludwig Gerstein decided his son had been right not to obey orders; *Gerstein*, pp. 205–06.

30. Joffroy, *Spy for God*, p. 225. In a letter to Bishop Otto Dibelius, Gerstein said: "These things must become the talk of the world" (Friedländer, *Gerstein*, p. 134).

31. Joffroy, *Spy for God*, pp. 220–21; Friedländer, *Gerstein*, p. 208.

32. Joffroy, *Spy for God*, pp. 217, 250, 282–83, 295.

33. Ibid., p. 221.

34. Ibid., pp. 12, 251–52.

35. Friedländer, *Gerstein*, pp. 225–26. On January 20, 1965, the premier of Baden-Württemberg made partial restitution by rehabilitating Gerstein's name on the grounds he had "resisted National Socialist despotism with all his strength and suffered consequent disadvantage."

36. Joffroy, *Spy for God*, p. 297. Gerstein was convinced that he was one of only four or five people who were not Nazis who had witnessed the atrocities and would be willing to give evidence. See Friedländer, *Gerstein*, pp. 209–10, 214–15.

37. Joffroy, *Spy for God*, p. 252.

38. Friedländer, *Gerstein*, pp. 209–10; Franz, *Kurt Gerstein*, p. 33.

39. Joffroy, *Spy for God*, p. 17; cf. Friedländer, *Gerstein*, p. 223.

40. Joffroy, *Spy for God*, p. 13.

41. Ibid., p. 260.

42. Ibid., p. 251.

43. Hochhuth, *Deputy*, p. 291; cf. Joffroy, *Spy for God*, p. 300.

44. Ibid.

45. Gandhi, *Works*, vol. 52, no. 359, p. 269.

46. Ibid., no. 618, p. 461.

INDEX

ILLUSTRATION CREDITS

The illustrations in this book were provided with the permission and courtesy of the following:

Eberhard Bethge: 317

Biblioteek der Rijksuniversiteit, Leiden: 42

Corbis-Bettmann: 22, 62, 184, 262, 338

Culver Pictures: 88, 208, 228

The Frick Collection, New York: 148

Alfred A. Knopf, Inc: 360

The New Yorker Magazine, Inc.: 300

The Pierpont Morgan Library/Art Resource, New York: 116